MACROECONOMICS

MACROECONOMICS

J. Carl Poindexter

North Carolina State University

The Dryden Press

Hinsdale, Illinois

To My Family

Chapter-Opener Photo Credits

1. Harold M. Lambert/Frederic Lewis Photographs   2.   Exxon
3. Samuel Kravitt/Frederic Lewis Photographs   4.   Harold M.
Lambert/Frederic Lewis Photographs   5.   Gerald L. French/Frederic
Lewis Photographs   6. New York Stock Exchange   7. Mac
Gramlich/Frederic Lewis Photographs   8. Ed Carlin/Frederic Lewis
Photographs   9. Harold M. Lambert/Frederic Lewis Photographs
10. Harold M. Lambert/Frederic Lewis Photographs   11. Grant
White/Frederic Lewis Photographs   12. Harold M. Lambert/
Frederic Lewis Photographs   13. Harold M. Lambert/Frederic
Lewis Photographs   14. Harold M. Lambert/Frederic Lewis
Photographs   15. Grant White/Frederic Lewis Photographs
16. Ed Carlin/Frederic Lewis Photographs

Editorial - Production Services provided
by COBB/DUNLOP, Inc.

Copyright © 1976 by The Dryden Press
A Division of Holt, Rinehart and Winston
All rights reserved
Library of Congress Catalog Card Number: 75-21322
ISBN: 0-03-089419-0
Printed in the United States of America
 6 7 8 9 032 9 8 7 6 5 4 3 2

Preface

This text is designed to provide a compact but comprehensive presentation of current mainstream macroeconomic theory, measurement, and policymaking. The empirical nature of modern economic analysis is effectively revealed and an effort is made to transmit the excitement generated by the controversies that provide progress in our efforts to understand and control the macroeconomy.

Macroeconomics is tailored to the needs of students in the upper level macroeconomics course—students who exhibit a substantial heterogeneity in background, interests, and motivation. No mathematical training past algebra is required for using and understanding this text. Still, footnotes provide frequent, conveniently available, simple calculus demonstrations of arguments that have been fully developed in the text so that those who have had calculus will be encouraged to use it as an analytical tool. The text in its current format has been extensively tested with quite favorable results in a classroom situation at the author's university.

The introductory chapter in the text requires students to formally recognize the scientific nature of economic analysis, clearly distinguishes between positive analysis and normative goals, acquaints students with the statistical technique most heavily relied on in modern macroeconomics, and finally, provides the logical foundation for undertaking the difficult analytical task of constructing models of the *macroeconomy* by discussing the goals of macroeconomic policy. Chapters 2 and 3 provide coverage of the data that are basic to macroeconomic analysis (the national income and product accounts, price indexes, and measures of employment and unemployment), critique those measures, and introduce students to new efforts to provide broader measures of economic welfare. While the primary focus of these chapters is on the conceptual foundations for the data series, students are exposed to the actual measures compiled for the United States.

Chapter 4 initiates the student's involvement in macroeconomic analysis as national accounts and income determination models are constructed for economic systems of differing degrees of complexity. Concern for policy making is maintained through application of the multiplier. While the limitations of the simple models developed in this chapter are explicitly recognized, the analysis in this chapter illustrates clearly the need for a firm empirical understanding of the components of aggregate planned spending. Chapters 5 and 6 provide theoretical explanations of consumption and investment spending and review the empirical evidence available on the consistency of the theories treated with observed behavior. Chapter 7 formally introduces money into the economic system, providing for determination of the interest rate. The forces that influence the interest rate are explained with attention focused on the bond market as well as on the demand for and supply of money. Again, theory is buttressed with empirical evidence on the nature of money demand.

In Chapter 8, the lessons provided by the partial equilibrium analysis in

earlier chapters are employed in constructing the Hicksian IS-LM model. Interest in policy is maintained by analyzing the impact of monetary and fiscal
policy actions in this model. The budget constraint that the government faces is
formally recognized and the monetary consequences of alternative methods of
government finance are addressed. Chapter 9 extends the IS-LM analysis, first
by considering the special Keynesian and classical regions of the LM schedule,
then by adding the labor market and aggregate production function to the general equilibrium model. The power of the resulting complete model is illustrated
through its application in analyzing the comparative static effects of a number
of disturbances, including an oil embargo by the OPEC countries. The exercises
employed in this chapter illustrate the role of *money illusion* in the standard
Keynesian model. The "stickiness" of money wages receives attention with the
search theory of labor markets offered as an explanation for a *slow* adjustment
of money wages in the face of an excess supply of labor. For those who want
more of an emphasis on *disequilibrium* analysis, an appendix is provided which
incorporates imperfect information in both the labor and commodity markets.

Chapter 10, entitled Great Debates, uses the general equilibrium model to
explain the major engagements that have taken place between Keynesians and
those critics of Keynesian analysis who owe their heritage to the classical economists. Monetarism is treated as a legitimate challenge to post-Keynesian ortho-
doxy even though the student will be well aware by this time that *Macroeconomics* is basically post-Keynesian. An appendix to Chapter 10 provides a
market by market comparison of Keynes's macro model with what he described
as the classical model and an exposition of the debates over the possibility of
equilibrium with less than full employment.

In light of the growing integration of world markets and the momentous
changes that have taken place in recent years in both trade patterns and the
international financial system, Chapter 11 provides a more comprehensive treatment of the macroeconomic role of international economic involvement than is
usually found in intermediate macroeconomic texts. Likewise, the inflationary
experience of recent years requires the extensive treatment of inflation that is
provided in Chapter 12. The dynamics of the "Phillips curve" relationship are
explored, programs for shifting the long-run Phillips curve leftward (or reducing
the *natural* rate of unemployment) are aired, and the influence of inflationary
expectations on the observed interest rate is examined in the complete aggregate
model. Chapters 13 and 14 continue the concern with dynamic analysis, treating
growth and business cycles.

Chapters 15 and 16 reinforce this text's substantial emphasis on policy
issues by considering in detail the real world application of monetary and fiscal
policy. In Chapter 15, a money supply model is carefully constructed and used
in explaining the tools that the central bank has available for controlling the
money supply. The difficulties which monetary policy makers may face because
of lags, uneven incidence, cooperation with the Treasury, international considerations, and so on are considered. Chapter 16 focuses on the application of

fiscal policy. The link between the state of economic activity and the budget balance is developed, requiring: (1) the standard distinction between automatic and discretionary fiscal responses to macroeconomic developments and, (2) the full employment surplus (deficit) as an indicator of changes in fiscal policy posture. A brief description of the congressional budgetary process is provided to underscore the standard concerns over lags in fiscal policy and overall budgets that are concocted without concern for their macroeconomic consequences. The Congressional Budget Reform Act of 1974 is reviewed with regard to its potential role in the budget-making process. Attention is also devoted to the burdens that government debt may impose, to the role of combination monetary-fiscal policies and, once again, to the monetary aspects of deficit (surplus) finance.

I have received valuable aid from a number of sources in developing this book. Several of my present and former colleagues have read and/or class-tested the text and have provided suggestions that measurably improved the final product. In this regard, Tom Grennes, John Lapp, Michael McElroy, and Richard Williamson deserve special thanks. Valuable suggestions were also provided by Robert Holbrook, Hartly Mellish, James Richardson, Frank Steindl, and, in particular, Donald A. Nichols. The text has also benefited from the comments of my students at North Carolina State University and from the typing assistance of Patti Griffin, Delilah Huber, and Pat Mangum. Regrettably, none of the above can be held accountable for any remaining shortcomings in this book.

Contents

Chapter 1
What Is and
What Should Be

Macroeconomics is the study of *aggregate* economic activity. In contrast to *microeconomics*, which focuses on explaining the economic behavior of small units, such as individual households, individual firms, and individual markets or industries, macroeconomics is concerned with the performance of the economic system *as a whole*. As such, it attempts to explain how, for the entire economic system, the level of employment and output, the level of prices, the rate of growth of output, and the rate of price level change are determined. Presuming that capability, macroeconomics proceeds to provide government policy prescriptions for *improving* the performance of the economic system.

The problems that macroeconomics deals with are among the most prominent concerns of the nation's leaders and the average citizen alike. The breadth of concern for macroeconomic problems is clearly reflected in newspaper headlines that announce: "Prices Rose at a 7 Percent Annual Rate in the First Quarter," "Unemployment Rises for Third Consecutive Month," "Balance of Payments Deficit Widens in Third Quarter," "Output Grew by Only 1.6 Percent in Last 12 Months." Of course, those who lose their jobs during periods of rising unemployment, those who graduate from college and fail to find employment during periods of retarded economic expansion, and those who suffer a reduction in economic well-being because of rising living costs hardly need a news media account of the significance of recession, anemic expansion, or inflation.

Because of their importance, macroeconomic problems are frequently responsible for major public policy actions. Federal budgets are made "expansionary" or "restrictive" in response to economic conditions, and deliberate alterations in the volume of money in circulation are undertaken in order to stimulate or retard economic activity. Meanwhile, always looking for political opportunity, the opposition political party can be expected to provide a critical review of any major macroeconomic policy action the government undertakes. Indeed, while both major political parties in the United States accept the notion that the government is duty bound to use the weapons it has at its disposal to contribute to the economy's vitality, some of the most prominent issues that divide our political parties reflect differences of opinion on how that responsibility should be met. But met it must be, as every candidate for a high federal office is aware.

Recognizing the political opportunity afforded him by several years of sluggish economic expansion during the 1950s, John Kennedy, pledging that he would revitalize the economy, was elected President in 1960. Most economists agree that the government policy actions that were subsequently implemented

1

under the guidance of Kennedy, and later, Lyndon Johnson, contributed substantially to a vigorous expansion of the U.S. economy that continued through
nearly the entire decade following the 1960 election—the longest unbroken expansion the U.S. economy has ever experienced. Still, the government policy engineered expansion of the 1960s must be rated as a qualified success. With the
rapid escalation of U.S. involvement in Vietnam during the mid-1960s, inflationary forces were aroused that have persisted into the mid-1970s. Richard
Nixon, pledging to stop inflation without raising unemployment, won the presi-
dential election in 1968. But much to the detriment of the common well-being,
the administrations of Richard Nixon suffered virulent inflation, excessive unemployment, international payments deficits, an energy crisis, and other economic woes.

   In spite of the policy actions the macroeconomic ills of the last decade have
elicited—and, many would argue, in part *because* of those actions—the economy's
performance has remained unsatisfactory since the late 1960s. As a consequence
of the duration and intensity of the macroeconomic difficulties we have endured,
the government's responses to the forces that have rocked the economy in the
last decade have been the subject of considerable public scrutiny. Reflecting the
general public's concerns, we might wish to ask: What causes an economy to
suffer the ills we have endured? How can we account for the kinds of federal
government intervention in the macroeconomy that we have witnessed in recent
years? Why are some of its policy actions successful and some not? What policies should our leaders undertake in the future?

   These are important questions that no informed citizen can ignore. Fortunately, they are questions that modern macroeconomic analysis can shed a
great deal of light on, even though some important disagreements on the answers
to these and related questions can be found among different analysts. This book
will help us untangle the complexities of modern macroeconomic analysis to
provide the answers that are now available. As a background for our upcoming
analytical journey, the remainder of this chapter concentrates, first, on outlining
the general nature of the analytical procedures employed in macroeconomics
and, then, on reviewing the goals we might want to set for the economy.

THE METHODOLOGY OF MACROECONOMICS— NORMATIVE VERSUS POSITIVE ECONOMICS

In the development of modern macroeconomics, economists have tried to separate
carefully their analysis of how the economic system functions to determine the
volume of output, the general price level, the rate of growth of output, and so on
from assertions about what values those variables *should* have. The first activity
falls in the realm of *positive economics*, often described as the study of "what is."
The second activity, dealing with questions of "what should be," falls in the
realm of *normative economics*. As an application of positive economic analysis,

using an understanding of the internal workings of the economy and the best data sources available, an economist might *predict* that unemployment in the United States will lie between 6 and 7 percent of the labor force next year. With positive analysis the economist might also predict how that unemployment rate could be changed through alternative government policy actions. But positive analysis cannot tell us whether society would be *better off* next year with some different unemployment rate. It is true, of course, that the economist who predicts a 6 to 7 percent unemployment rate might believe society would be better off with a different rate, such as 4 percent or 9 percent. If so, that economist might advocate government policies which positive analysis indicates would move the unemployment rate to the level he thinks *should* prevail for maximum social welfare. But his opinion of what the unemployment rate *should be* reflects his own preferences or value judgments on the link between unemployment and social welfare—that is, it rests on a normative judgment, rather than on objectively determined facts, since we have no way of objectively measuring human happiness.

The primary focus of this text, like the focus of most professional macroeconomists, is on positive analysis. Positive economic analysis has the responsibility of providing a set of generalizations or "laws" that can be used to make valid and useful predictions about the impact of various changes in circumstances. As is the case in all analytical endeavors, the generalizations positive economics provide take the form of "if A, then B" propositions. Such generalizations clearly imply *causality* since they tell us that with the occurrence of a specified event or set of circumstances (A), another specific event (B) will occur. The performance of positive economic analysis is judged by the consistency of its generalizations and their implications with experience. As in all scientific disciplines, a set of macroeconomic laws that yields conclusions (predictions) more consistent with experience will displace one that yields less consistent conclusions.

The Interaction between Positive Analysis and Normative Judgments

While our primary interest is in positive economic analysis, we cannot ignore an unavoidable interaction between positive economics and value judgments. That interaction begins early in the analytical process since the very choice of the problems we want to analyze rests on value judgments. Indeed, the clear-cut concern over unemployment, inflation, and sluggish growth that was voiced on the first page of this chapter reflects a set of normative judgments on the link between employment, price stability, and economic growth on the one hand and social welfare on the other.

Perhaps, more dramatically, but no more fundamentally, the normative concerns of macroeconomics are highlighted when macroeconomics is applied to the formal process of government policy making, for the major responsibility of normative economics is to select a set of government policy goals, the pursuit of which leads to an improvement in society's overall welfare (itself a normative policy goal). By necessity, a great deal of art is involved in selecting a set of goals that adequately reflects the collective desires of society at large, and economic analysis has little to contribute to policy makers' understanding of what society values. Still, the rational selection of a set of goals must rest heavily on the conclusions of *positive* economics since, without an objective understanding of how the macroeconomy functions, policy makers cannot know what potential policy goals are attainable nor the means through which chosen goals may be pursued. The useful application of macroeconomics clearly involves a blending of positive analysis with norms.

While modern macroeconomics involves a fundamental blending of positive analysis with social values, a student of economics should be able to distinguish normative from positive claims and should make a habit of doing so when evaluating economic statements, whether they appear in political speeches, in newspaper columns, or in the utterances of academic economists. Maintaining the important distinction that has been drawn between positive and normative economics, the next section of this chapter outlines the "methodology" employed in positive economic analysis. After that, the chapter concludes with a review of the normative goals policy makers in the United States are presumed to pursue in actual practice.

The Practice of Positive Economics

The practice of positive economic analysis begins when we confront an economic phenomenon we want to explain (changes in meat prices, unemployment, the price level, and so on). Providing an explanation requires: (1) the formation of hypotheses (tentatively accepted assumptions) about the behavior patterns involved, (2) accounting for any interrelationships among the hypotheses specified in step one, and (3) derivation of the implications or predictions logically deducible from the relationships constructed in steps one and two. On completion of step three, we have a *model* for explaining the economic phenomenon of interest. (4) The fourth step consists of testing the predictions our model provides against observed reality.

Probably the most demanding task in the practice of positive analysis is step one, the selection of a set of tentatively accepted assumptions that permits us to *explain* complex reality. The assumptions employed must always provide us with a simplified caricature of reality—that is, *an abstraction* from reality— for the maze of information that confronts us when we observe a real-world phenomenon we wish to explain obscures the fundamental causal relationships we seek. A good model will contain assumptions that capture the essential causal relations involved in producing the phenomenon we wish to explain, so that its predictions will be consistent with observed reality, while ignoring the maze of superfluous information with which reality confronts the observer.

As a simple, familiar, and compelling example of the skillful use of *simplifying* assumptions, we might recall the well-known Newtonian gravitational principle which states that, because of the force of gravity, a free body in space will fall with a constant rate of acceleration of some 32.2 feet per second. That law was developed for a body falling in a vacuum, attracted by just one other body. Still, the predictions it yields are impressively corroborated year after year by students dropping ball bearings in college physics labs. Clearly, the influence on the acceleration of the laboratory ball bearings of an atmosphere, of the gravitional pull of the sun, the moon, the stars and other heavenly bodies, and of the myriad of other things that might act on the ball bearing is small enough to be assumed away if we are seeking a basic understanding of the physics of gravitional attraction. Indeed, the presence of an atmosphere and of other heavenly bodies that can attract our laboratory ball bearings complicates and obscures the causal relationship we seek. The only viable method for obtaining an understanding of the behavior of falling bodies is that of constructing a model which abstracts from the many small forces that affect those bodies while concentrating on the major causal force(s).

Once the basic assumptions in our model have been specified and proper account has been taken of any relationships that link those assumptions, we must complete the model building process by logical deduction of the conclusions that flow from those assumptions. This step requires careful application of the rules of logic since any logical errors we commit can alter the conclusions our model provides. As a consequence, the resulting explanation of an observed phenomenon will be invalid no matter how skillfully the underlying assumptions were chosen. Presuming that we can successfully apply the techniques of logic, our model will provide us with a set of "if A, then B" predictions that we can compare to observed reality.

Familiar Economic Models. Now, if, by chance, our broad discussion of the process of economic model building has left you wondering whether economic analysis is not something practiced by witch doctors or some other modern form of mystic, brief reference to a couple of standard examples of economic models should convince you that you have already worked through the model building process in your basic economics courses. To begin with, you might recall the supply-demand market model you used for determining prices in microeconomics. The construction of that model required the specification of two hypothesized behavioral relations—a supply function and a demand function. On the supply side of the market the quantity of output offered for sale was assumed to be positively related to price, other things held constant, while on the demand side of the market the quantity of output purchased was assumed to be negatively related to price, other things held constant (step one of the analytical process). The hypothesized supply and demand functions were linked (step two of the analytical process) by the market equilibrium condition that requires equality of supply and demand. Completing the market model you were able to deduce (step three) what market price and quantity would prevail with the market in equilibrium and, more importantly, that model provided logical prediction of the impact on price and quantity of a change in circumstances. For example, a change in tastes that raised demand typically produced an increase both in price and in the quantity of output bought and sold.

Turning our attention from microeconomics to macroeconomics, it should be noted that macroeconomic models are distinctive only in that they concentrate on the behavior patterns of *aggregated groupings* of economic units. As such, we will spend a good deal of time analyzing separately the behavior of the household, business, foreign, and government *sectors* of the economy and, then, in examining the interactions among these groupings or sectors to see how the values of important aggregate variables such as output, employment, and the price level are determined. From your introductory macroeconomics course, you may recall the construction of a simple-minded income-determination model that did just that.[1] The simplest macroeconomic model you dealt with probably consisted of the hypothesis that aggregate consumption depends on the level of disposable income, the definition that total spending in a simple economy which has no government and no foreign trade is just the sum of consumption and investment spending, recognition that total spending and income in such an economy are identical, and the equilibrium condition that planned spending must be equal to output. That model allowed you to explain how the equilibrium levels of output and consumption are determined, to find their values, and to predict the impact on overall economic activity of any change in circumstances involving shifts in the consumption or investment functions.

Taxing your memory once more, you may recall that more complete macroeconomic models—those that took account of the economic role of government—not only allowed you to explain how the level of economic activity was determined but also permitted deduction of the aggregate influence on the economy of government policy actions. That is an important accomplishment because most capitalistic systems in the world today have governments that are macroeconomic activists—governments that use their economic muscle to deliberately influence economic aggregates. That activism could not be rationalized if we did not have models that allow us to evaluate the effects of the government's policy actions on economic activity.

No further discussion of the models dealt with in introductory economics should be necessary as evidence that you have already had experience with the model-building process employed in macroeconomics. To complete our discussion of the methodology of macroeconomic analysis we must look now at step four of the analytical process, the testing of our generalizations against observed reality.

---

1 If that basic macroeconomic model defies recall, you need not worry at this stage. It will be carefully reviewed in Chapter 4.

Econometric Models. Among the social sciences, economics is distinctly fortunate in that the phenomena with which it deals are generally quantifiable —that is, they can be measured. As illustrations, we can and do collect *numerical* observations on the level of unemployment, the level of output, the level and rate of change of prices, and a wide array of other variables that macroeconomic analysis deals with. Because economic analysis develops hypothesized relationships between concepts that are measurable, economists can employ the powerful techniques of modern statistics to *quantify* and *test* those hypothesized relationships. The combination of economic theory and statistical analysis, which allows the quantification and testing of economic models, is called *econometrics.*

In the four decades that have elapsed since macroeconomic analysis became a fashionable activity for economists, the theoretical models that macroeconomic analysts employ have been subjected to countless statistical tests. In fact, the reliance on econometric techniques has became so extensive that a full understanding of modern macroeconomics requires, at the least, a nodding acquaintance with those techniques. Of course, a full explanation of the econometric techniques that a skilled economic analyst might employ is outside the scope of this text. However, we can quite easily demonstrate what can be learned through econometric analysis and simultaneously develop an intuitive grasp of the most basic technique employed in econometrics.

As an example of econometric analysis, suppose a researcher sets out to ascertain what determines aggregate consumer spending. While recognizing that a number of other factors (perhaps the interest rate, wealth, family size, and so on) could have some effect on consumption, our researcher *hypothesizes* that aggregate consumption is positively related to the level of aggregate income with the magnitude of other influences on consumption small enough to be ignored. To test that hypothesis, suppose our researcher collects yearly data on aggregate income and aggregate consumption for, say, the period 1965-1975 and plots his income-consumption observations on a graph like Figure 1-1.

The plotted points in Figure 1-1 seem to indicate clearly that the level of aggregate consumer spending rises as the level of aggregate income rises. Further,

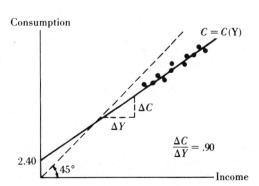

FIGURE 1-1 An Econometrically Fitted Income-Consumption Relation

it appears that a simple straight line "fitted" to the plotted data does a good job of representing the fundamental relationship between income and consumption within the range of observations on those two variables.

It would seem that our econometrician has shown that his hypothesis is consistent with observed reality. *In addition,* he has quantified the relationship between aggregate income and consumption. The vertical intercept of the straight line fitted to the 1965-1975 data points, which serves only as a reference point to indicate the *position* of the consumption function in Figure 1-1, is assumed to have a value of 2.40. The assumed slope (rise over run) of that line is $\Delta C/\Delta Y = .90$, indicating that a $1 million increase in aggregate income would raise consumption by $900,000. Thus, the equation of the straight-line relationship between income and consumption is $C = 2.40 + .90Y$. From the "actual" observations available on income and consumption, our researcher's econometric analysis has provided us with a quantified relationship that can be used to predict the level of consumption that would accompany any observed income level. For example, if income in 1976 should turn out to be $1,500 billion, our income-consumption relation tells us consumption would be $1,352.4 billion.

Since our straight-line function does not fit all the plotted data points perfectly, we should not be shocked if actual consumption in 1976 is a bit different from the predicted value. The fact that observed values of consumption differ from—or, as an econometrician would say, *deviate* from—the values predicted by our straight line suggests that one or more other factors besides income have some influence on consumption. By specifying what those other factors are and building them into our econometric model we might be able to improve its predictions. But, based upon the straight-line relationship in Figure 1-1, $1,352.4 billion is our best prediction of 1976 consumption.

Ordinary Least Squares Regression. The straight line plotted in Figure 1-1, which graphically displays the relationship between income and consumption, is called a *regression line*. The equation of that straight line, which represents the same relationship algebraically, is called a *linear regression equation*. The regression line (equation) fitted to the data points plotted in Figure 1-1 was selected visually; that is, it looked, to the author, like the one straight line that *best* fitted the data points plotted in that figure.

In actual econometric research, linear regression equations are most often fitted using a far more *objective* statistical technique called the *ordinary least squares technique*. In ordinary least squares regression, a set of formulas is employed to derive linear regression equations which, in a particular way, best fit our statistical data. The way in which our derived regression equations best fit can be demonstrated readily with an abbreviated form of our income-consumption example. Like before, we might hypothesize that the value of consumption (C) is dependent only on the value of income (Y). With observations on Y and C we can look for a regression line (or equation) that reveals that relationship. Now, supposing that we have only three observations on income and consumption, as

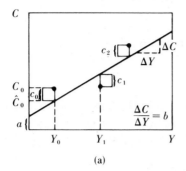
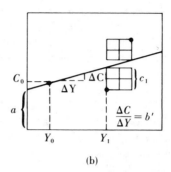

(a)   (b)

FIGURE 1-2 Effect on Sum of Squared Deviations of Altering the Values of the Slope and Intercept of the Regression Equation

graphed in both parts a and b of Figure 1-2, we must find the one straight line that best fits those data points. Of the unlimited number of different straight lines that could be fitted to those data points, two candidates are sketched in Figure 1-2.

Looking at part a of Figure 1-2, we see that when income is at level Y_0, actual observed consumption (C_0) differs or *deviates* from the value predicted by the regression line $(\hat{C}_0)$ by amount c_0; when income is at level Y_1, observed consumption deviates from that predicted by our regression line by amount c_1; and so on. Since we want our models to predict as accurately as possible, we want to choose the regression line (equation) using a criterion that, in some sense, minimizes errors of prediction. With the ordinary least squares technique we obtain the one regression line that *minimizes the sum of the squares* (thus, "least squares") of the deviations of actual observed values of the dependent variable from predicted values. Should the regression line sketched in part a of Figure 1-2 make the total area in the squares of deviations (the shaded squares) as small or smaller than the analogous area that would be associated with any other regression line, it would be the *linear ordinary least squares regression line* relating Y and C. The regression equation for that straight line would, of course, take the form $C_Y = a + bY$ where, with actual data on Y and C, a and b would be numerical constants.[2] The regression line in part b clearly cannot meet the

2 The mathematically inclined student who is interested in statistical techniques should be able to derive the formulas for fitting least squares regression lines to observed data. Suppose we believe any two variables X and Y to be linearly related so a regression equation fitted to the available data on X and Y would appear as $Y_x = a + bX$. Actual values of Y will deviate from the predicted values (Y_x), the amount of deviation for any one observation being $(Y - Y_x)$. It is the sum, over our n observations, of the squared values of all such deviations, that is,

$$\left[\sum_n (Y - Y_x)^2 \right],$$

that we wish to minimize. But, since $Y_x = a + bX$, we may claim we are minimizing $\sum_n (Y -$

least squares criterion since the sum of squared deviations associated with that line is more than twice as large as the analogous value for the regression line in part a. To explain fully why the least squares criterion is used in fitting regression equations would carry us far afield, but we can, in passing, note that it is because of the desirable statistical properties of our estimates of the constants a and b.

If the hypothesis that the value of C is determined by the value of Y is correct, we would expect our regression equation to do a good (statistically significant) job in predicting or *explaining* the variations in the dependent variable C as the independent variable Y varies. The *proportion* of the variation in the dependent variable explained by movement in the independent variable is called the *coefficient of determination*. If all the observations of C and Y values should fall exactly on our regression line, the coefficient of determination, usually denoted symbolically as R^2, would be one—our regression would permit *all* the variation in the dependent variable (C) to be explained by movements in Y. For a regression that explains 90 percent of the variation in Y, $R^2 = .9$; for a regression that explains 80 percent of the variation in Y, $R^2 = .8$; and so on.

If the hypothesized relationship between Y and C were invalid, we would expect our fitted regression equation to do a very poor job of explaining C so that the value of R^2 would be low, perhaps in the range of 0 to .30. However, one note of caution must be added here. The fact that a fitted regression line explains a large proportion of the variation in a variable in which we are interested does not always mean we have discovered a true causal relation between that variable and the independent variable in the regression. Instances of spurious, coincidental correlation are commonplace in economics. For example, it is frequently observed that movements in women's skirt lengths and in the Dow-Jones average of stock prices are closely correlated. It should not be concluded from that observation that changes in hem lengths *cause* changes in stock prices. Be-

---

$a - bX)^2$. Our immediate objective is to derive the a and b values that minimize this term. To do that, we need to take the partial derivatives of $\sum_n (Y - a - bX)^2$ with respect to a and b and

set them equal to zero. This yields,

$$\frac{\partial(\ )}{\partial a} = -2\sum_n (Y - a - bX) = 0$$

$$\frac{\partial(\ )}{\partial b} = -2\sum_n X(Y - a - bX) = 0.$$

Simplifying these equations yields the two equations (for n observations):

$$\sum_n Y = na + b\sum_n X$$

$$\sum_n XY = a\sum_n X + b\sum_n X^2.$$

With data on X and Y inserted, these two equations can be solved simultaneously for the values of a and b that provide the best fitting straight line through the available data points—that is, for the a and b values that provide the straight-line equation that minimizes the sum of squared deviations.

cause of the risk of just such a coincidental correlation, no empirical test can absolutely confirm a hypothesis we want to employ for economic analysis. At best, all that we can claim is that our test results are consistent with our hypothesis. To close our short discussion on the use of empirical tests in the analytical process used in economics, we must conclude that confidence in any hypothesis is attained only by finding that hypothesis consistent with experience in numerous alternative sets of circumstances.

While our primary concern in this text is with the construction of theoretical models, in later chapters we will at times want to support the use of specific behavioral functions in our models by referring to regression equations that have been fitted for those functions. As we have already indicated, in addition to serving as tests of the behavioral patterns we will assume to exist, those regression equations can give us valuable quantification of the assumed responses our models incorporate. While our explanation of regression analysis has been confined to an example in which only two variables were involved, we should note that the need to take account of additional explanatory variables is no cause for alarm. Our regression techniques can easily be extended to test for the importance of multiple explanatory variables.[3] Regression analysis is the most powerful technique we have for performing the tests that permit economics to be an empirical science. If you have developed an intuitive grasp of the nature of regression analysis from the discussion above, you should have no trouble understanding the regression results cited in this text, beginning in Chapter 5.

MACROECONOMIC GOALS

As our positive analysis of the economic system progresses, we will discover why a free market economy may be afflicted by extended periods of underemployment, anemic expansion, and inflation. We will also see just how the federal government can influence the economy's performance. But for now, with our broad summary of the methodology of macroeconomics completed, we must turn our attention to the aggregate economic *goals* our government presumably pursues.

The now-common view that government should try to improve the economy's performance was explicitly recognized by Congress just after World War II in a landmark piece of economic legislation known as the Employment Act of 1946. That act declared that ". . . it is the continuing responsibility of the Federal government to use all practicable means . . . to promote maximum employment, production, and purchasing power." Macroeconomic analysts have considered this act to be a *normative* mandate for active government efforts to maintain

---

3 For a complete treatment of regression analysis, including a discussion of the shortcomings of the ordinary least squares technique and of the sophisticated techniques available for overcoming those shortcomings, consult a standard econometrics text such as J. Johnston, *Econometric Methods* (New York: McGraw-Hill, Inc., 1963).

"full employment," "price stability," and "rapid economic growth." As we shall see, this list of goals is not exhaustive. However, these are generally assumed to be the primary concerns of macroeconomic policy.

Full Employment

Everyone has some notion of what the term *full employment* means. We will try to formalize those notions shortly. In the meantime, the burdens of failing to maintain full employment during much of our history should be vividly apparent. During the depths of the Great Depression, some 25 percent of the U.S. labor force was unemployed and unemployment remained above the 14 percent level throughout the 1930s. The families of the unemployed suffered a loss of current income, and, in most cases, a massive reduction in the savings they had accumulated during their lifetime. Even those workers who remained employed typically worked fewer hours and for lower wages than they would have under normal conditions so that their incomes, too, were reduced. Further, the psychological effect of the inability to find useful work which could provide support for one's family left permanent scars on many breadwinners. While these unfortunate effects of unemployment are most obvious during severe depression, similar effects result from every deviation of employment below the full employment level.

Employment and Output

It should be clear that employment and aggregate output are closely related. By recognizing their interdependence, we can readily develop crude aggregate measures of the economic costs of unemployment. Unemployment of labor is accompanied by idleness of plants and manufacturing equipment (that is, of capital). With productive labor and capital idled, aggregate output is reduced. In Figure 1-3, the movements in U.S. unemployment and output from 1955 through 1974 are charted. In addition, part a of that figure shows the Council of Economic Advisers' measure of *potential output*—the output level that could be achieved with full employment maintained.[4] The gap between actual and potential output crudely illustrates the loss in measured output society suffers from the failure to maintain continuous full employment. In 1962, the Council of

---

4   In the early 1960s, the Council of Economic Advisers chose a *measured* unemployment rate of 4 percent as its full employment target. The potential output measure plotted in Figure 1-3 is then obtained through the following calculation:

$$\text{Potential output} = \begin{pmatrix} 96 \text{ percent of} \\ \text{labor force} \end{pmatrix} \times \begin{pmatrix} \text{standard number} \\ \text{of work hours} \\ \text{per year} \end{pmatrix} \times \begin{pmatrix} \text{average value} \\ \text{of output} \\ \text{per man-hour} \end{pmatrix}.$$

The growth of potential output over time is determined by the growth of the labor force and the growth of labor's productivity.

Billions of dollars

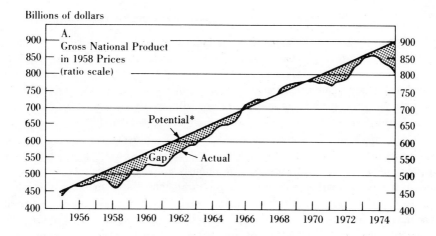

Percent

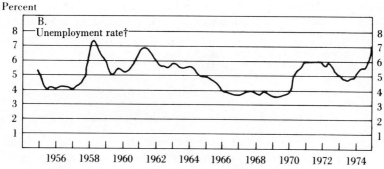

* Trend line of 3½ percent from middle of 1955 to 1962:4, 3¾ percent from 1962:4 to 1965:4, 4 percent from 1965:4 to 1974:4.

† Unemployment as a percent of civilian labor force; seasonally adjusted.

FIGURE 1-3 Gross National Product, Actual and Potential, and Unemployment Rate, 1955-1974. Sources: (Top) (*Business Conditions Digest;* (Bottom) Department of Commerce, *Survey of Current Business.*

Economic Advisers estimated that the cost of the four postwar recessions the United States had experienced to that date was some $172 billion in lost output (in 1958 prices). The data plotted in Figure 1-3 indicate that the loss from 1963 to 1974 was some $215 billion! It is no wonder the maintenance of full employment is a primary macroeconomic policy goal.[5]

5 For a critical review of the Council of Economic Advisers' technique of estimating the gap between actual and potential GNP and an alternative set of estimates of that gap, see Edward F. Denison, "Has the Potential Output of the U.S. Economy Been Misstated?" *Monthly Labor Review,* December 1974, pp. 34-42.

The Meaning of Full Employment

Having accepted full employment as an important policy goal, we must define precisely what full employment means. To begin with, we can define full employment as the absence of any *involuntary* unemployment. In turn, we will assert that involuntary unemployment exists when some workers who would willingly work at the prevailing wage employers are willing to pay cannot find employment. Thus, full employment exists when there are jobs available for all who are willing to work at the prevailing level of wages employers are willing to pay. With this definition of full employment, no economist would suggest that every member of the labor force must be continuously employed. It is recognized that, unlike the stock market and some agricultural commodity markets, the labor market is not a centralized auction market where offers to buy and offers to sell are readily matched. Because of imperfections in that market, notably the lack of readily available information on job vacancies and unemployed workers plus the lack of mobility on the part of labor, some unemployment must exist continuously if the labor market is to perform satisfactorily the socially desirable function of allocating labor to its most productive use. The important question for macroeconomics is how much measured unemployment we must tolerate at full employment due to those imperfections. Enroute to providing an answer to that question we will review the linkages between labor market imperfections and unemployment.

Search Unemployment and Structural Unemployment

No work seeker can know with certainty the wage offers that would be available to him from different employers. He can obtain information on job opportunities only by "searching" in the labor market—that is, by *sampling* job opportunities. Often an employed worker must quit the job he holds to search for more rewarding employment. In point of fact, a perusal of unemployment data typically shows that a large fraction of the pool of unemployed consists of individuals who have voluntarily quit their last job. Once a worker has terminated his previous employment and entered the unemployment pool, his self-interest would compel him to sample job openings as long as the expected return from an additional sample is greater than the loss of current income from not accepting the best job offer already received. The job search procedure takes time and during that time the job seeker will be counted as unemployed.

In addition to voluntary quits, we find many *laid-off* work seekers in the unemployment pool as a result of the normal functioning of a market economy. Shifts in demand for products which, in turn, reduce the need for labor in some industries while raising it in others; changes in production techniques that alter labor requirements; government imposition of restrictions on production that induce shutdowns; and a host of other disturbances that are normal occurrences in a modern economic system result in the involuntary termination of employment. Like the voluntarily unemployed job seeker, once a laid-off worker enters the unemployment pool it is in his own best interest to remain unemployed temporarily as he searches for a suitable job slot. The same can be said for new entrants into the labor pool. Job search time is demanded by self-interest and, while searching, a job seeker is counted as unemployed.

The kind of temporary unemployment just described, which coexists with unfilled job vacancies, has traditionally been labeled *frictional unemployment*. With growing frequency in recent years, it has been referred to as *search unemployment* in recognition of the basic justification for its existence. While search unemployment must always leave a significant fraction of the labor force unemployed, that unemployment cannot be considered an unmitigated evil either from an individual or a social perspective. The search process allows individuals to gravitate toward better employment opportunities—those in which they will be paid better because the *market value* of their production, reflecting society's evaluation of that production, is higher. Thus, the job search process provides higher wages to the work seeker and an enhanced value of production for society.

In addition to search unemployment, our summary measures of unemployment always reflect some *structural unemployment*. When shifts in product demand or changes in production techniques displace workers, who then cannot find alternative employment because they lack suitable skills or geographic mobility, those workers are structurally unemployed. Teenagers, the aged, the handicapped, and those who live in geographic areas well known for limited opportunity (such as Appalachia) are the common victims of this form of unemployment.

The Full Employment Level of Measured Unemployment

Because of the existence of structural and search unemployment, a positive level of measured unemployment must be accepted as full employment. But, determining the precise level of measured unemployment that we must tolerate as a reflection of the sum of structural and search unemployment is a difficult task. In the early 1960s, an "official" target unemployment rate of 4 percent was judged to be "reasonable and prudent" by the Council of Economic Advisers.[6] It was thought that a 4 percent unemployment rate could be achieved without producing significant upward pressure on prices. But, in view of changes in the structure of the labor market in recent years and our recent experience with inflation, the target value for unemployment has gradually been revised upward until a number of government officials and economists have suggested that an unemployment rate for the United States as high as 5 percent is acceptable and that any lower unemployment rate would arouse inflation forces.

6 *Economic Report of the President* (Washington, D.C.: U.S. Government Printing Office, 1962), p. 46.

While recognizing that it is impossible to pin down a precise numerical value for the full employment level of the measured unemployment rate, most every economic analyst would currently agree to a target unemployment rate somewhere between 4 and 5 percent of the labor force. The closer the economy presses to the lower limit of that range, the stronger we would expect upward pressures on the price level to become. Conversely, a movement of the unemployment rate toward the upper limit of that range arouses concern over the foregone production society could enjoy with unemployment reduced.

From a brief look at the postwar record, it is apparent that the economy's actual employment performance has frequently fallen short of our ideal. Between 1948 and 1974 unemployment averaged 4.8 percent of the labor force, but in 13 of those 27 years unemployment was above the 5 percent level. Of course, a primary concern of macroeconomic analysis is to explain why the actual unemployment rate is frequently above the level necessary to accommodate structural unemployment and an optimal volume of search unemployment. It is that additional unemployment which economy-stimulating government policy actions aim at eliminating.

Price Stability

Prices serve a resource allocation function of paramount importance in a capitalistic economic system. Rising prices in markets where demand exceeds supply call additional productive resources into those markets and reduce demand pressures. Falling prices in markets where supply exceeds demand serve as a signal for resources to leave such markets and for buyers to raise their purchases. It is clearly not the prevention of movements of individual prices or of what we refer to as *relative* prices that macroeconomic policy should seek since prices could not serve their allocative function in that case. Yet, it is a goal of macroeconomic policy to restrict movement in the average or *absolute* price level. Relative prices may be left free to change (for example, the price of oil may be rising while that of electronic calculators is falling) so that the allocative role of prices is served while the average price level remains reasonably stable. It remains for us to determine what reasonable price stability denotes.

From the end of the Korean War in 1954 until the middle of the 1960s, the U.S. price level *crept* upward at a moderate average rate of some 2 percent annually. That rate of *creeping inflation* evoked only mild concern. But during the late 1960s, the annual rate of price rise had accelerated to over 5 percent per year and concern over inflation become both widespread and intense. With "double digit" inflation rates in recent years, the goal of price stability has acquired a loftier status in the mid-1970s than it had enjoyed at any time since the start of the Korean War. Thus, judging from historical experience it appears that society and its policy makers are willing to tolerate a creeping inflation rate (say, 1 to 2 percent annually) while deeming higher inflation rates, like those we have experienced since the late 1960s, unacceptable. While we will have considerably more to say about controlling the price level as we proceed, it must be recognized that *reasonable* stability in the general price level is widely accepted as an important macroeconomic policy goal.

Rapid Economic Growth

Our third macroeconomic goal, rapid economic growth, has enjoyed an unquestioned position of importance for much of our history. With the rate of economic growth typically measured by the percentage rate of increase in output per capita, growth has been looked upon as synonymous with an improvement in society's well-being. It has been widely recognized that rising levels of per capita income allow the achievement of higher levels of private consumption; the provision of a larger volume of such public goods as education, national defense, and parks; the enjoyment of an increasing amount of the important commodity leisure as increasing productive capacity permits a reduction in the work-week; and the provision of resources for offering aid to less developed countries. In addition, we have long recognized that economic growth is closely tied to another of our goals, the maintenance of full employment. The labor force expands with the population, and labor-saving innovations tend to free labor from productive use. Maintaining full employment in the face of these forces has required the absorption of a volume of output that has grown briskly over time.

Still, in recent years the devotion to growth that we inherited from a simpler age has lost its near-universal grip. It has become increasingly apparent that economic growth, as traditionally measured, imposes some painful burdens on society as well as benefits. Polluted air and water; unsightly scars on the land where forests have been cleared and where minerals and rocks have been gouged out; beaches littered with cans, bottles, and oil residue; congested and noisy streets—these have been the by-products of rapid growth. With recognition of the unpleasant—indeed, some even life-threatening—by-products of growth, it has become fashionable to argue that far too much attention has been devoted to the production of *things* and too little attention to the quality of life. More dramatically, citing the environmental damage and mineral resource depletion that rising output levels portend, numerous ecologists have called for no-growth policies to preserve resources (including our scarce endowments of clean air and water).

The issues raised by the antigrowth forces are vital and cannot be ignored. Doubtless, it is true that for much of our history we have failed to recognize fully the overall costs that the pursuit of ever-higher levels of measured output has generated. Indeed, even now we know relatively little about the total environmental impact of most production processes. Still, we must recognize that a rational growth policy, one aimed at maximizing society's overall welfare, cannot ignore the heavy costs of environmental protection. Maintaining the cleanliness and purity of our air, water, and land requires a diversion of resources away from producing other goods and services which, as revealed by their positive market prices, society values. Likewise, slowing production to save our exhaustible mineral resources requires society to forgo valued current consumption. Rationality demands that we recognize these costs as well as the costs of environmental destruction. We cannot ignore the typical household's quest for a higher living standard—a quest which generally calls for the extra leisure time and additional manufactured goods that growth as traditionally measured provides.

There is, of course, no question but that we need to take account of the negative by-products of growth. Output growth can enhance society's welfare only if the value of that increased output more than covers the total cost to society of producing that output, including the value of the negative by-products generated in the production process or the cost of eliminating those by-products. Thus, if the ultimate concern of economic policy is social welfare, we should strive to permit output growth only in those lines of production that will provide a *net* benefit to society after provision for any unpleasant by-products of that growth. The value to society of increasing volumes of net output per capita still prevents us from relinquishing rapid growth as an important goal, but we now clearly recognize the need for new measures of output that adjust our production totals to allow for the destruction of our limited and exhaustible resources.

Other Policy Goals

There are, of course, additional socially desirable goals with which the informed citizen must concern himself. A partial list would include *balance-of-payments equilibrium*, an equitable distribution of income, and freedom of choice (both in economic and noneconomic matters). The goal of freedom of choice is not clearly macroeconomic in nature so the requirements for assuring that freedom will not be treated at any length in this text. However, it should be recognized that economic woes can and have contributed to dramatic losses of freedom. The Bolshevik Revolution in Russia, the rise of Hitler in depression-torn Germany, and the communist takeover in Cuba stemmed in large part from seething dissatisfaction with economic conditions.

Like freedom of choice, the goal of maintaining an equitable distribution of income is hardly an exclusive concern of macroeconomics. But government policy actions aimed at controlling the economy (particularly those that involve tax and government spending changes) do affect the income distribution, and choices among alternative policy actions are influenced by their distributional impacts. Certainly, no macroeconomic analyst can ignore the goal of equity in the distribution of income, and we will have occasion in this text to see how distributional concerns have impinged on actual policy actions.

To close our introductory discussion on the goals macroeconomic policy makers must concern themselves with, a brief discussion of the goal of balance-of-payments equilibrium is in order since, historically, macroeconomic policy actions have often been undertaken in order to affect the balance of payments, and since policies aimed at achieving other goals have frequently been constrained by balance-of-payments considerations. By allowing each country to specialize in the production of those commodities in which its relative efficiency is greatest, trade among countries allows total world production to increase. As a consequence, each trading country can enjoy a greater volume of real goods and services than would be possible without international trade. But for a country to continue enjoying a desirable volume of international trade, it must maintain *balance-of-payments equilibrium*.

While we do not need to involve ourselves in the complexities of the concept of balance-of-payments equilibrium at this point in time (that topic is treated in Chapter 11), we should note that under the system of international financial arrangements that prevailed until the late 1960s, balance-of-payments considerations were a fundamental concern of the nation's macroeconomic policy makers. Since the end of the 1960s, the international monetary system has been subjected to a traumatic and convulsive reordering that has, to a substantial extent, replaced the need for conscious macroeconomic policy actions aimed at balance-of-payments control with an automatic mechanism for maintaining balance-of-payments equilibrium. Still, the need for balance-of-payments equilibrium remains and the status of the balance of payments continues to receive a great deal of attention.

SUMMARY

As indicated in this introductory chapter, the remainder of this text will be concerned with explaining how public policy may contribute to the attainment of a number of important goals, including minimum unemployment (maximum output), price level stability, growth in per capita output, and, to some extent, balance-of-payments equilibrium. While such policy goals are sometimes complementary, as in the case of full employment and rapid growth, inconsistencies cannot be ruled out. There is substantial evidence, for example, that full employment and price stability are incompatible—that it may not be possible to achieve both of those goals. Moreover, to pursue any goal or set of goals the government must know how its policy actions affect the economy. Uncertainty with respect to the size and timing of impact of public policy actions limits government's ability to improve the economy's performance. Of course, the degree to which policy makers succeed in achieving the goals listed above is important to each of us since our individual as well as collective economic well-being depends heavily on the state of the economy as a whole.

It is worth reemphasizing the point that the methods through which government can pursue its chosen goals cannot be rationalized without understanding the functioning, at the macroeconomic level, of the economic system. To gain an understanding of how the system does work and, thus, of how government can affect the outcome of the economic process, we must build simplified models of the economy. The components of these models and the predictions the models provide must survive the scrutiny of careful statistical testing if we are to have confidence in our policy actions.

Taking a brief look ahead, in Chapter 2 we will become familiar with a set of aggregate production and income measures that macroeconomists have employed intensively in constructing, testing, and refining their models. Chapter 3 provides an intensive look at available measures of unemployment, employment, and the price level. Chapter 4 then begins our direct involvement in the process of macroeconomic model building.

QUESTIONS

1. What is the distinction between macroeconomics and microeconomics?
2. What is positive economics?
3. Try to determine whether the following statements are positive or normative and explain why.
   a. Smoking is bad for your health.
   b. According to the Brookings model of the U.S. economy, unemployment in 1978 will be 4.8 percent.
   c. The government should reduce taxes next year to stimulate the economy.
   d. The government should set strict emission limitations on automobiles.
   Do any of the statements mix norms and positive analysis?
4. The proposition that consumption depends on income is common to all macroeconomic models. How might you test this hypothesis?
5. Suppose that regressing consumption on income provided the function

   $$C = 31.4 + .73Y \text{ with } R^2 = .974.$$

   Explain these results.
6. Whose preferences should government's macroeconomic goals reflect, society's or those of the Council of Economic Advisers?
7. Select two macroeconomic goals and account for their importance.
8. Would you prefer to buy drinks in no-deposit bottles and cans or in containers that require payment of a deposit that is refundable? Why? What difference would it make in the overall level of U.S. output which kind of container was used?

SUGGESTED READING

Asimov, Isaac. *Asimov's Guide to Science.* New York: Basic Books, Inc., 1972, Chapter 1.

Blaug, Mark. *Economic Theory in Retrospect.* Homewood, Ill.: Richard D. Irwin, Inc., 1968, Chapter 16.

Bronfenbrenner, Martin. "A 'Middlebrow' Introduction to Economic Methodology," in S. R. Krup (ed.), *The Structure of Economic Science*. Englewood Cliffs, N.J.: Prentice-Hall, Inc., 1966, pp. 5-24.

"The Employment Act: Twenty Years of Policy Experience," *Economic Report of the President*. Washington, D.C.: U.S. Government Printing Office, January 1966, Chapter 7.

Friedman, Milton. *Essays in Positive Economics*. Chicago: University of Chicago Press, 1953, Chapter 1.

Huff, D. *How to Lie with Statistics*. New York: W. W. Norton & Co., 1954.

Johnston, J. *Econometric Methods*. New York: McGraw-Hill, Inc., 1963, Chapters 1 and 2.

Popper, Karl. "On the Sources of Knowledge and Ignorance," in *Conjectures and Refutations: The Growth of Scientific Knowledge*. New York: Harper & Row, 1968, pp. 3-30.

Robinson, Joan. *Economic Philosophy*. New York: Anchor Books, 1964, Chapter 1.

White, William H. "Econometric Models: General Considerations," in S. Mitra (ed.), *Dimensions of Macroeconomics*. New York: Random House, 1971, pp. 38-54.

Wonnacott, T. H., and R. J. Wonnacott. *Introductory Statistics for Business and Economics*. New York: John Wiley & Sons, Inc., 1972, Chapters 11-13.

Chapter 2
Measurement 1 –
the National Income
and Product Accounts

The most important data for macroeconomic analysis and policy making appear in the national income and product accounts compiled by the Bureau of Economic Analysis in the Department of Commerce.[1] These national accounts are of quite modern origin as they have been compiled and published on a regular basis only since World War II. While a number of other analysts contributed to the development of national income accounting, the U.S. accounts themselves were created under the guidance of Simon Kuznets.[2] In tribute to the importance of his creative efforts, Kuznets was awarded the Nobel prize in economics in 1971.

Like the accounting systems employed by private business firms, the national income and product accounts attempt to provide a summary description of economic performance—specifically, of the *production* performance of the aggregate economy. As such, the values of a number of variables in which we will be intensely interested—measures of national output, national income, consumption, investment, and so on—appear in those accounts. While the purpose of the national accounts is to measure and describe aggregate economic activity rather than to explain it, a skilled macroeconomic analyst can often gain valuable insights into the sources of economic disturbances with a quick review of the data in those accounts. For example, with a brief reference to the national income accounts we can often tentatively determine whether a decline in investment or a rise in private saving is responsible for a recession. Furthermore, when more refined analysis is required to explain macroeconomic events, the national income and product accounts typically serve both as the prime source of descriptive evidence on the nature of those events and as the source of data needed to test and quantify our theoretical explanations of those real-world events. Needless to say, government policy makers keep a close watch on the

---

1 National income and product statistics appear regularly in the *Survey of Current Business*, published monthly by the Department of Commerce. The July issue each year is a summary issue.

2 Kuznets' pioneering work on national accounts for the United States is recorded in his two-volume tome, *National Income and Its Composition, 1919-1938* (New York: National Bureau of Economic Research, 1941).

national accounts as they evaluate the success of past policy actions and formulate policy for the future. Likewise, the heads of business enterprises use the national accounts in their efforts to predict changes in general economic conditions and, thus, in the markets for their products. The obvious importance of the national income and product accounts compels us to become familiar with them even though studying the accounts can be somewhat tedious.

Our primary objectives in working with the national accounts will be, first, to gain an understanding of the conceptual foundations of national income accounting and, second, to familiarize ourselves with the format and content of the actual U.S. national accounts. As we work with the national accounts, we will find that a number of rather arbitrary decisions on the handling of specific items within those accounts must be made. Still, the presumptions employed in constructing the national income and product measures rest, for the most part, on sound analytical footing. If, while studying the national accounts, we can keep in mind the idea that their central objective is the measurement of the current *production* performance of the economy, some otherwise puzzling accounting decisions will make more sense.[3]

THE COMPONENTS OF CURRENT PRODUCTION

In organizing our measures of the economy's aggregate production and income, an unlimited number of classification schemes are possible. Income and output could be measured and reported on a regional basis, subdivided, say, into income and output originating in the Southeast, Southwest, Northeast, and Northwest. Alternatively, production and income could be classified according to industrial sources or according to whether it is generated during daylight hours or darkness. The classification scheme we employ must be dictated by the phenomena we want to explain and by our theoretical notions of how those phenomena occur.

The national income and product accounts were designed to provide data on those variables that macroeconomic theory tells us are important in explaining the overall level of economic activity, the course of price level changes, and the rate of economic expansion. The models most frequently employed in macroeconomic analysis subdivide the aggregate economy into four sectors: the household, business, foreign, and government sectors. Correspondingly, the measures of total output in the national income and product accounts are subdivided into consumption (by households), investment (by business firms), net exports in the foreign sector, and government purchases. Each of these component parts of aggregate output (the sum of which captures all of current output) is explained

---

3   Not infrequently, the measures of production provided in the national accounts are employed in roles for which they are ill suited. Most notably, production measures are often viewed as indicators of social welfare so that quantitative social welfare comparisons can be made between countries and across time. After describing the construction of the national accounts, attention will be focused on the limitations from which those accounts suffer.

below. On the income side of the national income and product accounts, aggregate income is divided according to type of income. That subdivision is formally explained beginning on page 36.

Consumption

Consumption, as measured in the national income and product accounts, consists of the market value of purchases of those goods and services that yield human satisfaction directly. For example, the value of a pound of hamburger bought by a private household counts as personal consumption spending. The same pound of hamburger bought by the local spaghetti parlor is not counted as consumption until its value is reflected in the price of a spaghetti dinner, which yields satisfaction directly.

While the economy's output of consumer products is measured by summing the expenditures made by all households and nonprofit institutions, it must be recognized that consumer spending does not, in every case, measure the true "using up" of consumer goods. The reason is that the household sector devotes a sizable fraction of its total spending to the purchase of *durable* goods like cars, home appliances, furniture, and so on. Since those commodities have service lives greater than our 1-year accounting period, households truly *use up* only a fraction of the consumer durables purchased during any selected accounting period. A household's purchase of a $4,000 automobile adds $4,000 to our measure of consumption when the purchase is made. However, if the car's life is 8 years, the household actually enjoys a stream of transportation services over that 8-year period. On average, only one-eighth ($500) of the value of the car is used up, providing transportation services, each year.

A true measure of the yield of consumer services that provide satisfaction directly should obviously count only the annual *use value* of consumer durables along with the full purchase value of those other *nondurable* consumer purchases which presumably are fully used up during the accounting period. But because of the insurmountable statistical difficulties that would be encountered in trying to measure the value of the services rendered each year by the massive accumulated stock of consumer durables, national income accountants treat durable purchases like other consumer expenditures, as though the durable goods acquired were fully consumed in one accounting period.

Investment

Investment is, essentially, the value of spending on newly produced, physical "capital goods" acquired for the purpose of providing a stream of productive services in the future. In the national income accounts, investment takes the form of spending on plants and equipment, inventories, and residential construction. Since the objective of the national accounts is the measurement of current production, only acquisitions of *newly produced* capital goods are counted as investment. The purchase by firm Z of an already existing plant, previously owned by firm X, reflects no current production. One firm's investment is matched by another firm's disinvestment. Similarly, purchases of stocks, bonds, and other interest-yielding *financial* assets, representing "financial investment," are excluded from the measure of investment recorded in the national income and product accounts since, again, such financial investment by a security buyer is offset by the equivalent disinvestment of the security seller (or issuer of *new* securities).[4]

The total expenditure in one period on newly produced, physical capital goods is labeled *gross investment*. A part of every period's gross investment is absorbed in the *replacement* of capital goods that wear out, become obsolete, or are accidentally destroyed during that period. The rest represents a net addition to the capital stock and is labeled *net investment*.

Net Exports

Net exports measures the difference in the value of exports and imports. U.S. exports consist of domestically produced goods and services which are sold abroad. Imports, on the other hand, consist of foreign produced goods and services bought by economic units in this country. U.S. exports must be included in the measure of U.S. production, while imports should be excluded. Since our measured values of household consumption, business investment, and so on include expenditures on imported items, total imports must be subtracted from our summary measures of the components of *domestic* output if those measures are not to overstate the level of that output.

Government Purchases

Government purchases consist of purchases by federal, state, and local government units. The government buys vast quantities of finished products including tanks and planes, bridges, schools, roads, and so on. In addition, it buys a substantial volume of productive factor inputs for use in its own "production" activities (think of the ink, paper, and manpower purchased by the Pentagon, your governor's office, and city hall). Unfortunately for the national income accountant, the "output" of most government operations is not exchanged in markets where a measure of its value (a market price) can be observed. The relatively small component of government production that does appear in markets, such as government produced electric power, transit service, and postal service, is valued at market prices just as is private business production. For lack of a better approximation, the rest is assumed to equal the factor cost of providing governmental functions. Thus, the value of most of that portion of the nation's production that is absorbed in government use is set equal to the sum of government spending on factor inputs and finished products.

---

4 In the process of buying and selling existing assets, real or financial, some commissions and fees, representing payments for services currently rendered, are typically generated. The value of such "production" is included in the national accounts.

GROSS NATIONAL PRODUCT—
ITS MEANING AND MEASUREMENT

Shifting our concern from the components of aggregate production to the most frequently cited summary measure of production, we need to take a close look at the concept of gross national product. As the name implies, *Gross National Product* (often abbreviated as GNP) is the broadest measure of an economic system's aggregate production performance. By definition, GNP is the total *dollar* value of all *final* goods and services produced by the economy during a specified time period, typically one year.

While this definition of GNP is straightforward, some elements of that definition are deserving of elaboration. First, it is worth noting that GNP must be measured in dollar terms because of the impossibility of adding physical quantities of different commodities. It is not meaningful, for example, to compute the sum of (3 apples + 4 dozen eggs + 5 autos).[5] In addition, great care is required to ensure that GNP figures measure just the value of *final* products, avoiding the problem of double counting. A *final good* is one that is produced during the observed accounting period but not resold during that period. Items purchased for resale, whether destined for additional processing or not, are *intermediate goods*. For example, water bought for household use is a final good. Water bought by a manufacturing firm, the cost of which will be reflected in the sales price of the firm's product, is an intermediate good. If we counted in GNP both the value of the firm's water purchases and of its output (the price of which includes provision for the cost of water used in production), we would be overstating the value of GNP. We would have, in fact, counted the value of water purchased by this firm twice. (Do the same claims hold for the household versus spaghetti parlor purchase of hamburger on page 25?)

Finally, the items counted in GNP must be actually *produced* during the accounting period. If a wave of nostalgia prompts me to purchase a 1950 Ford from you, that purchase entails no current production and must not be counted in GNP. In contrast, my purchase of a *new* Ford would reflect current production and must be counted in GNP.

Conceptual Techniques for Computing GNP

There are three important conceptual techniques that can be used to compute a value for GNP. They are commonly designated the *expenditure, income,* and *value added* techniques.

---

5 The term "National" in gross national product indicates that our interest is in measuring the output of the residents (nationals) of a particular country. Thus, U.S. measures of output include the production (reflected by their earnings) of Americans that occurs abroad while excluding some income earned in the United States by foreign residents.

The Expenditure and Income Techniques. If GNP is the dollar value of all final goods and services currently produced, we certainly should be able to measure GNP by adding up all spending on final products during the accounting period. Doing so provides an *expenditure approach* measure of production. Alternatively, since for every dollar of spending on final products there must be a dollar *received*, we should also be able to obtain a value for GNP by adding up all *incomes* generated during the accounting period—that is, by using the *income approach.*

The *circular flow* diagram in Figure 2-1 illustrates the validity of the expenditure and income approaches to measuring the value of output and also

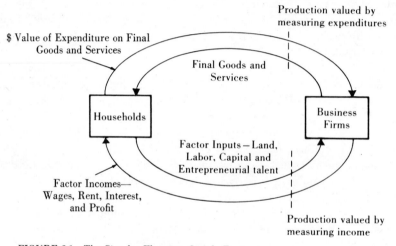

FIGURE 2-1 The Circular Flow in a Simple Economy

shows the basic equivalence of those two measurement techniques. In the simple economic system represented by Figure 2-1, there are only two sectors. All production activity is assumed to take place in business firms, which are consolidated in the *business sector*, while all output is shown absorbed by the *household sector*. Business firms combine factor inputs—land, labor, capital, and entrepreneurial talent—to produce a flow of final goods and services. Looking at the upper loop of the flow diagram, it is clear that the dollar flow of household expenditures on final products must be identical to the dollar value of the flow of final goods and services which businesses produce and sell to households. Even if it is difficult to measure output directly, we can measure its value indirectly simply by measuring total dollar spending on final products. But what becomes of those revenues which business firms receive from households? The lower loop of our flow diagram answers that question graphically. The factor inputs business firms use in the production process must be hired from households. In return for the factor services they provide, households receive a flow of income—wages for labor, rent for property, interest for money capital, and profit as the reward to entrepreneurial talent. Those income payments completely *exhaust* the business sector's revenues since any business revenues left over after payment of wages, rent, and interest are, by definition, fully absorbed by profit which is income accruing to the households that own business firms. Once again, it is easy to see that, even though a direct measure of output is difficult, we can readily measure the value of output indirectly, in this case by measuring the value of income generated in the production process.

For the simple economy represented by the flow diagram in Figure 2-1, the expenditure and income techniques provide equally valid measures of aggregate economic activity. Indeed, for that simple economy measured output and income are numerically identical. That identity is invalidated as we take account of the real-world complications (such as the existence of a government and foreign sector) that are reflected in the actual U.S. national accounts. But the expenditure and income approaches remain equally valid methods of measuring aggregate economic activity.

The Value Added Technique.   As well as employing basic factor inputs (land, labor, and so on), business firms purchase *intermediate* commodity and service inputs from other firms. In creating their own products then, firms *add value* to the intermediate inputs they receive from other firms. To measure one firm's contribution to current production, the value of the intermediate commodity and service inputs it purchases must be subtracted from the value of its own output, the difference being the firm's *value added*. As a simple example, a college bookstore that buys an economics text (an intermediate good) for $8 and resells it for $10 has contributed $2 worth of *value added* to the book.

Agriculture, mining, and similar basic industries provide huge volumes of raw material inputs to the U.S. economy. These basic inputs move through successive layers of industry which process them into new forms until, ultimately, they emerge transformed into homes, automobiles, clothing, machine tools, office buildings, and other *final* products. In each stage of the production process, value is added to the material and service inputs from the preceding stage. By simply adding up the amounts of value added at each production stage where market transactions take place, we can derive a measure of the total dollar value of current (final goods and services) production.

Table 2-1 provides a simple numerical example of a national income measurement task. In addition to demonstrating the equivalence of the expenditure, income, and value added techniques of measuring production, that concrete numerical example should make the national income accounting concepts we have reviewed more meaningful.

The economic system represented in Table 2-1 is very simple, producing only two final products. One of the products is an investment or capital good, say, a bread-making machine, with an unlimited life. The other is the consumer product, bread. Table 2-1 lists the various market transactions that take place

TABLE 2-1 DETERMINATION OF GNP BY EXPENDITURE, INCOME, AND VALUE ADDED TECHNIQUES

Good (1)	Seller (2)	Buyer (3)	Value of Transaction (4)	Value Added (5)	Expenditure on Final Good (6)	Factor Earnings (Incomes) (7)
Steel	Steel company	Producer of bread-making machines	$ 20	$20	—	$20
Bread-making machine	Producer of bread-making machines	Bread-making company	50	30	$50	30
Wheat	Wheat-growing farmer	Flour-producing mill	5	5	—	5
Flour	Flour-producing mill	Bread-making company	10	5	—	5
Bread	Bread-making company	Retail groceries	20	10	—	10
Bread	Retail groceries	Consumers	25	5	25	5
Total dollar value of transactions			$130			
Gross national product			—	$75	$75	$75

in producing these two final goods during the chosen accounting period. The first row shows the sale of $20 worth of steel to a firm that manufactures bread-making machines. The second row shows this manufacturing firm selling bread-making machines to the bread company for $50. The third row shows a wheat grower selling his product to a flour-producing mill, with the remaining rows showing the successive market transactions that take place in the process of producing and selling bread.

Column 5 shows the *value added* to purchased factor inputs as they are processed by the listed firms. The first entry shows, assuming that the steel company buys nothing from other firms, that its value added is $20. The company that manufactures bread-making machines buys steel for $20, and turns the steel into break-making machinery which it sells for $50. The value added by the bread-machine company then is $30. The value added by the wheat farmer, assuming he buys nothing from other firms, is the full $5 sales price of his wheat. The flour mill is shown paying $5 for the wheat which it turns into flour and resells for $10. The mill's value added then is $5. Continuing down column 5 yields value-added figures of $10 for the firm that transforms the flour into bread and $5 for the retailers who display and sell bread to consumers, the *final* purchasers of the bread. GNP, which is simply the sum of the value added contributions of all our firms, is $75.

By looking at column 6, we see that the same GNP figure can be obtained by adding up all expenditures on *final* goods and services. Again, there are only two items in our example that are final goods—goods produced during the accounting period but not resold—and they are bread-making machines and bread sold to consumers. Adding the $50 expenditure on bread-making machines to the $25 consumer expenditure on bread yields a value of $75 for GNP.

Finally, GNP can be computed by adding the factor payments (incomes) that appear in column 7. Interestingly, the factor income figures in any one row are identical to the value added figures in that row. That equality is not sheer coincidence—a moment's reflection on the entries in any row will explain that equality (or identity). The total revenue the flour mill in row 4 received for sales of flour was $10. However, $5 of that went into payments for the intermediate input of wheat purchased from the farmer in row 3. Only $5 was left for income payments to the factor inputs used by the mill. Out of that $5 must come wages for labor, rent for use of property, and interest for use of borrowed funds. Any leftover revenue is, by definition, fully absorbed by profit, which is another factor income payment. Thus, all of the difference between total revenues and payments to other firms for intermediate inputs (that is, the full amount of value added) goes to factor earnings.

In the actual U.S. accounts, there are, as we will see, a few complications that must be taken into account in computing GNP using the alternative techniques we have described. Nevertheless, GNP figures can be obtained using any of the three methods illustrated in our simple example. Before leaving that simple example, you should spend a few minutes looking at column 4 and thinking about the sources of double counting in the $130 total value of all transactions obtained by summing the entries in that column.

THE ACTUAL U.S. NATIONAL INCOME AND PRODUCT ACCOUNTS

We now need to concentrate our attention on the actual computation of the output and income values that appear in the national income and product accounts for the United States. We will concern ourselves only with calculating those values using the expenditure and income approaches. An actual sample account for the United States (1974 data) appears in Table 2-2.

GNP from the Expenditure (Product) Side

From the expenditure side of the accounts, we know that a value for GNP can be obtained by adding up all spending on final goods and services. Consistent with the classification scheme described earlier, our total expenditure measure of output can be broken up into consumption spending, investment spending, net exports, and government spending. Thus, for measured values of consumption

TABLE 2-2   THE NATIONAL INCOME AND PRODUCT ACCOUNTS (1974)

A.   GNP from the Expenditure Side
(in billions of dollars)

1. Personal consumption expenditures			876.7
2. Durable goods		127.5	
3. Nondurable goods		380.2	
4. Services		369.0	
5. Gross private domestic investment			209.4
6. Fixed investment		195.2	
7. Nonresidential	149.2		
8. Structures	52.0		
9. Producers' durable equipment	97.1		
10. Residential structures	46.0		
11. Change in business inventories		14.2	
12. Net exports of goods and services			2.0
13. Exports		139.9	
14. Imports		138.0	
15. Government purchases of goods and services			309.2
16. Federal		116.9	
17. National defense	78.7		
18. Other	38.2		
19. State and local		192.3	
20. Gross national product			1397.3

B. GNP from the Income (Factor Earnings) Side

(in billions of dollars)

21. Compensation of employees			855.8
22. Wages and salaries		750.7	
23. Supplements to wages and salaries		105.1	
24. Employer contributions for social insurance	53.6		
25. Other labor income	51.4		
26. Proprietors' income			93.0
27. Business and professional		61.2	
28. Farm		31.8	
29. Rental income of persons			26.5
30. Corporate profits and inventory valuation adjustment			105.9
31. Profits before tax		141.4	
32. Profits tax liability	55.8		
33. Profits after tax	85.7		
34. Dividends	32.7		
35. Undistributed profits	53.0		
36. Inventory valuation adjustment		−35.5	
37. Net interest			61.6
38. National income			1142.8
39. Indirect business tax liability and other minor adjustments			135.0
40. Net national product			1277.8
41. Capital consumption allowance			119.5
42. Gross national product from factor earnings			1397.3
43. Statistical discrepancy			.0
44. Gross national product from expenditures			1397.3

Source: Department of Commerce, *Survey of Current Business.*

(C), *gross* investment (I_G), net exports (net exports = exports minus imports = $X - M$), and government spending (G),

$$GNP \equiv C + I_G + G + (X - M).$$

Part A of Table 2-2 shows this breakdown of final spending with a further subdivision of each major component of spending. Total consumption spending, for example, is broken down into spending on durable goods (once again, cars, refrigerators, stoves, and so on), spending on nondurable goods (mainly food and clothing), and spending on services (housing, medical and dental treatment, domestic help, and so on).[6] While looking through the components of expenditure in Table 2-2 part A, it is worth noting that, in 1974, approximately 63 percent of GNP went into consumption, 15 percent into investment, and 22 percent was absorbed by government.

---

6 Commodities classified as consumer durables are those that generally last more than a year while nondurables generally last less than a year.

Other Measures of Output (Income)

As we have indicated before, GNP is our broadest measure of production. It is so comprehensive, in fact, that it fails to recognize the fact that some of the existing stock of capital is consumed in the production process. In any accounting period though, some capital is used up by being worn out, becoming obsolete, or by being accidentally destroyed. Subtracting the amount of "capital consumption allowance" from the GNP figure for our selected accounting period leaves the dollar value of *net* output available for society's use as a result of the productive efforts of all the factor inputs used in the production process. This measure of net output is labeled *net national product* (NNP).[7] Thus,

$$NNP \equiv GNP - D,$$

where D stands for the capital consumption allowance (essentially depreciation). Recognizing that the deduction of depreciation from gross investment leaves net investment (I_n), we also know that the measured value of NNP is

$$NNP \equiv C + I_N + G + (X - M).$$

Since part of the capital stock is used up in the act of production, it is clear that not all of GNP represents income *earned* by the factor inputs involved in the production process. We might, however, think of our *net* (after depreciation) measure of output as representing income earned by factor inputs. This is not the case in the U.S. economy, however. The dollar value of NNP still is larger than earned income because of some *nonfactor* payments business firms must make, the cost of which is reflected in our NNP figures. These nonfactor payments consist primarily of *indirect business taxes*. Included in this category of nonfactor payments are sales and excise taxes, property taxes, and franchise fees and fines collected by government agencies. A part of producers' sales revenues must be absorbed by these payments for which no specific productive service is rendered. Thus, the dollar value of NNP is larger, by the amount of indirect business taxes, than the value of income *earned* by the factors of production used

---

7 Conceptually, GNP is too broad a measure of true output because there is one source of double counting left unpurged in the GNP figure. The GNP figure includes all current spending on capital goods even though capital goods are used as inputs in the production of other goods and services. For example, the purchase in 1974 of a loom by a textile mill is included in GNP even though that loom will be used in 1974 in producing the final product cloth. As firms sell their final products, they include in their sales prices an allowance for the capital stock used up in the production process (that is, the price of final goods includes a charge for the capital embodied in those final goods). Thus, there is an element of double counting present in GNP figures, investment expenditures being counted twice. The deduction of depreciation charges eliminates this source of double counting, yielding that measure of net output which we call net national product. The GNP account includes this trouble-creating spending on investment goods as a final goods purchase only in order to better represent the *timing* of changes in the level of *production*.

in the production process. Deducting the value of indirect business taxes (T_i) from NNP then does yield a value for *earned* income, which is labeled *national income* (NI). Algebraically,

$$NI \equiv NNP - T_i,$$

or

$$NI \equiv GNP - D - T_i.$$

Going a step further, in the actual U.S. economy, income payments that are in fact *received* are typically smaller than the value of earned income. Why is not all of earned income paid out to the factor inputs involved in the production process? There are a number of reasons. First, a part of earned income typically takes the form of corporate profit against which the government levies a corporate income tax. That tax on profits reduces the dollar volume of profit income available for payment, in the form of dividends, to the owners (stockholders) of incorporated businesses. Further, firms typically pay out only part of their after-tax profits, keeping a portion (called *retained earnings*) for further internal expansion, enhancement of their liquid reserves, or acquisition of shares of other firms.

Another deduction from earned income is required to reflect the impact on received income of the social security system. Both employers and employees make (*required*) contributions to this *social insurance program*. The portion of earned income that is absorbed in the social security contribution is, consequently, not available for current income payments to our factors of production.

There is one final item that causes received income to differ from earned income. That item is the *transfer payment*—a payment for which no current productive service is rendered. Included in transfer payments are welfare payments, payouts on private and public (government) pension programs, including social security, and payments of interest on the national debt. Such payments make a positive contribution to received income though they do not reflect current *earnings* from the provision of productive services.

To transform national income into a measure of received income, denoted *personal* income, we must subtract from national income the amount of corporate taxes (T_b), retained earnings (R_t), and social security contributions (SS)—all components of income that are earned but not received—and we must add net transfer program payouts $(T_r,$ representing income received but not earned) to that value. Algebraically,

$$PI \equiv NI - (T_b + R_t + SS) + T_r,$$

where PI is personal income, our measure of received income.

To summarize briefly the accounting relationships developed in this section, we obtained GNP from the expenditure side of the accounts by adding consumption, gross investment, government spending, and net exports. The resulting GNP figures differed from our measures of net output, called net national product, by the amount of capital consumption. In turn, NNP differed from personal income, our measure of received income, because of indirect business taxes, the corporate profits tax, social security contributions, retained earnings and transfer payments. Can you write the equation that allows GNP figures to be converted to PI figures?

GNP from the Income Side

We should now be able to go to the income side of the national accounts and sum the values of income earned by each of the four basic productive factors—land, labor, capital, and entrepreneurial talent—to obtain values for GNP and the other output and income measures that appear in the national accounts. The measures derived should be comparable to those obtained from the product (expenditure) side of the accounts. While our discussion up to this point has implied that we should find total income subdivided into wages, rent, interest, and profit, a look at the income side of the actual national accounts (Table 2-2 part B) reveals a somewhat different breakdown. Each of the entries in Table 2-2 part B is discussed below.

Labor's Reward

Most of the income *earned* by labor is reflected in the first line of Table 2-2 part B, compensation of employees. The largest component of employee compensation—wages and salaries—includes (along with ordinary wages and salaries) executives' compensation, commissions, tips, bonuses, and payments in kind which represent earned income to the recipients. Supplements to wages and salaries include such items as employer contributions for social insurance (social security, federal and state unemployment insurance, and so on); employer contributions for private pension, health, unemployment, and welfare funds; compensation for injuries; and pay for military reserve duty. Labor's take-home pay is substantially smaller than its total earned income since part of its earnings take the form of *fringe benefits* of the type outlined here, part is withheld to meet personal income tax liabilities, and part is absorbed by each employee's own contribution to social insurance.

Rent (and Royalties)

Rental income of persons (line 29 of Table 2-2) consists of the earnings of persons from the rental of property, *except* the earnings of persons engaged in the real estate business as a primary source of income (in that case earnings from rent are reflected in the business sector's earnings); the *imputed* net rental value to owner-occupants of nonfarm dwellings;[8] and the royalties received by persons from patents, copyrights, and rights to natural resources.

Net Interest

Net interest (line 37) is the excess of interest payments by the business sector over its interest receipts. Interest paid by consumers and by government enterprises is excluded on the assumption that it does not represent a factor cost of production. A consumer's current interest payments on a loan he obtained a year ago to buy an auto reflects no current production; it is merely a transfer payment. Similarly, most of government's interest payments are to service debt incurred during past war periods and, thus, cannot be interpreted as payments for current productive use of money capital. The outstanding debt of business is, however, assumed to reflect current productive use of borrowed capital. Thus, the interest payments for use of that capital are counted as a component of GNP.

Profit

Profit is a residual. It is what is left over after, out of available revenues, all other expense items have been taken into account. In the national account in Table 2-2 part B, total profit appears under two headings: profit of corporations and profit of unincorporated enterprises—that is, of single proprietorships and partnerships. The earnings of the owners of unincorporated enterprises, denoted *proprietors' income* (line 26), include farm earnings and professional income (the income of doctors, lawyers, consulting engineers, and so on). The profit earned by corporations appears in line 30 and is labeled "corporate profits and inventory valuation adjustment." [9]

Both corporate profits and proprietors' income are modified by the *inventory valuation adjustment*. This adjustment is necessary to remove the impact on measured profit of changes in the level of prices. If prices rise during the accounting period, part of measured profit can represent simply a *markup* of the value of inventories that were bought at a lower price. If the inventory used in the production process was bought at prices lower than current replacement cost, firms' computed production costs (most frequently obtained using original purchase prices for inventory used) will be understated and their profits will be overstated. Conversely, during a period of price decline, production costs would

8   This imputation is necessary if we want to measure the actual value of housing services made available to society and do not want the value of those services to change every time a renter buys the house he has been renting.

9   In practice, it is impossible to judge what portion of proprietors' income is truly profit income and what portion is the reward for the proprietor's own labor, money capital, and property use. It is precisely because of the impossibility of disentangling the returns to the four basic factor inputs that the income side of our national accounts must be subdivided into the five earnings categories that appear in Table 2-2 part B.

be overstated and profits understated.[10] The inventory valuation adjustment attempts to remove the impact on profits (and on actual measured changes in inventories and GNP) of such changes in prices. Its value was unusually large in 1974, reflecting the unusually rapid increase in prices that year.

Earned Income and Its Relation to Our Other Income and Production Measures

By combining the components of earned income that appear in Table 2-2 part B (compensation of employees, rental income of persons, net interest, and proprietors' income plus corporate profit), we obtain a summary measure of the income *earned* by the factor inputs used in the process of production. The resulting value of earned income, labeled *national income*, appears in line 38 of Table 2-2 part B.

You should recall that by adding the value of nonfactor payments (basically the indirect business taxes shown in line 39) to national income we can obtain a value of NNP, and by adding the value of capital consumption to NNP we can obtain a value for GNP. Making these adjustments to the value of national income derived from the income side of the accounts yields a value for GNP of $1,397.3 billion with the adjustments required shown in lines 39 to 42 of Table 2-2 part B. Generally, the value of GNP derived from income measures can be expected to differ by a relatively small magnitude from the GNP value obtained from summing expenditures on final goods and services. Such *statistical discrepancies* are of a magnitude that can be attributed quite easily to statistical errors in independently compiling the data on earned income and expenditures.[11] In fact, there was no significant statistical discrepancy in 1974, as line 43 of Table 2-2 part B reveals (the statistical discrepancy in 1973 was $2.9 billion).

Moving in the other direction again, we have shown above that national income can be altered to provide a measure of actual received income (PI). Again, to obtain personal income values, national income was modified by the subtrac-

---

10   Correspondingly, the *product side* measure of inventory investment (a component of GNP), valued in money terms, will yield an overstatement of the actual physical change in inventories (thus in GNP) when prices are rising and an understatement when prices are falling. The size of the inventory valuation adjustment depends on the extent to which businesses rely on the FIFO [First In–First Out] or LIFO [Last In–First Out] methods of charging inventory usage against current sales. A simple demonstration of the implications of using these alternative methods of measuring inventories and of the need for an inventory valuation adjustment can be found in Sam Rosen, *National Income and Other Social Accounts* (New York: Holt, Rinehart and Winston, Inc., 1972), pp. 49-52.

11   The bulk of our income-side measures come from income tax returns and employment tax records. Data for the product-side measures come from records on sales, inventories, and product shipments. Generated, as they are, from two different data sets, the income- and product-side estimates of GNP will never be precisely equal. Usually the income-side estimate is the lower of the two, suggesting that income reported for tax purposes somewhat understates actual earnings.

tion of corporate income taxes, retained earnings, and social security contributions, and the addition of transfer payments.

The Disposition of Received Income

In the models macroeconomists construct, the manner in which the household sector of the economy disposes of its received income is crucial. A primary obligation that the recipients of money income must meet is the personal income tax liability.[12] The expendable income that is left after meeting this tax liability is labeled *disposable personal income*. It is income available to households to dispose of as they see fit. Thus,

$$Y_d \equiv \text{PI} - T_p,$$

where PI is personal income, T_p is personal income tax, and Y_d is disposable personal income.

Households can divide their disposable income between consumption and saving as they choose. That part of disposable income that is not consumed is, by definition, saved. Thus,

$$Y_d \equiv C + S,$$

or

$$S \equiv Y_d - C,$$

where C is consumption, S is personal saving, and Y_d, as before, is disposable income.

A Summary of National Income and Product Account Relationships

The accounting relationships we have developed can be summarized as in Table 2-3. Our ability to derive values for output or income from either the expenditures or the income side of the national income and product accounts should be apparent from a brief look at that table.

An understanding of the structure of the national income and product accounts will make the construction of models of the economic system much easier, and that chore awaits us. But before proceeding we should take note of a few of the special problems encountered in constructing the U.S. accounts and some of the limitations on those accounts.

---

12 In fact, most income recipients have a portion of their income "withheld" from their pay check to meet personal income tax liabilities.

TABLE 2-3 RELATIONSHIPS EMPLOYED IN THE NATIONAL INCOME AND PRODUCT ACCOUNTS

Σ Final expenditures =

    Consumption
 + Gross investment
 + Government spending
 + Net exports
─────────────────────
   Gross National Product

=

   Gross National Product
 − Capital consumption
─────────────────────
   Net National Product
 − Indirect business taxes
─────────────────────
   National income
 − Corporate profits tax
 − Retained earnings
 − Social security
 + Transfers
─────────────────────
   Personal income
 − Personal income tax
─────────────────────
   Disposable income
 − Consumption
─────────────────────
   Personal saving

=

   Compensation of employees
 + Rental income of persons
 + Net interest
 + Proprietors Income*
   & corporate Profits
─────────────────────
   National income

= Σ Earned income

* Both items modified by the inventory valuation adjustment.

40

THE NATIONAL ACCOUNTS—SOME NOTABLE COMPLICATIONS

While appropriate conceptual measures of a nation's economic activities may be readily formulated, the practical implementation of those conceptual measures is much more difficult. Compromises and approximations, some of which we have already touched upon, must frequently be tolerated. A number of the special difficulties involved in producing the U.S. national income and product accounts are reviewed below.

Depreciation

To know what is happening to the stock of capital and, correspondingly, to know the value of *net* output, we must know the rate at which the existing capital stock is being used up. Business firms' income statements provide a measure of depreciation but there are reasons for questioning the usefulness of that measure. If the dollar value of measured depreciation is exactly equal to current gross investment, our accounting definitions tell us that the capital stock is unchanged. But the newly produced capital goods will typically be technologically superior to the ones they replace and an improvement in the quality of the capital stock is equivalent, in terms of its impact on productive capacity, to an increase in the stock of capital with no quality improvement. Clearly, our measures of net investment which, in turn, tell us what is happening to the accumulated stock of capital over time, are somewhat misleading.

An additional problem exists because current depreciation charges are typically based on the original purchase prices of capital assets rather than on their replacement cost. Consequently, when prices are rising, the actual value of depreciation is understated. With depreciation understated, business profits are overstated and so is NNP. During a period of falling prices, depreciation would be overstated, resulting in an understatement of profits and NNP.

Finally, business firms' depreciation charges are mere bookkeeping adjustments. The depreciation lifetimes business firms *assign* to capital assets depend more heavily on the Internal Revenue Service's guidelines for "allowable lives" than on actual physical capital consumption. Hence, another possibility for error in our measurements of profit, net investment, and NNP arises.

Our measures of true capital consumption are clearly quite crude. In fact, many macroeconomic analysts prefer to work with GNP figures rather than NNP figures because of the potential inaccuracy in NNP introduced by shortcomings in the available measures of depreciation.

Capital Gains and Losses

The occurrence of capital gains and losses—changes in the market value of assets—also causes problems for the national income accountant. If I hire a contractor and have him build an addition onto my home which increases its market value, the value (cost) of the addition is included in our measures of output. If, however, the market value of my house is increased by a favorable shift in demand (for example, due to the opening of a new factory within easy commuting distance) or by a generalized inflation, no entry in the national accounts would reflect the capital gain I enjoy. The familiar reason is that no current production is involved in producing the latter type of increase in market value.

Similarly, if the value of a tract of land increases because of the discovery of oil or uranium ore, no record of that increase in national wealth appears in the national income and product accounts. But with the value of such discoveries omitted from our accounts, the depletion (using up) of natural resources must also be omitted—that depletion cannot be charged against current national output. Broadening our example, it must be recognized that no deterioration in the quantity or quality of natural endowments a nation is blessed with, including environmental quality, is directly reflected in the national income and product accounts. Our traditional measures of output and income clearly omit consideration of some economic activities that profoundly affect human well-being.

Nonmarket Production

The list of economic activities that are excluded from the national accounts can be extended with no difficulty. While GNP is defined as a measure of the dollar value of *total* production of final goods and services, there are a number of highly important productive activities that are not measured. The value of a housewife's performance of her duties as dietician, cook, housecleaner, chauffeur, baby sitter, and so on are omitted from the national income and product accounts. When those same services are performed for pay, their value does appear in GNP. If a man marries his hired housekeeper, GNP is reduced by the amount of her previous pay even though actual output has not changed.[13] In recent years, the proliferation of home gardening, home canning, and even do-it-yourself construction of cabin homes has attracted widespread attention. The value of the production these activities involve is not measured. Similarly, the value of lawn maintenance, plumbing, auto repairs and a host of other productive services performed by husband, wife, or child is omitted from GNP.

The omission of home production from GNP measures exists only because of the practical difficulty of valuing such productive activity for, typically, in-home production does not go through market channels to enable its value to be established. If two neighboring housewives should agree to do each other's housework, paying each other $8,000 yearly for the services provided, GNP will rise by $16,000 though actual production remains unchanged. It is worth noting that the same practical difficulty of measurement is also characteristic of the pro-

---

13 The value of a "typical" housewife's services as estimated by the research department of one of the nation's largest banks was, for 1970, $8,285.

duction of *externalities*.[14] For example, pollutants that enter the air or water are not "marketed" products. Thus, we are hard-pressed to value their *negative* contribution to output.

Illegal Activities

Incomes earned in illegal activities are also, and for obvious reasons, concealed. Still, such activities do provide services and commodities that some members of society desire. Those who like moonshine whiskey, marijuana, and the services of male and female prostitutes would certainly argue that the providers of those items are involved in *productive* activity. Still, such production is ignored in the computation of GNP. As long as illegal production is stably related to total production, its omission will not affect the usefulness of our output figures for measuring *changes* in production. The same can, of course, be said about the value of uncounted "housework."

Imputations

Some components of unmarketed production are judged to be sufficiently important and sufficiently easily valued that an *imputed* value is estimated for them. Imputed values are assigned to these items by using observed prices on similar or identical items that do pass through the market.

An imputed value is computed for farm production that is consumed on the farm. The imputed total value of retained output is counted as consumption on the expenditure side of the accounts and, on the income side of the accounts, an imputed net profit entry is made with any difference between the value of retained production and net profit credited to the appropriate expense items. For payments in kind, consumption expenditures and wages are increased by the same amount.

As indicated earlier, an imputation is also made for the value of productive services flowing from owner-occupied homes. Conceptually, each household is treated as a business enterprise which owns a home as a business and rents it to the household as a consumer. This imputation makes up a sizable proportion of the net rental figure that appears on the income side of the national accounts under rental income of persons. The net rent entry from this source falls short of total imputed rent by the amount of depreciation of the owner-occupied homes and the amount of indirect business taxes resulting from home ownership.

Other imputations are made for certain financial enterprises (such as banks, investment funds, and insurance companies) which produce services that have no observed market price or which have a price that does not cover the cost of

---

14 *Externalities* are production costs that individual producing firms do not have to bear but which are a cost to society.

providing the service (as is the case, for example, with commercial bank check-ing account services). Certainly, any of the imputations employed in the national accounts may give biased estimates of the true value of production they repre-sent. This would be the case if, for example, retained farm production differed in quality from marketed production. It would also be the case if the appearance on the market of retained goods and services would change the observed prices of those goods and services. However, even if the imputations are not precise, they would appear to adequately represent some important components of actual production which, without imputations, would have to be ignored.

While the list could be expanded substantially, our limited sample of the specific complications that national income accountants have to deal with is sufficient to provide a firm understanding of the nature of practical difficulties confronted in the construction of aggregate measures of economic activity. Be-cause of the practical impossibility of obtaining precise measures of aggregate economic activity, there are strict limitations on the uses of national income accounting data. The next section of this chapter focuses attention on those limitations.

RECOGNIZING OUR LIMITATIONS

As indicated repeatedly in this chapter, the national accounts were designed to measure the economy's productive performance and, presumably, it is the pro-duction of *real*, physical goods and services that we are interested in. However, our measures of output are in *nominal* (dollar) terms. If the general price level changes over time, our measures of output change even if real output stays con-stant. If, for example, prices had risen by 10 percent during 1974 while real output was constant, the measures of output discussed in this chapter would have shown a 10 percent increase. Fortunately, we do have devices, called *price in-dexes*, which allow us to convert all our *nominal* measures into *real* measures. We will take a critical look at the construction and use of price indexes in Chap-ter 3, but, for the moment, we will assume that price adjustments can be accu-rately performed to deflate nominal output and income measures.

Even when our measures of output are deflated by an appropriate price in-dex, they are still imperfect measures of production. As we have seen, a sub-stantial portion of output is ignored (homework, illegal production). Further-more, even when measured in terms of constant prices, output must still be valued in dollar terms since adding physical quantities of different goods and services is not meaningful. Thus, our measures of production provide little use-ful information in *absolute* terms. (How much output is represented by the $1,397.3 billion worth of output measured for 1974?) It is only the *change* in output that can have meaning for us and this only if we are willing to assume that omitted production is a stable proportion of total output.

Most analysts do have considerable confidence in the national accounts when they are used to provide measures of *change* in the level of economic activity over relatively short periods of time. When those accounts indicate that GNP is 3 percent smaller than last year's or 9 percent larger than its value two years earlier, we accept those figures. However, as the time interval across which comparisons of the level of production are to be made lengthens, faith in our measures of output change diminishes. Why? Because over time the fraction of production that is uncounted can change substantially and, also, because the very composition of output changes, tending to make output levels incomparable.

As an example of a *proportion* change in the composition of output, suppose we compare two market baskets of commodity production, one consisting of 100 turnips, 20 bicycles, and 500 ballpoint pens while the other consists of 80 turnips, 24 bicycles, and 470 ballpoint pens. Which basket is larger? The answer is certainly not obvious. Just the change in the proportionate composition of the two baskets makes their volume incomparable. You can readily see that changing the *kinds* of commodities produced (introduce autos, electric lights, and so on where they previously did not exist) makes comparisons even more difficult, as do changes in the *quality* of existing products. Expressing output values in dollar terms (even constant dollars) provides little relief from this dilemma.[15] We merely have to accept the fact that our measures of output changes are subject to more uncertainty as the time horizon we are working with lengthens. However, for purposes of monitoring those variables that are of fundamental concern in macroeconomic analysis, some of the limitations on available aggregate production measures are irrelevant. For the most part, the existence of nonmarket production (for example by households) and of omitted transactions has little to do with the functioning of the massive industrial complex that dominates modern economies. It is that complex which suffers from inflationary booms and employment-killing contractions and, hence, it is that complex that requires monitoring. The problems of inflation and unemployment are not the result of improper measurement of housewives' productive services.

International Comparisons of Production

The use of national income data for comparisons of output levels between countries is even more difficult than domestic comparisons across time. A major complication arises because the proportion of uncounted production varies from country to country. In more developed (industrialized) countries, uncounted home production is relatively less important. Also, the proportion of production that is uncounted because of its legal status varies markedly. Gambling is perfectly legal in England while outlawed in the United States (with local exceptions), and the French explicitly include a value for black market activities in

---

15 The problem in generating an index of output is one of correctly assigning price "weights" that reflect society's subjective estimates of the relative values of different items. As demonstrated in Chapter 3, there is no completely satisfactory way to deal with this problem.

computing output values. Even the influence of political ideology affects the proportion of total production captured in a country's income accounts, as shown by the complete omission of any entry for the value of services in the accounts of Russia and its satellites—their national accounts show only the production of *commodities*, the provision of services being deemed *nonproductive*.

The problem of differences in the composition of output also afflicts international comparisons of output figures, compounding the mechanical difficulties of expressing different countries' output levels in terms of a common currency. Major data adjustments are clearly necessary for meaningful international comparisons of production levels and even with adjustments and comparisons, at best, must be looked upon as crude approximations of the truth.

Aggregate Output as a Measure of Social Welfare

Despite limitations in the use of aggregate output data, even for measuring production, those data are often used in discussions of national welfare (some grand total of utility for society at large).[16] Rates of change of output are compared over two periods of time or between two countries, with conclusions derived on *progress* toward higher levels of social well-being. Levels of output are compared (again, both across time and between countries) to spot differences in standards of living. However, a moment's reflection will provide a healthy skepticism for conclusions drawn from such comparisons.

By forcing its labor force to work 25 percent longer each day, a country could substantially increase its per capita output. Would society be better off? (Would you recommend that policy for the United States?) Restricting our concern to a "free" society, even with accurate measurement, would all of the increase in U.S. per capita GNP between 1929 and 1974 represent an increase in economic welfare when some $79 billion was spent on national defense in 1974? Once again, the composition of output is clearly important.

Even in a free society in which the composition of output is unchanged, higher levels of measured output may not correspond to higher levels of social welfare. With measures of production that fail to take account of the negative effects on society's welfare of the extra air and water pollution, the noise and congestion, the destroyed scenery and other disamenities that may accompany additional production, not every increase in measured output represents a positive contribution to society's welfare. Reintroduce the practical difficulties in measuring total physical production and the use of output measures as welfare proxies becomes more suspicious still.

Further, with any redistribution of income accompanying an increase in the level of output, even if it leaves just one individual worse off than before, we are left unable to conclusively argue that total social welfare is enhanced by the in-

16 In fact, most comparisons of output levels implicitly treat output measures as proxies for the economic welfare of society at large.

come increase. We would have to be able to measure and sum up individual utility values to provide proof for that supposition—a task that is not now possible.

Finally, national income and product account measures are deficient for welfare-measuring purposes because they make no allowance for the value of leisure. Additional leisure time is one of the most sought consequences of increasing productive capacity. With no change in actual production of physical goods and services, society would undoubtedly consider its welfare increased with any increase in leisure time. Yet no measure of the value of extra leisure appears in national income and product accounts.

While the national income and product accounts have been invaluable as measures of the economy's production performance, those accounts must be used with care. Even as production measures the aggregate income and output totals require careful interpretation. When faced with the more demanding task of providing a summary measure of overall economic welfare, the national income totals are exceedingly crude.

Improved "Measures of Economic Welfare"

In recent years, recognition of the shortcomings in our national income accounts has prompted considerable interest in developing improved measures of output and economic welfare. The most prominent effort in that direction has been provided by James Tobin and William Nordhaus of Yale University.[17] Arguing that the ultimate purpose of economic activity is consumption, not production, Tobin and Nordhaus modify the currently used national income accounts data to provide a new index called the *measure of economic welfare* (MEW).

In broad terms, to obtain MEW gross national product totals are adjusted by: (1) reclassification of GNP expenditures into consumption, investment, and intermediate production where only consumption contributes to current economic welfare, (2) imputations of the value of the services of consumer capital, the value of leisure, and the value of household work, and (3) a negative correction for some of the disamenities of urbanization. While the list of specific modifications of GNP is quite long, prominent among the positive adjustments are the imputations for the value of leisure time and household production while notable negative adjustments are made for air and water pollution and for other forms of ecological damage not reflected in the traditional measures of GNP. With large entries for the value of leisure and household production, estimates of MEW are considerably larger than the corresponding GNP measures. However, while both the absolute and per capita values of MEW have been rising, GNP measures, which ignore the negative by-products of production and growth, have grown more rapidly.

---

17   William Nordhaus and James Tobin, "Is Growth Obsolete?" in *Economic Growth, Fiftieth Anniversary Colloquium V* (New York: National Bureau of Economic Research, 1972).

Tobin and Nordhaus themselves consider the measure of economic welfare a first, primitive attempt at providing an index of social welfare. They recognize the awesome practical problems involved in obtaining a broadly defined measure of consumption and, more fundamentally, they admit to an inability to correlate individual and collective happiness with consumption. Still, with creation of the MEW index the hard task of developing measures of the *quality of life* has been initiated. In the future, we can expect development of additional statistical indicators that will be used in conjunction with national income measures to provide *informed* judgments on the rate of economic progress.

SUMMARY

In this chapter, we have reviewed three conceptual techniques for obtaining a measure of the economy's output and, in the process, providing measures of a number of other variables of interest to economic analysts (including disposable income, consumption, investment, and so on). The three techniques are: (1) adding up all spending on final goods and services, (2) adding up all earned income, and (3) summing the "value added" that results from the production efforts of all producers. In practice, these three techniques must yield values for national output that, except for small statistical discrepancies, are identical.

We have also become familiar with the actual U.S. national income and product accounts. As is usually the case in series that attempt to measure economic activity, these accounts have shortcomings. They fail to measure some production; they measure production using an elastic yardstick (the dollar); and they do not provide an accurate measure of social welfare. We should not, however, be unduly critical of the national accounts. They were designed to measure production, not social welfare, and the Bureau of Economic Analysis which compiles those accounts presents them in just that light. For purposes of short-run analysis ("business cycle" analysis) and policy making, measured changes in output appear to be adequate if properly interpreted. Even more positively, data which appear in these accounts, despite their limitations, have helped macroeconomists bridge the gap between theory and policy practice. They have allowed the testing and refinement of economic theories and have provided quantification of the behavioral relationships used in modern models of the economic system.

Even when forced into uses for which they were not designed, such as measuring social welfare, measures in the national accounts have traditionally provided proxy measures superior to any alternatives available to us, and recent work suggests that GNP figures can be used as the basis for substantially improved (though not perfect) proxy measures of general economic welfare—we simply need to adequately add up the total flow of "goods" society has to enjoy and subtract the "bads." Despite its limitations, it would be hard to exaggerate the importance of the national income accounts to the progress of modern macroeconomics.

QUESTIONS

1. You are given the following scrambled data in billions of dollars:

Government and business transfers (T_r)	15
Indirect business taxes (T_i)	30
Gross National Product (GNP)	630
Social security contributions (SS)	20
Personal taxes (T_p)	25
Capital consumption (D)	80
Residential construction (RC)	70
Retained earnings (R_t)	0
Personal consumption expenditures (C)	390
Direct business taxes (T_b)	40

   (a) Work out in symbolic form (for example, $R_E - SS + CT = ?$) and calculate the numerical value of net national product (NNP), national income (NI), personal income (PI), and disposable income (Y_d).

   (b) Could you perform the same manipulations with data from the income side of the national accounts?

2. What is a transfer payment and why are such payments not included in our GNP measure?

3. There have been complaints about the use of GNP values as an indicator of the nation's well-being. Outline those complaints.

4. In terms of measured output, what difference does it make whether I repair my own car or hire a mechanic to do it? Is the difference important?

5. Suppose an infestation of pine trees west of the Mississippi by a fast spreading, tree-killing insect requires all pines in that region to be cut and burned. Let the cost of this program be $2 billion and assume some resources (including labor) are used which otherwise would have been idle. What happens to GNP? Is the nation's welfare improved because of the insect infestation?

6. Distinguish between gross and net national product, and between gross and net investment. What linkage do the investment measures have with estimates of aggregate output made using the expenditures approached.

SUGGESTED READING

Kendrick, John W. *Economic Accounts and Their Uses.* New York: McGraw-Hill, 1972.

Kuznets, Simon. *National Income and Its Composition, 1919-1938.* Vol. I. New York: National Bureau of Economic Research, 1941, Chapter I.

———. "National Income: A New Version," *The Review of Economics and Statistics.* Vol. XXX (1948), pp. 151-179.

National Bureau of Economic Research. *A Critique of the United States Income and Wealth,* Vol. XXII. Princeton, N.J.: Princeton University Press, 1958.

Nordhaus, William, and James Tobin. "Is Growth Obsolete?" in *Economic Growth, Fiftieth Anniversary Colloquium V*. New York: National Bureau of Economic Research, 1972.

Rosen, Sam. *National Income and Other Social Accounts*. New York: Holt, Rinehart, and Winston, Inc., 1972, Chapters 1-6.

Ruggles, Richard. "The U.S. National Accounts and Their Development," *American Economic Review*. Vol. 49, March 1959, pp. 85-95.

Shapiro, Edward. *Macroeconomic Analysis*, 3d edition. New York: Harcourt Brace Jovanovich, Inc., 1974, Chapters 2-5, pp. 11-74.

Stewart, Kenneth, "National Income Accounting and Economic Welfare: The Concepts of GNP and MEW," *Federal Reserve Bank of St. Louis Review*. Vol. 56, April 1974, pp. 18-24.

U.S. Department of Commerce, Office of Business Economics. "The National Income and Product Accounts of the United States, Revised Estimates, 1929-1964," *Survey of Current Business*. Vol. 45, August 1965, pp. 6-22.

———. "U.S. Income and Output," Supplement to the *Survey of Current Business*, 1958.

———. "The Economic Accounts of the United States: Retrospect and Prospect," *Survey of Current Business, 50th Anniversary Issue*. Vol. 51, July 1971.

Chapter 3
Measurement 2 – Nominal and Real Values, Price Indexes, and Employment-Unemployment Statistics

This brief chapter completes our survey of the summary statistical series available for monitoring and analyzing the aggregate performance of the U.S. economy. This chapter focuses attention on two sets of statistical series. The first set consists of measures of the level and rate of change of prices, while the second consists of measures of the economy-wide levels of employment and unemployment. Since full employment is a primary goal of macroeconomic policy, the employment and unemployment measures described in this chapter have long been closely watched indicators of the economy's health. Also closely monitored, especially so in the inflationary era that began in the late 1960s, the price level measures described in this chapter permit evaluation of the success (or failure) policy makers experience in the quest for reasonable price stability. Further, as suggested in Chapter 2, a properly measured index of price level change can be used to convert *nominal* measures of output into more meaningful *real* (price deflated) measures.

NOMINAL VERSUS REAL VALUES AND THE NEED FOR PRICE INDEXES

As indicated in Chapter 2, the important variables that appear in the national income and product accounts must be measured in dollar terms because of the impossibility of adding up the output of apples, oranges, autos, roller skates, haircuts, factory buildings, and the thousands of other products provided by a modern economy in anything other than money terms. With current output values in money terms, the total value of one year's output of a particular product is just the price (p) of that product times the quantity (q) produced that year or $p \cdot q$. In an economy which produces n different final products, the value

53

of total output (Y) is just the summed market value of the output of each of the n final products. That is, the total value of output, measured in dollar terms, is

$$Y = p_0 q_0 + p_1 q_1 + p_2 q_2 + \cdots + p_n q_n,$$

where $p_i q_i$ is the value of the output of the ith product, say, bicycles. It is abundantly clear that the measured, *nominal* values of output and the other variables (consumption, investment, and so on) that appear in the national accounts are altered both by changes in the *real*, physical volume of measured economic activity (production, consumption, and so on) and by changes in the general price level. Of course, measures of the real, physical volume of output are required for evaluating the production performance of the economic system, and separate measures of price level change are interesting in their own right. Thus, the need for a technique which separates the nominal changes recorded in the national accounts into real changes and price level changes is clear-cut. To understand the meaning and usefulness of the devices—called *price indexes*—which provide that separation, we need to know how those indexes are constructed.

Price Index Construction

Suppose we are interested in measuring the extent of change in the general price level between 1960 and 1970. Now, since any economic system produces a very large number of different products, it is immediately apparent that any price index which purports to reflect changes in the general price level must combine or *average* the movements in a number of different prices on different products. The price of oranges in 1970 will differ from what it was in 1960, the price of new Cadillacs will have changed between 1960 and 1970, and so on. The simplest way of obtaining a summary *index* measure of the general price level in 1970 *relative* to its level in 1960 would be to calculate the ratios of 1970 to 1960 prices for each product our economy provides, then take the simple average of all those ratios. If the economy were extremely simple that task would be easily accomplished. Suppose, for example, the economy produced only the two consumption goods bread and wine. In that case we would have to find only two price ratios and average their values to find what had happened to the *general* price level. If the price of bread (p_b) had doubled between 1960 and 1970 while the price of wine (p_w) had remained unchanged, the two ratios we would have to average would be

$$\frac{p_b \text{ in } 1970}{p_b \text{ in } 1960} = 2 \quad \text{and} \quad \frac{p_w \text{ in } 1970}{p_w \text{ in } 1960} = 1.$$

The simple average of those two ratios, our calculated price index, is just

$$(2 + 1)/2 = 3/2, \quad \text{or } 1.5.$$

According to this index, the general price level in our simple economy rose by one half, or 50 percent, between 1960 and 1970.

While the simple technique just used to calculate a price index cannot be dismissed as completely invalid, we can easily improve on our computational methods to provide more accurate measures of price level change. In the price index calculation above, each product was implicitly assigned the same weight (the same importance) in determining the extent of change in the general level of prices. But, in the simple and primitive two-good economy, it might be that wine is a very unimportant component of consumption, bread and *free* spring water providing the bulk of society's consumption needs. In that case, a sizable increase in the price of wine, while it would exert a strong upward push on our *calculated* price index, would have little effect on the true average price level society faces.

Since a simple average of price ratios assigns the same weight to every commodity, we have an obvious opportunity for development of improved measures of price level change. What is required, of course, is that we weight measure price changes in a way that more accurately accounts for the relative importance to society, or to an average consumer, of different products. In practice, individual product prices are often weighted by the number of units of the product actually purchased during a specified time period. Unfortunately for the purpose of measuring price level changes, the specific mix of products society consumes changes over time so that there remains some question about precisely which time period's purchase quantities should be used as weights in our price index calculations. We will note a bit later what difficulties arise from the lack of a universally valid set of quantity weights. Our next task is to review the standard methods that can be employed to calculate actual price indexes.

The Laspeyres Index

Virtually all of the price indexes that are calculated on a regular basis are *Laspeyres indexes* which use earlier year (*base* year) quantities as weights. The formula for computing a Laspeyres price index can be written

$$I_{2,1} = \frac{\sum\limits_{i} p_2\, q_1}{\sum\limits_{i} p_1\, q_1}, \qquad i = 1, 2, 3, \cdots, n,$$

where $I_{2,1}$ represents the value of the index in year 2 *based* upon year 1 prices, p_1 and p_2 represent prices of individual items bought in years 1 and 2 respectively, q_1 represents quantities of individual items bought in year 1, and $\sum\limits_{i}$ indicates that we are to sum the products of price and quantity over the n commodities that were bought in the base year (that is, in year 1). This index is really the ratio of two expenditure measures, the denominator being the actual base period expenditure required, in year 1, to buy the market basket of goods and services identified as "typical" in that year, while the numerator represents the amount of expenditure that would be required in year 2, at year 2 prices, to buy the same combination of items. With the combination of items bought held identical in both years (the quantity weights held constant), any change in the dollar volume of expenditure necessary to buy that *market basket* must be the result of a change in the price level.

The Paasche Index

An alternative form of price index is the *Paasche index*. The Paasche index uses latter period quantities (usually denoted *current* period) as weights. The formula for the Paasche index is

$$I_{2,1} = \frac{\sum\limits_i p_2 \, q_2}{\sum\limits_i p_1 \, q_2}, \quad i = 1, 2, 3, \cdots, n.$$

This index, too, is a ratio of two expenditures. The numerator in the Paasche index measures the actual, observed expenditure in year 2 (the current year) on a typical market basket of goods and services, while the denominator measures the amount of spending that would have been required in year 1, at year 1 prices, to buy the specific mix of items that composed the market basket in year 2.

Index Construction—A Simple Example

The mechanics involved in constructing both Laspeyres and Paasche indexes can be readily illustrated. Assuming that the world is only slightly more complicated than in our earlier example, suppose we have data on a "typical" household's actual expenditures, as recorded in Table 3-1. As indicated in that table,

TABLE 3-1 SPENDING DATA FOR 1960 AND 1970 FOR A TYPICAL HOUSEHOLD

	1960		1970	
Item	*Price*	*Quantity Bought*	*Price*	*Quantity Bought*
Wine	$2.00	80	$1.00	120
Bread	4.00	30	8.00	20
Song	1.00	40	2.00	30

our typical household consumes only three items: wine, bread, and song (which could be interpreted more broadly as food goods, other necessities, and luxuries).

It remains for us to determine what happened between 1960 and 1970 to the general level of prices our household was required to pay for the collection of items it purchased. The Laspeyres index tells us

$$I_{1970,1960} = \frac{\text{required spending in 1970 to get 1960 collection}}{\text{actual spending in 1960 on 1960 collection}} = \frac{\sum\limits_{i} p_2\, q_1}{\sum\limits_{i} p_1\, q_1}$$

$$= \frac{(1.00 \cdot 80) + (8.00 \cdot 30) + (2.00 \cdot 40)}{(2.00 \cdot 80) + (4.00 \cdot 30) + (1.00 \cdot 40)} = \frac{400}{320}$$

$= 1.25$ with a value of 1 assigned to the base year price level

or $\quad = 125\%$ with a value of 100% assigned to the base year price level.

It appears that the price level our typical household faces increased by 25 percent between 1960 and 1970.

Computing the Paasche index reveals:

$$I_{1970,1960} = \frac{\text{actual spending in 1970}}{\text{required spending in 1960 to get 1970 collection}} = \frac{\sum\limits_{i} p_2\, q_2}{\sum\limits_{i} p_1\, q_2}$$

$$= \frac{(1.00 \cdot 120) + (8.00 \cdot 20) + (2.00 \cdot 30)}{(2.00 \cdot 120) + (4.00 \cdot 20) + (1.00 \cdot 30)} = \frac{340}{350}$$

$= .971$ with a value of 1 assigned to the base year price level

or $\quad = 97.1\%$ with a value of 100% assigned to the base year price level.

According to the Paasche index, the price level facing our household *fell* nearly 3 percent between 1960 and 1970.

We must wonder, what is the true index number? Unfortunately, there is no simple answer to that question. All we can say is that the true index value lies somewhere between the two values yielded by computing Laspeyres and Paasche indexes. As you may have already noted, what our simple price index example has just succeeded in doing is to dramatically demonstrate what the lack of a universally correct set of quantity weights *can do* to measures of price level change. Quite simply, with standard weighting schemes (Laspeyres and Paasche) computed price indexes are biased. Perhaps fortunately, these indexes are biased in opposite directions so that (ignoring any other difficulties in price level construction) their values can be expected to bracket the true index value.

For expository purposes, our example permitted a marked difference between the Laspeyres and Paasche price index values. Fortunately, the difference in index values computed from actual data would be that striking only under exceedingly rare conditions. The actual price indexes calculated for the United States, despite some inherent biases, do contain important, usable information. After describing the most prominent price level measures that are calculated in the United States, we will try to gain some perspective on the quality of our price indicators by taking a formal look at the most serious criticisms that are lodged against those measures.

ACTUAL PRICE INDEXES

Computing a Paasche index on a regular basis would require the gathering of a new set of data on both current period sales quantities (current period weights) and current prices for every update of the index. The first burden, which in practice is quite costly, is avoided in computing the Laspeyres index, since only *base year* quantity weights are required for the latter. Primarily because of the practical difficulty of obtaining the sales data necessary for an updating of quantity weights each period, virtually all the price indexes that are compiled on a regular basis are of the Laspeyres type. While a large number of different price indexes are regularly calculated and reported in the United States, the lion's share of attention is focused on three—the *consumer price index*, the *wholesale price index*, and the *implicit price deflator*. The first two are calculated on the Laspeyres basis, while the implicit price deflator, which is derived in an indirect manner, is a Paasche index.

The Consumer Price Index

Of all the price indexes compiled in the United States, perhaps the most prominent in terms of public recognition is the consumer price index (CPI). Expressly designed to measure changes in the "cost of living," the CPI is particularly closely watched by government officials, union leaders, and consumer advocates. As protection against an erosion of their living standards through inflation, some 50 million U.S. residents, including some unionized workers, social security recipients, federal government pensioners, and food stamp recipients, have their incomes tied to the CPI.

The consumer price index is computed for a market basket of some 400 items which are intended to represent the typical mix of purchases of urban wage earners and clerical workers. The items included in that market basket fall into one of six broad groups: food, housing, apparel, transportation, health and recreation, and miscellaneous services. Of course, each of the items included in the index is weighted in proportion to its relative importance in the budget of the representative urban family. As might be expected, food and housing items make up a prominent portion of the market basket with some 33 percent of expenditures on the currently employed market basket going for housing and 25 percent for food.

The responsibility for gathering and processing the data which provide the consumer price index values resides with the Bureau of Labor Statistics (BLS) of the Department of Labor. Price observations on the items included in the urban wage earner or clerical worker's "market basket" are obtained through visits to around 18,000 selected retail outlets in 56 major cities across the country. Food prices are measured monthly while prices of most other items are updated quarterly.

The items to be included in the market basket, the retail outlets where those items are purchased, and the weights assigned to those items are determined through periodic surveys of the spending habits of a large sample of consumers. The last major survey was conducted in the period 1960-1961 and the current CPI calculations are based on the spending patterns revealed in that survey with minor modifications. The Bureau of Labor Statistics is currently involved in a Consumer Expenditure Survey, scheduled for completion in 1977, which will provide a new market basket of goods and services with new quantity weights. Moreover, the BLS intends, with the current survey, to broaden the coverage of the index to include the expenditures of professional and managerial workers, the self-employed, retired workers, and the unemployed.[1]

To end our brief description of the CPI, it is worth noting that, while computed values of the current CPI may measure very well changes in the general level of prices facing the average urban wage earner or clerical worker, it is likely to perform that feat less well for Howard Hughes, a U.S. Senator, a surgeon, a southern tobacco farmer, a college professor, a college student, or a ghetto dweller. There is no universally correct set of weights which can represent the spending patterns of different individuals and, consequently, there is no universally applicable cost-of-living index. A brief look at the price increases that have taken place over the last decade in each of the product groups that are included in the CPI indicates that the biggest increases have occurred in home prices, food prices, medical care charges, and in the prices of fuel oil and coal. A recent college graduate, facing home purchase and child-rearing expenses, might well feel that the CPI has understated the degree of inflation since 1965, particularly if he or she is a heavy eater and heats with oil or coal.

The Wholesale Price Index

The wholesale price index (WPI) covers some 2,300 commodities with their prices measured at the level of their first important commercial transaction. The commodities encompassed in the sample fall within three broad categories—farm products, processed foods and feeds, and industrial commodities. The base year weights currently employed in calculating this Laspeyres index were derived primarily from shipment values of commodities as recorded in 1963 industrial censuses. The price data used in generating the WPI are gathered monthly through mail questionnaires to a sample of representative manufacturers.

Because of the many commodities covered in the WPI and because changes in prices at the wholesale level have traditionally appeared later in retail prices, many analysts have looked at the WPI as a better measure of price movements than the consumer price index. However, the wholesale index completely omits the price level of services, and, at least in the last decade and a half, the increasing

---

1 For a brief discussion of the controversy ignited by this planned revision of the CPI, see "Modernizing an Inflation Barometer," *Morgan Guaranty Survey*, May 1974, pp. 11-13.

cost of services has been an important contributor to virtually everyone's cost of living. Moreover, in the 1973-1974 period, a persistent and dramatic divergence between the yearly price increases registered by the WPI and those indicated by other price indexes demonstrated that under some conditions the WPI provides highly misleading signals. In that period, price increases were not evenly distributed. The biggest increases were concentrated in products, such as wheat and petroleum, which have their first important commercial transaction at a very primitive stage of processing. Since products at all different stages of the production process have their prices reflected in the WPI, price changes that occur at early stages of the production process can be double and triple counted. As William Nordhaus and John Shoven have recognized, petroleum illustrates this difficulty particularly clearly. According to Nordhaus and Shoven, "Petroleum shows up in the WPI first as crude petroleum, then as refined petroleum products. The value of the petroleum products is then included again when they are sold as electric power, plastics and resins, and so on." [2] With the direct and indirect weights of crude products included repetitively in the WPI, that index is seriously biased in an uneven inflation when price increases are originating in the earlier stages of production (as was the case in the 1973-1974 period).

The Implicit GNP Deflator

With the same data that are used to compile the wholesale price index, a host of other measures of changes in the prices of detailed subgroupings of commodities are computed. For example, individual measures of price level change are kept for textiles, fuels, metals, machinery and equipment, nonmetallic minerals, and so on. Analogously, in addition to compiling values for the CPI, the Bureau of Labor Statistics compiles price index values for a detailed subgrouping of the goods and services consumers buy. In fact, for every one of a substantial number of subcomponents of GNP, a separate price index is maintained.

As previously suggested, price indexes permit the separation of changes in dollar magnitudes (the products of prices and physical quantities) into changes in *real*, physical units and pure price changes. With an understanding of the simple mechanics of making that separation—and, thus of deflating nominal quantities to convert them to real quantities—we will be ready to explain how the third important summary price index, the *implicit GNP deflator*, is calculated.

Suppose that the total dollar expenditures on machinery and equipment in 1970 were $65 billion. To be able to compare the real volume of machinery and equipment acquired in 1970 to the volumes in other years, each year's purchase must be expressed in terms of constant purchasing power dollars—deflated to

2 William Nordhaus, "Inflation 1973: The Year of Infamy," *Challenge*, May-June, 1974, pp. 14-22.

remove the effects of price level change. Simply dividing the 1970 dollar expenditure on machinery and equipment by the price index on that category of production accomplishes the desired deflation for 1970. If, for example, the index value for 1970 were 1.114 in terms of 1967 prices, the real value of 1970 machinery and equipment production would be $65B/1.114 = $58.35B valued at 1967 prices. This deflated value can be compared to any other year's output of machinery and equipment, also valued in 1967 prices, to see what has happened to real output.

To obtain the implicit price deflator, each of the components of GNP is deflated separately by its own price index. The resulting deflated measures are then combined to provide estimates of GNP and its four major expenditure components valued at *constant*, base-year prices. For 1974, the resulting estimates valued in 1958 prices were:

Gross national product	$821.1B
Personal consumption expenditures	539.5
Gross private domestic investment	126.7
Net exports of goods and services	8.9
Government purchases of goods and services	146.0

A quick reference to the sample national income accounts in Chapter 2 reveals that the 1974 GNP in *nominal* terms was $1,397.3B, markedly more than the deflated figure for 1974. Dividing the *inflated* nominal value of GNP by the constant price measure yields an implicit measure of the extent to which the price level has risen. The measure is the *implicit price deflator* for GNP. For our example the ratio of 1974 GNP at current prices to GNP at constant prices is $1,397.3/$821.1 ≃ 1.70, indicating that the price level rose by some 70 percent between 1958 and 1974. Derived indirectly from measures of GNP, our most aggregative measure of production, the implicit price deflator is the best measure we have of changes in the *general* price level. Postwar values for the implicit price deflator, along with values for the consumer and wholesale price indexes, are shown in Table 3-2. The divergence in the 1973-1974 period between price increases measured by the WPI and those indicated by the other price indexes in Table 3-2 is quite striking. In addition to price index values, nominal and deflated values of GNP are provided in that table to illustrate the magnitude of the adjustments necessary to separate *real* changes from price level changes.

PRICE INDEX LIMITATIONS

Clearly, price indexes are highly useful, indeed essential, if we want an accurate indication of the rate of price level change and if we want measures of the *real* performance of our economic system. It is no wonder so much attention is devoted to the regularly reported indexes. Of course, we expect our indexes to provide us with reliable price level measures. However, while most economists

TABLE 3-2   PRICE INDEXES AND GNP VALUES, 1947-1974

Year	Price Indexes (1967 = 100)		Implicit Price Deflator 1958 = 100	GNP in Current Dollars	GNP in Constant (1958) Dollars
	Consumer	Wholesale			
1947	66.9	76.5	74.6	231.3	309.9
1948	72.1	82.8	79.6	257.6	323.7
1949	71.4	78.7	79.1	256.5	324.1
1950	72.1	81.8	80.2	284.8	355.3
1951	77.8	91.1	85.6	328.4	383.4
1952	79.5	88.6	87.5	345.5	395.1
1953	80.1	87.4	88.3	364.6	412.8
1954	80.5	87.6	89.6	364.8	407.0
1955	80.2	87.8	90.9	398.0	438.0
1956	81.4	90.7	94.0	419.2	446.1
1957	84.3	93.3	97.5	441.1	452.5
1958	86.6	94.6	100.0	447.3	447.3
1959	87.3	94.8	101.6	483.7	475.9
1960	88.7	94.9	103.3	503.7	487.7
1961	89.6	94.5	104.6	520.1	497.2
1962	90.6	94.8	105.8	560.3	529.8
1963	91.7	94.5	107.2	590.5	551.0
1964	92.9	94.7	108.8	632.4	581.1
1965	94.5	96.6	110.9	684.9	617.8
1966	97.2	99.8	113.9	749.9	658.1
1967	100.0	100.0	117.6	793.9	675.2
1968	104.2	102.5	122.3	864.2	706.6
1969	109.8	106.5	128.2	930.3	725.6
1970	116.3	110.4	135.2	977.1	722.5
1971	121.3	113.9	141.6	1,055.5	745.4
1972	125.3	119.1	146.1	1,155.2	790.7
1973	133.1	134.7	153.9	1,289.1	837.4
1974	147.7	160.1	170.2	1,397.3	821.1

Source: Departments of Commerce and Labor.

and statisticians think the government does an admirable job of compiling price index values, the inherent complexities of real-world price index construction provide ample opportunities for the introduction of biases in price level measurement. We need to be aware of what the most prominent sources of bias are.

The Classic Index Number Problem

As our price index problem demonstrated, in measuring changes in the general price level the quantity weights assigned to each product price must be held constant, in effect, assuming that the quantities of each commodity consumed are the same in different periods. This requirement is the source of a systematic bias in all price index values, often referred to as the *index number problem*.

Traditional demand analysis indicates that price and quantity demanded are inversely related. In the price index example on page 56, the price of bread and song increased from 1960 to 1970 while that of wine decreased. With the price of bread and song increasing from 1960 to 1970 the quantity of those items demanded would be expected to fall (*ceteris paribus*) while, with the price of wine falling during that period, the quantity of wine demanded should have risen. Thus, wine would have become a more important part of the market basket of goods *actually bought* in 1972, the other two items becoming less important. But, to compute a Laspeyres price index, we used 1960 quantity weights, involving ourselves in a violation of the law of demand. Using base year weights to compute our price index caused us to weight too heavily the 1970 purchases of bread and song, the prices of which had risen, and caused us to weight too lightly the purchases of wine, the price of which had fallen. Generalizing, if tastes, incomes, and the other nonprice factors that affect demands for real goods and services should remain unchanged, any price index which uses base year weights (a Laspeyres index) gives too much weight to items that have experienced the greatest price increases (or smallest declines), and too little weight to those items that have experienced the smallest price increases (or greatest declines). Thus, these indexes would always be biased upward, overstating the true value of increases in the *general* price level or understating any fall in that level.

Conversely, price indexes computed with current year weights (Paasche indexes) would always attach too much weight to items that have experienced the smallest price increases (or greatest declines), and too little weight to items that have experienced the largest price increases (or smallest declines). Thus, Paasche indexes would always yield downward biased estimates of changes in the general price level. Consequently, we could expect to bracket the true change in the price level by computing both Laspeyres and Paasche indexes, since they are biased in opposite directions. Further, if the downward biased Paasche index indicated that the price level had risen, we could feel confident that, indeed, it *had* risen, while an indication from the upward biased Laspeyres index that the price level had fallen would be accepted with equal confidence. However, in reality we can expect tastes, incomes, and every other nonprice factor that affects demand to change over time so that we cannot be certain of the direction of price index bias that stems from the need of a fixed weighting scheme. For example, as a reflection of a change in tastes, we might see bicycle purchases multiplying. The increased demand for bicycles would likely cause an increase in bike prices with the *resulting* higher bike prices associated with a larger quantity of sales. With fixed quantity weights the importance of increased bike prices would be undervalued, introducing a *downward* bias in a fixed-weight index.

Quite clearly, if the composition of society's purchases changes over time, the necessity of using fixed quantity weights introduces biases into our price indexes. The direction of bias, though, depends on whether changes in prices are the dominant source of changes in the composition of purchases or whether changes in the other factors that affect prices are the dominant influence on purchases. At any rate, whatever the direction of bias imparted, most analysts think the degree of bias is small, particularly if price comparisons are made over relatively limited periods of time so that drastic changes in the composition of purchases are unlikely.

Quality Changes

An additional bias may be introduced if there are qualitative changes in the products included in the collection of goods and services used for computing a price index. Clearly, product quality can change in two directions. A more powerful or longer lasting auto engine with no increase in auto prices means more auto per dollar due to quality improvement. A reduction in the size of a "5-cent" candy bar is quality deterioration. Quality improvement (more car per dollar spent) is clearly equivalent to a "unit price" decline while quality deterioration (less candy bar per nickel spent) is equivalent to a "unit price" increase.

Product improvement is easy to spot in normal times. Quicker-to-fix and more nutritious frozen foods, quicker and safer appendectomies and sterilizations, safer and faster air trips—all these are examples of quality improvements. If such quality improvements are not accounted for in price index construction, the computed indexes will be biased upward. While efforts are made to adjust our indexes for qualitative changes, many such changes are subtle ones and may not be adequately incorporated into the computed indexes. A related problem results from the introduction of wholly new products. While new products typically raise living standards, their introduction is usually not properly accounted for in price index calculations, reinforcing the upward bias in price indexes.[3]

Other Problems

A number of other limitations on price indexes should be briefly noted. First, actual sales prices may differ from list prices. Where actual prices are available, price index calculations usually employ them. Often, however, actual prices, frequently discounted from list, are unavailable. Measured *changes* in the price level would not be affected by this problem if deviations from list prices stayed constant over time, but that is not likely to be the case. Discounts become increas-

---

3 For a discussion of this issue, see R. Ruggles, "The Problems of Our Price Indexes," *Challenge*, November 1961; and E. Clague, "Computing the Consumer Price Index," *Challenge*, May 1962. Both articles are reprinted in A. Okun, *The Battle Against Unemployment*, revised ed. (New York: W. W. Norton & Co., 1972).

To highlight the role of qualitative changes in affecting our price measures, you might ponder the following question: With $1,000 to spend, would you prefer to order exclusively from a 1958 Sears catalogue or exclusively from a 1974 Sears catalogue?

ingly important during business contractions and decreasingly important in expansions. Consequently, the lack of information on actual sales prices can introduce an upward bias in price indexes during recessions. Price indexes that suffer such a bias understate the size of both price declines and increases as the level of business activity fluctuates.

In addition, many prices vary systematically as the season changes (for instance, the price of lettuce, fresh strawberries, and construction service) so that price indexes that are not adjusted for such seasonal variations provide misleading measures of price level change during the year. Happily, the widely watched consumer price index is *seasonally adjusted*.

A further limitation on price indexes arises because the price figures used for computing those indexes are obtained by survey and represent a small *sample* of actual transaction prices. Of course, the sample may be biased. Finally, it is worth reemphasizing that there is no truly general price index. As indicated before, the consumer price index measures the price level of a basket of products purchased by "average" factory and clerical workers. Since my own purchasing patterns may differ substantially from those of factory and clerical workers, I would be likely to somewhat misrepresent changes in my real income by deflating changes in my money income by the consumer price index.

An Overview

Everyone recognizes that available price indexes have limitations. They cannot be perfectly general and most of them are likely to be biased upward to some degree so that real income figures obtained by deflating money income figures for price changes are biased downward. Unfortunately, the extent of bias in our indexes cannot be satisfactorily measured in any objective way. In years past, some analysts argued that the "creeping" inflation recorded in the late 1950s and early 1960s was illusory, that is, simply a failure of our price indexes to adequately recognize product improvements and changes in the composition of purchases. Others have contended there is no significant bias in our price indexes. Wherever the truth lies, no one claims that the inflation measured since 1966 has been an illusion and virtually everyone pays close heed to the latest recorded values of the price level measures the government compiles.

Over relatively brief periods of time, the composition of the market basket of products society purchases is rather stable, justifying the use of fixed weights in price index calculations. Moreover, normally product quality changes and the introduction of new products can be expected to occur quite gradually. Thus, the bias in available measures of price change over any short time period is likely to be small. In terms of calendar time, the year-to-year changes in price measures and the reported year-to-year changes in real (price deflated) GNP, NNP, consumption, and so on are likely to be close to actual values under normal conditions. As periods that are farther separated in time are compared, the accuracy of the price indexes employed and, thus, of the changes in real variables obtained with those indexes, is reduced. Still, even for comparisons over fairly extended time intervals, price adjusted data are, in most cases, more meaningful than unadjusted data. For example, we can be sure that real GNP in the United States did not rise by 391 percent between 1950 and 1974, though that is what the undeflated dollar figures in Table 3-1 indicate. We know that there was considerable inflation during that period, especially during the Korean War and the period since our Vietnam military involvement. The price deflated GNP figures tell us that the rise in real output was a much more modest 131 percent. Though this measure is likely to be somewhat biased, its value is sure to be a better indicator of the true change in real output than the unadjusted figures yield.

U.S. EMPLOYMENT AND UNEMPLOYMENT STATISTICS

We new need to shift our attention from price index values and their uses to the employment and unemployment measures compiled for the U.S. economy. These series, collected on a monthly basis for the Bureau of Labor Statistics by the Bureau of the Census, are based on a sample survey of about 50,000 households across the country. Like our other statistical series, these important measures have their own shortcomings.

Employment

According to the Bureau of Census definition, an individual is employed if, during the survey week, he was at work for any amount of time as a paid employee, or was self-employed, or worked unpaid in a family enterprise for 15 hours or more (as in a family business or farm). He is also counted as employed, even if he did not work during the survey week, as long as he had a job from which he was temporarily absent due to illness, labor dispute, vacation, bad weather, and so on.

This is clearly a crude measure of employment. An individual is counted as fully employed whether he works for pay on an average of 10 hours weekly or for 40 to 60 hours weekly. Realistically though, an individual who would like to work 40 hours weekly at the prevailing wage rate is three-fourths unemployed if he can only find 10 hours of weekly work. Because the average number of hours worked by employed individuals varies significantly with the level of overall economic activity—average work-weeks are lengthened when economic activity is buoyant and are shortened when economic activity is depressed—the employment statistics compiled by the Bureau of Labor Statistics tend to hide an increased volume of *underemployment* when the economy is depressed and obscure the existence of *overtime* work during boom periods.

In a similar vein, if a laid-off aerospace engineer takes a job as a short-order cook, he is not counted as unemployed. But when an individual is forced, by the state of health of the economy, to work in a job that does not fully utilize his abilities, he is in part unemployed or underemployed. When economic activity is depressed, the number of individuals forced to accept such underemployment multiplies. Further, seasonal variations in the number of workers on vacation and in the number temporarily out of work because of bad weather are not adequately represented if we want our employment data to measure the productive use of labor. While the official measure of employment generally can be expected to move in a roughly parallel fashion with a more refined measure of actual productive labor input, substantial improvements in the measure the Bureau of Labor Statistics provides are undoubtedly attainable.

Unemployment

An individual 16 years old or older, who was not employed during the survey week but who is currently available for work and has engaged in some specific job-seeking activity (interviewing a prospective employer, answering an ad, and so on) during the preceding four weeks, is counted as unemployed.[4] In addition, individuals waiting to be recalled to jobs from which they have been laid off and individuals scheduled to report to new jobs within 30 days are counted as unemployed. This definition of unemployment excludes those who would happily accept employment but who, after becoming convinced no job is available, have simply quit making *specific* efforts to find employment. Of course, such "discouraged" job-seekers are in every economically meaningful sense unemployed and they would resume active participation in the labor market if only they became convinced that favorable opportunities for employment exist. Moreover, there is evidence that housewives, retired workers, and students become more active participants in the labor force when, in the course of an economic expansion, attractive opportunities for employment become available. But like the discouraged worker, the *potential* worker receives no recognition in the U.S. unemployment statistics.

By counting workers whose skills are not fully utilized as fully employed, and by ignoring discouraged and potential workers, the official unemployment data *hide* or *disguise* a considerable volume of true unemployment.[5] In addition,

4   Being available for work does not require one to take any job offered. For example, a laid-off aerospace engineer is not *required* to take a job as a cook or a draftsman. He or she may refuse such jobs, remain unemployed, and still receive unemployment benefits for the normal duration of eligibility. However, if a job opening which is compatible with the individual's training and experience is refused, unemployment benefits may be terminated though he or she remains unemployed.

5   See T. Dernburg and K. Strand, "Hidden Unemployment, 1953-1962: A Quantitative Analysis by Age and Sex," *The American Economic Review*, Vol. 56, March 1966. According to this investigation, unemployment figures would be some 50 percent higher if discouraged workers were counted as part of the labor force. Of course, to the extent that discouraged workers are involved in nonmarket production, the economic loss from unemployment is less than the adjusted unemployment figures would suggest. Also, see J. Mincer, "Labor Force Participation and Unemployment: A Review of Recent Evidence," in R. A. Gordon and M. S. Gordon (eds.), *Prosperity and Unemployment* (New York: John Wiley & Sons, 1966).

that data series fails to reveal fully the unemployment changes brought about by cyclical swings in the overall level of economic activity. As the economy expands, the number of job opportunities increases. In response, discouraged workers and potential workers are enticed into becoming active participants in the labor force. With increased labor force participation, an increase in the number of job slots obviously cannot provide an equivalent reduction in unemployment and the measured reduction in unemployment understates the true impact of economic expansion. By the same token, when job opportunities become less abundant during a business contraction, frustrated work-seekers may abandon the job-search activities that make them an official part of the labor force. As a consequence, the measured increase in unemployment is an underestimate of the impact on true unemployment of a shrinkage in economic activity.

Another Overview

As just explained, the size of the labor force cannot be assumed to be constant since labor force participation is itself a function of the level of unemployment. During a business expansion employment opportunities expand and labor force participation is encouraged. During contractions, opportunities for employment shrink and labor force participation is discouraged as measured unemployment rises. We have also noted that available employment and unemployment data are on a job versus no-job basis, so that whether a worker is working parttime or overtime, at his "best" occupation or in one that does not fully utilize his abilities, he is counted as employed. Typically then, true unemployment (in, say, man-hours) is understated during recessions when parttime work becomes more commonplace and more labor is discouraged from participation in the labor force while, with overtime work common and labor force participation encouraged, the unemployment series might even overstate the extent of unemployment in periods of exuberant economic activity.[6]

Postwar data on employment, unemployment, and the unemployment rate—the percentage of the civilian labor force that is unemployed—are presented in Table 3-3. Despite their shortcomings, these data series are our best sources of information on the productive use of labor. As such, every monthly variation in each of these series, and most particularly in the unemployment rate series, is carefully scrutinized.

A quick look down the last column of Table 3-3 reveals variations in the unemployment rate that may or may not strike you as impressive. A moment's reflection will magnify their importance. The increase in the unemployment rate from 3.5 percent of the labor force in 1969 to 5.9 percent in 1971 means, of course, a 68-percent jump in measured unemployment—as the figures in column 3 of our table indicate, a measured increase of some 2.2 million workers un-

---

6   In the slack year 1961, the official unemployment rate was around 6 percent. Adjusting for parttime work, the full-time equivalent unemployment rate was around 9 percent. For a discussion of this adjustment, see *The Economic Report of the President* for 1962, p. 43.

TABLE 3-3 EMPLOYMENT AND UNEMPLOYMENT, 1929-1974

Year	Employment	Unemployment	Unemployment Rate—Percent of Civilian Labor Force
	Thousands of Persons Age 14 and Over		
1929	47,630	1,550	3.2%
1930	45,480	4,340	8.7
1931	42,400	8,020	15.9
1932	38,940	12,060	23.6
1933	38,760	12,830	24.9
1934	40,890	11,340	21.7
1935	42,260	10,610	20.1
1936	44,410	9,030	16.9
1937	46,300	7,700	14.3
1938	44,220	10,390	19.0
1939	45,750	9,480	17.2
1940	47,520	8,120	14.6
1941	50,350	5,560	9.9
1942	53,750	2,660	4.7
1943	54,470	1,070	1.9
1944	53,960	670	1.2
1945	52,820	1,040	1.9
1946	55,250	2,270	3.9
1947	57,812	2,356	3.9
	Thousands of Persons Age 16 and Over		
1947	57,039	2,311	3.9%
1948	58,344	2,276	3.8
1949	57,649	3,637	5.9
1950	59,920	3,288	5.3
1951	59,962	2,055	5.3
1952	60,254	1,833	3.0
1953	61,181	1,834	2.9
1954	60,110	3,532	5.5
1955	62,171	2,852	4.4
1956	63,802	2,750	4.1
1957	64,071	2,859	4.3
1958	63,036	4,602	6.8
1959	64,630	3,740	5.5
1960	65,778	3,852	5.5
1961	65,746	4,714	6.7
1962	66,702	3,911	5.5
1963	67,762	4,070	5.7
1964	69,305	3,786	5.2
1965	71,088	3,366	4.5
1966	72,895	2,875	3.8
1967	74,372	2,975	3.8
1968	75,920	2,817	3.6
1969	77,902	2,832	3.5
1970	78,627	4,088	4.9
1971	79,120	4,993	5.9
1972	81,702	4,840	5.6
1973	84,409	4,304	4.9
1974	85,936	5,076	5.6

Source: Department of Labor, Bureau of Statistics.

employed. And with what we already know about labor market responses to altered levels of economic activity, it should come as no surprise that a change in the measured unemployment rate can be associated with an even more striking change in output. In 1962 it was estimated that, in the United States, a 1-percent reduction in unemployment resulted in a 3-percent increase in output.[7] How can this be? As the number of unemployed falls the number employed rises even more because of increased labor force participation rates. Also, expansion of the number of employed workers typically is accompanied by an increase in the average work-week. Finally, labor's output per hour usually rises during expansions since employed workers are more fully utilized. A two-pilot airline crew may, for example, carry more passengers per flight as well as make more flights when business conditions improve. Our unemployment statistics appear to seriously understate the economic cost (in terms of measured output) of a slack economy since a substantial fall in national output can be accompanied by an increase in unemployment of an apparently small magnitude—for example, a 6-percent fall in output can accompany a 2-percent increase in unemployment. You should endeavor to remain aware of that bias as unemployment problems are analyzed in the remainder of this text.

SUMMARY

Among the goals of macroeconomic policy listed in Chapter 1, the maintenance of full employment and of reasonable stability in the general price level enjoyed lofty status. This chapter has reviewed the data series—price indexes and employment/unemployment statistics—which monitor our success or failure in achieving those goals. While both the price measures and the employment/ unemployment statistics compiled for the U.S. economy are subject to biases, they rank among the few most closely watched indicators of the macroeconomy's performance.

QUESTIONS

1.

Item	Prices		Quantities	
	1960	1975	1960	1975
Blue jeans	$ 3.00	$ 5.00	500	600
Drive-in movie tickets	1.25	1.75	400	450
Electronic calculators	150.00	55.00	40	120

7 See A. Okun, "The Gap Between Actual and Potential Output," reprinted in A. Okun, *The Battle Against Unemployment* (New York: W. W. Norton & Company, 1972), pp. 13-22.

(a) Calculate the Laspeyres index for 1975.

(b) Calculate the Paasche index for 1975.

(c) What biases would you expect in each of these index values?

(d) What practical advantages do you see in computing Laspeyres rather than Paasche price indexes?

2. Explain how price indexes can be used to deflate nominal values.

3. In a *Wall Street Journal* article on October 21, 1971, a number of criticisms were lodged against the CPI. As an example of the criticisms cited, that article said ". . . if tomatoes skyrocket in price and consumers thus switch to apples, the index may exaggerate the jump in the cost-of-living since it gives the unused tomatoes the same weight as before."

(a) Elaborate on the "exaggeration" in the rate of inflation cited in the *Wall Street Journal* article.

(b) Suppose tomatoes skyrocket in price because of a change in tastes— thence in demand. What bias would be introduced into the CPI?

(c) Cite two other likely sources of bias in the consumer price index and explain how they produce that bias.

4. How is the U.S. unemployment rate computed?

5. In what ways is the measured unemployment rate a biased measure of true unemployment.

6. In Chapter 1, we argued that full employment does not mean zero percent measured unemployment. Evaluate that assertion in light of the definition of unemployment you now have.

SUGGESTED READING

Clague, Ewan. "Computing the Consumer Price Index," *Challenge*. May 1962, reprinted in A. Okun (ed.), *The Battle Against Unemployment*, 1st edition. New York: W. W. Norton & Co., Inc., pp. 83-87.

Cullison, William E. "An Employment Pressure Index as an Alternative Measure of Labor Market Conditions," *The Review of Economics and Statistics*. Vol. LVII, February 1975, pp. 115-121.

Hailstones, T., B. Martin, and F. Mastrianna. *Contemporary Economic Problems and Issues*, 2d edition. Cincinnati: Southwestern Publishing Co., Chapter 2.

President's Committee to Appraise Employment and Unemployment Statistics. *Measuring Employment and Unemployment*. Washington, D.C.: U.S. Government Printing Office, 1962.

Ruggles, Richard. "The Problems of Our Price Indexes," *Challenge*. November 1961, reprinted in A. Okun (ed.), *The Battle Against Unemployment*, 1st edition. New York: W. W. Norton & Co., Inc., pp. 77-82.

Wallace, William. *Measuring Price Changes*. Richmond: Federal Reserve Bank of Richmond, 1972.

Wonnacott, T. H., and R. J. Wonnacott. *Introductory Statistics for Business and Economics*. New York: John Wiley & Sons, Chapter 23.

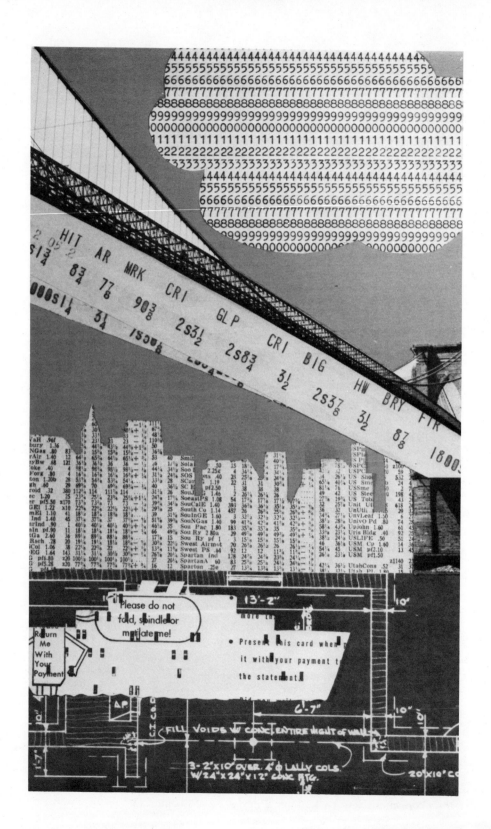

Chapter 4
Models of Simple
Economic Systems

The last two chapters surveyed the main sources of summary descriptive data available on the performance of the world's most complicated economic system. We are now ready to begin *analyzing* that economy's performance. To understand why the economy performs as it does and how its performance might be improved we have to build models of that complex system. As indicated in Chapter 1, such models are always simplified abstractions of reality for if our models did not vastly simplify the world, we could never hope to understand their workings (or, hence, the workings of the real world).

The models constructed in this chapter fall within the scope of what economists describe as *Keynesian models*. They owe their heritage to a revolutionary book, *The General Theory of Employment, Interest, and Money*,[1] written in 1936 by a British economist named John Maynard Keynes. Prior to the 1930s, economists placed great faith in the ability of a market economy to generate and maintain full employment automatically. While they recognized that the economy was subject to periodic slumps, pre-Keynesian economists believed that natural forces within the economy could be depended on to restore full employment within an acceptable time period.

But the experience of the *Great Depression* which began in 1929 required a reconsideration of the prevailing faith in an automatically adjusting economy. Unemployment hovered above 15 percent year after year with no evidence of any powerful forces working to restore full employment. Indeed, not until the mobilization for World War II was the economy freed from the lingering malaise that began a full decade earlier.

In marked contrast to the analysis of his predecessors, the model Keynes constructed in *The General Theory* argued that automatic forces within a market economy cannot be depended upon to maintain full employment or to restore full employment equilibrium once the economy has been rocked from that position. It follows that government intervention in the economy can, at times, be required to elicit a satisfactory performance from that system.[2] In the postwar era, the majority of economists have adopted the Keynesian framework for macroeconomic analysis.

1 Lord John Maynard Keynes, *The General Theory of Employment, Interest, and Money* (New York: Harcourt Brace Jovanovich, Inc., 1936).
2 Pre-Keynesian and Keynesian analysis is carefully compared and contrasted in Chapter 10 and Appendix 10A.

As a natural consequence of their birth during the Great Depression, Keynesian macroeconomic models focus attention on the determinants of aggregate *demand* for real goods and services. During the depression a skilled labor force and a massive store of factories and sales outlets languished in the face of pressing unfulfilled consumer needs. Business firms were shut down simply because their output could not be profitably sold; aggregate demand for real goods and services was just too weak to sustain full employment production.

With a major portion of the industrialized world's productive capacity idle, Keynes recognized the essentially passive role played in the depression by the supply side of the economy. His analysis emphasized the need for stimulating aggregate demand in order to return the economy to full employment. While we will have a great deal more to say about the supply side of the economy as our analysis progresses, the formal models developed in this chapter assume that the supply of real goods and services responds passively to changes in aggregate demand.

ANALYZING A SIMPLE ECONOMY

Since we are neophytes at model construction, we will begin our own model-building activities as painlessly as possible, putting together a model of the most basic kind of economic system. No modern real-world economy could be adequately represented by this first model, but the analytical sequence required for constructing such a model will be directly applicable to the construction of more sophisticated and realistic models. If you thoroughly understand the development of this simple model, you will be able to work through the more complex models developed in this chapter very quickly. Indeed, reflecting your rapidly developing skill as a model builder, you may conclude that the analysis in this chapter is unduly repetitious.

The simplest sort of economic system is *closed* (that is, it is involved in no economic transactions with agents of any other country) and has no government. Moreover, it can be assumed that all production takes place in the "business" sector of the economy with all resulting profits accruing to firms' owners,[3] that all consumption takes place in the "household" sector, and that there are no transfer payments. Reflecting our concern with the *real* performance of the economic system, all the magnitudes dealt with throughout this chapter are measured in *real* terms.

Measuring the Level of Production—
National Accounts for a Simple Economy

As a first step toward analyzing this simple economic system, let us see if we can create a correspondingly simple system of descriptive national accounts com-

---

3 In the case of incorporated business, this assumption requires all profits to be paid out to stockholders. These payments are cash *dividends*.

parable to the U.S. national income and product accounts. The broadest measure of production will again be GNP, which can be calculated using either the expenditure or the income (receipts) approach. From the expenditure side of the accounts, total GNP can be obtained by adding consumption spending by households and gross investment spending by business firms since, with no government and no foreign trade, government spending and net exports are nonexistent. From the income side, total received income will consist of the sum of wages, interest (paid by business to households), rent, and profit. This figure must be adjusted in the manner described below in order to provide a figure for GNP.

The *net* output generated in the production process still falls short of GNP by the amount of capital consumption, just as it did in the full accounts for the United States. Thus, net national product is still GNP minus capital consumption. Of course, it is also the sum of consumption and net investment spending.

At this point, our simple country's accounts begin to differ from those for the United States. With no government, there are no indirect business taxes. Thus, net national product is no different from national income (which represented *earned* income in the U.S. accounts). With no taxes on corporate profits, no social security system payments, no retained earnings by business, and no transfer payments, there is no difference between *earned* income and actual *received* income—that is, national income is the same as personal income for our simple economy. Finally, with no personal income taxes, all of received income is available to households as disposable income. We have clearly simplified the world. Households' disposable income is now identical to net national product. GNP figures can be obtained by adding up all consumption and investment spending or (from the income side) by adding to actual received income the amount of capital consumption. The national accounts for this economy are summarized algebraically as follows using the same symbols as in Chapter 2:[4]

$$\text{Expenditure Approach:} \left\{ \begin{array}{l} \Sigma \text{ spending on final} \\ \text{goods and services} \end{array} \right\} = C + I_G = \text{GNP} - D = \text{NNP} = C + I_N.$$

$$\text{Income Approach:} \left\{ \Sigma \text{ (wages, interest, rent, dividends)} \right\} = \text{NNP}$$

$$= \text{NI} \quad \text{since there are no } T_i$$
$$= \text{PI} \quad \text{since there are no}$$
$$\quad\quad T_b, SS, R_t, T_r$$
$$= Y_d \quad \text{since there are no } T_p.$$

The national account manipulations above demonstrate that, for *measured* values of the consumption, investment, and income terms,

$$Y \equiv C + I_N, \tag{4-1}$$

4 Those symbols are: $T_i =$ indirect business taxes, $T_b =$ taxes on corporate profits, $SS =$ social security contributions, $R_t =$ retained earnings, $T_r =$ transfer payments, NI = national income, PI = personal income, $Y_d =$ disposable income, $T_p =$ personal income taxes, and so on.

where Y is NNP, C is consumption, and I_N is net investment. Those manipulations also show that disposable income is identical to NNP. Since all of disposable income must be consumed or saved and disposable income is the same as NNP, for *measured* values of the variables,

$$Y \equiv C + S, \tag{4-2}$$

where S is personal saving by the household sector and the other variables retain their same definitions. Combining the accounting identities in Equations 4-1 and 4-2 yields the identity

$$S \equiv I_N. \tag{4-3}$$

Thus, the accounting identities for our simple world show that *measured* spending is always identical to the *measured* value of output (Eq. 4-1) and *measured* saving is always identical to *measured* investment (Eq. 4-3).

Why should measured saving always equal measured investment? A moment's reflection on one of our accounting identities (use Eq. 4-1) will make sense of this claim. Suppose the value of *net* output produced in the simple economy in 1974 was $1,000 billion (the value of income generated in the production process must, of course, also be $1,000 billion since, in the simple economy, any commodity's "value" or "price" is exhausted by factor payments—the sum of wages, rent, interest, and any residual profit). This $1,000 billion worth of output might have consisted of $200 billion worth of investment goods (goods produced to add *intentionally* to the existing stock of plants, equipment, and inventories held by the business sector) and $800 billion worth of output which business produced for consumption by the household sector. If during 1974 the household sector chose to consume out of its $1,000 billion of received income only $700 billion worth of goods and services, there would be an *unplanned* addition of $100 billion worth of goods and services to business inventories. Since additions to inventory count as investment, whether intended or not, *actual* or *measured* investment in 1974 would have been $300 billion, matching 1974's personal saving figure. The total $1,000 billion worth of output would be absorbed by *measured* consumption and investment. Counting the unplanned, unintended change in inventories as investment ensures the identity of measured saving with measured investment and of measured spending with output.[5]

While measured total spending must always be equal to the measured value of output (and income), the value of *planned* or *intended* total spending need not always be equal to output. In the example above, consumers *planned* to buy $700 billion worth of output and business *planned* to buy $200 billion worth.

5 It is also true that, for measured values, $Y_G = C + I_G$ and $Y_G = C + S_G$, where Y_G is GNP, C is consumption, I_G is gross investment, and S_G is "gross" saving, consisting of personal saving by households plus business saving in the form of depreciation funds. Therefore, $\cancel{C} + I_G = \cancel{C} + S_G$ so $I_G = S_G$. In the measured sense, gross spending $(C + I_G)$ must be equal to current gross output and gross investment must be equal to gross saving.

Also, business "bought" an *unplanned* addition of $100 billion worth of inventories. Analogously, while *measured* saving and measured investment are always equal, *planned* investment may differ markedly from *planned* saving (in our example, *planned* investment of $200 billion fell short of *planned* saving by $100 billion, resulting in an unintended increase in inventories of $100 billion). This distinction between planned and measured equalities is essential to macroeconomic analysis. As we shall see, equality of planned saving and investment (or of planned total spending and output) is necessary for our simple economic system to be in *equilibrium*. In contrast, measured equalities in the national income accounting measures tell us nothing about equilibrium.

Before proceeding to the next section, you should be certain you understand the distinction between planned and measured values of consumption, saving, and investment. To be sure that you do, repeat the exercise we have just been through but do it assuming that households choose to consume $900 billion worth of goods and services out of their $1,000 billion of received income.

Equilibrium in the Simplest Model

With the development of the descriptive national accounts for our simple economy completed, attention can be focused now on the requirements for equilibrium in that economy. An economic system is in *equilibrium*—at rest—when there are no forces tending to alter the prevailing levels of output, spending, and so on. For purposes of determining the specific requirements for an economy to be in equilibrium it is helpful to represent the flows of aggregate income (and spending) in that economy in a simple schematic diagram. For our basic economy, Figure 4-1 provides such a schematic description using the $1,000 billion figure for the assumed level of net output (Y).

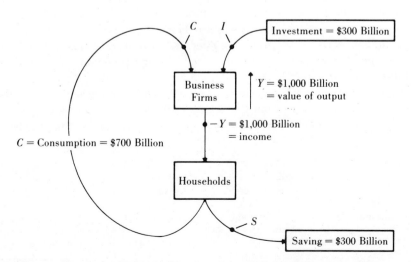

FIGURE 4-1 The Flow of Income (Spending) in a Closed Economy with No Government

Briefly relating what we already know to this flow diagram, we see again that output and income are identical. As we have previously indicated, the value of total output must be the same as total costs of production where those total costs include payments for wages, rent, interest, and the residual item profit. These payments for factor inputs by business are, of course, income to the owners (households) of the employed factor inputs.

Figure 4-1 shows households in the simple economy collectively spending part of their received income and saving part (in this case amounts $700 billion and $300 billion, respectively) with consumption plus saving equal to total received income. Our diagram clearly reflects the point that consumption spending absorbs part, but only part, of the total output of businesses (in this case, $700 billion of the $1,000 billion worth of output). But, if this economic system is to be in equilibrium, the remaining $300 billion worth of output must be *willingly* absorbed by that other component of spending, business investment in plants, equipment, and inventories (the necessary flow of planned investment spending is shown in the diagram). Total *planned* spending on output is, of course, the sum of *planned* consumption and *planned* investment spending $(C + I)$. This total of *planned spending* must be exactly equal to the value of output (income) for our simple economic system to be in equilibrium (that is, *it is required that* $Y = C + I$ *in the planned sense for equilibrium to exist*).[6]

Disequilibrium

But what happens if, at the $1,000 billion level of output, total *planned* spending $(C + I)$ is less than the value of output? For example, if this year output is $1,000 billion but planned $C + I$ is only $900 billion, what would we expect to happen? [7]

Clearly, $900 billion of spending cannot clear the market of $1,000 billion worth of output. Business inventories will be growing and this expansion of inventories is *unintentional*. Businesses would surely not continue to produce $1,000 billion worth of output period after period if only $900 billion worth is willingly purchased for final use each period, requiring the unintended addition of $100 billion of output to inventory each period. Eventually, firms would cut back production (output), reducing income generated in the production process equivalently. Generalizing from this example, if the value of output (income) exceeds the value of total planned spending $(C + I)$, output will fall. *The economy cannot be in equilibrium if unintended increases in inventory are occurring.*

---

6 Again, output and spending are always equal in value in the observed, measured, or "realized" sense.

7 To illustrate this question graphically, you can redraw Figure 4-1 replacing the flow of $300 billion of measured investment with $200 billion of *planned* investment, making total *planned* spending equal to $900 billion (planned $C + I = $700 billion + $200 billion = $900 billion).

Similarly, if total planned spending or *aggregate demand* exceeds the value of output (for example, if planned $C + I = \$1,100$ billion while $Y = \$1,000$ billion), inventories will suffer an unplanned shrinkage. If firms observe such an unintended decrease in their inventories, period after period, they are likely to respond by increasing their rate of production if they have any unused capacity to produce. Thus, if the value of total planned spending exceeds the value of output, output (income) will rise. *The economy cannot be in equilibrium if unintended decreases in inventory are occurring.*

The basic rule we have drawn from our discussion of disequilibrium will be valid for every model we construct no matter how complicated. *The market for goods and services can be in equilibrium only if there are no unintended increases or decreases in inventory.*

An Alternative Statement of the Formal Equilibrium Condition

Again, the basic equilibrium requirement of no unintended change in inventory will be met if all of received income is spent (that is, if total planned spending is identical to the value of output, or $Y = C + I$). Referring to Figure 4-1 again, we can see that there is an alternative way of stating this rule. Total spending will remain equal to the value of output as long as any *leakage* from the circular flow of income (such as the $300 billion of saving) is exactly offset by an identical *injection* of spending into the income stream (such as the $300 billion of investment). That is, total planned spending will equal the value of output $(Y = C + I)$ if leakages equal injections. For the simple economy we are analyzing, saving is the only leakage from the income stream and investment is the only injection into that stream. Thus, equilibrium will prevail if planned saving is equal to planned investment, or $S = I$. Since our two fundamental equalities are fully equivalent statements of the same equilibrium condition, in addition to both holding true when the simple economic system is in equilibrium they both must be violated when that system is in disequilibrium. Glancing back at Figure 4-1, it is easy to see that when planned spending falls short of current output $(C + I < Y)$, planned saving must exceed planned investment $(S > I)$. In this case, inventories will experience an unplanned growth, and production will be reduced. When planned spending exceeds current output $(C + I > Y)$, planned saving will be less than planned investment and, with inventories shrinking unexpectedly, business firms will step up the rate of production.

A QUANTITATIVE ESTIMATE OF EQUILIBRIUM INCOME

We now know what condition(s) must hold if an equilibrium income level is to prevail in the simple economic system, but we do not know what the value of equilibrium income will be. To find out we need to introduce some specific quantitative information about the spending behavior of the households and business firms in the simple economy. Specifically, estimates of planned consumption and planned investment are needed. Simple Keynesian models hypothesize that the volume of consumption spending society plans to undertake during any period is directly related to the volume of income it has to spend. Typically, consumption is taken to be a linear function of disposable income so that the *consumption function* in our model can be written algebraically as

$$C = a + bY,$$

where Y is the value of aggregate income (net output), and the coefficients a and b are behavioral constants. The second coefficient, b, which measures the slope of the straight-line consumption function, is called the *marginal propensity to consume*. It is a measure of the response of aggregate consumption per dollar of change in disposable income.[8] The first coefficient, a, is just the intercept of the straight-line consumption function.

With data on aggregate consumption, C, and income, Y, over time, linear regression analysis can be used to ascertain the values of a and b in the consumption function (review Chapter 1, pp. 7-11 if this assertion is not clear). In the process of fitting the hypothesized consumption function, we would be testing the validity of the simple hypothesis that consumption is linearly related to income. If the linear consumption function appears to adequately capture the linkage between income and consumption, the fitted function could be used as a predictor of the level of consumption society would *plan* to undertake at any selected level of income.

We can now turn our attention to accounting for planned investment spending. Unfortunately, explaining what determines planned investment is relatively complex. To keep our model-building efforts as simple and straightforward as possible, we will avoid that complexity for now by assuming that the volume of planned investment in the time period with which we are concerned is a constant, the value of which is *given* (say, through a survey of businessmen's investment plans). In the jargon of economic analysis, we are assuming that the value of planned investment is *exogenous* to our model—that is, its level does not depend on the value of any variable in the model we are building but is determined by forces outside the scope of that model. In contrast, the value of income and of consumption (which depends on income) are to be determined within our model. Thus, those variables are *endogenous*.

We are now ready to solve for the quantitative value of equilibrium output. Restating our two equivalent formulations of the equilibrium condition, plugging

---

8   As we have already demonstrated, society must either consume or save all of its disposable income. If only a fractional portion of any $1 dollar increase in income is consumed, the remaining fraction must be saved. Thus, the response of saving per dollar of change in income, the so-called *marginal propensity to save*, is $(1 - b)$.

in our "behavioral hypotheses" for consumption and investment, and solving algebraically for the equilibrium level of output (income) yields the following results:

Form 1:

Aggregate demand = value of output (income),

or

$Y = C + I.$

With $C = a + bY$ and $I = \bar{I}$ (the bar indicating exogenous), the equilibrium condition becomes

$Y = a + bY + \bar{I},$

so the equilibrium level of income $(Y_{eq.})$ is

$$Y_{eq.} = \frac{1}{1-b}(a + \bar{I}). \tag{4-4}$$

Form 2:

Leakages (saving) = injections (investment),

or

$S = I.$

With

$S = Y - C$

$\quad = Y - a - bY$

$\quad = -a + (1-b)Y,$

the equilibrium condition becomes

$-a + (1-b)Y = \bar{I}$

so the equilibrium level of income is

$$Y_{eq.} = \frac{1}{1-b}(a + \bar{I}). \tag{4-5}$$

Since the two forms of the equilibrium condition are equivalent, the level of income that satisfies either statement of the equilibrium condition must be the same $[Y_{eq.} = (1/1 - b)(a + \bar{I})$ for this model].

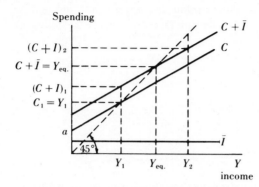

FIGURE 4-2 Equilibrium Income—
Total Spending Equal to Income

Graphical Solutions

We can also solve this simple algebraic system graphically. Plotting our assumed consumption and investment functions would yield schedules C and $\bar{I}$ in Figure 4-2. Total demand (planned spending) in this model is, again, just $C + I$. Graphically summing the C and I schedules vertically in Figure 4-2 yields the aggregate demand schedule $C + \bar{I}$. Since this schedule lies above the consumption schedule by amount $\bar{I}$ at every income level, it has the same slope as the consumption schedule.

The 45° line in Figure 4-2 is purely a reference line. With the same dollar scale on the horizontal and vertical axes of our diagram, this reference line simply serves to identify points where spending is equal to the value of income (output). For example, when income is Y_1, consumption (C_1) is exactly equal to income, as the intersection of the consumption schedule with the 45° reference line demonstrates.

For equilibrium, we know total planned spending must be equal to the value of income $(Y = C + I)$. The reference line identifies the *one level* of income where this equality holds as $Y_{eq.}$ in Figure 4-2. As we can also readily see from that diagram, if the business sector incorrectly anticipates the strength of aggregate demand there will be unplanned inventory investment prompting an adjustment in output (income). For example, if the business sector produces a volume of output smaller than the equilibrium quantity (such as Y_1 in Figure 4-2), planned spending $(C + I)$ will exceed the value of output [by $(C + I)_1$ minus Y_1], resulting in an unplanned depletion of inventories. As inventories suffer an unintended decline, business firms will step up production raising the level of output toward $Y_{eq.}$.

On the other hand, if the business sector overestimates the strength of aggregate demand and produces a volume of output larger than $Y_{eq.}$ (say, Y_2), not all of current output will be willingly purchased. There will be unintended inventory investment which will prompt business firms to cut back on production. Only at

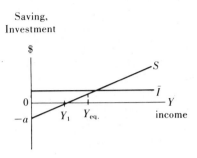

FIGURE 4-3 Equilibrium Income—
Leakages Equal to Injections

output level $Y_{eq.}$ is there neither unintended inventory accumulation nor depletion.

We can also produce a graphical solution for this system by plotting leakages (saving) and injections (investment) against income. These schedules are,
respectively, S and I in Figure 4-3. Recall from Figure 4-2 that, as a mathematical
proposition, consumption was amount a when income was zero, so that all consumption at that unlikely income level would be provided by *dissaving*. That is,
saving at $Y = 0$ is $S = Y - C = 0 - a - b \cdot 0$ or $S = -a$. When income was Y_1,
consumption was equal to income (saving was zero) as reflected by point Y_1
in Figure 4-3. By knowing any two points on the linear saving schedule we can,
of course, plot the entire schedule as we have in Figure 4-3. The investment
schedule plotted in that figure is the same one employed in Figure 4-2.

The relationship that must hold between leakages and injections for there to
be equilibrium is that leakages and injections must be equal $(S = I)$. This
equality holds only for $Y_{eq.}$ in Figure 4-3 ($Y_{eq.}$ in Figure 4-3 must, of course, be
the same as $Y_{eq.}$ in Figure 4-2). With output below $Y_{eq.}$, the investment injection
into the income stream exceeds the saving leakage from that stream so aggregate
demand must exceed the volume of output. Consequently, inventories would
suffer an unplanned depletion prompting an increase in production. With output
above $Y_{eq.}$, the saving leakage is larger than the investment injection indicating
that output exceeds planned spending. Thus, there would be an unplanned swelling of inventories prompting a production cutback.

With statistical estimates of the behavioral constants (a and b) in the consumption function and with an estimate of planned investment ($\bar{I}$) we could
solve for the specific numerical value of equilibrium income. If, for example,
statistical analysis showed $a = \$100$ billion, $b = .60$, and $\bar{I} = \$300$ billion, the
equilibrium level of income would be $\$1,000$ billion. *Prove this result both
algebraically and graphically.*

The exercise you have just been through is a clear-cut application of the
methodology of macroeconomic analysis. For several decades, economists have

involved themselves in similar exercises, building models and, then, using statistical analysis to test and quantify their models. Quite probably you are thinking: "Is that all there is to macroeconomic analysis? This model must be too simple for practical application." Your concern is well founded; the model *is* too simplistic. However, introducing real-world complexities into the analytical framework we have just constructed is straightforward and easily understood if you have a firm grasp of the basic model. The rest of this chapter is devoted to constructing more complex models of the market for real goods and services (what is often labeled the *commodity market*) and to demonstrating the use of those models for predicting not only the level of output but also the changes in output that would result from various shocks to the economic system.

MODEL II—A CLOSED ECONOMY WITH A GOVERNMENT SECTOR

Perhaps the one most important modification we could undertake to make our product market model more realistic is the introduction of a government that has the power to collect taxes and spend. Through its expenditures and tax levies the government plays an important role in determining the overall level of aggregate demand. Indeed, through changing its levels of spending or tax collections, the government can and does exert control over the economy—as we indicated in Chapter 1, employing expansionary or restrictive "budgets" as it judges necessary for enhancing the economy's performance.

The impact of the introduction of such a government on our original income flow diagram (Figure 4-1) is reflected in Figure 4-4. When there is a government that collects taxes, the value of income available to be disposed of as households see fit (disposable income) is no longer the same as received income Y. Instead, disposable income is received income less taxes ($Y_d \equiv Y - T$) and it is this reduced level of income that households have available to consume or save as they choose as indicated schematically in Figure 4-4. To accommodate government spending, it must be recognized that such spending comprises an additional source of demand for the output of the business sector as also shown in that diagram.

For equilibrium in this more complicated economic system, the same *basic* condition must hold as for the economy without a government—*there must be no unintended changes in inventories.* Total planned spending ($C + I + G$) must be just sufficient to clear the market of the current level of output (Y) or, in algebraic terms, we must have $Y = C + I + G$ for equilibrium in this closed (no foreign sector) model with a government that taxes and spends.

As was the case with our simpler model, for aggregate demand to be just equal to the value of output, any leakage from the circular flow of income must be precisely offset by an equal injection into the income stream. But in this model, there are two sources of leakage [private saving (S) and tax collections

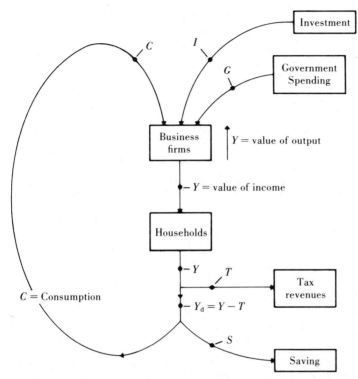

FIGURE 4-4   The Flow of Income (Spending) for a Closed Economy

(T)] and two sources of injections into the spending stream [investment (I) and government spending (G)]. For equilibrium, then, it is also necessary that $S + T = I + G$.

A Quantitative Estimate of Equilibrium Income

With the equilibrium condition(s) for this model in hand, we can now solve for a quantitative estimate of the equilibrium level of income if we have the necessary quantitative information on planned consumption, investment, taxes, and government spending. Suppose our information on the consumption function indicates that the simple straight-line form of the consumption function we have already employed can be retained. In this case, the only modification needed in the treatment of consumption in order to accommodate the role of government is the explicit recognition that consumption depends on *disposable income* (Y_d) rather than received income Y. We will also retain the same value for investment assuming, again, that this variable is exogenously determined. Finally, we will assume that the levels of government spending (G) and tax collections (T) are exogenously determined (they are government policy decisions). In summary, our model of income determination has become:

$$\left.\begin{array}{l} Y = C + I + G \\ \text{or } S + T = I + G \end{array}\right\} \text{ the equilibrium condition(s)},$$

$$C = a + bY_d \quad \text{where } Y_d \equiv Y - T \text{ by definition,}$$

$$\left.\begin{array}{l} I = \overline{I} \\ G = \overline{G} \\ T = \overline{T} \end{array}\right\} \text{ bar indicates values determined exogenously.}$$

Once again, we can solve our model algebraically for the equilibrium level of income beginning with either of our two equivalent statements of the equilibrium condition. Doing so yields:

Form 1:

Aggregate demand = value of output

or

$$Y = C + I + G.$$

Substituting for C, I, and G,

$$Y = a + bY_d + \overline{I} + \overline{G}$$

$$= a + b(Y - \overline{T}) + \overline{I} + \overline{G}$$

$$\therefore Y_{\text{eq.}} = \frac{1}{1-b}(a + \overline{I} + \overline{G} - b\overline{T}) \tag{4-6}$$

Form 2:

Leakages = injections,

or

$$S + T = I + G.$$

Substituting for S, T, I, and G yields

$$(Y_d - C) + \overline{T} = \overline{I} + \overline{G},$$

so

$$Y_d - a - b(Y - \overline{T}) + \overline{T} = \overline{I} + \overline{G},$$

or

$$Y(1-b) = a + \overline{I} + \overline{G} - b\overline{T}.$$

$$\therefore Y_{\text{eq.}} = \frac{1}{1-b}(a + \overline{I} + \overline{G} - b\overline{T}). \tag{4-7}$$

As you can corroborate easily, with $a = \$100$ billion, $b = .60$, and $\overline{I} = \$300$ billion as before, and with $\overline{G} = \$100$ billion and $\overline{T} = \$83.3$ billion (the government budget $\$16.7$ billion in *deficit*), the equilibrium level of income is $\$1,125$ billion.

Graphical Solutions

A solution for the equilibrium level of income can also be obtained graphically as illustrated in Figure 4-5. In the upper portion of that diagram, the aggregate demand schedule is obtained by summing, vertically, the consumption, investment and government spending schedules. The equilibrium output level, where aggregate demand and output are equal, is $Y_{eq.}$. The government's tax levies can be seen influencing aggregate demand (hence equilibrium output) by reducing consumption spending out of net national product by amount $b\overline{T}$, the volume of tax collections times the fraction of those tax revenues that would be spent if left in the hands of consumers.

In the lower portion of Figure 4-5 total injections into the spending stream are obtained by summing the exogenous investment and government spending schedules, $\overline{I}$ and $\overline{G}$. Total leakages are the sum of saving out of *after-tax* income

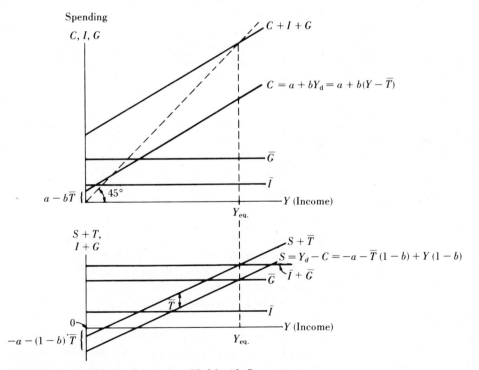

FIGURE 4-5   Equilibrium Income in a Model with Government

and exogenous tax levies $\overline{T}$. Equilibrium prevails, at output level $Y_{eq.}$, where total leakages and total injections are equal. While graphical solutions to the equation systems we have constructed to represent simple economies remain possible, it should be clear that the graphical technique becomes intractable quite rapidly as our models become more complicated.

MODEL III—A CLOSED ECONOMY WITH GOVERNMENT; INVESTMENT AND TAX REVENUES ENDOGENOUS

Our model of the economy can be made still more realistic by introducing some simple but compellingly sensible modifications in the investment and tax revenue schedules we employ. Dealing first with the investment function, it should be noted that the extent of utilization of existing plants and equipment is positively related to the level of income. Furthermore, businessmen's expectations of future business conditions are likely to be more optimistic when the economy is healthy. With these notions in mind, many macroeconomic analysts allege that business investment in new productive facilities is a positive function of income. A simple investment function that allows investment to change with income, but still accounts for the existence of an *autonomous* component of investment spending *not influenced by the level of economic activity*, is the straight-line function $I = \overline{I} + cY$ where $\overline{I}$ is the autonomous component of investment (representing, for example, investment that results from innovations); c, which could be called a "marginal propensity to invest," represents the *induced* response of investment to changes in the level of income; and Y is aggregate income as usual.

Turning now to the tax function, in practice government tax policy typically specifies not the total volume of tax receipts to be collected but the structure of tax *rates* instead, with the revenues generated by the tax system changing as the level of income changes. A simple tax function which permits this behavior of tax receipts is the linear relationship $T = \overline{T} + tY$ where $T =$ total tax revenues, $\overline{T}$ is the autonomous component of taxes, t is the marginal tax rate representing the response of tax collections to a change in income, and Y is total received income.

Altering the form of our tax and investment functions has little impact on the analytical framework we have employed for finding the equilibrium value of income. The schematic income flow diagram for our new model is the same as for the preceding model (Figure 4-4) since no new sources of leakages or injections have been introduced into that model. Thus, the basic conditions that must hold for equilibrium are the same (that is, for equilibrium $Y = C + I + G$ or, equivalently, $S + T = I + G$).

Retaining the same behavioral assumptions for our other schedules, but employing the modified investment and tax schedules, our model can be algebraically summarized as:

$$\left.\begin{array}{l} Y = C + I + G \\ \text{or } S + T = I + G \end{array}\right\} \quad \text{the equilibrium condition(s)}$$

$$\left.\begin{array}{l} C = a + bY_d \\ I = \overline{I} + cY \\ G = \overline{G} \\ T = \overline{T} + tY \end{array}\right\} \quad \text{spending and tax functions.}$$

Plugging into the first form of the equilibrium condition for this model, a solution for the equilibrium level of income can be obtained as follows:

$$Y = C + I + G \text{ for equilibrium}$$
$$\text{so } Y = a + bY_d + \overline{I} + cY + \overline{G}$$
$$= a + b(Y - T) + \overline{I} + cY + \overline{G}$$
$$\text{or } Y = a + b(Y - \overline{T} - tY) + \overline{I} + cY + \overline{G} \quad \text{where } Y_d = Y - T \text{ and } \overline{T} = T + tY.$$

Collecting the Y terms and moving them to the left side of our equality yields

$$Y(1 - b - c + bt) = a + \overline{I} + \overline{G} - b\overline{T},$$

and solving for Y alone yields

$$Y_{\text{eq.}} = \frac{1}{1 - b - c + bt}(a + \overline{I} + \overline{G} - b\overline{T}) \tag{4-8}$$

$$\text{or } Y_{\text{eq.}} = \frac{1}{1 - b(1 - t) - c}(a + \overline{I} + \overline{G} - b\overline{T}).$$

With numerical values for a, b, c, $\overline{I}$, $\overline{G}$, t, and $\overline{T}$, we could solve for the numerical value of equilibrium income. You should be able to prove that the same value for the equilibrium level of income can be derived from the alternative form of the equilibrium condition $(S + T = I + G)$.

There are many additional modifications that could be introduced into our income determination models. For example, as a next logical step the economy could be *opened* to permit international trade—the export of domestically produced goods and services and the import of their foreign produced counterparts (indeed, a foreign sector will be built into the macro model in Chapter 11). However, the prime objective of the first half of this chapter has been to provide familiarity with the model-building process as applied in the construction of simple Keynesian income-determination models, and no further complexities need be entertained to acquire that familiarity. As our exercises have already demonstrated, the introduction of additional complexities in no way alters what we have determined to be the basic requirement for equilibrium in the market for goods and services. For equilibrium, there must be no unintended inventory changes (requiring equality of planned spending with output and of planned injections with planned leakages). With unplanned additions to inventories, business firms will reduce output and with the unplanned shrinkage of inventories they will endeavor to raise production. With no more than a comprehension of the basic requirement for commodity market equilibrium and an ability to visualize income and spending flows, as we have done schematically in this chapter, you can construct models of surprising complexity which, with information on planned spending totals, can be used to predict income.

MULTIPLIER ANALYSIS

We have now seen that we can build simple, mathematical models of the product market and solve for the equilibrium level of income with those models. But, a question which is of more direct importance to policy makers is: What happens to the level of income if equilibrium is disturbed by a change in some parameter in the system (for example, if equilibrium is disturbed by a shift in the consumption, investment, government spending, or tax schedule)? The macroeconomist's construction that is concerned with the impact on equilibrium income of such shocks to the system is called the *multiplier*.

The Multiplier for Model I—A Closed Economy without Government

To develop the multiplier concept, let us return to our simplest model of the product market. In that model, there was no government and no foreign sector, consumption was a function of received income $(C = a + bY)$ since there were no taxes, and investment was exogenous $(I = \bar{I})$. From Equation 4-4 or 4-5, the equilibrium level of income in that model was:

$$Y_{eq.} = \frac{1}{1-b}(a + \bar{I})$$

or, in specific "numerical" terms,

$$Y_1 = \frac{1}{1-b}(a_1 + \bar{I}_1)$$

for the particular *numerical* values of a and I of $a = a_1$ and $\bar{I} = \bar{I}_1$. That equilibrium level of income appears in Figure 4-6 corresponding to the solid aggregate demand schedule $C_1 + \bar{I}_1$.

Suppose now this equilibrium is disturbed by the shock of an increase in planned investment spending reflected by the upward shift in the investment demand schedule from $\bar{I}_1$ to $\bar{I}_2$ in Figure 4-6. What happens to the equilibrium level of income as a result of this shift in the investment schedule?

An upward shift in the investment schedule requires an equivalent upward shift in the aggregate demand schedule (to $C_1 + \bar{I}_2$ in Figure 4-6) since aggregate demand is the sum of C and I. With the aggregate demand schedule at $C_1 + \bar{I}_2$,

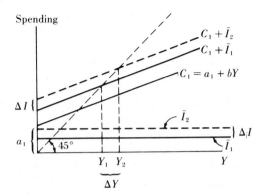

FIGURE 4-6 Impact on Income of a
Change in Investment

the equilibrium level of income becomes Y_2. Thus, the increase in investment in
amount ΔI results in an increase in the equilibrium level of income of ΔY. The
ratio of ΔY to ΔI (the *change* in income that results from a specified *change* in
investment) gives the value of the *investment multiplier* (K_I). If the schedules
in our graph were accurately constructed, by measurement of ΔY and ΔI we
could obtain a numerical estimate of this multiplier's value.

Equivalently, and with less effort, the value of this investment multiplier
can be obtained algebraically. Solving our equilibrium income condition using
specific values of the consumption function intercept and investment $(a = a_1$
and $I = \bar{I}_1)$ gave us the specific value of equilibrium income

$$Y_1 = \frac{1}{1-b}(a_1 + \overline{I}_1).$$

If we now let investment rise from $\bar{I}_1$ to $\bar{I}_2$, the equilibrium level of income becomes

$$Y_2 = \frac{1}{1-b}(a_1 + \bar{I}_2).$$

The *change* in income is

$$Y_2 - Y_1 = \frac{1}{1-b}(a_1 + \bar{I}_2) - \frac{1}{1-b}(a_1 + \bar{I}_1).$$

Collecting terms provides the measure of income change

$$\Delta Y = \frac{1}{1-b}(\cancel{a_1} + \bar{I}_2 - \cancel{a_1} - \bar{I}_1)$$

$$= \frac{1}{1-b}(\bar{I}_2 - \bar{I}_1)$$

or, $\Delta Y = \dfrac{1}{1-b}\,\Delta I.$

Since the investment multiplier is just $K_I = \Delta Y / \Delta I$, this expression for ΔY can be rearranged to yield,[9]

$$K_I = \frac{\Delta Y}{\Delta I} = \frac{1}{1-b}. \tag{4.9}$$

If the value of b were .75, the investment multiplier would have a value of 4 indicating that a \$10 billion increase in investment would increase the equilibrium level of income by \$40 billion (a *multiple* of the original shift in the investment schedule). The justification for the name "multiplier" for this concept should be clear. What effect would a decrease of \$10 billion in investment spending have on equilibrium income?

An Autonomous Shift in the Consumption Function

With planned investment unchanged, suppose our original equilibrium was disturbed by a parallel shift in the consumption function (a change in the autonomous component of consumption as a result, for example, of a change in consumer preferences). The impact of an upward shift in the consumption function by amount Δa is shown in Figure 4-7. A parallel upward shift in the consumption function shifts the aggregate demand schedule $(C + \bar{I})$ upward by the same vertical distance. As a result, the equilibrium level of income increases from Y_1 to Y_2 (by ΔY).

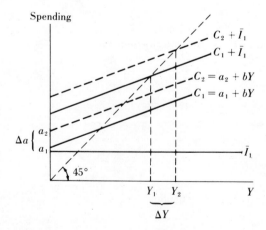

FIGURE 4-7 Impact on Income of a Shift in the Consumption Function

---

9 Students who have had differential calculus should recognize that attempting to find the *change* in the value of income that results from a *change* in investment requires simply the differentiation of the expression for equilibrium income with respect to investment. Thus, if $Y_{eq.} = [1/(1-b)] (a + \bar{I})$, then $K_I = dY/d\bar{I} = 1/(1-b)$.

We can easily solve algebraically for the impact on income of the shift in the consumption function. Following a familiar sequence we know

$$Y_1 = \frac{1}{1-b}(a_1 + \bar{I}_1) \quad \text{for } a = a_1$$

and,

$$Y_2 = \frac{1}{1-b}(a_2 + \bar{I}_1) \quad \text{for } a = a_2.$$

Hence,

$$\Delta Y = Y_2 - Y_1 = \frac{1}{1-b}(a_2 + \bar{I}_1) - \frac{1}{1-b}(a_1 + \bar{I}_1)$$

$$= \frac{1}{1-b}(a_2 + \bar{I}_1 - a_1 - \bar{I}_1)$$

or $\Delta Y = \frac{1}{1-b}\Delta a.$

Dividing this expression for ΔY by Δa to obtain the consumption multiplier yields

$$K_a = \frac{\Delta Y}{\Delta a} = \frac{1}{1-b}, \tag{4-10}$$

the same value that we obtained for the investment multiplier.[10] Indeed, it does not matter whether the original autonomous change in spending is in consumption or investment, the impact on income is the same.

The Logic of the Multiplier

So far, we have established the existence of the multiplier in a mechanical manner without attempting to explain the economic logic of the process by which an autonomous change in some spending schedule generates a multiple expansion of income. To illuminate that process, suppose we again disturb equilibrium in our model by letting investment increase, then trace the individual rounds of income expansion which ensue. Let businessmen increase their spending on plants, equipment, and inventories (that is, on investment goods) by some specified amount, say, $1. A $1 increase in investment spending means $1 of extra income to the recipients of that spending. The typical recipient of this new $1

---

10 Differentiating the equilibrium condition with respect to a, with $Y_{eq.} = [1/(1-b)](a + \bar{I})$, the consumption multiplier is $K_a = dY/da = 1/(1-b)$.

flow of income will spend part of the $1 and save part, passing on a reduced increment of new income ($1 × MPC) to the recipients of spending in this second round of the expansion process. The recipients of this new income from second-round spending will spend part and save part, and so the process goes *ad infinitum*.

The process of adjustment, tracing both the expansion of spending (income) and saving, is summarized in Table 4-1. The numerical values in each round are generated assuming an MPC of .75. As shown there, summing the changes in spending and saving that take place in each round of adjustment yields an overall increase of $4 in total spending and $1 in saving in response to the original increment of $1 in investment spending. These mathematical results are perfectly consistent with our understanding of the requirement for macroeconomic equilibrium, equality of leakages from and injections into the income stream. With a marginal propensity to save of .25, income must rise by $4 to *induce* a sufficient increase in the saving leakage to offset the original $1 increase in investment.[11] Keeping in mind this spending expansion process which is responsible for the multiplier effect, we can proceed to develop multiplier formulas for our more complicated models of the economic system. In the meantime, it should be recognized that the multiplier we have developed for the simplest sort of economic system sheds light on some important policy issues. For example, with the economy in equilibrium at an output level that is $40 billion below full employment the multiplier can reveal the amount by which planned investment by business firms or planned consumption by households would have to increase to restore full employment.

MULTIPLIERS FOR MODEL II—A CLOSED ECONOMY WITH A GOVERNMENT SECTOR

Our second model of income determination was built for a closed economic system, but one that had a government with the power to collect taxes and spend.

---

11 Values for the total change in spending and saving can be derived algebraically quite easily by summing, over all rounds of adjustment, the increments in spending and saving respectively. For spending, the total change is (for $\Delta I = \$1$) :

Total $\Delta Y = \$1(1 + \mathrm{MPC} + \mathrm{MPC}^2 + \mathrm{MPC}^3 + \cdots + \mathrm{MPC}^n + \cdots)$.

From a well-known formula in algebra, the value of the sum of a geometric series of the form in parentheses is $1/(1 - \mathrm{MPC})$ for MPC < 1. Thus, $\Delta Y = \$1[1/(1 - \mathrm{MPC})]$, implying that the multiplier $(\Delta Y/\Delta I = \Delta Y/\$1$ in this case) is $1/(1 - b)$, as we have shown previously.

For saving, the total change is

$\Delta S = \$1 \cdot (1 - \mathrm{MPC})(1 + \mathrm{MPC} + \mathrm{MPC}^2 + \mathrm{MPC}^3 + \cdots + \mathrm{MPC}^n + \cdots)$.

Again, the value of the sum of the geometric series in parentheses is $1/(1 - b)$. Thus,

$\Delta S = \$(1 - \mathrm{MPC}) \cdot$

$= \$1(1)$

$= \$1$

TABLE 4-1 EXPANSION OF INCOME THROUGH THE MULTIPLIER

Round	Change in Spending (Income)	Change in Saving
1	$1 = $1 (the original increase in investment)	—
2	($1) MPC $= .75$	($1) MPS $= \$1(1 - \text{MPC}) = .25$
3	($1) MPC$^2 = .56$	($1) (MPC) MPS $= (\$1)$ MPC $(1 - \text{MPC}) = .19$
4	($1) MPC$^3 = .42$	($1) (MPC^2) MPS $= (\$1)$ MPC^2 $(1 - \text{MPC}) = .14$
5	($1) MPC$^4 = .32$	($1) (MPC^3) MPS $= (\$1)$ MPC^3 $(1 - \text{MPC}) = .10$
$\cdot \cdot \cdot 8$	$\cdot \cdot \cdot$	$\cdot \cdot \cdot \cdot$
Total	$\$1 \cdot \dfrac{1}{1 - \text{MPC}} = \$4.00$	$\$1 \cdot \dfrac{(1 - \text{MPC})}{(1 - \text{MPC})} = \$1.00$

The addition of government spending and taxes makes this second model far more interesting than the simple model for, as we have indicated, the government exerts a large part of its control over the economy through alterations in the levels of its spending and tax revenues. With investment, government spending, and total tax revenues determined exogenously, the equilibrium level of income for this model was

$$Y_{eq.} = \frac{1}{1-b}(a + \bar{I} + \bar{G} - b\bar{T}) \tag{4-11}$$

as indicated earlier in Equations 4-6 and 4-7.

The Spending Multipliers

For the specific values of the autonomous terms $a = a_1$, $\bar{I} = \bar{I}_1$, $\bar{G} = \bar{G}_1$, and $\bar{T} = \bar{T}_1$, equilibrium income in this second model is

$$Y_1 = \frac{1}{1-b}(a_1 + \bar{I}_1 + \bar{G}_1 - b\bar{T}_1).$$

If investment should rise from $\bar{I}_1$ to $\bar{I}_2$, income would become

$$Y_2 = \frac{1}{1-b}(a_1 + \bar{I}_2 + \bar{G}_1 - b\bar{T}_1).$$

Subtracting Y_1 from Y_2 yields

$$\Delta Y = Y_2 - Y_1 = \frac{1}{1-b}(a_1 + \bar{I}_2 + \bar{G}_1 - b\bar{T}_1) - \frac{1}{1-b}(a_1 + \bar{I}_1 + \bar{G}_1 - b\bar{T}_1)$$

or $\qquad \Delta Y = \frac{1}{1-b}\Delta I.$

Thus, the investment multiplier must be

$$K_I = \frac{\Delta Y}{\Delta I} = \frac{1}{1-b}, \tag{4-12}$$

the same value that was obtained for the simple model (model I) without government. This is a sensible conclusion for, just as in model I, the only spending response that is induced by an income change in this model is a change in consumption. Repeating this derivation for a change in the autonomous component of consumption spending *or for a change in government spending* would yield the same result; like the investment multiplier, the consumption multiplier and the government spending multiplier for model II have a value of $1/(1-b)$. It makes no difference whether the original change in spending is in the form of a change in investment, consumption, or government spending, the impact on income is the same.[12] Any first-round change in spending, no matter what its source, generates the same series of induced increments in spending. Thus, there is only one value for a particular model's *spending* multiplier and there is no necessity to distinguish between consumption, investment, and government spending multipliers.

The impact of a change in one spending schedule, a change of amout ΔG in the government spending schedule, is illustrated graphically in Figure 4-8.

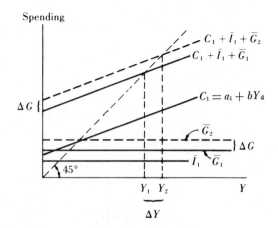

FIGURE 4-8 Impact on Income of a Change in Government Spending

As shown, an increase in government spending of ΔG leads to an increase in the equilibrium level of income of ΔY. As we already know, the value of the ratio $\Delta Y/\Delta G$, the spending multiplier for this model, is $1/(1-b)$. With that knowledge, the change in government spending required to produce any selected change in the equilibrium level of output can be determined easily as $\Delta G = \Delta Y(1-b)$ or $\Delta G = \Delta Y / K_{\text{spending}}$.

The Tax Multiplier

In addition to wielding control over its expenditures, the government in our second model has the power to change the "lump sum" amount of tax revenues it collects. If it does so, the equilibrium level of income changes. Beginning with

---

12 With differential calculus we can quickly show this. If

$$Y_{\text{eq}} = \frac{1}{1-b}(a + \bar{I} + \bar{G} - b\bar{T}),$$

then

$$K_a = \frac{dY}{da} = K_{\bar{I}} = \frac{dY}{d\bar{I}} = K_{\bar{G}} = \frac{dY}{d\bar{G}} = \frac{1}{1-b}.$$

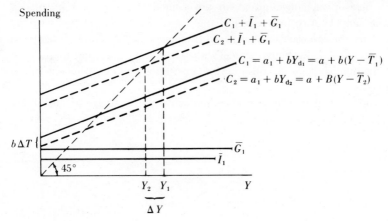

FIGURE 4-9   Impact on Income of a Change in Taxes

the economic system in equilibrium at income level Y_1, as shown in Figure 4-9, what will be the impact of an increase in taxes from $\overline{T}_1$ to $\overline{T}_2$ dollars?

An increase in taxes reduces disposable income by the amount of the increase in taxes (recall that $Y_d = Y - T$). Since consumption is a function of disposable income (Y_d), an increase in taxes that reduces disposable income would reduce consumption at every level of received income (Y). Graphically, this means a downward shift in our plotted consumption function.

By how much would the consumption function shift? By $\$\Delta T \cdot \text{MPC}$ at every level of income; that is, by the change in disposable income resulting from the tax change times the fraction of that income that would have been spent had it been left in the hands of consumers. The new consumption function (C_2) is shown in Figure 4-9. The parallel downward shift in the consumption function requires an equivalent downward shift in the aggregate demand schedule establishing a new equilibrium level of income at Y_2 in Figure 4-9. Thus, an increase in tax receipts by amount ΔT leads to a *decrease* in income of ΔY. The ratio $\Delta Y / \Delta T$ can be called the tax multiplier, K_T.

Clearly the tax multiplier $(K_T = \Delta Y / \Delta T)$ is negative in value. We can readily demonstrate this fact and simultaneously derive a formula for finding the size of the tax multiplier by employing the same algebraic procedure we have used to evaluate spending multipliers.

For $a = a_1, I = \overline{I}_1, G = \overline{G}_1,$ and $T = \overline{T}_1$, equilibrium income is

$$Y_1 = \frac{1}{1-b}(a_1 + \overline{I}_1 + \overline{G}_1 - b\overline{T}_1).$$

Similarly,

$$Y_2 = \frac{1}{1-b}(a_1 + \overline{I}_1 + \overline{G}_1 - b\overline{T}_2)$$

for $a = a_1$, $I = \bar{I}_1$, $G = \bar{G}_1$, and $T = \bar{T}_2$ which is greater than $\bar{T}_1$ by amount ΔT. Subtracting Y_1 from Y_2,

$$\Delta Y = Y_2 - Y_1 = \frac{1}{1-b}(a_1 + \bar{I}_1 + \bar{G}_1 - b\bar{T}_2) - \frac{1}{1-b}(a_1 + I_1 + G_1 - b\bar{T}_1)$$

or $\Delta Y = \dfrac{-b}{1-b}\,\Delta T$.

Dividing through by ΔT to obtain the tax multiplier yields

$$K_T = \frac{\Delta Y}{\Delta T} = -\frac{b}{1-b} \tag{4-13}$$

or

$$K_T = -b\left(\frac{1}{1-b}\right). \tag{4-14}$$

The tax multiplier is indeed negative and its value is smaller than that of the spending multiplier. For an MPC of .75, the tax multiplier has a value of -3.

In fact, in absolute size it is only b times as large as the spending multiplier. The reason for the smaller size of the tax multiplier can be readily seen by recalling our discussion of the logic of the multiplier. Unlike a shift in a spending schedule, which means an equivalent change in first-round spending in the multiplier adjustment process, a change in taxes alters first round spending by only the MPC times the change in taxes. With the impact on first-round spending of a change in taxes only b times as large as the impact of an equal change in investment, consumption, or government spending, the overall change in income will be reduced to a value b times as great as the spending multiplier.

Government Transfers

At this point, we can easily expand our comprehension of government's impact on economic activity by recognizing that, in essence, government transfer payments are negative taxes. Like taxes, transfer payments do not directly affect aggregate demand but, instead, alter the volume of disposable income. A $100 increase in transfer payments generates first-round spending of $100 \cdot \text{MPC}$, which is then subject to the normal multiplier expansion process. Hence, the algebraic expression for a "transfer" multiplier $[K_{TR} = b/(1-b)]$ shows that it is equal in magnitude but opposite in sign to the tax multiplier.[13]

---

13 To the extent that the recipients of transfer payment have different MPCs from those of taxpayers, the aggregate impact of a $1 change in taxes may differ from the impact of an equivalent change in transfers. It is, in fact, commonly alleged that recipients of transfer payments (social security payments, welfare payments, unemployment compensation, and so on),

In the interest of simplicity of exposition, we will consolidate our positive and negative tax collections in one variable which, if you like, can be thought of as *net* tax collections (total tax revenues minus transfers). The value of this variable will always be positive (taxes always exceed transfers) but will change in response either to tax revenue or transfer payment changes. We will continue to use the letter T to represent (net) tax revenues.[14] What would be the impact on equilibrium income of an equal increase in both tax revenues and transfer payments?

THE BALANCED BUDGET MULTIPLIER

Having considered the independent effects of both government spending and tax alterations, we can now ask: What would be the impact on the equilibrium level of income of an equal change in government spending and tax revenues? Since the spending multiplier has a value of $K = 1/(1-b)$, a change in government spending changes income by $\Delta Y = 1/(1-b) \cdot \Delta G$. Also, since the tax multiplier is $K_T = \Delta Y/\Delta T = -b/(1-b)$, a change in tax revenues changes income by $\Delta Y = -b/(1-b) \cdot \Delta T$. The total impact on income of a simultaneous change in both government spending and taxes is simply the sum of the two separate effects, or,

$$\Delta Y = \frac{1}{1-b} \cdot \Delta G - \frac{b}{1-b} \cdot \Delta T.$$

Since a "balanced budget" change in taxes and government spending requires an equal change in taxes and government spending ($\Delta G = \Delta T = \Delta B$ where ΔB is the

---

occupying the lower range of the income distribution, consume most or all of any change in income (that is, their MPC $\simeq 1$). As a consequence, the numerical magnitude of the transfer multiplier would be closer to that of the government spending multiplier than to the tax multiplier. At this juncture, however, there is no need for us to distinguish between taxpayers and transfer recipients in our models.

14 We are defining net taxes as tax revenues minus transfers. That is,

$T = R - tr$

where T is net taxes, R is tax revenues, and tr is transfers. The introduction of transfer payments has made the value of disposable income in our model equal to earned income minus taxes plus transfers, or,

$Y_d = Y - R + tr$

which is simply

$Y_d = Y - T.$

Thus, we have done nothing to alter the form of any of the models developed in this chapter. To make the models relevant for analysis of a system that has transfer payments, we simply need to think of our tax variable as a measure of *net* taxes, affected both by tax collections and transfers.

"balanced" change in the size of the budget), we can substitute the common term (ΔB) for ΔG and ΔT. Doing so yields

$$\Delta Y = \frac{1}{1-b} \cdot \Delta B - \frac{b}{1-b} \cdot \Delta B$$

$$= \Delta B \cdot \frac{1-b}{1-b}$$

or $\Delta Y = \Delta B$.

The balanced budget multiplier must have a value of 1 no matter what the value of the marginal propensity to consume! That is,

$$K_B = \frac{\Delta Y}{\Delta B} = 1. \qquad (4\text{-}15)$$

Quite logically, because the tax multiplier has a value that is 1 less than the government spending multiplier, equal changes in government spending and tax revenues will change equilibrium income by precisely the same dollar amount no matter what the size of the MPC and no matter what the initial state of balance or imbalance in the budget. Tax collections reduce society's purchasing power, but if tax revenues are respent, the purchasing power in the hands of consumers is exactly restored and the sequence of consumer spending is unaltered. Thus, total production is increased by the volume of additional goods and services government purchases when it enlarges its budget in a balanced fashion.[15] This same conclusion holds even in models which provide an induced increase in taxes as income rises (as our model III does) so long as the increase in government spending is matched by the total increase in tax revenues when equilibrium has been restored.[16]

While *real-world* complications, like possible differences in the MPCs of taxpayers and government spending recipients, weaken the conclusion that the

---

15 An equal change in government spending and tax revenues generates the following series of income changes in the model we are working with:

(1) ΔY from an increase in $G = \Delta G + \Delta G \cdot \text{MPC} + \Delta G \cdot \text{MPC}^2 + \cdots + \Delta G \cdot \text{MPC}^n + \cdots$

(2) ΔY from an increase in $T = -[0 + \Delta T \cdot \text{MPC} + \Delta T \cdot \text{MPC}^2 + \cdots + \Delta T \cdot \text{MPC}^n + \cdots$

If $\Delta G = \Delta T$, all the terms on the right-hand side of the two series are the same except the term ΔG. Combining the two series for $\Delta G = \Delta T$ shows that overall $\Delta Y = \Delta G = \Delta T$.

16 When taxes are a function of income, the *total* change in tax revenues when the size of the government's budget is altered consists in part of an autonomous change in taxes and in part of a change in tax revenue that occurs as income changes. A mathematical proof that the balanced budget multiplier has a value of 1 in this case can be found in T. F. Dernburg and Judith D. Dernburg, *Macroeconomic Analysis* (Reading, Mass.: Addison-Wesley Publishing Co., 1969), pp. 17-20.

balanced budget multiplier has a value of precisely 1, the conclusion that equal changes in government spending and tax revenues exert a strong influence on the equilibrium level of output has played an important role in economic policy making. A notable illustration of the application of the balanced budget multiplier concept occurred in 1964. Early that year Congress enacted an $11 billion tax cut to stimulate the economy. Prior to its passage, opponents of the tax cut said they would favor the bill if government spending were cut by an equal amount. In response, the Council of Economic Advisers argued that cutting taxes and government spending by the same amount would not only fail to stimulate the economy but would result in a sharp contraction.

MULTIPLIERS FOR MODEL III—INVESTMENT AND TAX REVENUES ENDOGENOUS

We attempted to make our third model of income determination more realistic by allowing investment and tax revenues to respond positively to changes in the level of income. The functional relationships employed in that model were

$$C = a + bY_d$$

$$I = \bar{I} + cY$$

$$G = \bar{G}$$

$$T = \bar{T} + tY$$

with the variables defined as before. As it originally appeared in Equation 4-8, the equilibrium level of income for this model was

$$Y_{eq.} = \frac{1}{1 - b - c + bt}(a + \bar{I} + \bar{G} - b\bar{T}). \tag{4-16}$$

The value of the spending multiplier for this model is

$$K_{spending} = K_a = K_{\bar{I}} = K_{\bar{G}} = \frac{1}{1 - b - c + bt} \tag{4-17}$$

or

$$K_{spending} = \frac{1}{1 - b(1 - t) - c}, \tag{4-18}$$

a result you should be able to prove.[17] The multiplier for a change in taxes

---

17 The calculus proof is simple:

$$K_{spending} = \frac{dY}{da} = \frac{dY}{d\bar{I}} = \frac{dY}{d\bar{G}} = \frac{1}{1 - b - c + bt}.$$

through a change in the autonomous component $(\overline{T})$ of tax collections is

$$K_{\overline{T}} = -\frac{b}{1-b-c+bt} = -b\left(\frac{1}{1-b-c+bt}\right) \tag{4-19}$$

or,

$$K_{\overline{T}} = \frac{-b}{1-b(1-t)-c}. \tag{4-20}$$

Again, the impact of a change in taxes is weaker than, and opposite in direction to, the impact of an equivalent autonomous change in spending.[18]

It is important to note, as some unfamiliar terms appear in the denominators of our multiplier expressions, that the sizes of both the spending and the tax multipliers for this model are different from the sizes of those respective multipliers derived for models I and II. We can readily account for the differences. If investment is a positive function of the level of income, an autonomous shift in any spending schedule will induce a spending response from investment as income changes as well as from consumption. With both consumption and investment responding to movements in income, it is not surprising that the total change in spending brought about by an antonomous increment in spending is larger than if only consumption responds to such movements. That the multiplier is larger with this positive investment response to income changes is apparent from the presence of the c term in the denominator of the multiplier formula (the c term makes the denominator smaller, thus the value of the multiplier larger).

In probing the logic of the multiplier process, we noted that when equilibrium was disturbed income would always have to adjust by enough to generate a change in leakages from the spending stream sufficient to offset the increment in injections into the spending stream. If tax receipts respond positively to changes in income, a *smaller* change in income is sufficient to generate

18   We might also be interested in the impact on equilibrium income of a change in the *marginal* tax rate (t). Of course, raising the marginal tax *rate* increases the total volume of taxes collected at any specified income level, inducing a contraction in equilibrium income, while reducing the tax rate lowers total tax collections stimulating income. Moreover, the first-round change in spending produced by a tax rate change depends on the initial level of income so that the total multiplier effect of a tax rate change varies positively with the level of income. Differentiating the expression for equilibrium income with respect to t yields

$$\frac{dY}{dt} = -\frac{b(a+\overline{I}+\overline{G}-b\overline{T})}{(1-b-c+bt)^2}$$

or $\quad \dfrac{dY}{dt} = -\dfrac{b}{1-b-c+bt} \cdot Y_{\text{eq.}} \quad$ since $\quad Y_{\text{eq.}} = \dfrac{a+\overline{I}+\overline{G}-b\overline{T}}{1-b-c+bt}.$

The size of the impact on Y of a change in t clearly depends on the level of income at which the economy is initially operating.

the leakages (saving plus taxes) necessary to offset any increment in spending injections. That the multiplier is indeed weaker with taxes responding to income changes is apparent from the presence of the positive term bt (which appears only because taxes are assumed to respond to income changes) in the denominator of the multipliers derived in this section. Factors that decrease the size of the multiplier are frequently called *automatic stabilizers* in economic analysis. Such factors stabilize the economy in the sense that for any shock to the system (any shift in a spending schedule), whether expansionary or contractionary, the size of the resulting *change* in aggregate output is reduced by their presence. The tax structure in this model would be such a stabilizer.

EQUILIBRIUM INCOME, THE MULTIPLIER, AND EMPLOYMENT

As our last major task in this chapter, by introducing the concept of an aggregate production function, we can relate the changes in income that our multiplier analysis has dealt with to changes in employment. The aggregate production function is simply the relationship between aggregate output and the inputs necessary to produce that output. Letting N be hours of labor and A the volume of nonlabor inputs (capital, land), the production function in algebraic terms is $Y = Y(N, A)$ with output (Y) positively related to both the number of hours of labor and the volume of nonlabor resources employed. In the short run, the total stock of nonlabor inputs can be assumed to be constant and technological change can be ignored. Thus, the only way to get a changed volume of output is through changes in the volume of labor employed. For the short run, then, the production function can be rewritten as $Y = Y(N)$. If the economy is operating with substantial excess capacity (that is, with underemployment of both labor and nonlabor inputs), a given percentage change in output could be associated with an approximately equal percentage change in *properly measured* employment. That is, we might expect essentially constant returns to *fully utilized* labor and capital inputs as larger volumes of those inputs are put to work since idle labor could be put to work with existing but idle nonlabor inputs. Of course, to the extent that business firms *hoard* partially idle labor during periods of depressed economic activity, an expansion of employment as measured in the United States can yield an even greater percentage increase in output. In fact, as we indicated in Chapter 3, output per hour of measured employment typically does rise during economic expansions as employed workers are more fully utilized and, as a consequence, total output expands by a larger percentage than employment. As the level of economic activity expands toward full utilization of nonlabor factors of production, larger increments in labor utilization become necessary for attaining ʳified additions to output (we are in the region of diminishing returns). To ˑˑrecisely the impact on employment of any particular change in the level ˑˑˑˑwe would need empirical knowledge of the exact form of the production function. At the moment, however, it is sufficient to note that wherever our multiplier analysis tells us that output is increasing, it is also telling us that employment is increasing.[19] It should be apparent that if the government wants to alter the level of employment (or unemployment) it can do so by changing government spending, taxes, or both.

The Size of the Multiplier

By estimating the size of the behavioral parameters in our multiplier models (the MPC, the marginal tax rate, and so on) we can obtain numerical values for our multipliers. Keynes himself believed the spending multiplier for the United States had a value between 2.5 and 3.[20] Other investigators have typically found multiplier values for periods of normal economic activity to lie between 2 and 3. Paul Davidson's estimate of the spending multiplier yields a value of 2.11.[21] Arthur Okun, one-time member of the President's Council of Economic Advisors, has estimated the spending multiplier to have a value of 3.[22] The value of the tax multiplier is, of course, one less than the value of the spending multiplier in the simple commodity market models constructed in this chapter. Complicating matters, the multiplier's value is likely to change over the business cycle as businesses' *investment* response to changes in aggregate demand vary with the stage of the cycle. One study of a short-run recession spending multiplier placed its value in 1957 at 1.34.[23]

If the government budget is to be used deliberately to alter the level of economic activity, good estimates of multiplier values are a necessity. If, for example, aggregate output is $25 billion below the full employment level and we want to know how much to change government spending or tax collections to achieve full employment, we need to know the values of the government spending and tax multipliers. With those values the required dose of budget adjustment can be prescribed. If the spending multiplier were 2.5, a $10 billion increase in

19   It is also worth recalling from the discussion in Chapter 3 that every increase in measured employment need not decrease measured unemployment. It would if the labor force were constant, but it is not. Instead, the size of the measured labor force itself depends on the rate of unemployment. If additional employment opportunities become available, tending to lower unemployment, labor force participation tends to increase—that is, housewives, teenagers, and other categories of "discouraged workers" will actively enter the labor force as employment opportunities improve. See T. Dernburg and K. Strand, "Hidden Unemployment, 1953-1962; A Quantitative Analysis by Age and Sex," *The American Economic Review*, Vol. 56, March 1966, pp. 71-95.

20   See J. M. Keynes, *The General Theory of Employment, Interest, and Money*, pp. 127-128.

21   P. Davidson, "Income and Employment Multipliers, and the Price Level," *The American Economic Review*, Vol. 52, September 1962, pp. 738-752.

22   *State of the Economy and Policies for Full Employment*, Hearings Before the Joint Economic Committee, 87th Congress, 2nd Session, 1962, p. 199.

23   J. S. Duesenberry, O. Eckstein, and G. Fromm, "A Simulation of the United States in Recession," *Econometrica*, Vol. 28, October 1960, pp. 749-809.

government spending would increase output to the full employment level (remember, $K_G = \Delta Y / \Delta G$ or $\Delta Y = K_G \cdot \Delta G$). What change in taxes would provide full employment?

With the correct set of fixed numerical values for the tax and spending multipliers, the policy maker's task of prescribing government spending and tax programs for altering aggregate output and employment would be a straightforward arithmetic exercise. Unfortunately, not enough is known about the empirical structure of the economy to provide a foolproof set of multiplier values. That is so even though a great deal of research effort with models of varying degrees of complexity has focused on the economy's response to changes in spending and tax levies. This note of humility should serve to reinforce our earlier suggestion that the models constructed in this chapter are simplistic. Even the most complex model in this chapter treated the supply of real goods and services as passive, ignored international trade, and took no account of the economic impact of changes in the supply of money. Multipliers that are to be used for *real-world* policy making must take account of these complications. Further, for policy purposes we must know more than the impact on *equilibrium* income of a specific government expenditure or tax policy action, for it takes time for the economy to adjust from one equilibrium to another. We need to know the timing of the income response to policy actions as well as the size of that response.

The Price Level

So far we have also failed to discuss any price level response to changes in the level of output. That omission has been possible only because it has been tacitly assumed that the economic systems we are analyzing are operating with substantial excess capacity. In that case, any increase in aggregate demand can be satisfied by an increase in real output with little or no change in the price level. However, as the economy approaches full employment it becomes increasingly difficult to meet growing demand with an increase in output. Clearly, if the economy were operating at full capacity so that output could not expand, any increase in aggregate demand would have to result in an increased price level. There is much more that we need to say about the behavior of the price level. We will, however, delay any involved discussion of that topic to Chapter 9.

SUMMARY

In this chapter attention has been focused on one market—the commodity market. We have built models of the commodity market for economic systems of varying complexity to find: (1) how the equilibrium level of income is determined and value is, and (2) how the equilibrium level of income changes in response to autonomous changes in consumption, investment, government spending, and tax collections. Equilibrium in these models could exist only when total planned spending was just exactly equal to the value of output (when any leakages out of the spending stream were offset by equal injections). The equilibrium level of income was increased by an increase in consumption, investment, or government spending, or by a decrease in taxes. Conversely, income was reduced by a reduction in C, I, or G, or by an increase in taxes. The size of the multipliers depended on the values of the MPC, the marginal propensity to invest (MPI), and the marginal tax rate (t), with their size enlarged by a bigger MPC and MPI but reduced by a larger t. We also showed that with estimates of these parameters we could solve for values of the spending multiplier and the tax multiplier, constructs that have important implications for government policy.

While the mechanics of model construction presented in this chapter are essential to the construction of macroeconomic models suitable for policy application, we cannot claim to have constructed such models at this time. Our models still have not taken account of the role of international trade and they have completely ignored the role of the nation's money supply. Further, our behavioral assumptions have not been quantified using observed values of income, consumption, investment, and so on. Quantification would suggest that the multiplier processes we have reviewed take a substantial amount of calendar time and might convince you that the level of aggregation has been pushed too far. But whatever the shortcomings of the models we have constructed, they clearly demonstrate the paramount importance of planned spending in determining the level of economic activity. In deference to this role, a substantial portion of this text is devoted to explaining the behavioral relations that generate final spending on consumption, investment, government purchases, *and* net exports.

Taking a quick look ahead, Chapter 5 examines the determinants of personal consumption in a complex modern economy. While a number of potential determinants of consumption including wealth, interest rates, and the distribution of income are considered, disposable personal income remains the key consumption determining variable, as it was in this chapter.

Chapter 6 examines the determinants of business investment in plant and equipment. The arguments in Chapter 6 will indicate that we must, in any serious attempt at modeling a modern economy, rely on an investment demand relationship that is considerably more complicated than the one employed in this chapter.

Chapter 7 allows the introduction of the role of money into our analysis by focusing on the role the interest rate plays in determining the level of economic activity. The following two chapters, which rely on information from Chapters 4-7, build fairly sophisticated income determination models. As was the case with the simple models in this chapter, the more sophisticated models constructed in Chapters 8 and 9 will be "Keynesian" or "post-Keynesian" models.

Over the years, Keynesian analysis has had, and continues to have, its critics, many of them prominent economists. And modern macroeconomics has been influenced to a substantial degree by *non-Keynesians*, as we shall see in future chapters. Yet, mainstream macroeconomic analysis has been dominated by the analytical framework developed by Keynes in *The General Theory*. As though he could predict the influence his analysis would have even long after his death, in his own "modest" appraisal of *The General Theory*, Keynes asserted:

> I believe myself to be writing a book on economic theory that will largely revolutionize—not, I suppose, at once but in the course of the next ten years—the way the world thinks about economic problems.[24]

QUESTIONS

1. At one point in this chapter, we claimed that measured saving and investment are always equal while at other times we argued the equality of saving and investment is necessary for the economy to be in equilibrium. Explain this apparent inconsistency.

2. A change in inventory investment is the adjustment mechanism that assured equality of realized saving and investment in our simple model. Explain.

3. In the table below, there is data on planned consumption and investment for a closed economy with no government.

Income	Consumption	Investment
$ 0	$ 50	$25
100	125	25
200	200	25
300	275	25

   (a) Find the equilibrium value of income for this model both algebraically and graphically.

   (b) Derive the spending multiplier formula and calculate its value.

   (c) Determine the equilibrium values of consumption, saving, and investment.

   (d) Explain the adjustment that would occur should current income be less than equilibrium income.

4. The last problem you had to solve ignored the existence of government. Suppose we introduce a government sector into the model of problem 3 letting the government spend $50 billion and collect $50 billion in taxes.

---

24 Letter from J. M. Keynes to George Bernard Shaw, New Year's Day, 1935. For an excellent description of the process through which Keynesian analysis came to be embraced in America, see John K. Galbraith, "How Keynes Came to America," *The New York Times Book Review*, May 1965. Reprinted in Paul Samuelson, *Readings in Economics*, 7th ed. (New York: McGraw-Hill, Inc.), pp. 91-96.

(a) Using whatever parameter values you need from your solution to problem 3, find the new equilibrium value of output.

(b) Derive the formulas for the government spending and tax multipliers and calculate their values.

(c) Find the equilibrium values for C, S, and I.

5. Assume the government spending multiplier has a value of 3 and the tax multiplier a value of -2.

(a) Find the impact on equilibrium income of a $20 billion increase in government spending. Of a $20 billion reduction in tax collections.

(b) If equilibrium output is $30 billion below the target (full employment) level, what change in government spending could eliminate the gap? What change in tax collections would have the same effect?

(c) How would a $15 billion reduction in both tax revenues and government spending affect output? How do you know?

6. See if you can sketch the flow diagrams and identify the equilibrium conditions for:

(a) A closed economy with a government that taxes but does not spend,

(b) A closed economy with a government that spends but does not tax,

(c) An *open* economy (one with exports and imports) with no government.

7. What difference does it make whether investment depends on the level of output or not? Explain.

8. What difference does it make whether net tax revenues depend on the level of aggregate income or not? Explain.

9. How would a step-up in military spending affect economic activity? A cutback in military spending? What tax policies could be used to offset those government spending changes?

10. Since in reality tax revenues vary with the level of income, an autonomous shift in any spending schedule results in a change in tax revenues. For example, a fall in investment lowers income through the multiplier, in turn reducing tax revenue. Analyze the implications of requiring the government to maintain a balanced budget (tax revenue and spending equal) in the face of shifts in nongovernmental spending schedules. Is that requirement likely to enhance or reduce economic stability?

SUGGESTED READING

Council of Economic Advisers. "The Workings of the Multiplier," in A. Okun (ed.). *The Battle Against Unemployment.* Revised edition. New York: W. W. Norton & Co., 1972.

Friedman, Milton. "Weak Links in the Multiplier Chain," *Capitalism and Freedom.* Chicago: University of Chicago Press, 1962. Reprinted in A. Okun (ed.). *The Battle Against Unemployment*. Revised edition. New York: W. W. Norton & Co., 1972.

Goodwin, Richard M. "The Multiplier," in Seymour E. Harris (ed.). *The New Economics*. New York: A. A. Knopf, 1947, pp. 482-499.

Heller, Walter W. *New Dimensions in Political Economy*. New York: W. W. Norton & Co., 1967, Chapter 2.

Machlup, Fritz. "Period Analysis and Multiplier Theory," *Quarterly Journal of Economics*, Vol. LIV, Nov. 1939, pp. 1-27. Reprinted in *Readings in Business Cycle Theory*. Philadelphia: Blakiston Co., 1944, pp. 203-234.

Musgrave, Richard. *The Theory of Public Finance*. New York: McGraw-Hill, Inc. 1959, Chapter 18.

Samuelson, Paul A. "The Simple Mathematics of Income Determination," in *Income, Employment, and Public Policy, Essays in Honor of Alvin H. Hansen*. This selection is reprinted in M. G. Mueller (ed.). *Readings in Macroeconomics*. Second edition. New York: Holt, Rinehart, and Winston, Inc., pp. 24-36.

Chapter 5
The Consumption
Function

The models of income determination developed in the last chapter demonstrated that planned consumption plays an integral role in the determination of aggregate demand and thus income. That role is retained in all Keynesian income-determination models, including the most sophisticated variants. It goes without saying that to construct Keynesian macroeconomic models which can be relied on to predict economic developments and to tailor policy prescriptions to the economy's needs, a clear understanding of the consumption function is needed —we must know what the determinants of consumption are and how consumption responds to changes in its determinants. That is the primary focus of this chapter. By explaining the behavior of consumption, we will be simultaneously explaining the behavior of saving, since any income that is not consumed is, by definition, saved. Thus, we can discuss the consumption function and the saving function simultaneously and interchangeably.

INCOME-CONSUMPTION AND INCOME-SAVING FUNCTIONS

The models constructed in Chapter 4 employed a simple, linear consumption function. Although some repetition of effort is involved, the analysis in this chapter will begin by looking a bit more intensively at that simple function.

While we have ignored the point up to now, there are obviously other factors besides income that can affect consumption demand. Thus, the simple linear relationship we assumed to hold between income and consumption in Chapter 4 must be qualified. The formal hypothesis we implicitly employed there was that *ceteris paribus* (other things held constant), *real* consumption spending[1] is a linear function of *real* disposable income as reflected in the equation

$$C = a + bY_d.$$

---

1 For some purposes a different concept of consumption would be more appropriate. If our objective was to measure the actual using-up (consumption) of final products, we would be better off to break down aggregate expenditure into spending on nondurables (eggs, bacon, balloons, and so on) and spending on durables (autos, refrigerators, washing machines, and so on). Since only a part of a durable good is used up in a typical accounting period (one-fifth of an auto if the accounting period is 1 year and the auto's life is 5 years), actual consumption (using-up of products) is the sum of expenditure on nondurables and depreciation (using-up) of durables, not total expenditure on final products.

Since saving is income less consumption, it follows that saving is also a linear function of real disposable income. Algebraically, saving must be:

$$S = Y_d - C$$
$$= Y_d - (a + bY_d)$$

or $S = -a + (1-b) Y_d$.

As shown in Chapter 4, with a positive value for the intercept (a), and with a value of the slope (b) that is positive but less than 1, the consumption and saving functions would plot like those in Figure 5-1. The slope of the consumption function, which is labeled the marginal propensity to consume (MPC), measures the response of real consumption spending to a change in real income. Symbolically, that response is

$$MPC \equiv \frac{\Delta C}{\Delta Y_d} = b.$$

The slope of the saving function, labeled the marginal propensity to save (MPS), measures the response of saving to changes in income. Symbolically, the MPS

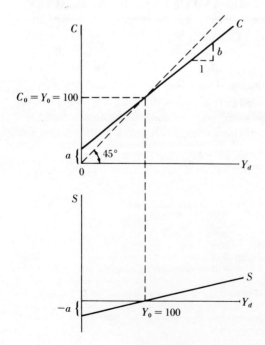

FIGURE 5-1 Consumption and Saving Functions

is MPS $\equiv \Delta S/\Delta Y_d = (1-b)$.[2] Further, since every one dollar change in income must either be consumed or saved, the MPC and the MPS must sum to one. That is, since

$$\Delta Y_d = \Delta C + \Delta S,$$

dividing through by ΔY_d yields

$$1 = \frac{\Delta C}{\Delta Y_d} + \frac{\Delta S}{\Delta Y_d}$$

or $1 = MPC + MPS$.

We also need to define *average* propensities to consume and save. The average propensity to consume (APC) is simply the portion of the average dollar of income that is consumed, symbolically represented as

$$APC \equiv \frac{C}{Y_d}.$$

The average propensity to save (APS) is the fraction of the average dollar of income that is saved. Thus,

$$APS \equiv \frac{S}{Y_d} \equiv \frac{Y_d - C}{Y_d} \quad \text{since } S \equiv Y_d - C.$$

Making the division indicated in this expression for the APS yields,

$$APS = 1 - \frac{C}{Y_d},$$

or $APS = 1 - APC$,

reflecting the fact that the portion of the average income dollar that is not spent must be saved.

With values for the parameters a and b, we can formally graph the consumption and saving functions, trace those schedules in tabular form, or just leave them in algebraic form. For example, with $a = 20$ and $b = .8$, consumption is $C = 20 + .8Y_d$ and saving is $S = -20 + .2Y_d$. These are the specific functions that were used to plot the schedules in Figure 5-1. In addition, these schedules

---

2 Students with a calculus background will recognize that the marginal propensities to consume and save are the first derivatives of the consumption and saving functions respectively with respect to disposable income. For $C = a + bY_d$, $MPC = dC/dY_d = b$ and for $S = -a + (1-b)Y_d$, $MPS = dS/dY_d = (1-b)$.

were used to provide the values for consumption, saving, and the propensities to consume and save entered in Table 5-1. Quite apparently, what is known about consumption and saving behavior can be conveyed in a number of different formats with no loss of information. You might also note that for the particular consumption and saving functions represented in Table 5-1, the MPC and MPS are constant while, with an increase in income, the APC falls and the APS rises.

TABLE 5-1 PROPENSITIES TO CONSUME AND SAVE FOR A SPECIFIC (SAVING) FUNCTION

Y_d	$C =$ $(20 + .80Y_d)$	$S =$ $(-20 + .20Y_d)$	APC $= \left(\dfrac{C}{Y_d}\right)$	APS $= \left(\dfrac{S}{Y_d}\right)$	MPC $= \left(\dfrac{\Delta C}{\Delta Y_d}\right)$	MPS $= \left(\dfrac{\Delta S}{\Delta Y_d}\right)$
0	20	−20	—	—		
50	60	−10	1.2	−.2	.8	.2
100	100	0	1.0	0	.8	.2
150	140	10	.93	.07	.8	.2
200	180	20	.90	.10	.8	.2

Other Forms of Consumption and Saving Functions

While the consumption function we have employed up to this point served us well in the simple models of Chapter 4, it should be recognized that other forms are possible—perhaps even more realistic. Two alternative, but still simple, consumption functions are plotted in Figures 5-2 and 5-3. The function in Figure 5-2 is a variant of the linear function which has a zero vertical intercept. For such a function the APC and MPC are equal to each other and are constant as income changes.

We could also have a nonlinear function like the one plotted in Figure 5-3, reflecting the tendency of both the MPC and APC to fall as disposable income rises. The possibility that this shape is the appropriate one for the aggregate consumption function is ominous, for as income grows over time a larger *frac-*

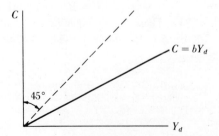

FIGURE 5-2 A Linear Consumption Function with Zero Intercept

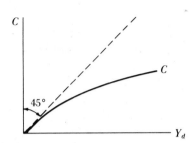

FIGURE 5-3   A Nonlinear Consumption Function with Zero Intercept

tion of income is saved.[3] To avoid *stagnation* in economic activity due to slack aggregate demand, this growing proportional difference between income and consumption would have to be made up by some other form of spending (for example, private investment or government spending). The higher income becomes, the greater the burden imposed on nonconsumption spending. In the immediate post-depression period of the 1930s a number of prominent economists were concerned that the U.S. propensity to save would outrun the inducement to invest, resulting in a chronic depression of economic activity.[4] Happily, the dour predictions of the stagnationists have not been fulfilled.

It is apparent that different forms of the consumption function are possible, and that these differences in form can give rise to important differences in implications for government policy. The rest of this chapter reviews what economists have learned about the precise form of the aggregate consumption function beginning with Keynes' own description of that function.

THE APPROPRIATE FORM
OF THE CONSUMPTION FUNCTION

Keynes' own view of the consumption function is described quite succinctly in *The General Theory*. According to Keynes:

> The fundamental psychological law, upon which we are entitled to depend with great confidence both *a priori* from our knowledge of human nature and from the detailed facts of experience, is that men are disposed, as a rule and on the average, to increase their consumption as

3   It is also true for the function graphed in Figure 5-1 that the fraction of income saved rises as the level of income rises. However, for the function graphed in Figure 5-3, the gap between income and consumption widens at an increasing rate as income rises.

4   This *stagnation* thesis is most often associated with Alvin H. Hansen. See A. H. Hansen, "Economic Progress and Declining Population Growth," *American Economic Review*, Vol. 29, March 1939, pp. 1-15. Reprinted in M. G. Mueller, *Readings in Macroeconomics* (New York: Holt, Rinehart and Winston, 1971), pp. 265-276.

their income increases, but not by as much as the increase in their income. . . .

Apart from short-period *changes* in the level of income, it is also obvious that a higher absolute income will tend, as a rule, to widen the gap between income and consumption. For the satisfaction of the immediate primary needs of man and his family is usually a stronger motive than the motives toward accumulation, which only acquire effective sway when a margin of comfort has been attained. These reasons will lead, as a rule, to a greater *proportion* of income being saved as real income increases.[5]

Thus, for Keynes,

$$C = f(Y_d) \quad \text{such that } 0 < \text{MPC} < 1.$$

The APC was expected to fall as income rose. With which of the specific forms of the consumption function discussed above is this hypothesis consistent?

This was a firmly stated if not very restrictive hypothesis which, with data on disposable income and consumption, could be statistically tested. But unfortunately, adequate observations on the levels of aggregate income and consumption that the economy had enjoyed *over time* were not available in the 1930s. Without appropriate time series data, empirically oriented economists in the late 1930s and the early World War II years had to rely heavily on cross-section data for testing and quantifying consumption function hypotheses. Specifically, from cross-sectional family budget surveys of the population conducted in 1935-1936 and again in 1941-1942, there were observations on the level of disposable income and the associated level of consumption spending for *individual families*. Until the World War II era, economists employed those cross-section surveys in empirical studies of the consumption function. If the families surveyed in the budget studies are divided into groups by income level (for example, those with incomes between $3,000 and $3,500 per year could constitute one group), a plot of average *family* consumption spending versus average disposable income for the selected ranges of disposable income yields an income-versus-family consumption curve of the form shown in Figure 5-4. While this function is consistent with Keynes' requirements, we should place little reliance on this evidence from cross-section data as corroboration of a Keynesian-form consumption function. The consumption-income relationship we need is one that tells us how *aggregate* consumption (by all families) depends on *aggregate* disposable income (received by all families). The function plotted in Figure 5-4 tells us how *different families*

---

5 Keynes, *The General Theory, op. cit.*, pp. 96-97.

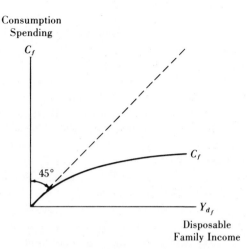

FIGURE 5-4   The Family (Budget
Study) Consumption Function

Disposable
Family Income

at different levels of income divide their income between consumption and saving.[6]

By the early 1940s, enough annual measures of aggregate income and consumption had become available (such figures were compiled beginning in 1929) to provide a much-needed time series test of the Keynesian consumption function hypothesis. As shown in Figure 5-5, the time series data available through 1941

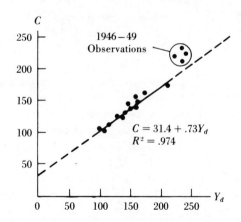

FIGURE 5-5   The Consumption Function from Time Series Data, 1929-
1941 (Data in Billions)

6   To conclude that the results from budget study data provide strong support for the Keynesian consumption function we would have to be willing to accept some rather strong presumptions. Most notably, we would have to assume that families are quite homogeneous in terms of spending desires across broad ranges of income levels, and we would have to assume that *relative income* (a concept to be developed later in this chapter) is unimportant as a determinant of consumer behavior.

provided support for a simple, linear consumption function consistent with Keynesian presumptions. Consumption was shown to rise with income, but by less than the income rise, and the proportion of income consumed appeared to decline with income growth.

Seemingly supported by both time series and cross-sectional data, the simple, linear consumption function, exhibiting a gap between income and consumption that widened with income growth, was widely employed in macroeconomic forecasts made during the middle 1940s. However, faith in that function was short-lived. With a postwar cutback in government spending anticipated, many economists predicted a severe economic slump at war's end. But, in fact, there was a postwar boom fueled by a volume of consumption spending substantially larger than the level predicted by extrapolating the consumption function in Figure 5-5 forward to higher income levels. (The levels of actual consumption and disposable income for 1946-49 are plotted in Figure 5-5 for comparison.)

Extrapolating the aggregate consumption functions that had been fitted to *interwar* data backward also provided highly suspicious predictions for consumption spending. In fact, with the consumption function in Figure 5-5, at any income level below $116 billion consumption exceeds current output—a possibility only if society consumes its accumulated wealth, and it is hard to imagine society doing that on an extended basis. Moreover, during World War II Simon Kuznets generated additional annual observations on disposable income and saving (consumption) backward in time to 1869, and that data indicated there had been no long-run change in the proportion of income consumed even though income had quadrupled between 1869 and 1929.[7]

We can readily update the conclusions from time series data that the crude empirical investigations conducted through the early 1940s provided. When regression analysis is employed to fit a consumption function to aggregate data over a long time span (including the span from 1869 to the present) a straight-line function that emanates from a point near the origin results (just like the hypothetical consumption function in Figure 5-2). As you already know, the marginal and average propensities to consume are equal and constant for such a function, as are the marginal and average propensities to save.

Clearly, the long-run or *secular* consumption function is inconsistent with Keynes' belief that a larger proportion of income would be saved as the level of aggregate income rose. However, we can also fit consumption functions to shorter time periods (like the interwar and postwar periods). Doing so yields flatter consumption functions (functions with positive intercepts), each of which

---

7 See Simon Kuznets, *Uses of National Income in Peace and War* (New York: National Bureau of Economic Research, 1942). Similar results were obtained later by Raymond Goldsmith for consumption and *personal* income. According to Goldsmith, a "main enduring characteristic [of saving behavior is] long-term stability of aggregate personal saving at approximately one-eighth of income." See Goldsmith, *A Study of Saving in the United States*, Vol. 1 (Princeton, N.J.: Princeton University Press for the National Bureau of Economic Research, 1955), p. 22.

by itself is consistent with the Keynesian specification of the income-consumption relationship.

A graph of consumption functions fitted to an extended time period (denoted by C_s for secular consumption function) and to shorter time periods (denoted by C_c for cyclical consumption function) would appear as shown in Figure 5-6A. It appears that the short-run (cyclical) consumption function, marked with a c subscript, is flatter than the long-run relationship, with the short-run function somehow shifting upward over time to yield the observed long-run function. The differences in the properties of secular and short-run consumption functions are exaggerated for expository purposes in Figure 5-6A. In Figure 5-6B, the short-run consumption function from Figure 5-5 is replotted along

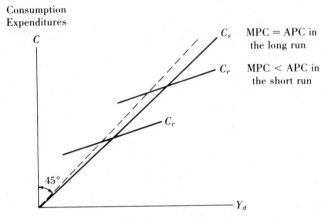

FIGURE 5-6A   The Long-Run and Short-Run (Secular and Cyclical) Consumption Functions

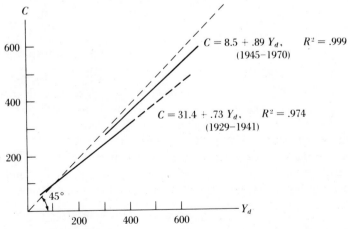

FIGURE 5-6B   Actual Cyclical Consumption Functions for 1929-1941 and 1945-1970 (Values Measured in Billions of 1958 Dollars)

with another cyclical function fitted to data from 1945-1970. Comparing the postwar function to the extension of the prewar schedule makes it apparent that the short-run function has shifted upward substantially. Modern research on consumption functions has focused on reconciling the apparent conflict between short- and long-run evidence and on providing a theoretically more satisfying consumption behavior model than that implied by the simple Keynesian hypothesis.

RECONCILING THE CONFLICT

Economists have traveled a number of different paths in their efforts to improve our understanding of consumption behavior and, hence, to reconcile the conflicting evidence provided by short- and long-run investigations of the consumption function. Some studies have tacitly assumed that the basic income-consumption linkage is nonproportional, as suggested by short-run data. Emphasizing the *ceteris paribus* nature of the income-consumption relationship, these investigations rely on changes in one or more factors other than income to shift the consumption function upward over time so that consumption remains a constant proportion of income in the long run. Other studies have assumed that the income-consumption relationship is proportional, with short-run data simply showing cyclical deviations from the basic relationship. While many of the early efforts to improve our understanding of the behavior of consumption casually added nonincome variables to consumption function regressions, more recent efforts have concentrated on the construction and testing of formal and sophisticated models of consumer behavior. After briefly looking at several factors that might produce a secular shift in a nonproportional short-run consumption function, we will turn our attention to the modern consumption function hypotheses that have played a dominant role in the construction of macroeconomic models in the last decade and a half.

Income Distribution

The first nonincome determinant of consumption we will consider is the distribution of income.[8] It has long been contended that budget study data show both the average and marginal propensities to consume falling as the level of family income rises. As a consequence of that behavior pattern, a reduction in income inequality should shift the consumption function upward. Why? Suppose, with aggregate income unchanged, there is a redistribution (transfer) of $1 billion of income from families in the top 10 percent of the income distribution to families in the lowest 10 percent. For families in the top 10 percent of the income dis-

---

8 Keynes himself provided a more exhaustive list of factors that could change the propensity to consume than we will review here. See *The General Theory, op. cit.*, Chapters 8 and 9.

tribution a substantial portion of any increment in income is absorbed by saving (the MPC of this group is relatively small, say .4). With a small MPC, a loss of $1 billion of income would reduce consumption spending by much less (by .4 billion with an MPC of .4). In contrast, the MPC of low income groups is typically quite large. If the MPC for the low income group were .9, a $1 billion increase in income for this group would raise its consumption spending by $.9 billion. Total consumption spending out of a given level of aggregate income would be increased by $.5 billion as a result of our hypothetical transfer. With a significant difference in the MPCs for low- and high-income groups, any equalization of the distribution of income, since that requires some reshuffling of income from higher to lower income groups, would increase the volume of total consumption spending out of any given volume of aggregate income.

If the distribution of income has become more nearly equal over time, we have identified one factor that might produce the kind of secular upward drift in the short-run consumption function necessary to hold the long-run APC constant. There has indeed been some tendency toward income equalization in the United States. This tendency was most significant during the period from 1929-1944. Outside of that period, however, there has been very little change in the distribution of income. Thus, the historical pattern of change in income distribution does not appear capable of generating the kind of even and sustained pattern of upward shifts in the consumption function necessary to maintain a secularly constant APC.[9]

Wealth

It is frequently contended that the greater a consumer unit's net wealth (assets minus liabilities) the less is the pressure to accumulate (save) and, thus, the larger the fraction of a given level of income that consumer unit will spend. If that contention is correct, we would expect to see the aggregate consumption function shift upward over time as aggregate wealth increases. While Keynes himself recognized that changes in wealth could affect the consumption function,[10] the potential role of wealth in linking the short-run and long-run consumption

---

9 Moreover, the strength of the impact on consumption of a redistribution of income is open to substantial question. Lubell has argued that a complete equalization of incomes in 1941 would have increased consumption by 5.82 percent, a value which implies that the kind of reduction in income inequality we have observed historically in the United States would have little impact on consumption. See Harold Lubell, "Effects of Redistribution of Income on Consumers' Expenditures," *The American Economic Review*, Vol. 37, March 1947. See also M. Bronfenbrenner, T. Yamane, and C. H. Lee, "A Study in Redistribution and Consumption," *The Review of Economics and Statistics*, May 1955, pp. 154-156.

For data on income distribution patterns over time in the United States, see *Survey of Current Business*, U. S. Department of Commerce, April 1964.

10 According to Keynes, changes in wealth "... should be classified amongst the major factors capable of causing short-period changes in the propensity to consume." *The General Theory, op. cit.*, p. 93.

functions was first clearly outlined by James Tobin in 1951.[11] Tobin's empirical work revealed the significant positive relationship between wealth and consumption necessary for reconciliation of short- and long-run evidence. Since then, wealth has received a great deal of attention in explanations of consumer behavior.

Demographic Factors

Demographic factors, such as movements of population from rural to urban areas, changes in family size, and changes in the average age of the population, can also cause the aggregate consumption function to shift over time. Other things being the same, families in urban areas have a larger APC than similar families in rural areas so that a net migration of families from rural to urban areas should shift the aggregate consumption function upward. Just such a redistribution of population has occurred over time in the United States.

Larger families tend to exhibit higher APCs so an increase in the average size of families could shift the consumption function upward. Family size has tended, however, to decrease in the United States during this century and that change would *lower* the aggregate APC.

The APC can also be altered by changes in the age distribution of the population. Consumer units in the 18-24 year age bracket typically find it difficult to save any sizable portion of their incomes. Indeed, those consumers are often dissavers, the APC for such units exceeding unity. The same is true of consumer units past retirement age, as these units consume past savings. Between these extremes consumer units, on the average, have APCs considerably less than unity. In the early 1960s, the U.S. population saw a large increase in the number of families in the 18-24-year-old bracket (the result of the World War II "baby boom") and in the number of family units in the retirement age bracket. Both of these developments would raise the aggregate APC. What would you expect to happen to the APC as the bulge of war babies ages? [12]

---

11   James Tobin, "Relative Income, Absolute Income, and Saving," *Money, Trade and Economic Growth* (New York: Macmillan, 1951), pp. 135-156.

At times, it is important to concentrate on the role of that component of wealth called "consumer durables" (autos, refrigerators, washing machines, and so on). During World War II, even though income was rising rapidly, stocks of consumer durables were depleted. At the end of the war, with reconversion of production facilities from wartime to peacetime uses, consumers went on a buying spree so that the APC was extremely high relative to prewar standards. Pent-up demand for unavailable durable goods, in conjunction with an abnormally high level of liquid wealth (particularly in government bonds), no doubt played an important role in this consumption function shift.

In more normal times it is harder to assess the role of durable goods stocks. However, the existence of such goods, the purchase of which can be accelerated or postponed at the consumer's whim, does serve to make consumption demand more unstable than it would otherwise be.

12   Careful consideration of the values of these demographic factors and data on the behavior patterns involved are provided in Milton Friedman, *A Theory of the Consumption Function* (Princeton: Princeton University Press for the National Bureau of Economic Research, 1957).

The Price Level and Price Expectations

Changes in the general price level, by altering the real value of some of the assets that society holds, may affect consumption. In particular, an increase in the general price level reduces society's wealth by reducing the purchasing power embodied in its holdings of government-issued bonds and money since both of those assets are fixed in nominal value. Of course, a persistent *decline* in prices, steadily increasing society's wealth, would be required to continuously shift the consumption function upward over time, and we can scarcely claim to have had that experience. Moreover, empirical evidence indicates that the impact on consumption of the changes in real wealth resulting from movements in the price level are small enough to be ignored for practical purposes.[13]

A second influence on consumption may arise from the effect that observed price changes have on consumer expectations. For example, if experience convinces consumers that prices are destined to rise in the future, a higher-than-normal proportion of current income may be devoted to consumption in order to "beat the expected price increase." While this linkage between price increases and consumption spending is of academic interest, the moderate inflation rate the United States has experienced over most of the extended period for which we have national income accounting data provides no significant role for price expectations in shifting the consumption function.

There are other factors that can cause shifts in the consumption function and that, consequently, *might* produce the kind of systematic upward drift of a basically nonproportional consumption function necessary to yield a secularly constant APC. Without any extention of our list, however, it should be recognized that to maintain a *constant* APC over extremely long periods of time (such as the 100-plus years we have observed) implies a remarkable coincidence in timing of changes in a factor (or combination of factors) of the type we have been discussing.

The Interest Rate and Consumption

Before turning our attention to more sophisticated, post-Keynesian consumption models, we need to look at one more variable which, in *pre*-Keynesian analysis, was assumed to play an important role in determining the level of consumption and saving. That variable is the interest rate. Keynes' predecessors argued that consumption spending was quite sensitive to changes in the interest rate. In their analysis, interest was the reward for saving (not consuming). With a positive interest return on savings which are loaned out, 1 dollar of current saving can provide more than a dollar's worth of future consumption. The larger the reward for saving (the higher the interest rate) presumably the bigger the vol-

---

13 As a theoretical matter, changes in wealth that result from price adjustments can be quite important, as will be demonstrated in Chapter 10.

ume of saving and, consequently, the smaller the volume of consumption expected to flow from any given level of income. In contrast, Keynes' analysis played down the sensitivity of consumption to interest rate changes by assuming that consumption and saving are directly affected very little, if at all, by changes in the interest rate. Indeed, some analysts have even provided arguments that rationalize a *negative* link between the interest rate and the level of saving. For example, if households save with particular *targets* in mind (for example, $20,000 by 1985 for Junior's education, or $50,000 by 1990 for a retirement fund), a higher interest rate permits attainment of the savings goal with a *lower* annual flow of saving. With no convincing evidence on even the direction of impact of interest rate variations, despite its inclusion in numerous empirical investigations, the interest rate continues to enjoy the same negligible *direct* role in altering consumption as it was accorded by Keynes.

MODERN CONSUMPTION FUNCTION HYPOTHESES

The so-called "new" or "modern" consumption function hypotheses attempt to reconcile the apparent conflict between long- and shorter-run consumption functions without depending on *coincidental* changes in nonincome factors (wealth, income distribution, and so on) to conveniently shift the short-run consumption function. To justify the intellectual effort required in working with these more complicated consumption theories, we need to remind ourselves that it is our understanding of the determinants of consumption demand that allows us to predict future consumption and to design policy prescriptions for controlling the level of consumption demand.

Past and Relative Income

One of the first models to offer a systematic resolution of the conflict between long- and short-run consumption functions was developed by James Duesenberry shortly after World War II.[14] Duesenberry's consumption model involves a skillful combination of two hypotheses about human consumer behavior—the *relative income hypothesis* and the *past income hypothesis*. Rejecting a basic tenet of standard consumption theory—the assumption that household consumption is independent of the actions of other households—the relative income hypothesis treats man as a social animal. As such, his behavior, including the economic behavior of consuming, is assumed to depend very heavily on the actions of members of his peer group (his neighbors, business associates, and so on). If consumers are concerned with social status and if income, or, more precisely, consumption expenditure as a demonstration of income, is an accepted

---

14   J. S. Duesenberry, *Income, Saving, and the Theory of Consumer Behavior* (Cambridge, Mass.: Harvard University Press, 1949).

guide to social position, the proportion of income a consumer unit spends will depend heavily on its relative income position.

Suppose we are observing the behavior of individual consumer units in a peer group with average income Y_m. For a unit with income below the average $(Y < Y_m)$, we could expect to find an APC above the average as the lower-income family tries to "keep up with the Joneses." On the other hand, those with above-average incomes can consume a smaller fraction of their incomes and still maintain their social status. Hence, we should expect to find a nonproportional cross-sectional consumption function for our sample of families, just as family budget study data revealed. Formally stated, the relative income hypothesis indicates that, for the ith individual consumer unit, the APC is

$$\text{APC}_i = \frac{C_i}{Y_i} = f\left(\frac{Y_i}{Y_m}\right)$$

where

$C_i =$ real consumption by the ith consumer unit,

$Y_i =$ real income for the ith consumer unit,

$Y_m =$ average income of the relevant peer group.

Applied to the economy as a whole, this hypothesis contends that families with below-average incomes will have larger APCs than those who enjoy above-average incomes.

The APC for a consumer unit will change only if his percentile position in the income distribution changes. For example, if a consumer unit's income rises more slowly than average income over time, its APC would be expected to rise while, if its income rises faster than Y_m, its APC would be expected to decline. But if everyone's income is rising over time, and at the same rate, relative income positions would be unchanged and there would be no reason for any consumer unit's APC (or, therefore, for the aggregate APC) to change. The aggregate APC (total consumption/total income) would change only as a result of a significant change in the overall distribution of income. If the distribution of income is stable over time, the aggregate APC should be stable over time. Thus, the long-run (trend) constancy of the APC can be rationalized if the hypothesis that a consumer unit's APC depends only on his percentile position in the relevant peer group is accepted.

As we know, though, there are cyclical movements in aggregate income and consumption and cyclical (short-run) deviations of the APC from its trend value which must be explained. To do that, Duesenberry employs the past income hypothesis. According to the past income hypothesis, when there are cyclical movements in income, consumption expenditures depend not only on the current level of income but also on the highest level of income attained in the past. According to Duesenberry:

The fundamental psychological postulate underlying our argument is that it is harder for a family to reduce its expenditures from a high level than for a family to refrain from making high expenditures in the first place.[15]

A family with a high income, given time for adjustment, will become accustomed to an accordingly elevated standard of living. If income moves cyclically, in response to a fall in income such a family would attempt to maintain its standard of living at the expense of saving. Thus, "past income" is an important determinant of consumption expenditures as well as current income. The precise past income figure which Duesenberry thinks important is the previous peak income. "The peak year's consumption sets the standard from which cuts are made (provided the peak did not represent a mere spurt in income)."[16] Duesenberry relied on both the relative and the past income hypotheses to attempt to reconcile the long- and short-run consumption/income relations.

According to Duesenberry, if income increases along a steady trend path, the aggregate APC would be affected only by changes in income distribution (the relative income hypothesis rules). If the income distribution stays the same over time, then we should expect to obtain the long-run consumption function, $0C_{LR}$ in Figure 5-7, along which consumption is proportional to income.

If, however, income varies cyclically (as well as increasing secularly),

Consumption
Expenditures

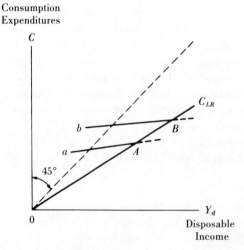

FIGURE 5-7 Duesenberry's Secular and Cyclical Consumption Functions

15 Duesenberry, *op. cit.*, pp. 84-85.
16 Duesenberry concedes that a weighted average of past income levels might be better but claims that too few observations are available to statistically estimate the weights.

Duesenberry would expect deviations from the secular path $0C_{LR}$. With cyclical movements, the past income hypothesis comes into play and consumption at any point in time would be expected to depend not only on current income but also on the highest level of income previously attained.

Suppose we are at point A in Figure 5-7. If consumption depends only on current income, a decline in income would result in a movement back along $0C_{LR}$ (the APC constant). If the past income hypothesis holds, however, such a cyclical fall in income would be met first with a sacrifice in saving—a movement back along the flatter short-run consumption schedule aA. Along this schedule, the APC falls as income rises and declines as income grows.

As the economy passes through the trough of the income cycle and income rises, consumers would first restore the desired level of saving until point A (corresponding to previous peak income) were reached. As income continues to increase, a more "normal" saving ratio can be restored since previous peak income has lost its sway. Consequently, the economy would move along the proportional schedule $0C_{LR}$ until the next cyclical downturn, at which point we would again see a movement along a flatter consumption function such as bB. A nonproportional, short-run (cyclical) consumption function is perfectly consistent with a proportional long-run consumption function.[17]

Duesenberry's consumption model has enjoyed prominence in the evolutionary development of macroeconomic analysis as the first of the systematic reconciliations of observed long- and short-run income/consumption relations. However, because Duesenberry's model is not derived through the direct application of traditional consumer behavior theory—indeed, it rejects some of the basic tenets of that traditional theory—it has never been fully accepted by the economics profession as a general explanation of aggregate consumption behavior. Economists have responded with considerably more favor to consumption function hypotheses that are derived assuming utility maximization by rational households who are not imprisoned by habitual consumption patterns or social pressures. Such households save to make the time pattern of their consumption more gratifying with both current and future consumption contributing to utility. Milton Friedman's *Permanent Income Hypothesis* fits this mold.[18]

---

17   Duesenberry fitted a simple linear relation of the form $S_t/Y_t = a(Y_t/Y_0) + b$ to aggregate data for the years 1923-1940, obtaining

$$S_t/Y_t = .166(Y_t/Y_0) - .066 \qquad (R^2 = .9).$$

This relationship can account for both secular and cyclical behavior in saving.

   (a) Secular: looking at the trend of income, Y_t/Y_0 can be, say, 1.03 (reflecting a 3-percent annual growth in income) since Y_0 is the previous year's income in any year t if only a smooth upward trend of income levels is relevant. In this case, $S_t/Y_t = .166(1.03) - .066 = .105 = 10.5\%$ = APS or APC $= 1 - $ APS $= 89.5\%$, a value consistent with Kuznets' data on the secular value of the APC.

   (b) Cyclical: as income falls the ratio (Y_t/Y_0) falls so that S_t/Y_t falls (APS↓, APC↑), as cyclical data typically demonstrate.

18   Milton Friedman, *A Theory of the Consumption Function, op. cit.*

The Permanent Income Hypothesis

Duesenberry's attempt at explaining consumption behavior implicitly assumes that the national income and product accounts definitions of income and consumption are the appropriate ones for explaining consumer behavior. In Friedman's treatment of the permanent income hypothesis that assumption is rejected. According to the permanent income hypothesis, a consumer's spending behavior during this period depends not only on this period's income, but also on the future stream of income the consumer *expects* to receive. Current consumption may be practically independent of current income! Further, observed consumption *spending* does not measure true consumption—for example, only part of an auto is consumed during a year. Friedman would argue that the appropriate consumption variable we should try to explain with a fitted consumption function would count only an imputed value of the services of such durable goods in addition to the value of spending on nondurable consumer goods.[19]

When the appropriate modifications for removing the most obvious deficiencies of existing data on income and consumption are completed,[20] one additional step is required to formalize the relationship between observed values of income and consumption and their proper theoretical counterparts. This step requires breaking observed income and consumption into two components, a "permanent" component and a "transitory" component. That is, let

$$Y \equiv Y_p + Y_t \qquad \text{where} \qquad Y = \text{observed income}$$
$$Y_p = \text{permanent income}$$
$$Y_t = \text{transitory income}$$

and

$$C \equiv C_p + C_t \qquad \text{where} \qquad C = \text{observed consumption}$$
$$C_p = \text{permanent consumption}$$
$$C_t = \text{transitory consumption.}$$

"The permanent component [of income] is to be interpreted as reflecting the effect of those factors that the unit regards as determining its capital value or wealth." [21] Thus, Y_p is a measure of expected expendable income available to be

---

19 Just where the line should be drawn between consumer durable goods and nondurables is clearly a matter that contains an element of uncertainty.

20 Additional suggested modifications include deducting cash expenditures that occur as a cost of earning income from income data (cost of clothing, transportation to work, and so on), switching from cash accounting to an accrual technique, and so on.

21 Friedman, *A Theory of the Consumption Function, op. cit.*, p. 21.

spread over the consumer's life.[22] Envision a consumer unit who, this period, intends to sell the rights to its future earnings from working for an immediate lump-sum payment. Add to the market value of its future labor earnings the current value of its accumulated property wealth, providing a sum which the consumer unit can contract to lend at interest. The yearly interest income, which the consumer unit could spend each year without reducing its capital (wealth), is permanent income. Permanent consumption (C_p) is that consumption which the consumer unit systematically chooses to enjoy based upon its permanent income.

Y_t and C_t are unexpected, "chance" movements in income and consumption respectively. Microeconomic examples would include income loss due to an unexpected illness, gains due to an unexpected inheritance, and losses due to a crop failure for Y_t, and such items as unexpectedly good opportunities to make purchases, and spending due to an unexpected illness for C_t. The possibility of transitory disturbances at the aggregate level and their role in aggregate consumption behavior is explored in the next section.

The Formal Hypothesis

Friedman's formal hypothesis states that the systematic relationship which we should look for between consumption and income is the relationship between the permanent components C_p and Y_p. He hypothesizes that the true relationship is proportional with the proportion (the APC) affected by several factors other than income. That is:

$$C_p = k(i, w, u) \cdot Y_p.$$

The factors affecting the size of k are i, the rate of interest (or a set of rates); w, a proxy variable that measures the relative importance of property and nonproperty income; and u, a catch-all variable included to capture the impact on k of such factors as tastes, the size and age of consumer units, and so on.[23] With no significant secular tendency for the interest rate to change, and with no demonstrated empirically significant role for w and u in altering the value of k at the aggregate level, the secular income-consumption relationship for the economy should exhibit a fairly constant APC.

To make the hypothesis testable (subject to refutation), Friedman assumes that "the transitory components of income and consumption are uncorrelated

---

22 Realistically, Friedman's empirical work implies that the consumer's time horizon is more limited in duration, close to 3 years.

23 Since it is easier to borrow against nonhuman wealth than human wealth, the higher the value of w (the higher the ratio of "property" to "nonproperty" wealth) the weaker the motivation to accumulate (save) and the larger the value of k. How would k be related to i and u?

with one another and with the corresponding permanent components." [24] *The substantive implication of the formal hypothesis is that a change in observed income would systematically affect consumption (if at all) only to the extent that it affects the value of permanent income.*[25] If a consumer has a long time horizon, a change in the level of income currently received could have little impact on his "permanent" income level and, thus, would have little effect on his consumption behavior.

At the aggregate level then, *transitory* (cyclical) swings in current, measured income would have little effect on aggregate consumption. Faced with a decline in current income to a *subnormal* level during recessions, consumers would reduce their saving rate without significantly reducing consumption, *which is based on permanent income.* Hence, in recessions an increased fraction of current measured income would be consumed. On the other hand, in boom periods measured income rises more rapidly than historical experience tells us is normal. Households, continuing to base their consumption on what they perceive as normal or permanent income, save an unusually large fraction of the transitory increase in earnings. As long as income varies cyclically in addition to growing steadily over the long run, we should expect flat (nonproportional) short-run consumption functions to coexist with a proportional long-run income-consumption relationship. The corresponding macroeconomic policy implications are striking for, according to the permanent income hypothesis, a change in received income stemming from a government policy action (for example, a change in tax collections) that is *temporary* would have a negligible impact on consumption spending. Thus the *explicitly temporary* increase in tax collections imposed under Lyndon Johnson in 1968 (in the form of a 10-percent income tax surcharge), having little impact on permanent income, could not have been expected to depress consumption very substantially. Appearing to support that view, aggregate demand remained at an inflationary level through 1968 and 1969. But, of course, statistical series cannot unequivocally reveal what *would have happened* without the tax surcharge.[26] In the same vein, advocates of the permanent income hypothesis would argue that the one-time 10-percent rebate on personal income tax liabilities, which Congress provided in 1975 as part of a stimulative fiscal program, would generate relatively little additional consumption.

Though Friedman's application of the permanent income theory to numerous

---

24   Friedman, *A Theory of the Consumption Function, op. cit.*, p. 26. The assumption in rigorous terms is $\rho_{Y_t Y_p} = \rho_{C_t C_p} = \rho_{Y_t C_t} = 0$, where ρ is the partial correlation coefficient between the variables indicated by subscripts.

25   That is, if $C_p = f(Y_p)$, then $\text{MPC} = dC_p/dY = \partial C_p/\partial Y_p \cdot (dY_p/dY)$ with the size of dY_p/dY declining as the consumer's time horizon lengthens.

26   For an explanation of the "weak" effects of the 1968 surcharge see R. Eisner, "Fiscal and Monetary Policy Reconsidered," *The American Economic Review*, Vol. 59, December 1969, pp. 897-905. Other economists have argued that the tax surcharge was effective in reducing consumer spending. See A. Okun, "The Personal Tax Surcharge and Consumer Demand, 1968," *Brookings Papers on Economic Activity*, Vol. 1, 1971, pp. 167-200.

empirical situations has demonstrated its consistency with real-world observations in a broad array of circumstances, there are studies that have failed to support the hypothesis. An investigation by Bodkin[27] found that the MPC out of unexpected (transitory) income from National Life Insurance dividends in 1950 fell between 0.72 and 0.97, values considerably larger than allowable in Friedman's model.[28] Friedman's own empirical work with time series data for the years 1905 through 1951 has yielded a function of the form $C = 0.88Y_p$. For this function the APC is clearly a constant proportion of permanent income (thus both the average and marginal propensity to consume out of permanent income is 88 percent). Since there is no direct way to observe permanent income, as a proxy for permanent income Friedman used a weighted average of current and past values of observed income.[29] The presumption is that individuals base their expectations of future income on past and current experience. But expectations of future income levels certainly can incorporate information that is not included in current and past income observations. Thus, reliance on a weighted average of observed income values to predict permanent income and consumption builds a degree of momentum into those predictions which can result in sizable errors when turning points in consumption occur. But, in spite of difficulties like this one, which must be tolerated in the empirical application of the permanent income hypothesis, that hypothesis plays a dominant role in modern discussions of aggregate consumption behavior. The fundamental conclusion that income changes which are viewed as temporary (transitory) have a significantly weaker effect on consumption than those that are perceived as permanent is aired commonly now, even in newspaper discussions of proposed tax policy changes. More controversially, Friedman and his most ardent supporters emphasize the notion that the multiplier is an undependable tool for

---

27   R. Bodkin, "Windfall Income and Consumption," *The American Economic Review*, Vol. 49, September 1959, pp. 602-614.

28   If the appropriate time horizon for consumers is 3 years, as Friedman's estimates have indicated, the MPC out of windfalls should be approximately one-third. A shorter horizon is obtained in an investigation by R. Holbrook, "The Three-Year Horizon: An Analysis of the Evidence," *Journal of Political Economy*, Vol. 75, October 1967, pp. 750-754. Negative results have also been produced by H. Houthakker, "The Permanent Income Hypothesis," *The American Economic Review*, Vol. 48, June 1958, pp. 396-404; and by R. Jones, "Transitory Income and Expenditures on Consumption Categories," The American Economic Association *Proceedings*, Vol. 50, May 1960, pp. 584-592. Evidence that supports the hypothesis has been obtained by M. Krainin, "Windfall Income and Consumption—Additional Evidence," *The American Economic Review*, Vol. 51, June 1961, pp. 310-324.

29   Friedman uses a weighted average of incomes for the previous 17 years with weights declining rapidly as the observation becomes more distant in time (current year's income has a weight of .33, the previous year's income a weight of .22, and so on). With this weighting scheme a $100 change in *current* income changes Y_p by $33. The MPC out of current income is $dC/dY = \partial C/\partial Y \cdot dY_p/dY = .88(.33) = .29$. Clearly, with an MPC of .29, this short-run aggregate consumption function is flatter (nonproportional) than the long-run function. Approximately one-third of a measured change in current income is currently consumed. Hence, it is argued that, on the average, increments to income appear to be spread out over an approximate 3-year planning horizon.

policy making and forecasting because households have to translate observed income changes into permanent and transitory components. In an effort to control the economy, the government can alter taxes and its spending levels, in both cases altering disposable income. According to Friedman, however, policy makers cannot know how much of the income change a fiscal policy action produces will be considered permanent and how much transitory. Hence, they cannot know the MPC (or the multiplier) and they cannot reliably predict the impact of fiscal actions.

The Life-Cycle Hypothesis

A hypothesis similar in implications to Friedman's permanent income hypothesis is the so-called *life-cycle hypothesis*. The central theme of this hypothesis is that men are "forward-looking animals." [30] Accordingly, "there need not be any close and simple relation between consumption in a given short period and income in that same period. The rate of consumption in any given period is a facet of a plan which extends *over the balance of the individual's life,* while the income accruing within the same period is but one element which contributes to the shaping of such a plan." [31]

For the typical individual, income is low during the early years of life, rises toward a peak in the late years of full-time employment, then returns to a low level in the late years of life. But with current income only a relatively minor determinant of current consumption, the life-cycle hypothesis suggests that an individual will spread out his consumption in a pattern much smoother than that of his income stream. The predicted form of behavior is shown in Figure 5-8

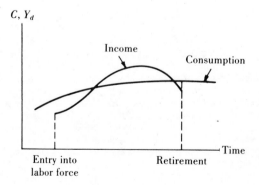

FIGURE 5-8   Life-Cycle Income and Consumption

30   See F. Modigliani and Richard Brumberg, "Utility Analysis and the Consumption Function: An Interpretation of Cross-Section Data," in K. Kurihara (ed.), *Post Keynesian Economics* (New Brunswick, N.J.: Rutgers University Press, 1954). Also, A. Ando and F. Modigliani, "The 'Life Cycle' Hypothesis of Saving," *The American Economic Review,* Vol. 53, March 1963, pp. 55-84.

31   F. Modigliani and Richard Brumberg, *op. cit.,* pp. 391-392.

with our individual saving during his peak earning years and dissaving in his low-income years.[32]

In summary terms, the life-cycle hypothesis indicates that an individual's consumption in any period depends on the total resources he has to spend over his remaining life (once again on his total *wealth*, consisting of the value of the property he owns plus the market or *discounted* value of the future stream of income he expects to earn by working)[33] and the number of years he expects to live. The greater an individual's wealth or the shorter his expected life, the larger his yearly consumption will be, according to the life-cycle model.

In formal terms, Modigliani's hypothesis suggests that in a simple setting a consumer would spend the same proportion of what he perceives to be his total wealth each year, no matter what the level of received income is in that one year. That is, for an individual consumer consumption is[34]

$$C_t = \frac{1}{L_t} V_t$$

where

C_t = consumption in year t;

L_t = the consumer's expected remaining life in year t (in years);

V_t = the consumer's total wealth in year t.

With an individual's total wealth in year t dependent on the value of his property wealth at the beginning of year t, the income he earns from his labor efforts in year t, and his expected stream of labor income receipts over the remaining years till retirement age, the individual's consumption function can be rewritten as

$$C_t = C(Y_t, Y_t^e, a_t)$$

where

Y_t = labor income in year t;

Y_t^e = income expected from working in the consumer's remaining earning years $(Y_{t+1}, Y_{t+2}, \ldots)$;

a_t = net value of assets owned by the consumer at the beginning of year t.

---

32   This is the pattern of behavior assumed in the discussion of the age distribution of the population early in this chapter.

33   The process called *discounting* allows us to convert a stream of expected future income receipts into an equivalent value of wealth held currently as a stock. The mechanics of discounting are covered in Chapter 6.

34   The model was first developed, in the form used here, assuming a zero interest rate, then extended to a world with a positive interest rate.

An increase in current income above the expected level increases the individual's net worth. But according to the life-cycle hypothesis, if the increase in that 1 year's income is not perceived as permanent, the resulting *small* increase in net worth, spread evenly over the consumer's remaining life with equal additions to consumption in each period, would have a *small* impact on current consumption. For the typical individual then, the marginal propensity to consume out of current income would be small relative to the average propensity to consume. However, the larger the impact of an unanticipated increase in current income on the level of income *expected* in the future (and thus on the consumer's net worth) the larger the response in consumption and, of course, the larger the MPC. The implications of the hypothesis for an individual's consumption behavior are clearly quite similar to those of the permanent income hypothesis. Once again, an explicitly temporary change in current income, for example, because of a temporary income tax change, would be expected to have little influence on consumption.[35] On the other hand, a change in current income that is viewed as reflecting a shift in the entire time stream of future income receipts (for example, a *permanent* change in tax rates) would have a far larger impact on consumption.

To employ the life-cycle hypothesis in explaining aggregate consumption behavior, we need to recognize that the proportion of aggregate income society would consume in any period would change with the age distribution, rising as the proportion of the population in the early and late stages of life increases. However, the life-cycle hypothesis does not rely on changes in the population's age distribution to reconcile the behavior patterns observed in short-run and long-run studies of the consumption function.

Holding the age composition of the population constant, the life-cycle hypothesis implies that aggregate consumption depends on society's current income, its expected future labor earnings, and the value of its assets. In linear form then, aggregate consumption in period t is expected to be

$$C_t' = b_1 Y_t' + b_2 Y_t^{e'} + b_3 a_t'$$

where the superscript ($'$) indicates the variables are *aggregate* measures (of consumption, current labor income, expected labor income, and assets).

---

35 If N is the number of remaining working years for our consumer, Y^e is the average yearly value of labor income expected in the future, the other variables are defined as before, and the interest rate is zero, then

$$C = C(Y, Y^e, a, t) = 1/L_t(Y) + N/L_t(Y^e) + 1/L_t(a),$$
so $\partial C/\partial Y = 1/L_t + N/L_t(dY^e/dY).$

If an unexpected change in received income has no impact on income expected in the future, then the second term disappears leaving $\partial C/\partial Y = 1/L_t$, which typically would be extremely small in value. If, as is more reasonable, an unexpected change in income causes expected future income to change in the same direction $(dY^e/dY > 0)$, then the MPC will be larger. How much larger it would be depends on the size of dY^e/dY.

Unfortunately for purposes of testing this model, future expected income cannot be measured. But if expected income depends on current income (let expected income be $Y_t^{e'} = ZY_t'$), our consumption function can be rewritten as

$$C_t' = b_1 Y_t' + b_2 Z Y_t' + b_3 a_t',$$

or

$$C_t' = b_4 Y_t' + b_3 a_t', \; (b_4 = b_1 + b_2 Z),$$

allowing predictions of changes in consumption based just on changes in the observable variables, current labor income (Y_t') and asset holdings (a_t'). Moreover, this equation can be readily employed to reconcile short- and long-run patterns of consumption behavior. In the short run, the value of assets remains virtually unchanged so that the short-run income-consumption relationship is nonproportional, its intercept $(b_3 a_t')$ dictated by the value of assets, as shown in Figure 5-9. With a steady growth of property wealth in the long run, the value of the intercept of the short-run function is steadily increased, shifting the consumption function upward in the manner necessary for generating a proportional long-run consumption function.[36] Wealth, which we identified early in this chapter as a candidate for explaining observed consumption patterns, plays a crucial role in the life-cycle hypothesis.

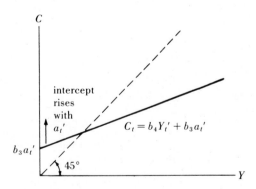

FIGURE 5-9 The Life-Cycle Consumption Function

36   Ando and Modigliani fitted a number of empirical forms of this hypothesis to time series data for the United States. A representative result is the equation

$$C_t' = 0.7 \, Y_t' + .06 \, a_t',$$

where Y_t' is labor income, a_t' is the value of property wealth, and C_t' is consumption. This equation says, of course, that the MPC out of current income is .7 and the MPC out of assets is .06. For short-run, or cyclical movements in income, a_t' is near constant. Thus, the short-run consumption function is nonproportional with a virtually fixed intercept (an intercept value of $.06 a_t'$). As the time period lengthens, saving will result in growth of the value of accumulated

SUMMARY

The discussion of consumption in this chapter began with Keynes' rough "psychological law" that consumption is a positive function of the absolute level of current disposable income with a marginal propensity to consume smaller than the average propensity to consume and also less than one. As demonstrated, this crude hypothesis is not supported unequivocally by available data on income and consumption, is incapable of reconciling the conflict between short-run and secular time series data, and is open to criticism on theoretical grounds.

Three formal hypotheses that have been developed to try to overcome the shortcomings of the Keynesian *absolute income hypothesis* are the Duesenberry *relative (and past) income hypothesis*, the Friedman *permanent income hypothesis*, and the Modigliani *life-cycle hypothesis*. Each of these appears to be more general and, thus, more satisfying theoretically than the Keynesian function. Each is capable of reconciling the conflict between long-run and short-run consumption functions. Making a choice between these hypotheses on purely *a priori* grounds is impossible, though the fact that Duesenberry's consumption model is not firmly grounded in standard consumer behavior theory has prevented its general acceptance by economists. It is also difficult to make a clear-cut choice on empirical grounds since all three hypotheses yield consumption functions that fit the data quite well (that is, all three functions yield high R^2 terms when fitted to data on income and consumption).[37]

It is frustrating that available test methods are unable to identify the one *best* model from the several logical constructions that are capable of reconciling the conflict between short- and long-run evidence on the consumption function.

---

assets. As property wealth increases, the short-run consumption function will shift upward since its intercept is simply $.06a_t'$ and the value of a_t' is growing.

Dividing the fitted consumption function by total disposable income (Y_d') to provide a measure of the APC yields

$$\text{APC} = \frac{C_t'}{Y_d'} = .7\frac{Y_t'}{Y_d'} + .06\frac{a_t'}{Y_d'}.$$

Clearly, the APC can remain constant over time if labor's share of total income (Y_t'/Y_d') stays constant *and* if wealth grows at the same trend rate as income (keeping a_t'/Y_d' unchanged). Both those conditions have held approximately in the United States.

37 The very high measured correlations between income and consumption in fact do not provide compelling evidence that income changes *cause* consumption changes. While the income level no doubt does influence consumption, in turn consumption spending is by far the largest component of aggregate spending (income). Whether consumption is high because income is high or whether income is high because consumption is high cannot be ascertained from the statistical tests reported in this text. The statistical difficulties that result from correlating one variable, (C), with another variable, (Y), of which the first is a component part, are beyond the scope of this text. However, it should be recognized that a "spuriously" high correlation results. D. B. Suits has suggested that with consumption comprising near 90 percent of income, the correlation between income and consumption should be expected to be around .9 even if income changes do not cause consumption changes. See D. B. Suits, "The Determinants of Consumer Expenditure: A Review of Present Knowledge," *Impacts of Monetary Policy* (Englewood Cliffs, N.J.: Prentice-Hall, 1963).

But, for our purposes it is sufficient to note that all of the empirical investigations we have reviewed agree on the basic form of the income-consumption relationship. Both the proportional long-run function and the nonproportional short-run function have important applications in macroeconomic analysis. For short-run analysis, which is the primary concern of this text, a nonproportional function of just the form employed in Chapter 4 $(C = a + bY_d)$ is appropriate. On the other hand, for analyzing the long-run growth of the economy, as we will do in Chapter 14, a proportional consumption function is appropriate. Moreover, there is basic agreement between the two consumption function hypotheses that are most intensively employed in current research (the life-cycle hypothesis and the permanent income hypothesis) on the impact of government budget changes. Most notably on this score, both hypotheses agree that changes in government outlays or tax collections that are perceived as *temporary* will have a significantly smaller impact on current consumption, and hence on overall demand, than those that are perceived as *permanent*. As a consequence, great care is required in attempting to devise fiscal policy actions that will have the desired effect on aggregate spending.

In light of the indicated weakness of explicitly temporary income tax changes, a few economists have recently suggested that the government could more effectively control the level of consumption spending by applying (or relaxing) a temporary *sales tax* on consumption goods. Such a temporary tax would alter the relative cost of current as opposed to future consumption. You should be well equipped now to provide a theoretical evaluation of the impact on aggregate consumption of such a tax levy and to compare its effects to those that would stem from a permanent change in the sales tax rate (be careful!).

Finally, it is worth noting that the government still looks upon income tax changes as a basic tool for controlling consumption spending. In the spring of 1975 Congress instituted a personal income tax cut to spur anemic consumption demand in the midst of a steep contraction in economic activity. Combining a 10-percent rebate on 1974 income tax liabilities with a 1-year cut in tax obligations, that tax cut package was designed to materially increase disposable income in 1975. How should consumption have been expected to respond?

QUESTIONS

1. Suppose you have the observations presented in the table below generated by a consumption function of the form: $C = a + bY + cA$.

Year	C	Y	A
1	670	800	800
2	750	900	900
3	770	900	1000
4	850	1000	1100
5	910	1100	1100

From the data, find the constant a and the marginal propensity to consume out of Y and A. What is consumption when Y (income) is zero? When Y is zero and A is 1000?

2. From the *Survey of Current Business* plot the real consumption and real disposable income figures for 1960 through last year. Using a straight-edge, draw the straight line that, by eye, seems to fit best through your plotted observations.

 (a) Is your plotted line a usable short-run consumption function?

 (b) From your consumption line, find the approximate value of the marginal propensity to consume.

 (c) What does your MPC make the value of the multiplier in models I and II of Chapter 4?

3. Suppose you are given the hypothetical consumption function $C = a + bY + cW + di + eE$ in which C is real consumption spending, Y is real disposable income, W is real wealth, i is the interest rate, and E is a measure of the equality of income distribution. Explain how C would respond to changes in each of these variables and why.

4. By extrapolating short-run or cyclical consumption functions (like C_c in Figure 5-6B) fitted to prewar data, economists predicted a growing gap between consumption spending and full employment output after World War II. With government spending expected to decline with the war's end predictions of massive recession were commonplace. But, in fact, consumers went on a buying spree after the war and inflation was more of a problem than stagnation. Account for the major error in forecasting consumption that gave us misleading forecasts of postwar economic performance.

5. In recent years, the government has increased social security payments to the aged and has provided that group with medical care. With these programs financed through general tax revenues and increased social security contributions, what impact should we expect these programs to have on aggregate consumption spending?

6. In the Biblical story about the 7 good years and 7 bad years, a community stored up grain during 7 years of extraordinarily good harvests and was thereby enabled to live "normally" during 7 subsequent years of crop failure. Identify a consumption function hypothesis that accommodates the behavior described above and briefly explain the logical foundation of that function.

7. In her last album *Pearl*, recorded by Columbia Records, the late Janis Joplin sang:

 "Lord, won't you buy me a Mercedes Benz?
 My friends all have Porsches, I must make amends." *

* Lyrics from "MERCEDES BENZ" by Janis Joplin, Michael McClure, and Bobby Neuwirth. © 1970. Strong Arm Music. Reprinted by Permission of the Publisher. International Copyright Secured. All Rights Reserved.

Identify the consumption function hypothesis that reflects the sentiment expressed in the song and explain how economists have used that hypothesis to account for observed consumer behavior.

8. What do the permanent and life-cycle consumption function hypotheses have to say about the effect on consumption of a temporary income surtax?

SUGGESTED READING

Ando, Albert, and Franco Modigliani, "The 'Life-Cycle' Hypothesis of Saving: Aggregate Implications and Tests," *American Economic Review.* Vol. 53, March 1963, pp. 55-84.

deLeeuw, Frank, and Edward Gramlich. "The Federal Reserve—MIT Econometric Model," *Federal Reserve Bulletin.* Vol. 54, January 1968, pp. 11-13 and 21-25.

Duesenberry, James S. *Income, Saving, and the Theory of Consumer Behavior.* Cambridge, Mass.: Harvard University Press, 1949.

Farrell, M. J. "The New Theories of the Consumption Function," *Economic Journal.* Vol. 69, December 1959, pp. 678-695. Reprinted in M. G. Mueller (ed.). *Readings in Macroeconomics,* 2d edition. New York: Holt, Rinehart and Winston, Inc., pp. 77-92.

Ferber, Robert. "Research on Household Behavior," *American Economic Review.* Vol. 52, March 1962, pp. 19-63.

Mayer, Thomas. *Permanent Income, Wealth, and Consumption: A Critique of the Permanent Income Theory, the Life-Cycle Hypothesis, and Related Theories.* Berkeley: University of California Press, 1972.

Suits, D. B. "The Determination of Consumer Expenditure: A Review of Present Knowledge," *Impacts of Monetary Policy,* Commission on Money and Credit. Englewood Cliffs, N.J.: Prentice-Hall, 1964.

Tobin, James. "Relative Income, Absolute Income and Saving," in *Money, Trade and Economic Growth: Essays in Honor of J. H. Williams.* New York: Macmillan, 1951, pp. 135-156.

Chapter 6
Investment

Like consumption, investment was a key determinant of the level of economic activity in the simple income determination models of Chapter 4. Nonetheless, to simplify the analysis of that chapter we took investment to be exogenous to our models. We now need to lay the groundwork for more sophisticated models by identifying the forces that determine aggregate planned investment—by providing for the endogenous determination of investment.

While investment is a far smaller component of aggregate spending than consumption (net investment rarely exceeds 12 percent of aggregate output), analysis of its determinants and attempts to predict its level have received a disproportionate share of economists' attention. This is so for several reasons. First, investment has attracted analytical attention because of its volatility. Since aggregate demand is the sum of investment demand and some other components of planned spending, sizable variations in investment demand can produce magnified changes in aggregate demand and, thus, in the level of output and employment. Second, some of the important weapons the government has for influencing the level of economic activity work through altering the level of planned investment. Accurate predictions of the response of investment to policy actions are essential for the design of those policy actions. Finally, the exploration of investment behavior has engaged the economics profession because of the difficulty of adequately explaining that behavior. In spite of the sophistication of modern explanations of investment, there is ample room for improvement in the reliability of our predictions of that component of aggregate demand.

Before embarking on an analysis of what determines aggregate investment, we need to recall (from our treatment of the national income and product accounts) that the term *investment* applies only to the purchase of *new, physical* assets, not to the purchase of existing physical assets nor to the purchase of financial assets (stocks, bonds, and so on). The acquisition of an existing physical asset represents investment to the purchaser but, in the aggregate, is offset by an equal amount of disinvestment by the previous owner. The same can be said for exchanges of financial assets. In neither case do the exchanges reflect *current production* (except for the services of the broker in the exchange process).

We should also recall that total investment spending (so-called *gross investment*) is composed of two components—*replacement investment* (that part of gross investment required to replace the capital consumed during the production process) and *net investment* (the net addition to the existing stock of capital). Investment may take the form of new plants, new machines, changes in inventory, and new housing.

THE INVESTMENT DECISION

Directing our attention now to the task of explaining investment, we need to familiarize ourselves with the rudiments of the decision-making process business firms engage in as they consider additions to their existing stocks of capital assets. As we all know, firms invest in new, productive assets (new machinery, a new store, a new office building, and so on) only because they expect that investment to be *profitable*. More specifically, a firm will buy a new capital asset because it expects that asset to yield a future stream of receipts sufficient to cover all direct costs involved in production utilizing that asset (labor costs, energy costs, and so on) and still leave revenues sufficient to amortize (pay the depreciation costs on) the asset and provide a residual representing the *return on capital investment*.

We can clarify these ideas and set the stage for further development of the investment decision-making process by looking at a simple example. Suppose I am considering investing in a peanut stand for this year's county fair. Before I can rationally decide whether this investment is worthwhile (that is, if it will be *profitable*), I need to develop estimates of the revenues I can expect to receive and of the costs that will be involved in establishing, maintaining, and operating the peanut stand. Such estimates may range from rough, crude, intuitive "guesstimates" to precise, sophisticated estimates supported by data generated and analyzed by engineers, accountants, and business forecasting specialists. The quality of such estimates will typically vary with the size of the company, the sophistication of its managers, the size of the investment project being considered, and so on.

Regardless of the technique of estimation I employ, suppose I determine the

TABLE 6-1 DATA FOR INVESTMENT DECISION ON A CAPITAL ASSET
WITH A 1-YEAR LIFE

Original cost of equipment (peanut stand)		$1,000
Expected life of equipment	1 year	
Total revenue expected from operation of stand (total revenue = number of bags of peanuts sold x price per bag)		1,500
Operating expenses (expenses other than depreciation and interest)		400
Labor	$300	
Franchise fee	50	
Raw materials	50	
Expected gross revenue from investment before depreciation and interest charges (total revenue minus operating expenses)		$1,100
Depreciation cost		1,000
Net revenue before deduction of interest cost		$ 100

set of values in Table 6-1 as my best estimates of revenue and costs. Deducting the $400 of operating expenses from the $1,500 of expected revenues leaves receipts of $1,100 to amortize my investment and provide a residual return on investment. With an expected life of 1 year and no salvage value on my peanut stand, the depreciation charge is the full $1,000 of original cost, leaving $100 as the net return on investment. You should note that no interest charges have been entered in Table 6-1. Typically, investment decision analysts compare the net return on a proposed investment (ignoring interest costs) to the interest cost of that investment in order to decide whether the project will be profitable. In our example, if I had to borrow $1,000 for 1 year to finance the peanut stand investment, the interest cost of the investment would be $1,000 times the rate of interest I had to pay on the loan. With a market interest rate of 9 percent, interest charges would be $90. With net revenue of $100 before interest charges, $10 would be left after paying interest costs. I would be $10 better off making the investment than if I did not make it. If the interest rate I had to pay were 10 percent, interest costs would have completely exhausted pre-interest net revenue. And, if the interest rate should exceed 10 percent, I would clearly be worse off making the investment than if I did not invest. An investment in the peanut stand should be made only if the expected revenues from using the peanut stand would cover all direct costs involved in peanut sales and still leave sufficient revenue to cover the depreciation cost of "using up" the stand plus a residual, representing the return on capital, which must exceed the interest cost of the investment.

Generalizing from this example, the investment decision is made by comparing the net return on investment before interest charges to those interest charges. Typically, both figures are expressed in percentage terms rather than in absolute figures. In our example, the percentage rate of return on investment *before* interest charges is 10 percent (net revenue ÷ original investment = $100 ÷ $1,000 = .10 or 10%). If the cost of capital (the market rate of interest) is less than 10 percent, the project should be undertaken. If the interest rate is greater than 10 percent, it should not.

Our conclusions are unchanged if the investment is to be financed out of our own funds instead of by borrowing, for we can lend as well as borrow at the market interest rate. Unless the expected rate of return on our physical investment project exceeds the interest rate at which we can lend (or borrow), we will not invest in that project.

While the mechanics of investment decision making for the peanut stand example are clear-cut, to handle more complicated projects some of the concepts introduced only by implication in that example must be extended. However, the decision rule developed for the peanut stand investment has general validity. If the rate of return on investment exceeds the going interest rate (the cost of capital to the firm considering the investment project), the investment should be undertaken. If the rate of return on investment is less than the interest rate, the project should not be undertaken.

THE MARGINAL EFFICIENCY OF CAPITAL

The pre-interest-cost *rate* of return on investment derived in our example is what investment analysts often call the *internal rate of return on investment*. It is what Keynes chose to call the *marginal efficiency of capital*, defined as "that rate of discount which would make the present value of . . . [net receipts] expected from the capital-asset during its life just equal to its supply price."[1] We can readily develop an understanding of this definition of the marginal efficiency of capital (denoted hereafter as the MEC) through the example above.

In our example, $1,000 invested in a 1-year project yielded pre-interest-cost revenues of $1,100. That is, $1,000 invested for 1 year grew in value to $1,100. The internal rate of return on that investment is 10 percent. Clearly, with investment opportunities that yield a 10-percent rate of return available to the business firm, $1,000 in the present is precisely equivalent to the receipt of $1,100 1 year from now.

So far, all we have done is illustrate that there is a *time value* of money. $1,000 in the present is worth more than $1,000 to be received 1 year from now simply because the $1,000 now can be invested at a positive rate of return. Finding the equivalent value *now*—the so-called *present value*—of expected future income receipts is called the *discounting* of those future receipts. In investment analysis the percentage *rate of discount* that makes the cost of an investment project just equal to the present or discounted value of the future receipts expected to result from that project is its internal rate of return or, in Keynes' terms, MEC. Since in our example a $1,000 investment grew to $1,100 at the end of 1 year, the MEC, the rate of discount that made the present value of the expected earnings equal to the $1,000 cost of the asset was 10 percent.

In algebraic terms, the equation $1,000(1 + .10) = $1,100 demonstrates the equivalence of $1,000 in the present with $1,100 a year hence when investments yielding 10 percent annually are available. Generalizing from our example, the equivalence of $C invested in the present with revenues of $R one year later, when investments yielding rate of return r are available, is illustrated by the equation $C(1 + r) = R$. Of course, this equation can be rearranged, for example, to appear as $C = R/(1 + r)$. Clearly, there is some percentage rate of return—some discount rate—that will make these equalities hold. In our example, with $C = $1000 and $R = $1,100, the solution value for r is 10 percent.

Investment Projects with Lives of More Than 1 Year

When the investment project being considered has a life greater than 1 year, the necessity of allowing for compound interest makes the computation of the internal rate of return on investment slightly more complicated. Suppose a project

---

1   Keynes, *The General Theory, op. cit.*, p. 135.

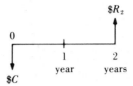

FIGURE 6-1   Cash Flows for a Project with a 2-Year Life

is being considered that costs C dollars, has a life of 2 years, and is expected to return revenues in the amount of $\$R_2$ in one lump payment at the end of its 2-year life. The stream of relevant money flows can be schematically represented as in Figure 6-1. What is the rate of return on this project or, asking the same question in a different form, at what rate must $\$C$ grow to become amount $\$R_2$ in 2 years? $\$C$ invested at rate of return r would be worth $\$C(1+r)$ after 1 year and, with compound interest, would be worth $[C(1+r)\cdot(1+r)]$ or $\$C(1+r)^2$ after 2 years. If $\$C(1+r)^2$ must grow to value $\$R_2$ [that is, $C(1+r)^2 = R_2$] and we have estimates of C and R_2, we can solve for r, the internal rate of return. Again, it is the rate that allows $\$C$ to grow to value $\$R_2$ in 2 years or it is the rate that can make the present discounted value of $\$R_2$, received 2 years hence, equal to $\$C$ now:

$$\left[C = \frac{R_2}{(1+r)^2} \right].$$

The relevant cash flows for an asset that has a life of 3 years, costs $\$C$, and promises to pay a lump sum of revenue of $\$R_3$ at the end of its 3-year life can be schematically represented as in Figure 6-2. For such a project, the internal rate of return can be obtained by solving the equation $C = R_3/(1+r)^3$ for r. In this case, the lump revenue payment must, of course, be discounted back three periods. What relationship would you use to find the MEC on a project with a life of 4 years? 6 years? 10 years?[2]

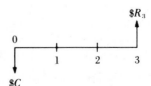

FIGURE 6-2   Cash Flows for a Project with a 3-Year Life

2 The investment of $\$C$ in an n-year project promising to pay $\$R_n$ at the end of its life must satisfy the equality $C(1+r)^n = R_n$ or $C = R_n/(1+r)^n$.

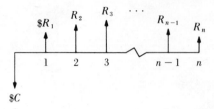

FIGURE 6-3   Cash Flows for a Project with an n-Year Life

The MEC for the General Investment Problem

Typically, an investment project may be expected to yield a stream of receipts throughout its life rather than one lump sum of receipts at a single point in time. A cash flow schematic for this more typical investment project, with a life of n years, would appear as in Figure 6-3, with each year's receipts assumed to accrue at the end of the respective year. For this project, how do we find the MEC, the rate of discount that will make the discounted (present) value of the future stream of receipts equal to $\$C$, the current cost of the capital asset? As shown earlier, the present value of R_1 can be found by discounting R_1 back 1 year, the present value of R_2 can be found by discounting R_2 back 2 years, and so on. For the project in Figure 6-3, the MEC can be found from the equality

$$C = \frac{R_1}{(1+r)} + \frac{R_2}{(1+r)^2} + \frac{R_3}{(1+r)^3} + \cdots + \frac{R_n}{(1+r)^n}. \tag{6-1}$$

With estimates for the cost of the asset (C) and for expected receipts $(R_1, R_2, \ldots, R_n)$ there is only one unknown, r, which can be found by trial and error.[3]

No matter what the specific time pattern of revenue flows, with estimates of those flows and of the cost of the asset that provides them, a value for the MEC on that asset can be computed. This computed rate of return can be compared to

---

3 If our investment project yields a *uniform* stream of annual receipts, that is, $R_1 = R_2 = R_3 = \cdots = R_n = R$, Equation 6-1 can be rewritten as

(a) $C = \dfrac{R}{1+r} + \dfrac{R}{(1+r)^2} + \cdots + \dfrac{R}{(1+r)^n}$

$$= R[(1+r)^{-1} + (1+r)^{-2} + \cdots + (1+r)^{-n}].$$

Multiplying both sides of this expression by $(1+r)^{-1}$ yields

(b) $C(1+r)^{-1} = R[(1+r)^{-2} + (1+r)^{-3} + \cdots + (1+r)^{-(n+1)}].$

Subtracting (b) from (a) yields

$$C[1 - (1+r)^{-1}] = R[(1+r)^{-1} - (1+r)^{-(n+1)}]$$

which, multiplied by $(1+r)$, yields

(c) $C = \dfrac{R}{r}[1 - (1+r)^{-n}].$

With values for R and C this single equation can be solved for the rate of return (r), which the cost of funds to the firm in order to determine whether the project should be undertaken. If the MEC exceeds the market rate of interest, the project should be undertaken. If the MEC is less than the interest rate, the project should not be undertaken. Of course, the rate of return on an investment project will be higher the larger the expected future receipts from that project or the smaller the cost of that project. On the other hand, with smaller expected revenues or with a higher acquisition cost the rate of return on a capital asset is reduced. A moment's reflection may also suggest that the *timing* of the stream of receipts a capital asset provides has an important influence on its MEC, a point which will be investigated later in this chapter.

An Alternative Approach

The method of investment decision making just reviewed is called the *internal rate of return technique*. An alternative approach is provided by what is known as the *present value technique*. We saw above that we can solve for the MEC— the discount rate that makes the discounted value of anticipated revenues from an investment project equal to its acquisition cost. If, alternatively, expected receipts are discounted using the *market rate of interest* as the discount factor, the present value obtained reflects the *current market value* of the expected stream of receipts.

The purchase of a capital asset gives the purchaser the right to the stream of receipts expected from its use. Going back to the peanut stand example, our investment provided revenues of $1,100 at the end of 1 year. With a market interest rate of 10 percent available, the present value of that expected revenue is $1,000. A firm would be willing to pay up to $1,000 for the peanut stand since at any lower acquisition price the rate of return earned would exceed the market interest rate. At a purchase price of exactly $1,000, the firm should be just indifferent between buying the peanut stand and lending at the 10 percent market interest rate—in either case, $1,000 in the present grows to $1,100 in 1 year. The firm would, of course, be reducing its profits by paying more than $1,000 for the peanut stand.

In general terms, the present value of an asset with a life of n years, which is expected to yield receipts $R_1, R_2, \ldots, R_n$ in years 1 through n, is

$$V = \frac{R_1}{1+i} + \frac{R_2}{(1+i)^2} + \cdots + \frac{R_{n-1}}{(1+i)^{n-1}} + \frac{R_n}{(1+i)^n}, \tag{6-2}$$

---

equates the discounted value of future receipts generated by a capital asset with its acquisition cost.

Should the stream of uniform payments from an asset continue forever, equation (c) reduces (as $n \rightarrow \infty$) to

(d) $C = \dfrac{R}{r}.$

Once again, with R and C known, the rate of return can be found.

where V is present value, i is the market rate of interest, and R_j is the expected net revenue in year j.[4]

What general investment rule should a profit-maximizing firm, using present value calculations, follow in its investment decision process? The present value calculation tells the firm what the *right* to the expected stream of earnings from an asset is worth *now* (that is, the present value of the earnings expected from use of the asset). The firm also knows, or has an estimate of, the price it must pay for the asset now. If the present value of the expected receipts made available to the firm by buying an asset exceeds that asset's purchase price, the firm should invest. Conversely, if the purchase price of the right to those receipts (the asset) exceeds the present value of the receipts, the firm should not undertake the investment project.

For our purposes, it can be assumed that the decisions made on potential investment projects using the present value technique are always the same as those obtained using an internal rate of return calculation.[5] To see the basic equivalence of the two techniques, compare Equations (6-1) and (6-2) assuming, initially, that the market rate of interest is the same as the MEC ($i = r$) for the investment project under consideration. With $i = r$, the present value of the project is equal to the original cost of the asset being considered. But, with the market rate of interest higher ($i > r$), the internal rate of return decision rule would tell us not to undertake the project. Looking at Equation (6-2) tells us that as i is increased, making $i > r$, the present value of the asset under consideration falls, making $V < C$, which also tells us not to undertake the project. With $i < r$, so that an investment project appears profitable on the basis of the internal rate of return decision rule, we will find $V > C$, making that project appear favorable on the basis of the present value-cost comparison.

To summarize, the decision rules for these two alternative techniques of investment analysis are shown in Table 6-2. The interest rate (i), prices of capital assets (C), and the expected size and time pattern of net receipts (the Rs) are important determinants of business firms' investment decisions. A change in any of these factors will affect the level of investment by individual firms and, thus, aggregate investment spending.

Our primary concern in the next section of this chapter will be with the relationship between the market rate of interest and the *aggregate* level of investment. But, before progressing to that topic, a brief discussion of the precision with which individual firms' investment decision calculations can be made is in

---

4   For an asset with an infinite life which is expected to yield net receipts of the same size each period throughout its life, the present value is $V = R/i$.

5   In a number of special cases of investment problems, the internal rate of return rule breaks down. Among the reasons for failure are the assumption of an interest rate that remains constant over time and the mathematical possibility of multiple rates of return for the same capital asset. For a discussion of the conditions under which the internal rate of return criterion fails see J. Hirschleifer, *Interest, Investment, and Capital* (Englewood Cliffs, N.J.: Prentice-Hall, 1970), especially pp. 74-81.

TABLE 6-2   INVESTMENT DECISION RULES

Decision Technique Employed			
Internal rate of return versus interest rate comparison	$i < r$	$i > r$	$i = r$
Present value versus cost comparison	$V > C$	$V < C$	$V = C$
Fate of project	should be undertaken	should *not* be undertaken	indifferent

order. Investors' estimates of the original cost of a prospective investment project are frequently quite precise (though this is not always the case). Their estimates of future net receipts are, however, subject to considerable uncertainty since they typically reach across an extended time horizon. Future net receipts may differ from estimates because of changes in demand (thus in product price and quantity sold) or because of changes on the supply side (changes in current operating costs due to changes in wage rates, materials costs, and so on).

Forecasts of future movements in demand and costs, and thus in net receipts from and the rate of return on a new capital asset, are often crude and quite subjective.[6] The subjective element in those forecasts can lead to substantial volatility in businessmen's estimates of the profitability of new investment projects and, hence, in investment expenditures. Business confidence is frequently assumed to be so sensitive as to cause a revision of profitability estimates in response even to political developments (for example, the switch from a conservative to a liberal government). Keynes emphasized the delicate nature of profit expectations in the following passage:

> If the fear of a Labour Government or a New Deal depresses enterprise, this need not be the result either of a reasonable calculation or of a plot with political intent;—it is the mere consequence of upsetting the balance of spontaneous optimism. In estimating the prospects of investment, we must have regard, therefore, to the nerves and hysteria and even the digestions and reactions to the weather of those upon whose spontaneous activity it largely depends.[7]

Investment decision making, appearing as a precise art in an example in which future net receipts are known with certainty, is fraught with uncertainty and subjectivity in practice.

6   Such estimates can be quite misleading. Where did the Edsel go?
7   Keynes, *The General Theory, op. cit.*, p. 162.

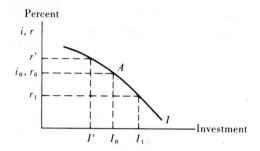

FIGURE 6-4   Investment Demand

The Rate of Interest and Aggregate Investment Behavior

Assuming that business firms attempt to maximize profits and that to do so they employ investment decision techniques like those discussed above, Keynes alleged that there was an aggregate investment demand schedule that slopes downward from left to right, as shown in Figure 6-4. The schedule in that figure shows the percentage rate of return that could be expected on *new* investment, during a specified time period, for any level of investment expenditure. It indicates, for example, that if investment in this period were taking place at rate I_0, at the margin the rate of return on investment would be r_0.

In what sense is schedule I in Figure 6-4 a demand curve? A *demand curve* relates the cost of an item to the quantity of that item demanded, and schedule I does just that. The price of capital goods—the "cost of capital"—is the market rate of interest at which the firm can borrow and lend. Thus, the schedule in Figure 6-4, which shows what volume of real investment (the rate of purchase of capital goods) will take place at every possible market interest rate we might observe, serves as a demand curve for investment. If the interest rate (i) were just equal to internal rate of return r_0, businesses would choose collectively to invest amount I_0. With any smaller volume of investment, the rate of return on investment at the margin would be higher, hence, greater than the cost of capital. For example, at investment level I', the rate of return on investment would be r'. Total profits of any firm are, of course, always increased by investing, even if the firm must borrow to finance that investment, as long as the return on investment exceeds the market interest rate. Thus, there would be an incentive for investment to be increased as long as r exceeds i. Only when investment has increased sufficiently to drive the rate of return on investment down to equality with the rate of interest (as at point A in Figure 6-4 for an interest rate equal to i_0) does the inducement to increase investment disappear.

Analogously, if the market rate of interest remained equal to i_0 but investment exceeded I_0 (for example, increased to I_1), the rate of return on investment (r_1 if $I = I_1$) would be less than the cost of capital. Firms would be reducing the size of their total profits by this overinvestment and would be induced to contract investment expenditures sufficiently to allow the rate of return on investment to return to equality with the market interest rate $(i = r_0)$. It should be clear that for any rate of interest the investment demand schedule can tell us the equilibrium (profit-maximizing) rate of real investment expenditure.

The Downward Slope of Investment Demand

So far, we have not indicated why there should be an inverse relationship between the level of investment and the rate of return on investment (that is, why the investment demand curve slopes downward from left to right). Keynes mentioned two reasons for this downward slope. According to Keynes:

> If there is an increased investment in any given type of capital during any period of time, the marginal efficiency of that type of capital will diminish as the investment in it is increased, partly because the prospective yield will fall as the supply of that type of capital is increased, and partly because, as a rule, pressure on the facilities for producing that type of capital will cause its supply price to increase; the second of these factors usually being the more important in producing equilibrium in the short run, but the longer the period in view the more does the first factor take its place.[8]

To make sense out of the two reasons for the inverse relationship between investment and the rate of return on investment suggested in the quote from Keynes, we need to develop both a capital (stock) theory and an investment (flow) theory. The capital stock is the existing physical accumulation of productive facilities in the form of factories, machinery, office buildings, sales outlets, and so on. As the simple example developed early in this chapter suggested, the rate of return on capital goods depends upon the value of sales revenues that can be generated through their use and on the operating costs associated with their use. Further, as the concept of *diminishing returns* suggests for any other factor of production, an increase in the capital stock, with the size and quality of the existing labor force, the technique of production, and the stock of natural resources and land given, should lead to a lower return at the margin on additions to the capital stock. Thus, the schedule which we shall call the *marginal efficiency of capital stock* (MEK) slopes downward from left to right, as in Figure 6-5, reflecting, due to diminishing returns, a fall in the expected return to capital assets as the stock of capital increases.

8 Keynes, *The General Theory, op. cit.*, p. 136.

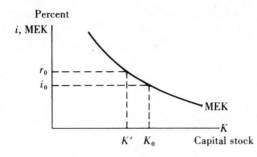

FIGURE 6-5   The Demand for Capital

Given the marginal efficiency of capital stock schedule and the market rate of interest there will be one unique *equilibrium stock* of capital. For example, if the interest rate is i_0, the equilibrium capital stock in Figure 6-5 is K_0. A smaller capital stock, like K', could not be an equilibrium stock because the return on additions to the capital stock (r_0) would exceed the cost of capital (i_0). Thus, additional investment would take place, increasing the capital stock until the return to capital is driven down to equality with the market rate of interest. Similarly, a capital stock larger than K_0 could not be an equilibrium stock with a market rate of interest equal to i_0 since the return on capital would be less than the return available for lending. Net disinvestment in capital assets would occur until the capital stock had shrunk to size K_0.

Once investment has equated the actual stock of capital with the desired (profit-maximizing) stock, as long as no shocks are allowed to disturb equilibrium (nothing happens to change the position of the MEK curve and the interest rate stays constant) the capital stock will remain unchanged. Net investment will be zero since no change in the size of the capital stock is desired. Gross investment must, however, be positive with a magnitude equal to the value of capital consumption allowances.[9]

The Interest Rate and the Equilibrium Capital Stock

If the market interest rate changes, the equilibrium value of the capital stock changes. The capital stock demand (MEK) schedule shows the impact of a change in the market rate of interest on the equilibrium capital stock. The MEK schedule in Figure 6-6 shows a fall in the rate of interest from i_0 to i_1, increasing the equilibrium capital stock by amount ΔK. It indicates nothing, however, about how rapidly the desired adjustment in the size of the capital stock will take place. That is, it tells us nothing about the level of *net investment* we can expect to observe during the adjustment process initiated by the change in the market rate

---

9   As indicated in Chapter 2, capital consumption encompasses the depreciation, obsolescence, and accidental destruction of capital assets.

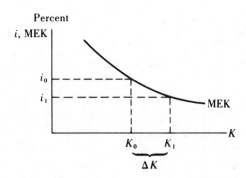

FIGURE 6-6   Changes in the Demand for Capital

of interest. We must develop an investment (flow) model to discern the relationship between the market interest rate and the *flow* rate of aggregate investment.

The Interest Rate and Investment

If the existing capital stock is equal to the desired capital stock (that is, there
is equilibrium in our capital stock model), there will be no net investment. The
only investment taking place will be *replacement* investment. Since this investment just maintains the existing capital stock, the return (at the margin) on
that investment will be equal to the return on capital stock. With the capital
stock at level K_0 in Figure 6-7, the rate of return on the last dollar of replacement
investment is $r_0 = i_0$. Hence, if we wish to plot the rate of return on *net investment* (and the market interest rate) against the level of *net investment*, we know
one observation: when net investment is zero (gross investment = capital consumption = replacement investment), the rate of return on investment is $r_0 = i_0$,
as illustrated by point A in the investment diagram in Figure 6-7.

Net investment will have a value other than zero only if the existing capital
stock differs from the *desired* capital stock—that is, only if there is *disequilibrium*

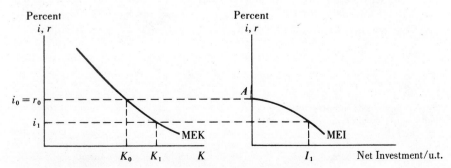

FIGURE 6-7   Capital Stock Disequilibrium and Investment Demand

in our capital stock model. If the rate of interest should fall from i_0 to i_1, as shown in Figure 6-7, capital stock K_0 would no longer be the desired stock. The desired stock of capital would be K_1, requiring net investment (an increase in the capital stock) to take place to restore equilibrium. What we do not know as yet is the rate at which the desired adjustment in capital stock will be made.

The higher the rate at which the adjustment of the capital stock takes place —that is, the higher the level of net investment—the higher the original purchase price of capital goods will become. Why? Simply because, given the productive capacity of the capital goods industry, the marginal cost of producing capital goods rises as the volume of output rises, and the price of capital goods can be expected to increase with the marginal cost of production.[10] Since an increase in the purchase price of a capital asset lowers the internal rate of return on that asset,[11] the rate of return on aggregate investment falls as the level of investment rises. Thus, the return on investment schedule, which we will label the *marginal efficiency of investment*, must slope downward from left to right, as shown in the right-hand portion of Figure 6-7. Given the marginal efficiency of investment (MEI) schedule in Figure 6-7, the level of net investment will be zero if the market rate of interest is i_0, I_1 if the interest rate is i_1, and so on. Clearly, not all of the desired change in capital stock resulting from a fall in the interest rate will take place in a short period following the interest rate change. Net investment (the change in capital stock) in any period will be pushed only to the point where the return on investment is, at the margin, equal to the market interest rate.

The Dynamics of Capital Stock Adjustment

Let us now backtrack to our original capital stock equilibrium, reintroduce the *shock* to that system (the interest rate reduction from i_0 to i_1), and attempt to trace the complete adjustment in capital stock (from K_0 to K_1). Recall that before the interest rate fell the capital stock in place matched the *desired* capital stock so that no *net* investment was taking place. When the market interest rate fell from i_0 to i_1, K_0 was no longer an equilibrium capital stock. The desired stock suddenly became K_1 requiring positive net investment to take place. The original MEI schedule (MEI$_1$ in Figure 6-8) shows the level of net investment (I_1) that will take place in the first period after the interest rate decline.

---

10 If the capital goods producing industry were perfectly competitive, price would be equal to marginal cost so that an increase in marginal cost would require an identical increase in price. If the capital goods industry were not perfectly competitive, an increase in marginal cost due to higher output would typically be accompanied by higher prices.

The MEK schedule is constructed for a constant acquisition cost of capital that would prevail if net investment were zero. Hence, its position can be considered to be unaltered by those capital goods price changes that are induced by changes in the level of investment.

11 See Equation (6-1) on page 148.

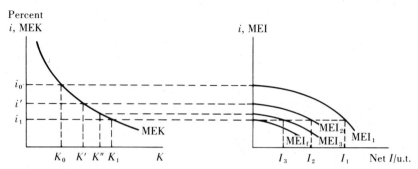

FIGURE 6-8   The Path of Adjustment of the Capital Stock

By definition, net investment is the change in capital stock per unit of time. Thus, after one period of positive net investment the capital stock will have increased by the amount of net investment that period. With a downward-sloping MEI schedule, investment in any period will be small in value relative to the value of the capital stock in place. Thus, the increase in capital stock in period 1 in our example must be "small" (say, to K' in Figure 6-8). But, because of diminishing returns, any increase in the capital stock will be accompanied by a decrease in the return to capital (to i' in Figure 6-8 for capital stock K'). Thus, in the second period of capital stock adjustment, the return to replacement investment will be lower than in the first period following the disturbance of equilibrium (equal to i' instead of i_0). For the second period, then, we will have a new MEI curve (MEI_2) that is lower than the period 1 curve. It has shifted down because the increase in capital stock during period 1 pushed us farther into the domain of diminishing returns.

In period 2 investment will take place at rate I_2. Hence, at the end of period 2 the capital stock will have increased once more (say to K''), again pushing down the rate of return to capital. The MEI curve for period 3 will be MEI_3 and investment will take place at rate I_3. This process of adjustment will continue until the capital stock has grown to value K_1.[12] At that point the return to replacement investment and the return to capital stock will equal the new market rate of interest. Equilibrium will have been reestablished; there will be no inducement for net investment (positive or negative) to take place.

Summarizing what our analysis of aggregate investment has accomplished at this point, we first demonstrated that the MEI schedule is the demand curve for a flow of investment spending. That demand curve displays an inverse relationship between the interest rate and the level of planned investment because the

---

12   For simplicity of exposition the capital stock adjustment has been described in incremental terms. In reality, the adjustment takes place continuously with the capital stock changing gradually through time rather than in discrete lumps at specific points in time.

marginal cost of providing capital goods rises with their flow rate of production. Moreover, we have shown that as positive *net* investment takes place the MEI curve shifts downward since an enlargement of the stock of capital pushes the economy farther into the realm of diminishing returns. While our primary focus has been on the link between the interest rate and the level of investment, with interest rate changes causing movements *along* an investment demand schedule, we must not forget that there are other factors (including the size of the capital stock) that can alter the level of investment by shifting the entire MEI schedule. Indeed, in developing the model that provided our aggregate MEI schedule a number of the other variables that have an important influence on investment were identified. Changes in those variables shift the MEI schedule.

Determinants of the Position of MEI

As demonstrated above, the position of the MEI curve depends on the position of the MEK schedule and on the size of the existing stock of capital. In turn, the position of the MEK schedule is determined by (1) businessmen's collective expectations about future receipts from product sales *after* deduction of the direct costs of production and (2) the purchase price of capital assets.

If expectations about future sales improve, raising the expected rate of return on any increment to the capital stock, the MEK schedule shifts outward increasing the desired stock of capital at any rate of interest. This shift in the MEK schedule results in a rightward shift of the MEI schedule, increasing the equilibrium level of investment accompanying any given rate of interest. Such an adjustment is shown in Figure 6-9. Beginning with marginal efficiency of capital schedule MEK_0 and market interest rate i_0, the equilibrium capital stock is K_0. With the actual capital stock equal to its desired level (K_0), net investment is zero (the marginal efficiency of investment schedule would be MEI_2).

With the shift toward more optimistic future sales expectations, the marginal efficiency of capital schedule shifts upward (to MEK_1, in Figure 6-9), reflecting the expectation of higher returns on capital. With the market rate of interest

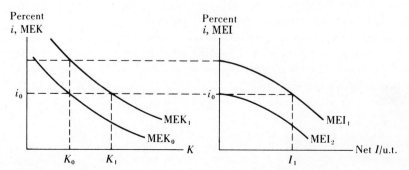

FIGURE 6-9   The Adjustment to an Improvement in Sales Expectations

remaining at i_0, the desired stock of capital becomes K_1 and net investment will take place.

With capital stock K_0 and the new marginal efficiency of capital schedule MEK_1, the marginal efficiency of investment schedule is MEI_1—that is, the rate of return on the first unit of expenditure on net investment is equal to the marginal efficiency of capital at capital stock K_0. Thus, in the first period after the shift in sales expectations we would expect net investment of I_1, which partially closes the gap between the desired capital stock (K_1) and its actual level (K_0). The complete capital stock adjustment proceeds as explained above. Of course, a shift toward pessimism in businessmen's expectations of future sales would lower the desired stock of capital, inducing disinvestment as the existing capital stock depreciates until the actual capital stock coincides with the desired level.

Shifting our focus, should direct production costs fall, say, as a result of technological innovation, expected revenues after deduction of those costs would grow. The increased revenue from any size capital stock means a higher return to capital—a higher MEK schedule. Again, an upward shift in the MEK schedule raises the MEI schedule, stimulating net investment. In contrast, an increase in production costs lowers the expected return on capital (shifting the MEK and MEI schedules downward) and reduces investment spending.

Finally, we need to look a little more closely at the role of the capital stock itself as a determinant of the position of the MEI schedule. As already demonstrated, because of diminishing returns an enlargement in the stock of capital lowers the return on capital and shifts the MEI schedule downward. Conversely, with a smaller capital stock, the rate of return on capital is raised. However, the problems with which macroeconomic analysis deals are frequently short-run problems. If our analysis is confined to short time periods (1 year, one phase of the business cycle), net changes in the capital stock will be very small relative to the stock of capital in place so that no significant change in the return on capital will arise from diminishing returns. Consequently, we can reasonably ignore the effects of changes in the stock of capital and deal with a single marginal efficiency of investment schedule. In this case, the return on investment declines as the level of investment rises only because of rising prices on capital assets.

A Summary of the Investment Model

The important variables determining the level of aggregate net investment appear to be the market interest rate (i), expected revenues after deduction of direct operating expenses (R), and the existing stock of capital (K).[13] Net investment

---

13 The change in the price of capital goods *induced* by a change in the level of investment is fully captured by—indeed, is responsible for—the downward slope of the MEI schedule. If there are *autonomous* changes in capital goods prices, then such changes will shift the investment demand schedule. An *autonomous* increase in capital goods prices would shift the MEK and MEI schedules downward and an *autonomous* fall in capital goods prices would shift those schedules upward.

spending should respond positively to changes in expected net revenues and negatively to changes in the interest rate and capital stock. That is,

$$I_{net} = I(i, R, K) \qquad (6\text{-}3)$$

such that
$$\frac{\Delta I}{\Delta i} < 0$$

$$\frac{\Delta I}{\Delta R} > 0$$

$$\frac{\Delta I}{\Delta K} < 0.$$

Over relatively short periods of time (1 year, one-half of a business cycle) changes in the capital stock can be ignored for practical purposes since such changes are likely to be very small relative to the existing stock. Hence, the investment function reduces to

$$I = I(i, R). \qquad (6\text{-}4)$$

Since "expected net revenues" are not observable in the real world, for empirically testing investment functions some proxy variable that is thought to be closely related to expected net revenues must be relied on. A variable that has frequently been assumed to exhibit the necessary close association with expected revenues is the current level of sales (output). If current output is a reasonable proxy for expected revenues, then we can employ the function

$$I = I(i, Y), \qquad (6\text{-}5)$$

where i is the market interest rate and Y is the output level, as our aggregate investment schedule. This simple investment function has been supported by a number of empirical tests, and, as a reasonable, basic model of investment behavior this function is commonly employed in simple models of the economic system such as the ones that will be constructed in this text beginning in Chapter 8.

Unfortunately, recent empirical research on investment demand involves complexities that prevent us from being able to look directly at fitted regression equations for evidence on the response of investment to changes in output and the interest rate. However, a simple summary of that evidence may be helpful. There is widespread agreement from recently conducted studies that investment demand is positively related to the level of output and negatively related to the interest rate. In a survey of results generated from data on manufacturing industries, Evans has concluded that: (1) "A change of 1 percent in output will produce an average change of $1\frac{1}{2}$ to 2 percent in investment over a two-year period," and (2) "A change of one *point* in the long-term interest rate, say from 4 to 5 percent, will change investment from 5 to 10 percent over a two-year period." [14] Little of this impact is generated until over a year has elapsed, according to Evans, since an interest rate change does not affect projects that are already under way.

THE ACCELERATION PRINCIPLE

The roles of two variables that we have identified as determinants of the position of the MEI schedule, output and the existing stock of capital, can be vividly and formally demonstrated by various forms of a construct known as the *accelerator model*. In its simplest form, the accelerator principle is a mechanical model based on the assumption that there is a fixed, *technical* or *engineering* relationship between the *flow* of output and the *stock* of capital necessary to produce that flow.[15] As a simple microeconomic example, we might assume that it takes one loom of a particular type to produce 1,000 yards of woolen cloth per year. To produce and sell 3,000 yards of such cloth a firm would have to possess three such machines. With technology constant, to meet an increase in cloth sales to a new rate of 6,000 yards per year the firm would have to double its *stock* of looms from three to six. Converting our measures of output and capital stock into constant-dollar terms does not disturb the simple technical relationship between output and the capital stock. If the cloth in our example sells for $1 per yard and looms sell for $2,000 apiece, $2,000 worth of capital stock would be required for $1,000 worth of yearly cloth output; $4,000 worth of capital would be required for $2,000 of yearly cloth output; and so on. The required stock of capital is proportional to the value of output. Letting K be the value of capital stock (looms) and O the value of the firm's output, for any period t,

$$K_t = AO_t \tag{6-6}$$

where the proportionality constant (A) is the *accelerator coefficient* linking the level of output to the stock of capital required to produce that output.[16] If output

14 Michael Evans, *Macroeconomic Activity: Theory, Forecasting, and Control* (New York: Harper & Row, 1969), p. 138. Chapters 4 and 5 provide an extensive review of the modern empirical literature on investment demand.

15 For the classical exposition of the basic acceleration principle, see J. M. Clark, "Business Acceleration and the Law of Demand: A Technical Factor in Economic Cycles," *Journal of Political Economy*, Vol. XXV, March 1917, pp. 217-235. Focusing on the technical link between output and the stock of capital, as we shall see the basic accelerator model relates the level of investment to *changes* in the level of output. With the time rate of change of output a determinant of investment, reliance on the simple accelerator to explain investment converts static equilibrium models of income determination into *dynamic* models of the business cycle, the topic of Chapter 14.

16 It should be clear that the value of A will change if the period of production is changed. For example, if the output variable is measured in quarterly rather than yearly terms, the A value will be increased by a factor of four.

increases from O_t in period t to a larger value (O_{t+1}) in period $t+1$, then the required capital stock in period $t+1$ becomes

$$K_{t+1} = AO_{t+1}. \tag{6-7}$$

Subtracting Equation (6-6) from (6-7) yields:

$$K_{t+1} - K_t = AO_{t+1} - AO_t \tag{6-8}$$

or

$$\Delta K_t = A \, \Delta O_t.$$

Since net investment is nothing but the change per period in the capital stock (ΔK per period), net investment is

$$I_t = A \, \Delta O_t \tag{6-9}$$

Equation (6-9) is the simple accelerator model.[17] For our simple numerical example, the value of A in Figure 6-9 is 2, indicating that a \$1,000 increase in cloth output requires \$2,000 of investment.

Although we have developed the accelerator relationship for a single firm, it can be applied equally well to an entire industry or, as is necessary for purposes of macroeconomic analysis, to the economy as a whole. Repeating the accelerator model for this last use, the net *aggregate* investment that is induced by changes in aggregate output is

$$I_{\text{net}} = A\Delta Y$$

where ΔY is the change in aggregate output and A is the aggregate accelerator coefficient.

Several features of this simple accelerator model are important. First, with an accelerator coefficient value greater than one, a change in the rate of growth of output will induce an even larger change in the level of investment (in our example, twice as large). No wonder that investment is such a volatile component of total spending!

Secondly, inspection of Equation (6-9) shows that, in the simple accelerator model, the level of investment depends not on the level of output but on the *rate*

---

17   In differential calculus terms, if $K_t = AO_t$, then

$$I_t = \frac{dK_t}{dt} = A \frac{dO_t}{dt}.$$

While no effort has been made in the derivation of the accelerator model to demonstrate its consistency with accepted microeconomic doctrine, Eckaus has shown that under certain conditions the accelerator is implied by the neoclassical theory of the firm. With constant returns to scale and the relative prices of factor inputs unchanged, a profit-maximizing firm would alter the volume of all factor inputs it employs (including the stock of capital) in proportion to its increase in production. See R. S. Eckaus, "The Acceleration Principle Reconsidered," *Quarterly Journal of Economics*, Vol. 67, May 1953, pp. 209-230.

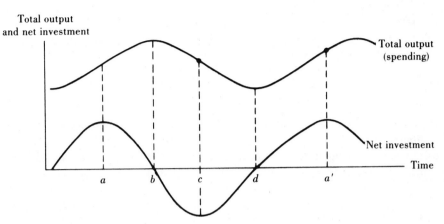

FIGURE 6-10   Movements in Output and Investment

of change of output. The resulting patterns of movement in output and investment are quite curious, as is shown in Figure 6-10. In that figure, investment is
at a maximum when the *rate of change* in output is greatest (points *a* and *a'*).
When output is at its maximum value, investment is zero (point *b*). When output is falling at its maximum rate (point *c*) net investment attains its greatest
negative value, and when output is at its minimum (point *d*) investment is once
again zero. Note from Figure 6-10 that cyclical peaks and troughs (turning
points) in investment occur *before* the accompanying peaks and troughs in output. It appears that changes in investment (the *result* of changes in output) are
a leading indicator of changes in output (the *cause* of the changes in investment).[18] When two variables are causally related, observed lead-lag relationships
cannot be trusted to identify the direction of causation between those variables.

Replacement Investment

The simple accelerator model can be modified readily to make allowance for replacement investment. We know that the sum of replacement investment (I_r) and
net investment (I_n) is gross investment (I_g). With the reasonable assumption
that a constant proportion (d) of the existing capital stock (K) is worn away
and replaced each year, aggregate gross investment is

$$I_g = I_n + I_r \underline{\qquad} \tag{6-10}$$

or

$$I_g = A\Delta Y + dK.$$

---

18   If the investment process is time consuming, because of time delays in the investment decision-making process or because of the time-consuming nature of the actual process of producing
investment goods, aggregate data need not show changes in investment leading changes in output.

According to this equation, gross investment is increased by an *acceleration* in the rate of output growth or by an enlargement of the capital stock. On the other hand, gross investment is reduced by a decline in the rate of growth of output or by a reduction in the size of the capital stock.

A Critique of the Simple Accelerator

Despite its plausible basis—a technological link between output and the desired capital stock—an abundance of empirical tests have shown that the simple accelerator model cannot explain movements in investment spending adequately. While an extended list of reasons for the failure of the simple accelerator can be compiled,[19] the major complaints focus on the implied assumptions in the model regarding excess capacity, business expectations, and the role of monetary variables. In summary those criticisms are:

1. If a firm is operating with substantial excess capacity, it is unlikely to invest in additions to its capital stock even when its sales are increasing. Firms invest to add to productive capacity only when sales are straining existing capacity. For the aggregate economic system, there is likely to be substantial excess capacity—idle capital—except during advanced stages of the expansion phase of the business cycle. Thus, the simple accelerator may yield poor predictions of investment except during this limited portion of the cycle.

    Similar considerations call into question the symmetry of investment behavior predicted by the simple accelerator. According to that model, the *absolute* value of net investment will be the same for a particular rate of change in output whether the output change is positive or negative. The maximum rate of disinvestment is constrained, however, by the rate of deterioration and obsolescence of the existing capital stock—that is, business firms do not simply destroy those capital assets that are left idle by a decline in sales. Hence, the simple accelerator yields absurd values for disinvestment during rapid declines in the level of output.

2. In the simple accelerator model, under conditions of no excess capacity an increase in the output of final goods and services implies an increase in the capital stock to the new desired level *during the same period* in which the increase in output occurs. Without substantial excess capacity in the capital goods producing sector of the economy, providing for an increase in capital goods production with no increase in capital goods prices (hence a horizontal MEI schedule), such a quick adjustment would be impossible. It would appear that for the simple accelerator to work at the aggregate level there must be massive excess capacity in the investment goods sector of the econ-

---

19 See S. C. Tsiang, "Accelerator, Theory of the Firm and the Business Cycle," *Quarterly Journal of Economics*, Vol. 65, 1951, pp. 325-341.

omy and zero excess capacity in all other sectors. Such a fortuitous combination of circumstances is not likely to occur.

3. The simple accelerator also indicates that the capital stock will be modified in response to every change in output. Realistically, we should expect to see business firms alter their productive capacity only in response to changes in output they *expect to be permanent.*[20] The simple accelerator assumes, by implication, that all observed changes in output are permanent. This is highly unlikely, as illustrated by an obvious but familiar example. Most bookstores that serve colleges are "overcrowded" at the beginning of each semester. It is clear to all of us why the managers of such stores do not call for an expansion of facilities after the opening week of school each fall and spring.

4. The simple accelerator model ignores the impact on investment of the unavailability of investable funds and changes in the (interest) cost of investable funds. This omission may be quite serious in periods of substantial credit restriction or expansion.

A More General Accelerator Model

In light of the importance of the link between the level of output and the desired (profit-maximizing) stock of capital, modern attempts to explain investment behavior have continued to employ an accelerator relationship. However, the accelerator models now used are considerably more flexible than the simple accelerator and, hence, are free of some of the shortcomings of that basic model. One simple but prominent variant of the accelerator model, often called the capital *stock adjustment* model, can be easily constructed. In the stock adjustment model, we can continue to assume that the desired stock of capital depends upon the level of output so that

$$K_t^* = AO_t \tag{6-11}$$

where K_t^* is the desired stock of capital in period t, O_t is current output (replace O_t with Y_t if applying the model to the aggregate economy), and A is the desired capital to output ratio.

Consistent with our earlier theoretical treatment of investment, net investment is called for in the stock adjustment model only when the desired capital stock differs from the actual stock in place. Further, recognizing that to fully close the gap between the actual and desired capital stock in one period might well be technically impossible and, in general, would be economically undesirable, the stock adjustment model explicitly assumes that only some fraction of that

20   For an attempt to develop an accelerator model in which investment responds only to permanent changes in output, see R. Eisner, "Investment: Fact and Fancy," *The American Economic Review*, Vol. 53, May 1963, pp. 237-246.

gap is closed each period. In algebraic terms, net investment in period t is given by the expression

$$I_{\text{net}_t} = B(K_t^* - K_{t-1}) \tag{6-12}$$

where K_t^* is, once again, the desired capital stock, K_{t-1} is the actual capital stock in place at the beginning of period t (end of period $t-1$), and B is the *partial adjustment coefficient* representing the *fraction* $(O < B \leq 1)$ of the gap between the desired and actual capital stock that is filled each period by net investment.

Since the value of the desired capital stock is known [from Equation (6-11), $K_t^* = AO_t$], Equation (6-12) can be rewritten as

$$I_{\text{net}_t} = BAO_t - BK_{t-1}. \tag{6-13}$$

According to this accelerator formulation, the level of net investment is positively related to the *level* of output (not the rate of change of output) and negatively related to the size of the existing capital stock. In terms of the capital and investment theory developed in this chapter, increases in output can be thought of as shifting the MEK and associated MEI schedules upward, thus raising investment. In a similar vein, an increase in the stock of capital, moving the economy down along an existing MEK schedule, reflecting an advance into the realm of diminishing returns, shifts the MEI schedule downward and reduces investment. While this more flexible accelerator model still suffers from some shortcomings—our model still uses current output as an indicator of the *permanent* output level and still fails to explicitly account for the financing of an investment program—it should be apparent that the stock adjustment framework can tolerate substantial variations in the specification of the determinants of the optimal capital stock. For example, the desired capital stock might be related to a weighted average of recent levels of output instead of just to current output to obtain a better estimate of the *permanent* level of future sales. In addition, the interest cost of capital can be reintroduced in the stock adjustment model as a determinant of the desired stock of capital. With the desired stock of capital inversely related to the interest rate, investment would again be an inverse function of the interest cost of capital. In fact, a number of variants of the stock adjustment model have been tested, and the empirical results cited on page 160 stem from regression models that incorporate a flexible accelerator relationship.[21]

21 An interesting and relatively complete assortment of investment functions that employ an accelerator model can be found in D. Jorgenson and C. Siebert, "Theories of Corporate Investment Behavior," *The American Economic Review*, Vol. 58, September 1968, pp. 681-712. Also see R. Eisner, *op. cit.*

Summary on the Accelerator

As we have seen, in its simplest form the accelerator model assumes that a determinate amount of capital is required (for technical or engineering reasons) to produce a specified volume of output. Such a model has serious shortcomings which prevent it from serving as a complete explanation of investment. Yet, the simple accelerator does contain an important element of truth that is likely to be useful in attempting to explain and predict investment. Given the state of technology, a firm's profit-miximizing (cost-minimizing) mix of factor inputs (labor, capital, and so on) depends on relative factor prices (wages, the interest rate, and so on). For a permanent increase in the level of output with relative factor prices constant, an increase in the stock of capital would be expected for a profit-maximizing firm. If firms view their current sales as an indicator of future demand, then an observed increase in sales may well lead to an increased level of investment as firms attempt to obtain the profit-maximizing stock of capital for the expected optimal future level of sales. It is this phenomenon that the accelerator attempts to capture. If the MEK curve developed earlier in this chapter captures the effect on the optimal capital stock of changes in the interest rate, the accelerator model can be interpreted as an explanation of shifts in that schedule (and thus in the MEI schedule). As such, the accelerator contributes a substantial element of instability to the investment schedule, although other factors can also be expected to affect the actual level of investment. Of course, we know that a complete model of investment behavior cannot ignore movements in any factor input price since changes in relative price ratios require a profit-maximizing firm to switch to more or less capital-intensive techniques of production.

To close our discussion of the role of the accelerator in modern economic analysis it must be noted that in a substantial majority of the investment functions that have been statistically fitted in recent years an accelerator relationship has been employed. Generally, the accelerator relationships employed have been more flexible than the simple accelerator—the stock-adjustment model developed on pages 165-166 is a representative example of current practice—and interest costs of capital have been included with output measures as a determinant of the desired stock of capital.

THE TAX TREATMENT OF BUSINESS INCOME AND INVESTMENT

While little remains to be added to the basic structure of the investment analysis developed in this chapter, we have not yet exhausted the array of factors that may influence investment spending. Probably the most important potential determinant of investment that has not been explicitly acknowledged thus far is the tax treatment of business income. The concern of businessmen when they are making an investment decision is with the after-tax profitability of that investment—that is, the stream of expected net receipts upon which they base their investment calculations is the after-tax stream. An increase in the tax rate on business income will lower expected after-tax receipts, shifting the MEK and MEI schedules downward and thus depressing investment.[22] Conversely, a reduction of business income tax rates would shift the MEK and MEI schedules outward and stimulate investment.

In addition, since with existing Internal Revenue Service rules depreciation costs are deductible as current expenses, a change in depreciation rules will alter a firm's current expenses and, thus, its total profit. Moreover, since it is a firm's profit that determines its direct tax liability, after-tax profits will be altered by changes in depreciation rules.

When depreciation rules are altered to allow a firm to depreciate a capital asset more rapidly, the current, *measured* expenses from using that asset are raised in the early years of its life, lowering taxable profits in those years. That is, *accelerated depreciation* can lower a firm's tax liability in the early years of the asset's life by raising the costs it reports for tax purposes. In the later years of the asset's life taxable income and the firm's tax liability will be increased equivalently (the asset will be fully depreciated before its economically useful life is ended). Thus, the overall effect of accelerated depreciation rules is to allow an alteration of the *time pattern* of the firm's tax liabilities, permitting it to pay lower taxes in the early years of a capital asset's life and higher taxes in the later years. This, of course, alters the time pattern of the after-tax stream of revenues expected from use of a capital asset, raising the values of the after-tax Rs expected from that asset during the depreciation period and lowering the values expected in the later years of the asset's life. Changing the time pattern of expected revenues in this manner raises the present value of the asset (or, *ipso facto*, raises the internal rate of return on that asset) since, taking account of the time value of money, a dollar's revenue in the near future is worth more now than a dollar's revenue in the more distant future. Thus, a shift to accelerated depreciation rules should stimulate investment while a shift to a less liberal set of depreciation rules should reduce investment.[23] Accelerated depreciation was adopted in 1954 and liberalized in 1962. More recently, a further shortening of allowable depreciation lives on equipment was provided at the beginning of 1971.

22   This shift will be smaller the greater the ability of producing firms to pass the tax increase on to the public in the form of higher prices. Even if tax increases are fully passed on to the public ultimately, the required price adjustments take time and expected after-tax receipts will be depressed during that interval.

23   Tilting the time pattern of expected after-tax revenues does not alter the total undiscounted dollar value of those revenues. If the rate of interest were zero, changing the time pattern of the after-tax Rs would not affect the present value of a capital asset and, thus, would not affect investment.

In 1962, a special form of tax reduction was introduced in the United States in an effort to stimulate investment. The provision, usually labeled the *investment tax credit*, allowed business firms to deduct, as a credit against their tax liabilities, 7 percent of the amount of their new investment spending during the accounting period. In effect, this provision lowered the purchase price of any prospective capital asset by the amount of tax saving that asset purchase entailed, and thus raised the after-tax rate of return projected for that asset. Hence, introducing a tax credit or raising its effective rate stimulates investment while removal of such a credit or reducing its rate reduces investment.[24] The 7 percent tax credit was suspended in 1966 in an effort to slow economic expansion, reinstated in 1967, and suspended again in 1968. More recently, the tax credit was reinstated with minor modification in August of 1971 and in the spring of 1975 the tax credit rate was boosted to 10 percent for a 2-year period in an effort to stimulate investment.

OTHER FACTORS AFFECTING INVESTMENT

There are a number of other, for our purposes "minor," potential determinants of investment spending. A brief discussion of a small sample of such factors follows.

Credit Rationing or Availability

It is sometimes argued that investment depends not only on the interest rate firms have to pay on borrowed funds but also on the availability of credit. The central argument is that "nonprice" rationing of loan funds may prevent some investment projects from being undertaken. For nonprice rationing of credit to be important, the interest rate must, for some reason, be prevented from rising to a market clearing level.

The one component of investment that is likely to be most affected by credit rationing is residential construction. Legal ceilings on mortgage interest rates and legal ceilings on the rates that can be paid to depositors by those financial institutions that specialize in mortgage loans result in a flight of lendable funds

---

24   For a test of the impact on investment of tax policy changes, see D. Jorgenson and R. E. Hall, "Tax Policy and Investment Behavior," *The American Economic Review*, Vol. 57, June 1967, pp. 391-414. According to Jorgenson and Hall, both the liberalization of depreciation guidelines and the introduction of a tax credit substantially stimulate investment, net investment enjoying a temporary increase and gross investment permanently increasing due to an enlargement of the optimal capital stock. To a sizable extent, however, the Jorgenson and Hall results are built into their investment model. Alternative and more modest appraisals of the impact of tax policies on the level and timing of investment appear in G. Fromm (ed.), *Tax Incentives and Capital Spending* (Washington, D.C.: Brookings, 1971).

away from the mortgage market and toward higher-yielding alternatives during periods when market interest rates rise above those ceiling levels. In such circumstances, borrowable funds for residential construction may simply not be available, even for the legal maximum interest price, and investment in such assets will be diminished.

Proxies for Expected Profitability of Investment

The current level of output is not the only variable that can be chosen as a proxy for expected revenue or expected profitability from investment spending. To cite one alternative, some analysts have suggested that current profit is a better predictor of investment than output. While the two variables are closely correlated (when output rises profits typically rise), empirical tests seem to favor an income variable as a superior indicator of changes in investment.

Cash Flow

Our theoretical analysis suggests that in making an investment decision it is immaterial whether the funds to be invested are borrowed or whether they come from the savings (retained earnings and depreciation funds) of the firm. The interest cost (explicit or "opportunity" cost) is the same and, thus, the same investment decision should be made. However, there is some empirical evidence that investment spending is positively related to the flow of internally generated funds. Such a relationship suggests that firms do not consider the true cost of internally generated funds to be as high as that of funds generated by borrowing (which raise a firm's fixed obligations) or funds generated by stock issue (which dilute management's control).[25]

SUMMARY

As the material in this chapter suggests, the determination of the aggregate level of investment is quite complex. However, with a thorough grasp of the methods by which individual firms make their investment decisions we were able to build a fairly sophisticated model for explaining investment spending; a model that was capable of telling us the direction of investment response to changes in the interest rate, the size of the capital stock, the confidence of businessmen, tax policy, and so on. Of course, all the specific factors that can alter investment in the short run do so by affecting the expected profitability (the stream of future

---

25 See Locke Anderson, "Business Fixed Investment: A Marriage of Fact and Fancy," *The Determinants of Investment Behavior* (New York: National Bureau of Economic Research, Columbia University Press), pp. 413-425.

Rs) of capital or its interest cost. Hence, we were able to summarize our investment model in the simple algebraic form

$$I_{\text{net}_t} = I(Y, i)$$

with current output (Y) providing a proxy measure for expected business conditions and i the market interest rate. While we will employ this somewhat simplified investment function in the income determination models we construct in later chapters, the role of the several specific determinants of investment discussed in this chapter cannot be forgotten. Perhaps most importantly, we must remain mindful of the impact on investment of changes in the tax treatment of business income since the government possesses discretionary control over tax regulations and uses tax changes to stimulate or retard planned investment.

As a final point, it may be noted that the highly aggregative treatment of investment developed in this chapter was based on an analysis of business firms' decisions on investment in *plant and equipment*. No special theory of inventory investment or investment in residential housing has been provided. Fortunately, that is only a minor limitation on your understanding of the determinants of investment, which can be quickly eliminated by a brief look at the *special* nature of those two components of investment. Since inventories are held to meet anticipated sales requirements, the desired stock of inventories may be expected to vary roughly in proportion to the level of expected sales. While differences in the rate of inventory turnover, distance from suppliers, storage bulk, and so on may result in variations among firms in the desired inventory-sales ratio, in the aggregate the desired inventory-sales ratio can be expected to be relatively stable. Hence, an accelerator model can be employed to link net inventory investment with the appropriate sales (output) variable. With current sales employed as a measure of expected sales, empirical evidence indicates that over a year's time actual inventory investment largely reflects desired changes in inventories. Hence, with annual data the simple accelerator provides a suitable explanation of inventory investment, mirroring the considerable volatility of that component of aggregate investment. For shorter time periods, a stock-adjustment form of the accelerator is clearly superior. In no case is there any compelling evidence that inventory investment is influenced significantly by changes in the interest cost of maintaining inventories.[26]

The remaining category of investment, investment in residential housing, is highly sensitive to credit market conditions. By and large, residential housing purchases are mortgage-loan financed. Since houses are durable, their purchase can be postponed easily if the interest cost of mortgage loans rises (that tendency should be particularly pronounced if interest rates on mortgages are expected

---

26   See Evans, *op. cit.*, Chapter 8.

to go down in the future). Moreover, as indicated earlier there are reasons for expecting the availability of mortgage funds to change dramatically as market interest rates vary. At the same time, the income variable that influences households as they consider the long-term commitment to buy a house is surely permanent income. The influence of current income on home purchases is sufficiently small that residential investment typically varies countercyclically, increasing during contractions (when interest rates decline and the availability of mortgage funds increases) and shrinking as expansions persist.[27] As with the other components of investment, empirical investigations of residential investment rely heavily on stock adjustment forms of the accelerator with close attention paid to permanent income, population, and credit market conditions as determinants of the desired stock of housing at any point in time.

QUESTIONS

1. Suppose, as a personal investment, you have the opportunity to purchase a suburban lot for $10,000. You estimate that in 5 years you will be able to sell the lot for double its purchase price. You now own $10,000 worth of corporate bonds which are yielding a 10-percent annual rate of return. Should you sell the bonds and buy the lot?

2. Suppose the Belchmore Cola Company has the opportunity to invest in a new cola plant that costs $272,500 and has a life of 3 years. The company expects the plant to generate annual net revenues of $100,000, $500,000, and $150,000 at the end of the first, second, and third years, respectively. The market interest rate is 4 percent.
   (a) Find the present value of this project and determine whether it should be undertaken.
   (b) Use the internal rate of return calculation to make that decision.
   (c) Make the same calculations you made in (a) and (b) but assuming the expected net revenue stream is reversed. What difference does this change in the *timing* of net revenues make? What does this have to do with the tax treatment of business profits?

3. How would the outbreak of all-out war between Japan and China affect the marginal efficiency of investment in the United States?

4. Our investment theory provides an inverse relationship between the market interest rate and the level of investment. But, in reality, we typically find

27 See J. M. Guttentag, "The Short Cycle in Residential Construction," *The American Economic Review*, Vol. 51, June 1961, pp. 275-298. Also, William E. Gibson, "Protecting Home-Building from Restrictive Credit Conditions," *Brookings Papers on Economic Activity*, 1973:3, pp. 647-699.

that the level of investment is high when the interest rate is high, and low when the interest rate is low. Can our investment theory be correct? Explain.

5. Suppose, in a new empirical study of investment, you find investment explained by the regression equation:

$$I_t = .25(K_t^* - K_{t-1})$$

with $K_t^* = a + b_1 Y_t + b_2 i_t$

where K_t^* is the desired capital stock in period t, K_{t-1} the actual capital stock in the preceding period, Y_t is real income in period t, and i_t is the interest rate in period t. Explain the investment theory represented.

6. Explain how the investment tax credit and changes in the depreciation rules business firms are allowed to employ can be used to alter investment.

7. Use the simple accelerator model to explain changes in the demand for college teachers. What is wrong with that model?

8. It is frequently observed that during periods of generally exuberant economic activity, with interest rates at relatively high levels, residential construction is depressed while other components of gross investment remain strong. Account for the special behavior of residential construction.

SUGGESTED READING

Ackley, Gardner. *Macroeconomic Theory.* New York: Macmillan, 1961, Chapter XVII.

Anderson, W. H. L. "Business Fixed Investment: A Marriage of Fact and Fancy," *The Determinants of Investment Behavior.* New York: National Bureau of Economic Research, Columbia University Press, pp. 413-425.

Eckaus, R. S. "The Acceleration Principle Reconsidered," *Quarterly Journal of Economics.* Vol. 67, May 1973, pp. 209-230.

Eisner, Robert. "Investment: Fact and Fancy," *The American Economic Review.* Vol. 53, May 1963, pp. 237-246.

———, and R. H. Strotz. "Determinants of Business Investment," in Commission on Money and Credit. *Impacts of Monetary Policy.* London: Prentice-Hall, 1963, pp. 60-333.

Evans, Michael. *Macroeconomic Activity: Theory, Forecasting, and Control.* New York: Harper & Row, 1969, Chapters 4 and 5.

Hirshleifer, J. *Investment, Interest, and Capital.* Englewood Cliffs, N.J.: Prentice-Hall, 1970.

Johnson, Harry G. *Macroeconomics and Monetary Theory.* Chicago: Aldine Publishing Co., 1972, Chapter 5.

Jorgenson, Dale W. "Anticipations and Investment Behavior," in J. Duesenberry,

G. Fromm, L. Klein, and E. Kuh (eds.). *The Brookings Quarterly Model of the United States.* Chicago: Rand McNally and Co., 1965, pp. 35-92.

―――. "Capital Theory and Investment Behavior," *The American Economic Review.* Vol. 53, May 1963, pp. 247-259.

―――. "Investment Behavior and the Production Function," *The Bell Journal of Economics and Management Science.* Vol. 3, Spring 1972, pp. 220-251.

―――, and R. E. Hall. "Tax Policy and Investment Behavior," *The American Economic Review.* Vol. 57, June 1967, pp. 391-414.

―――, and C. D. Siebert. "A Comparison of Alternative Theories of Corporate Investment Behavior," *The American Economic Review.* Vol. 58, September 1968, pp. 681-712.

Keynes, J. M. *The General Theory of Employment, Interest, and Money.* New York: Harcourt Brace Jovanovich, Inc., 1936, Chapters 11 and 12.

Witte, James G. "The Micro-Foundations of the Social Investment Function," *Journal of Political Economy.* Vol. 71, October 1963, pp. 441-456.

Chapter 7
Money and the
Interest Rate

The simple income determination models of Chapter 4 showed that investment is an important determinant of the level of economic activity. Through the multiplier, it was shown that an increase (decrease) in the level of planned investment results in an even-larger expansion (contraction) in the equilibrium level of output. In turn, the analysis in Chapter 6 indicated that the interest rate is one of the important determinants of the level of planned investment. The relationship between investment and the interest rate was shown to be an inverse one with low rates of interest stimulating investment (*ceteris paribus*) and high interest rates retarding investment. Clearly, interest rate changes can have an impact on the overall level of economic activity which cannot be ignored in a comprehensive model of the macroeconomy. Logically, it would appear that we now must turn our attention to discovering what forces determine the value of the interest rate and, hence, cause the interest rate to change. With that objective in mind, this chapter introduces the *financial sector* of the economy, consisting of a money market and a bond market.

THE RATE OF INTEREST

As the first step in analyzing the financial sector of the economy, a close look at a familiar yet frequently misunderstood term is in order. As always, to understand complex reality we must construct simple representations of that reality. *The rate of interest* is just such a simple, abstract, representation. There is no such item in the real world, as a glance at the financial pages of any of the country's major newspapers can verify. Indeed, in every actual economic system one observes not one rate of interest but many. At one point in time there is one rate of interest on each of the alternative forms of time deposits at your local bank, another set of rates on U.S. government bonds, a different rate on the credit extended by the local furniture store, and so on. It is not obvious that any one of these observed rates can be singled out as *the rate of interest*.

Observed interest rates should be thought of as *gross* interest rates, which include charges for risk, administrative costs, and the *pure* rate of interest.[1] It is this last component of observed interest rates that we can take as our measure of *the interest rate*.

---

1 In addition, where capital markets are not perfectly competitive, there will be an additional charge representing pure profit or monopoly rent earned by lenders in the market.

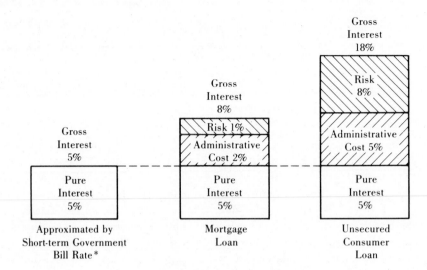

* Short-term U.S. government bonds are virtually riskless since the government has effective tax-levying power. Also, since government bonds are sold in large valued "lots" the per unit administrative cost is very low. Thus, the observed interest rate on short-term U.S. debt provides a close approximation of the pure rate of interest.

FIGURE 7-1 Components of Observed Interest Rates on Different Types of Loans

The pure rate of interest is the rate that would be observed on a perfectly riskless asset, in a purely competitive market, if administrative costs were zero. Since that interest rate is the opportunity cost of holding noninterest-yielding money, it must be the reward to wealth holders that is just sufficient to entice them to sacrifice the convenience yielded by money balances and hold their wealth in the form of bonds. Although this pure rate of interest is not observable, it is present (and equal in value) in every observed gross interest rate. In a competitive financial market, differences in observed interest rates are the result of differences in administrative costs or risk allowances, as shown in Figure 7-1. Since the pure rate of interest is a component of every gross rate, a change in the pure rate of interest will change every observed interest rate. That is, an increase in the pure rate of interest, our measure of *the interest rate*, raises the entire structure of interest rates and a decrease in the pure rate lowers the entire structure of interest rates. The models developed in this chapter demonstrate how this pure interest rate is determined and how changes in that rate—and, thus, in the entire structure of interest rates—can occur.[2]

2 As a practical matter a weighted average of the array of observed interest rates can be used as a measure of the interest rate or, if all market interest rates move together, any one of them can be used as an index of overall interest rate movements. Macroeconomic analysts most often look at movements in long-term bond rates and in the "prime rate" at which banks lend to their best commercial customers for indexes of interest rate movements.

THE KEYNESIAN LIQUIDITY PREFERENCE THEORY

In the well-developed financial markets in the United States, a household, business firm, or government unit can easily borrow money to enhance its current purchasing power. Interest is the price paid for the borrowed funds. At the same time, interest payments constitute the reward which lenders receive for abstaining from current commodity purchases and lending. For the financial sector to be in equilibrium, the prevailing interest rate must equate borrowers' demands for credit with lenders' supplies. Apparently, the determinants of the equilibrium interest rate can be analyzed in a model consisting of credit supply and demand schedules. But, the interest rate is also the opportunity cost of holding money (which pays no interest), so the interest rate which provides financial sector equilibrium must also equate society's *demand for money balances with the available money stock*. Hence, analysis of the determinants of the interest rate can also be conducted concentrating on the supply of and demand for money. The *liquidity preference theory* of interest rate determination, developed by Keynes in *The General Theory*, employs this second approach.[3]

To identify those forces that alter money supply or demand, and hence influence the interest rate, we certainly need to know what should be counted as money. Thus, the first order of business in developing the liquidity preference model entails providing an *appropriate* definition of money. According to a frequently accepted definition, money is anything that is generally accepted as a medium of exchange. While in different times and places gold, silver, jewelry, cigarettes, stones, and other things have served as money, in the United States today only currency (both paper currency and coins) and demand deposits (checkbook money) are generally accepted as a means of payment. But, in addition to serving as a medium of exchange, money also functions as a store of value and as a standard or measure of value. Of course, both of these functions are performed as well by a number of other financial assets. Time deposits, for example, serve as a store of purchasing power and a measure of value just as efficiently as do currency and demand deposits. However, time deposits are not generally accepted as a medium of exchange. Short-term government securities also serve as an excellent store of purchasing power even though their value is not strictly fixed in dollar value at every point in time. Yet, government securities are certainly not generally accepted as a medium of exchange.

Clearly, different financial assets possess different degrees of "moneyness" or "liquidity." Time deposits are slightly less liquid than currency and demand deposits; short-term government securities are less liquid than time deposits; and other financial assets (long-term government bonds, corporate bonds, and so on) are less liquid than short-term government securities. Since there is a continuum

---

3 Keynes, *The General Theory, op. cit.*, Chapter 13. The tight link between the money market and the market for credit (bonds) is developed more fully later in the chapter.

of financial assets which offer differing degrees of liquidity, the selection of a dividing point in the liquidity spectrum for determining which assets are money and which are not involves some element of arbitrariness. To be consistent with the mainstream of macroeconomic analysis, which emphasizes the role of money as a medium of exchange, we must choose the division so as to exclude from the money stock all assets except currency and demand deposits, the two assets that are readily accepted as a medium of exchange. That definition (or any other) is satisfactory if it permits the derivation and statistical estimation of *stable* money demand and supply functions which can be relied on for predicting interest rate changes.

Money Supply and Demand Functions

To build a model that determines the interest rate, we now must develop functions for the supply of money and the demand for money. Dealing with the supply function first, we will assume that the *nominal* supply of money is exogenously determined and constant at the level selected by the central bank. More specifically, we are assuming that the central bank (in the case of the United States, the Federal Reserve System) has control over the total number of dollars held by the public so that once it has selected a desired level for the *nominal* money stock it can hit and maintain that target stock with substantial precision.[4] Turning to the demand side of our money market, we have to begin by noting that money demand in the liquidity preference model is broken into three components: *transactions demand*, *precautionary demand*, and *speculative demand*.

Transactions Demand

Transactions demand is demand for money balances to bridge the gap between the receipt and disbursement of income. If all income receipts were instantaneously spent, the value of transactions balances could always be zero. Such a coincidence of receipts and disbursements is, of course, not achieved in reality, so some positive volume of cash balances must, on average, be held to avoid the difficulties that arise from running out of money. To take a simple example, think of an individual who receives a monthly income of $300 which he spends at the uniform rate of $10 per day during the 30-day month. On average, this individual would hold $150 of money balances ($300 at the beginning of the month and $0 at the end) for transactions purposes.

Like households, business firms are continually receiving and making money payments. They, too, need positive transactions money balances during the in-

---

4   Chapter 15 looks at the mechanics of money supply control more closely in order to explain the assertion that the central bank can and does control the stock of money.

terval between the receipt of income (sales revenue) and its disbursement for wages, rent, interest, raw materials, and so on.

Transaction Demand and Income

What determines the dollar volume of transactions balances held? Without trying, at present, to provide a complete answer to that question, we can safely say that the most important determinant is the dollar volume of transactions which must be financed. For both individuals and business firms, a higher dollar value of transactions will require a higher average dollar volume of transactions balances to be held. Since the dollar volume of transactions rises and falls with income, an increase in the nominal level of aggregate income (thus of both individuals' and firms' incomes and expenditures) will increase aggregate transactions demand for money, while a reduction in aggregate income will decrease that demand.

Of course, the nominal value of income can change either because of a change in real income or because of a change in the price level. In both cases, transactions demand will change in the same direction as income.[5]

Transactions Demand and the Interest Rate

Though Keynes' original analysis deemphasized the role of the interest rate in determining the demand for transactions balances, it is likely that, as this opportunity cost of holding such balances rises, both individuals and business firms make some effort to economize on their holdings of noninterest-yielding money. The higher the interest rate, the more of their "portfolio" we would expect wealth holders to want to hold in interest-yielding form and the less we would expect them to want to hold in money form. Of course, as cash is needed for transactions the income-earning assets held can be sold, but with the inconvenience and explicit money costs associated with converting wealth from money to income-yielding form and back, an increase in the interest rate would be required to encourage efforts to economize on cash holdings. Thus, the transactions demand for money balances might appear like line M_t in Figure 7-2, showing some sensitivity to the interest rate. An increase in the level of income would shift this schedule to the right (as to M_t') and a decrease in income would shift it left-

5 The specific quantitative impact on transactions demand of a given change in the nominal level of income may vary depending on whether that change in income is the result of a change in real income (physical sales volume) or whether it results from price changes. A doubling of money income as a result of an increase in the price level may double the demand for transactions balances. In contrast, modern analysis suggests that a doubling of physical sales volume with prices constant will lead to a less than doubled demand for money balances as opportunities for scale economies in the holding of an inventory of money arise. This possibility is demonstrated in footnote 19 in this chapter.

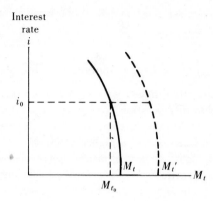

FIGURE 7-2 Transactions Demand for Money

ward. As is the case with demand for any item, a change in price (the interest rate) results in a movement along a given transactions demand curve.

Institutional Determinants of the Transactions Demand for Money

There are other factors that affect the demand for transactions balances that for purposes of business cycle analysis can usually be ignored (that is, assumed constant). These include institutional considerations, such as the established average frequency of income payments, the degree of integration of industry, and the extent to which credit is used to finance transactions.

If income payments are made more frequently, the demand for transactions balances may diminish. If our hypothetical income earner, who held all his received income in money form, were paid his $300 monthly income in biweekly $150 increments rather than in one monthly payment and maintained the same spending pattern (1/30 of monthly income spent each day), he would hold (demand) average transactions balances of $75. Thus, a change in the average frequency of income payments could change the demand for transactions balances, with a switch to more frequent payments shifting the entire transactions demand schedule leftward and a change to less frequent income payments shifting the transactions demand schedule rightward.

In addition, the extent of credit usage affects transactions demand. The greater the use of credit in financing transactions as an alternative to cash purchases the less the demand for transactions balances. No doubt, the proliferation of retail store credit and credit card usage in recent years has, by itself, been responsible for a substantial decline (leftward shift) in the transactions demand schedule.

Finally, it should be noted that operating as separate firms an auto producer and a steel plant would need cash transactions balances to pay each other for sales between themselves. If the auto firm purchased the steel firm (or vice versa), vertically integrating, internal bookkeeping entries could be used to record transfers of steel to the auto producing facility and autos to the steel producing facility. The demand for money for financing such transactions would then disappear. Thus, the greater the degree of integration of industry, the smaller the transactions demand for money balances.[6]

The *institutional* arrangements that affect transactions demand for money are likely to change rather slowly over time. While their role is important in determining the course of changes in money demand over long periods of time, for short-run, income-determination analysis, changes in institutions can generally be ignored. For short-run analysis then we will assume at present that the transactions demand for money is a function primarily of the level of income with some sensitivity to changes in the interest rate possible.

Precautionary Demand

Precautionary demand for money balances exists because there is uncertainty—uncertainty with respect to the timing and size of future income receipts and necessary expenditures. An individual never knows with certainty what his future income will be. He may unexpectedly become disabled or be laid off from his job. He never knows with certainty what expenditures he will need to make in the future. He may have unexpected medical bills, may stumble into unexpectedly favorable opportunities to make purchases, and so on.

Similarly, business firms never know with certainty what future receipts and production costs will be. Revenues may fall temporarily or permanently as a result of shifts in demand (for example, demand for lawn sprinklers may evaporate during an unusually rainy summer). Costs may rise, for example, because of unexpectedly successful wage bargaining efforts by labor unions. To avoid the pecuniary and nonpecuniary (embarrassment?) costs of running out of money as a result of unforeseen events, both individuals and firms are likely to maintain some precautionary balances.

The demand for precautionary balances is likely to be a positive function of the level of income (the higher an individual's income, the larger the safety margin he can afford to hold and the larger unexpected transactions needs may be). In addition, precautionary demand, too, may be sensitive to the interest rate. As in the case of transactions balances, an increase in this opportunity cost of holding noninterest-bearing money balances may induce an effort to economize on the size of those balances. Finally, institutional factors may be expected to influence precautionary money demand just as they do transactions demand. Hence, the spread of credit card usage could substantially reduce precautionary

---

6 While this example is one of *vertical* integration of industry, the effect on money demand is the same if *horizontal* integration is taking place (for example, the merger of two trucking companies that previously employed one another's services).

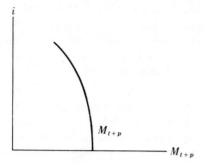

FIGURE 7-3 Demand for Transactions-Precautionary Balances

money demand, as could the expansion of the volume of outstanding claims (like time deposits) that can be readily converted into money.

In the short run, with institutions unchanged, a graphical representation of precautionary demand would look like the demand schedule for transactions balances sketched in Figure 7-2. *Lumping together transactions and precautionary demand for money balances yields a demand function for money with income as the primary determinant and with the interest rate as an additional, though (according to Keynes) perhaps weak influence.*

Algebraically, our transactions-precautionary demand for money function would be $M_{t+p} = M(P \cdot Y, i)$ where $P \cdot Y$ is the dollar value of income (real income Y valued at price level P), i is the interest rate, and M_{t+p} is nominal money demand. Such a function is plotted in Figure 7-3. Once again, a change in the level of income would induce a shift in the demand curve in the same direction as the change in income while a change in the interest rate would require a movement along the given demand schedule, an increase in the interest rate reducing the quantity of money demanded and a fall in the interest rate increasing the quantity demanded.

Speculative Demand

The third component of demand for money balances represents demand for money *to hold as an asset.* This *speculative demand* for money clearly distinguishes the Keynesian theory of interest rate determination from that of his precursors who, emphasizing the role of money as a medium of exchange, dealt only with transactions or transactions-precautionary demand for money. Keynes emphasized the proposition that after an individual has made a decision about what part of his income to spend and what part to save he has an additional decision to make. He has to decide what form to hold his savings in—whether to use his savings to buy interest-yielding securities (in Keynes' terminology "bonds") or whether to hold it in the form of idle, noninterest-yielding money balances.

Presumably, an individual will choose to hold that asset (money or bonds) that maximizes his economic well-being. Since bonds pay a positive interest yield and money does not, he will hold his savings in cash form only if he expects bond prices to fall. As such, speculative demand for money can be characterized as demand for money to hold as an asset in order to avoid capital losses on bonds.

Suppose an individual has $100 of savings and is trying to choose the best form to hold this savings in. Like Keynes, we can simplify our discussion of the portfolio decision this saver faces by assuming that there are only two financial assets available, money and long-term bonds. While we are already familiar with money, the alternative asset deserves some explanation. Basically, bonds are contractual agreements that obligate a borrower (the bond-issuer) to pay *fixed* sums of money at stated time intervals. Typically, over the life of a bond the issuer is obligated to make semiannual or annual *interest* payments while, upon maturity, the *face* or maturity value of the bond must be paid. As an example, a 3 percent, $1,000 bond due in 20 years would pay $15 semiannually (or $30 annually) for 20 years, plus $1000 at the end of the 20 years.

Less common than bonds with specified maturity dates, some bonds are designed never to mature but to provide a perpetual stream of equal semiannual or annual interest payments. Such *perpetual* bonds are particularly easy to work with computationally and, hence, can be conveniently employed in examining the speculative demand for money. Returning to the individual with $100 of savings, suppose the choices he has available for holding that savings in are money and a $100 perpetual bond currently paying a 10 percent annual *coupon* yield ($10 per year in interest payments). Now whether he chooses to hold $100 of speculative money balances or the bond depends on what our wealth-holder *expects* to happen to the market rate of interest in the future. If he expects the market interest rate to rise, say, to 12 percent in the next year, he will keep his savings in money form rather than buy the bond, for with an increase in the market interest rate from 10 to 12 percent the market price of a perpetual bond paying $10 yearly would fall from $100 to $83.33.[7] The loss in capital (market) value of $16.67 on the bond more than offsets the $10 coupon payment our saver would receive in 1 year as a bondholder, so he clearly would be worse off holding the bond than if he kept his $100 savings in idle, money form. Certainly, any individual who expects a substantial rise in the market interest rate, which means

7   At a price of $83.33, our saver's perpetual bond would be yielding a 12 percent rate of return like all other securities in the bond market. Of course, this equilibrium market price is just the present value of the bond, obtained using the 12 percent market interest rate as the discount rate applied to future income receipts generated by that bond. From the section on present value calculations in Chapter 6, you may recall that the present value of an asset that yields a perpetual stream of uniform payments (as the perpetual bond does) is $V = R/i$ where R is the yearly payment and i is the market interest rate.

a corresponding fall in bond prices, would choose to hold his savings in money rather than bonds in order to avoid capital losses.[8]

If, on the other hand, an individual expects the interest rate to fall (bond prices to rise), he would prefer to hold his savings in the form of bonds since he would enjoy a capital gain in addition to the coupon interest payment. Thus, it is the individual's *expectation* of future interest rate movements which governs his choice between speculative money balances and bonds.

To provide an explanation of expected interest rate changes, Keynes suggested that every individual has some notion of what the "normal" rate of interest is (for example, from historical experience, I might think that the normal rate of interest for the United States is close to 6 percent). If the currently observed market rate exceeds an individual's notion of what the normal rate is, he would expect to see market rates fall (bond prices rise) in the future and would prefer to hold bonds rather than money. Conversely, if the market rate is below his concept of the normal rate, he would expect market rates to rise (bond prices to fall) and would choose to hold speculative money balances instead of bonds. Of course, with experience an individual's notion of what the normal interest rate level is can change, but that possibility in no way alters our conclusions about the portfolio choice a wealth-holder will make at one point in time. We now must explore the *aggregate* speculative money demand schedule that is provided by individual portfolio decisions.

If, among the millions of participants in the money (bond) market, there is a diversity of opinion with regard to what the normal rate of interest is, for typical market interest rates we would find some individuals who expect interest rates to rise and some who expect market rates to fall.[9] Thus, for interest rate i_0 in Figure 7-4, we would expect to find some positive demand for speculative money balances (say M_{sp_0}) since those who expect a substantial interest rate rise would prefer to hold their savings in money balances rather than bonds.

If the market interest rate were higher (say, i_1), there would be fewer individuals who expect the interest rate to rise and more who expect it to fall. Thus, the quantity of idle speculative balances demanded would be less (say, M_{sp_1}) than for interest rate i_0.

---

8 To be more specific, the total yield from bond holdings consists of the interest yield plus any capital gain (loss) from a change in bond prices. The percentage yield is:

$$\% \text{ yield} = i + \frac{1}{B}\frac{\Delta B}{\Delta t}$$

where i is the interest yield at the price the buyer purchases the bond and B is the bond price, making $1/B(\Delta B/\Delta t)$ the percentage rate of capital gain yield. As long as wealth-holders expect the overall yield to be positive $[i > -1/B(\Delta B/\Delta t)]$, they prefer to hold bonds rather than money, according to the Keynesian analysis. But, if bond prices are expected to fall (interest rates rise) at a rate that exceeds the interest yield on bonds, wealth-holders would be better off holding their savings in money form.

9 In popular investor jargon, an individual who expects interest rates to fall (bond prices to rise) is a *bull* and one who expects interest rates to rise (bond prices to fall) is a *bear*.

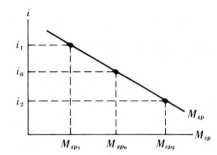

FIGURE 7-4   Speculative Money Demand

Analogously, for an interest rate below i_0 (say, i_2), more individuals would expect the interest rate to rise and fewer would expect it to fall. Thus, more individuals would choose to hold their savings in the form of money balances and fewer in the form of bonds, increasing the quantity of money balances demanded (say, to M_{sp_2}). As shown in Figure 7-4, then, the aggregate demand for speculative balances is an inverse function of the interest rate.

Total Money Demand

The total demand for money is simply the sum of the transaction-precautionary and speculative demands. Since speculative money demand is definitely an inverse function of the interest rate and, also, since transactions-precautionary demand for money may exhibit some negative interest sensitivity, the total money demand function slopes downward from left to right when plotted against the interest rate, as shown in part (c) of Figure 7-5.

In graphic terms, the total money demand schedule is obtained by simply summing horizontally the transactions-precautionary and speculative demand

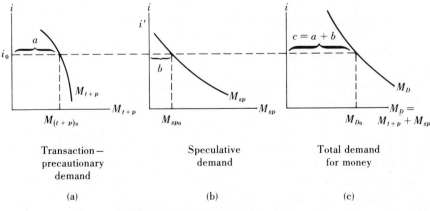

Transaction—precautionary demand	Speculative demand	Total demand for money
(a)	(b)	(c)

FIGURE 7-5   Total Demand for Money

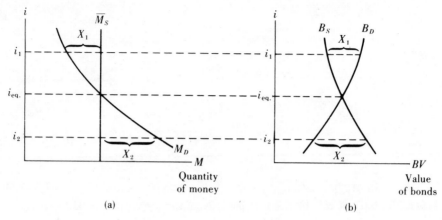

FIGURE 7-6 The Equilibrium Interest Rate

schedules (that is, total $M_{D_0} = M_{(t+p)_0} + M_{sp_0}$ as shown in Figure 7-5). Accepting the Keynesian argument that transactions-precautionary demand for money is primarily a function of money income $\{M_{t+p} \simeq M_1(P \cdot Y)\}$ and speculative demand is sensitive to changes in the interest rate $\{M_{sp} = M_2(i)\}$ *total nominal money demand is a function of both the level of money income and of the interest rate* $\{M_D = M_{t+p} + M_{sp} = M_1(P \cdot Y) + M_2(i)\}$, *with changes in money income causing shifts in the money demand schedule and changes in the interest rate inducing movements along an existing demand schedule.*

The Equilibrium Interest Rate

For one particular income level there is a single, interest-elastic money demand function, like schedule M_D in part (a) of Figure 7-6. Adding a completely interest-inelastic nominal money supply schedule to that figure—vertical schedule $\overline{M}_S$ since we have assumed the nominal money supply to be exogenously determined—permits determination of the equilibrium interest rate (like any other competitively determined price) at the intersection of the market supply and demand schedules. Hence, $i_{eq.}$ is the equilibrium interest rate consistent with money demand schedule M_D.

Moreover, since in the simple Keynesian model savers have only two financial assets in which they can hold their accumulated savings—idle money and long-term bonds—the interest rate that makes wealth-holders just satisfied to hold the existing stock of money in their portfolios must also make them just satisfied to hold the existing stock of bonds. Illustrating that point, the market for bonds is depicted in part (b) of Figure 7-6 with bond supply and bond demand equated at interest rate $i_{eq.}$.

Briefly focusing attention directly on the bond market representation in part (b) of Figure 7-6, you should notice that our bond supply and demand schedules have an unusual appearance—the bond supply schedule (B_S) slopes *downward* from left to right and the bond demand schedule (B_D) slopes *upward*. The apparent reversal of the normal slopes of those schedules is the result of plotting bond supply and demand against the interest rate instead of against bond prices (remember, bond prices are inversely related to the interest rate). Also, for consistency with part (a) of Figure 7-6, the horizontal axis of the bond market diagram shows the *value* of bonds supplied and demanded. Since the bonds in our analysis have been assumed to be *perpetuities*, the market value of every bond is $V = R/i$ and, if there are B bonds in existence, the total market value of the existing stock (supply) of bonds is $B \cdot V = B \cdot R/i$. With an increase in the interest rate, the market value of every bond, hence of the entire existing supply of bonds, falls as reflected in the bond supply schedule B_S. On the other hand, since an interest rate increase convinces more wealth-holders that their savings should be held in bonds rather than in money, the bond demand schedule slopes upward.[10]

With the aid of the bond market, we can now corroborate the claim that $i_{eq.}$ is the equilibrium interest rate and, furthermore, we can demonstrate that it is a *stable* market-clearing rate. Suppose that the actual market interest rate should somehow rise to level i_1. With more wealth-holders wanting to hold their accumulated savings in bonds and fewer wanting their savings in money form at this elevated interest rate, there would be an excess supply of money and an excess demand for bonds. Further, since our wealth-holders are confined to placing their wealth either in money or bonds, the excess supply of money must be equal in value to the excess demand for bonds (value X_1 in both the money and bond markets). But despite the efforts of those individuals who hold larger money balances than desired to reduce those money hoards through the purchase of bonds, the total stock of money balances which society must hold remains unchanged. What will change is the interest rate, for the excess demand for bonds, which must accompany an excess supply of money, will drive bond prices upward. As bond prices rise (the interest rate falls), the quantity of money demanded increases, closing the gap between money demand and the constant supply of money. Likewise, the fall in the interest rate (increase in bond prices) closes the gap between bond supply and bond demand. Clearly any excess supply of money (excess demand for bonds) will set in motion forces that depress the interest rate toward the equilibrium rate—a rate that makes society willing to hold the *existing stock* of money.

Should the interest rate somehow get below the equilibrium level, say, to level i_2 in Figure 7-6, there will be an excess demand for money and, correspondingly, an excess supply of bonds. The resulting effort by society to build up its money balances by selling the alternative asset, bonds, will not change the total money stock but will raise the rate of interest (lower the price of bonds) sufficiently to make society satisfied with the available supply of money balances.

---

10 Since our analysis is basically short run, we can ignore the *flow* change in bond supply which will be negligible compared to the existing physical stock of bonds.

The Extreme Cases for Speculative Demand

Returning now to our focus on the money market,[11] you should recall that the existence of a smooth, continuous, downward-sloping speculative demand for money schedule depends on the existence of a diversity of opinion with respect to what the normal rate of interest is. In generating a speculative demand schedule, we assumed that, as the observed market interest rate falls, more and more savers become convinced that the market rate is below the normal rate and will rise in the future (bond prices fall). Thus, speculative demand for money balances is increased by an interest rate reduction. But what would happen to speculative demand for money balances if the market rate of interest falls to a level so low that *everyone* becomes convinced the observed rate is blow the normal rate? In this extreme situation, since everyone would be expecting the interest rate to rise (bond prices to fall), everyone would prefer to hold his savings in the form of money balances rather than bonds. Society would be willing to absorb a virtually unlimited volume of idle money balances rather than use those money balances to buy bonds. Consequently, the speculative demand for money would become highly elastic at this low interest rate.

Figure 7-7 shows a speculative demand schedule which, at the low interest rate i_{LT}, becomes highly elastic. The elastic portion of the speculative demand schedule is what Keynesian literature calls the *liquidity trap*—at this low interest rate society would willingly absorb unlimited volumes of liquid money balances rather than buy bonds which are expected to decline in value in the future. Keynes himself believed that the liquidity trap would manifest itself at interest rates in the 1 to 2 percent range.

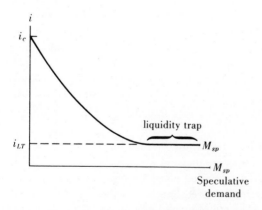

Speculative demand

FIGURE 7-7   Speculative Demand with the Liquidity Trap

---

11   Since the bond market in the Keynesian model is virtually a mirror image of the money market, with both representing the same events (an excess supply of money must be an excess demand for bonds and vice-versa), we need only to keep one of those markets for construction of macroeconomic models. By convention, the money market is retained.

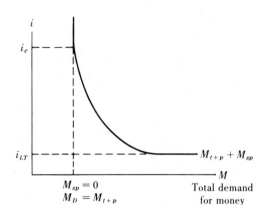

FIGURE 7-8 Total Money Demand with the Liquidity Trap

If the speculative component of total demand for money becomes perfectly elastic at some low interest rate, the total demand schedule $(M_{t+p} + M_{sp})$ must also display that property. Thus, total demand for money would become perfectly elastic at interest rate i_{LT}, as shown in Figure 7-8.

Briefly shifting attention now from low to high interest rates, if there can be some interest rate so low that everyone believes that rate will rise, there can also be some rate so high that everyone expects the interest rate to fall (bond prices to rise). At any interest rate equal to or above this rate (rate i_c in Figures 7-7 and 7-8) speculative demand for money would be zero and total money demand would be interest-elastic only if transactions-precautionary demand is interest-elastic. If the transactions-precautionary demand for money exhibits a negligible interest-sensitivity, the money demand schedule would be vertical above rate i_c.

To complete our presentation of the basic interest rate determination process, the liquidity preference model is represented graphically in Figure 7-9. Since this money-market model will play an integral role in the development of complete aggregate income-determination models, you should be sure you can ex-

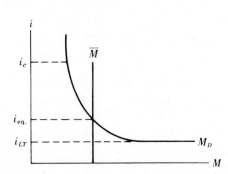

FIGURE 7-9 The Equilibrium Interest Rate

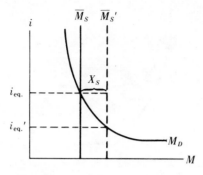

FIGURE 7-10 Response of the Interest Rate to an Increase in Money Supply

plain the shapes of the money supply and demand schedules and account for the forces that establish and maintain the equilibrium interest rate before proceeding.

Changes in the Interest Rate

The equilibrium interest rate can change only as a result of a shift in either money supply or demand. Suppose the central bank chooses to increase the nominal money supply from $\overline{M}_S$ to $\overline{M}_S'$ as shown in Figure 7-10. This *shift* in the money supply function immediately creates an excess supply of money balances of amount X_S. Society, unwilling to hold the enlarged money stock $\overline{M}_S'$ at interest rate $i_{eq.}$, would try to draw down its money balances by exchanging money for bonds (remember, in this model an excess supply of money means an equivalent excess demand for bonds). Of course, society cannot succeed in reducing its actual money holdings but it will succeed in driving the interest rate down (bond prices up) to a level that makes it just willing to hold the existing stock of money balances. That is, the interest rate must fall from $i_{eq.}$ to $i_{eq.}'$ in response to the increase in money supply.

If the central bank reduces the money supply, the opposite result occurs as the reduction in money balances creates an excess demand for money. Society, in response, would try to build up its money balances by selling the alternative asset—bonds (an excess demand for money must be accompanied by an equivalent excess supply of bonds). The volume of money balances held will not change as a result of the public's efforts but the interest rate must rise sufficiently to make society willing to hold just the reduced volume of money balances that the central bank has provided.

Shifting our focus to the demand side of the money market, suppose with the money supply fixed something happens to increase money demand from M_D to M_D', as in Figure 7-11. The resulting excess demand for money balances (excess supply of bonds) would drive the interest rate up to $i_{eq.}'$. Conversely, a decrease in the demand for money would result in a fall in the interest rate. In this regard, it must be emphasized that any one money demand schedule is valid only

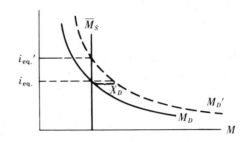

FIGURE 7-11   An Increase in Money
Demand

for one income level. A change in the level of income shifts the money demand
schedule, rightward for an income increase and leftward for an income decline.
What else would cause the demand for money to change?

The Liquidity Trap and the Equilibrium Interest Rate

If the money market is in equilibrium in the liquidity trap ($i_{eq.}$ in Figure 7-12),
sizable shifts in the money supply or money demand schedule can occur without
altering the equilibrium interest rate. Several alternative positions for our money
supply and demand functions appear in Figure 7-12, with every supply-demand
intersection providing the same, liquidity-trap interest rate level.

This is an important point in Keynesian analysis, for if the economy is in
the liquidity trap, even if the central bank engineers an increase in the money
supply, all that increase will be completely absorbed in idle cash balances with
no investment-stimulating reduction in the interest rate.

Nominal versus Real Money Demand and Supply

So far, the money supply and demand functions we have developed are *nominal*
schedules, dealing just with the number of dollars supplied and demanded. As
such, as demonstrated earlier in the chapter, total money demand is a function of

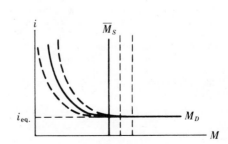

FIGURE 7-12 Equilibrium in the
Liquidity Trap

the *nominal* value of income and the interest rate. That is, nominal money demand is

$$M_D = M(P \cdot Y, i)$$

where $P \cdot Y$ is nominal income and i is the interest rate. As indicated on page 180, nominal money supply has been assumed to be exogenously determined so that

$$M_S = \overline{M}_S.$$

But if, as is usually assumed in macroeconomic analysis, a once-and-for-all change in the price level brings about an equiproportionate change in the total nominal demand for money, the nominal money demand function we have developed can be rewritten as

$$M_D = P \cdot M(Y, i)$$

where, as before, P is the general price level and Y is the level of real income (that is, nominal income deflated by the price level).[12] To convert this function from a demand function for *nominal* money balances to an equivalent demand function for *real* money balances, we need simply to divide through by P, yielding

$$\frac{M_D}{P} = M(Y, i).$$

The real value of the money supply is simply the nominal money supply divided by the price level, or $M_S/P = \overline{M}_S/P$.

Our explanation of the process of interest rate determination is little changed by the conversion from nominal money supply and demand functions to

---

12 In technical terms, we are assuming that total nominal money demand is "linearly homogenous" in prices. This assumption remedies a difficulty in the original Keynesian analysis which is reflected in our discussion up to this point. The Keynesian analysis seems to imply that transactions-precautionary demand for nominal money is affected by the price level but speculative demand is not. That is, $M_D = P \cdot M_1(Y) + M_2(i)$, implying that individuals try to maintain the command over goods and services embodied in their M_1 holdings as prices change but allow the purchasing power of their M_2 balances to change at the whim of price movements, as though they are unaware that the purchasing power embodied in those balances is altered, Assuming away the "illusion" in speculative demand by making speculative demand linearly homogenous in P yields:

$$M_D = P \cdot M_1(Y) + P \cdot M_2(i) = P[M_1(Y) + M_2(i)] = P \cdot M(Y, i) \quad \text{with}$$

$$\frac{\Delta M_D}{\Delta Y} > 0, \frac{\Delta M_D}{\Delta i} < 0, \text{ and } \frac{\Delta M_D}{\Delta P} > 0.$$

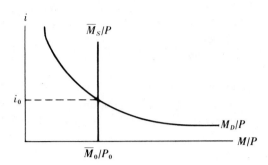

FIGURE 7-13 Demand for and
Supply of Real Money Balances

their real (price deflated) counterparts. For equilibrium, money demand (now
in real terms) must equal money supply—that is, $\overline{M}_S/P = M(Y,i)$ for equilibrium. The properties of the supply and demand functions are, likewise, unchanged. Since the central bank can control the nominal money stock, $\overline{M}_S$, it
can also directly control the real money supply ($\overline{M}_S/P$) as long as the price
level is constant. Real money demand rises (the schedule shifting rightward)
with an increase in *real* income, and the quantity of real money balances demanded is inversely related to the interest rate. A change in the price level (Y
and i unchanged) causes an equiproportionate change in *nominal* money demand
but leaves real demand unchanged while the real money stock is inversely related to the price level. Graphically, the market for real money balances appears
as in Figure 7-13. As before, any factor which increases money demand (shifts
M_D/P outward) raises the interest rate, and any factor that reduces money demand lowers the interest rate. Any increase in the real money stock lowers i, and
any decrease raises i (except in the liquidity trap region).

While we have now drawn attention to the influence of a permanent change
in the price level on the equilibrium interest rate, we have not considered the
impact of a continuing price level adjustment (inflation or deflation) which produces the *expectation* of further price changes. We will postpone that task temporarily and turn our attention to the empirical testing of money demand functions.

A GLIMPSE AT THE EMPIRICAL LITERATURE ON
MONEY DEMAND FUNCTIONS

There is a sizable volume of empirical literature that has attempted to test and
quantify theoretical money demand models. Concentrating on periods during
which the general price level was fairly stable, a large portion of this literature
has provided statistically fitted money demand functions similar to the form we
have developed—that is, with money demand dependent on income and the in-

terest rate. Some examples of the results obtained are presented in Table 7-1.[13] Column 3 of that table shows money demand's elasticity of response to changes in income and the interest rate.[14]

The studies cited were for different time periods, used different measures of the interest rate (for example, some used a long-term "bond" rate and some a short-term "bill" rate for the interest variable), and fitted functions which differ in precise algebraic formulations. While the resulting measures of response in money demand to changes in income and the interest rate differ in size, all agree

TABLE 7-1 EMPIRICAL EVIDENCE ON THE MONEY DEMAND FUNCTION

(1)	(2)	(3) Elasticities		(4)	(5)
Authors	General Form of Demand Function	Interest	Income	Period of Study	R^2
Bronfenbrenner-Mayer	$M = M(Y,i,NW)$ $NW =$ Net Worth or "Wealth"	−.33	1.23	1919-1956	.91
Latané	$M = M(Y,i)$	−.89	1.00	1909-1958	n.a.
Christ	$M = M(Y,i)$	−.58	1.00	1892-1959	.76
Teigen	$M = M(Y,i)$	−.05	.51	1946-1959	.99
Heller	$M = M(Y,i)$	−.104	1.076	1957-1958	.92
Lee	$M = M(Y,i)$	−.75	1.076	1951-1965	.94

13 The equations in the table are found in M. Bronfenbrenner and T. Mayer, "Liquidity Functions in the American Economy," *Econometrica*, Vol. XXVII, October 1960, pp. 810-834; H. Latané, "Income Velocity and Interest Rates: A Pragmatic Approach," *Review of Economics and Statistics*, Vol. XLII, November 1960, pp. 445-449; C. Christ, "Interest Rates and 'Portfolio Selection' Among Liquid Assets in the U.S.," in Christ, *et al., Measurement in Economics* (Stanford, Cal.: Stanford University Press, 1963), pp. 201-218; R. Teigen, "The Demand for and Supply of Money," in R. Teigen and W. Smith (eds.), *Readings in Money, National Income and Stabilization Policy* (Homewood, Ill.: Richard D. Irwin & Co., 1965), pp. 44-76; H. R. Heller, "The Demand for Money: The Evidence from the Short-Run Data," *Quarterly Journal of Economics*, 1965, pp. 291-303; Tong Hun Lee, "Alternative Interest Rates and the Demand for Money: The Empirical Evidence," *The American Economic Review*, Vol. 57, December 1967, pp. 1168-1181.

Other important contributions to the literature on empirical tests of money demand functions include K. Brunner and A. Meltzer, "Some Further Evidence on Supply and Demand Functions for Money," *Journal of Finance*, Vol. 19, May 1964, pp. 240-283; M. Friedman, "The Demand for Money—Some Theoretical and Empirical Results," *Journal of Political Economy*, Vol. 67, June 1959, pp. 327-351; D. Laidler, "The Rate of Interest and the Demand for Money—Some Empirical Evidence," *Journal of Political Economy*, Vol. 74, December 1966, pp. 545-555; and Stephen Goldfield, "The Demand for Money Revisited," *Brookings Papers on Economic Activity* (1973:3), pp. 577-646.

14 To refresh your memory, price elasticity is percentage change in quantity divided by percentage change in price and income elasticity is percentage change in quantity divided by percentage change in income. The interest rate is the price of holding money. You might also note that the Christ and Latané studies employed regression models which constrained the income elasticity of money demand to be unitary.

that there is a significant positive relationship between income and money demand and a significant inverse relationship between money demand and the interest rate. The preponderance of evidence in Table 7-1 suggests that the elasticity of money demand with respect to income is close to one. Equally important, while the interest elasticity of money demand varies with the specific choice of an interest rate variable, the algebraic formulation of the demand function, and so on, empirical evidence suggests that the response of money demand to interest rate changes is *stable* through time so that our interest rate determination model can be useful for analytical and predictive purposes.

A BRIEF SUMMARY

So far in this chapter attention has been focused on developing a simple money supply and demand model (the liquidity preference model) that can be used to predict the interest rate response to a number of disturbances in the financial sector of the economy. In building that model of the money market it has been assumed that, on the supply side of the market, the central bank has precise control over the nominal stock of money and, consequently, over the real stock *as long as the price level is constant.*

On the opposite side of the money market, while institutional arrangements were recognized as important determinants of money demand in a long-run analysis, for the short run we concluded that income and the interest rate are the major determinants of desired money holdings. The propositions that money demand is positively related to the level of income and inversely related to the interest rate were found to be quite consistent with the conclusions drawn from extensive empirical testing of money demand functions.

While our analysis showed that a model of the money market could be constructed either in nominal or in real terms, the real formulation is more convenient in complete macroeconomic models and will be stressed in the remainder of this text. In either formulation of the money market model, the interest rate was lowered by an increase in money supply or a decrease in demand and raised by a reduction in money supply or an increase in money demand. In the real formulation of the model, demand for real money balances is positively related to the level of real income and inversely related to the interest rate, but unaffected by *once-and-for-all* changes in the price level. The real stock of money is inversely related to the price level but, with prices constant, is altered in proportion to changes in the nominal stock of money which the central bank controls. As suggested before, through the interest rate-investment linkage, shifts in the supply and demand functions for real money balances will play an important role in our complete income determination models.

While money supply and demand functions of precisely the form developed in this chapter will be utilized in constructing more complete models of the aggregate economy, our discussion of money and the interest rate is not yet complete. It remains for us, first, to review two notable post-Keynesian refinements in the theoretical explanation of money demand and, second, to explore the impact on our analysis of *anticipated* price changes.

POST-KEYNESIAN MONEY DEMAND MODELS

While it is majority opinion among economists that the form of the aggregate money demand function constructed in this chapter is appropriate, shortcomings in the Keynesian derivation of that function have prompted economists to offer a number of alternative explanations of money demand. Two of the alternatives are treated below.

Unrealistic Individual Behavior in the Keynesian Theory

The Keynesian liquidity preference theory of interest rate determination provides an aggregate demand function for money balances which involves an inverse relationship between the interest rate and money demand. However, a smooth, continuous, functional relationship between the interest rate and money demand is possible only if there is a diversity of opinion about the value of the "normal" rate of interest among the millions of individual demanders of money. That is, there is no comparable smooth, continuous, interest response in individual money demand functions since in Keynes' analysis every individual would want to hold *all* of his speculative wealth either in money (expecting bond prices to fall) or in bonds (expecting bond prices to rise), never part in each. This kind of behavior is reasonable if individuals feel *certain* they know the future path of movement of the interest rate (bond prices). However, the real world rarely allows individuals to hold expectations about the future with certainty. The existence of uncertainty or *risk* is likely to prompt an individual to hold wealth in both money and securities, that is, to *diversify* his portfolio. The arguments below show that, in a world characterized by uncertainty or risk, an individual's speculative money demand can be a continuous inverse function of the interest rate. As a consequence, a smooth aggregate relationship between the interest rate and money demand is possible without appeal to a diversity of opinion that would gradually erode as the interest rate rests at a near-constant level for substantial time periods.

Risk and Money Demand [15]

We know that individuals hold diversified portfolios (for example, one individual might be observed holding money, stocks, bonds, and savings deposits simul-

---

[15] See James Tobin, "Liquidity Preference as Behavior Toward Risk," *Review of Economic Studies*, Vol. XXV, February 1958, pp. 65-68.

taneously). This would not be the case if there were *certainty* with respect to yields on various assets. Instead, individuals would hold only one asset—that one that offers the highest yield.

In a Keynesian world where there are only two liquid assets, money and long-term bonds, an individual can increase the expected yield on his portfolio of wealth holdings only by increasing the proportion of his portfolio held in the form of interest-yielding bonds. However, if interest rates (thus bond prices) are subject to *unexpected* movements, raising the proportion of the portfolio held in bonds increases the *risk* of capital loss the individual wealth-holder faces. With all bonds assumed to be identical, we can graphically describe the risk-yield trade-off available to an individual, as in Figure 7-14. In that figure, the expected percentage yield on the individual's total portfolio of liquid assets is measured on the vertical axis while the total portfolio risk he is exposed to is measured on the horizontal axis. As indicated by the straight-line trade-off schedule, with identical bonds both expected yield and risk increase in direct proportion to the allocation of speculative wealth to bond holdings. If an individual's entire portfolio is held in money form (point A in Figure 7-14), there is zero yield and zero risk. In contrast, with a specific total stock of liquid wealth in the portfolio, both expected yield and risk attain their maximum values of i_{max} and R_{max} respectively when the entire portfolio is held in the form of bonds (point B in Figure 7-14).

If the typical wealth-holder finds risk unpleasant—is *risk averse*[16]—he will be willing to hold a higher-risk portfolio of assets only if compensated by a higher expected yield on that portfolio. We can represent an individual's *willingness* to trade yield for risk by a set of indifference curves, as shown in Figure 7-15. By definition, an individual is indifferent between alternative positions on any one indifference curve. For example, an individual would feel equally well off

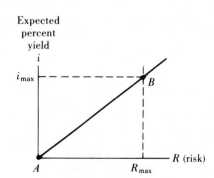

FIGURE 7-14 Risk-Yield Trade-off
Available to a Wealth-Holder

16 Individuals who are *risk averse* would prefer to receive $100 with certainty to having a 50-percent probability of receiving $0 and a 50-percent probability of $200, the *expected value* of which is $100.

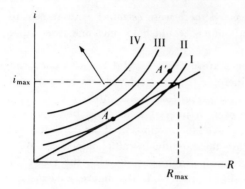

FIGURE 7-15 Portfolio Equilibrium

at position A or A' on indifference curve II. However, a movement to a higher indifference curve provides an unequivocal improvement in the individual's well-being (in our diagram, a movement to a higher indifference curve provides a higher expected yield with no increase in risk or equal yield with lowered risk).

As indicated earlier, a risk-averse individual will accept a riskier portfolio only if compensated for the accompanying disutility by a higher expected rate of return. Further, it is usually assumed that the higher the level of risk the portfolio is subject to, the larger must be the compensatory addition to the expected yield on the portfolio. It is this set of assumptions that dictates the shape of the indifference curves in Figure 7-15. Our utility-maximizing individual would choose to hold the one determinate *mix* of money and bonds that would place him on the highest attainable indifference curve (point A on curve II), given the initial endowment of wealth that constrains the size of his portfolio, the interest rate, and the degree of uncertainty with respect to future interest rates (bond prices).

Now, suppose the market interest rate (thus the expected percentage rate of return on bond holdings) rises with no change in the perceived riskiness of bonds. This change in the expected percentage yield on bonds would rotate the

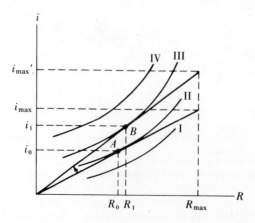

FIGURE 7-16 An Increase in the Interest Yield on Bonds

available risk-yield trade-off schedule counterclockwise, as shown in Figure 7-16. As a consequence, our utility-maximizing individual would change the composition of his portfolio to move from point A to point B. The new portfolio (point B) could be subject to more risk (R_1 instead of R_0) only if the proportion of the portfolio held in bonds were to increase and, therefore, if the proportion held in money were to decrease. Thus, for the individual represented by Figure 7-16, we have shown that an increase in the interest rate can reduce the speculative demand for money.[17] Direct aggregation of such individual speculative demand schedules would generate a *market* speculative money demand function exhibiting the same property of inverse interest-sensitivity without relying on a diversity of opinion about a normal interest rate in the process. Other indifference map patterns that yield different conclusions about the response of money demand to interest rate changes can be constructed. But if the Tobin analysis is a correct explanation of speculative money demand, the widespread empirical support for an inverse interest-sensitivity in aggregate money demand suggests that the behavioral response represented by Figure 7-16 is the dominant pattern.

Interest-Sensitive Transactions Demand for Money

Both the Keynesian and Tobin liquidity preference models rationalize the existence of a strong interest-sensitivity in the aggregate money demand function by demonstrating an interest-sensitivity of speculative demand. They do so, however, in an artificial world which has only two assets: money, the value of which is constant, and long-term bonds, the value of which varies with changes in the interest rate.

In the real world, wealth can also be held in stocks, short-term bonds, savings bonds, savings accounts, and so on. The existence of a significant speculative demand for money in such a world has been seriously questioned since individuals who fear bond price declines can still hold their wealth in an interest-bearing form, rather than in money, with little or no fear of capital losses—for example, in a savings account or in 90-day-maturity Treasury "bills," both assets being essentially risk-free and virtually instantly convertible into money or other assets.

If interest rate changes do not induce a shift in speculative wealth between bond holdings and money, total money demand can be interest-sensitive only if transactions demand is interest-sensitive. That a significant interest-sensitivity in transactions demand should be expected has been demonstrated by both William Baumol and James Tobin.[18]

---

17 We have not shown that the speculative demand for money is an inverse function of the interest rate for every individual in every range of possible interest rates. In fact, you can and should construct sets of indifference curves that show a positive response of speculative demand to interest rate changes.

18 W. Baumol, "The Transactions Demand for Cash: An Inventory Theoretic Approach," *Quarterly Journal of Economics*, Vol. LXVI, November 1952, pp. 545-546, and J. Tobin, "The Interest-Elasticity of Transactions Demand for Cash," *Review of Economics and Statistics*, Vol. XXXVIII, August 1956, pp. 241-247.

Baumol's analysis suggests that transactions money holdings should be treated as an inventory from which gradual drains occur. There are costs involved in maintaining this inventory (as in the case with every inventory), and it is in the interest of any individual or business firm to minimize the costs of maintaining an inventory of money that allows transactions needs to be met.

Let us look at an individual's inventory control task assuming, for simplicity, that his purchase transactions are perfectly foreseen and occur in a steady stream. If, at the beginning of each time period, money balances in amount w are acquired and steadily expended through the period until exhausted at the end of the period, average transactions balances held will be $w/2$. Such a flow pattern is graphed in Figure 7-17.

There are two components of the total cost of maintaining the inventory of money balances from which the individual draws. First, if i is the available market interest rate, then the value of one cost component each period, the foregone interest income on an average volume of money inventory of $w/2$, is simply $i \cdot w/2$. In addition, each time a cash acquisition occurs there are noninterest transactions costs, such as brokerage fees for converting securities into cash, postage, bookkeeping expenses, and transportation costs to a bank or broker. If T is the value of transactions that must be financed in our selected time period and w is the size of withdrawals, then T/w is the number of cash acquisitions (withdrawals) required. If the dollar transactions cost of making one cash acquisition or withdrawal is n, then the noninterest cost of money inventory management in our selected period is $N = n \cdot T/w$.

Thus, the total cost of money inventory management is $tc = i \cdot w/2 + n \cdot T/w$, the interest cost plus transactions (withdrawal) cost. If an individual holds large cash balances, there will be few withdrawals and $n \cdot T/w$ will be small. Foregone interest costs will be large, however. Conversely, small average cash balances will result in relatively high transactions costs and low interest costs. Only one size of withdrawal (thus of average cash balances) will minimize the total cost of maintaining an adequate cash inventory.

Figure 7-18 shows how the interest and transactions costs of maintaining an inventory of transactions balances vary with the size of withdrawal. Vertically

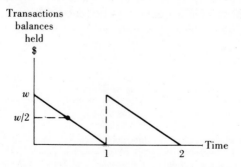

FIGURE 7-17 The Time Path of Transactions Balances

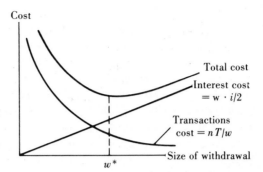

FIGURE 7-18   The Costs of a Cash
Inventory for a Specified Volume of
Transactions per Period

summing these two components of inventory cost yields the total cost schedule
plotted in that figure. The size of withdrawals that minimizes the total cost of
maintaining an inventory of cash balances sufficient to finance our T dollars of
transactions per period is w^*. In this example then, average money balances
would be $w^*/2$.

An increase in the interest rate would rotate the interest-cost schedule
counterclockwise, shifting the total cost curve upward and leftward. The leftward
shift of the total cost schedule would reduce the cost-minimizing size of cash
withdrawal and, thus, reduce the average volume of desired transactions balances.
Quite simply, the increase in the interest cost of holding an inventory of transactions balances induces a reduction in the quantity of dollars demanded for that
purpose.

An increase in the volume of transactions to be financed during our observation period would shift the transactions cost schedule upward since more withdrawals of any selected size would be required to meet transactions needs. As a
result, the total cost schedule would be shifted rightward, increasing the optimal
size of withdrawal and average size of transactions balances.[19]

19   The *formula* for the optimal size of withdrawal is $w = \sqrt{2nT/i}$. This formula makes it
clear that the optimum size withdrawal and corresponding average cash inventory ($w/2$) varies
inversely with the interest rate. It also suggests that transactions demand for money is proportional to the *square root* of the volume of transactions, implying that there are some *scale economies* in cash holding. Empirical evidence that there are such scale economies is provided in
Stephen Goldfeld, "The Demand for Money Revisited," *op. cit.*, pp. 580-589.
The derivation of the optimal withdrawal formula is a straightforward application of the
classical calculus maximization process. If the total cost of maintaining the cash inventory is

$$tc = \frac{i}{2} \cdot w + n \cdot \frac{T}{w},$$

the rate of change (first derivative) of total cost with respect to withdrawal size is

$$\frac{d(tc)}{dw} = \frac{i}{2} - n\frac{T}{w^2}.$$

Setting the rate of change equal to zero (an extreme value of the total cost function) and solving for the withdrawal size yields the formula above. The second derivative of the total cost
function is positive, indicating that the extreme value for total cost is a minimum value.

The inventory model argues then that transactions demand for money is positively related to the volume of transactions and inversely related to the interest rate. These conclusions have general applicability since our model was developed to analyze either individual or business firm behavior. That is not to say, however, that we should expect to see the average individual investing a fraction of his monthly salary in interest-yielding securities which he *expects* to exchange for cash during the following month in order to meet his transactions needs. For most individuals, the fixed cost of converting cash into securities and, later, back into cash exceeds the interest income that could be earned during the period between income receipts. On the other hand, a large business firm that must accumulate sizable cash balances to pay annual employee bonuses or to meet quarterly tax liabilities may well profit from investing those funds temporarily in interest-earning securities.

It should be apparent that the inventory model provides an aggregate money demand function that is qualitatively equivalent to the Keynesian money demand model. According to either model, aggregate money demand is a positive function of the income level and an inverse function of the interest rate. Significantly though, the inventory model can explain the empirically observed interest sensitivity of money demand without resort to a speculative demand for money.

Price Expectations and the Market Interest Rate

In analyzing the determination of an equilibrium value for the interest rate we have allowed once-and-for-all changes in the general price level. However, we have not entertained the possibility of a *continuing*, nonzero rate of price change. Hence, we have been able to tacitly assume that the general price level is *expected* to remain unchanged in the future.

When no change in the general price level is anticipated, the *nominal* interest rate which is observed in the money (bond) market measures the expected *real* interest yield on bonds. But when the general price level is expected to change, the real (price adjusted) yield on bonds can differ substantially from the observed interest rate, requiring us to distinguish between the *nominal* and *real* rate of interest.

Without attempting at the moment to explain how those expectations are generated, suppose that borrowers and lenders have come to expect an increase in the price level. With prices rising over time, the purchasing power of money shrinks. Hence, lenders (bond holders), whose financial claims for interest and principal payments are fixed in dollar terms, would suffer capital losses while borrowers (bond issuers) would enjoy equivalent capital gains. Of course, instead of lending savers could exchange their savings for real property (land and commodities), the dollar value of which rises with the general price level. With this option available, savers who anticipate inflation would be willing to lend their savings (buy bonds) only if the nominal interest yield is sufficient to both compensate for the loss of purchasing power of the dollar repayments they receive and provide the (real interest) reward they require to forego the current use of funds. By the same token, borrowers who anticipate inflation would be willing to pay a higher nominal interest rate since they expect their future interest and principal payments to be made in depreciated dollars.

If lenders and borrowers share a common expected rate of change in the general price level, the nominal interest rate will differ from the real rate by that expected rate of price change. In algebraic terms, with prices expected to change at the rate $\Delta P^e/P$ each period, the nominal interest rate would be

$$i = \rho + \frac{\Delta P^e}{P}$$

where ρ is the real rate of interest—the percentage interest rate that would prevail if no change in the price level were expected.[20] If, with no price level change expected, the equilibrium interest rate (nominal and real) were 4 percent, with prices expected to rise by 4 percent per period, the nominal interest rate which we observe would be 8 percent; if prices were expected to rise 6 percent per period the market interest rate would be 10 percent; and so on. If the substantial inflation the United States began experiencing in the mid-1960s produced the expectation of continuing inflation, the record-high interest rates witnessed in the United States in recent years may have largely reflected the price expectations term in the equation above rather than a rise in the real rate of interest. But what portion of observed interest yields does, in fact, represent an inflation premium must remain to some extent a matter of conjecture since we can observe neither the real interest rate nor the value of expected price changes.[21]

To complete our current discussion of the role of expected changes in the price level, we must determine whether it is the nominal or the real rate of interest which our previous analytical efforts have identified as an important determinant of both money demand and planned investment spending. First, for

20 To be mathematically complete, our expression for the nominal interest rate should be written as

$$i = \rho + \frac{\Delta P^e}{P} + \rho \frac{\Delta P^e}{P}$$

where the last term $[\rho(\Delta P^e/P)]$ measures the expected change in the real value of interest payments. Since this term is quantitatively negligible, it is normally ignored in attempts to explain movements in the nominal interest rate.

21 For the most part, the few existing investigations of the formation of price expectations conclude that expectations are modified only very slowly in response to experienced price level movements. For example, see T. J. Sargent, "Commodity Price Expectations and the Interest Rate," *Quarterly Journal of Economics*, Vol. 83, February 1969, pp. 127-140; and W. E. Gibson, "Price Expectations Effects on Interest Rates," *The Journal of Finance*, Vol. 25, March 1970, pp. 19-34. A shorter adjustment period is found in W. P. Yohe and D. S. Karnosky, "Interest Rates and Price Level Changes," *Federal Reserve Bank of St. Louis Review*, Vol. 51, December 1969, pp. 19-36.

the holders of money balances, the *nominal* interest rate is relevant for it is the nominal interest rate that must be sacrificed when one holds money instead of bonds. In contrast, it is the *real* interest rate that determines the level of investment spending. To justify that claim, consider an inflationary period—a period in which the prices business firms would receive for the goods and services they produce would be rising. At the same time, during a generalized inflation the production costs firms face would be rising in the same proportion as their prices. Hence, the net revenues firms would *expect* to flow from any investment they undertake would be increased by just the expected rate of inflation. Since the nominal interest cost of investment would also be increased by just the expected inflation rate, the same investment decisions would be made no matter what the size of the inflation premium built into the nominal interest rate. That is, the level of investment must depend on the real interest rate.

SUMMARY

The primary concern of this chapter has been to explain the determination of the interest rate. While indicating that the forces which determine the interest rate can be accommodated within the confines of either the money market or the bond market, we followed Keynesian tradition by focusing attention on the supply of and demand for money. The model of the money market that was constructed in this chapter took the stock of nominal money balances to be exogenously determined. In contrast, the first explanation of money *demand*, the Keynesian liquidity preference theory, argued that money demand is a positive function of the level of income and inversely related to the interest rate. The positive linkage to income reflected the demand for transactions-precautionary balances while the interest response was attributed in the main to speculative demand for money. From a small sample of empirical studies, it was easy to see that our hypothesized money demand function was consistent with observed aggregate behavior. But despite its agreement with empirical observation at the aggregate level, in the post-Keynesian era there has been some dissatisfaction with the Keynesian derivation of a money demand function and, as a consequence, alternative money demand models have been formulated. One of the alternatives, the inventory model of transactions demand, provided an aggregate money demand function that was the qualitative equivalent of the Keynesian function. Again, money demand was positively related to the level of income (volume of transactions) and inversely related to the interest rate. Notably though, this model provided an interest sensitivity in money demand without reliance on a speculative demand for money.

The other money demand model analyzed in this chapter, the Tobin portfolio model, was concerned only with explaining the speculative demand for money. That model demonstrated that *individual* speculative money demand functions can exhibit a continuous inverse response to interest rate changes. As in the Keynesian case, by combining interest-sensitive speculative demand with income-determined transactions demand, we obtain a complete money demand function—one that calls for money demand to change in the same direction as the output level and in the opposite direction from interest rate movements. It is worth noting, however, that the portfolio model focuses attention on another variable, the accumulated stock of wealth, as a constraint on the size of the portfolio of liquid assets. Thus, if there is a demand for money to hold as an asset, we would need to consider wealth as a possible determinant of total money demand.

To complete our discussion of money and the interest rate, we introduced the expectation of a nonzero rate of change in the general price level, concluding that observed interest rates would differ from the *real* rate by the expected rate of price level change. Of course, as long as no change in the general price level is expected, the nominal and real rates of interest are identical. Since it is convenient to develop models of the aggregate economy without having to distinguish between those measures, all of the analysis in the next two chapters tacitly assumes that no change in the general price level is expected. But, with the groundwork provided in this chapter, we will be able to assess easily the role of nonzero inflation (deflation) expectations in the model developed in those two chapters. In Chapter 12 on inflation we will undertake that task.

QUESTIONS

1. It is often alleged that the central bank can control either the money supply or the interest rate but not both simultaneously. Explain.
2. You are considering buying a bond that has a maturity value of $1,000, a life of 5 years, and provides an annual (coupon) payment of $40. With the market interest rate 5 percent, what will the price of this bond be? Explain the intrinsic link between bond price changes and interest rate changes.
3. Consider a bond with 10 years to run until maturity and a $5,000 face value, which pays an annual coupon rate of 6 percent. Find the price of this bond when the market interest rate is 4 percent. Is this bond selling at a discount or a premium?
4. From the *Wall Street Journal* or *The New York Times*, select a government bond that has 15 or more years until maturity, and use the yield rate of that bond as your measure of the market interest rate.
   (a) Use the observed market interest rate to determine the market value of a bond like the one in Question 2.
   (b) Make your one best prediction of what the market interest rate will be 1 year from now and use that predicted interest rate to determine the market value of our bond.
   (c) Would you be better off holding the bond or money, given your prediction of the interest rate a year from now?
5. Suppose the President, by executive order, decreed that all workers should

be paid monthly instead of weekly or semiweekly. What would you expect to happen to the interest rate?

6. Suppose the election of a liberal government, by reducing confidence in future economic stability, increases liquidity preference. What would happen to the interest rate?

7. How does a central bank engineered increase in the money supply affect the interest rate if:
   (a) We are in the liquidity trap?
   (b) Interest rates are so high that everyone expects them to fall in the future?
   (c) We are in the normal or intermediate region of the money demand curve?

8. Suppose the market interest rate should remain in a narrow range between 7 and $7\frac{1}{2}$ percent for several years. What would be the impact of this experience on the diversity of opinion assumed in the liquidity preference theory and what is the implication for the shape of the aggregate money demand function?

9. For a risky world, build a model that shows an individual increasing his speculative demand for money as the interest rate rises. Is this possible?

10. To finance $400 worth of transactions per month, find the cost-minimizing volume of transactions balances with the cost of converting securities to money equal to $2 per conversion and an interest yield on securities of .01 (1 percent) per month.

11. You are given the following information:

Money Market
$$\begin{cases} \text{Money Supply} & \dfrac{\overline{M}}{P} = \$250 \\[2mm] \text{Money Demand} & \dfrac{M_D}{P} = 1/3Y + \dfrac{2}{i} \end{cases}$$

Goods and Service Market
$$\begin{cases} \text{Consumption} & C = 20 + 4/5Y_d \\[2mm] \text{Investment} & I = 20 + \dfrac{.8}{i} \\[2mm] \text{Government Spending} & \overline{G} = 60 \\[2mm] \text{Tax Revenue} & \overline{T} = 0 \end{cases}$$

You should inspect these simplified equations to make sure they represent (roughly) the behavioral patterns we would expect to observe for the aggregate economy.

To anticipate one of the tasks we will face in the next chapter, see if you can solve this algebraic (simultaneous equation) representation of the economy for the equilibrium values of income, the interest rate, consumption, investment, and saving.

12. On a $100 loan for a 5-year period, with both principal and interest to

be paid in a lump sum at the end of the 5 years, the lump payment would be

$R = \$100(1 + .04)^5 = \$121.70.$

Now, suppose that the lender who is satisfied with a 4 percent *real* annual return comes to expect a 5 percent annual inflation rate. Calculate the dollar payment at the end of 5 years that would make him willing to lend the $100, then calculate the *nominal* interest rate he would have to charge to compensate for the anticipated inflation.

SUGGESTED READING

Baumol, William. "The Transactions Demand for Cash: An Inventory Theoretic Approach," *Quarterly Journal of Economics*. Vol. LXVI, 1952, pp. 545-556.

deLeeuw, Frank, and Edward Gramlich. "The Federal Reserve—MIT Econometric Model," *Federal Reserve Bulletin*. Vol. 54, January 1968, pp. 11-40.

Friedman, Milton. "The Demand for Money—Some Theoretical and Empirical Results," *Journal of Political Economy*. Vol. 67, August 1959, pp. 327-351.

Gibson, William E. "Price Expectations Effects on Interest Rates," *Journal of Finance*. Vol. 25, March 1970, pp. 19-34.

Goldfeld, Stephen M. "The Demand for Money Revisited," *Brookings Papers on Economic Activity*. 1973:3, pp. 576-646.

Humphrey, T. "Evolution of the Concept of the Demand for Money," *Federal Reserve Bank of Richmond Monthly Review*. Vol. 59, December 1973, pp. 9-19.

Keynes, J. M. *The General Theory of Employment, Interest, and Money*. New York: Harcourt Brace Jovanovich, Inc., 1936, Chapter 13.

Laidler, David E. W. *The Demand for Money: Theories and Evidence*. Scranton, Penn.: International Textbook Company, 1969.

Meltzer, Allan H. "The Demand for Money: The Evidence from the Time Series," *Journal of Political Economy*. Vol. 71, June 1963, pp. 219-246.

Teigen, Ronald. "The Demand for and Supply of Money," in W. L. Smith and R. L. Teigen (eds.), *Readings in Money, National Income, and Stabilization Policy*, 3rd edition. Homewood, Ill.: Richard D. Irwin, Inc., 1974, pp. 68-103.

Tobin, James. "Liquidity Preference as Behavior Toward Risk," *Review of Economic Studies*. Vol. 25, February 1958, pp. 65-86.

Yohe, William P., and Dennis S. Karnosky. "Interest Rates and Price Level Changes," *Federal Reserve Bank of St. Louis Review*. Vol. 51, December 1969, pp. 19-36.

Chapter 8
Money In a Keynesian System— The Constant Price *IS·LM* Model

In Chapter 4, we built several models of macroeconomic systems that could be solved for equilibrium values of income. Though these models differed in complexity and sophistication, they shared one important trait—they all dealt exclusively with the behavior of the commodity market (the market for goods and services), completely ignoring the existence of the money market and, for all practical purposes, the labor market, as though the behavior of those markets would have no effect on the equilibrium level of income. Chapters 5 and 6 looked in considerable detail at the determinants of consumption and investment, the major private sector (as opposed to government) components of demand for real goods and services. Since it was demonstrated that the interest rate is an important determinant of investment spending, Chapter 7 was devoted to introducing the financial sector of the economy. The forces that influence the interest rate were analyzed, concentrating on the money market.

PUTTING IT ALL TOGETHER

In this chapter, the commodity and money markets are formally combined so that the fundamental interactions between those markets can be explicitly and systematically included in our analysis of the macroeconomy. Since the resulting models have two markets, the commodity market and the money market, when we speak of our system being in equilibrium we will mean that both of those markets are in equilibrium. As we proceed, we will try to take full advantage of what was learned about consumption and investment demand in Chapters 5 and 6. However, detail will be added gradually as we proceed from the construction of very simple models to models that are fairly complex. The first model constructed will be for a closed economy with no government expenditures or taxes. In developing this model it is assumed that the price level is constant. In fact, that convenient but unrealistic assumption is employed throughout this chapter. In Chapter 9 the restrictive assumption of no price level changes is removed.

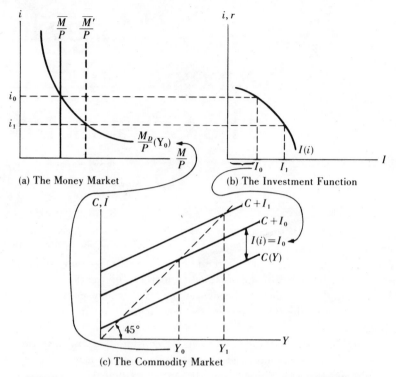

(a) The Money Market

(b) The Investment Function

(c) The Commodity Market

FIGURE 8-1   A Graphical Summary of a Two-Market Macroeconomic Model

A Graphical Summary of What We Know

Figure 8-1 graphically summarizes the component parts of the model of the macroeconomy which has now been developed (again, ignoring government spending and tax collections). In part (a) of that figure, interest rate i_0 is shown equating money supply and demand. In turn, given the investment demand schedule plotted in part (b) of that figure, the equilibrium level of investment at interest rate i_0 is I_0. Finally, in part (c) of Figure 8-1 investment demand of I_0 is combined with a nonproportional consumption function to yield the equilibrium level of income labeled Y_0. If the money demand and investment demand schedules plotted in Figure 8-1 are the schedules which correspond to income level Y_0, Figure 8-1 provides a completely satisfactory graphical representation of our model of the economy *in equilibrium.* (We are about to discover the magnitude of that "if.") But, that graphical summary of the component parts of the macroeconomy is of far less use in assessing the full response of the economic system to any of the shocks it must endure. To illustrate that claim, suppose equilibrium (at i_0, I_0, Y_0) is disturbed by an increase in the stock of money. Were the real money stock to expand to level $\overline{M}'/P$, the interest rate would have to fall to level i_1 for money market equilibrium to be maintained. At that lower interest rate, the equilibrium volume of investment would be increased to I_1 and, through the multiplier, that increase in planned investment would raise equilibrium income to level Y_1. But, with income increased, the demand for money would be increased, raising the equilibrium interest rate at least part of the way back toward its initial level.[1] In turn, with the interest rate raised investment would be reduced leading, through the multiplier, to a lower equilibrium level of income, hence a reduced demand for money, a lowered interest rate, and so it goes *ad infinitum*. With developments in the commodity market causing adjustments in the money market, and money market adjustments, in turn, having feedback effects on the commodity market, the task of searching out the new equilibrium values of income and the interest rate could be quite tedious if we had to rely on the graphical summary in Figure 8-1 of what we know about the macroeconomy. But, thanks to the efforts of a British economist named John Hicks,[2] what we *already know* about the macroeconomy can be presented in a far more convenient format. To construct that alternative format for a simple economic system we will focus formal attention first on the commodity market, then on the money market.

COMMODITY MARKET EQUILIBRIUM—THE *IS* CURVE

For a closed economy with no government spending or taxes, expenditures on goods and services can only exist in the form of household expenditures on consumer goods and business expenditures on investment goods. The analysis in this chapter continues to assume that real consumption spending is a positive function of real income with a marginal propensity to consume between 0 and 1. That is, real consumption is given by

$$C = C(Y) \qquad \text{such that } 0 < \frac{\Delta C}{\Delta Y} < 1.$$

In Chapter 6 on the determinants of investment, it was argued that aggregate investment is a positive function of the level of income and an inverse function of the interest rate. For the analysis in this chapter a simplified form of the investment function will be used, one that reflects the interest sensitivity of investment but ignores any link between investment and the level of income. Consequently, the investment function takes the form

$$I = I(i) \qquad \text{such that } \frac{\Delta I}{\Delta i} < 0.$$

1 The investment demand schedule would also be shifted rightward if investment is a positive function of the output level. However, to avoid an excessive number of complications, investment's response to income changes can be ignored for the time being without altering our conclusions.

2 See J. R. Hicks, "Mr. Keynes and the 'Classics': A Suggested Interpretation," *Econometrica*, Vol. V, April 1937, pp. 147-159.

In Keynesian models of the economy it is primarily through this interest rate-investment linkage that developments in the money market have their influence on the commodity market.

For an economy without a government, we know that for commodity market equilibrium total planned spending (planned $C + I$) must equal the real value of output (Y) or, *ipso facto*, planned saving must equal planned investment (thus the designation $I = S$ or *IS* curve for the commodity market equilibrium relationship we are developing). Substituting the behavioral relationships for consumption (saving) and investment into either of the two equivalent forms of the commodity market equilibrium condition,

$$Y = C + I$$

or

$$S = I,$$

yields respectively

$$Y - C(Y) = I(i)$$

or

$$S(Y) = I(i).$$

These equilibrium conditions are the fundamental ingredient in the arguments that follow.

If any one value for the interest rate is arbitrarily selected, the investment schedule $[I(i)]$ defines the accompanying equilibrium value of investment. Since saving is a function of income, there is some income level that will generate a saving flow that is precisely equal to the flow of investment, permitting commodity market equilibrium to be restored. Suppose, for the particular investment and saving (consumption) functions prevailing in our simple economy, such a

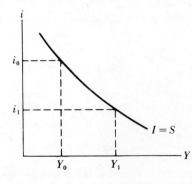

FIGURE 8-2 Commodity Market Equilibrium: The *IS* Curve

saving-investment equality holds for $i = i_0$ and $Y = Y_0$, as shown in Figure 8-2. This is one *equilibrium* combination of i and Y. Suppose now that the interest rate falls, say, to i_1. Since the investment function indicates that a fall in the interest rate increases investment, for our equilibrium conditions to continue to hold after the interest rate declines, saving $[S(Y)$ or $Y - C(Y)]$ must rise. To induce a rise in saving, Y must increase. Thus, *any* fall in the interest rate, which increases aggregate planned spending through its stimulative effect on investment, would have to be accompanied by an increase in income (say, to level Y_1 for a drop in i to i_1) if commodity market equilibrium is to be maintained. For our specified saving and investment schedules, a curve showing all the possible combinations of i and Y that yield equilibrium in the commodity market (the $I = S$ or *IS* curve) slopes downward from left to right as Figure 8-2 shows.[3]

3 The *IS* curve is frequently derived graphically with a four-part diagram such as shown below. Employing simple linear functions, part (a) of the diagram below is a plot of the investment function (the MEI); part (c) plots the saving function; part (b) is simply a 45° identity line; and part (d) plots the commodity market equilibrium or *IS* curve.

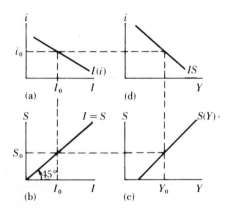

Picking an initial interest rate level (say, i_0) fixes the level of investment (at I_0) and, thus, the volume of saving (S_0) necessary for equilibrium. Given the volume of saving required, the saving function defines the level of income (Y_0) necessary for equilibrium. This establishes one point on the *IS-LM* schedule. Altering the initial interest rate selected by any amount and tracing through the diagram counterclockwise yields another point on the *IS* curve. The resulting *IS* curve will slope downward from left to right as shown.

The downward slope of the *IS* curve can also be quite easily demonstrated mathematically. For equilibrium, $Y - C(Y) = I(i)$. Differentiating with respect to Y yields

$$1 - \frac{\partial C}{\partial Y} = \frac{\partial I}{\partial i} \frac{di}{dY}. \text{ Thus}$$

$$\frac{di}{dy} = \frac{1 - \partial C/\partial Y}{\partial I/\partial i}.$$

Since $0 < \partial C/\partial Y < 1$, the numerator of this expression is positive and, by assumption, the denominator is negative requiring di/dY, the slope of the *IS* curve, to be negative.

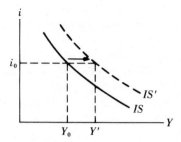

FIGURE 8-3   Shifts in the *IS* Schedule

Shifts in the *IS* Schedule

Maintenance of commodity market equilibrium requires the entire *IS* curve to shift if there are shifts in the investment or consumption (saving) schedules. An autonomous increase in investment (a rightward shift in the investment demand schedule) means a higher level of investment spending at *any* interest rate, such as i_0 in Figure 8-3. For equilibrium, the higher level of investment must be matched by an increase in saving. Since saving increases only if income increases, to maintain equilibrium the autonomous increase in investment must be associated with an increase in income—an increase large enough to generate extra saving in an amount equal to the increase in investment. An autonomous increase in investment then implies a rightward shift in the *IS* schedule, as shown in Figure 8-3. Conversely, an autonomous reduction in investment implies a leftward shift in the *IS* schedule.[4]

Shifts in the consumption function have similar effects. An autonomous upward shift of the consumption function (an increase in the value of the intercept) is the same as an autonomous downward shift of the saving function—the volume of saving at any level of income is reduced. To maintain sufficient saving to offset the investment that takes place at any selected interest rate, the level of income would have to rise. Since commodity market equilibrium at any selected interest rate could be maintained only with income increased, this shift in the consump-

---

4   These shifts in the *IS* curve will be parallel shifts, the magnitude of which is equal to the autonomous change in investment times the investment multiplier. This result is easily proved. For equilibrium, $Y = C(Y) + I(i)$. Taking the total differential of this expression yields

$$dY = \frac{\partial C}{\partial Y} dY + \frac{\partial I}{\partial i} di + dI$$

where dI is an *autonomous* change in investment. Holding the interest rate constant $(di = 0)$ and recognizing that $\partial C/\partial Y$ is the MPC, we have

$$dY(1 - \text{MPC}) = dI \quad \text{or} \quad dY|_{i=\text{const.}} = \frac{1}{1 - \text{MPC}} \cdot dI.$$

This expression tells us the required change in income, holding the interest rate constant at *any* level, to restore equilibrium after an autonomous increase in investment. In this expression we can readily recognize $1/(1 - \text{MPC})$ as the simple spending multiplier for a closed economy in which investment and tax revenues are independent of the level of income.

tion (saving) function implies a rightward shift of the *IS* schedule. Conversely, an autonomous decrease in consumption (increase in saving) implies a leftward shift of the *IS* schedule. You should prove that the shift is a parallel one with a magnitude equal to the shift in the consumption function times the spending multiplier. You may do this with the four-part diagram in footnote 3 or mathematically. Alternatively, you may *shift* the consumption function employed in any specific algebraic representation of the commodity market (such as the one in Question 11 in Chapter 7) and algebraically or graphically trace its impact on the *IS* schedule.

In brief, the *IS* curve is a schedule showing every possible combination of the interest rate and income level that can yield commodity market equilibrium. Its position and slope depend on the positions and slopes of the investment and consumption (saving) functions that underlie it. By itself, the *IS* schedule cannot reveal which combination of i and Y will prevail as the overall or *general* equilibrium combination.

MONEY MARKET EQUILIBRIUM—THE *LM* CURVE

For economy-wide or general equilibrium it is necessary that we also have equilibrium in the money market. This will occur, of course, when money supply and money demand are equal. Continuing to assume that the nominal money supply is exogenously determined, the real money supply is also an exogenously given constant as long as the price level is constant. Based on the analysis in Chapter 7, it is assumed that the real demand for money is an inverse function of the interest rate and a positive function of real income. Thus, in algebraic form our real money supply function is

$$\frac{M_S}{P} = \frac{\overline{M}}{P}$$

and our real money demand function is

$$\frac{M_D}{P} = M(i, Y)$$

with $\Delta M/\Delta i < 0$ and $\Delta M/\Delta Y > 0$. For equilibrium, money supply must equal money demand or

$$\frac{\overline{M}}{P} = M(i, Y).$$

Now, let us suppose we know one combination of i and Y (i_0 and Y_0 in Figure 8-4) that will produce equilibrium in the money market. Then, letting the interest rate rise by any selected amount, say, to i_1, we must ascertain how Y has to change if money market equilibrium is to be maintained. An increase in the

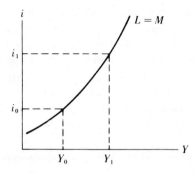

FIGURE 8-4   Money Market Equilibrium: The *LM* Curve

interest rate reduces money demand tending to create an excess supply of money. The public would be willing to absorb these excess funds in transactions balances (and thus be willing to hold the given real money stock $\overline{M}/P$) only at a higher level of income (say, Y_1). Thus, a rise in the interest rate must be accompanied by a rise in the level of real income if money market equilibrium is to be maintained. Clearly the money market equilibrium curve (the $L=M$ or *LM* curve where L represents money demand and M money supply) must slope upward from left to right. That schedule shows all the combinations of i and Y that produce equilibrium (equality of supply and demand) in the money market.[5]

5   The *LM* schedule is frequently derived graphically using the four-part diagram below. The schedule in part (b) of the diagram represents transactions-precautionary demand for money, assuming that demand to be proportional (with proportionality constant k) to Y. The schedule in (d) represents speculative demand for money. The schedule in (c) is simply an identity line that mechanically divides the total money supply into transactions-precautionary and speculative components. That part of total money balances ($\overline{M}/P$) not held in one form must be held in the other. The schedule in (a) is the *LM* curve.

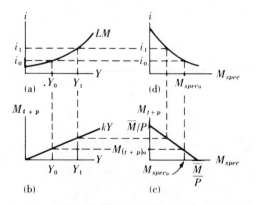

Beginning in (d), with a known interest rate (assume it is i_0), the volume of speculative demand is defined [$M_{(spec)_0}$]. Given the total money supply ($\overline{M}/P$), that portion not held as

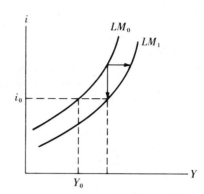

FIGURE 8-5   Shifts in the *LM* Schedule

Shifts in the *LM* Schedule

The *LM* schedule will shift in response to shifts in the underlying money supply or money demand functions. Beginning in equilibrium, an increase in the supply of money would create an excess supply of money requiring either an increase in Y (thus in transactions demand) or a decrease in i (thus a rise in speculative demand) for the additional real money balances to be willingly absorbed. This means, of course, a rightward shift of the *LM* curve, as shown in Figure 8-5. Conversely, a reduction in money supply requires a leftward shift of the *LM* function.[6]

---

speculative balances must be held in transaction balances $[M_{(t+p)_0}]$ as shown in (c). The schedule in (b) shows what level of real income (Y_0) must prevail in order to get the public to willingly absorb the money available for transactions balances in that form. Thus, as we see in (a), for interest rate i_0 the only possible money market equilibrium value for income is Y_0. Should the interest rate rise to i_1, the only possible equilibrium level of income would be Y_1 as we can see by again starting in (d) and proceeding clockwise through our diagram. Thus, the *LM* curve slopes upward from left to right.

This proposition can be quickly proved mathematically. For money market equilibrium the real money supply must equal real money demand—$\overline{M}/P = M(i,Y)$. With a fixed real money supply, total differentiation of this equilibrium conditions yields

$$0 = \frac{\partial M}{\partial i}\, di + \frac{\partial M}{\partial Y}\, dY$$

so that

$$\frac{di}{dY} = -\frac{\partial M/\partial Y}{\partial M/\partial i}.$$

The numerator of this expression is positive while the denominator is negative. Thus, di/dY, the slope of the *LM* schedule, is positive.

6   The shifts will be parallel shifts with a magnitude (measured horizontally) equal to the change in real money supply times the "velocity of circulation," where the velocity of circulation measures the number of times per accounting period each dollar of transactions balances is, on average, used for an income payment. This makes intuitive sense—for all of the change in money supply to be absorbed in transactions balances, at a given interest rate spending on final goods and services (which is the same as income) must have changed by the increment in money supply multiplied by the number of times each new dollar is, on average, spent on final goods and services. Can you prove this proposition mathematically? Hint: If you assume $M_{t+p} = kY$, then $1/k = Y/M_{t+p}$ is the velocity of circulation of transactions balances.

An autonomous increase in the demand for money would create an excess demand for money which could be eliminated only by a rise in the interest rate or a fall in income. Thus, an increase in the demand for real money balances means a leftward shift of the *LM* schedule. Conversely, a decrease in money demand would mean a rightward shift of the *LM* schedule. As suggested in Chapter 7, money demand will shift with a change in the degree of integration of industry, a change in the frequency of income payments, a change in expectations, and so on.

Clearly, the shape and position of the *LM* schedule depends on the shapes and positions of the underlying money supply and demand schedules, a shift in either of those schedules shifting the *LM* curve. As was the case with the *IS* curve, although the *LM* curve shows all the combinations of i and Y that can yield an equilibrium in the money market, it cannot tell us which combination will prevail as the equilibrium combination when there is system-wide or general equilibrium.

GENERAL EQUILIBRIUM

General equilibrium requires simultaneous equilibrium in both the commodity and money markets. By combining the commodity and money market equilibrium schedules (the *IS* and *LM* curves) as in Figure 8-6, we can see that only one combination of i and Y (the combination i_0 and Y_0) can simultaneously clear both the money and commodity markets.[7] That is, given the money supply and

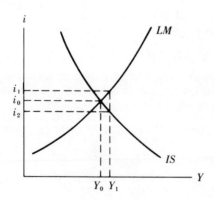

FIGURE 8-6 General Equilibrium: *IS* and *LM* Combined

---

7 The *IS* schedule and *LM* schedule are just graphical representations of single equations in the two unknowns i and Y. With the two equations in i and Y we can solve simultaneously for the values of i and Y that satisfy both these equations. This is, of course, what we are doing graphically in Figure 8-6.

The equilibrium conditions represented in Figure 8-6 [$\overline{M}/P = M(i,Y)$ and $S(Y) = I(i)$] could be written in simple linear form as $m = kY + ni$ and $a + sY = I + vi$ where $m = \overline{M}/P$ and $k, n, s,$ and v are the coefficients measuring the responses of transactions demand for money, demand schedules that underly the *LM* curve and the consumption and investment schedules that underlie the *IS* curve, the only possible equilibrium values of i and Y are the combination at the *IS-LM* intersection. At any other combination of an interest rate and an income level the commodity market, or the money market, or both markets will be in disequilibrium. If, for example, the level of income should rise (say to Y_1), the rate of interest determined in the money market (i_1) would exceed the interest rate that is necessary (i_2) to stimulate sufficient investment to make Y_1 the equilibrium level of income in the commodity market. With excess supply in the commodity market, income would be forced downward. If income should ever fall below Y_0, the money market interest rate would fall below the level that would restrict investment to a volume small enough to produce equilibrium in the commodity market. That is, planned investment would exceed planned saving and income would rise. A formal mathematical proof that stability of equilibrium is always ensured by the forces that are aroused whenever the existing i and Y combination differs from the *equilibrium* combination is beyond the scope of this text.[8] However, there is little question but that stability of equilibrium is provided by those forces.

Using the Model

We now have a simple macroeconomic model which can be used to trace the impact of various economic disturbances on an array of important economic variables. Specifically, we can introduce shocks into the system (changes in money supply or demand, changes in consumption, or changes in investment) and trace the impact of those shocks on income (output), the interest rate, consumption (saving), investment, and, if we wish to make the distinction, transactions and speculative demand for money.

To illustrate the use of our simple *IS-LM* model, suppose general equilibrium is disturbed by an autonomous increase in the money supply. According to our analysis an increase in money supply, which immediately creates an excess supply of money (excess demand for bonds), reduces the interest rate and stimulates investment spending. In Figure 8-7, the increase in money supply is represented by a rightward shift of the *LM* schedule (from *LM* to *LM'*), providing the new equilibrium at reduced interest rate (i_1) and higher income level

---

speculative demand for money (if that is the only source of interest sensitivity), saving, and investment, respectively, to changes in income, the interest rate, income, and the interest rate. Solving these two equations simultaneously for the two unknowns i and Y yields:

$$Y = \frac{1}{s + vk/n}\,(-a + \overline{I} + vm/n) \text{ and } i = -\frac{1}{s + vk/n} \cdot \frac{k}{n}(a + \overline{I} - ms/k),$$

specific values for i and Y.

8   The dynamic issue of stability is dealt with in T. F. Dernburg and J. D. Dernburg, *Macroeconomic Analysis* (Reading, Mass.: Addison-Wesley Publishing Co., 1969), pp. 7-8 and Chapter 12.

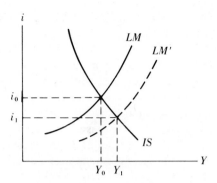

FIGURE 8-7 A Change in General
Equilibrium from a Shift in the *LM*
Curve

(Y_1). Since consumption and saving are positive functions of income, the values
of both of these variables will be greater in the new equilibrium. Transactions
demand for money will also have increased due to the increase in income. The
lower interest rate results in a higher level of investment spending and an increase in speculative demand for money. What would be the impact of a reduction in money supply?

Shifting attention to the demand side of the money market, an increase in
the frequency of income payments or an increase in the fraction of transactions
that are credit financed could reduce the transactions demand for money, resulting in an excess supply of money (excess demand for bonds). In that case, the
unchanged stock of money would be willingly held only at a lower interest rate
or higher income level. Thus, these *institutional changes* would shift the *LM* curve
rightward and the interest rate would fall, stimulating investment and, hence,
raising the equilibrium level of income.[9]

Equilibrium is also disturbed by shifts in the *IS* schedule. Suppose the
initial equilibrium in Figure 8-8 (i_0 and Y_0) is disturbed by an autonomous increase in investment. This shock would shift the *IS* curve rightward to a position
like that of IS_1, showing that the increase in investment provides higher equilibrium values of both the interest rate and income (i_1 and Y_1).

Why does the equilibrium level of income not increase by the full amount
of the horizontally measured shift in the *IS* curve (that is, by $Y_0 - Y_2$) which
is the amount of change in income that the simple multipliers in Chapter 4
would predict in response to our hypothetical increase in investment? The reason is that the interest rate rises as income rises, tending to reduce the amount
of investment spending. The initial increase in investment spending starts the
multiplier process working. However, as income rises, transactions demand for

9 To be precise, these institutional changes would rotate the *LM* schedule in the clockwise
direction since, for example, a halving of the volume of transactions balances that must be held
to finance each dollar's worth of transactions would double the volume of transactions that any
given volume of money balances could support.

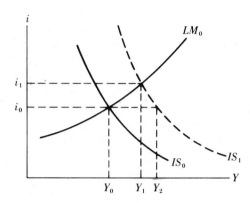

FIGURE 8-8 A Change in General Equilibrium from a Shift in the *IS* Curve

money rises creating excess demand in the money market (excess supply in the bond market). This results in a rise in the interest rate that *damps* (reduces) the volume of investment, tending to reduce the size of the multiplier effect on income. This feedback phenomenon, which appears because the monetary sector of the economy has been combined with the commodity market, can be labeled the *monetary dampener*. It acts to reduce the size of any spending (or tax) multiplier and, as such, it serves as an automatic stabilizer originating in the monetary sector of the economy.[10]

What has happened to the other variables in our model? With income up, consumption and saving will have risen along with the transactions demand for money. There was an initial increase in investment, then a negative investment response to the rising interest rate. However, the overall level of investment must end up higher than before the autonomous shift in the investment schedule. Otherwise, there would be no reason for income, the interest rate, and so on to end up with any values other than their initial values. The rise in the interest rate would, of course, reduce any speculative demand for money. What would be the impact of an autonomous decrease in investment? Of an autonomous shift in the consumption (saving) function?

GOVERNMENT IN THE *IS-LM* MODEL

As always, the basic objective of the effort we have expended in constructing the *IS-LM* model of the economy was that of providing a simplified representation of reality, permitting us to make conditional (if *a*, then *b*) predictions about real

---

10   You should have noticed by now that in the *IS-LM* framework the interactions between the money and commodity markets are no longer a major source of confusion as we search for new equilibrium values of *i* and *Y*.

world events. As demonstrated above, our *IS-LM* model predicted that *if* invest-ment should experience a once-and-for-all increase, *then* the equilibrium values of income, consumption, saving, and the transactions demand for money would increase while speculative demand for money would decrease. In like fashion, our basic *IS-LM* model permitted analysis of the impact of all the other shocks that could shift either the *IS* schedule or the *LM* schedule—an autonomous shift in the consumption function, an autonomous change in money demand, or a change in the size of the money supply. But among the forces that affect the macroeconomy those that emanate from the government's economic activities are probably the most important, and the model we have constructed in this chapter has certainly not provided an adequate role for government. So that we will be able to assess the aggregate impact of government's economic activities, as the next step in our analysis we must formally recognize the existence of government and build the relevant activities of government into the *IS-LM* model.

We will continue to assume that the central bank, which you now may recog-nize as an agent of the government, has complete control over the stock of nominal money balances so that, with this control and a constant price level, it can make the stock of real money balances $(\overline{M}/P)$ what it wants it to be. Con-sequently, no changes in the behavioral relationships in the monetary sector of our model are necessitated by the introduction of a government. The demand for real money balances is still a function of real income and the interest rate and, for equilibrium, real money supply must equal demand. *The* LM *curve is un-affected by the introduction of a government.*

The introduction of a government in the commodity market is more involved but follows a familiar path. In Chapter 4 a government was introduced into models of the commodity market and that government was allowed to spend and to collect taxes. In terms of the behavioral functions in the commodity market, as in Chapter 4 we must recognize government as a source of spending on final goods and services and we must recognize the dependence of household consump-tion on the level of real *disposable income,* which differs from total (received) income by the amount of tax collections.

Equilibrium in the commodity market with government included in the *IS-LM* model requires equality of planned spending with output or, alternatively stated, equality of total leakages from the spending stream (saving plus taxes) with total injections into the spending stream (investment plus government spending). That is, the commodity market equilibrium conditions with govern-ment are

$$Y = C(Y) + I(i) + G$$

or

$$S(Y) + T = I(i) + G.$$

The general properties of the *IS* curve are unchanged. It still slopes downward from left to right since a fall in the interest rate still stimulates investment, requiring a higher level of income to generate sufficient leakages (now saving plus taxes) from the income stream to offset the volume of injections (now investment plus government spending) into that flow. Further, the *IS* curve is still shifted rightward by an autonomous increase in consumption or investment and leftward by a fall in either of those functions. In addition, however, with government included in our model the *IS* schedule will be shifted by any change in government spending or tax collections. Starting at any point on the *IS* schedule, an increase in government spending would create an excess demand for commodities, requiring a higher interest rate or an enlarged volume of output (income) to maintain equilibrium. Thus, an increase in government spending has the same effect on the *IS* curve as an increase in consumption or investment—they all shift the *IS* curve rightward. Conversely, a decrease in government spending, resulting in an excess supply of commodities, shifts the *IS* leftward just as a fall in consumption or investment does.[11]

An increase in taxes, because it reduces disposable income and thus consumption spending, shifts the *IS* curve leftward. Conversely, a reduction in taxes, by raising disposable income and consumption, shifts the *IS* curve rightward. A given dollar volume change in tax collections shifts the *IS* curve by a smaller amount than an equivalent dollar change in government spending, since first-round spending in the tax change case is altered only by the change in tax collections times the marginal propensity to consume, not by the full amount of the tax change.[12]

A Brief Glance at Monetary and Fiscal Policy

It should be apparent by now that government, by altering its spending, its tax receipts, or the money supply, can affect the equilibrium position of the economy. What, specifically, are the changes it can bring about?

---

11   The shifts due to changes in government spending are parallel and have a magnitude equal to the change in government spending times the spending multiplier, as you can demonstrate using the method illustrated in footnote 4 of this chapter.

12   That is, the magnitude of the shift in the *IS* curve resulting from a change in tax collections is the *tax* multiplier times the change in taxes. Explicitly introducing tax revenues into the consumption function, equilibrium income is $Y = C(Y - T) + I(i) + G$. Taking the total differential of this expression yields

$$dY = \frac{\partial C}{\partial (Y - T)}(dY - dT) + \frac{\partial I}{\partial i}\, di + dG.$$

Holding the interest rate and government spending constant $(di = dG = 0)$, and recognizing that $\partial C/\partial (Y - T) = \text{MPC}$, we have $dY(1 - \text{MPC}) = -\text{MPC} \cdot dT$ or

$$\frac{dY}{dT} = \frac{-\text{MPC}}{1 - \text{MPC}},$$

the simple tax multiplier for a closed economy in which investment and tax revenues are independent of the level of income.

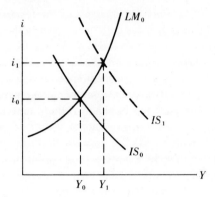

FIGURE 8-9 The Effect on Equilibrium of an Increase in Government Spending

Beginning with our model in general equilibrium (position i_0, Y_0 in Figure 8-9), let the government increase its spending. The increase in government spending shifts the IS curve rightward (say, to IS_1) raising the equilibrium level of income to Y_1 and of the interest rate to i_1.[13] The increase in income will result in a rise in consumption, saving, and transactions demand for money while the rise in the interest rate will result in reduced investment (the monetary dampener

13 To prove this mathematically, assume that both government spending and tax collections are autonomous so that the money and commodity market equilibrium conditions are

$$\frac{\overline{M}}{P} = M(Y, i) \quad \text{and} \quad S(Y) + \overline{T} = I(i) + \overline{G}.$$

Differentiating both equilibrium conditions with respect to G yields

$$\frac{\partial M}{\partial Y}\left(\frac{dY}{dG}\right) + \frac{\partial M}{\partial i}\left(\frac{di}{dG}\right) = 0$$

and

$$\frac{\partial S}{\partial Y}\left(\frac{dY}{dG}\right) - \frac{\partial I}{\partial i}\left(\frac{di}{dG}\right) = 1.$$

Solving simultaneously for dY/dG and di/dG yields:

$$\frac{dY}{dG} = \frac{\dfrac{\partial M}{\partial i}}{\dfrac{\partial S}{\partial Y}\dfrac{\partial M}{\partial i} + \dfrac{\partial M}{\partial Y}\dfrac{\partial I}{\partial i}}$$

and

$$\frac{di}{dG} = \frac{-\dfrac{\partial M}{\partial Y}}{\dfrac{\partial S}{\partial Y}\dfrac{\partial M}{\partial i} + \dfrac{\partial M}{\partial Y}\dfrac{\partial I}{\partial i}}.$$

Both the numerator and denominator of dY/dG are negative making dY/dG positive, while di/dG is positive since a negative sign prefixes the negative ratio expression (positive numerator and negative denominator) for di/dG. Thus, both income and the interest rate respond positively to changes in government spending.

effect) and reduced speculative money demand. Trace the effects of a decrease in government spending on your own.

An increase in tax collections, which reduces disposable income and hence consumption, would shift the *IS* curve leftward lowering income, the interest rate, consumption, savings, and transactions demand for money. Investment and the speculative demand for money would increase. These results are reversed for a reduction in tax receipts.

Clearly, if government wishes to change the level of income by the use of *fiscal policy*—that is, through discretionary changes in government spending and/or tax collections—it can do so. In addition, the government can use monetary policy—alterations in the quantity of money held by the public—to alter the economy's equilibrium position. The effects of money supply changes are those spelled out beginning on page 221, an increase in the money stock raising income and reducing the interest rate. It goes without saying that monetary and fiscal policies can also be used together to pursue the government's policy goal(s). For a particular income target, the equilibrium level of our other variables—the interest rate, consumption, investment, and so on—will differ with the particular *mix* of monetary and fiscal policy actions employed.

The Source of Income Changes

With the model constructed in this chapter, we can readily acquire a summary comprehension of the nature of a major, unsettled debate among economists. That debate is over the source of economic instability. Some economists believe that economic instability stems primarily from the *monetary* sector of the economy. Typically, they argue that central bank mismanagement of the money supply must shoulder the blame for the lion's share of unwanted fluctuations in economic activity. Another group, arguing that economic instability stems primarily from the *real* sector, frequently cites the volatility of investment expenditure and, on occasion, the large-scale changes in government spending associated with wars in explaining the volatility of aggregate income.

In the model constructed in this chapter, the real sector of the economy is represented by the commodity market equilibrium (*IS*) schedule while the monetary sector is represented by the money market equilibrium (*LM*) schedule. If this model is an adequate representation of the economy, we can use it to distinguish between real and monetary sources of income change.[14] A real disturbance—an autonomous change in consumption, investment, government spending, or tax collections—shifts the *IS* schedule in our model, while a monetary disturbance—an autonomous change in money supply or demand—shifts the *LM* curve.

14   See J. L. Stein, "A Method of Identifying Disturbances Which Produce Changes in Money National Income," *Journal of Political Economy*, Vol. 68, 1960, pp. 1-16.

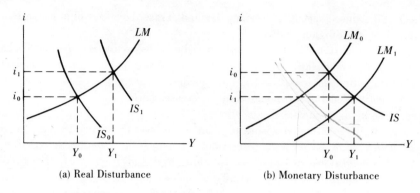

(a) Real Disturbance   (b) Monetary Disturbance

FIGURE 8-10   Real versus Monetary Sources of Income Change

Figure 8-10 part (a) uses the *IS-LM* model to show the impact of a real disturbance—a shift in the *IS* curve. A glance at that diagram reveals that income and the interest rate change in the same direction when the *IS* curve shifts. Figure 8-10 part (b) shows the impact of a monetary disturbance—a shift in the *LM* curve. In this case, income and the interest rate move in opposite directions.

Unfortunately, we will find as our model building progresses that there are not infrequent conditions under which no simple comparison of the directions of movement of i and Y can be used to identify the source of disturbance. That, of course, is the reason that debate over the source of particular income movements continues.

THE MONETARY EFFECTS OF FISCAL OPERATIONS

The *IS-LM* model with government has allowed us to evaluate easily the effects of monetary and fiscal policy actions. Money supply changes produced shifts in the *LM* curve with no impact on the *IS* curve while fiscal actions (a change in government spending or in tax collections) shifted the *IS* curve with no impact on the money supply and thus no effect on the *LM* curve.

To avoid the confusion that has led to some pointless debate in recent years we should take care to label the policy actions we have analyzed in this chapter *pure* monetary and fiscal policies. A pure monetary policy alters the money supply without directly affecting the current flow of income, while a pure fiscal operation, which does directly affect the income stream via a change in government spending or tax collections, leaves the money supply unchanged.

While the standard operational methods of money supply control that are available to the central bank[15] provide pure monetary policy actions, fiscal

15   Those methods are described in Chapter 15.

operations can and often do have an accompanying effect on the money supply. The potential for having a monetary effect accompany a fiscal operation is easy to see. Suppose the Treasury makes a $1,000 payment to a presidential aide. Mechanically, the Treasury would make that payment with a check drawn on its account with the central bank, a check with the presidential aide would take to his own bank for deposit or for conversion to currency. In either case, the publicly held stock of money would be increased by this $1,000 *fiscal* operation unless the monetary effect were offset by a compensatory reduction in the publicly held money stock. Whether it is offset or not depends on the method employed to finance the $1,000 expenditure.

When the government collects tax revenues, in addition to reducing disposable income, it also reduces the publicly held money stock by the amount of tax collections. Consequently, the monetary effect of a $1,000 government expenditure would be offset if the expenditure were tax financed. A tax-financed fiscal operation is a *pure* fiscal operation.

Similarly, if the government finances an expenditure program by selling government bonds to the public, the fiscal operation is pure. In this case, the public swaps money for government bonds but has its money stock just restored by the bond-financed government expenditure. Whenever we are discussing fiscal policy in this text, it is to be understood that any government deficit is financed by borrowing from the public (that is, the public sale of newly issued government bonds) and that any surplus (which would otherwise reduce the money stock) is used to retire publicly held government bonds.

The Treasury *can* finance a deficit by borrowing from (selling bonds to) the central bank. In this case, there is no offset to the monetary effect of the expenditure. Thus, an increase in the level of government expenditure financed by bond sales to the central bank would constitute a combination monetary-fiscal operation. In fact, the resulting one-shot rightward shift in the *IS* curve would be accompanied by a continuing rightward shift in the *LM* curve if, in every subsequent period, the deficit is central bank financed and, hence, increases the money stock.

SUMMARY

In this chapter, a simple model of the economy that takes account of the interactions between the money market and the market for goods and services has been developed. That model enabled us to assess the impact on a broad array of important macroeconomic variables of a number of common economic disturbances. Still, that model suffers from a number of limitations.

In order to concentrate on the mechanics of the *IS-LM* model, we omitted some of the richly detailed information on the behavior of consumption, investment, and interest rate determination that was developed in Chapters 5 to 8.

Listing the major omissions, we have ignored the link between investment and income, failed to allow for the liquidity trap or zero demand for speculative balances, and, by assuming a constant price level, we have failed to provide an explanation of price level determination. In addition, we have virtually ignored the entire supply or production side of the economy—hence, the link between equilibrium output and employment (unemployment). Finally, no account has been taken of the role of international trade. Each of these shortcomings will be dealt with in future chapters.

QUESTIONS

1. The *IS-LM* model in this chapter assumes a constant price level. Discuss the reasonableness of that assumption.
2. Use the *IS-LM* model to analyze the impact on income, the interest rate, consumption, saving, investment, and if your instructor wants to make the distinction, on transactions and speculative demand for money, of the disturbances listed below:
   (a) A change (+ or −) in government spending,
   (b) a change (+ or −) in tax revenues,
   (c) an increase in society's "thriftiness,"
   (d) an autonomous increase in liquidity preference,
   (e) a central-bank-engineered reduction in the money supply,
   (f) an autonomous reduction in the price level,
   (g) a simultaneous increase in the money supply and reduction in government spending.
3. Explain the impact that consideration of the role of the money market had on the multiplier analysis developed in Chapter 4.
4. How would the model developed in this chapter be altered if:
   (a) investment spending were unaffected by changes in the interest rate?
   (b) the demand for money were insensitive to interest rate changes?
   How would the strength of monetary and fiscal policy actions be affected?
5. If you have sufficient mathematical background, derive, for the *IS-LM* model with government:
   (a) the slopes of the *IS* and *LM* schedules,
   (b) the size of the shift in the *IS* schedule that stems from an autonomous change in spending and the size of shift resulting from an autonomous change in tax collections,
   (c) the size of the shift in the *LM* schedule stemming from a change in the real money supply,
   (d) the system-wide impact of an autonomous change in any spending schedule, the tax schedule, or the money supply.

SUGGESTED READING

Hicks, John R. "Mr. Keynes and the 'Classics': A Suggested Interpretation," *Econometrica*. Vol. V, April 1937, pp. 147-159.

Keynes, J. M. *The General Theory of Employment, Interest, and Money*. New York: Harcourt Brace Jovanovich, Inc., 1936, Chapter 18.

Ritter, Lawrence S. "The Role of Money in Keynesian Theory," in Deane Carson (ed.). *Banking and Monetary Studies*. Homewood, Ill.: Richard D. Irwin, Inc., 1963, pp. 134-50. Reprinted in M. G. Mueller, *Readings in Macroeconomics*, 2d edition. New York: Holt, Rinehart and Winston, Inc., 1971, pp. 161-172.

Chapter 9
More Sophisticated
Aggregative Models

Chapter 8 attempted to provide an understanding of the mechanics of *IS-LM* analysis and, hence, of the interactions between the markets for commodities and for money. As the first task in this chapter, the *IS-LM* apparatus will be refined and generalized to enhance its usefulness as a tool for dealing with real-world economic problems. But, an even more important contribution of this chapter is the addition of the market for labor to the basic macroeconomic model. With this addition our analysis can deal explicitly with interactions between the labor market and the commodity and money markets. Thus the resulting *complete* macroeconomic model will permit us to explain how the level of unemployment is determined and how unemployment can be reduced, key concerns of the public and economic policy makers alike. The addition of a formal model of the labor market also permits relaxation of the assumption of a constant price level and *determination* of the general price level within the aggregate model. Directing attention now to the first task of this chapter, we need to modify the treatment of the money market provided in Chapter 8 to allow for the *special Keynesian* liquidity trap and the *special classical* interest-insensitive segments of the money demand function developed in Chapter 7.

IS-LM ANALYSIS—PURE KEYNES AND PURE CLASSICAL CASES

Since our first refinement of the *IS-LM* model focuses on the money market, we will begin by briefly reviewing the treatment of that market in Chapter 8. As reflected in that chapter, with the price level constant money market equilibrium requires the real value of the autonomously determined money supply to equal demand for real money balances. With the demand for real money holdings a function of both real income and the interest rate, the money market equilibrium condition can be written as

$$\frac{\overline{M}}{P} = M(Y, i)$$

with $\Delta M/\Delta Y > 0$ and $\Delta M/\Delta i < 0$. A rise in the interest rate, which reduces the real quantity of money demanded, must be accompanied by an increase in real income, which raises money demand, in order for money market equilibrium to

233

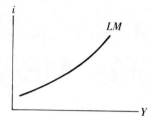

FIGURE 9-1 Money Market Equilibrium—The *LM* Curve

be maintained. Thus, our standard money market equilibrium or *LM* schedule appears as in Figure 9-1 with its slope dependent on the responses of money demand to changes in the interest rate and the income level.[1]

The Generalized Money Demand Function

In our discussion of the full-blown Keynesian money demand function in Chapter 7 we noted that Keynes entertained the possibility of a liquidity trap—a perfectly elastic speculative demand for money at an interest rate so low that everyone expected it to rise (bond prices fall) in the future. The Keynesian analysis also implied that there could be some interest rate so high that everyone expected it to fall and, consequently, preferred his or her *wealth* holdings to be in bonds rather than money. With zero speculative demand for money at interest rates above that level, any interest-sensitivity of money demand would have to stem from the interest-sensitivity of transactions demand. *If* that sensitivity is inconsequential, the money demand function can be written as

$$\frac{M_D}{P} = M_t(Y) + M_{sp}(i)$$

with $M_t(Y)$ representing transactions (or transaction-precautionary) demand for money and $M_{sp}(i)$ speculative demand. Such a function is plotted in Figure 9-2.

Since, with the interest rate above i_c speculative demand for money is zero,

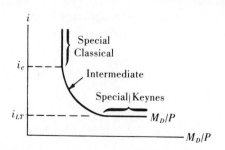

FIGURE 9-2 The Generalized Real
Money Demand Function

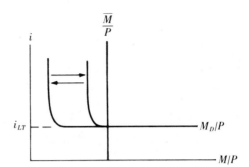

FIGURE 9-3 Money Market Equilibrium in the Liquidity Trap

in this region of the demand curve money is held only for transactions (or transactions-precautionary) purposes as assumed by the "classical" economists who preceded Keynes. This *special classical* region is the vertical segment of the demand schedule in Figure 9-2, reflecting the presumption of no significant interest sensitivity in transactions demand. The alternative special case, the *special Keynesian* liquidity trap region, is the horizontal segment of the demand schedule.

The Generalized *LM* Curve

What must we do to the *LM* curve we have derived in order to accommodate the extreme Keynesian and extreme classical features of the money demand function? As shown in Figure 9-3, when operating within the liquidity trap region, a sizable fall (rise) in the level of income, which shifts the money demand curve leftward (rightward), would leave the interest rate unaltered. Within this liquidity trap region, the *LM* schedule is horizontal—any volume of transactions balances freed by a reduction in income is willingly absorbed in speculative balances with no change in the interest rate. No one would use the released transactions balances to buy bonds because *everyone* expects bond prices to fall. By the same token, the increased demand for money which a rise in the level of income elicits can be accommodated readily out of idle speculative balances if the economy is in the liquidity trap.

On the other hand, when operating within the special classical region, the *LM* curve is vertical. To demonstrate that claim, Figure 9-4 shows the money

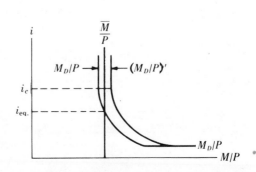

FIGURE 9-4 Equilibrium in the Classical Region

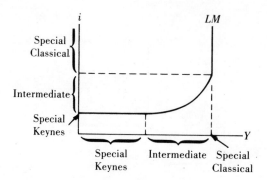

FIGURE 9-5 A Generalized LM Curve

market initially in equilibrium with the market interest rate *just below* the rate (i_c) which demarks the special classical portion of the money demand curve. With a "small" increase in the level of income, the money demand schedule would shift rightward to position $(M_D/P)'$ creating an excess demand for money. The public would try to increase its money balances by selling securities, driving down the price of securities and raising the interest rate. However, since at interest rates above i_c we have ruled out any sensitivity in either money supply or demand, the rising interest rate cannot eliminate the excess demand for money. Thus, with no feedback help from the commodity market, the interest rate could rise without limit as a result of our initial small increase in income (thus money demand), implying that the LM schedule is vertical at interest rates above i_c.

The generalized LM schedule we have rationalized is plotted in Figure 9-5. Labeled in conformity with the generalized money demand function, the horizontal region of the LM curve reflects the existence of the special Keynesian liquidity trap, and the vertical region reflects the interest-insensitive classical portion of the money demand function. The remaining intermediate region is a blending of the two extremes. A general theory of income determination must accommodate the entire spectrum of behavioral patterns reflected in this generalized LM schedule.

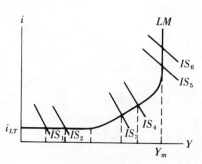

FIGURE 9-6 Changes in i and Y in a General Model of Income Determination

Equilibrium with the Generalized *LM* Curve

General equilibrium requires simultaneous equilibrium in both the money and commodity markets. Combining the generalized *LM* schedule with a group of standard commodity market equilibrium (*IS*) schedules as in Figure 9-6 immediately illuminates two important conclusions. First, given a constant stock of money, there is a maximum attainable level of real income (Y_m) and, secondly, there is a minimum attainable interest rate (i_{LT}), regardless of the position of the *IS* schedule.

Changes in Equilibrium

As before, the *IS* curve shifts in response to a autonomous change in consumption, investment, government spending, or tax collections. But the impact of those disturbances on income, the interest rate, and the other variables with which macroeconomists are concerned can differ markedly depending on the particular range of the *LM* curve in which the economy is operating. As revealed in Figure 9-6, a shift in the *IS* curve in the pure Keynesian *liquidity trap* region (for example, from IS_1 to IS_2) leaves the interest rate unchanged. While such a rightward shift of the *IS* curve indicates an increase in income, and consequently, in the transactions demand for money, the increase in transactions demand can be met readily out of idle speculative balances with no upward pressure on the interest rate. Thus, the magnitude of the income change that stems from an autonomous change in spending or tax collections is given by the simple commodity market multiplier—there is no monetary dampener effect in the special Keynesian region.

As we already know, a shift in the *IS* curve in the intermediate region of the *LM* curve produces a change in both income and the interest rate. The change in income will be smaller than the value predicted by simple multiplier analysis due to the investment-retarding effect of the monetary dampener in this region.

Finally, in the interest-insensitive *special classical* region the monetary dampener effect is so powerful that no shift in the *IS* schedule can alter equilibrium income. Beginning in equilibrium in this region, an increase in any spending schedule, which tends to raise Y, would cause a condition of excess demand in the money market which, within the confines of the money market, could not be alleviated by any increase in the interest rate. But, as people try to increase their money balances by selling securities the interest rate would rise, eventually by enough to reduce planned *investment* spending by an amount equal to the original increase in planned spending. At this point, equilibrium is reestablished at the original income level and at a higher interest rate (note the *IS* curve shift from IS_5 to IS_6).

The Strength of Fiscal Policy

Fiscal policy actions—changes in the level of government expenditures and tax collections—shift the *IS* curve, a rightward shift being produced by an increase in government spending or a decrease in taxes and a leftward shift by a decrease in government spending or an increase in taxes. Clearly, the impact on income (and thus employment) of a specific fiscal policy action will be largest in a depression situation (that is, in the special Keynesian region). The impact on income would become progressively smaller and that on the interest rate progressively larger as we move toward the extreme classical region and, once we have reached that vertical range of the *LM* curve, fiscal policy is completely powerless to alter income! Any first-round change in spending due to a fiscal policy action would cause the interest rate to change sufficiently to induce an exactly offsetting change in investment spending. Thus, for example, an increase in government spending would "crowd out" an exactly equal volume of investment leaving equilibrium income (and thus employment) unchanged.

The Strength of Monetary Policy

The implications of the generalized *LM* curve for monetary policy can be seen in Figure 9-7. As that diagram shows, the impact on income of a monetary policy action—a change in the supply of money—is strongest in the pure classical region. In fact, through its effect on investment an increase in the money supply in this region would increase total spending (income) by the change in money supply times the velocity of transactions money holdings.[2]

Immediately following a money supply increase, there would be an excess supply of money balances. Society would try to reduce its money holdings by purchasing securities, driving security prices up and the interest rate down. With no speculative demand for money and with transactions demand assumed to be insensitive to the interest rate, no interest rate decline can increase money

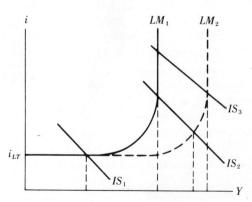

FIGURE 9-7 The Impact of Monetary Policy in the General Model

2 That is, it would increase total spending by the full amount of the shift in the *LM* curve, the magnitude of which was described in footnote 6, of Chapter 8.

demand to restore money market equilibrium. However, the interest rate decline will stimulate investment, increasing total income and, thus, the transaction demand for money. As long as excess supply prevails in the money market, the interest rate will fall. Only when transactions demand for money is swollen to absorb the full increase in money supply will money market equilibrium be restored. Thus, with the economy operating within the vertical segment of the *LM* curve, the income level must grow by the increase in money supply times the velocity of turnover of transaction money balances.

With the economy operating in the familiar intermediate portion of the *LM* curve, a change in the money supply would still affect the level of income. However, the impact would be smaller than in the pure classical region since the public, which *is* willing to hold speculative balances in this region, would allow part of any change in the money supply to be absorbed in (or come out of) speculative balances.

Finally, with the economy operating in the pure Keynesian liquidity trap monetary policy is powerless. Since a change in the money supply cannot alter the interest rate, investment and income cannot be affected by monetary policy. Suggesting that the liquidity trap is characteristic of deep depression, Keynes argued in the 1930s that monetary policy could not be counted on to restore full employment and called for the vigorous use of fiscal stimulation to end the Great Depression. [*Note:* Can you trace the impact of fiscal and monetary policy actions on the variables inside the *IS-LM* model—that is, on consumption, investment, transactions demand for money, speculative demand for money, and velocity?]

Briefly repeating our conclusions on the strength of monetary and fiscal policy in the special classical region, in that vertical segment of the *LM* curve fiscal policy is powerless to alter the level of income and employment while monetary policy has its greatest influence on aggregate demand. In modern terminology, for an economy operating under special classical conditions, "only money matters." In stark contrast, for an economy operating in the Keynesian liquidity trap region monetary policy is powerless while fiscal policy has its greatest strength. In that case, "money doesn't matter" and fiscal policy must be relied on if the government is to influence the level of economic activity. Between the special classical and special Keynesian extremes, both monetary and fiscal policy can be used to regulate economic activity.

THE LABOR MARKET AND AGGREGATE OUTPUT

With our generalization of the *IS-LM* model completed, we can now direct our attention to adding to our summary model of the macroeconomy the third and last important market, the market for labor. The maintenance of full employment and price stability are the key concerns for macroeconomic policy makers. The forces that determine the employment level must do so by influencing the market for labor services. Moreover, it is often argued that forces emanating from the labor market can cause inflation. Certainly, an analytical model designed to explain the functioning of the aggregate economy cannot be judged complete unless it includes the labor market, and the addition of that market is our immediate task.

Once again, our efforts to broaden and enrich the basic macroeconomic model require a development of market supply and demand schedules, in this case schedules for the supply of and the demand for labor. Of couse, in reality a country's labor force includes cooks, steeplejacks, welders, doctors, secretaries, bulldozer operators, and a host of other categories of skilled and unskilled workers. Likewise, the job slots that employers offer differ in skill requirements, working conditions, levels of pay, forms of pay, and so on. As always though, concern for explaining the broad forces that influence the *aggregate* economy requires us to forego detailed examination of the many submarkets where labor is employed. Our attention must be focused on those common, pervasive forces which affect the supply of and demand for *labor in general* and, hence, influence the *general* wage level and the *aggregate* employment level. To that end, our development of the labor market, at least for now, can be thought of as dealing with *homogenous* labor which sells its services at a common wage economy-wide.

The Aggregate Production Function and Labor Demand

By first focusing attention on the *technical* link between employment and output we will be able to provide a straightforward explanation of the aggregate demand for labor. In general, we can expect a country's aggregate output to be positively related to the quantity of capital and labor employed (given the quality of the labor force and the state of technology). At a given point in time then, a country's aggregate *production* function would take the form $Y = Y(K, N)$ where K is the stock of capital and N is the number of hours of labor services employed. For short-run analysis, the stock of capital is constant so output can change only if there is a change in the quantity of labor services firms utilize. As firms hire more labor, the volume of real output is increased as shown in the top half of Figure 9-8. Thus, in the short run output is a positive function of labor employment or $Y = Y(N)$ with $\Delta Y/\Delta N > 0$. The downward concavity of the short-run aggregate production function reflects the presence of *diminishing returns*—while output rises as employment rises, it is assumed that the output growth takes place at a decreasing *rate* as the existing capital stock is spread out over more and more hours of labor input. Eventually output would attain a maximum value and then begin to fall if enough labor is crowded into employment with the fixed stock of plants and equipment.

The *marginal product of labor*, the *extra* output provided by a unit addition of labor input, is simply the slope of the aggregate production function ($\Delta Y/\Delta N$ in Figure 9-8). By inspection of the production function in Figure 9-8, we can see that the assumption of diminishing returns requires the marginal product of labor to fall as employment increases.

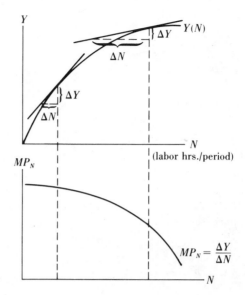

FIGURE 9-8 The Aggregate Production Function and the Marginal Product of Labor

We can now explain what determines the quantity of labor input individual firms hire and use that information to explain the aggregate demand for labor. For simplicity, that explanation will be developed for firms that operate in competitive markets. As a firm increases the quantity of labor employed, it increases output by $(\Delta Y/\Delta N)\Delta N$, the marginal product of labor times the increase in employment. Since competitive firms face a given product price level, the dollar revenue increase from extra labor input is $\Delta R = (P \cdot \Delta Y/\Delta N)\Delta N$, the *value* of labor's marginal product times the increase in employment. Of course, with more labor employed a firm's total costs are increased. The extra dollar costs faced by a firm employing ΔN additional units of labor is just $\Delta C = W \cdot \Delta N$, the market-determined money wage rate times the increase in employment. A profit-maximizing firm will always increase its labor input as long as the increase adds more to revenue than to cost. Thus, for equilibrium, employment must be increased until the extra revenue generated by the last increment of labor employment just covers the cost to the firm of employing that last increment—that is, until $\Delta R = \Delta C$. If, in equilibrium, *marginal revenue* (ΔR) must equal *marginal cost* (ΔC), then

$$P \cdot \frac{\Delta Y}{\Delta N} \cdot \Delta N = W \cdot \Delta N$$

or, canceling the common ΔN terms,

$$P \cdot \frac{\Delta Y}{\Delta N} = W$$

where, once again, $P \cdot \Delta Y/\Delta N$ is the value of labor's marginal product and W is

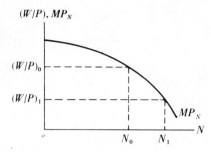

FIGURE 9-9 The Real Wage and the Level of Imployment

the money wage. Rearranging this equality in a form that is more useful for our purposes we obtain

$$\frac{\Delta Y}{\Delta N} = \frac{W}{P}.$$

In this expression $\Delta Y / \Delta N$ is the marginal product of labor and W/P is the *real* wage of labor. For any specific prevailing values of the money wage and price level the real wage is determined and any one competitive firm will strive to employ that volume of labor that equates the marginal product of labor with the real wage. Should the real wage fall, either through a fall in money wages or a rise in the price level, firms will find it profitable to increase the volume of labor employed. For the collection of all firms, this implies the aggregate labor demand function in Figure 9-9 which is nothing more than the aggregate marginal product of labor schedule from Figure 9-8. According to this schedule, at real wage $(W/P)_0$ the business sector will employ N_0 units of labor. Should the real wage be reduced to $(W/P)_1$, the business sector would find it profitable to increase employment for, at wage rate $(W/P)_1$, the marginal product of labor would exceed the real wage of labor for every level of employment less than N_1. Thus, business firms' profits would be increased by adding to employment until employment level N_1, the new equilibrium level which equates the marginal product of labor and the real wage, is established.

Labor Supply

To complete our model of the labor market, we need to know what determines the number of hours of labor that will be *supplied* to the business sector. To begin with, we will assume that labor clearly perceives the impact of price level changes on the purchasing power embodied in its money wage—that it is the *real* wage that influences labor's work-leisure decision. Thus, we start with the classical aggregate labor supply schedule sketched in Figure 9-10 which assumes

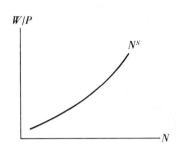

W/P

N^S

N

FIGURE 9-10   Aggregate Labor Supply

that a rise in the real wage induces labor to forego leisure and offer more hours
of labor service to employers.[3]

Labor Market Equilibrium

With labor supply a positive function and labor demand a negative function of
the real wage, there is one real wage rate that clears the labor market, real wage
rate $(W/P)_f$ in Figure 9-11. Market clearing is tantamount to full employment
in our labor market model since it leaves no involuntary unemployment—labor
is selling all the hours of labor services it wishes at the real wage $(W/P)_f$. Thus,
employment level N_f represents full employment. If for some reason the real
wage were fixed above the market-clearing level [say at $(W/P)_1$], persistent involuntary unemployment (excess supply of labor) could exist since business
firms would be unwilling to hire the volume of labor services being offered at
that higher wage. Indeed, at real wage $(W/P)_1$ firms would employ only N_1
units of labor while N_2 units of labor would be willingly supplied.

As illustrated in Figure 9-11, since with a particular aggregate production
function and accompanying marginal product of labor (labor demand) schedule
the real wage determines the volume of employment, it also dictates the volume
of real output. Thus, at real wage $(W/P)_1$, employment is N_1 and output Y_1,
while at the lower real wage $(W/P)_f$ employment is higher at N_f and output
is Y_f.

If the labor market is competitive and there are no restrictions on wage
movements, in response to an excess supply of labor the money wage rate would
fall as unemployed labor offered its services at reduced rates. Conversely, an excess demand for labor would raise the money wage as frustrated employers
attempted to add to their labor force by offering a higher price for labor services.

---

3   A rigorous derivation of the aggregate labor supply schedule, assuming utility-maximizing
behavior on the part of laborers, can be found in W. H. Branson, *Macroeconomic Theory and
Policy* (New York: Harper & Row, 1972), pp. 103-106.

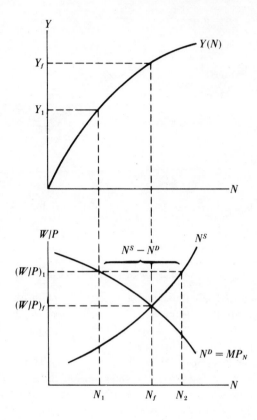

FIGURE 9-11 The Labor Market and Aggregate Output

Hence, we might be tempted to argue (as the classical economists did) that disequilibrium in the labor market automatically generates those adjustments in real wages (through money wage changes) that are required for restoring full employment. But, as we shall see as our analysis progresses, movements in the money wage rate may or may not affect the *real* wage which determines the level of employment. Moreover, there are real-world imperfections in the labor market which keep money wages from responding freely to a divergence between the quantity of labor supplied and that demanded.

A COMPLETE KEYNESIAN MODEL

We can now readily combine what we have learned about the labor market with the *IS-LM* model to provide an expanded representation of the aggregate economy. An algebraic summary of the resulting complete model consists of the following familiar commodity and money market relationships (which yield the *IS* and *LM* schedules respectively) and the new labor market relationships.

$$C = C(Y_d) \qquad 0 < \frac{\Delta C}{\Delta Y_d} < 1$$

$$I = I(i) \qquad \frac{\Delta I}{\Delta i} < 0$$

$$G = \bar{G}$$

$$T = T(Y) \qquad 0 < \frac{\Delta T}{\Delta Y} < 1$$

$$Y = C + I + G \text{ in equilibrium}$$

$\left.\rule{0pt}{80pt}\right\}$ commodity market

$$\frac{M_S}{P} = \frac{\bar{M}}{P}$$

$$\frac{M_D}{P} = M(Y,i) \qquad \frac{\Delta\left(\dfrac{M_D}{P}\right)}{\Delta Y} > 0, \frac{\Delta\left(\dfrac{M_D}{P}\right)}{\Delta i} < 0$$

$$\frac{\bar{M}}{P} = M(Y,i) \text{ in equilibrium}$$

$\left.\rule{0pt}{70pt}\right\}$ money market

$$N^s = N\left(\frac{W}{P}\right) \qquad \frac{\Delta N^s}{\Delta\left(\dfrac{W}{P}\right)} > 0$$

$$\frac{\Delta Y}{\Delta N} = \frac{W}{P}$$

$$Y = Y(N) \qquad \frac{\Delta Y}{\Delta N} > 0$$

$\left.\rule{0pt}{70pt}\right\}$ labor market

For a given aggregate production function, labor demand schedule, and labor supply schedule, there is only one real output level that is consistent with full employment (look back at Figure 9-11). That output level is superimposed on an *IS-LM* model as the broken vertical schedule Y_f in Figure 9-12. In that figure, the *IS* and *LM* schedules have been drawn so that they intersect (establish simultaneous commodity and money market equilibrium) at a level of output

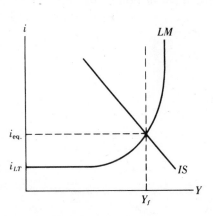

FIGURE 9-12 Full Employment Output in an *IS-LM* Model

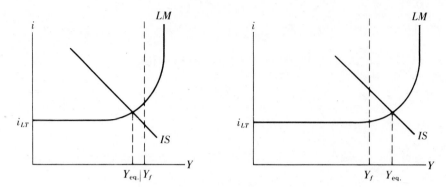

FIGURE 9-13   Alternative "Equilibrium" Positions

equal to the full employment level. However, Keynesian analysis suggests that such a condition is, in the real world, unusual and fortuitous. It is much more likely for the level of *aggregate demand*, determined by money and commodity market interaction, to lie above or, as Keynes was most concerned with, below the full employment level. These possibilities are shown in Figure 9-13.

Relaxing the Constant Price Assumption

To facilitate comprehension of the mechanics of *IS-LM* analysis, we have so far assumed that the price level is constant in the face of sizable shifts in the *IS* and *LM* schedules. As a consequence, all income changes indicated by those shifts were *real* income changes. Consistent with our analysis to this point, until recent years macroeconomic analysis frequently assumed that changes in aggregate demand would result in changes in real output, with little impact on the price level, as long as the economy was operating with substantial unemployment. Once full employment was reached it was assumed that any further increase in aggregate demand (from a rightward shift of *IS* or *LM*) would be met with rising prices on an unchanged volume of real output. Thus, the aggregate supply function was

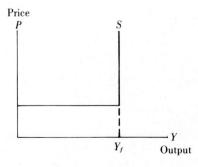

FIGURE 9-14   A Simplified Aggregate Supply Function

assumed to have the L-shape shown in Figure 9-14 with Y_f the full employment level of output.

The aggregate supply function in Figure 9-14 may reflect an often-convenient simplifying assumption. But a supply schedule of that form is not compatible with what we know about the functioning of the labor market. According to the analysis of the labor market provided in this chapter, for the economy to be at rest at a less-than-full-employment output level the real wage must be kept above the market-clearing level [as at level $(W/P)_1$ in Figure 9-11]. That is possible, at the prevailing price level, only if money wages are not bid down by workers *competing* for jobs—that is, only if there are *imperfections* in the labor market which prevent the money wage from falling in the face of involuntary unemployment. In that case, since the marginal product of labor declines with an increase in the quantity of labor employed, firms will increase employment (and output) only if the price level rises to reduce the real wage. As a consequence, the aggregate supply curve must look like the schedule plotted in Figure 9-15, allowing prices to rise with output well before the full employment level of output is reached. Only if both the marginal product of labor and the money wage were constant until full employment is reached could the aggregate supply schedule have the shape shown in Figure 9-14.

Why are money wages "sticky" downward when there is unemployment? Over the years, a number of answers to that question have been offered. For example, it has been argued that with extensive unionization of the labor force money wages are set by contract for extended periods into the future. Those contracts are not invalidated by a price decline in a recession. Minimum wage laws may also be called upon as a bar to competitive money wage reductions, and it can be argued that labor refuses to take money wage cuts, even when the general price level is falling, because a goodly portion of its own contracted expenditures (including rental payments, mortgage payments, auto payments, insurance premiums, and the like) are fixed in money terms. As the issues we confront require, we will have more to say about the downward "stickiness" of money wages and the nature of the aggregate supply schedule. But for now our analysis can proceed tacitly accepting the assumption, well embedded in tradi-

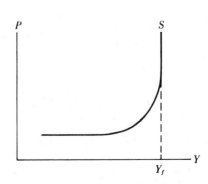

FIGURE 9-15 A More Realistic
Aggregate Supply Function

tional Keynesian analysis, that money wages are inflexible in the downward
direction.

Henceforth, our models will permit the price level to vary—to be *determined*
within the aggregate model. As a consequence, we must recognize the effect on
the *LM* curve of price level changes. Quite simply, a price increase reduces the
real stock of money, $(\bar{M}/P)$, shifting the *LM* curve leftward, while a price decline increases the real money stock shifting the *LM* curve rightward. With this
last bit of background information, we are now ready to make *practical use* of
the *complete* Keynesian model.

USING THE COMPLETE KEYNESIAN MODEL

The complete Keynesian model we have constructed is laid out in graphical form
in Figure 9-16. With the 45° identity line in part (c) of that figure our graphical

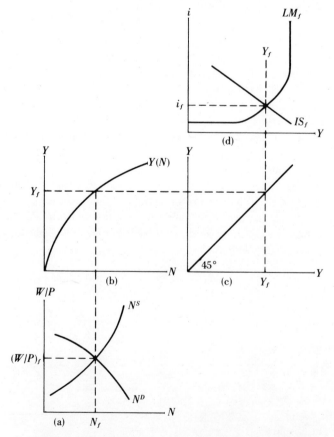

FIGURE 9-16 General Equilibrium in a Complete Keynesian Model

representation of a complete three-market model (the money, commodity, and labor markets) links aggregate supply (output) from the labor market with the demand for output dictated by the interaction of the money and commodity markets. In this first case, the model represents an economic system in full employment equilibrium since all three markets are cleared with the volume of output supplied (Y_f) equal to the volume that provides money and commodity market equilibrium.

A Fall in Aggregate Demand

Suppose now that full employment equilibrium is disturbed by an autonomous decline in some component of aggregate planned spending, which generates the leftward shift of the IS curve from IS_f to IS_1 in Figure 9-17. With no immediate change in the real wage, the level of employment and real output would be unchanged while the reduced level of aggregate demand would clear the commodity

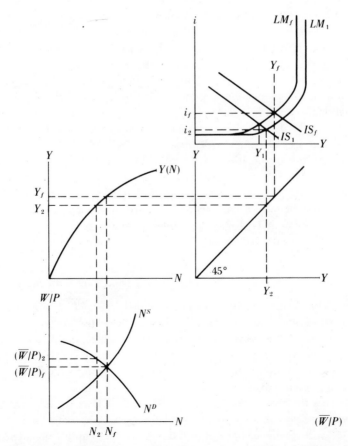

FIGURE 9-17   The Effect of an Autonomous Leftward Shift in the IS Curve

market of only the reduced volume of output Y_1 (that is, aggregate demand has fallen to Y_1). With excess supply in the commodity market, there would be an unintended increase in inventories and downward pressure on the now-flexible price level. As long as there is excess supply in the market for goods and services prices will decline, tending to raise the real wage above the full employment level $(W/P)_f$. Any rise in the real wage above $(W/P)_f$ creates an excess supply of labor (involuntary unemployment) as employers move leftward along the labor demand schedule and households increase the quantity of labor services they offer. In the Keynesian analysis, the excess supply of labor does not produce a fall in the money wage, for that wage $(\overline{W})$ is assumed to be inflexible in the downward direction.

As the real wage rises, reducing the quantity of labor hired, aggregate output falls from Y_f *toward* Y_1. However, the price decline that raises the real wage also increases the real money supply (shifting the LM schedule rightward). The increase in real money supply reduces the interest rate, which stimulates investment and, thus, increases aggregate demand. When shrinking output and growing demand meet, the system will settle at a new equilibrium position, as shown in Figure 9-17 with employment and output reduced (N_2 and Y_2 respectively), the interest rate reduced (i_2), and the real wage increased [to $(\overline{W}/P)_2$] by the price level fall. In turn, the fall in income will have reduced consumption and saving while the reduced interest rate will have raised investment. But, since we did not specify the source of the original leftward shift of the IS curve (it could have been an autonomous reduction in planned investment), we cannot know whether investment is increased or reduced overall. Finally, with the nominal money stock unchanged but the dollar value of output reduced (both Y and P have declined), the velocity of circulation, $P \cdot Y/\overline{M}$, must have declined.

Whatever the explanation of downwardly inflexible money wages—labor union pressure, long-lived wage contracts, minimum wage laws or what-have-you—with that rigidity there is no automatic tendency for our system to return to full employment once a contraction of aggregate demand has depressed the level of economic activity. Relief from unemployment requires the active use of expansionary monetary and/or fiscal policy.

Monetary and Fiscal Policy in the Full Model

Beginning with an excess supply of labor at real wage $(\overline{W}/P)_2$ in Figure 9-18, the use of an expansionary pure fiscal policy is illustrated. An increase in aggregate demand through a fiscal policy action (an increase in government spending or reduction in tax collections) shifts the IS curve rightward so that aggregate demand exceeds output. With excess demand driving prices up, the real wage falls stimulating employment and raising output. At the same time, the rise in prices reduces the real money supply shifting the LM curve leftward. Starting with unemployment, there is some fiscal policy action (some shift in the IS curve) that will restore our model to full employment equilibrium. The original and final equilibrium positions are shown in Figure 9-18 with 2 subscripts indi-

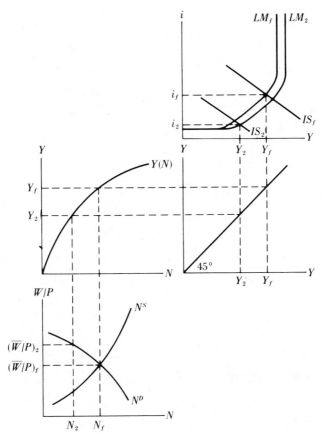

FIGURE 9-18   Restoring Full Employment Equilibrium Through Fiscal Policy

cating original equilibrium values and f subscripts denoting the final values. Clearly the necessary shift in the IS curve (the necessary fiscal policy action) is larger than would be required if the resulting adjustment process did not entail a rising price level that, by reducing the real money supply, shifts the LM curve leftward. In summary, the expansionary fiscal policy action will have, in essence, reversed the changes that resulted from the autonomous contraction of aggregate demand analyzed immediately above with the aid of Figure 9-17. In this expansion case, income, employment and the interest rate will have increased and the real wage will have fallen. Both saving and consumption will have increased with income while the rising interest rate would reduce investment. With the nominal money stock fixed and the dollar value of output increased (both Y and P have increased), the velocity of turnover of the money stock will have increased. As a note of historical interest, the Great Depression which began in 1929 must have convinced nearly every adult who experienced it that the economic system was not self-adjusting, for on through the 1930s the level of economic activity remained woefully depressed. But, with the massive increase in government spending necessitated by preparation for World War II, unemployment shrank and production soared. In short order, full employment was restored as a by-product of the preparation for war. Of course, it was not because of war itself that the economy was returned to full employment but simply because of the massive increase in government spending. An equal increase in spending for any other purpose, including building schools and highways, planting or clearing forests, even building pyramids, would have had a like effect on the overall level of economic activity.

Obtaining relief from unemployment through a monetary policy action would require an increase in the money supply. There is some increase in money supply (some rightward shift of the *LM* curve) exactly the right size to relieve a given level of unemployment. The impact of such a monetary policy action is shown in Figure 9-19 with 1 subscripts on the original equilibrium values and

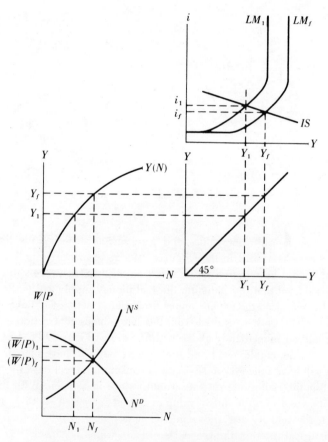

FIGURE 9-19 Restoring Full Employment Equilibrium Through Monetary Policy

f subscripts on the final, full-employment-equilibrium values. Beginning with unemployment, an increase in the money supply (shifting the *LM* schedule rightward) drives down the interest rate, stimulating investment and, thus, creating excess demand in the commodity market. The resulting rise in prices reduces the real wage, increasing employment and output. The rising price level also shifts the *LM* curve leftward, indicating that the original policy shift in the *LM* curve must have moved it to the right of its final, full employment equilibrium position (LM_f). In summary, this expansionary monetary policy will have resulted in a higher income level with higher consumption and saving, a lowered interest rate, increased investment, increased employment, a lowered real wage, and increased money holdings. The impact on velocity is uncertain since both the nominal money stock and the dollar value of output increased.

While both monetary and fiscal policy actions were capable of restoring full employment equilibrium in the two situations we just analyzed, you should note that in both of those cases the economy was operating in the intermediate region of the *LM* curve. The task of analyzing the impact of fiscal and monetary policy actions in the special regions of the *LM* curve is left to you. Continuing to suppose that the economy is initially at rest in an underemployment position, your analysis should provide predictions consistant with those derived earlier in this chapter when we focused exclusively on the demand side of the economy. In the liquidity trap region fiscal policy will have its most powerful effect on income (and employment) while monetary policy is powerless. In the pure classical region, fiscal policy will have no effect on the overall level of economic activity while monetary policy will have its strongest effect.

Money Illusion in the Labor Market

As an interesting corollary of the exercises we have just been through with our *Keynesian* model it is often argued that Keynesian analysis implies the existence of *money illusion* in the labor market. Labor, faced by unemployment, refuses to allow its real wage to fall by reducing its own money wage. But labor willingly accepts a fall in the real wage when the real wage decline results from a price level rise, that price level increase the result of an expansionary monetary or fiscal policy. That is, labor establishes and adamantly maintains a fixed money wage without regard to changes in the price level and, thus, in its real wage. The issue of whether labor is acting irrationally by not accepting money wage cuts even as unemployment is increasing will be discussed at some length after we have used our complete model to analyze a few more of the disturbances which the economy faces from time to time.

The Impact of Changes in Labor Supply

Suppose full employment equilibrium is disturbed by an increase in the supply of labor. For our model's purpose, an increase in labor supply could result from immigration, the maturation of a bumper crop of postwar babies, or a flooding of the labor market by ex-G.I.s returning from a foreign military engagement. Can the increased supply of labor be employed (without displacing already employed workers) or must chronic unemployment result as it would if there were only a fixed number of jobs available in our economic system? Indeed, particularly in debates over immigration laws, this question has a long and prominent history. Through the 1800s and into the present century strict limits on immigration have been favored by countless organizations, including the American Federation of Labor, the American Legion, and the National Grange. A common concern, voiced most insistently by organized labor, has been that "The immigrant, with his low rate of wages, drives out of his trade men formerly employed therein. . . ." [4]

Our aggregate model can shed some light on this issue. Beginning with our model representing an economic system in full employment equilibrium, an increase in labor supply would shift the labor supply curve rightward (say, from N_f^s to N_1^s in Figure 9-20), creating involuntary unemployment (an excess supply of labor) at the original real wage $(\overline{W}/P)_f$. As long as money wages cannot fall, and in the short-run analysis we have confined ourselves to that situation, there will be no mechanism within the economic system we have modeled to eliminate the new excess supply of labor (unemployment). The system is again in a position of persistent unemployment *precisely of the type we have just finished analyzing.* Moreover, while we might at this juncture recognize that ultimately, after some protracted time period, a sizable excess supply of labor would tend to depress money wages in a manner that could allow the increase in the labor force to be gradually absorbed, our earlier analysis has shown that the government has the tools necessary for moving the economy to full employment (now employment level N_f' and output level Y_f' in Figure 9-20) without an extended delay. Either expansionary monetary or fiscal policy can be used to raise aggregate demand to the level (Y_f') that allows the increased supply of labor to be absorbed. There is no fixed volume of remunerative work to be done in any economy and, with appropriate monetary and fiscal policys implemented, no country need accept a condition of massive unemployment.

Macroeconomic Effects of an Oil Embargo

Late in 1973, the oil producers (primarily Middle Eastern) that have provided the bulk of a growing volume of U.S. oil imports in recent years shut down the

---

4 John Mitchell, *Organized Labor: Its Problems, Purposes and Ideals* (Philadelphia, Penn.: American Book and Bible House, 1903). Mr. Mitchell was president of the United Mine Workers of America. The notion that there is "only so much work to be done" has also been responsible for organized labors' efforts to prevent the employment of women and children and for the widespread fear that adoption of machine production techniques would *displace* labor. A fascinating discussion of these venerable "working-man's" explanations of unemployment can be found in W. B. Catlin, *The Labor Problem* (New York: Harper & Row, 1926), Chapter III.

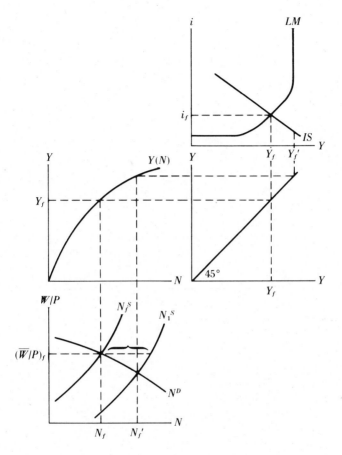

FIGURE 9-20   The Impact on General Equilibrium of an Increase in the Supply of Labor

supply lines. Given the importance of oil as a basic productive input in the industrialized U.S. economy, the resulting reduction in the overall flow of available oil could have been expected to significantly impair the U.S. economy's performance. And indeed, through 1974 symptoms of illness were easy to find. Quarter after quarter the economy's vital signs showed deterioration as real output fell, real wages and labor's productivity fell, unemployment swelled (exceeding 7 percent by the end of 1974), prices increased (actually rose at a quickened rate), and market interest rates soared to record levels. As this chapter's last detailed application of the aggregate model we will use that model to see what events we could have expected to stem from the oil embargo.

Figure 9-21 shows the economy in full employment equilibrium (f subscripts) prior to the oil embargo. With the embargo, the economy was confronted

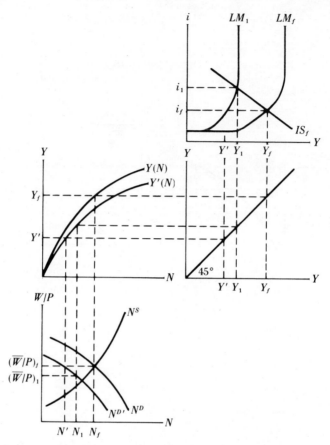

FIGURE 9-21   The Impact of an Oil Embargo

with "... supply restraints, [with] shortages and bottlenecks. ..."[5] To use our model to predict the impact on the economy of the oil shortage we must recall that the production function drawn in Figure 9-21 represents the relationship between employment of labor and real output *given* the quantity and quality of other factor inputs used in the production process. If labor has a smaller volume of any other important factor input to work with (and oil would appear to be important) labor will produce less. In Figure 9-21 the aggregate production function is rotated clockwise and the labor demand schedule (the marginal product of labor which is just the slope of the production function) is shifted downward to reflect the reduction in labor's productivity.

With the fall in labor demand, business firms would willingly employ only

---

5   Walter Heller, "The Case for Fiscal Stimulus," *Wall Street Journal,* March 11, 1974. Dr. Heller was chairman of the Council of Economic Advisors under Presidents Kennedy and Johnson.

the amount of labor N' at the original real wage $(\overline{W}/P)_f$. With employment at N', the equilibrium level of output would be at level Y' on the *new* production function while the equilibrium level of demand would remain at level Y_f. As always, the resulting excess demand for real goods and services must raise the price level. As prices rise, the real supply of money is reduced (shifting the *LM* curve leftward), raising the interest rate and, by depressing planned investment spending, lowering total demand. At the same time, the rising price level would be decreasing the real wage, increasing employment along the new labor demand curve $(N^{D'})$ and, hence, increasing output. When shrinking demand and growing supply are equated, as at output level Y_1, the economy would be back in equilibrium. Our model has predicted an adjustment to a lower level of real output (with consumption and saving reduced accordingly), a higher interest rate (hence reduced investment), a reduced level of employment (increased unemployment), and a lower real wage to accompany the reduction in labor's productivity. Moreover, during the adjustment, prices were rising in our model, indicating that the oil embargo would have temporarily accelerated any ongoing inflation. This last conclusion is worth emphasizing for it demonstrates that with no expansion in aggregate demand (no shift in the *IS* or *LM* schedule) a rise in the general price level can result from a change in the *supply* of real goods and services, a point that will receive detailed attention in the discussion on inflation in Chapter 12.

A Summary of Predicted Responses to Macroeconomic Disturbances

Our complete aggregate model has been used to analyze only a small number of specific shocks to the economy. A list of some additional autonomous disturbances of equilibrium in the Keynesian model and the impact of those disturbances on several important variables appears in Table 9-1. For each of the listed disturbances, it is assumed that the system starts with some unemployment

TABLE 9-1 SOURCE OF DISTURBANCE OF EQUILIBRIUM AND IMPACT IN A KEYNESIAN INCOME DETERMINATION MODEL WITH DOWNWARD INFLEXIBLE MONEY WAGES AND UNEMPLOYMENT

Source of disturbance	Impact on: (− means decrease, + increase, 0 no change, ? uncertain)								
An autonomous:	i	I	C	S	Y	N	W/P	P	V^*
Increase in government spending	+	−	+	+	+	+	−	+	+
Decrease in taxes	+	−	+	+	+	+	−	+	+
Increase in consumption	+	−	+	−	+	+	−	+	+
Increase in investment	+	+	+	+	+	+	−	+	+
Increase in money supply	−	+	+	+	+	+	−	+	?
Increase in money demand	+	−	−	−	−	−	+	−	−
Increase in labor supply	0	0	0	0	0	0	0	0	0
Increase in labor productivity	−	+	+	+	+	?	+	−	?

* V is velocity of circulation of money.

and that money wages are inflexible in the downward direction. The student should practice deducing these results with the model we have developed.[6]

Generalizing the Investment Function

We have seen that an increase in aggregate demand which stems from the real side of the economic system (from a rightward shift of the *IS* curve) generally raises the interest rate as income expansion increases money demand. As indicated in Table 9-1, when the increase in aggregate demand stems from an autonomous upward shift of the investment schedule, after the economy has adjusted to its new equilibrium both investment and the interest rate are increased. Symmetrically, an autonomous contraction in planned investment spending results in a reduction of the interest rate and investment when equilibrium is restored. Since planned investment is the one most volatile component of aggregate demand, we should not be surprised to find investment and the interest rate frequently moving in the same direction as a consequence of shifts in the investment function (even though, *ceteris paribus*, investment is an inverse function of the interest rate). However, shifts in other components of aggregate demand do occur. And, our model indicates that with an increase in any other component of aggregate demand the resulting interest rate increase reduces investment below its original level in the face of a strong expansion of business activity in general. By the same token, our model indicates that a contraction in any *noninvestment* component of aggregate demand generates an increase in the level of investment as the interest rate falls, even though existing capital is idled by production cutbacks. These conclusions frequently bother students whose intuition and experience (supported by the arguments of Chapter 6) suggest a strong positive causal link between business activity and investment. It should bother them! Indeed, a casual look at data on investment and general business activity suggests a positive link between the two so strong that even a highly volatile investment function is hard pressed to provide a full explanation of that association. Our aggregate model has predicted a behavior pattern that may be inconsistent with historical experience because of the overly simplistic treatment of the determinants of investment in that model. A model's predictions can only reflect the assumptions built into that model!

Falling back on the analysis of Chapter 6, it was concluded that the best aggregate net investment function for short-run analysis (capital stock constant) was $I_{net} = I(Y, i)$ with investment positively related to the level of output and inversely related to the interest rate. However, for purposes of constructing our aggregate model as easily as possible, the simpler behavioral function $I_{net} = I(i)$ was employed in Chapter 8 and, up to now, in this chapter. If that simple invest-

---

6 The last shock, the increase in labor productivity, can be assumed to shift the labor demand schedule rightward and raise the production function. The conclusions in the table are, again, deduced for an economy operating in the intermediate region of the *LM* curve.

ment function is replaced by the alternative which our analysis of investment concluded was more reasonable, the aggregate model generates conclusions on the behavior of investment that are more agreeable.

Since the investment function plays a crucial role in determining the interest rate and output values that permit commodity market equilibrium, we need to explore the implications of introducing the more general investment function into our model of the commodity market. Commodity market equilibrium still requires equality of output and total planned spending. That is, for equilibrium $Y = C(Y) + I(i, Y) + G$. Once again, the commodity market equilibrium condition is a single equation in the two unknowns Y and i.

As before, suppose we know one interest rate and output combination (say, i_0, Y_0 in Figure 9-22) that satisfies the equilibrium condition above. Now let the interest rate fall from i_0 to i_1. As before, a fall in the interest rate stimulates investment spending, creating excess demand in the commodity market that can be offset only by an increase in output. Unlike before, as output rises investment is further stimulated, producing an additional expansion of aggregate demand. As long as the growth in output exceeds the induced growth in planned spending,[7] there is some income increase that will restore commodity market equilibrium. The required increase is larger (say, to Y_1' rather than Y_1) than would be required if investment were not positively related to income. Thus, the *IS* curve is more *interest-elastic* if investment is a positive function of the output level.

As before, the *IS* curve will shift in response to autonomous changes in spending and tax collections.[8] Further, there have been no changes in the money

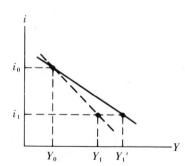

FIGURE 9-22   The *IS* Curve with Investment a Function of Income

---

7   That is, as long as the *marginal propensity to spend* $= \Delta C/\Delta Y + \Delta I/\Delta Y$ is less than unity.

8   The size of the horizontally measured shift in the *IS* curve will now be

$$\Delta Y|_i = \frac{1}{1 - \text{MPC} - \text{MPI}} \cdot \Delta a$$

where MPI is the marginal propensity to invest and Δa is the autonomous change in spending. The presence of the MPI in the denominator of the expression above raises the value of ΔY— an autonomous increase in spending requires a larger rise in income to generate the leakages necessary to offset a volume of injections that grows as income grows.

supply or demand functions nor in the labor market relationships incorporated in the aggregate model—thus, the rest of the aggregate model is unaffected by employing the more general investment function.

Beginning with some unemployment, there are, as before, monetary and fiscal policy actions that will restore full employment equilibrium. Suppose we once again trace the adjustment process through which an expansionary fiscal policy restores equilibrium. Draw your own graph to track the adjustment using Figure 9-17 as a pattern. If your model's appearance differs from before, it should only be in the slope of the *IS* curve that the change appears.

Implementation of an expansionary fiscal policy creates excess demand in the commodity market, raising the price level. As before, the rising price level reduces the real wage, stimulating employment and the quantity of output supplied. At the same time, the price rise reduces the real money stock, shifting the *LM* curve leftward. With the "correct" original shift in the *IS* curve (the right amount of fiscal stimulus), equilibrium will be restored at full employment. As a result of the expansionary policy, income, employment, the interest rate, and the price level will have increased, just as before. The real wage will have fallen and both consumption and saving will have risen with income. There are influences on the level of investment that act against each other—the interest rate increase tends to reduce investment while the increase in output stimulates investment. However, observation suggests that the response of investment to the income expansion must outweigh its response to the interest rate rise. Thus, we would expect investment to increase. You are invited to go through the disturbances listed in Table 9-1 to see how our predictions are changed by using the model with the more general investment function.[9] In addition, as a prelude to the discussion of inflation in Chapter 12, see if you can work out the implications of an increase in aggregate demand beginning with full employment equilibrium.

MORE ON WAGE RIGIDITY, UNEMPLOYMENT, AND FULL EMPLOYMENT

In developing the Keynesian income determination model in this chapter, we have followed tradition by assuming that money wages are not free to fall even in the face of substantial unemployment. In our model, a contraction in aggregate demand permitted prices to fall, raising the real wage so that employers cut back on employment and output. Even though labor's *real* wage would not be reduced if money wages were permitted to fall in step with prices, labor steadfastly maintained its money wage as though suffering from an irrational "money illusion." Labor appeared willing to accept reductions in employment rather than permit its money wage to fall.

---

9 If anything except the signs of the first three rows of column 2 are changed, you should try again.

This Keynesian treatment of wages has frequently been criticized. We know that in prolonged periods of depressed economic activity (like the Great Depression) money wages have fallen, albeit slowly. Thus, the assumption of downwardly rigid money wages can only be taken as a first approximation of short-run wage behavior. Moreover, even if unemployment does not result in any substantial fall in money wages over short time intervals, recognition of the existence of wage rigidity does not explain that rigidity. Neither do the traditional appeals to union wage contracts, minimum wage laws, and the like provide a satisfactory explanation of wage rigidity, for wages have never declined by much during recessions, even those that occurred prior to the 1930s when only a small part of the labor force was unionized and minimum wage laws were nonexistent.[10] (Even now, less than 25 percent of the U.S. labor force is unionized and relatively few workers are employed at the legal minimum wage.)

Further, whatever is responsible for labor's refusal or inability to accept a wage cut to stimulate employment, it is not obvious that labor is behaving irrationally. As we will show below, it is often rational for labor *not* to react to short-run changes in job opportunities by altering its wage requirements—at least not if those changes are expected to be temporary.

Because of the shortcomings in the traditional Keynesian treatment of wages, economists have recently developed a new theory of wage behavior that implies money wage rigidity as a natural consequence of optimizing behavior.[11] Offering a plausible explanation for the *ad hoc* Keynesian assumption of downward inflexible money wages, it appears probable that some form of this new theory will displace the traditional Keynesian treatment of wages.

The Fragmented Labor Market

In the Keynesian treatment of the labor market presented in this chapter, homogeneous labor was offered for hire in a centralized market where supply and demand were matched with little friction. However, as briefly argued back in Chapter 1 and, again, upon introduction of the labor market in this chapter, the labor market is actually quite fragmented. In fact, it is sensible to think of the labor market as segmented into many submarkets for labor distinguished by geographical location, industry group, skill requirements, and so on. Analogously, labor itself exhibits substantial heterogeneity in skills, geographic preference, and so on. Consequently, there is no single, easily observed wage rate received by all workers but rather a myriad of different wage rates paid on different jobs. If we wish to talk about *the* wage rate, as we have in the past, we must now

10 Clarence Long, "The Illusion of Wage Rigidity: Long and Short Cycles in Wage and Labor Costs," *Review of Economics and Statistics*, Vol. XLII, May 1960, pp. 140-151.

11 A. A. Alchian, "Information Costs, Pricing, and Resource Employment," *Western Economic Journal*, Vol. VII, June 1969, pp. 109-28.

recognize that rate to be a weighted average of the many different wage rates actually received in the aggregate labor market.

In this new theory of labor market behavior, labor is assumed to act rationally on the basis of available information—to pay attention to the *perceived* real value of wages when determining how much labor to supply to employers. As the perceived real wage rises, the quantity of labor supplied is expected to increase as employed workers accept more overtime work and begin to moonlight, and as secondary workers (primarily housewives and students) are enticed into the labor force.

As before, given the stock of capital and the production function (thus, the marginal product of labor), the quantity of labor employers demand is inversely related to the real wage. Except for the labeling of the vertical axis, our labor market model, which is presented graphically in Figure 9-23, looks like the model we have used all along. But, by taking account of the rich variety of job opportunities available in a large economy, we have immeasurably complicated labor's job search task.

Imperfect Information and the Natural Rate of Unemployment

As we have previously argued, a worker cannot know with certainty what job openings (wage offers) are available to him. He can obtain information on job opportunities only by *searching* in the labor market—by sampling job opportunities. In point of fact, the essential difference between the new search theory of the labor market and the traditional treatment of that market which we have relied on up to now is the lack of freely available, perfect information.

The actual job search process includes reading help wanted ads, interviewing prospective employers, and so on. Frequently, to search the job market optimally, an employed worker must quit the job he has. Clearly, the job search process is costly, the bulk of the cost of search for an unemployed worker being the wage (opportunity) cost of the most attractive job opportunity he has been offered but has not accepted. The longer a worker searches, presumably the

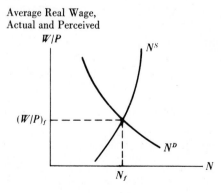

FIGURE 9-23 The Aggregate Labor Market

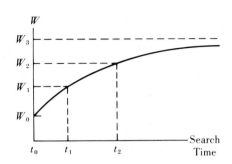

FIGURE 9-24 Search Time and Wage Offers

better the job offer he can find. Still, the expected increase in wage offers from extending the search period must shrink as the search period is incrementally lengthened. Figure 9-24 graphs the presumed relationship between search time and the maximum money wage offer a job seeker might *expect* to receive.

According to Figure 9-24, by accepting wage offer W_0, a job seeker could obtain employment with virtually no time spent in search. However, if the wage offer he is willing to accept (his *reservation* wage) is above W_0, he will have to spend some time searching the labor market. By searching for time period t_1, he can obtain a highest wage offer of W_1. By searching for the additional time period $(t_2 - t_1)$, he may obtain a best wage offer of W_2. An optimizing individual will continue sampling job opportunities until the *expected* return (the present value of the expected wage increase) from additional search time just covers the cost of that extra search time.

While individuals search the job market, they are *voluntarily* unemployed. Still, they are counted in U.S. unemployment statistics and, in some cases, the duration of unemployment may be quite lengthy. For example, an individual with some (possibly incorrect) notion of the distribution of job offers available in the labor market might enter that market with a reservation wage equal to W_3 in Figure 9-24. However, if the schedule in that diagram represents the opportunities available to him, he would never be employed at that reservation wage. As he searches, he gradually comes to realize that wage W_3 exceeds what he can *expect* to receive. In response, the rational individual will reduce his reservation wage. Still, if expectations are "slow" to change, he will expend substantial search time (during which he is counted as unemployed) before he accepts a job offer at a reduced reservation wage.

The unemployment explained by the theory briefly reviewed here is what we called *frictional* or *search unemployment* in Chapter 1. If, looking at Figure 9-24 once again, we can think of some job seekers whose reservation wages (like W_3) always exceed the wage offers available to them, we can explain the "hard-core" or "structural" component of unemployment mentioned in that introductory chapter too. For individuals with skills that have little market value, the effective reservation wage at which firms can hire those workers may be held above the value of their marginal product by minimum wage laws, welfare programs, the higher rewards from criminal activity, and so on. Such individuals are apt to remain chronically unemployed.

Because of frictional and structural unemployment, we know that the labor supply-demand intersection in Figure 9-23 does not represent a zero-percent-unemployment equilibrium in the labor market. Rather, for the U.S. economy a 4-5 percent unemployment rate is usually thought to be consistent with full-employment labor market equilibrium. This *natural rate* of unemployment is believed to be consistent with the absence of any upward or downward pressure on money wages and, with commodity market equilibrium providing a stable price level, with an absence of pressures tending to change the real wage.

Unemployment and Aggregate Wage Rigidity

Beginning with full employment equilibrium, let us suppose that aggregate demand for goods and services declines. With excess supply in the commodity market there will be downward pressure on output prices. Employers would be willing to continue using the same quantity of labor only at money wage rates that are reduced in step with prices (keeping real wages constant). Workers, however, may rationally refuse to accept money wage cuts given the information about market conditions available to them from past, and now obsolete, experience. An individual worker knows with certainty only that the money wage his employer is willing to pay him has declined. He may think he would be better off leaving his current job and searching for alternative employment that offers a wage above his reservation wage rather than accepting the money wage cut. However, since the reduction in aggregate demand has induced other firms to cut back on their wage offers, he (and the other workers who behave like him) may spend a considerable time period unemployed, searching for a job offer that meets his reservation wage. Thus, the reduction in aggregate demand would initially result in reduced employment (increased *search* unemployment) with little or no reduction in money wages, just as the Keynesian model in this chapter indicated.

Eventually, the workers who chose unemployment instead of money wage cuts would revise their expectations (and reservation wages) as their search efforts provide more accurate information on what has happened to the demand for labor. Hence, money wages would fall and unemployment might be reduced to its original level with the real wage restored to its original level. However, such an adjustment must be painfully slow,[12] justifying the use of expansionary monetary and/or fiscal policy to pursue the full employment goal.

---

12 Recent research suggests that wage demands of unemployed workers fall very slowly, perhaps at a .27-percent monthly rate. See Charles Holt, "Job Search, Phillips Wage Relation and Union Influence: Theory and Evidence," in Phelps *et al.*, *Microeconomic Foundations of Employment and Inflation Theory* (New York: Norton, 1970), pp. 96-101.

The notion of *information* costs can also be applied to the commodity market, resulting in "sticky" prices in that market. Some interesting implications follow from such an integration of search theory into the *IS-LM* model as the appendix to this chapter reveals.

SUMMARY

In this chapter, a fairly sophisticated income determination model has been developed—a model that accommodates the money, commodity, and labor markets. With that model we were able to evaluate the impact of a number of disturbances on an extensive list of important macroeconomic variables including output, the interest rate, the level of employment, and the price level. That model also allowed the prescription of fiscal and monetary policy cures for the economic ills (such as excessive unemployment) that might plague the economy the model represents.

The model we developed is clearly a Keynesian model. While it is a tribute to Keynes that modern macroeconomic analysis still relies so heavily on the ideas that he offered economists in 1936, we did find shortcomings in the *modern* Keynesian treatment of the labor market that justified a brief review of the new job search theory of labor market behavior. This new theory rationalizes the existence of substantial (though not complete) downward rigidity of money wages without implying that labor behaves irrationally. As our analysis proceeds to deal with inflation in Chapter 12, we will again make use of both the Keynesian analytical framework developed in this chapter and the job search theory of the labor market.

QUESTIONS

1. Table 9-1 summarizes the impact on the key variables in the Keynesian model of a number of disturbances. Repeat the exercises performed in Table 9-1:
   (a) with the economy assumed to be operating in the liquidity trap,
   (b) with the economy assumed to be operating in the special classical region of the *LM* curve.
2. Discuss the comparative effectiveness of monetary and fiscal policy in the special Keynesian, special classical, and intermediate regions of the *LM* schedule.
3. The depletion of a major source of the nation's flow of energy reserves might be expected to reduce the volume of output produced at any given employment level.
   (a) Without referring to the text, see if you can use the Keynesian model to predict the impact of such a "one-shot" reduction in the flow of energy inputs.
   (b) How would predictions differ if monetary and fiscal policy were used to prevent a price increase?
   (c) How would predictions differ if monetary and fiscal policy were used to try to maintain the initial level of employment?
   (d) Can fiscal and monetary policy be used to maintain society's living standard?

4. What suggestions can you offer for improving the functioning of the labor market so that the full-employment unemployment rate might be reduced?

5. Unemployment compensation may serve to increase measured unemployment. Explain that contention and evaluate the desirability of unemployment compensation.

6. With adoption of the job search theory for explaining wage stickiness, we must replace the concept of a deterministic level of full employment with a full-employment *zone* which, in the short run, can permit different levels of measured employment and unemployment. Explain.

SUGGESTED READING

Ackley, Gardner. *Macroeconomic Theory*. New York: The Macmillan Co., 1961, Chapter XIV.

Alchian, Armen A. "Information Costs, Pricing, and Resource Unemployment," *Western Economic Journal*. Vol. VII, June 1969, pp. 109-128.

Clower, Robert W. "The Keynesian Counter-revolution: A Theoretical Appraisal," in F. H. Hahn and F. P. R. Brechling (eds.). *The Theory of Interest Rates*. International Economic Association Series: Macmillan, Chapter 5. Reprinted in R. W. Clower (ed.). *Monetary Theory: Selected Readings*. Middlesex, England: Penguin Books, 1969, pp. 270-297.

Keynes, J. M. *The General Theory of Employment, Interest and Money*, New York: Harcourt Brace Jovanovich, Inc., 1936, Chapters 18 and 20.

Leijonhufvud, Axel. *On Keynesian Economics and the Economics of Keynes*. Oxford: Oxford University Press, 1968, Chapter 5, Section 3.

Phelps, Edmund, *et al. Microeconomic Foundations of Employment and Inflation Theory*. New York: W. W. Norton, 1970, Introduction and Part 1.

Smith, Warren L. "A Graphical Exposition of the Complete Keynesian System," *Southern Economic Journal*. Vol. XXIII, October 1956, pp. 115-125.

Appendix to Chapter 9
Macroeconomic
Disequilibrium Analysis[1]

In Chapter 9 we explained wage inflexibility in the labor market as a logical consequence of imperfect information. In a similar fashion, in any market where information is costly, available only through a time-consuming *search* process, rational decision making by the transactors in that market will result in price inflexibility. In this brief appendix, imperfect information is formally introduced into a second market in the macroeconomic model, the commodity market, so that *sticky* commodity prices coexist with sticky money wages. As before, no stickiness in interest rate adjustments is assumed since information costs are thought to be relatively inconsequential in the money (bond) market. Distinctively, the securities market is a virtual auction market where changes in supply or demand are reflected in newspaper financial columns within a day as changes in security prices (hence, interest yields).

Using our familiar graphical apparatus, Figure 9A-1 shows the economy initially at rest with full employment in the labor market (initial equilibrium values of variables indicated by f subscripts). Now, as we have before, suppose there is an autonomous reduction in planned investment spending as businessmen's expectations of future profits become more pessimistic. With the reduction in planned investment, real aggregate demand falls to a level like Y' with the *IS* curve shifted to position *IS'*. As in our previous analysis, with the real wage unchanged at $(W/P)_f$, immediately after the decline in aggregate demand the volume of output produced is unchanged and would exceed demand by $Y_f - Y'$. In contrast to our earlier analysis, we now must take heed of the role of information costs in the commodity market as each firm sees its sales reduced.

Individual firms, while they may quickly recognize that their sales have fallen, cannot immediately know that there has been a "permanent" decline in the demand schedules they face. Since price changes are costly, rather than immediately cutting prices in response to a sales decline that may be temporary, firms may rationally choose to hold the line on prices while cutting back production through labor layoffs. Thus, increased unemployment is the natural consequence of a fall in demand for commodities, and, with money wages inflexible downward because of imperfect information in the labor market, the rise in unemployment does not immediately result in a decline in money wage rates. Collectively, busi-

1 See Pon Patinkin, *Money, Interest, and Prices*, 2d ed. (New York: Harper & Row, 1965), Chapter 13; Robert W. Clower, "The Keynesian Counterrevolution: A Theoretical Appraisal" in *The Theory of Interest Rates*, H. Hahn and F. P. R. Breckling (eds.) (London: Macmillan and Co., Ltd, 1965), pp. 103-25; Axel Leijonhufvud, *On Keynesian Economics and the Economics of Keynes* (Oxford: Oxford University Press, 1968).

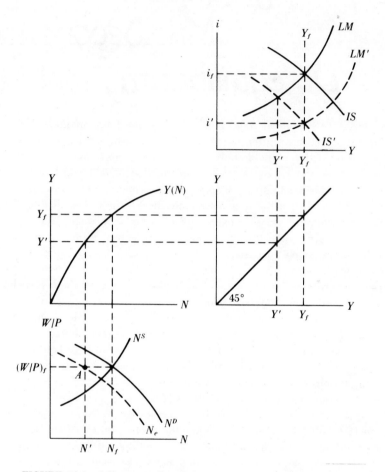

FIGURE 9A-1   A Keynesian Contraction in a General Disequilibrium Model

ness firms might rationally cut output to equality with the reduced level of aggregate demand (Y'). That is true even though, with real wages unchanged at level $(W/P)_f$, the *comparative static* analysis we employed to construct our labor market indicates that the optimal (profit-maximizing) level of output for all firms collectively is still Y_f with employment level N_f. Labor is off of both the labor supply and labor demand schedules plotted in Figure 9A-1.

The labor demand schedule plotted in Figure 9A-1, derived explicitly to show the *static equilibrium* relationship between the real wage and the quantity of labor demanded, assumes that the commodity market is in equilibrium—that the general price level is appropriate to allow the volume of output which profit-maximizing firms choose to produce at the current money wage level to be purchased. But in fact, the commodity market is not in equilibrium (even though planned saving and investment are equal so that the economy is on the *IS* curve).

With commodity prices sticky downward, a reduced level of aggregate demand results in the *involuntary underproduction* of commodities. And, since firms can produce the reduced volume of output with less labor, the *effective* demand for labor schedule must pass through point A in Figure 9A-1. The usual labor demand schedule (N^D), which is valid when the commodity market is in equilibrium, is what Clower calls the *notional* demand for labor schedule to distinguish it from the schedule which is *effective* when the commodity market is in *disequilibrium*. Analogously, the *effective* supply of output (Y') may be distinguished from the *notional* supply (Y_f) which business firms would like to provide at real wage ($W/P)_f$.

As long as money wages and prices stay at their original levels, involuntary unemployment will persist and business firms will have excess capacity. But unemployed workers will be searching the labor market for jobs and business firms will be seeking information on the permanence of the decline in the demand schedules they face. While information is costly, the search process will gradually reveal the generalized and permanent nature of the decline in demand for commodities and, hence, labor. In response, unemployed labor will reduce its reservation wage and firms with excess capacity will lower their product prices. Purely for simplicity, we might assume that money wages and prices decline in step with the real wage staying at level ($W/P)_f$. In the meantime, as prices fall the real value of the money stock increases, driving down the interest rate (shifting the LM curve in Figure 9A-1 rightward). The declining interest rate stimulates investment which, through the multiplier, raises aggregate demand. With the real demand for output growing, the *effective* demand for labor is shifting rightward toward the notional labor demand schedule (N^D). Ultimately, full employment equilibrium will be restored with *notional* and *effective* schedules identical, but only when money wages and prices have declined by an amount sufficient to shift the LM schedule to position LM', providing the new equilibrium interest rate i'.

In the analysis just presented it must be granted that full employment equilibrium is restored, finally, by forces within the economy. But the adjustment period required for the *automatic* restoration of equilibrium, during which firms suffer from excess capacity and labor from involuntary unemployment, is quite extended, as Keynesian analysis indicates. And, as we know, Keynesian analysis concludes that we do not have to wait for automatic forces to lead the economy back to the desired state of full employment equilibrium. For example, the leftward shift of the IS curve (due to reduced investment) which initiated the contraction we just analyzed could be offset by an expansionary fiscal policy that returns the IS schedule to its original position. Alternatively, instead of waiting for a price decline to increase the real money stock (shifting the LM curve to LM'), the central bank could quickly increase the nominal money supply. Logically, it should be apparent that the exercise just completed could easily be repeated for a contraction that stems from a money supply reduction, a tax increase, a cut in government spending, and so on.

One final point remains that we should note. In the comparative static analysis in Chapter 9, labor stayed on its demand curve through contractions and expansions. Hence, in a contraction real wages increased while in an expansion they declined. This pattern of real wage changes is inconsistent with empirical observations on real wage changes over the business cycle and that fact has been responsible for some harsh criticism of Keynesian analysis.[2] But with imperfect information incorporated in the treatment of both the labor and the commodity markets, the inconsistency with observation is eliminated. As shown above, a contraction in output and employment may occur with no increase in the real wage, and a subsequent expansion of output and employment may take place with no decline in the real wage required.[3]

2 For evidence on the relationship between movements in employment and in real wages see L. Tarshis, "Changes in Real and Money Wages," *Economic Journal*, Vol. 49, 1939, pp. 150-154; and J. T. Dunlop, "The Movement of Real and Money Wage Rates," *Economic Journal*, Vol. 48, 1938, pp. 413-434. A response to his critics on this issue appears in J. M. Keynes, "Relative Movements in Real Wages and Output," *Economic Journal*, Vol. 48, 1939, pp. 34-51.

3 See Robert J. Barro and Herschel I. Grossman, "A General Disequilibrium Model of Income and Employment," *The American Economic Review*, Vol. 61, March 1971, pp. 82-93.

Chapter 10
Great Debates

Like all major revisions in accepted theory, the Keynesian *revolution* in macro-economic analysis has involved numerous engagements on the battlefield of academic debate. The battle lines for debate between Keynes and his antagonists were first clearly drawn with publication of the *General Theory* as in that book Keynes launched a frontal attack on what he took to be the macroeconomic model of his predecessors, the *classical* economics. Of course, the classical economists did not accept Keynes' representation and criticism of their analysis without reply. Indeed, debate between the supporters of Keynesian analysis and *its* critics, which began in the 1930s, continues even today.

This chapter looks at a sample of the major macroeconomic issues that have occupied economists since publication of the *General Theory*. In studying the conflicting explanations of macroeconomic behavior aired in this chapter, the student should be mindful that through the confrontation of *alternative theories* economic analysis is refined to yield a better understanding of real-world economic problems.

A CLASSICAL INCOME DETERMINATION MODEL

With very little difficulty, we can alter the analytical framework constructed in Chapter 9 to provide a model that generates classical conclusions. Then we will be able to point out clearly the disagreements between Keynesian and classical analysis.[1] To build our *classical model*, we will assume that labor is concerned only with its real wage and that money wages and prices are flexible in both the upward and downward direction. Also, we will initially assume that the economy is operating in the *intermediate* portion of the *LM* curve. None of the other behavioral relationships employed in Chapter 9 will be altered. Thus, our classical model would appear in the familiar graphical format shown in Figure 10-1. While the money and commodity markets are initially in equilibrium with $i = i_1$ and $Y = Y_1$ in Figure 10-1, we have shown the labor market in disequilibrium— that is, there is substantial involuntary unemployment (excess supply of labor) at real wage $(W/P)_1$. Can this unemployment persist?

Equilibrium with Flexible Money Wages and Prices

In the Keynesian analysis of the last chapter, the excess supply of labor at real wage $(W/P)_1$ in Figure 10-1 would have no effect on the money wage in the

---

1 For a market-by-market comparison of the Keynesian and classical models, see the appendix to this chapter.

273

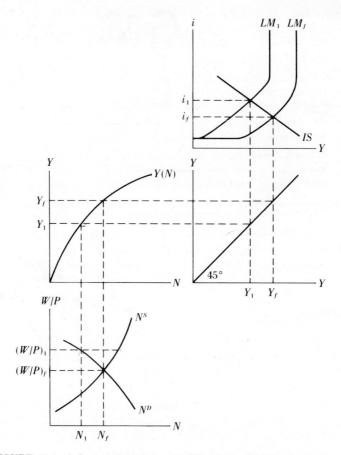

FIGURE 10-1   A General Equilibrium Model with Flexible Wages and Prices

short run and there would be no automatic system-wide adjustment that tended to reduce unemployment. However, if money wages are free to fall and labor competes for jobs, excess supply in the labor market results in a fall in money wages. Any resulting tendency for real wages to fall increases employment and output. With no shift in aggregate demand though, not all of *any* increase in output would be bought since we have assumed the marginal propensity to spend to be less than one. Thus, *any increase* in output would lead to an unintended increase in inventories (excess supply in the commodity market) resulting in a fall in the flexible price level. If the aggregate commodity demand schedule should stay unchanged, prices would have to fall as much as money wages leaving real wages, employment, and real output unchanged because there is only one output level, the initial one, which will clear the commodity market. However, commodity demand will not stay unchanged. The falling price level increases the real supply of money (shifting the *LM* curve rightward) which lowers the market interest rate. As the market interest rate falls, investment is stimulated, raising aggregate demand for commodities and, thus, preventing prices from falling as much as money wages. With money wages reduced by a larger proportion than prices, the real wage is reduced, allowing employment and output to grow. Wages will continue to fall (prompting a lesser fall in output prices and a rightward shift of the *LM* curve) as long as there is excess supply in the labor market. Eventually, full-employment equilibrium will be established as indicated by the *f* subscripts in Figure 10-1.

In this *classical* model, unemployment is *automatically* eliminated by forces within the economic system. We must adopt a Keynesian assumption like the premise of downwardly rigid money wages for persistent unemployment to plague our modeled economy—a possibility that the classicals themselves recognized!

The Role of Money with Flexible Money Wages and Prices

The foregoing analysis suggests that, with money wages and prices free to fall when there is unemployment, full employment is automatically maintained. In this case, unemployment appears to be a temporary, transitional phenomenon. Over the past few decades, considerable effort has been expended in assessing the role of money in such an economy. The primary concern has been determining whether the classical economists were correct in arguing that money was *neutral* —that a change in the nominal money stock would change only nominal values (the price level thus the *dollar value* of consumption, investment, income, and so on) leaving real quantities unchanged (real output, consumption and investment, employment, the real interest rate, and the real wage). This issue can be readily dealt with by altering the nominal money supply in our classical model and tracing the impact on the equilibrium values of the array of variables determined in that model.

Undertaking that project, a doubling of the money supply shifts the *LM* schedule in our model rightward (to LM_1 as shown in Figure 10-2). With no other immediate changes there would be excess demand in the commodity market (the increased money supply drives the market interest rate downward, stimulating investment and raising aggregate demand to Y_1) prompting a rise in the price level. A rise in the price level would tend to reduce the real wage. However, any fall in the real wage, no matter how small, creates excess demand in the labor market driving money wages upward. Thus, with flexible money wages, the rise in the price level cannot significantly reduce real wages and, consequently, cannot alter the level of employment and output.

The rising price level, by reducing the real value of the money supply, will shift the *LM* curve leftward, gradually reducing excess demand in the commodity market. As long as there remains excess demand in the commodity market, prices

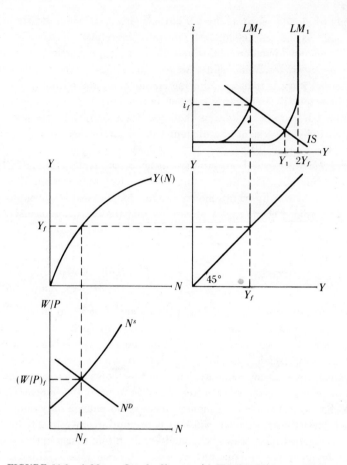

FIGURE 10-2   A Money Supply Change with Flexible Wages and Prices

(and money wages) will be rising, shifting the *LM* curve leftward. Hence, excess demand will exist until the *LM* curve has shifted back to its original position, restoring commodity market equilibrium (thus ending the price movement) at the original real income and interest rate levels. What price change is necessary? With real income and the interest rate returned to their original values, demand for real money balances would be at the original level requiring, for money market equilibrium, that the real money supply be at its original level. With the *nominal* money supply doubled, the price level must have doubled to restore real money balances to their initial level:

$$\left(\frac{\overline{M}}{P} = \frac{2\overline{M}}{2P} \right).$$

That is, the price level must have doubled to provide society with the real volume of money balances it demands at the full employment levels of income and the interest rate.

Full employment equilibrium then reigns again with real wages, employment, real income, the real money stock, and the interest rate at their original levels. With the price level doubled, *nominal* wages will have doubled as will have the *dollar* value of consumption, investment, and income. With money income increased by the same proportion that the money stock has risen, velocity will have returned to its original value. Indeed, money appears to be neutral. A doubling of the money supply in our model doubled prices (thus nominal values) and left real values unchanged. It is also worth noting that, with the *IS* schedule unaffected by our monetary policy action, there is only one interest rate (i_f) consistent with full employment output (Y_f). The equilibrium interest rate is then fixed by the determinants of the position of the *IS* curve—as the classicists would have said, the interest rate is a real variable, the value of which depends on the "productivity of capital" (our marginal efficiency of capital) and "thrift" (the propensity to save).

The Quantity Theory of Money

The limited role of money in our classical model can be adequately represented in what is known as the *quantity theory of money*. The framework for analysis in the quantity theory is a simple *identity* called the *equation of exchange*. The equation (identity) of exchange can be written as $MV \equiv PY$ where M is the nominal money supply, V is velocity, P is the price level, and Y is real output.

The product MV in the equation of exchange, the number of dollars in circulation times the average frequency with which dollars are used to finance final purchases, is just total spending on final goods and services. The product PY, the price level times the volume of real output, represents just total receipts from the sale of final goods and services. The identity says simply that total spending equals total receipts.

As we have shown, with the classical assumption of flexible wages and prices, full employment equilibrium is automatically maintained. Thus, the classicists took output as fixed at the full employment level when analyzing the impact of money supply changes. With one additional proposition, an explanation of the value of velocity, the classicists transformed the simple $MV \equiv PY$ identity into a theoretical explanation of the role of money. That proposition was that velocity, determined by *institutional* arrangements including the customary income payments period, the degree of integration of industry, and the extent of credit usage, could be treated as *constant* when assessing the impact of money supply changes since institutions change very slowly.

With V and Y fixed, the quantity theory of money tells us that any change in the stock of money must be accompanied by an equivalent proportional change in the price level. That is, $(\lambda M) \cdot \overline{V} = (\lambda P) \cdot \overline{Y}$ for any value of λ. Money affects only the price level and nominal values of income, consumption, and so on, leaving all real values unchanged. Such quantity theory conclusions clearly rest on the theory of velocity determination.[2]

It appears that we have provided strong support for the classical analysis. Moreover, we generated classical quantity theory conclusions on the role of money even though we employed the Keynesian money demand (velocity) theory that takes account of the interest cost of holding money.[3] Yet, Keynes argued that faith in the classical analysis was misplaced and sought to destroy that faith. The *special Keynes* liquidity trap was an important element in Keynes' critique of accepted doctrine.

Flexible Wages, the Liquidity Trap, and Unemployment Equilibrium

Granting the fundamental classical assumption of money wage and price flexibility, suppose our economy is characterized by unemployment in the labor market while the money and commodity markets are in equilibrium with the interest rate at the liquidity trap level. This situation is illustrated in Figure 10-3 with 1 subscripts denoting initial values.

With flexible wages and competition in the labor market, the excess supply of labor would result in a fall in money wages. However, unless aggregate demand for commodities changes, only real output level Y_1 can clear the market. Since Y_1 will be produced only at real wage $(W/P)_1$, a falling money wage rate, with no change in aggregate demand, must be accompanied by an equiproportional decline in the price level.

What would be happening in the commodity and money markets during this process? The declining price level results in an increasing real value of the money supply which shifts the LM curve rightward (to LM_2, LM_3, ...). Yet, commodity market equilibrium is unaffected! As long as the economy is in the liquidity trap there is no increase in the real money supply that can lower the interest rate and, thus, no increase in money supply that can increase demand in the commodity market. In just this manner, Keynes demonstrated the theoretical possibility of the economy being condemned to a continuing downward spiral of money wages and prices with no resulting reduction in unemployment.

---

2 The equation of exchange, $MV = PY$, can easily be rewritten as $M = 1/V \cdot PY$ or $M = kPY$ where $k = 1/V$ is the proportion of money income (PY) society wants to hold command over in money form. A theory of velocity, then, is a theory of money demand. If velocity is constant, then $k = 1/V$ is constant and an increase in money *supply* must be accompanied by an equal proportional increase in the price level if the extra money is to be willingly held (demanded) by society.

3 Like Keynes, the best of the classical economists recognized that an increase in the supply of money drives down the interest rate and reduces velocity. As we have shown though, in the classical model this effect is temporary. Once the system has fully adjusted to the increased money stock, velocity is unchanged (restored to its original level). Since the classicists were only concerned with equilibrium positions, they simply assumed velocity to be constant.

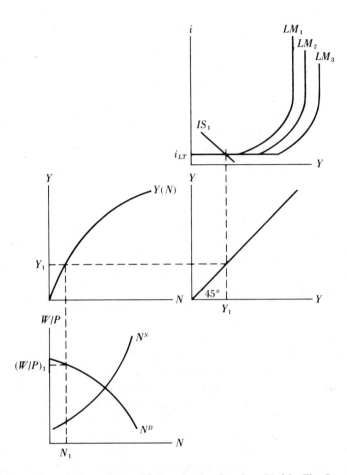

FIGURE 10-3   Unemployment Disequilibrium in the Complete Model—The Liquidity Trap Case

Just as an increase in real money supply due to a falling price level is power-less to relieve this unemployment, a real money supply increase through monetary policy action will be powerless. Again, the rightward shift of the *LM* curve would leave aggregate demand unaffected. It should be clear, however, that fiscal policy, which alters the position of the *IS* curve, can be effectively used even in the face of a liquidity trap. In fact, there would be no monetary dampener if the economy were confined to the liquidity trap region so that fiscal policy could increase in-come by the full value of the rightward shift of the *IS* curve.[4]

---

4   Similar conclusions result if, instead of assuming a liquidity trap, we assume that invest-ment is completely insensitive to changes in the interest rate (the *IS* curve vertical). In this case, an increase in the real money supply (either from a monetary policy action or a general

The Real Wealth Effect and Unemployment

The Keynesian liquidity trap or interest-insensitive investment schedule arguments soon elicited a *neoclassical* response. It was claimed that in his attack on the classical analysis Keynes had ignored an important element in the macroeconomic adjustment process which was implicitly built into the classical analysis.[5] Defenders of classical analysis suggested that faith in the ability of wage and price flexibility to provide the automatic establishment of full employment, even if there is a liquidity trap and even if investment is insensitive to changes in the interest rate, could be restored by taking account of what we will call the *real wealth effect.*

It was argued that the classicists assumed that consumption and saving were functions not just of income but of the real value of household wealth as well. An increase in real wealth, by reducing the pressure on households to accumulate wealth by saving, was assumed to raise the level of consumption spending (reduce saving) out of any income level.

If the real value of any component of households' wealth is affected by a change in the general price level, a price level decline would raise the real value of household wealth providing, through the *real wealth effect,* a stimulus to consumption spending. With an adequate increase in consumption (thus aggregate) demand, full employment equilibrium could be restored. What assets do households own that might provide the real wealth effect we have described? Only one class of asset qualifies—the household-held obligations of government that are fixed in dollar value. There are two forms of government debt that can meet this requirement, interest-bearing (bond) and non-interest-bearing (currency) government debt.

In contrast, private debt plays no clear-cut role in the real wealth effect. While private creditors' real wealth is increased by a fall in the price level, private debtors' wealth is reduced by an equivalent amount. For the aggregate household sector of the economy, a price level change would generate no net change in the wealth that households own (and owe) in privately issued security form. Thus stocks, privately issued bonds, interest-bearing commercial credit, and even demand deposits are ruled out as contributors to a real wealth effect.[6] Likewise, physical property wealth plays no role. If the dollar value of property

---

decline in money wages and prices) does reduce the interest rate, but that falling interest rate has no impact on investment or, consequently, on aggregate demand. Again, wages and prices would decline indefinitely with no relief from unemployment.

Keynes suggested that in periods of depression, when there would be substantial idle productive capacity, no fall in the interest rate could be expected to stimulate much investment in new productive capacity.

5 See G. Haberler, *Prosperity and Depression*, 3rd ed., pp. 242, 389, 403, 491-503; A. C. Pigou, "The Classical Stationary State," *Economic Journal*, Vol. 53, December 1943, pp. 343-351.

6 For a possible exception to this general rule see B. Pesek and T. Saving, *Money, Wealth, and Economic Theory* (New York: The Macmillan Co., 1967), Chapter 4.

changes in step with the general price level, the real value of society's property wealth remains constant.

Returning to our consideration of household-held government debt, a halving of the price level would double the real value of the currency and government bonds households own, increasing total consumption. Of course, a halving of the price level also doubles the real value of government debt. However, unlike private consumption, government economic activity is assumed to be unaffected by changes in government's net worth so government's real spending is assumed to be unaffected by a changed *level* of prices.

In Figure 10-4, we have let the economic system initially be afflicted with involuntary unemployment while the commodity and money markets are cleared at the liquidity trap interest rate level (initial position indicated by 1 subscripts).

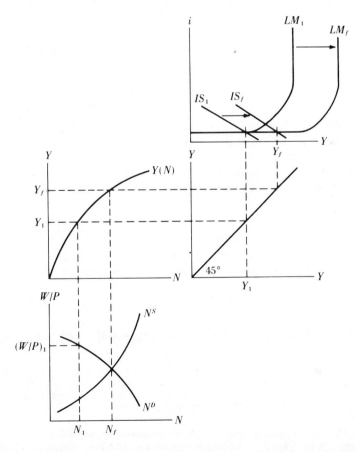

FIGURE 10-4 Automatic Restoration of Full Employment—The Role of the Real Wealth Effect

With flexible money wages, the excess supply in the labor market would prompt a fall in money wages. Again, if no change in aggregate commodity market demand occurs, the fall in money wages would be accompanied by an equiproportional fall in prices. As before, any price level reduction increases the real supply of money, shifting the *LM* curves rightward. In *addition*, if there is a real wealth effect, the price level decline will stimulate consumption, shifting the *IS* curve rightward. Even with the interest rate at the liquidity trap level, the increase in consumption demand, reflected in the rightward shift of the *IS* curve, would prevent prices from falling as much as wages.[7]

As long as there is unemployment, wages and prices will fall. As long as prices are falling the *LM* and *IS* curves will be shifting rightward as the level of aggregate demand for goods and services increases. There must be some fall in wages and prices sufficient to shift the *IS* and *LM* curves rightward to an intersection at the full employment level of output (indicated by *f* subscripts in Figure 10-4).[8] Thus, full employment is achieved automatically, even with the pure Keynes assumption of a liquidity trap (or interest-insensitive investment), as long as money wages are flexible. With the real wealth effect, labor, by bidding down the money wage, *can* reduce its real wage allowing full employment to be established.

Downward Inflexible Money Wages

If money wages are kept from falling in the face of unemployment, there is no automatic tendency to full employment even with the real wealth effect. The economy is stuck in a condition represented by the initial values in Figure 10-4. Once again, active use of fiscal and monetary policy (only the first would work if in the liquidity trap) would be required to relieve unemployment.

The Outcome of the Debate

The logic of the neoclassical analysis is hard to fault. If wages and prices are flexible, the essential classical proposition that the economy is self-regulating is supported. Moreover, as a matter of lesser practical importance but considerable theoretical interest, if a full set of classical assumptions is granted (including the restrictive assumption that currency is the only government debt), money is *neutral* or, as the classicists often suggested, "money is a veil" which only ob-

---

7   That is, any increase in aggregate demand requires increased output for the commodity market to be cleared. Output can increase only if real wages are reduced. Thus, the fall in money wages due to excess supply in the labor market must be accompanied by a less than proportional fall in the price level.

8   This is true even with investment completely insensitive to the interest rate. The only change in our graphical analysis necessary to accommodate that possibility is the alteration of the slope of the *IS* curve—the *IS* curve would be vertical but still shift rightward as the price levels falls.

scures the *real* forces that determine the equilibrium values of such *real* variables as employment, output, the interest rate, real consumption and saving, real money balances, and real investment. Money is relegated the relatively minor long-run role of determining the general price level while, exclusively in the short run, it can act more perniciously as a cause of *temporary* movements of the economy away from full employment equilibrium.

With less restrictive and seemingly more realistic assumptions, money generally cannot be considered neutral and prices need not change in precisely the same proportion as the nominal money stock. For example, if society holds government-issued bonds as well as currency, and looks upon these bonds as a component of its net wealth, a change in the money supply cannot change prices and nominal values in the same proportion with no effect on real variables. As a specific example, a doubling of the nominal money supply would not double prices and leave the interest rate and other real variables unchanged. To prove that claim, suppose that with a doubling of the nominal money supply the price level and the money wage rate did double. The real wage, the volume of employment, and the level of real output would be unchanged. Moreover, the real money supply would be unchanged and, with real output and the interest rate unchanged, the money market could be back in equilibrium. Also, with the interest rate unchanged, real investment would be at its original level. But, with the price level doubled, the real value of the government bond debt which society owns would be halved and, with society less wealthy, real consumption would be below its original level. Hence, there would be an excess supply of real goods and services which would depress prices (below the doubled level), increasing the real value of the money supply and driving down the interest rate. With the economy returned to equilibrium, the real wage, employment, and real output would be restored to their original levels (the economy still automatically returns to full employment). But, the interest rate (a *real* variable) would remain below its original level, more of the full employment level of output would be flowing into investment and less to consumption, the price level would be less than doubled, and the real money stock held would be increased.

The debate between Keynesians and the neoclassicists provided a vital service in refining our understanding of the role of money, clarifying the conditions under which money is or is not neutral. But, the most fundamental lesson from the debate was that Keynes' attack on the classical analysis was flawed. While Keynes claimed to have demonstrated the possibility of underemployment "equilibrium," even with flexible wages and prices, incorporation of the real wealth effect in the aggregate model negates that claim. Still, if wages or prices adjust only *slowly* in the real world, unacceptably high levels of unemployment could endure for extended periods following deflationary disturbances. It is the turtle-like pace of wage and price adjustments that calls for the application of Keynesian-prescribed monetary and fiscal policy actions.

What overall conclusion can we draw from the Keynes versus classicists debate? We might be tempted to agree with the following assessment: "... The model which Keynes had the gall to call his 'general theory' is but a special case of the classical theory, obtained by imposing certain restrictive assumptions on the latter, and the Keynesian 'special case,' while theoretically trivial, is none-theless important because it so happens that it is a better guide in the real world...." [9] This statement suggests that the honor for elegant theoretical de-velopment should go to the classicists (or their post-Keynesian defenders, the neoclassicists) while the special case treated by Keynesian analysis was conceded to be relevant for policy formulation.

With this uneasy truce, economists who oppose permitting price increases in order to stimulate employment and those who are ideologically opposed to the activist government involvement in economic activity required by discretionary stabilization policy could be expected to emphasize the benefits of policies aimed at encouraging wage-price flexibility. Vigorous prosecution of antitrust regula-tions to ensure product price flexibility and the extension of application of those regulations to unions to encourage wage flexibility could be advocated—the need for wage and price flexibility for the economy to be self-regulating requires sup-porters of the classical propositions to advocate fighting monopoly tooth and nail wherever it might appear. Minimum wage laws that prevent wage declines and fair trade laws that restrict price movements are anathema.

However, the modern job search theory of wage determination discussed in the last chapter indicates that wages would decline very gradually in the face of unemployment even if institutionalized restraints on wage and price movements were nonexistent. The lack of perfect information on general wage and price movements provides a strong justification for Keynesian stabilization policy rather than traditional classical policies to promote wage-price flexibility.

In addition, the recent formal recognition of the role of imperfect informa-tion in economic decision making provides for a new interpretation of Keynesian analysis—an interpretation that agrees with Keynes' contention that he had pro-vided a more general analytical framework than that inherited from the classi-cists.[10] According to the new interpretation, classical conclusions are generated relying on a very *special* assumption—the assumption that the price at which transactions take place in any market is determined as it would be in an *auction market*. In each market, the "autioneer" accepts buy and sell orders (for goods, labor services, money, or bonds) at a trial price. If the trial price is not an equilibrium (market-clearing) price, no transactions take place. Instead, the auctioneer tries a new price requiring buyers and sellers to "recontract" (submit new orders). This groping process is assumed to continue until the auctioneer

9 This brief summary of the outcome of the debate, though not representing the author's own view, is presented in A. Leijonhufvud, *On Keynesian Economics and the Economics of Keynes* (Oxford: Oxford University Press, 1968), p. 7.

10 This new interpretation of Keynes stems, in large part, from the efforts of Robert Clower and A. Leijonhufvud. For an introduction to the new interpretation, see R. Clower, "The Keynesian Counter-Revolution: A Theoretical Appraisal," in F. H. Hahn and F. P. R. Brechling (eds.), *The Theory of Interest Rates*, International Economic Association Series (New York: Macmillan, 1965), Chapter 5.

finds the market-clearing price at which time contract offers are made binding and actual market transactions take place.

In the real world, however, most markets are not auction markets and market transactions do take place in markets that are not in equilibrium. The new interpretation of Keynes claims that Keynes' analysis was primarily concerned with the behavior of macroeconomic markets that are in *disequilibrium*. Thus, Keynesian analysis is theoretically more general because it does not rely on the special assumption of auctioneer-regulated markets that permit transactions only at equilibrium prices. It recognizes that information is a scarce and costly resource.

This is an important distinction. Beginning with equilibrium, assume an autonomous decline in aggregate demand resulting in an excess supply of commodities. The economy is in disequilibrium. Without an auctioneer to ferret out the new equilibrium values for the price level, the wage rate, and the interest rate, transactors must *search* for the new values that will restore equilibrium. This is a time-consuming process during which transactions will occur.

The typical business firm will not know whether its decline in sales is temporary or permanent. Until management can acquire some reliable *information* on the nature of the decline in demand, the firm may leave its product prices unchanged, simply cutting back on the employment of labor[11] (and other variable inputs) to avoid an unwanted accumulation of inventories.

Such cutbacks raise unemployment. While displaced labor could, presumably, lower its *reservation* wage sufficiently to quickly become reemployed, it may choose not to do so. If displaced labor thinks the reduction in labor demand is temporary or that it afflicts only a subsector of the economy with general labor demand unchanged, it may rationally refuse to lower its reservation wage. *Time* is required for labor to search the job market before it can recognize the demand shift as economy-wide and permanent.

With wages and prices declining sluggishly, the reduction in aggregate demand will generate a Keynesian contraction in employment and output. Even though full employment equilibrium would ultimately be restored by the decline in money wages and prices, the adjustment period necessary for establishing the new equilibrium values of money wages and prices is long.[12]

THE MODERN MONETARIST CHALLENGE

In recent years, a modernized version of the classical quantity theory has challenged orthodox Keynesian analysis. Like the old classical analysis, the modernized quantity theory emphasizes the role of money in determining the *dollar*

---

11 This is so even with real wages unchanged.

12 The appendix to Chapter 9 provides a more detailed exposition of the *Keynesian* contraction which follows a fall in product demand when information is a scarce resource in both the commodity and labor markets.

value of output. Unlike the old analysis, however, the modern theory is willing to recognize the existence of unemployment so that the money income changes prompted by a change in money supply can consist of changes in real production as well as changes in the price level.

While the equation of exchange $(MV = PY)$ always holds, in the new quantity theory an increase in the money supply that raises MV (that is, that increases *spending*) may result in an increase in P, Y, or both. Like the Keynesian analysis then, the new quantity theory focuses on explaining changes in the level of aggregate demand with the supply side of the economy playing a dominant role in determining how money output's response is divided between real output and price level changes. In addition, in the new quantity theory *velocity can change* as the market interest rate changes just as it does in Keynesian analysis.[13]

What then distinguishes the new quantity theory from Keynesian theory? The major differences are quantitative. Because of differences in judgment on the empirical properties of a number of behavioral relationships, supporters of the new quantity theory identify money supply changes as the dominant cause of changes in aggregate demand, while Keynesian analysts, though recognizing an important role for money, continue to attribute major significance to changes in the marginal efficiency of investment, revisions in the government budget, shifts in the consumption function, and changes in net exports. Because of their emphasis on the dominant role of money, the modern quantity theorists are labeled *monetarists*.[14]

The Transmission of Money Supply Changes

While both Keynesians and monetarists believe money supply changes alter spending, there is a significant difference between the models in the *transmission mechanism* through which those money supply changes affect aggregate demand. In the familiar Keynesian model, a money supply increase drives down the market rate of interest. With investment spending on plant and equipment inversely related to the interest rate, the money supply increase is *transmitted* to the capital goods industry. Through the multiplier, the increased level of investment induces an increase in consumption.

In this Keynesian analysis, all of the effects on aggregate spending stem from a *portfolio* readjustment as the initial excess supply of money prompts

13 The modern quantity theory has leaned heavily on the lessons learned from Keynesian analysis and often appears to be more similar to Keynesian theory than to the old classical theory. This kinship is clearly spelled out in Don Patinkin, "The Chicago Tradition, the Quantity Theory, and Friedman," *Journal of Money, Credit and Banking*, Vol. 1, February 1969, pp. 46-70.

14 For a brief and lucid comparison of Keynesian and monetarist analysis from a monetarist's viewpoint, see L. C. Anderson, "The State of the Monetarist Debate," *Federal Reserve Bank of St. Louis Review*, Vol. 55, September 1973, pp. 2-8. The accompanying "Comments," especially the one by Lawrence Klein, are also instructive.

households and firms to try to draw down their money balances by exchanging them for interest-yielding securities. Changes in consumption spending occur only as an *indirect* result of the portfolio adjustment as, through the interest rate-investment linkage, the level of income is altered.

In the monetarist model, an increase in the money stock again creates a portfolio imbalance with society initially holding a larger stock of real money balances than it desires. In this case, however, society is assumed to undertake the readjustment of its portfolio not just by attempting to swap money for securities but by *directly* raising its expenditures on commodities (primarily consumer durables) as well. In this case, a money supply change is transmitted directly into final expenditures rather than just indirectly through the Keynesian interest rate-investment linkage.

The difference in transmission mechanism reflects a difference in empirical judgments. The Keynesian analysis assumes that financial securities are close *substitutes* for money while the other assets in which households can hold their wealth (including all manner of consumer durables) are not. The monetarist model does not make that distinction, reflecting the empirical judgment that society will attempt to swap excess money balances for physical as well as financial assets.

The Speed of Adjustment

Differences in the assumed speed with which the economy adjusts to monetary disturbances also distinguish the Keynesian and monetarist models. In the Keynesian model, an increase in the supply of money drives the interest rate downward for an extended period of time. As a result, society is willing to absorb a part of the increased money supply in idle money balances (velocity is reduced). Thus, in the *short run* (which may extend for several calendar years), money income is not expected to increase in proportion to the increase in money stock. Since modern Keynesians do recognize the internal forces that, given sufficient time, tend automatically to restore full employment equilibrium (with the full employment interest rate, real wage, and so on), as a long-run proposition Keynesians are hostile neither to the monetarist claim that money income rises in proportion to money supply changes nor to the claim that money is essentially neutral in its effects on the interest rate (thus velocity), the real wage, real output, and other real variables. However, the Keynesian believes that in the *policy relevant* short run, money is not neutral and money income need not change in proportion to a money supply change.

In contrast, the monetarist believes the economy adjusts rather quickly. While a money supply increase may temporarily depress the interest rate and reduce velocity, the monetarist believes that within a policy relevant time interval (a matter of months) the interest rate will have returned to near its earlier level, restoring velocity's original value and raising nominal income in proportion to the increase in nominal money stock.

The Crowding-out Effect

Keynesians and monetarists also disagree on the impact of fiscal policy. The Keynesian analysis developed in this text indicates that an increase in government spending is expansionary, lifting the equilibrium level of income. In contrast, monetarists argue that an increase in government purchases "crowds out" an approximately equal amount of private expenditures so that aggregate demand (thus equilibrium income) is changed little, if any, by an expansionary, *pure* fiscal policy. Analogously, while Keynesian analysis indicates that a tax cut is expansionary, monetarists argue that any resulting increase in consumption spending crowds out some other component of private spending leaving aggregate demand unchanged.

These conclusions can be easily generated within the confines of the analytical framework we have developed *if* we are willing to impose certain restrictions (most of which we have already seen in one context or another) on our analysis. To begin with, a crowding-out effect will occur if money wages and prices are highly flexible so that full employment equilibrium is automatically maintained. In this case, an increase in government spending creates excess commodity demand (shifting the *IS* curve rightward), raising output prices. The increase in prices reduces the real money stock (shifting the *LM* curve leftward), raising the interest rate and reducing investment. For equilibrium to be restored (requiring aggregate spending once again to be equal to *full employment* output), investment must decline by the full value of the increase in government spending, leaving real aggregate spending (and output) unchanged. Quite simply, resources will have been reallocated from private investment use to government use. We could just as easily trace the effects of a cut in taxes. In that case, consumption spending would be increased at the expense of investment leaving real output unchanged.

While this full-employment exercise is instructive, it fails to capture the full thrust of the monetarist indictment of fiscal policy since the monetarist claim that fiscal policy is very weak is not restricted to full-employment situations. But what are the conditions under which their more powerful claims are valid? Leaning on a simple and already-familiar argument, fiscal policy actions will crowd out an approximately equivalent volume of private spending, leaving aggregate demand unaltered even when there is substantial unemployment, if money demand exhibits little or no interest sensitivity.[15] This should come as no great surprise—we have already deduced that conclusion in our discussion of the pure classical region of the LM schedule (page 237 in Chapter 9).

In evaluating the role of fiscal policy in the pure classical region of the *LM* schedule, we argued that an increase in government spending (which shifts the

---

15 It is also required that money supply show little interest sensitivity, a property of the money supply schedule that we have, so far, been willing to accept. That assumption is briefly reconsidered later in this chapter and discussed in some detail in Chapter 15.

IS curve rightward) would raise the market interest rate until a volume of private spending (investment) approximately equal to the original increase in government spending is choked off. While monetarists would find this proposition agreeable, a monetarist's explanation would sound a bit different from the Keynesian account presented on page 237 of Chapter 9.

In analyzing the effect of an increase in government spending, monetarist reasoning would pay close attention to the technique used to finance that spending. The monetarist description would then proceed as follows: If an increase in government spending is financed by bond sales to the public (a *pure* fiscal policy), the public's portfolio of assets is being transformed with a higher proportion of its portfolio held in bonds. Society must be enticed into accepting that revision of its portfolio by an increase in the reward for holding bonds, the interest rate. Of course, an increase in the interest rate reduces investment and, if saving shows little or no sensitivity to interest rate changes, all of the funds borrowed by government must come from a reduction in private investment with the government's new bond issue replacing private issue. Hence the increase in government spending can *crowd out* an approximately equal volume of private (investment) spending.

Similar arguments can be made concerning the impact of tax changes. If the government cuts taxes and sells bonds to the public to provide financing for its unchanged level of spending, society again must accept an increase in the proportion of its portfolio held in bonds. The interest rate increase required for public acceptance of the portfolio revision crowds out investment, once again leaving total spending virtually unchanged.

In contrast, if the financing needs created by an increase in government spending or a decrease in taxes are accommodated by a *new money* issue, real income will rise. In this case, however, the monetarists would attribute the income growth to the swelling of the money stock—money supply is the prime mover of economic activity.

Most economists would not be convinced by the vertical *LM* argument we have reviewed. If the demand for money exhibits a strong interest sensitivity, and nearly all empirical studies of money demand, like those reviewed on page 196 of Chapter 7, suggest that this is the case, the *LM* schedule is interest-elastic implying that fiscal stimulation *does not* leave aggregate spending unchanged. However, a monetarist would retort that our analytical framework is too restricted—that in the confinements of *IS-LM* analysis the portfolio revision which fiscal deficits financed by public bond sales require must result in a leftward shift of the *LM* schedule. Any leftward shift of the *LM* schedule that is generated by the financing of a budget deficit weakens the effect of the expansionary fiscal policy that produces that deficit and a large enough shift of the *LM* curve would completely offset the expansionary effects of the deficit-producing fiscal action. In Figure 10-5, the "expansionary" fiscal policy which shifts the *IS* schedule from IS_0 to IS_1 is offset as the financing of the fiscal action shifts the *LM* schedule leftward from LM_0 to LM_1. As in the vertical *LM* case, the portfolio revision re-

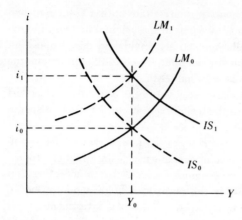

FIGURE 10-5   Crowding-out Through a Shift in the *LM* Curve

quired to get the increase in outstanding bond debt absorbed raises the interest rate and reduces investment spending (in Figure 10-5 by an amount equal to the original fiscal stimulus to total spending leaving equilibrium output unchanged).

The monetarist adjustments in the money and bond markets that permit the crowding-out effect to occur are shown in Figure 10-6.[16] Those markets are initially at equilibrium at interest rate i_0 (schedules $\overline{M}_S/P$, $(M_D/P)_0$, B_0^S, and B_0^D). To finance a *one-period* deficit, the government must issue new bonds, shifting the bond supply schedule rightward to position B_1^S. The interest rate must rise to level i_1 to restore bond market equilibrium. In the money market,

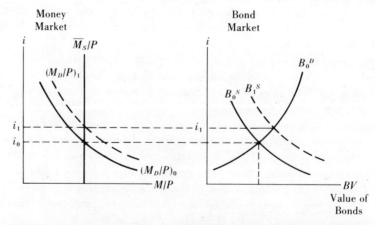

FIGURE 10-6   Monetarist Effects of a Deficit in the Money and Bond Markets

16 Note again the odd appearance of the bond supply and bond demand schedules. To refresh your memory of the structure of the bond market, review pp. 188-190, Chapter 7.

restoration of equilibrium requires the money demand schedule to shift to position $(M_D/P)_1$. In effect, the monetarist analysis includes the volume of government debt in the determinants of money demand so that an increase in society's holdings of government bond debt increases money demand.[17] Such an increase in money demand shifts the *LM* schedule leftward. In every period that the government continues running a deficit financed by bond sales to the public, the supply of bonds (and the demand for money) increases, raising the interest rate and reducing investment. Clearly, it is technically *possible* for the immediate expansionary effects of an increase in government spending or a decrease in taxes to be completely offset by the financing needs of the resulting budget imbalances.

While the monetarists' claims for the crowding-out effect represent serious attacks on the modern Keynesian analysis, their empirical importance is not established. The specific behavioral linkages through which crowding-out occurs have not been clearly spelled out (or even worked out by the monetarists) and, consequently, cannot be tested for consistency with reality.[18]

Summary Tests of the Monetarist Model

Monetarists have produced a number of statistical investigations that offer *summary* evidence on the validity of the new quantity theory. For the most part, these investigations have tried to test directly for the relative effectiveness of monetary and fiscal policy in controlling the level of economic activity. Typically, regression tests have been performed with movements in aggregate income "explained" by changes in the money supply and changes in the government's fiscal posture. The roles of fiscal and monetary variables have been judged by: (1) comparing the correlation between changes in income and changes in money supply with the correlation between changes in income and fiscal variables (for example, changes in government spending and tax revenue measures) and (2)

17 For completeness, the volume of government debt society holds in its portfolio, representing wealth to society, must also contribute to determining the volume demanded of bonds themselves. Hence a bond-financed deficit would shift the bond demand schedule rightward as well as the bond supply schedule. However, since only a fraction of the wealth increase in bond form could be expected to be willingly taken in bond form, the rightward shift of the bond demand schedule will be small relative to the shift in the bond supply schedule. Hence, it is ignored in Figure 10-6.

18 More complete treatments of the possibilities of crowding-out can be found in W. Silber, "Fiscal Policy in *IS-LM* Analysis: A Correction," *Journal of Money, Credit and Banking*, Vol. II, November 1970, pp. 461-472; and C. Christ, "A Simple Macroeconomic Model with a Government Budget Restraint," *Journal of Political Economy*, Vol. 76, January 1968, pp. 53-67. Also worth noting are reports that some of the leaders of the monetarist movement are currently putting together formal models of the macroeconomy. For discussion of an analytical framework offered as an alternative to the standard *IS-LM* model, see K. Brunner and A. Meltzer, "Money, Debt, and Economic Activity," *Journal of Political Economy*, Vol. 80, September/October 1972, pp. 951-977.

by the relative strengths of response in income (the size of regression coefficients) to changes in monetary and fiscal variables.[19]

These tests have revealed strong correlations between movements in the money supply and changes in the level of economic activity while, at the same time, yielding weak correlations between movements in economic activity and measures of fiscal policy. Monetarists tout these test results as compelling support for the belief that money plays a dominant causal role in determining the value of aggregate income. As we have noted before, however, a high correlation between two variables (in this case between money supply movements and aggregate income) cannot establish a causal role for either of the variables. The high correlation between money supply changes and income changes is consistent with the monetarist contention that money supply changes *cause* changes in money income. However, it is also consistent with the hypothesis that money plays a *passive* role in the economic process—for example, that changes in income *cause* changes in the money supply. Many Keynesians give credence to the latter argument. As income expands, they argue, the demand for money is increased putting upward pressure on the interest rate. As interest rates rise, the cost to commercial banks of not fully utilizing their lendable funds (deposits) is increased, prompting banks to economize on idle deposit *reserves* through a more aggressive loan policy. This action raises the publicly held money stock. It is also possible that the nonbank public itself can contribute to this induced rise in money supply by swapping some of its *currency* holdings for interest-yielding assets (time deposits in banks) as yields rise, raising commerical banks' lending ability.

In addition, if the central bank uses interest rates as a measure of monetary restraint or ease, its response to interest rate changes can result in a high correlation between movements in income and movements in the money supply even with money acting quite passively. With monetary policy directed to maintaining a *target* interest rate, any tendency for the interest rate to rise during an expansion could be met by a central bank administered increase in the supply of money.

In contraction periods, declining income reduces the demand for money putting downward pressure on the market interest rate. Reversing the arguments above, we would conclude that income and the quantity of money would contract together with the money supply change the *result* of contraction rather than its cause. In economists' jargon, these Keynesian arguments suggest that money

19 Interest in summary tests of monetarist and Keynesian explanations of the income determination process has been extensive since publication by Milton Friedman and David Meiselman of a study of the relative stability (thus predictive ability) of the Keynesian multiplier and the classicists' monetary velocity. See M. Friedman and D. Meiselman, "The Relative Stability of Monetary Velocity and the Investment Multiplier," in Commission on Money and Credit, *Stabilization Policies*, Prentice-Hall, 1963, pp. 165-268. The economic research staff at the St. Louis District Federal Reserve Bank is maintaining an ongoing test of the relative effectiveness of monetary and fiscal policy. For a sample of their test results see L. Anderson and J. Jordan, "Monetary and Fiscal Actions: A Test of Their Relative Importance in Economic Stabilization," *Federal Reserve Bank of St. Louis Review*, Vol. 50, November 1968, pp. 11-24.

supply changes cannot be treated as *exogenous* but that the money supply is *endogenously* determined. When the endogenous response of the money supply is built into tests of the relative effectiveness of monetary and fiscal policy, both sets of stabilization tools appear to exert a strong influence on the level of economic activity.[20]

SUMMARY

Beginning with Keynes' attack on the classicists, this chapter has traced briefly the major confrontations that occupied macroeconomists from the 1936 publication of *The General Theory* until the present. While many issues have been resolved in the macroeconomic debates of the last 40 years, others have emerged that, as of now, await resolution. Perhaps in the future you will contribute to improvements in our understanding of the functioning of the macroeconomy. In the meantime, this chapter has shown you what paths economists have trod, permitting you to comprehend the frequent and highly publicized exchanges between Keynesians and monetarists.

As sophisticated as the tools of statistical analysis available to economists are, they have not been able to determine the direction of causal link between money and economic activity. High correlations between movements in those two variables are consistent with both monetarist and Keynesian models. Indeed, instead of settling the debate between monetarists and Keynesians, the summary tests of monetary and fiscal policy effectiveness seem to have broadened it by highlighting an important methodological disagreement. Keynesians have regarded macroeconomic theory's task as the full specification of the *structure* of the economic system (its behavioral relationships, identities, and equilibrium conditions). However, Friedman, Meiselman, Anderson, and other monetarists have rejected this methodology. Claiming that the structural link between income and its ultimate determinant (money) is stable, they argue that we do not need to know what is going on inside the "black box" (the structure of the economy) but only the (presumably stable) link between income and its ultimate, exogenous determinants. Keynesian economists argue that until the channels through which money wields the *dominant* influence monetarists accord it are identified and subjected to statistical tests little reliance should be placed on policy prescriptions based on the monetarists' summary tests. Judging from the historical record, the monetarist versus Keynesian debate is destined to continue for the indefinite future.

---

20 See R. E. Lombra and R. G. Torto, "Measuring the Impact of Monetary and Fiscal Actions: A New Look at the Specification Problem," *Review of Economics and Statistics*, February 1974, pp. 104-107. Also, for a sophisticated theoretical critique of the monetarist practice of looking at correlations and "lead-lag" relations in attempting to demonstrate causality see J. Tobin, "Money and Income: Post Hoc Ergo Propter Hoc," *Quarterly Journal of Economics*, May 1970, pp. 299-329.

QUESTIONS

1. Explain how, under *ordinary* circumstances, forces within the economy would restore full employment equilibrium after some disturbance has created unemployment.
2. Use the classical model to evaluate the impact of:
   (a) the discovery of sizable deposits of energy resources,
   (b) a halving of the nominal money stock,
   (c) the arrival of a sizable number of immigrants or the return of military personnel at the end of a war.
3. Even with flexible wages and prices, there are circumstances under which the economy is not self-regulating. Name and explain two prominent cases where this contention applies. How does the existence of a real-wealth effect alter your arguments.
4. Does "money matter"? Does "fiscal policy matter"? Use the *IS-LM* model to answer these questions. What do your answers have to do with the interest elasticity of money demand?
5. The quotation on page 284 suggests that classical economists deserve more credit than Keynes for their theoretical analysis while Keynes' model is a better "practical" guide. Explain.
6. A number of highly aggregative, summary tests of the importance of monetary and fiscal policy in controlling the level of output have shown stronger correlations between movements in money and income than between government budget posture and income. Critically analyze those tests.
7. Distinguish between the old quantity theory and the modern quantity theory.
8. In what sense is Keynes' *General Theory* more general than the neoclassical theory?

SUGGESTED READING

Ackley, Gardner. *Macroeconomic Theory*. New York: Macmillan Co., 1961, Chapters V-VIII, XV.

Anderson, Leonall. "The State of the Monetarist Debate." Also the accompanying "Commentary" by L. Klein and K. Brunner in *St. Louis Federal Reserve Bank Review*. Vol. 55, September 1973, pp. 2-14.

———, and Jerry Jordon. "Monetary and Fiscal Actions: A Test of Their Relative Importance in Economic Stabilization," *Federal Reserve Bank of St. Louis Review*. Vol. 50, November 1968, pp. 11-24.

Ando, Albert, and Franco Modigliani. "The Relative Stability of Monetary Velocity and the Investment Multiplier," *American Economic Review*. Vol. 55, September, 1965, pp. 693-728.

Brunner, Karl, and Allan Meltzer. Predicting Velocity, Implications for Theory and Policy," *Journal of Finance*. Vol. XXVIII, May 1963, pp. 319-354.

Carlson, Keith M., and Roger W. Spencer. "Crowding Out and Its Critics," *Federal Reserve Bank of St. Louis Review*. Vol. 57, Dec. 1975, pp. 2-17.

deLeeuw, F., and J. Kalchbrenner. "Monetary and Fiscal Actions: A Test of Their Relative Importance in Economic Stabilization—Comment," *Federal Reserve Bank of St. Louis Review*. Vol. 51, April 1969, pp. 6-11.

Friedman, Milton. *The Optimum Quantity of Money and Other Essays*. Chicago: Aldine Publishing Co., 1969, Chapters 2, 3, 5-7, and 9.

———, and D. Meiselman. "The Relative Stability of Monetary Velocity and the Investment Multiplier in the United States, 1897-1958," in E. C. Brown *et al. Stabilization Policies*. Englewood Cliffs, N. J.: Research Studies for the Commission on Money and Credit, 1963.

Goldfeld, Stephen M., and Alan S. Blinder. "Some Implications of Endogenous Stabilization Policy," *Brookings Papers on Economic Activity*. Vol. 3, 1972:3, pp. 585-640.

Gramlich, E. "The Usefulness of Monetary and Fiscal Policy as Discretionary Stabilization Tools," *Journal of Money, Credit and Banking*. Vol. III, May 1971, pp. 506-532.

Johnson, Harry G. "Monetary Theory and Policy," *American Economic Review*. Vol. 52, June 1962, Parts I and II, pp. 335-357.

———. "The Keynesian Revolution and the Monetarist Counter-Revolution," *American Economic Association, Papers and Proceedings*. Vol. LXI, May 1971, pp. 1-14.

Lombra, R. E., and R. G. Torto. "Measuring the Impact of Monetary and Fiscal Actions: A New Look at the Specification Problem," *Review of Economics and Statistics*. Vol. 56, February 1974, pp. 104-7.

Patinkin, Don. "Price Flexibility and Full Employment," in American Economic Association, *Readings in Monetary Theory*. Homewood, Ill.: Richard D. Irwin, 1951, pp. 252-283.

———. "The Chicago Tradition, the Quantity Theory, and Friedman," *Journal of Money, Credit and Banking*. Vol. 1, February 1969, pp. 46-70.

Pigou, A. C. "The Classical Stationary State," *Economic Journal*. Vol. LIII, December 1943, pp. 343-351.

Rasche, Robert H. "A Comparative Static Analysis of Some Monetarist Propositions," *St. Louis Federal Reserve Bank Review*. Vol. 55, December 1973, pp. 15-23.

Spencer, R. W., and W. P. Yohe. "The 'Crowding Out' of Private Expenditures by Fiscal Policy Actions," *Federal Reserve Bank of St. Louis Review*. Vol. 50, November 1968, pp. 12-24.

Silber, W. L. "Fiscal Policy in *IS-LM* Analysis: A Correction," *Journal of Money, Credit and Banking*. Vol. II, November 1970, pp. 461-472.

Teigen, Ronald. "A Critical Look at Monetarist Economics," *Federal Reserve Bank of St. Louis Review*. Vol. 54, January 1972, pp. 10-25.

Appendix to Chapter 10
The Straw Man
Classical Model,
The Keynesian Revolution,
and the Neoclassical Retort[1]

The essence of the classical model of income determination which Keynes attacked is captured in a proposition known as *Say's Law*. Briefly summarized, Say's Law claims that "supply creates its own demand," that the very act of production increases demand by an amount equal to the increase in output so that a condition of overproduction, inducing a persistent contraction of output and employment, could not occur.

The logic of Say's Law seems clear for a barter economy. An individual increases his output of some product only in order to trade the extra output (over and above his own demand) for products produced by others. An increase in output carries with it an identical increase in demand in real terms.

An elegantly simple, formal, mathematical statement of Say's Law can be readily provided. While there is no money—that is, no one item that is generally used as a medium of exchange—in a barter economy, for simplicity suppose that there are "accounting prices" for every product. These prices reflect the rate at which any commodity will exchange for another—for example, the rate at which shoes exchange for cloth. Since any individual might produce one or more commodities, in general the *value* of any individual's production of n different commodities (measured at accounting prices) is

$$p_1 s_1 + p_2 s_2 + \ldots + p_n s_n. \tag{10A-1}$$

He produces so that he can demand commodities for his own use. The total *value* of the commodities he demands is

---

1 For an excellent expository discussion of the straw-man classical model, see E. Hagen, "The Classic Theory of the Level of Output and Employment," *Six Chapters on the Theory of Output, Income, and the Price Level.* Reprinted in M. G. Mueller (ed.). *Readings in Macroeconomics,* 2d edition (New York: Holt, Rinehart, and Winston, Inc., 1971), pp. 3-15.

$$p_1 d_1 + p_2 d_2 + \ldots + p_n d_n. \tag{10A-2}$$

If an individual produces only for his own use or for exchange with other producers then it must be the case that

$$p_1 s_1 + p_2 s_2 + \ldots + p_n s_n \equiv p_1 d_1 + p_2 d_2 + \ldots + p_n d_n. \tag{10A-3}$$

The value of his production (of one commodity or n commodities) is identical to the value of his total demand for goods and services. With this identity holding for any and every individual then *the value of aggregate supply must be identical to the value of total demand,* or

$$\sum_{i=1}^{n} p_i S_i \equiv \sum_{i=1}^{n} p_i D_i, \tag{10A-4}$$

where S_i is the *aggregate* output of commodity i from all individuals and D_i is the *aggregate* quantity of commodity i demanded by all individuals. Equation (10A-4) allows one or more commodities to be in excess supply at existing accounting prices, while, for some one or more other commodities, there is excess demand. But Equation (10A-4) requires the total value of excess supplies to be matched by the total value of excess demands. Output *in general* cannot differ in value from the level of demand since the act of supplying commodities is, at the same time, the act of demanding commodities.

A Money Economy

But what about the case of a money economy where exchanges are made using money and individuals can *save* a portion of their money income? In this case, since part (or all) of any increase in income may be saved in money form, an increase in income (output) may not imply an increase in spending sufficient to clear the market of the increased level of output. How would Keynes' classical predecessors respond to this point?

They would claim that the introduction of money makes no difference. Total spending would always be sufficient to clear the market of any specified level of output (income). In a monetary economy, however, the mechanism that ensures equality of income and spending is a flexible interest rate, a rate that can equate aggregate demand and supply (or *ipso facto,* investment and saving) at any level of income.

The Commodity Market

In our classical model, investment is an inverse function of the interest rate since the classicists assumed that the return on investment fell as the level of investment rose. The level of saving out of any specified level of income was a positive function of the interest rate. Further, it was assumed to be irrational for anyone to hold his savings as idle money balances if there was any positive yield available from lending. Thus, any saving was promptly loaned. An interest return (which allows net worth to grow permitting increased future consumption) was the reward for abstinence—that is, for not consuming. The higher the reward, the larger the fraction of income saved. With both investment and saving quite sensitive to the interest rate, it was believed that interest rate adjustments would always allow saving and investment to be equal at any level of income. Thus, for any selected level of income, the classical saving and investment functions are

$$I = I(i) \qquad \text{s.t.} \quad \frac{\Delta I}{\Delta i} < 0$$

and

$$S = S(i) \qquad \text{s.t.} \quad \frac{\Delta S}{\Delta i} > 0 \qquad\qquad (10A\text{-}5)$$

with

$$S = I \text{ always.}$$

These schedules are plotted in Figure 10A-1.

An increase in thriftiness (a shift to the right of the saving function such as shown in Figure 10A-1) with the interest rate at level i_0 would leave an excess supply of saving, with some savers frustrated in their attempt to earn a reward (i_0) for abstaining from consumption. If any of these savers offer to lend their savings at a reduced rate, the interest rate must fall (competitive market). Thus, the interest rate is flexible and adjusts to maintain the equality of S and I. Clearly, any level of income can be an equilibrium level. The level of income must be determined elsewhere. Only the interest rate, the proportion of income consumed (and saved), and the level of investment are determined here in the commodity market. Note, again, that the interest rate is a real variable determined in the commodity market with its value dependent on the "productivity of capital" (our marginal efficiency of investment) and "thrift" (the saving schedule).

Similarly, a shift in the investment function would require a change in the equilibrium interest rate with an increase in investment (a rightward shift of

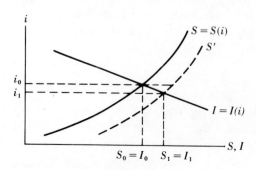

FIGURE 10A-1 Commodity Market Equilibrium

the investment function) raising the interest rate and a decrease in investment lowering it. Once again, the level of income does not need to change to maintain the equality of investment and saving needed for commodity market equilibrium. The flexible interest rate mechanism assures that equality.

The Labor Market

Say's Law, even extended to a money economy, allows *any* level of income to be an equilibrium level. It says nothing about what level of income will actually be established. In our simple classical model the level of output is established in the labor market by the demand for and supply of labor.

The classical economists assumed that the quantity of labor supplied and the quantity demanded depended on the real wage. Labor supply was a positive function of the real wage. The higher the reward for foregoing leisure, the larger the quantity of labor services offered.

Demand for labor was a derived demand as indicated by standard marginal productivity theory. Additional labor would be hired by a firm (and thus by the economy as a whole) as long as the marginal product of labor exceeded the real wage of labor. Given the stock of land, the capital stock, the state of technology, and the quality of the labor force, with diminishing returns to the *quantity* of labor employed the demand schedule for labor sloped downward from left to right.

Thus,

$$N^s = N\left(\frac{W}{P}\right) \qquad \frac{\Delta N^s}{\Delta\left(\frac{W}{P}\right)} > 0$$

$$N^D = N\left(\frac{W}{P}\right) \qquad \frac{\Delta N^D}{\Delta\left(\frac{W}{P}\right)} < 0$$

(10A-6)

and $N^s = N^D$ in equilibrium.

The classical labor supply and demand schedules appear in Figure 10A-2.

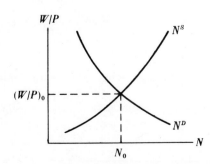

FIGURE 10A-2   Labor Market Equilibrium

That figure shows that unemployment can exist only if the real wage is above $(W/P)_0$. If labor actively competes for employment, the classicists argued, unemployment could not persist. By bidding down the money wage, labor could bid down its real wage (prices are determined elsewhere!), reducing the quantity of labor supplied and increasing the amount demanded until any excess supply is eliminated.

Clearly, competitive forces are sufficient to ensure full employment equilibrium! Any change in the labor supply or demand schedules can only temporarily disturb full employment equilibrium. Thus, the equilibrium level of employment is established at the full employment level. Further, given the production function, which describes the relationship between employment and output, equilibrium output is determined. That is,

$$Y = Y(N) \quad \text{so that for} \quad N = N_0, \ Y = Y(N_0) = Y_0. \tag{10A-7}$$

Prolonged unemployment could exist only if for some reason, such as the existence of powerful labor unions or minimum wage laws, labor is unable to reduce its real wage by bidding down the money wage.

Thus, all real variables (W/P, N, Y, r, C, S, and I) are determined in the *real* sectors of the economy—that is, in the commodity market and the labor market. The only role left for the money market is the determination of nominal values.

The Money Market

The role of money was analyzed through the well-known *equation of exchange* which states that:

$$MV = PY \tag{10A-8}$$

where:

$M =$ money supply;

$V =$ velocity, the number of times each dollar is, on average, used to buy final goods and services during any given time period;

$P =$ the average price of goods and services sold;

$Y =$ the quantity of output or the level of output in real terms.

The equation of exchange is an identity which recognizes that:

Total spending $(MV) =$ receipts or value of goods purchased (PY).

The equation of exchange becomes a theory with causal content, *the quantity theory of money,* when a theory of velocity is introduced.[2] A frequent classical assumption was that velocity was determined by institutional factors such as the frequency of income payments maintained by tradition, contract, and so on along with the degree of integration of business firms. Hence, it was assumed that velocity was constant (at least in the short run since institutional arrangements change only gradually over time if at all).

With velocity constant and the level of real output established at the full employment level by the labor market, money supply and the price level (and thus the nominal value of income and output) are directly related. An increase in M must lead to a proportional increase in P, but can have no permanent impact on any *real* variable. Thus, the quantity of money determines the price level and nominal values of Y, C, S, I, and W, but the real values of these variables are determined in the labor and commodity markets.

The only way for equilibrium income to change in this classical model is for a shift to occur in the labor supply or demand curve. For example, an autonomous increase in labor supply would lower the real wage, raise employment and output, and thus raise consumption, saving, and investment. In contrast, an autonomous fall in consumption (rise in saving), which would cause a contraction of income and employment in a Keynesian model, results, in the classical model, in a fall in the interest rate which stimulates additional investment to maintain equilibrium in the commodity market. Income and employment would remain unaffected.

KEYNES' CRITICISM OF THE STRAW-MAN MODEL

Our classical model suggests, then, that competitive forces are sufficient to maintain full-employment equilibrium. A shift in any schedule brings about adjustments (notably, in real wages or the interest rate) which allow the level of income to remain at a full employment level.

This Keynes denied. He claimed that it might frequently be *income* that has to adjust to establish equilibrium and that the equilibrium established might not be at a full employment income level. We need now to look inside the Keynesian model to see what analytical differences are responsible for these different conclusions.

---

2 As indicated earlier, a theory of velocity is the equivalent of a theory of the demand for money. Assume that the volume of money demanded for transactions purposes is proportional to the level of income with proportionality constant k. That is,

$$M_D = kPY.$$

For money market equilibrium money demand must, of course, equal money supply.

From the equation of exchange in the text,

$$MV = PY,$$

we see that $M = (1/V)PY$. Thus, $1/V$ and k (or *ipso facto*, $1/k$ and V) are identical. A theory that explains the value of V also explains the value of k.

Saving, Investment, and the Interest Rate

The classical analysis of the commodity market suggested that, with a flexible interest rate, saving was always equal to investment so that any income level was always an equilibrium level. Keynes claimed that saving was a function of income rather than of the interest rate (it might in fact be inversely related to i) and that investment might sometimes be quite insensitive to interest rate changes. What are the implications of these assumptions? Starting with equilibrium at $i = i_0$ in Figure 10A-3, suppose the saving schedule (S) shifts outward to S'. Here there would be no positive intersection of S and I. With the storage costs of holding idle money balances close to zero, no one would be expected to lend his idle money balances and pay the recipient to use them. Thus, a negative interest rate is an impossibility making the intersection of S' and I in Figure 10A-3 unattainable. What must happen? Income must fall to allow S' to shift leftward before equilibrium can be reestablished.

Suppose the intersection of the saving and investment schedules occurred at an interest rate of 1 percent. Would equilibrium reign? To answer this question we need to look into Keynes' treatment of the money market. He argued that the interest rate is determined in the money market by money supply and interest-sensitive money demand. He suggested that at low interest rates (2 percent?) money demand might become perfectly elastic (there was a liquidity trap!) so that the interest rate could never fall below that level.

Thus, the existence of a nonnegative intersection of the saving and investment schedule in the commodity market is not sufficient to establish equilibrium if the required interest rate is unattainable (below the liquidity trap level). Again, income must change to reestablish equilibrium.[3]

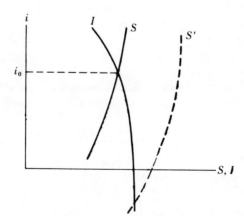

FIGURE 10A-3 An Unattainable Equilibrium

3 In the general case, a shift outward of the saving schedule (a fall in consumption demand) would free some transactions balances. Holders of excess transactions balances might buy bonds driving the interest rate down. However, if total money demand is elastic and the response of investment to changes in the interest rate is small, the resulting change in investment is not likely to be sufficient to offset the increase in saving. Income must change!

The Money Market

The assumed behavior of the Keynesian money market is quite different from the classical model where all money demand was for transactions purposes and was highly interest insensitive. In the Keynesian analysis money demand is for multiple motives and can be highly interest sensitive. It is no longer irrational to hold *idle* money balances in Keynes' two-financial-asset (money and bonds) world since doing so may allow the avoidance of capital losses that accompany a rise in the interest rate.

Changes in the Money Supply and Speculative Money Demand

In the Keynesian model part of any increase in the money stock could go into transactions balances and part into speculative balances. An increase in the money supply (from, say, $\overline{M}/P$ to $\overline{M}'/P$ in Figure 10A-4) would drive the interest rate down, increasing the speculative demand for money sufficiently to allow the increase in money supply to be absorbed. Since speculative money balances have a velocity of zero, overall velocity must fall. No longer can velocity be assumed to be institutionally determined. It now depends on the interest rate and, thus, on money supply.

Also, changes in the money supply can affect real output. If money demand is not perfectly interest elastic, a change in money supply will change the interest rate and, thus, investment and the level of output. (If at less than full employment, real output is affected. If at full employment, the changes may be just price changes.) If the economy is in the liquidity trap, then a change in money supply will not affect the interest rate and, thus, will have no impact on income. In this case, velocity is the only other variable to change in response to a change in money supply.

The Labor Market

Keynes denied the classical claim that downward flexibility of money wages could ensure full employment equilibrium. He recognized that a general reduction in money wages would not only lower costs to firms *but would also reduce con-*

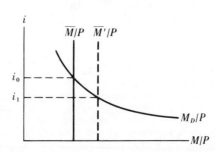

FIGURE 10A-4 Money and the Interest Rate

sumption demand for aggregate output and, thus, the derived demand for labor. Would a fall in money wages lower the real wage rate? Quite possibly not. A fall in money wages might be matched by an exactly proportional fall in prices. (Any fall in W not matched by a proportional fall in P lowers real wages which would raise employment and thus Y. However, with the MPC < 1, all of the extra output would not be bought so inventories would mount leading to a fall in P and Y.) Thus, the only result of downward flexibility of money wages might be a downward spiral of wages and prices with no change in real wages or employment.

Any impact on employment from falling wages and prices would have to come about by an indirect route. A fall in wages and prices reduces business and individual transactions demand for money. Redundant transactions balances would be used to buy securities driving the interest rate downward, stimulating investment and thus raising Y. However, even this indirect help would not occur if the economy were in a liquidity trap situation or if investment were insensitive to i.[4] Furthermore, Keynes recognized and accepted the fact that money wages are not very flexible in the downward direction.

The Keynesian system then, can be summarized algebraically as follows:

$$\left.\begin{aligned} S &= S(Y) \\ I &= I(i) \\ S &= I \quad \text{only in equilibrium} \end{aligned}\right\} \text{commodity market}$$

$$\left.\frac{\overline{M}}{P} = M_1(Y) + M_2(i) \quad \right\} \text{money market}$$

$$\left.\begin{aligned} N^s &= N\left(\frac{W}{P}\right) \\ \frac{\Delta Y}{\Delta N} &= \frac{W}{P} \quad \text{or} \quad N^D = N\left(\frac{W}{P}\right) \\ W &= \overline{W} \text{ (the bar indicating} \\ &\qquad \text{downward sticky)} \\ Y &= Y(N) \end{aligned}\right\} \text{labor market}$$

In this system, competitive forces are not sufficient to maintain full employment. Chronic unemployment is a distinct possibility.

---

4 There are other indirect effects. In an open economy in which foreign trade is an important component of economic activity (for example, Great Britain), a fall in domestic prices would stimulate exports and reduce imports, thus raising aggregate demand. On the other hand, a fall in wages and prices might tend to redistribute real income away from wage earners toward other segments of the population (receivers of profits and rents). If the propensity to consume is higher for wage earners than for the other groups, this redistribution would reduce consumption demand and, thus, aggregate demand.

THE NEOCLASSICAL RETORT

The classical system of analysis has been defended by Haberler, Pigou, Patinkin, and others.[5] These authors claim that the straw-man classical model attacked by Keynes does not represent sophisticated classical analysis: that it leaves out a mechanism, implicit in classical analysis, that allows full employment to be maintained *automatically*. The mechanism is the *real balance effect*. The classicists, according to these authors, assumed that consumption and saving were functions, not just of income and the interest rate, but of the value of *real balances* as well. That is, saving and consumption are given by

$$S = S\left(Y, i, \frac{M}{P}\right)$$

and

$$C = C\left(Y, i, \frac{M}{P}\right),$$

where M is the dollar value of cash balances held by the public, P is the price level, and the other variables are defined as before.

Real money balances are a form of wealth. Clearly an individual's accumulated real wealth in the form of cash balances can be increased by an increase in M (the dollar value of cash balances he holds) or by a fall in P which increases the command over real goods and services embodied in each dollar's worth of cash balances. Presumably, an increase in the real wealth an individual holds in the form of cash balances would induce him to consume a larger fraction (save a smaller fraction) of his income since the pressure to accumulate wealth by saving is reduced as wealth increases. Thus, a fall in the price level, which raises the real value of cash balances, would stimulate consumption and reduce saving both at the individual and the aggregate level.

How was this real balance effect employed in classical analysis? Assume that the economy is in full employment equilibrium when the saving schedule shifts, autonomously, to the right, producing a saving-investment intersection at an unattainable interest rate (as illustrated in Figure 10A-3).[6] Since saving would exceed investment at any attainable interest rate, the Keynesian analysis would require the equilibrium level of income to fall, resulting in an unemployment equilibrium. If, however, wages were free to fall, unemployed labor would bid the nominal wage rate down. If prices fell with wages (as Keynes argued

5 See G. Haberler, *Propensity and Depression*, 3rd edition, *op. cit.*, pp. 242, 389, 403, 491-503; A. C. Pigou, "The Classical Stationary State" *Economic Journal*, Vol. 53, December 1943, pp. 343-351; D. Patinkin, "Keynesian Economics, the Classics, and the Keynesians," *American Economic Review*, Vol. 38, September 1948, pp. 543-584.

6 Recall that a commodity market equilibrating interest rate would be unattainable if it were negative or if it fell below the liquidity trap rate.

they would if wages were free to fall), then the real value of the cash balances held by the public would rise. As the value of cash balances rose, the saving schedule would shift leftward. *As long as there was any unemployment in the labor market the nominal wage, thus prices, would continue to fall. As long as prices fell the real value of cash balances would rise, shifting the saving schedule leftward. As a theoretical proposition, there must be some fall in the price level sufficient to shift the saving schedule leftward far enough to produce an intersection of the saving and investment schedules at an attainable rate of interest.*

Thus, equilibrium at less than full employment is impossible *as long as wages and prices are free to fall.* According to this analysis, if there is persistent unemployment it is the result of imperfections in the labor or product markets that prevent downward flexibility of wages and prices. And this is true regardless of the strength of the real balance effect (that is, regardless of the size of impact on saving of a change in real balances) as long as it is not zero.[7] To relieve persistent unemployment, then, the classicists would suggest the removal of imperfections in labor and product markets—that is, the reduction of the power of labor unions, the removal of minimum wage laws, the reduction of monopoly power in product markets, and so on.

One important question remains concerning the real balance effect. That is, of what do real balances consist? As indicated in Chapter 10, our answer is that they consist of all the obligations of government to society that are fixed in dollar value and only of these obligations. That is, they consist of government debt to the public.

Private debt cannot be included. Though private creditors' real wealth is increased by a fall in the price level, private debtors' wealth is reduced by an equivalent amount. Any stimulus to consumption by creditors would be offset by a reduction in consumption by debtors. Thus stocks, bonds, interest-bearing commercial credit, and even demand deposits are ruled out as components of real balances. In each case the total real value of wealth society holds in such assets is exactly equal to the real value of society's private debt. A change in the price level leaves the total real value of wealth in this form unchanged.

In contrast, a change in the price level does affect the real value of society's total wealth held in the form of government debt, the value of which is fixed in dollar terms. This is true for both interest-bearing (bond) and non-interest-bearing (currency) government debt. A halving of the price level would double the real value of the currency and government bonds society holds increasing total consumption spending (reducing saving). The halving of the price level also doubles the real value of government debt. However, unlike private consumption, government economic activity is typically assumed to be unaffected by changes in the government's *net worth.* A fall in the price level then increases

---

7 This is also true regardless of the size of the interest elasticities of the saving and investment schedules.

consumption without reducing any other component of aggregate demand.[8] There must be some fall in the price level, even if it means a price level approaching zero where real balances become limitless, sufficient to reduce saving to a level that produces a saving-investment intersection at a full employment level of output. This holds true even under the Keynesian assumption of a liquidity trap. Thus, *as the classicists always argued*, it is the strong Keynesian assumption of downward inflexibility of wages (thus of prices) that permits the existence of unemployment equilibrium in his model.

SUMMARY

The classical model allowed the real values of all important macroeconomic variables (the real wage, employment, income, the interest rate, consumption, and investment) to be determined in the "real" markets—the labor and commodity markets. The only role left for money was the relatively unimportant one of determining the price level, thus the nominal values of wages, income, consumption, and investment. The only way persistent unemployment could exist in the classical world was for the nominal wage rate to be inflexible in the downward direction—that is, to be held above the equilibrium wage rate, according to the classical economists by powerful and intransigent labor unions, minimum wage laws, and the like. In the face of persistent unemployment, the classicists would recommend policies to eliminate those imperfections in the labor market—policies of reducing union power, eliminating minimum wage floors, and so on.

Keynes, in his attack on classical macroeconomics, claimed to have established the existence of less than full employment equilibrium even with flexible wages and prices. Removal of market imperfections was not a cure for recession. Instead, active government manipulation of aggregate demand through monetary and fiscal policy was required to relieve and avoid recessions.

The neoclassical retort to Keynesian analysis demonstrated that, if consumption (saving) responded positively to the growth in real balances that resulted from a price decline, equilibrium at less than full employment was impossible— with flexible wages and prices there was an *automatic* mechanism for restoring the economic system to full employment equilibrium. Thus, the Keynesian indictment of the classical analysis was misleading. The only way Keynes' system could produce persistent unemployment was the same way that the classical system produced persistent unemployment. Namely, by fixing the nominal wage at a level too high to allow full employment.

---

8   We should also include in real balances the debt of the central bank to member commercial banks. This inclusion does not alter our conclusion. In recent years there has been some debate over exclusion of demand deposits as a component of real balances. Their inclusion is advocated by B. Pesek and T. Saving in *Money, Wealth, and Economic Theory* (New York: Macmillan, 1967).

Where then does this leave modern macroeconomic analysis and policy? It appears quite certain that the response of consumption to changes in real balances is positive though small so that, if wages and prices were free to fall, persistent unemployment might not be a problem, even without government intervention in economic activity. However, wages and prices are, as Keynes recognized, *not free* to fall. Even in periods of considerable slack in economic activity they decline only very slowly if at all.[9] Thus, the time necessary for the economic system to recover automatically from a contraction is, in the minds of most economic policy makers, too long. Aggregate demand is deliberately manipulated by changes in government spending, taxes, and transfer payments as well as by alterations of the money stock by the central bank.

9 Look again at Chapter 9, pages 260-264.

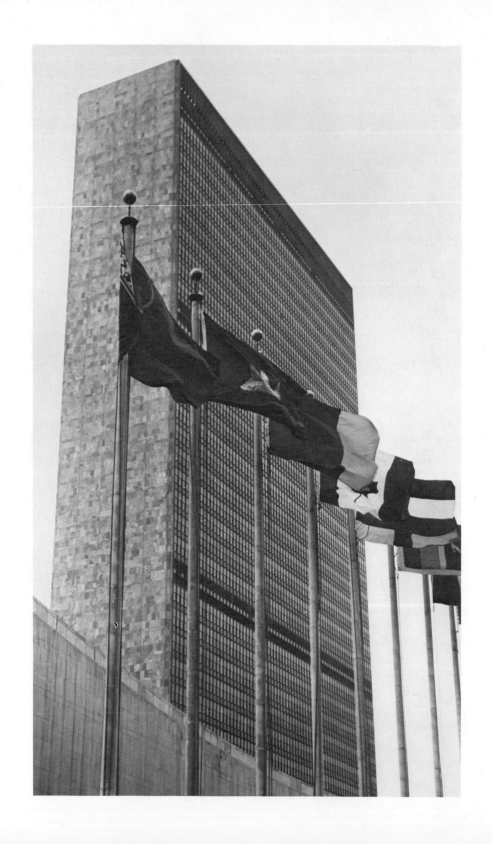

Chapter 11
International Economic Relations and Macroeconomic Equilibrium

Up to now we have worked with models of closed systems, paying scant attention to the foreign sector of the economy. But when there is trade among nations the domestic economies of those nations are linked together so that economic conditions in one country are affected by conditions in the rest of the world. Our understanding of how one country's level of economic activity is determined cannot be complete until we provide for these international linkages.

The importance of U.S. participation in the world economic community has been highlighted in the past decade by a highly publicized U.S. gold drain and, in recent years, by two formal devaluations of the dollar, experimentation with floating exchange rates, and an embargo on oil shipments to the U.S. from the OPEC countries. Happily, an analysis of these headline-winning phenomena and of the overall role of the foreign sector of the economy can be accommodated readily in the *IS-LM* framework we have already developed. Beginning that task, we will first analyze the direct effects of international trade on the domestic level of economic activity by demonstrating the impact of the foreign sector on the commodity market component of the *IS-LM* model.

FOREIGN TRADE AND THE COMMODITY MARKET

The introduction of foreign purchasers of U.S. produced goods and services simply adds one more component, export sales, to U.S. aggregate demand. With this addition, domestic output is absorbed by consumption, investment, government, and *exports*. However, part of U.S. consumption, investment, and government purchases will be foreign produced (imported) goods. To cite some common examples, consumption spending on French wines and Japanese radios and investment expenditures on German machine tools do not contribute directly to demand for domestically produced output. Therefore, all spending on imports must be deducted from the total of final expenditures on consumption, investment, and government purchases in deriving a measure of aggregate demand for *domestic* production. Total demand for U.S. output then is

$$(C + I + G - M) + X,$$

311

where C is consumption, I investment, G government spending, X exports, and M imports. Rearranging, aggregate demand is

$$C + I + G + (X - M)$$

where the role of foreign trade in determining aggregate demand is captured in the *net exports* or *trade balance* term $(X - M)$.

For commodity market equilibrium it is still necessary for planned spending to be equal to output,

$$Y = C + I + G + (X - M),$$

or for leakages to equal injections,

$$S + T + M = I + G + X.$$

And just as before, the appropriate behavioral relationships must be plugged into these equilibrium conditions to provide a solvable income determination model. To be able to do that, we must specify the determinants of the volumes of exports and imports in usable (mathematical) form.

Exports (Sales) to and Imports (Purchases) from the Rest of the World

Foreign agents buy U.S. produced goods and services when they cannot buy the same items from other sources at a lower delivered price. Foreign purchases of domestic output must depend then on international price differences as well as on tastes and income in the purchasing country. For purposes of building the foreign sector into our *IS-LM* model, it will be assumed that the foreign domestic price ratio does not vary with changes in U.S. output. Then once the complete model with a foreign sector is constructed, that model will be used to analyze the impact of price disturbances. Also, it will be assumed initially that changes in U.S. output have a negligible effect on the income level in the rest of the world.[1] These simplifying assumptions allow us to treat our exports as *exogenously determined*.

Imports on the other hand must be treated as endogenously determined, even in the absence of a change in domestic and foreign price levels. With increases in income, consumption spending on both domestic and foreign produced goods and services rises. Also, with increased output producing firms purchase larger

---

1 A change in the U.S. output (income) level will change U.S. import purchases. Unless offset by the domestic stabilization policies of our trading partners, an increase in their exports to the United States would stimulate their economies. Assuming this response is negligible is tantamount to assuming that our trading partners pursue their own domestic policy goals in a manner that offsets any undesired change in their foreign sector's net sales.

volumes of inputs including foreign produced inputs (transistors, shipping services, and so on). Thus, *imports are a positive function of aggregate income.* The marginal propensity to import has a value between zero and one, and for simplicity we can assume its value to be constant.

The *IS* Curve with Foreign Trade

With the addition of the export and import functions to the existing catalogue of behavioral relations we have developed for modeling the aggregate economy, our analysis of international trade will employ a commodity market equilibrium (*IS*) schedule based on the following functions:[2]

Saving	$S = S(Y)$
Investment	$I = I(i)$
Exports	$X = \bar{X}$
Imports	$M = M(Y)$
Government Spending	$G = \bar{G}$
Taxes	$T = \bar{T}$

For commodity market equilibrium, leakages must equal injections or, in algebraic form,

$$S(Y) + \bar{T} + M(Y) = I(i) + \bar{G} + \bar{X}.$$

In Figure 11-1, suppose we know one combination of an interest rate and an in-

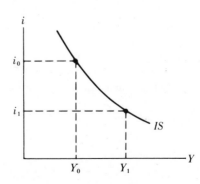

FIGURE 11-1 The *IS* Curve for an
Open Economy

2 Some of the behavioral functions are more simplistic than those we have previously worked with. For example, the responses of investment and taxes to changes in the income level are ignored. Using these simple functions makes the exposition of this section easier without requiring us to sacrifice any understanding of the role of the foreign sector. In the same spirit, explicit inclusion of the labor market in our graphical analysis is foregone.

come level (i_0, Y_0) which provides commodity market equilibrium (that is, we know one point on the *IS* curve). At the lower interest rate i_1, investment (thus total injections with $\overline{G}$ and $\overline{X}$ fixed) would be larger requiring leakages to be enlarged if product market equilibrium is to be maintained. Leakages, saving and imports, are a positive function of income implying that some increase in income (say, to Y_1) is sufficient to restore the equality of leakages and injections. The *IS* curve again slopes downward from left to right just as before. However, the slope of the *IS* curve is greater for the open economy than for the closed economy. A fall in the interest rate stimulates investment leading, through the multiplier process, to a higher level of income. But, with the import leakage response added to the saving response of the closed system, a smaller increase in income will suffice to reestablish the equality of leakages and injections required for equilibrium.[3]

Shifts in the *IS* Curve

As was the case for our closed systems, the *IS* curve is shifted rightward by any autonomous increase in spending on domestically produced output and leftward by any decrease. In addition to autonomous changes in domestic consumption, investment, or government spending, changes in exports will also generate such a shift—foreign purchases are no different from domestic purchases in their effect on output. An increase in exports shifts the *IS* curve rightward (increased aggregate demand must be matched with increased output for equilibrium to be maintained) and a decrease shifts it leftward. Likewise, a reduction in spending on imports, if that spending were redirected to purchases of domestic output, would shift the *IS* curve rightward while a redirection of spending away from domestic goods and into imports would shift the *IS* curve leftward.

---

3 For commodity market equilibrium in the open economy,

$$Y = C + I + G + (X - M)$$

or, using simple linear forms of our behavioral functions,

$$Y = a + bY + \overline{I} + I(i) + \overline{G} + \overline{X} - \overline{M} - mY.$$

Differentiating this equilibrium condition yields:

$$dY = b \cdot dY + \frac{\partial I}{\partial i} di - m \cdot dY$$

or

$$dY (1 - b + m) = \frac{\partial I}{\partial i} di.$$

The slope of the *IS* curve is

$$\frac{di}{dY} = \frac{1 - b + m}{\dfrac{\partial I}{\partial i}}.$$

This slope must be greater with the positive marginal propensity to import (m) present in the numerator.

The size of the shift in the *IS* curve generated by an autonomous spending change, measured at a constant interest rate, will be smaller for an open economy. That, again, is because any income adjustment results in a larger change in leakages when import purchases are sensitive to income changes than when they are not. The numerical value of the parallel shift in the *IS* curve is given by the product of the simple multiplier (assuming no interest rate change and, thus, no monetary dampener) and the autonomous change in spending.

Just as before, an increase in tax collections shifts the *IS* curve leftward and a tax reduction shifts the *IS* curve rightward. To anticipate an important concern that will be dealt with more fully later, you might pause to think about the impact in the commodity market of an increase in the domestic price level relative to the foreign price level. If such a price change affects our export or import functions, the *IS* curve will shift.

Equilibrium Income

The modified *IS* curve can be combined with the standard *LM* (money market equilibrium) schedule to determine *internal* or *domestic* equilibrium values of the interest rate, the level of income, employment, consumption, investment, and so on. The intersection of IS_0-LM_0 in Figure 11-2 depicts an economy with domestic equilibrium at the income and interest rate levels Y_0 and i_0 respectively.

An autonomous increase in net exports would shift the *IS* curve rightward to a position like IS_1, raising the domestic equilibrium values of income, the interest rate, consumption, saving, and employment, while reducing investment in this model.[4] Conversely, an autonomous fall in net exports would shift the *IS* curve leftward, reducing the domestic income and interest rate levels and so on. What would be the direct effect on equilibrium of an increase in the U.S. price level relative to that of our trading partners? A generally accepted answer is easy to provide. A rise in U.S. prices relative to those in other countries would prompt

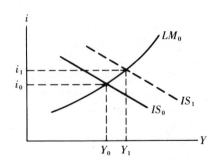

FIGURE 11-2 The Domestic Impact of an Autonomous Change in Net Exports

4 Recall that we have assumed away the response of investment to income in this model.

a substitution of imported products for domestic purchases while, with U.S. goods and services more costly, U.S. exports would decline. With exports reduced and imports increased, aggregate demand is reduced (the *IS* curve shifted leftward), prompting a contraction in economic activity. What would be the effect of an increase in the level of income in other countries? Of a change in tastes with vacations in Europe, foreign cars, and imported clothes and wine becoming more fashionable in the United States? Of legislation that raises tariffs (tax levies) on imports while providing subsidies to exports? You must provide your own detailed answers to these questions, but any disturbance that raises exports or shifts expenditures from imported to domestic production raises aggregate demand (shifts the *IS* curve rightward), stimulating economic activity. Conversely, any disturbance that reduces exports or shifts spending from domestic to imported production reduces aggregate demand, fostering a contraction in the domestic economy.

Balance of Payments Concerns

With only minor modifications in the *IS-LM* apparatus, we have been enabled to analyze the direct effects on the domestic economy of disturbances that impinge on a country's foreign trade balance. In addition, the modified *IS-LM* model can provide some important insights into the role of foreign trade in determining the state of a country's *balance of payments*. To initiate our concern with the balance of payments it must be noted that any domestic equilibrium position (*IS-LM* intersection) that could be located in Figure 11-2 *might* be consistent with *external* or balance of payments equilibrium. However, under a system of fixed international exchange rates, such as have prevailed in one form or another for most of this century (until February 1973), such a result would be sheer coincidence. The probability is large that domestic equilibrium (an *IS-LM* intersection) will be accompanied by disequilibrium—a surplus or deficit—in the balance of payments. Indeed, as a case in point the United States experienced a chronic balance of payments deficit in the era between World War II and the early 1970s.

The size of a balance of payments surplus or deficit is altered of course by autonomous changes in exports or imports, an issue to which we will return momentarily. But in addition, the expansions and contractions in economic activity which stem from domestic sources produce systematic changes in the balance of payments. Consider, for example, an economic expansion fueled by an autonomous increase in domestic investment. As output (income) rises, imports are stimulated aggravating any existing balance of payments deficit or reducing a previous surplus. In addition, as output rises prices may also rise, making domestic output more expensive relative to foreign production. As prices rise, imports are encouraged and exports discouraged so the balance of payments response to an income increase may be reinforced by any accompanying price increase. Similar arguments may be offered for economic expansions fueled by increased domestic consumption or government purchases. On the other hand, an economic contraction that stems from a fall in domestic consumption, investment, or government spending will enlarge a balance of payments surplus or reduce a deficit. Again that must be so because imports fall with income, providing a balance of payments response that may be reinforced by any decline in domestic (relative to foreign) prices during the contraction.

An autonomous increase in exports would shift the balance of payments toward surplus. But, an increase in exports raises the equilibrium level of income and, as income rises, imports rise. This induced import response must partially offset the effect on the balance of payments of the autonomous increase in exports and the remaining gap may be partly closed if the domestic expansion prompts an increase in prices. Conversely, an autonomous decline in exports would lower income (and perhaps domestic prices relative to foreign prices) inducing a partial offset in the balance of payments to the initial contraction in export sales. In a similar vein, any autonomous change in imports will induce further changes in imports (as income changes) which partially offset the balance of payments impact of the autonomous change—a tendency reinforced by any price level change that accompanies the change in economic activity.

Quite obviously, since the balance of payments is affected by changes in the level of income (the trade balance being inversely related to income), the use of stabilization policies to pursue domestic goals may result in balance of payments disequilibrium. If balance of payments equilibrium is itself a desirable end, our ability to pursue the domestic goals of full employment and price stability may be seriously constrained. For example, if a full employment level of output results in an unacceptable balance of payments deficit, policy makers may have to accept a lower level of output and employment to maintain balance of payments equilibrium. There are alternatives, including direct intervention in foreign trade (employing tariffs, quotas, export subsidies, and exchange controls which limit the right to exchange domestic for foreign currency), that can and have been relied on in efforts to reconcile domestic and external goals. But unmistakably, a balance of payments disequilibrium cannot persist indefinitely without a corrective adjustment and the requirements of balance of payments equilibrium can seriously hinder the pursuit of domestic goals.

Thus far, our accomplishments from opening our model of the economy to permit foreign trade are fundamental. We have shown the direct effect of export sales and import purchases on aggregate demand and, hence, on equilibrium income. In addition, we have demonstrated the interdependence between the domestic equilibrium level of income and the balance of payments—an interdependence that can be quite troublesome since efforts to achieve full employment may result in balance of payments disequilibrium. With these accomplishments our introduction to the macroeconomic role of international economic linkages is complete. But a comprehensive view of the macroeconomic consequences of involvement in the world economic community requires further analysis. At the outset, it must be recognized that the state of the balance of payments is not determined only by the balance of trade. Capital flows between countries (from investment, loans, grants, and the like) are also determinants of the overall state of the balance of payments. Furthermore, it must be recognized that a balance of payments surplus or deficit has important feedback effects on the domestic economy which, as we shall see, can manifest themselves in shifts in the *LM* curve. To permit illumination of the balance of payments feedback, en route to a comprehensive assessment of the influences of our international economic involvement, familiarity with the international monetary system is imperative.

THE INTERNATIONAL MONETARY SYSTEM

To permit efficient settlement of the net credits (credits minus debits) generated by international transactions, there is an elaborate international monetary system. The original foundation for the postwar system was established in 1946 with creation of the International Monetary Fund (IMF), an institution that now includes in its membership nearly all of the free-world nations.

With the establishment of the IMF, the domestic currencies of the *member* countries had their par values defined in terms of gold. For years (in fact, from 1934 until August 1971), the official dollar price of gold was $35 an ounce. With the official British pound sterling price of gold at 14.58 pound sterling per ounce, the official dollar-pound exchange rate was $2.40 per pound. It should be clear from this example that defining national currency values in terms of gold also defines their values relative to one another.

With clearly defined exchange ratios between different national currencies, individual transactions that take place across the borders are simple to accommodate financially. A tire maker in Akron, Ohio, wants to receive dollar payments for his sales in Texas. Likewise, he wants dollar payments for his sales abroad. In turn, a British exporter will want, ultimately, to have payment for his exports in the form of pounds sterling. In general, private transactions across borders can be and are ultimately settled in national currencies.

A U.S. firm that imports British sports cars may remit payment for those imports in dollars or pounds (or even in some third currency). If payment is made in dollars, the British exporter can sell those dollars to his bank at the prevailing exchange rate, receiving credit for deposits of pounds in exchange. To remit payment in pounds, the U.S. importer could, at the prevailing exchange rate, swap his dollar deposits for a bank draft denominated in pounds. But how are the exchange rates relied upon determined and what happens to foreign currency deposits sold to domestic banks (for example, any dollars sold to the British exporter's bank)?

A Two-Country Model of the Foreign Exchange Market

To answer the questions posed above and to ensure an understanding of the functioning of the international monetary system, we will analyze a simple, two-country example of a "foreign exchange" market. Let the two countries be the United States and England, and let us suppose that all debt payments between the countries are made in pounds. The foreign exchange market for the two-country example encompasses those institutions through which dollars and pounds are exchanged for each other. Included are private banks in the United States and Britain, foreign exchange dealers, and central bank agencies of both countries.

In this simple two-country world, there are a variety of British products and marketable assets that Americans demand. That is, Americans are willing to exchange some of their dollar purchasing power for English linen and china, English shipping services, stock in English companies, English real estate, and so on. Since English suppliers want to be paid in pounds let us place on American importers the burden of exchanging their dollars for the pounds they need. The demand for British goods, services, and capital assets then generates a demand for pounds (and a supply of dollars to pay for them) in the foreign exchange market. The higher the exchange value of pounds (the more dollars that must be given up to acquire a pound), the higher is the dollar price of British purchases to American buyers. With the dollar price of purchases increased, Americans will buy less from Britain, reducing the quantity of pounds demanded (dollars supplied) in the foreign exchange market.

Similarly, English demand for American goods, services, securities, and real estate creates a supply of pounds (in exchange for dollars) in the foreign exchange market since American suppliers want to be paid in dollars. The higher the value of pounds (the more dollars a British importer can get in exchange for a pound), the larger the quantity of pounds supplied in the foreign exchange market since each pound would buy a larger volume of American goods, services, or securities.[5] The foreign exchange market for pounds might appear as depicted in Figure 11-3 with the market-clearing exchange rate $2.40 = £1. Changes in supply or demand would lead to changes in the market-clearing exchange rate. For example, an increase in American demand for British goods and thus for pounds, reflected in the rightward shift from demand schedule D to demand schedule D_1 in Figure 11-3, raises the market-clearing exchange rate to $2.80 = £1. What would be the impact of an increase in British demand for American goods? [6]

---

5   To be more precise, a rise in the exchange rate will definitely increase the dollar volume of British purchases from America. Whether, with more dollars available per pound of expenditure, this results in an increased quantity of pounds supplied depends on the elasticity of British demand for U.S. purchases. The statement in the text implicitly assumes that this demand is elastic.

6   With international payments also made in dollars, there would also be a market for dollars in England. The price (exchange rate) determined by supply and demand in that market would have to match the price determined in the market for pounds. Why? To offer an analogy that may be familiar to you, if the price of eggs (or pounds) in two regions differs, *arbitragers* will enter the market buying in the low-price market (increasing demand and pushing the price up there) while selling in the high-price market (increasing supply and forcing the price down in that market) until no price differential from which they can profit remains.

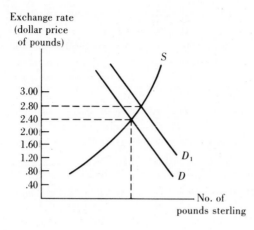

FIGURE 11-3 A Foreign Exchange Market

Flexible Exchange Rates

If demand and supply are left free to determine the foreign exchange rate, that rate will be forced to the market-clearing level. In that case if, at an exchange rate of $2.40 = £1, Americans are demanding more pounds for purchases from Britain than the British are supplying through their purchases from the United States (that is, there is an excess demand for pounds for foreign exchange), the exchange rate will rise. How far? To the level where U.S. demand for pounds is reduced to equality with the enlarged supply of pounds—that is, to the market-clearing level. A movement in the exchange rate from $2.40 = £1 to $2.80 = £1 as in Figure 11-3 would reflect such an adjustment. An exchange rate change of this sort would be referred to as a *depreciation* of the dollar relative to the pound or as an *appreciation* of the pound. The currency that was previously *undervalued* (the pound) has risen in foreign exchange value and the currency that was previously *overvalued* (the dollar) has fallen in value.

What would happen if suddenly the United States should decide to send more troops abroad or if we should find British cars more attractive because of a fall in their prices? Either of these disturbances would increase the demand for pounds in our two-country world and thereby raise the exchange rate. On the other hand, domestic (U.S.) inflation would make our goods and services more expensive relative to those in England. This would increase U.S. demand for British goods (thus U.S. demand for pounds) and would reduce British demand for U.S. goods (thus reducing the supply of pounds in the foreign exchange market). With increased demand for pounds and reduced supply, the exchange rate would be driven upward.

Fixed Exchange Rates

The flexible exchange rate system discussed above has direct current relevance. Yet, most of the post-World War II period has been characterized by *fixed* ex-

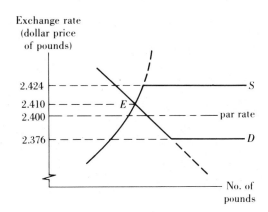

Exchange rate
(dollar price
of pounds)

FIGURE 11-4 The Stabilized
Pound Market—No Intervention
Required

change rates—rates which were initially agreed to at the 1944 meeting at Bretton
Woods, New Hampshire, in which the postwar international monetary apparatus
was created. Under the original Bretton Woods agreement, exchange rates were
fixed as countries were required to take the steps necessary to keep exchange
rates from varying more than 1 percent from specified par values.

The steps that are necessary for achieving such stabilization of exchange
rates can be illustrated using our two-country example. Suppose, beginning with
a $2.40 = £1 exchange rate, that Britain has responsibility for maintaining the
value of the pound within 1 percent of par. With that responsibility, a tendency
for the dollar price of pounds to rise above the legal limit must be met by Britain
with the offer of pounds (for dollars). Conversely, downward pressure on the
exchange rate would require the British government to absorb pounds by fur-
nishing dollars. Figure 11-4 shows the foreign exchange market with Britain responsible for stabilizing the pound. As that figure shows, the Bank of England,
as England's monetary agent, must stand ready to supply pounds (for dollars)
perfectly elastically at the *upper band* price of $2.424 (= $2.40 × 1.01) and
must be willing to buy pounds in whatever quantities offered (by selling dollars)
at the *lower band* price of $2.376 (= $2.40 × .99).

With the market situation as depicted in Figure 11-4, no intervention by the
Bank of England is required. The free-market equilibrium price of $2.41 = £1
(point *E*) is well within the bands of allowable exchange rate variation. In this
case, the supply of pounds resulting from U.S. sales to Britain is matched by
U.S. demand for pounds to pay for purchases from Britain.

This situation can change quickly. Suppose U.S. demand for British goods
and thus for pounds increases, shifting the demand schedule for pounds to D_1 in
Figure 11-5. With floating (flexible) exchange rates, the exchange rate would rise
to $2.45 = £1. However, under the postwar IMF system, Britain would have to
limit the rise to the upper band value of $2.424. The number of pounds supplied
to the foreign exchange market as a result of purchases from the United States is
quantity 0*A* in Figure 11-5 while the number of pounds demanded for financing

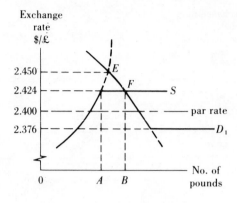

FIGURE 11-5 The Stabilized Market. Bank of England Supplying Pounds

U.S. purchases from Britain is OB. The difference (AB) is the number of pounds the Bank of England would have to supply in exchange for dollars offered in the foreign exchange market. In this case, the Bank of England's dollar holdings clearly would be growing.

As the obvious counter-example of exchange rate stabilization, suppose the demand for pounds had shifted leftward to position D_2 in Figure 11-6. In this case, Britain would be absorbing pounds in volume CD by providing dollars out of its accumulated stock of dollar *reserves*. That is, the supply of pounds from British purchases from the United States (OD) would exceed the U.S. demand for pounds (OC) for making payments to Britain. Out of its dollar reserves the Bank of England would have to exchange dollars for the excess pounds in order to prevent the exchange rate from falling below the permissible lower band value. Clearly, in order to provide this support for the pound, the Bank of England would need substantial reserves either in the form of dollars or in assets that can be exchanged for dollars.

Typically, the reserves that a central bank possesses would have been accumulated during a period of balance of payments surplus (like that in Figure

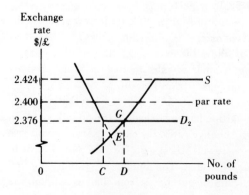

FIGURE 11-6 The Stabilized Market. Bank of England Absorbing Pounds

11-5). Figure 11-6, on the other hand, shows Britain in a balance of payments deficit situation where she is required to use accumulated reserves to absorb pounds in order to meet her IMF responsibility for maintaining the exchange rate.

In our two-country example then, Britain would have met her responsibility to the IMF by buying or selling pounds (dollars) as required to keep the exchange rate stabilized within the allowable range around par. The United States would have met its obligation by readily buying *gold* from or selling *gold* to Britain at $35 per ounce.

With the United States stabilizing the price of gold and Britain stabilizing the foreign exchange rate, there is a fixed relationship between both national currencies and gold. With these arrangements, when Britain has a balance of payments surplus (accumulating reserves), she can hold those reserves in a number of forms. They could be held in idle (noninterest-yielding) dollar deposit form; in the form of gold; or in the form of short-term, interest-bearing, U.S. securities. Either gold or dollars serve equally well as reserves in this two-country system. As such, total (two-country) world reserves would be increased either by new gold being introduced into monetary usage or by the United States running a balance of payments deficit settled by Britain's acceptance of the excess supply of dollars in reserves.

Extend our simple system to accommodate some 125 countries instead of two and we will have captured the essential features of the real-world international monetary system as established at Bretton Woods. With the currencies of all member countries of the IMF defined in gold, par values between those currencies were defined. In the post-Bretton Woods era, countries other than the United States kept their exchange rates within the allowable bands around par value with the dollar by exchanging their currencies for dollars. The United States, in turn, by exchanging gold for dollars at $35 per ounce, maintained the required link between the dollar and gold and, consequently, between all other national currencies and gold. In this system the dollar, "as good as gold" in the early postwar period, served as a basic reserve asset.

Adjustments for Fundamental Disequilibrium

While the fixed exchange rate system worked well enough to allow an unprecedented postwar growth in world trade, it did permit periodic monetary crises that threatened worldwide economic progress. The major crises stemmed from persistent balance of payments deficits in Britain and, more importantly, the United States.

Looking first at the British case, beginning with British purchases from the rest of the world in balance with purchases from Britain (so Britain was neither gaining nor losing reserves), assume that Britain experiences a domestic inflation at a rate exceeding that in the rest of the world. With fixed exchange rates, the relative price of British goods, services, and securities would be rising in world markets. Thus, world purchases from Britain (and demand for pounds) would fall and British purchases from the rest of the world (and the supply of pounds) would be increasing. The result, as in the situation depicted in Figure 11-6, is a balance of payments deficit requiring Britain to absorb pounds by exchanging its reserves (of other national currencies or gold) for those pounds.

A persistent deficit would gradually exhaust the deficit country's reserves if allowed to persist. However, the Bretton Woods agreement included provision for a country with such a chronic deficit (a country in *fundamental disequilibrium*) to alter its exchange rate to make its products more competitive in world markets. By redefining the gold value of the pound, making each pound worth less in terms of gold (an action called *devaluation*), Britain could *depreciate* the pound against other currencies (lower the exchange rate.)[7] With that *official* devaluation, Britain would have to intervene in the foreign exchange market (selling or absorbing pounds) at the new set of allowable exchange rates. With dollars, marks, francs, pesos, and so on exchangeable for more pounds, purchases from Britain are made less dear in the rest of the world while British purchases from the rest of the world are made more costly. With a suitable devaluation (and resulting depreciation of the pound against other currencies), a balance of payments deficit could be eliminated or reversed.[8]

The pound sterling has, in fact, been a weak link in the international monetary system and, as a prelude to the tremors that have reordered world monetary arrangements in recent years, was subjected to devaluation in 1967. Devaluation of the pound was disruptive primarily because the pound has been held as a reserve currency by the commonwealth countries. Of course, a depreciation of the pound reduced the purchasing power in world markets embodied in those reserves and hence reinforced the reluctance of the world community to hold reserves in a form other than gold or a *strong* (generally balance of payments surplus) currency. When the confidence-shaking devaluation of the pound occurred, the dollar was anything but *strong*.

The Dollar

As suggested earlier, in the wake of the Bretton Woods agreement, the dollar was the "key currency" in terms of which international trade and finance were

7 A depreciation of the pound against other currencies is an appreciation of those other currencies relative to the pound. The surplus countries could appreciate their currencies relative to the pound by *revaluing* (raising their currency's value in terms of gold). However, this technique has been used rarely to combat balance of payments difficulties.

8 Recognizing the increase in living costs suffered in the devaluation, the British could react to the increase in the pound price of imports by demanding higher incomes. Higher income payments, however, require higher product prices. By raising the domestic price level sufficiently, the effects of the devaluation (both on living costs and on the balance of payments) could be negated. For a full discussion of the impact of devaluation on the balance of payments, see H. G. Johnson, "Toward a General Theory of Balance of Payments" in Johnson, *International Trade and Economic Growth* (London: George Allen and Unwin, 1958).

implemented. Both private and government reserves were held, to a large extent, in dollar form (in cash, bank deposits, and short-term U.S. securities). With world trade growing rapidly after World War II, a limited volume of international gold reserves made the world happy to hold, as reserves, the large outflow of *safe, stable* dollars that a chronic U.S. balance of payments deficit provided. In fact, there was an international "dollar shortage" during that period. But, toward the end of the 1950s the demand for dollar reserves appears to have been satiated and the surplus dollars the continuing U.S. deficit provided were, increasingly, sold back to the U.S. central bank for gold reserves.

As we progressed into the 1960s, U.S. gold reserves were being depleted at a substantial rate.[9] The 1967 devaluation of the pound ended the pretense that reserve currencies were "as good as gold." With worldwide confidence in reserve currencies shaken, there followed a period of intense pressure on the dollar (a *run* into gold). The intense upward pressure on the price of gold (downward pressure on the dollar) resulted in establishment of a two-tier price structure for gold. In the "free market" tier, jewelers and dentists, industrial users, Arab Sheiks, and European speculators bid for gold in an unconstrained market.[10] In the official tier, international debts were still cleared with $35 an ounce gold.

With the U.S. balance of payments deficit growing explosively in 1970 and 1971, another massive crisis arose with a 1971 run against the dollar in favor of the strong German mark and Japanese yen. On August 15, 1971, President Nixon was prompted to abandon gold convertibility, a cornerstone of the system created at Bretton Woods.

In December, an emergency meeting of the main IMF members at the Smithsonian Institute in Washington produced an interim realignment of currency values. The dollar was devalued (the official price of gold was raised from $35 an ounce to $38 an ounce) and a number of other currencies were *revalued*. The overall impact was to depreciate the dollar relative to most European currencies by something under 10 percent while the German mark ended up with a relative appreciation of 14 percent and the Japanese yen appreciated 17 percent. In addition, the "bands" which demark the allowable outside limits on exchange rate variations were widened from 1 percent on either side of par to 2½ percent.

The Smithsonian agreement provided only temporary peace in the foreign exchange market. Under crisis conditions once again, the dollar was devalued to $42.22 per ounce of gold in February 1973 and, shortly thereafter, *official intervention in foreign exchange markets was ended*. Thus, early in 1973 the world was shuttled to a system of floating exchange rates. Since that time, limited cen-

---

9 From a high of $29 billion in 1949, the U.S. gold stock was halved by the mid-1960s and, with the deficit not merely continuing but growing, that gold stock had shrunk to near $10 billion by August 1971 when gold convertibility was abolished.

10 Since central bank intervention in the gold market ceased, free-market gold has sold for prices far above the previously effective $35 per ounce price. As of the completion of this text in the summer of 1975 gold had sold for as much as $198 per ounce.

tral bank intervention in foreign exchange markets has resumed but on a scale that leaves us on an essentially floating exchange rate system.

THE BALANCE OF PAYMENTS ACCOUNT

On our path back to the central concern of this chapter, the role of international involvement in shaping domestic macroeconomic conditions, we can add precision to our understanding of the transactions we have reviewed by taking a brief formal look at the U.S. balance of payments account which summarizes those transactions. Formally, the balance of payments account is just a summary representation of all the international economic transactions of a country and its citizens during a prescribed time period, typically a year. The U.S. balance of payments account for 1973 appears in Table 11-1. In this account, credit items (those with positive signs) represent the export of something: a commodity, a service, a security, a bank deposit, or gold. In return, such transactions provide residents with claims on the foreign exchange balances of foreigners. Debit items (those with negative signs) reflect an import from the same array of items and, hence, create claims by foreign residents on domestic funds.

The balance of payments is divided into three basic component accounts— the *current account*, the *capital account*, and *net gold and reserve asset movements*. Basically, the current account shows the difference between our exports of commodities and services and our import of them, though in some countries' accounts (as revealed in the U.S. account in the table above) transfer payments are included. U.S. commodity exports range from raw agricultural products to sophisticated electronic devices. Service exports include shipping, transportation on U.S. airlines, insurance, and the services of U.S. capital and technology abroad (from these last two items, we receive investment income—item 6 in Table 11-1—and royalties, respectively). Total revenues from exports appear in the national income and product accounts as exports (line 13 of Table 2-2 in Chapter 2, pp. 32-33). Total U.S. expenditures on imported goods and services appear in the national income and product accounts designated imports (line 14 of Table 2-2 in Chapter 2, pp. 32-33). The difference between exports and imports, designated net exports $(X - M)$, is the balance on goods and services in the overall balance of payments account (item 8 in Table 11-1).

The *capital account* measures the international purchase and sale of assets. Foreign lending and investment by U.S. citizens or businesses is tantamount to the *import* of securities or IOUs. As such, my purchase of a Swiss bond and General Motor's acquisition of a truck plant in Spain appear as debit items in the capital account (providing claims against U.S. foreign exchange reserves). The U.S. export of securities or IOUs, private or government (constituting foreign lending and investment in the United States), is a credit item. The balance on capital account (the sum of items 14 and 19 in Table 11-1) shows a deficit of $8,055 million in 1973. That is the amount by which U.S. loans and investments abroad exceeded foreign loans and investments in the United States, augmenting foreign-held claims on domestic funds, during 1973. Combining the *current account* and *capital account* balances, and adding the $2,302 million of liquid transfers from foreign holders of dollars to their central banks (item 21), we

TABLE 11-1 U.S. BALANCE OF PAYMENTS, 1973 (IN MILLION OF DOLLARS)

	Credits	Debits	Net
I. Current Account			
1. (Private) merchandise trade balance			+471
2. Exports	+70,277		
3. Imports		−69,806	
4. Military transactions, net			−2,266
5. Travel and transportation, net			−2,710
6. Investment income, net			+5,291
7. Other services, net			+3,540
8. Balance on goods and services (1 + 4 + 5 + 6 + 7)			+4,327
9. Remittances, pensions, and other transfers			−1,943
10. U.S. government grants (excluding military)			(−3,876) −1,933
11. Balance on current account (8 + 9 + 10)			+$ 450
II. Capital Account			
12. Long-term private capital flows, net (long-term loans and investments)			+62
13. U.S. government capital flows including long-term borrowing from foreign residents			−1,538
14. Net long-term capital flows abroad (12 + 13)			− 1,476
15. Balance on current account and long-term capital (11 + 14)			−$1,026
16. Nonliquid short-term private capital flows, net			−4,276
17. Allocations of Special Drawing Rights (SDRs—a form of "paper gold") —none after 1972			
18. Errors and omissions, net			−2,303
19. Total short-term capital movements (16 + 17 + 18)			− 6,579
20. Net liquidity balance (15 + 19)			−$7,606
21. Liquid private capital flows (from foreigners to their central banks)			+ 2,302
22. Official reserve transaction balance (20 + 21)			−$5,304
III. Net Gold and Reserve Assets Movements			
The official reserve transactions balance was financed by changes in:			
23. Liquid and nonliquid liabilities to foreign official agencies			+5,095
24. U.S. official reserve assets (gold, convertible currencies, etc.)			+209
25. Total (23 + 24)			+$5,304

Source: *Survey of Current Business.* Apparent computational errors due to rounding.

have the balance on official reserve transactions of —$5,304 shown in item 22. This deficit must be "financed" by movements of U.S. reserve assets. Thus, in 1973 we lost official international reserves and incurred reserve liabilities to foreign central banks in the amount of $5,304 million. It should be noted that like all balance sheets, Table 11-1 exhibits overall balance since the $5,304 million accretion of reserve assets to foreign official agencies just covers the official reserve transactions deficit. But this accounting balance says nothing about the presence or absence of balance of payments equilibrium. It is the unsustainable growth or shrinkage of a country's stock of reserve assets that indicates a balance of payments disequilibrium, and it is the balance on the current and capital accounts which augments or diminishes that stock. With those two component parts of the balance of payments account in mind, we can proceed to identify the fundamental determinants of the state of the balance of payments.

MAINTAINING OVERALL BALANCE OF PAYMENTS EQUILIBRIUM

Early in this chapter we discussed the determinants of the state of balance of the *current account*. We argued that imports are a positive function of the level of domestic income while exports can be treated as exogenous. Thus, net exports (the balance on current account) were an inverse function of the level of income. By adding an explanation of the state of balance of the capital account, we can now specify the conditions under which a country will find its stock of international reserves neither growing nor dwindling.

Loans and investments are attracted by higher interest returns. The higher are foreign interest yields relative to U.S. yields, the larger the fraction of any increment in U.S. wealth that will be loaned or invested abroad and the smaller the fraction of any increment in foreign wealth that will be loaned or invested in the United States. A rise in U.S. yield rates relative to foreign rates would attract an inflow of capital into U.S. assets (or, on balance, would reduce the size of any net outflow). Thus, the *net* outflow of capital (the balance on capital account) is an inverse function of the U.S. interest rate. Algebraically,

$$F = F(i) \quad s.t. \ \frac{\Delta F}{\Delta i} < 0,$$

where F is the net capital outflow and i is the U.S. interest rate.

Balance of Payments Equilibrium

A country's international reserve position will be unchanged in any period if, for that period, any surplus (deficit) in the current account is offset by an equal deficit (surplus) in the capital account. As we have indicated before, for our purposes such a period can be described as one of balance of payments equilibrium. With net exports a function of income and the net capital outflow dependent on

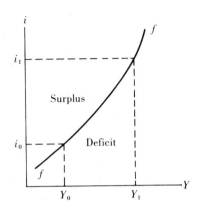

FIGURE 11-7 Combinations of i and Y That Provide Balance of Payments Equilibrium

the interest rate, there is always some interest rate level which can be paired with a specified income level to yield an overall balance of payments equilibrium.

Suppose we know one income and interest rate combination that provides balance of payments equilibrium (i_0, Y_0 in Figure 11-7). An increase in the level of income (say, to Y_1) would, by stimulating imports, reduce net exports and move the current account toward a larger deficit (or smaller surplus). Overall balance of payments equilibrium could be maintained only if an increase in the capital account surplus (or decrease in its deficit) could be obtained. With capital flowing toward attractive interest yields, there is some increase in the U.S. interest rate (say, to i_1) that would generate the increase in capital inflows necessary to maintain overall balance of payments equilibrium. Schedule ff in Figure 11-7 plots all the combinations of i and Y that permit balance of payments equilibrium, its upward slope showing, again, that deterioration in the current account balance caused by a rise in the level of income requires a capital-inflow-stimulating rise in interest rates if overall equilibrium in the balance of payments account is to be maintained. The larger the response of import purchases to any change in the domestic income level, the larger the capital-flow-inducing interest rate increase required to maintain balance of payments equilibrium—that is, the steeper will be the ff schedule. In contrast, the stronger is the capital flow response to a change in the domestic interest rate, the larger the required import-generating change in the income level—the flatter the ff schedule must be. In fact, with a "perfect" world capital market—foreign assets perfect substitutes for domestic assets, no transactions costs in shifting between foreign and domestic assets, no government controls on international capital flows, and so on—the ff schedule would be horizontal. The smallest change in the domestic interest rate would prompt massive international capital flows (inflows for an interest rate increase and outflows for a decline in the domestic interest rate). But, since imperfections (including transactions costs and government controls on capital flows) do exist in the international market for capital, a horizontal ff schedule is not realistic.

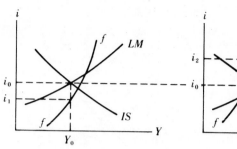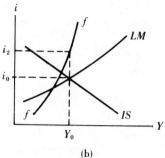

FIGURE 11-8   Internal Equilibrium and External Disequilibrium

With all the interest rate-income combinations that provide balance of pay-ments equilibrium represented by the *ff* schedule, every other *i*, *Y* combination must provide a balance of payments surplus or deficit. Any combination of *i* and *Y* that falls below the *ff* schedule yields a balance of payments deficit since the interest rate is too low to provide a capital inflow large enough to offset the accompanying deficit on current account. Conversely, any combination of *i* and *Y* above *ff* yields a balance of payments surplus.

By plotting the *ff* schedule in the same diagram with the *IS-LM* model, we can tell (for a given exchange rate and given domestic and foreign price levels) whether any *internal equilibrium* point (*IS-LM* intersection) will yield a balance of payments surplus or deficit. Figure 11-8a shows a domestic equilibrium that would be accompanied by a balance of payments surplus since the domestic equilibrium interest rate (i_0) is above the level needed for balance of pay-ments equilibrium (i_1) at income level Y_0. In contrast, Figure 11-8b shows a domestic equilibrium that would be accompanied by a balance of payments deficit. In this case, the interest rate would have to be raised to level i_2 to pro-duce balance of payments equilibrium at income level Y_0.

Systematic Shifts in the *ff* Schedule

A change in the domestic price level relative to the foreign price level will shift the *ff* schedule as will any change in the foreign exchange rate. As previously argued, an increase in the domestic price level will stimulate U.S. purchases from abroad as foreign goods, services, and capital assets become relatively cheaper, while reducing foreign purchases from the United States since U.S. goods, services, and assets are made more costly by the price increase. A domes-tic inflation at a rate that exceeds that of our trading partners then shifts the *ff* schedule leftward, requiring a higher interest rate (to attract capital inflows) or a lower income level (to boost net exports) to maintain balance of payments equilibrium. Of course, the *IS* schedule is also shifted leftward as net exports decline.

A fall in foreign prices while the U.S. price level stays constant would have the same effects since U.S. purchases from abroad would be made less costly and foreign purchases from the U.S. would be made relatively more costly. On the other hand, a fall in the U.S. price level or a rise in the foreign price level would shift the *ff* schedule (and the *IS* schedule) rightward.

An increase in the foreign exchange rate, like a fall in the domestic price level or a rise in the foreign price level, shifts the *ff* curve downward. As an illustration from our two-country world, suppose the dollar is depreciated from an exchange rate of $2.40 = £1 to $2.80 = £1. This depreciation raises the dollar price of U.S. purchases from Britain and lowers the pound price of British purchases from the United States. Domestic equilibrium positions (*IS-LM* intersections) that provided balance of payments equilibrium prior to the depreciation (that fell on the original *ff* curve) would provide surpluses afterward as U.S. purchases from Britain are reduced and British purchases from the U.S. increased. On the other hand, a reduction in the foreign exchange rate (an appreciation of the domestic currency) would shift the *ff* curve upward so that domestic equilibrium positions which previously yielded balance of payments equilibrium would produce deficits after the exchange rate alteration. Before continuing to the next section, you should be sure you can account for the impact on *both* balance of payments equilibrium and commodity market equilibrium of changes in the exchange rate and changes in the domestic price level relative to the foreign price level.

AUTOMATIC RESPONSES TO BALANCE OF PAYMENTS DISEQUILIBRIUM

Early in this chapter we indicated that a balance of payments disequilibrium produces important feedback effects on the domestic economy. With what we now know about the determinants of the balance of payments and the nature of alternative exchange rate systems, we can direct our attention to the automatic responses that balance of payments disequilibria produce. Since the nature of the adjustments differs, we must look at the response to a balance of payments disequilibrium with both flexible and fixed exchange rates.

The Flexible Exchange Rate Case

With flexible exchange rates, the adjustment to a balance of payments disequilibrium requires little explanation. In fact, you already know that if the exchange rate is determined by a free market, neither surpluses nor deficits in the balance of payments can persist no matter what the domestic equilibrium position. Supply and demand would force a floating exchange rate to that level that equates the volume of foreign currency demanded for domestic purchases of foreign goods, services, and assets with the available supply.

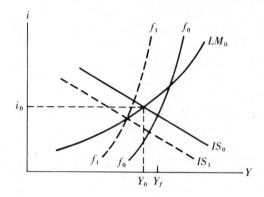

FIGURE 11-9 Adjustment to a Balance of Payments Surplus with Flexible Exchange Rates

Figure 11-9 illustrates the macroeconomic adjustment prompted by the appearance of a balance of payments surplus (due, say, to an exogenous increase in foreign investment). Interest rate-income combination i_0-Y_0 denotes the initial domestic equilibrium position, schedule $f_0 f_0$ is the initial balance of payments equilibrium schedule, and, for reference, the full employment output level is labeled Y_f. With the volume of foreign currency being provided by foreign purchases of domestic goods, services, and assets exceeding domestic demand for that currency, the domestic currency will appreciate (the foreign currency depreciate) making foreign purchases from our economy more costly and reducing the cost of domestic purchases from abroad. As a result, exports will fall and imports increase, shifting both the ff and IS schedules leftward. This adjustment must continue until both domestic and external equilibrium prevails, as at the intersection of IS_1, $f_1 f_1$, LM_0. Since a flexible exchange rate provides balance of payments equilibrium at any domestic equilibrium position, domestic policy makers are free to use monetary and fiscal policy to pursue the domestic goals of price stability and full employment (the latter of which now appears to need some attention), unfettered by balance of payments concerns.

The Fixed Exchange Rate Case

For most of our history, exchange rates have not been free to vary continuously but have been fixed. With fixed exchange rates, persistent balance of payments surpluses and deficits can be generated and those surpluses and deficits can affect the domestic economy in a manner that has not been explored yet.

With a balance of payments surplus, the domestic commercial banking system and the central bank will be experiencing an increase in reserves. With U.S. buyers offering fewer dollars in world markets than foreigners demand for financing their purchases from the U.S., commercial banks in the United States will be receiving for deposit a net inflow of funds (currency and checks) de-

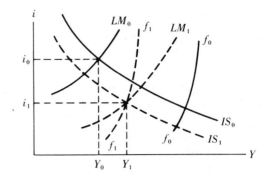

FIGURE 11-10 Adjustment to a
Balance of Payments Surplus with
Fixed Exchange Rates

nominated in foreign currencies. When the commercial banks turn these checks
over to the central bank, they have their reserve accounts with the central bank
credited in the appropriate dollar amount (given the current exchange rate) and
the central bank can use the foreign-drawn checks to obtain currency, bank deposits, short-term securities, or gold from the issuing country.

Our main concern now is with the impact of the change in domestic commercial bank reserves. As long as the central bank permits a balance of payments
surplus to increase commercial banks' reserves, those banks will be expanding
the domestic money supply, shifting our LM curve rightward. Thus, the economy
represented in Figure 11-10 by schedules IS_0, LM_0, f_0f_0 cannot be in full equilibrium at i_0, Y_0.

The balance of payments surplus generated with the economy at i_0, Y_0 would
increase the domestic money supply, shifting the LM curve rightward. The resulting increase in aggregate demand would induce an increase in the level of
income and an increase in the price level (preventing the LM schedule from
shifting rightward as far as it would with prices constant). A rising domestic
price level, by increasing the relative cost of U.S. products in the world market,
would reduce net foreign purchases from the United States, shifting the IS curve
downward.[11] At the same time, with foreign purchases of U.S. goods, services,
and assets depressed by increases in U.S. prices, the balance of payments (ff)
schedule would be drifting leftward as prices rise. Eventually, full equilibrium
would be reached at a point like i_1, Y_1 with income and prices above their original levels and the interest rate reduced. Clearly, the domestic money supply
response to a balance of payments surplus will, if permitted, eliminate that surplus even with exchange rates fixed. Likewise, a balance of payments deficit
could, through its impact on the LM curve, ultimately eliminate itself, but only
after a fall in domestic income and prices and a rise in the interest rate.

11 In addition, any real balance effect on consumption would reinforce this downward shift.

MONETARY AND FISCAL POLICY IN AN OPEN ECONOMY

As we have shown for both flexible and fixed exchange rates, without government intervention there are automatic adjustments that will eliminate a balance of payments disequilibrium. But, in doing so, those automatic adjustments produce changes in domestic output and employment levels, the price level, and the interest rate—changes that, in general, cannot be expected to be consistent with domestic policy preferences. For example, few countries are apt to welcome a sizable increase in unemployment in order to combat a balance of payments deficit or a domestic inflation to cure a surplus. Domestic policy makers will want to continue the pursuit of full employment and price stability in the face of a balance of payments surplus or deficit.

In both of the adjustment processes analyzed above, the economy ended up with commodity and money market equilibrium and with balance of payments equilibrium. But in both cases there remained unemployed labor at the end of the adjustment process. If an excess supply of labor results in a fall in money wages, further adjustments would take place that ultimately provide full employment too. A fall in money wages would permit the price level to fall, shifting the LM and ff schedules rightward (the IS schedule also with a real-wealth effect) until equilibrium is achieved at full employment. But if money wages did not fall, or fell so slowly that waiting for an automatic return to full employment would be unacceptable, policy makers would want to use monetary and fiscal policy actions to pursue full employment. In a similar vein, with money market, goods market, and balance of payments equilibrium at an output level above the full employment level, a price rise would permit reestablishment of full employment with stable prices. But if the price rise is unwanted, monetary and fiscal actions may be taken to reduce aggregate demand. We need to assess the effectiveness of fiscal and monetary policy in an open economy.

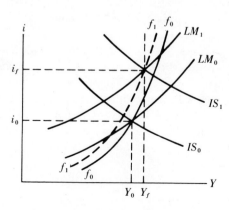

FIGURE 11-11 Fiscal Stimulus with Fixed Exchange Rates

Fiscal Policy with Fixed Exchange Rates

In Figure 11-11 the economy is represented with the money market, commodity market, and balance of payments in equilibrium at i_0, Y_0. The full employment level of output is Y_f so an expansionary fiscal policy (increase in government spending or cut in taxes) would appear to be in order. Fiscal stimulus (a rightward shift of the *IS* curve) would raise the level of income and, since the trade balance is inversely related to income, push the balance of payments into a deficit. However, the expansion of income would raise the interest rate as money demand is increased, and the interest rate increase would attract capital inflows, pushing the balance of payments back toward equilibrium. Should the capital flow attracted by the higher interest rate not fully offset the trade balance deficit, leaving an overall balance of payments deficit, the central bank would have to provide the needed additional foreign currency, swapping that currency for domestic currency (otherwise the excess supply of domestic currency in the foreign exchange market would produce an unallowable change in exchange rates). As domestic currency is absorbed by the central bank, the domestic money supply falls (shifting the *LM* curve leftward), raising the interest rate until capital inflows are sufficient to restore balance of payments equilibrium.[12] The final equilibrium would occur at a position like that denoted by i_f, Y_f with external equilibrium and domestic equilibrium at full employment. The *ff* schedule is shown shifted to the left of its original position to allow for the effect on the balance of payments of any price increase that accompanies the economic expansion. With fixed exchange rates, fiscal policy remains effective.

Monetary Policy with Fixed Exchange Rates

Earlier we demonstrated that with a balance of payments deficit and the central bank committed to maintaining a fixed exchange rate, the money supply automatically contracts until balance of payments equilibrium is restored. By implication, with money supply control subservient to the requirements of maintaining a fixed exchange rate, a second master—domestic stabilization—cannot be served. A corroborative demonstration of the indicated impotence of monetary policy when exchange rates are fixed is easily provided. With the economy at rest below the full employment level (at i_0, Y_0 in Figure 11-12) let the central bank attempt to increase the level of income by increasing the money supply (shifting the *LM* curve rightward to position *LM'*). In Figure 11-12, the money supply increase is shown reducing the domestic interest rate to level i'. But, we

---

12   As indicated earlier, the more mobile is international capital, the flatter is the *ff* schedule. If the capital inflows that the interest rate rise induces are greater than the trade imbalance induced by the expansion, providing a balance of payments surplus, the domestic money supply will grow and depress the interest rate until balance of payments equilibrium is restored. Fiscal policy in this case is reinforced by an induced monetary expansion.

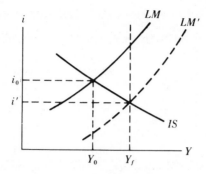

FIGURE 11-12   Monetary Policy with Fixed Exchange Rates

have not yet taken account of the international reaction to a reduced domestic interest rate.

As soon as the domestic interest rate falls, a capital outflow will begin—dollars will be rapidly withdrawn from domestic assets for reinvestment in foreign assets which offer a more attractive interest yield. To buy those foreign assets, dollars (the domestic currency) must be exchanged for other currencies. Of course, as additional dollars appear on foreign exchange markets there will be a downward pressure on the dollar in those markets. But, under a system of fixed exchange rates, the central bank must support the value of the dollar, swapping foreign currencies (or gold) for dollars at the allowable (fixed) exchange rate. As dollars are swapped for other currencies, the domestic money supply shrinks, shifting the *LM* curve leftward and reducing aggregate demand. If capital were perfectly mobile internationally (a possibility we have briefly encountered before), the capital outflow and the resulting shrinkage of the domestic money supply would continue as long as the domestic interest rate remained below the interest rate prevailing in other countries. Thus, with other central banks maintaining unchanged interest rates in their countries, the U.S. capital outflow would return the *LM* curve to its original position when the central bank has bought, in the foreign exchange market, the money it attempted to pump into the domestic economy. With perfect capital markets only one interest rate can prevail worldwide and the slightest change in any rate would call forth a shift in funds that equalizes all rates.

For monetary policy to have any domestic impact in a fixed-exchange-rate world with *perfectly* mobile capital, it would have to alter interest rates worldwide. To do that, massive monetary policy actions that are not offset by foreign central banks would be required for *small* domestic effects. Of course, foreign assets are not perfect substitutes for domestic assets, and there are transactions costs involved in shifting from one set of assets to another. Hence, complete equalization of interest rates between countries is not required in reality and individual central banks do have some power to influence their domestic economies.[13] But the limits which fixed exchange rates place on the central bank's ability to pursue an independent monetary policy have compelled countries to seek additional control tools, as we shall see below.

Monetary and Fiscal Policy with Flexible Exchange Rates

As we already know, with flexible exchange rates it is the exchange rate itself (rather than the domestic money supply) that adjusts to maintain balance of payments equilibrium. Hence, both monetary and fiscal policy can be used to pursue domestic goals with flexible exchange rates. (You should provide a graphical demonstration of this claim.) In effect, the flexible exchange rate serves as an additional policy instrument, maintaining balance of payments equilibrium so that our monetary and fiscal tools are free to serve other masters.

ADDITIONAL BALANCE OF PAYMENTS CONTROL INSTRUMENTS

Historical experience with a fixed exchange rate system has demonstrated clearly the reluctance of countries to sacrifice the pursuit of national ends for maintaining external equilibrium. Often, quite extraordinary measures have been taken to insulate domestic economies from the automatic adjustments that payments imbalances provoke. As we have already shown, with fixed exchange rates a balance of payments deficit prompts a contraction in the domestic money supply and, hence, in the level of economic activity. But, if the monetary authorities are unwilling to tolerate an economic contraction, they can "sterilize" the international flow of currency by returning to circulation every dollar that is absorbed by support actions in the foreign exchange market. Likewise, a payments surplus can be sterilized by removing from circulation every dollar that the surplus adds to the domestic money supply. Of course, with sterilization a balance of payments disequilibrium will persist—the use of monetary policy for domestic goals negates its use in pursuing any other goal. Thus, a payments deficit which would ultimately exhaust a country's available reserve assets could persist, as could a payments surplus that adds continuously to the idle stock of reserve assets accumulated by the country experiencing that surplus. Certainly, sterilization efforts in a fixed exchange rate system can only postpone adjustments that can provide balance of payments equilibrium.

13 See W. Branson, "The Minimum Covered Interest Differential Needed for International Arbitrage Activity," *Journal of Political Economy*, Vol. 77, November/December 1969, pp. 1028-1035. According to Branson, the U.S. interest rate can enjoy a swing of .36 percent without enticing short-term capital movements between the United States and Canada or the United States and Britain.

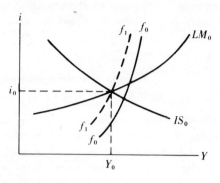

FIGURE 11-13 Exchange Rate Adjustment to Combat a Surplus

Altering "Fixed" Exchange Rates

Figure 11-13 depicts a country with a balance of payments surplus. If this country thinks its current domestic equilibrium position is optimal, and wishes to avoid both the inflation that would allow the surplus to bring about its own end and the accumulation of idle foreign currency that sterilization of the surplus requires, it could lower its foreign exchange rate (appreciate its currency relative to other currencies) to eliminate the surplus. The appropriate *appreciation* of the domestic currency would shift the ff curve leftward to $f_1 f_1$ so that the original domestic equilibrium could be maintained.[14] Germany, persistently in surplus, appreciated the mark in 1961 and again in 1969.

To avoid domestic contraction, a country with a persistent deficit can depreciate its currency relative to other currencies, shifting its ff curve rightward. As we have mentioned earlier, England devalued the pound in 1967, producing a sizable depreciation of the pound relative to most other currencies,[15] and the United States undertook two devaluations in the early 1970s.

Exchange rate adjustments are simple and straightforward. Yet, from the Bretton Woods meeting until 1971 exchange rate adjustments were infrequently used, usually being called on only under crisis conditions. While there are a number of reasons (not all rational) for reluctance to alter exchange rates, the most prominent concerns seem to have been the following:

1. A depreciation means an increase in the cost of purchases from abroad, thus, in the cost of living. For countries that depend heavily on imports, like

---

14 Maintaining equilibrium at i_0, Y_0 would also require some shift toward more expansionary fiscal policy since the currency appreciation will reduce net exports and, thus, domestic aggregate demand. It should be clear that with fiscal, monetary, and exchange rate policy, we could place the full equilibrium position (the IS-LM-ff intersection) at any point we wish in Figure 11-13.

15 A number of Commonwealth countries devalued with England so that the pound was neither depreciated nor appreciated relative to their currencies.

Britain and the Netherlands, the impact is conspicuous (and politically costly). In real terms, a country that is experiencing a balance of payments deficit can be enjoying a greater flow of real goods and services than the domestic economy produces, a privilege that is hard to give up.

2. National pride is often cited as a reason for avoiding devaluation as though some monumental loss of national face would be generated by a realignment of currency values. In the past, our own political leaders seem to have been smitten by an irrational concern for "cheapening the dollar."

3. While the threat of exhausting its international reserves imposes a balance of payments adjustment requirement on deficit countries, no comparable incentive afflicts a country with a surplus (which it can sterilize). With well-entrenched, politically powerful export- and import-competing industries, which would see their sales reduced by appreciation of the undervalued domestic currency, we would not expect to see frequent currency revaluations.

Other Practical Adjustment Techniques

In lieu of exchange rate alterations, a host of other direct restrictions on international trade and capital flows can be deployed to combat a balance of payments disequilibrium. By shifting the external balance schedule such direct restrictions serve as an additional policy instrument. Commonly employed direct controls include tariffs and quotas to limit imports, subsidies to exports making it possible for domestic firms to sell their products abroad at more attractive prices, restrictions on foreign aid, and quotas or taxes on foreign capital flows. Exchange controls which limit the volume of foreign exchange made available to domestic firms and households have also been employed by some countries.

There are many familiar illustrations of the application of direct controls. A common ploy is to limit tourist spending abroad. The techniques range from exhortations to "see America first" to restrictive limits on the value of goods tourists may bring home duty-free, to the prescription of maximum daily travel allowances while abroad. Exports are subsidized in a number of European countries where a domestic *value added tax* is rebated on exports and levied on imports. Foreign aid transfers are frequently tied to expenditures on the donor country's products, and, in the 1970s the United States, which has shouldered a large share of the world's burden both for development aid and for worldwide defense, has asked the other developed free-world nations to assume a larger share of those burdens. In the capital flow arena (which has displayed a chronic deficit in the United States as a result of foreign investment), direct controls on U.S. foreign investment by banks and nonfinancial institutions were imposed in 1965. These controls reinforced the restraint provided by an $11\frac{1}{2}$ percent *interest equalization tax* on all American purchases of foreign stocks and long-term bonds (these restrictions were lifted in 1973).

Needless to say, direct controls distort the trade and capital flows that would be observed in unfettered world markets wherein each country would emphasize production of those items in which it enjoyed a relative cost advantage. Instead, with direct controls the total volume of world trade is reduced, requiring some decline in the efficiency and material well-being of the world community. While *protectionist* direct controls are officially denounced by Western governments that ostensibly recognize the gains in production efficiency and world consumption offered by free trade, those governments all maintain some (primarily tariff and quota) barriers to the free flow of goods, services, and capital.

COORDINATED MIXES OF MONETARY AND FISCAL POLICY

For completeness, we need to extend our discussion of the techniques countries have for overcoming conflicts between domestic goals and balance of payments equilibrium by considering the use of alternative *combinations* of monetary and fiscal policies. For example, let us once more consider an economy that suffers from a balance of payments deficit when operating at full employment (domestic) equilibrium. Such an economy is represented in Figure 11-14 with Y_f the full employment level of output and i_0 the equilibrium interest rate. Now, with domestic equilibrium at output level Y_f balance of payments equilibrium would prevail if only the interest rate were i_1 instead of i_0. Logically, a reduction in the domestic money supply (shifting the LM curve to LM') could be employed to lift the interest rate and attract capital inflows.[16] But, to maintain full employment an

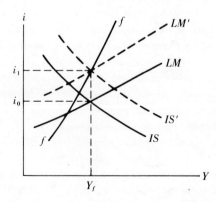

FIGURE 11-14 Combination Policies to Maintain Internal and External Equilibrium

16 As we have already indicated, with the passage of time a balance of payments deficit would automatically reduce the domestic money supply (*ceteris paribus*), shifting the LM curve leftward until balance of payments equilibrium is restored. But, the central bank can reduce the money supply without waiting for the domestic currency outflow to produce a domestic money stock contraction.

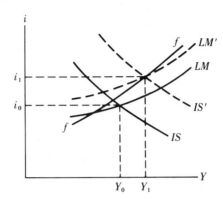

FIGURE 11-15 A Cure for Unemployment and a Balance of Payments Deficit

expansionary fiscal policy (shifting the *IS* curve to *IS'*) would have to accompany the *restrictive* monetary policy.

More generally, if the economy were suffering from both a depressed level of economic activity and a balance of payments deficit (as at Y_0, i_0 in Figure 11-15), it is still theoretically possible for an appropriate combination policy to achieve both full employment and balance of payments equilibrium. Once again, expansionary fiscal policy (shifting the *IS* curve to *IS'*) could be used to pursue the domestic goal of full employment while monetary policy is employed to achieve external balance (shifting *LM* to *LM'*).

Leaving graphical proofs to you, we need to acknowledge that it is also theoretically possible to employ mixed monetary-fiscal policies to deal with the combination of underemployment and a balance of payments surplus, with inflation (domestic demand greater than full-employment output) and a balance of payments surplus, inflation and a balance of payments deficit, and so on. In each case, with capital flows between countries sensitive to interest rate changes, monetary policy bears the responsibility for external balance (the subservience of monetary policy to the requirements of external balance is illustrated again) while fiscal policy must be used to achieve and maintain full employment. Unfortunately, the government generally must pursue more than two policy goals so that simple combination policies of the type we have illustrated may not be of much use. For example, the provision of a rapidly expanding stock of housing is usually accorded a high priority (at least in the United States). But, residential construction is suffocated by the high interest rates a monetary-fiscal policy mix aimed at combating a balance of payments deficit requires. More generally, high interest rates depress all investment plans, slowing the growth of productive capacity in general. It is quite logical that governments typically look for additional instruments for reducing a deficit that limit the reliance on high interest rates. Moreover, even when some simple mixed monetary and fiscal policy is appropriate, proper application of such a policy would require rather precise knowledge of the strength and timing of impact of both monetary and fiscal actions—knowledge that is not available now. It is no wonder that direct controls on international transactions have enjoyed such popularity.

The Future of the International Monetary System

Quotas and tariffs, export subsidies, restrictions on capital flows, indeed all manner of direct control techniques for combating a balance of payments disequilibrium are stop-gap measures which carry a heavy cost in that they disrupt efficient patterns of world resource utilization. But as we have seen they were quite naturally relied on, increasingly through the 1960s and into the 1970s, until the final breakdown of the Bretton Woods system in the spring of 1973. What is needed now is basic structural reform of the international monetary system.

As indicated earlier, the breakdown of the old order resulted in a system of flexible exchange rates.[17] While this system has allowed some fairly wide swings in exchange rates, it has survived the serious challenges generated by the massive balance of payments imbalances that have accompanied a worldwide protein shortage in early 1973 and the oil crisis that began in the fall of 1973—both developments that likely would have been far more disruptive of world financial order under a system of fixed exchange rates. Encouraged by that experience, the negotiating members of the IMF appear convinced (judging from the lack of movement toward a formal new world monetary system) that, with the current system (1975) of floating exchange rates, ample time is available for deliberating the future of the international financial system without the spectre of imminent worldwide monetary collapse haunting them.[18]

While the specific form of the financial arrangements that the IMF will finally adopt for the future remains uncertain at this time, some requirements are clear. First, the system adopted will have to provide considerably more freedom in exchange rate adjustments than was inherent in the Bretton Woods agreement and, second, it will have to include an inducement for balance of trade adjustments by surplus countries as well as by those in deficit.

While freely floating exchange rates provide for automatic maintenance of balance of payments equilibrium, freeing domestic stabilization tools to pursue domestic goals, it is often argued (especially by bankers and the world business community) that freely floating exchange rates are fraught with too much *uncertainty* and, hence, are disruptive of long-term sales and investment commitments. To focus on the essential concern, with floating exchange rates a U.S. firm cannot know the dollar value of the pound payments it will receive 1, 2, or 5 years from now on delivery of a shipment of wheat or a complex computer installation. In re-

---

17 Central banks can and still do intervene in foreign exchange markets, providing for a *managed float* of currency values.

18 In fact, world trade has continued to grow vigorously under the flexible exchange rate system.

sponse to that charge, it can be argued that firms can guarantee the domestic currency values of their foreign contracts by selling those contracts in international currency markets known as *futures* markets (for example, a U.S. firm can exchange pounds to be received in the future for dollars). But, to the extent that flexible exchange rates do increase uncertainty, ensuring the domestic value of contracts will raise the transactions costs firms face, reducing the volume of international trade.

Whether the uncertainties with floating exchange rates will be judged sufficiently costly to require a return to a system of fairly tight restriction on the exchange rate changes permitted in a specified time period remains an unsettled issue. The most frequently advocated compromise system that would restrict exchange rate adjustments is the so-called *crawling peg* system. Under this system, a country experiencing a balance of payments deficit (surplus) would have its currency depreciated (appreciated) by no more than a maximum stipulated amount per year, say, 1 or 2 percent. This system would permit substantial exchange rate adjustments over a decade (up to 22 percent with a 2-percent annual limit) to counter the effects on different countries' balances of payments that stem from such sources as differing rates of change in domestic price levels, changes in interest rates and income levels, and changes in the pattern of world resource prices. Under normal conditions, such a system should allow the external balance (*ff*) curve to track movements in the internal equilibrium position (*IS-LM* intersection) fairly closely so that, as with flexible exchange rates, domestic economic policy is unconstrained. At the same time, it is argued that the limits on the annual rate of adjustment in exchange rates would eliminate much of the uncertainty that might dampen the business community's interest in long-term sales and investment commitments.

SUMMARY

In this chapter, we have tried to provide a fairly comprehensive understanding of the macroeconomic ramifications of international trade and finance. Accommodating the role of exports and imports of goods and services was straightforward since net exports are a component of aggregate, commodity market demand. An increase in net exports shifted the *IS* curve rightward in the *IS-LM* model, stimulating the domestic economy, while a reduction in net exports shifted the *IS* schedule leftward, inducing a domestic contraction.

By extending our analysis to look at international financial flows, we were able to analyze a second, indirect way (or set of ways) in which the domestic level of economic activity may be affected by involvement in the world marketplace. When international transactions produce a surplus in the balance of payments (a net acquisition of reserve assets or foreign issued claims exchangeable for those assets), the net inflow of foreign currency deposits into the commercial banking system raises commercial bank reserves. The commercial banks' reaction increases the domestic money supply, shifting the *LM* curve rightward and stimulating the domestic economy. On the other hand, a balance of payments deficit drains commercial bank reserves, producing a reduction in the domestic money supply. The accompanying leftward shift in the *LM* curve results in a domestic contraction.

The automatic response to balance of payments disequilibrium in a fixed exchange rate world can, however, be postponed (the balance of payments disequilibrium perpetuated) if the central bank sterilizes the international deposit flows that accompany the disequilibrium. Central banks have, in fact, frequently short-circuited the automatic adjustment mechanism since the internal changes in income, prices, and interest rates that are necessary for automatic elimination of a balance of payment disequilibrium are typically inconsistent with domestic policy objectives. Still, concern for disequilibrium, at least in the deficit case where ultimate exhaustion of reserves is a threat, has all too often resulted in the imposition of a host of controls on trade, tourism, and capital flows. In addition, there is little doubt that domestic policies in the postwar period have, on occasion, been seriously constrained by balance of payments difficulties.

A glimpse at postwar experience suggests that the main shortcoming of the Bretton Woods system was the operational inflexibility of official exchange rates. Under that system, currency parities were changed only infrequently and always under crisis conditions—after the existence of fundamental disequilibrium was clearly confirmed. With the breakdown of the Bretton Woods system in 1973, we can look forward to a future system that is certain to provide more flexibility in exchange rates, perhaps a system that will provide for small but frequent changes in exchange rates with responsibility for exchange rate adjustments resting more evenly on both deficit and surplus countries. If the reformed system permits the *ff* curve to track closely movements in domestic equilibrium (as the freely floating exchange rates we now have do), macroeconomic policy will be free to pursue the goals set for the primary target variables of macroeconomic policy which include the levels of output, employment, and prices. Further, the reformed system should free us from the necessity of living with inefficient and cumbersome controls on trade and capital flows.

QUESTIONS

1. Draw the flow diagram appropriate for an open economy's commodity market and write out the equilibrium condition(s) for that market. Explain how commodity market equilibrium is affected by:
    (a) an increase in foreign income,
    (b) depreciation of the domestic currency,
    (c) an increase in the domestic price level.

2. Explain the slope of the ff curve. Explain how that schedule is affected by:
   (a) appreciation of the domestic currency,
   (b) foreign inflation,
   (c) import controls,
   (d) export subsidies,
   (e) exhortations to "see America first."
3. Explain how the exchange rate is determined under a system of floating exchange rates. Why have we relied on fixed rather than floating exchange rates?
4. Suppose, to combat a balance of payments deficit, import restrictions are imposed. Analyze the impact on income, employment, the interest rate, and the balance of payments.
5. Suppose a devaluation is utilized to reduce a balance of payments deficit. What fiscal policy should accompany that devaluation if no domestic income change is wanted?
6. We have assumed that the volume of export sales is independent of domestic income. Critically evaluate that assumption.
7. Suppose, under a system of fixed exchange rates, a country is considering two alternative policies to improve its balance of payment: (1) a formal devaluation and (2) an income reduction through restrictive monetary and fiscal policy. Which policy would you recommend? Why?
8. Evaluate the effectiveness of using monetary policy to raise the level of domestic employment:
   (a) with fixed exchange rates,
   (b) with flexible exchange rates.

SUGGESTED READING

Caves, R. E. "Flexible Exchange Rates," *American Economic Review*. Vol. LIII, May 1963, pp. 120-129.

Friedman, Milton. "The Case for Flexible Exchange Rates," in *Essays in Positive Economics*. Chicago: University of Chicago Press, 1953, pp. 157-203.

Krueger, Anne O. "Balance of Payments Theory," *Journal of Economic Literature*. Vol. 7, March 1969, pp. 1-26.

Machlup, Fritz. *Remaking the International Monetary System: The Rio Agreement and Beyond*. Baltimore: Johns Hopkins Press, Committee for Economic Development, 1968.

Meade, J. E. *The Balance of Payments*. London: Oxford University Press, 1951, Chapter 10.

Mundell, Robert A. "The Appropriate Use of Monetary and Fiscal Policy for External and Internal Balance," *IMF Staff Papers*. Vol. IX, March 1962, pp. 70-79.

————. "The Monetary Dynamics of International Adjustments Under Fixed and Flexible Exchange Rates," *Quarterly Journal of Economics.* Vol. 74, May 1960, pp. 227-257.

Smith, Warren. *Macroeconomics.* Homewood, Ill.: Richard D. Irwin, 1970, Chapters 22-24.

Wallich, Henry C. Statement in *The United States Balance of Payments.* Hearings Before the Joint Economic Committee, Part 3, The International Monetary System: Functioning and Possible Reform, 88th Congress. Reprinted as "In Defense of Fixed Exchange Rates," in Lawrence S. Ritter (ed.). *Money and Economic Activity: Readings in Money and Banking,* 3rd edition. Boston: Houghton-Mifflin Co., 1967, pp. 442-445.

Yeager, Leland. *The International Monetary Mechanism.* New York: Holt, Rinehart and Winston, 1968.

Chapter 12
Inflation

Inflation, a sustained *rise* in the general price level, is a phenomenon that U.S. society has been keenly aware of in the last decade. Indeed, in 1974 when the inflation rate crossed the threshold from a single-digit to a double-digit rate, inflation was conceded the distinction of being "Public Enemy Number 1" by President Ford. While the front page newspaper space currently devoted to monthly updates of the wholesale and consumer price indexes highlights the nationwide concern over inflation, we should not let those headlines or our own experience convince us that the current generation faces unprecedented inflationary forces. In fact, the United States has had a good deal of historical experience with inflation. As measured by wholesale price changes, the price level rose by some 25 percent annually during the Civil War, by more than 15 percent annually in the World War I era, and by nearly 9 percent per year between 1940 and 1948.[1]

In every inflationary period, there has been widespread and vocal concern over inflation suggesting that a rising price level imposes a heavy burden on society. Moreover, during every inflation period efforts have been made to identify the *villains* responsible for the inflation. Business leaders point accusing fingers at labor unions; labor points to avaricious, profit-chasing management; and every group saves some of its ire for governmental mismanagement of the economy.

In this chapter, we will try to sort out the issues that inflation raises—to explain how inflation occurs (and thus identify who the culprits are), to spell out the burdens inflation imposes on society, and to present the stabilization policy options available to government. We have already constructed macroeconomic models that explain the determination of the equilibrium price level. We now need to focus on the forces that produce changes in that price level. While our arguments up to this point have relied on *static* models, the analysis of inflation initiates our involvement in tracing the *dynamic* (time paths of) adjustments in our models of the economy.

THE EFFECTS OF INFLATION

What are the costs that society bears because of inflation and what benefits, if any, does society reap from inflation? The vocal public response to inflation leaves the impression that rising prices reduce living standards across the board by reducing the purchasing power of received income. This, however, cannot be

---

1 See Milton Friedman, "Price, Income, and Monetary Changes in Three Wartime Periods," *American Economic Review*, Vol. 92, May 1952, p. 629.

349

the case since, in the aggregate, money income is equal to real output times sales price. If inflation does not cause real output to fall, then the price level and *aggregate* money income can only rise together. It seems though that individuals are often unwilling to attribute their increases in nominal income to generalized inflationary forces. They appear to feel that their money income increases are *earned* while the increasing prices they have to pay for goods and services stem from the avaricious actions of some other individuals or groups.

Inflation and the Distribution of Income and Wealth

But even if aggregate money income rises with prices, inflation can benefit some groups at the expense of others—it can redistribute income and wealth. As we all know, anyone whose money income rises more rapidly than prices during periods of inflation enjoys an increasing real income level, and anyone whose money income rises more slowly than the general price level suffers a reduction in real income. But what individuals or groups does inflation affect in these distinctive ways? While conclusive evidence is hard to come by, it has long been asserted that profit earners gain and wage earners lose from inflation because wage costs of production typically lag behind increases in selling prices. And indeed, at least in the unionized sector of the economy where wages are set by contract, there appears to be some lag between price level increases and money wage adjustments. However, while adjustments in wages do appear to lag behind movements in the price level during the early stages of an inflation, wages tend to catch up in later periods as inflation premiums are built into new wage agreements. Thus, any inflation-induced redistribution of income from labor to profit earners is likely to be transitory.[2]

Tradition also holds that the salaries of white-collar workers adjust to price level changes with a long lag, permitting inflation to reduce the real income those workers enjoy. For some salaried workers, notably state and local government employees (including teachers) the reduction in real income from inflation is commonly alleged to be long-lasting since their salaries are notoriously slow to adjust to changes in prices. Of course, as long as government salary adjustments lag behind increases in the cost of living, income is redistributed from government workers to taxpayers.

For some individuals, inflation results in a permanent reduction in real purchasing power. Anyone who is dependent on an income that is not just slow to adjust to price level changes but is absolutely fixed in nominal terms will suffer a permanent purchasing power reduction when prices rise. Since bonds offer

---

2 Evidence that real wages and employment tend to peak together during inflationary expansions appears in R. G. Bodkin, "Real Wages and Cyclical Variations in Employment," *Canadian Journal of Economics*, Vol. II, August 1969, pp. 353-374. Also, see G. L. Bach and J. B. Stephenson, "Inflation and the Redistribution of Wealth," *The Review of Economics and Statistics*, Vol. LVI, February 1974, pp. 1-13.

coupon and principal payments that are fixed in dollar amount, bondholders suffer a reduction in real purchasing power as prices rise. Similarly, the beneficiaries of fixed value annuities from pension and life insurance programs have their real purchasing power reduced by inflation. Unlike a wage earner, a retired individual living off such fixed payments cannot bargain for catch-up increases in his income receipts. As a result, past savings that were thought to be ample to meet future needs (say, for retirement) can end up being woefully inadequate because of inflation. Partially relieving the impact of inflation on the living standards of the retired, Congress in recent years has provided a number of boosts in social security benefits. Moreover, since 1972 social security benefits have been tied to the price level by an *escalator* formula that automatically increases those benefits with increases in the consumer price index.[3]

Inflation can also alter the distribution of *wealth* between creditors and debtors. While debtors are benefited by inflation since their debts are fixed in dollar terms, the real value of which is diminished by the price level increase, creditors are damaged. An individual (debtor) who buys a $30,000 house with a $24,000 (80 percent) mortgage might welcome inflation. If prices should rise by 50 percent, the market value of his house would be $45,000 while his mortgage remains at $24,000. While inflation has increased the buyer's equity in the house more than threefold (from $6,000 to $21,000), the lender has suffered a one-third reduction in the real value of the mortgage debt due to him. Should all mortgaged homeowners favor inflation? Not necessarily. Most individuals are both creditors and debtors. Most have some savings which typically are *loaned* out (to a bank in a savings account, to government through bond purchases, and so on). The real value of the wealth they hold in the form of dollar claims is eroded as prices rise. With a large volume of outstanding debt, the wealth redistribution from creditors to debtors that inflation causes can be quite substantial. While unequivocally identifying debtor and creditor groups is difficult, older people are more frequently net creditors and younger people net debtors.

What broad conclusions on the equity of the redistributive effects of inflation have we outlined? No hard and fast generalization on the general nature of redistribution, on whether there is redistribution from poor to rich or *vice versa* as a result of inflation, is justified.[4] It is clear though that some groups,

---

3 While Congress in recent years has provided boosts in social security benefits to offset the effects of inflation, the real value of payments on bonds, insurance, and other fixed-dollar assets retirees often rely on has fallen substantially. With the potential for loss of real income on fixed-nominal-value annuities highlighted by recent experience, a number of variable-payment retirement programs have been made available in recent years.

4 Again, see Bach and Stephensen, *op. cit.* Also, for a discussion of the problems involved in evaluating the redistributive effects of inflation, see G. L. Bach and A. Ando, "The Redistributional Effects of Inflation," *Review of Economics and Statistics*, Vol. XXXIX, February 1957, pp. 1-13; and O. Brownlee and A. Conrad, "Effects upon the Distribution of Income of a Tight Money Policy," in *Stabilization Policies* (Englewood Cliffs, N.J.: Prentice-Hall, Research Studies of the Commission on Money and Credit, 1963), pp. 499-558.

like retired individuals living on pensions and other annuities, have suffered real income cuts through inflation as have the employees of state and local governmental units and of educational and religious institutions. In addition, it is clear that inflation can produce large wealth redistributions *within* groups when there are both net creditors and net debtors in those groups. Any redistributive effects from inflation, no matter what their breadth of incidence, are highly arbitrary and would be consistent with socially determined norms for income and wealth redistribution only by coincidence.

Learning to Live with Inflation

It is important to note that the potential redistributive burdens we have discussed arise as a result of *unanticipated* inflation. If the rate of inflation is correctly anticipated by the general public, the redistributions of income and wealth we have outlined above need not occur. With inflation anticipated, workers will demand contracts which include money wage or salary adjustments to offset the anticipated price increases and retirement plan purchasers will demand retirement benefits that are tied to the price level. In addition, nominal interest rates on bonds will rise to compensate lenders for the erosion of purchasing power that inflation imposes on fixed money payments. As we argued in Chapter 7, if an individual who would normally lend at a 4-percent annual interest rate expects prices to rise at a 5-percent annual rate over the life of the loan, he will demand a 5-percent inflation premium in the nominal interest rate he requires for lending —that is, he would lend only if he could receive a 9-percent or higher nominal interest rate. A borrower who expects prices to rise by 5 percent annually would be willing to pay the 5-percent inflation premium because he knows he will repay the loan in dollars that have lost purchasing power at a 5-percent annual rate.

Of course, it is unreasonable to expect all of society to properly anticipate episodes of inflation and, with the extraordinarily rapid inflation of the early 1970s, there emerged a great deal of interest in institutional changes that could limit the uneven and arbitrary redistributive effects which an unanticipated inflation engenders. Attracting the most attention were proposals for universal *indexation*—the attachment of inflation escalator clauses to all forms of contractual arrangements involving money transfers. Already, escalator clauses that employ the consumer price index as a measure of changes in the purchasing power of the dollar protect the real wages of some 5 million union workers and the real food purchasing power of some 18 million food stamp recipients along with the real value of the pensions of some 31 million social security recipients. With a comparable indexation of all loans, insurance premiums and benefits, long-term purchase agreements, rents, taxes, and so on, we might "learn to live with inflation," blunting its harshest redistributive effects.

On the other hand, it can be contended that learning to live with inflation through indexation is a sure-fire way of perpetuating and even accelerating inflation. With broad if not universal protection from inflation, the public and political support necessary for the sometimes harsh policies necessary to control inflation might well evaporate. Moreover, universal indexation would build momentum into any episode of inflation that an unavoidable, random disturbance might initiate as automatically escalated wages and prices chase each other upward. Because of such concerns universal indexation is supported by relatively few economists.[5]

It should also be noted that while correct inflationary expectations or widespread indexing can largely prevent the redistributive impact of inflation, there is one social cost of inflation that cannot be circumvented as long as interest (which rises to compensate lenders for expected inflation losses) is not paid on money holdings. Even with correct inflation expectations or widely dispersed escalator agreements, inflation still reduces the real value of any individual's cash balances. Recognizing the increased cost of holding money which inflation creates, the public will try to reduce its money holdings below the desired level that would prevail if no inflation were anticipated. Economizing on the use of money balances does reduce the "inflation tax" on money holdings but, at the same time, it entails a sacrifice of the convenience yield of the additional money balances.

Effects on Production and Growth

There are conflicting views on inflation's connection to real production and output growth. Some contend that price stability is essential for maximum production and rapid growth. It is argued that the expectation of further price increases nurtured by inflation experience causes a reduction in the propensity to save (that is, an upward shift in the consumption function) as individuals, expecting prices to rise, *buy now* to beat the price increases. Since it is only by saving (not consuming) that resources can be freed for the investment which will increase the stock of capital and, thus, future production capacity, any reduction in the propensity to save may limit the growth in output. Further, the expectation of inflation may divert substantial energy away from production activities and into speculative activities as individuals search for assets that can protect their accumulated wealth from erosion due to price increases.

The opposition view holds that gradual increases in the price level have a beneficial effect on economic activity or, at least, that such price increases are symptomatic of the existence of those forces that produce maximum output and rapid growth. According to this view inflation occurs only when, because of buoyant demand, productive capacity is fully utilized. The combination of inten-

5 There is considerably more support for indexing the federal income tax system so that mere inflation would not push taxpayers into higher percentage tax brackets when they have enjoyed no real income gain. Basically, indexing the income tax would involve tying the dollar value of personal exemptions, deductions, and income brackets to a broad measure of the price level.

sive utilization of existing productive facilities and rising prices (which producers are likely to read as a sign of strong demand) is assumed to spur business investment. This, in turn, adds both to current demand for output and, as time goes on, to the economy's productive capacity. Those concerned with the distribution of income also claim that in periods of rapid expansion low productivity labor is drawn into the work force and given skills, through on-the-job training, which permanently raise its income stream.[6]

In point of fact, general prosperity and rapid growth have been observed historically during periods in which prices have been rising, falling, or stable. Thus, no generalization on the implications of different rates of inflation for economic vitality can be unequivocally established, at least not for the limited range of rates of price change which the United States has experienced.

Inflation and the Balance of Payments

We can complete our survey of the effects of inflation with a brief look at the link between inflation and the balance of payments. Under a system of fixed international exchange rates, if a country has a rate of inflation which exceeds that of its trading partners, its balance of payments is likely to suffer. If domestic prices rise more rapidly than prices in other countries, domestic products become more expensive relative to those produced in other countries. As a result, exports are likely to fall and imports rise, aggravating any balance of payments deficit.[7] Hence, the role of inflation in weakening the balance of payments in a fixed-exchange-rate world can add to the official concern over inflation. However, as explained in Chapter 11, after many years of continuing U.S. balance of payments deficits, the world trading community adopted a system of flexible exchange rates in 1973. Under that system, differential rates of inflation in different countries bring about automatic changes in exchange rates to maintain balance of payments equilibrium.

While our list of the by-products of inflation is not exhaustive, it is representative of the lines of reasoning followed in discussions of the costs of inflation. Moreover, it is sufficient to rationalize the common acceptance of general price stability as a national policy goal.

THE INFLATIONARY PROCESS

Our next task is to explain how inflation occurs. In broad terms, the price level is determined by the interaction of aggregate supply and aggregate demand so

---

6 Evidence on the connection between inflation and improved employment prospects for the unskilled poor appears in L. Thurow, *Poverty and Discrimination* (Washington, D.C.: The Brookings Institution, 1969).

7 While there are some possible offsets to this "current account" response to inflation, it is generally believed that inflation results in deterioration in the balance of payments.

price level changes must be the result of changes in aggregate supply or demand. By directly applying the aggregate model we have already constructed (in Chapter 9), we can trace the adjustments in aggregate supply and demand that are capable of generating inflation.

The aggregate model is reproduced in Figure 12-1, initially at rest at interest rate i_0, output level Y_0, and employment level N_0 (there is involuntary unemployment in the labor market) at real wage $(\overline{W}/P)_0$. If money wages are assumed to be inflexible in the downward direction, even in the face of unemployment, no automatic adjustment takes place to alter the initial values (0 subscripts) of income, the interest rate, employment, the real wage, and so on.

If we now let this initial equilibrium be disturbed by an autonomous increase in aggregate demand stemming from the real sector (we could as easily raise aggregate demand through an increase in the money stock), then let the system return to equilibrium, what will have happened to the equilibrium levels of output

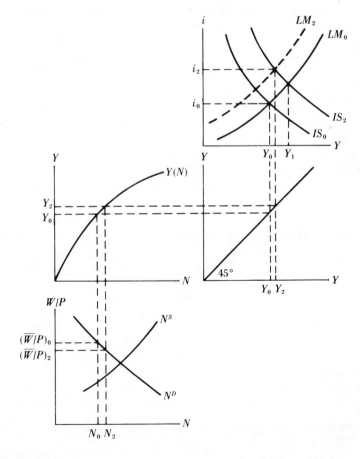

FIGURE 12-1 Real Output and the Price Level in the General Model

and prices? Already, in Chapter 9, we have looked at a disturbance of this nature. The autonomous increase in aggregate demand creates excess demand in the commodity market $(Y_1 - Y_0)$, resulting in a rise in prices. As long as prices rise, the real value of the money stock is reduced (shifting the LM curve leftward), raising the interest rate. The increased interest rate reduces investment. Thus, after the initial disturbance, total demand will be contracting as the price level rises.[8] In the meantime, any price increase not matched by a money wage increase lowers the real wage, allowing an increase in employment and thus in output. Equilibrium will be restored when reduced total demand and increased output meet at a level like Y_2 in Figure 12-1. At that point, with neither excess supply nor excess demand in the commodity market, the price level will become *stable at the new higher level* ending the adjustment process. Clearly, the initial increase in demand results in an increase in real output (quantity supplied) accompanied by a once-and-for-all increase in the equilibrium price level. With both real output and the price level increased, the dollar value of output (spending) is increased. To accommodate this increase in the dollar value of total spending with a fixed nominal money stock, velocity must be increased since, by definition, $MV = PY$. For velocity to increase, there is an increase in the interest rate.

If, beginning with the new equilibrium position (2 subscripts), we again let aggregate demand increase autonomously, we would again obtain an increase in both output and prices. If aggregate demand continues expanding, output and prices would continue to rise together *until* we reach the full employment level of output. At that point, any further autonomous increase in aggregate demand would result in an increase in the price level and in money wages, but the real wage, the level of employment, and the volume of real output would not be changed.[9] The relationship between output and prices that we have traced, the "aggregate supply function" implied by our complete model, would appear as in Figure 12-2. As that schedule shows, as long as the economy is operating with excess capacity, a higher price level will be accompanied by a higher level of output.[10] Once full employment is reached, however, output cannot increase no matter what happens to prices.[11]

In addition to the aggregate supply schedule of Figure 12-2, our aggregate

8 If there is a significant real wealth effect, this shrinkage of demand as prices rise will be reinforced by a reduction in consumption spending (shifting the IS curve leftward). Likewise, in an open economy operating in a fixed-exchange-rate world, an increase in the domestic price level reduces net exports (shifting the IS curve leftward) reinforcing the shrinkage of demand.

9 You should be able to prove this conclusion with the model in Figure 12-1, concentrating on the impact of price level changes in the labor market. Review Chapter 9 if you cannot.

10 In fact, the greater the degree of excess capacity, the smaller the decline in the marginal product of labor required for a given increase in output and, thus, the smaller the increase in price level (required to reduce the real wage) we would expect to see accompanying the output increase.

11 This is assuming that labor has full information on money wage and price movements so that money wages rise to eliminate any excess demand for labor.

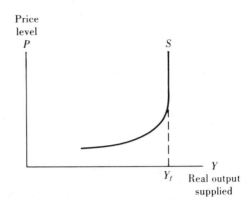

FIGURE 12-2 The Aggregate Supply Function

analysis has also provided us with a simple aggregate demand function. As the
price level rises, reducing the real value of the money stock, the interest rate
rises damping investment. Hence, an increase in the general price level reduces
the quantity of aggregate output demanded, providing the aggregate demand
function sketched in Figure 12-3.[12] The summary aggregate supply and demand
schedules that are implied by our full model provide a convenient vehicle for
explaining the processes that can produce inflation, the concern of this chapter.
(They also are convenient for analyzing the disturbances dealt with in Chapter 9
using the full model. You were forced to work with the full model in that chapter
to become familiar with the interactions between the money, commodity, and
labor markets as the economy adjusts from one equilibrium position to another.)

Demand-Pull Inflation

Demand-pull or *excess demand* inflation is, as the labels imply, an inflation
(*rising* price level) that results from aggregate demand exceeding the volume of

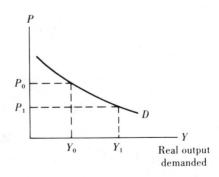

FIGURE 12-3 The Aggregate Demand Schedule

12 Footnote 9 of this chapter is equally applicable here. Also, with a negative real wealth effect
or with net exports reduced by the domestic price increase, the shrinkage in demand would be
reinforced.

output. Often, this variety of inflation has been described as resulting from "too many dollars chasing too few goods." Combining the aggregate supply and aggregate demand schedules illustrated in Figures 12-2 and 12-3, Figure 12-4 depicts an economic system initially at equilibrium in the position characterized by 0 subscripts. In developing the aggregate demand schedule, we allowed the price level to change (to rise in our exercise) while assuming that all the other factors that affect the positions of the IS and LM curves remained unchanged. It should be clear then that a change in any of those factors (the nominal quantity of money, the level of autonomous consumption and investment, government spending and tax collections, or any other *nonprice* determinant of aggregate demand) will alter the position of the aggregate demand schedule. For example, an autonomous increase in consumption (decrease in saving), which shifts the IS curve in the full model rightward, results in a higher level of aggregate demand at any given price level (that is, in a rightward shift of the aggregate demand schedule). The same would be true of an autonomous increase in investment or government spending, or of an autonomous decrease in tax collections. An autonomous rightward shift of the LM schedule, due to an increase in money supply or an autonomous decrease in money demand, would likewise shift the aggregate demand schedule rightward.

What happens if the initial equilibrium in the economic system represented in Figure 12-4 is disturbed by a rightward shift of the aggregate demand schedule, say, to the position of schedule D_1? With no change in the price level, total demand after the shift would be Y_1 while output would be at the initial level Y_0. Thus, excess demand would exist pulling the price level upward. The *rising* price level would, as we have already demonstrated, induce an increase in the level of output supplied (by reducing the real wage, stimulating employment) along with a decrease in the quantity of output demanded (by reducing the real money supply, raising the interest rate and reducing investment) as long as prices are

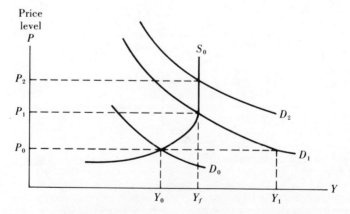

FIGURE 12-4 The Effects on Real Output and the Price Level of Shifts in the Aggregate Demand Schedule

rising. Equilibrium would be restored when output and demand match at level Y_f and the price level is at the new higher level P_1. During the adjustment process (while the price level is rising) we would be experiencing demand-pull inflation. However, it would be an inflation that results in a *once-and-for-all* increase in the price level and a *once-and-for-all* increase in the level of output and employment. This adjustment process requires, of course, a finite period of calendar time.

Suppose, at the new equilibrium position (P_1,Y_f), aggregate demand once more shifts autonomously rightward to position D_2. Since, in this case, we start with the economy operating at its capacity output position, the increase in aggregate demand will result in an increase in the price level (to P_2) with no change in the level of output (output remains at capacity level Y_f). While the adjustment process is taking place we would be experiencing inflation. Once the price level rises to P_2, inflation halts. For pure demand-pull inflation to persist indefinitely, demand would have to continue shifting rightward indefinitely. This would require a continuing autonomous: (1) increase in spending (C, I, or G); (2) reduction in taxes; (3) increase in money stock; or (4) reduction in demand for money. Further, if the *LM* schedule becomes interest inelastic at high interest rates, a money supply increase would be required to permit any price level increase in the resulting vertical segment of the *LM* schedule.[13]

Cost-Push or Seller's Inflation

While traditional explanations of inflation have emphasized the role of demand pressure on the price level, in the post-World War II period there has been widespread interest in theories that focus on the role of aggregate supply in the inflation process. The simultaneous appearance of both inflation and excessive unemployment in the postwar period suggests, as we shall see, that inflation *can* stem from a leftward or upward shift of the aggregate supply curve. An inflation that stems from such a shift, labeled a *cost-push* or *seller's inflation*, has usually been attributed to sellers of labor services or products raising their prices when there is no generalized excess demand for labor or output.[14]

---

13 It should have occurred to you that we have already worked out the demand-pull inflation process with our full model. Again, all we have done in this section is draw out of our full model the aggregate supply and demand functions that can be used to quickly identify the impact on real output and the price level of shifts on the supply or demand side of the economy. To fully explain the inflation process, market by market, you must employ the full model.

14 The suggestion that inflation can result from supply or *cost* sources is not really new. In their review of inflation theory, Bronfenbrenner and Holzman acknowledge precedent for this explanation saying:

> Cost inflation has been the layman's instinctive explanation of general price increases since the dawn of the monetary system. We know of no inflationary movement that has not been blamed by some people on "profiteers," "speculators," "hoarders," or workers and peasants "living beyond their station."

M. Bronfenbrenner and F. Holzman, "Survey of Inflation Theory," *American Economic Review*, Vol. 53, September 1963, p. 613.

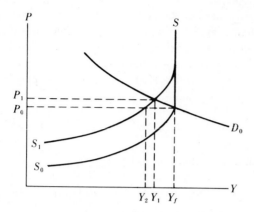

FIGURE 12-5 An Upward Shift of the Aggregate Supply Curve—Cost-Push Inflation

    With an upward shift of the aggregate supply curve, the business sector will continue supplying any selected volume of real output only at a higher price level. In Figure 12-5, our aggregate supply-demand model is reproduced with the economy initially at full employment equilibrium with output Y_f and price level P_0. An upward shift in the aggregate supply function to position S_1 creates excess demand for output $(Y_f - Y_2)$ at original price level (P_0) and, as usual, excess demand raises the general price level. As the price level rises, reducing the real value of the money supply and raising the interest rate, aggregate demand shrinks along the original demand schedule (D_0) while supply grows along the new aggregate supply schedule (S_1) as the real wage declines. Thus, the price increase closes the gap between supply and demand permitting equilibrium to be restored at an increased price level (P_1) and reduced output level (Y_1). With output reduced, employment must be reduced. Should the aggregate supply curve continue shifting leftward the price level would continue rising and output (and employment) would continue falling. Clearly, cost-push inflation not only can accompany unemployment but, in fact, can cause unemployment.

Shifting the Supply Curve Upward

To *explain* upward shifts in the aggregate supply schedule, cost-push inflation theories have traditionally relied on the exploitation of monopoly power for the motive force that generates those shifts. Such monopoly power resides, according to the subscribers to the cost-push theory, in the hands of organized labor and big business.

    An inflation that results from labor exerting its market power to bid up wages is typically labeled a *wage-push inflation*. However, not all increases in wage rates are inflationary. In order for wage increases to be inflationary, the rate of wage increases must exceed the rate of growth of labor productivity.

    If unionized labor bargains successfully for a 3-percent increase in money wages over a 1-year period and, during that same period, labor productivity

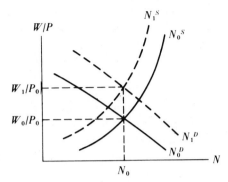

FIGURE 12-6 A Noninflationary
Wage Increase

increases by 3 percent, the wage increase is not inflationary. Figure 12-6 shows
the labor market initially in equilibrium with real wage W_0/P_0 and full employment at N_0. By bargaining for an increased money wage, labor shifts its supply
schedule upward, for example to N_1^S. If labor's *marginal* productivity is increased in the same proportion as the wage increase, the labor demand schedule
shifts upward (N_1^D) and intersects the new labor supply schedule at an unchanged employment level (remember that the labor demand schedule is nothing
but the marginal product of labor schedule). Profit-maximizing firms (which
equate the real wage and the marginal product of labor) can continue to hire the
same, full employment volume of labor (N_0) with the price level unchanged at P_0
while labor's real wage and productivity have increased together. Of course, with
labor's marginal productivity raised an unchanged level of employment would
produce an increased volume of real output, requiring a full employment stabilization policy to keep the price level from changing. But, this minor complication
leaves our general conclusion unchanged. If the money wage rate and labor's
marginal productivity grow at the same rate, the wage increase is noninflationary
in the sense that an unchanged volume of employment may be maintained (including full employment) with no price level rise. If money wages rise faster
than labor's marginal product, an unchanged level of employment could be
maintained only with higher prices.[15]

Returning to our numerical example and altering our focus to look at unit
production costs, with both money wages and output per man-hour (the *average*

---

15 Competitive, profit-maximizing firms hire the volume of labor that equates the real wage
and the marginal product of labor—$W/P = MP_N$. Thus, the price level is given by $P = W/MP_N$.
With money wages rising in the same proportion as labor's marginal product, the price level
remains unchanged—$P = (1 + \lambda)W/(1 + \lambda)MP_N$. But if prices rise faster than labor's marginal product, say at rate γ, then the price level must rise if employment is to remain unchanged—in that case.

$$P = (1 + \gamma) \cdot \frac{W}{(1 + \lambda)} \cdot MP_N = \left(\frac{1 + \gamma}{1 + \lambda}\right) \cdot \frac{W}{MP_N}.$$

product of labor) increased by 3 percent, the unit cost of output is unchanged. The same total output could be produced with 3 percent fewer labor hours, each receiving a 3-percent higher wage rate so that total labor outlay is unchanged at any selected output level. However, if unions should win a 5-percent wage boost during a period when productivity rises by 3 percent, unit labor costs would rise by 2 percent. If firms' profit margins are to be maintained at the before-wage-boost level, prices would have to rise, allowing the increase in unit production costs to be passed on to buyers. Thus, producers would be willing to provide any specified volume of aggregate output only at an increased price level—the aggregate supply schedule is shifted upward producing cost-push inflation.

Alternatively, if cost-push inflation stems from business firms' use of the monopoly power they enjoy in product markets to directly raise product prices, the inflation can be termed a *profit-push inflation*. With firms charging higher prices on any output volume, the aggregate supply curve has shifted upward. No matter which group is held responsible for the upward shift of the aggregate supply schedule in our model, as prices rise there is cost-push inflation.

ANTI-INFLATION POLICY

In theory, curing an inflation that results purely from demand pressure would be quite simple. Since, in that case, inflation occurs only because aggregate demand exceeds supply, all that is necessary to stop inflation is a reduction in demand until the dollar value of demand equals the value of supply at the existing price level. To prevent demand-pull inflation, it is sufficient to have demand grow at the same rate as supply. As we know, the necessary tools for controlling aggregate demand are available. Both restrictive monetary policy, entailing a reduction in the money stock or in its rate of growth, and restrictive fiscal policy, entailing a shift toward a smaller deficit or larger surplus, are able to effectively combat the pure demand-pull inflationary forces in our model.

Unfortunately, as a practical matter a number of (often essentially political rather than economic) difficulties stand in the path of an inflation abatement program. A reduction in government spending may require cutbacks in programs that have high social priorities; a restrictive monetary policy may raise interest rates to distastefully high levels; and tax increases are always unpopular measures. We will have more to say about these *practical* difficulties later. But practical difficulties aside, it is easy to see that treating a pure demand-pull inflation would be simple compared to providing a cure for cost-push inflation. As already indicated, beginning with full employment and stable prices the appearance of cost-push pressures shifts the aggregate supply curve upward, resulting in both a higher price level *and a higher level of unemployment*. Cost-push pressures are shown shifting the aggregate supply curve from position S_0 to S_1 in Figure 12-7. If increased unemployment is deemed unacceptable, fiscal and/or monetary policy actions must be undertaken to maintain full employment. However, to

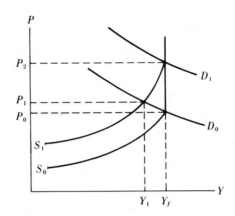

FIGURE 12-7 Policy Choices in a
Cost-Push Inflation

maintain full employment the demand schedule would have to be shifted to D_1 resulting in a further rise in the price level to P_2. With prices increased, those responsible for the initial cost-push pressures might be expected to again push for higher (wage or profit) returns, continuing the inflationary process. By allowing aggregate demand to grow as rapidly as necessary to maintain full employment in the face of a cost-push inflation, government would be ratifying or validating the uses (or abuses) of market power which were responsible for the inflation rather than allowing the inflation process to terminate itself.

If, on the other hand, the government chooses not to allow (via permissive monetary and fiscal policies) any increase in aggregate demand, the result is no more satisfying. If demand is maintained at level D_0 while cost-push pressures force the supply schedule upward, there will be some increase in the price level accompanied by an increased level of unemployment. The longer cost-push pressures are maintained in our model (that is, the further upward the supply schedule is pushed), the greater the resulting sacrifice in employment and sales. There is, presumably, some level of excess capacity which would induce the possessors of monopoly power to stop those actions (attempted wage or profit boosts) which result in greater excess capacity. Thus, restrictive monetary and fiscal policies could stop or prevent a cost-push inflation. However, the employment cost of that policy stance could be deemed a heavy price to pay for price stability.

Identifying the Source of Inflation

The convenient distinction in the discussion above between inflations that result from an upward shift in the aggregate demand curve and those that stem from a shift in the aggregate supply curve suggests that the source of inflation can be identified by looking at the change in employment as prices rise. With a pure cost-push inflation, unemployment rises with prices. However, in a typical inflation both the aggregate demand and aggregate supply schedules shift upward so following the course of changes in unemployment cannot unequivocally identify either the supply or the demand side of the economy as the original source of the inflation. Further, comparing changes in prices and factor earnings (wages and profits) cannot fix the blame for initiation of an inflation since prices and factor rewards tend to rise together during the inflation process. Even observed lead-lag relations between prices and factor earnings are of little help. By altering the point in time picked for reference, it is generally possible to reverse the observed lead-lag sequence. Even an increase in prices which clearly precedes an increase in wages (a case which might seem to suggest demand-pull inflation) could result from recognition of an imminent increase in wages due to the exercise of union power rather than from recognition of excess demand in the product market or might simply reflect profit-push pressures. Further, wage increases could outrun price increases in a demand-pull inflation situation if labor was the factor in most restricted supply or if firms, say, for public relations purposes, break their intended price increases into small increments spread over an extended period of time.

While we have no direct observations that can untangle demand-pull and cost-push pressures on the price level, standard economic theory can illuminate the conditions necessary for inflation to be the result of wage-push or profit-push forces. Indirect evidence is available to determine whether these conditions are met. Though we have clearly shown the theoretical possibility of wage-push or profit-push inflation, many economists doubt that labor and business firms actually behave in the manner required for inflation to stem from the supply side of the economy. Looking first at business behavior, firms with monopoly power in the product market will sell at higher prices than they would if prices were competitively determined. However, higher prices are not *rising* prices. With a given degree of monopoly power there is only one price that maximizes a firm's profits. It would be self-defeating for a firm to continue raising prices once that price had been established. On these grounds, critics of the cost-push model argue that for profit-push pressure to be responsible for a sustained increase in the general price level the degree of monopolization of industry would have to rise continuously over time. The evidence available on the extent of monopoly power in the U.S. economy suggests that in recent decades there has been no tendency for increased monopolization.[16]

Shifting attention to the labor market, if unionized labor succeeds in bargaining for a money wage increase that lifts its real wage, it does so at the cost of reduced employment. Workers, of course, are interested in both their real wage and the volume of available employment. With a trade-off between real wages and employment, there must be one optimal real wage rate and employ-

16 An excellent review of the empirical evidence on changes in U.S. market structure appears in F. M. Scherer, *Industrial Market Structure and Economic Performance* (Chicago: Rand McNally and Co., 1970), Chapter 3. That evidence shows no significant overall increase during this century in measures of monopoly power in the U.S. product market.

ment combination for labor. Once the optimal real wage is attained, further union efforts to increase real wages would be self-defeating. Thus, it can be argued that a sustained upward shift in the aggregate supply schedule (hence in prices) stemming from wage-push pressures would require a continuing expansion of the extent of unionization of the labor market. In fact, for a number of years the fraction of the U.S. labor force that is unionized has declined leaving less than one-quarter of the labor force unionized today.

One More (Contemporary) Explanation of Upward Shifts in the Aggregate Supply Schedule

Before abandoning our focus on the aggregate supply curve, we can profit from recognizing that a number of special factors that have little to do with traditional wage-push and profit-push forces can influence the price level by shifting the aggregate supply function. We considered one such special factor—the embargo on oil shipments to the United States by Middle Eastern oil producers—in Chapter 9. That embargo produced shortages and bottlenecks in production, reducing the volume of real final goods and services that could be profitably produced at any price level. In our summary aggregate supply and demand model the embargo simply shifted the supply schedule leftward, prompting both a shrinkage in real output and a rise in the price level.

In the same vein, the sharp increase in oil prices charged by the cartelized OPEC countries when oil shipments were resumed in 1974 raised U.S. production costs. Facing higher petroleum product costs, firms could continue producing any particular volume of real output profitably only with their higher costs covered by higher prices. The aggregate supply curve is shifted upward by such an externally imposed increase in the price of basic production materials.[17] With no government intervention, the price level would experience a once-and-for-all increase and output would fall. The imposition of pollution abatement laws which require firms to modify their plants or their manufacturing processes in ways that lower technical production efficiency and add to costs would also shift the aggregate supply schedule upward. So, too, would the requirements of safer working conditions, successive poor years for world food production, and so on. The *transitory* inflation prompted by such special factors would be superimposed on any ongoing continuing inflation process, temporarily accelerating that inflation. In fact, it was the combination of an ongoing inflation process and a one-shot price rise prompted by just the special factors listed above that pushed the U.S. inflation rate into the double-digit range in 1974.

As with any other source of cost-push pressure on the price level, the special

17 The increase in oil prices would also cause an important change in relative prices with that production that is more heavily dependent on petroleum product inputs becoming relatively higher-priced. Our immediate concern, however, is with short-run changes in the general price level.

factors that affect aggregate supply confront policy makers with a dilemma. With no policy response to an upward shift in the aggregate supply curve, prices would rise and output would contract. To avoid the price increase, restrictive fiscal or monetary actions that accentuate the contraction would be required. On the other hand, stimulative policies aimed at cushioning the contraction caused by the supply shift would result in an even larger one-shot increase in prices. There is no easy escape from this dilemma.

EXPECTATIONS AND THE INFLATION PROCESS— AN INFLATION SCENARIO

In limiting the price level changes prompted by supply schedule shifts to essentially one-shot changes in the price level (transitory and self-terminating inflation), we have by implication placed heavy responsibility for producing sustained episodes of inflation on demand. Nevertheless, once inflation is under way, there are systematic responses from the supply side of the economy which contribute significantly to the inflationary experience. The explanations of pure demand-pull and cost-push inflations developed earlier assume that inflation is not expected or anticipated. As a consequence, the clear distinction drawn between demand-pull and cost-push inflation is somewhat artificial. When inflation occurs, business firms' managers and laborers form *expectations* about future price level movements, based on their inflationary experience, and their actions are influenced by those expectations. Taking account of those expectations (formed on the basis of *imperfect* information) in the framework of the *search theory* of imperfect markets, we can outline an inflation theory in which the supply side of the economy plays an active and ultimately pernicious role. We will develop that inflation theory by tracing the adjustments that could take place during an extended inflation.

The Gradual Adjustment to Excess Demand

To begin our description of an extended episode of inflation, assume that the economy is in full employment equilibrium with no significant price level adjustment under way—it is important to remember that our concept of full employment (the real wage and employment at the levels where labor supply and labor demand intersect) corresponds to a measured unemployment rate of some 4 to 5 percent of the U.S. labor force with that measured unemployment reflecting structural and search unemployment. Now suppose that the government, perhaps to escalate a military involvement, increases its expenditures in order to garner a larger share of the economy's capacity output and does so without levying an offsetting increase in tax collections (just what the United States did in the middle 1960s).

With government spending raised, aggregate demand exceeds full employment output. Bringing to bear the arguments of the search theory, producers, faced with increased demand, watch their inventories shrink as they try to determine whether the increase in demand for their products is permanent. We know it is and producers will determine this too as their inventories continue to decline. As producers recognize the permanent nature of the increase in demand for their products, they will begin raising their prices (inflation has begun). They will also try to increase employment in order to raise output. But for all firms to raise their employment levels they will have to raise their money wage offers as they compete for *scarce* labor. How does labor respond? Initially, with imperfect information, laborers do not recognize that the general price level has risen. Further, they perceive the higher *money* wage offers they are receiving as isolated instances of good fortune which should be accepted rather than the result of a generalized increase in the wage level. Thus, with unchanged reservation wages based on now obsolete experience, convinced that their real wages are increased, job seekers spend less time in search and labor collectively moves outward along the labor supply curve to the right of the full employment position (N_0) in Figure 12-8.

Again, with the price level increase business firms, which are directly involved in marketing goods and services and only need to know what has happened to their own product price, quickly recognize the profitable opportunity for adding to their work force when demand is increased. If the price increase should lower the real wage to W_0/P_1 in Figure 12-8, in the aggregate firms would want to hire N_1 units of labor services. But since firms have to offer higher money wages to attract an increased quantity of labor, the real wage would fall not to W_0/P_1 but to a level like W_1/P_1. Since, with labor as yet unaware of the general price level increase, more hours of labor services are offered as the *money* wage rises, business firms' demand for labor can match supply at an employment level, like N_2, which is above *full* employment. At that point job search time is reduced with job seekers accepting offers which they perceive as pro-

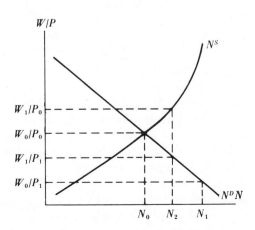

FIGURE 12-8 The Labor Market.
Adjustment to Excess Demand

viding higher real wages. Total measured unemployment is reduced by the shrinkage in search unemployment. Labor's real wage at this point would be (W_1/P_1) while labor *thinks* it is receiving real wage (W_1/P_0).

This kind of increase in employment (reduction in search unemployment) will prove temporary. Labor will gradually discover that there has been a general price level increase which has reduced its real wage and, as it makes that discovery, it will move back down the labor supply schedule reducing the hours of labor services offered and permitting a reappearance of excess demand for labor. Individual workers are also apt to be discovering that the higher money wage offers they have received are not isolated instances of good luck but reflect a general rise in wage offers. In response, they will raise their nominal reservation wages and will go back to spending a more extended time in the job search process.

With labor moving back down its supply curve excess demand for labor re-emerges and money wages will rise. To close the gap between labor demand and supply, money wages must rise faster than prices until real wage (W_0/P_0) is restored, nominal wages having risen by the same proportion as prices. At that point, search unemployment is back to its normal or "natural" rate and output is back to its full employment level.

It appears that with imperfect information, (unanticipated) inflation can temporarily raise employment and output above the *normal* full employment level (lower measured unemployment by reducing search unemployment). As experience provides a more accurate understanding of what is happening in the economy, employment and output are reduced. If, in the long run, the price level adjustment is *perfectly* perceived, the economy returns to full employment with a normal or *natural* amount of search unemployment remaining. Thus, pure inflation would be the prominent ultimate result of the government spending increase. It is important to note that a full adjustment of the variety just traced would take a substantial period of time. By the time the adjustment is complete both labor and employers may have become convinced that inflation will continue—that is, *inflationary expectations* may have taken root.

Steady-State Inflation at the Expected Rate

Suppose that during the period of adjustment to increased demand prices rise at an annual rate that averages 5 percent. Furthermore, let us assume that labor and employers gradually *adapt* their expectations to experience during the adjustment until both come to expect a 5-percent annual rate of inflation by the time full employment is restored. Then labor will demand its usual (stable price) yearly money wage increase for productivity growth plus a 5-percent annual cost-of-living increase. Employers, sharing labor's inflation expectations, will be willing to grant the 5-percent premium in wage contracts expecting the higher wage costs to be easily passed along in higher prices, leaving real wages unchanged. As long as monetary and fiscal policy are used to maintain aggregate demand at the full employment level (requiring *nominal* spending to rise in step with prices), inflation expectations are verified. We can have a pure inflation at the expected rate with full employment maintained. In this wage-price spiral, the supply side of the economy is an active participant. With labor pushing money wages up faster than productivity growth, just to compensate for expected inflation, the aggregate supply schedule shifts upward—in step with aggregate demand in this steady-state wage-price spiral.

The Adjustment to an Anti-Inflation Policy

Now let us suppose that, faced with a 5-percent inflation rate that does not appear transitory, government chooses not to validate inflation expectations but to restrict aggregate demand in an effort to slow inflation. The ensuing adjustment can be painful as efforts to slow inflation in the United States have demonstrated vividly. As aggregate demand falls below the full employment level of output, inventories mount. Over time, business firms come to recognize that a permanent reduction in demand has taken place and, in response, they allow output prices to fall (or rise at a reduced rate) and lower their money wage offers to labor. Many individual laborers, not recognizing the slowed rate of inflation nor the general nature of the decline in wage offers but assuming they are experiencing isolated episodes of misfortune, will quit their jobs and search for alternative employment that will provide a wage that grows to compensate for the 5-percent inflation rate labor still anticipates. Collectively, labor moves back along the labor supply curve to the left of the market-clearing level of employment thinking, incorrectly, that the reduced money wage offers being received represent a real wage decline. Thus, labor's money wage demands can continue to rise faster than productivity, shifting the aggregate supply schedule upward in the face of growing search unemployment while holding the real wage above its full employment value.

Gradually, labor-market search will convince workers that there has been a general reduction in money wage offers. In addition, labor will be learning that the inflation rate is falling. In response, workers will lower their (reservation) wage requirements and spend less search time before accepting wage offers. With money wage requirements reduced, firms have lower *costs* to pass along in prices, reinforcing the slowing of the inflation rate even while search unemployment is shrinking.

As long as labor's wage requirements hold the real wage above the full employment level, there will be downward pressure on those wage requirements forcing money wages to fall relative to prices. If, in the long run, the price level adjustment is fully perceived, full employment will be restored at the market-clearing real wage. If, during the adjustment process, government pursues a sufficiently restrictive policy, the new full-employment equilibrium can be noninflationary with money wages rising only as rapidly as productivity and full employment output just cleared from the product market. Unfortunately, with inflationary expectations deeply ingrained, the adjustment process must be long with the twin evils of both inflation and unemployment plaguing society during the transition.

UNEMPLOYMENT AND INFLATION—THE PHILLIPS CURVE

While there is little doubt that expectations are adjusted in the light of experience, it is not yet clear whether price adjustments are perfectly perceived in any meaningful long-run period. If they are not, then an inflation, which raises money wage offers, may *permanently* reduce unemployment below the so-called natural rate by reducing the real wage (with labor, not fully perceiving the price level increase, thinking its real wage is increased). If price adjustments are perfectly perceived in the long run, then changes in the inflation rate can only produce temporary, short-run changes in employment.

The empirical nature of the actual link between the inflation rate and the level of unemployment has been the subject of intensive debate since the late 1950s. As an outgrowth of an investigation reported in 1958 by a British economist named A. W. Phillips,[18] economists have generated a large body of empirical evidence on that link. In Figure 12-9, we have sketched a schedule, called

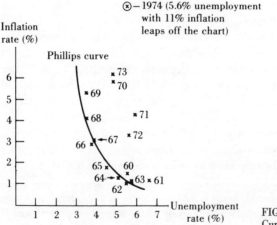

FIGURE 12-9 The U.S. Phillips Curve, 1960-1974

18 A. W. Phillips, "The Relationship between Unemployment and the Rate of Change of Money Wage Rates in the United Kingdom, 1861-1957," *Economica*, New Series, Vol. XXV, November 1958, pp. 283-299. As indicated in the title, Phillips' original investigation was concerned with the link between unemployment and the rate of change of money wage inflation, not with unemployment versus the rate of change of prices in general. However, the shift to the latter concern is simple and straightforward and the label "Phillips curve" is generally applied to both relationships. A follow-up study which emphasized the unemployment-price change link using U.S. data was provided in P. Samuelson and R. Solow, "Analytical Aspects of Anti-Inflation Policy," *American Economic Review*, Vol. L, May 1960, pp. 177-194.

a *Phillips curve*, relating the U.S. unemployment and inflation rates for 1960-1974. The data points plotted in that figure fit our Phillips curve quite convincingly—*until the end of the 1960s* (a point that we will return to shortly).

What our plotted Phillips curve seemingly shows is that full employment and price stability are not compatible goals—that there is a *trade-off* between unemployment and inflation. To have restricted inflation to an inconsequential rate in the 1960s (say, to just over 1 percent annually) it appears we would have had to accept a 5½-6 percent unemployment rate. To reduce unemployment, it appears we must tolerate an increased rate of inflation. For example, to squeeze unemployment to 4 percent of the labor force, the Phillips curve plotted in Figure 12-9 suggests that the United States would have had to tolerate an inflation rate of near 3 percent annually.

In the early 1960s, the Phillips curve was thought to represent a "menu of choices" available to policy makers. Weighing the social costs of both unemployment and inflation, policy makers were to choose, from the unemployment-inflation combinations that the Phillips curve showed were available, that one combination that would maximize social welfare. It now appears though that the mildness and brevity of the inflation episodes which generated the Phillips curve plotted in Figure 12-9 provided for a misleading notion of the employment-inflation trade-off. The recent inflation-unemployment observations (from 1970 onward in Figure 12-9), generated during a period of fairly rapid and sustained inflation, question the stability of the simple Phillips curve of Figure 12-9.

Price Expectations and the Natural Rate of Unemployment

As a first approximation, we can assume that the plotted Phillips curve in Figure 12-9 represented the trade-off (for the 1960s) between employment and inflation *when no significant inflation was anticipated*. But such a schedule cannot, in any long-run sense, represent a stable menu of policy choices for the economy. If stabilization policy aims at reducing unemployment, it will, moving *along* the Phillips curve, increase the inflation rate. As society perceives that the inflation rate has risen and builds that perception into its expectations, the Phillips curve will shift.

A sizable group of economists (for the most part monetarists) believe that price expectations adjust with sufficient accuracy to eliminate *any* long-run trade-off between employment and inflation. The observed Phillips curve trade-off, they argue, is a purely transitory phenomenon that results from imperfect information—from labor recognizing a general increase in prices and money wage offers only with a substantial lag. In the long run, they contend, past price level changes will be fully perceived and any ongoing inflation fully anticipated. At that time (the steady-state inflation case in our inflation scenario), unemployment can only be at the natural rate represented by the vertical schedule in Figure 12-10. Once again, this natural rate of unemployment reflects only the search (or search and structural) unemployment that corresponds to equilibrium in the

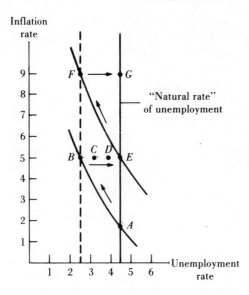

FIGURE 12-10   The Natural Rate of Unemployment

labor market. With equilibrium at the natural rate of unemployment, labor bargains for a real wage and adjusts its money wage for every price level change without delay.[19]

Beginning with such a steady-state equilibrium (point A in Figure 12-10),[20] if an increase in aggregate demand causes prices to rise more rapidly than anticipated, money wage adjustments will fall behind price adjustments, reducing the real wage while labor thinks its real wage has risen. We are on familiar ground! The unanticipated inflation *temporarily* reduces unemployment, say, to the 2.5 percent level corresponding to point B in Figure 12-10. We have generated a simple Phillips curve showing a trade-off between inflation and unemployment. But, as we argued previously, the apparent trade-off may be temporary. As labor recognizes that prices have risen and perceives the general nature of the increase in money wage offers, it will raise its money wage requirements and gradually push its real wage back up toward the full employment level. As the real wage rises (money wages growing more rapidly than prices), unemployment grows (to the levels corresponding to points C, D, and so on) even as inflation continues. *If* price adjustments are fully perceived in the long run, unemployment returns to the natural rate (say, at point E) with a continuing, steady-state, pure inflation possible after the adjustment is complete.

---

19   See E. Phelps, "Money-Wage Dynamics and Labor Market Equilibrium," *Journal of Political Economy*, Vol. LXXVI, July/August 1968, pp. 678-711; and M. Friedman, "The Role of Monetary Policy," *American Economic Review*, Vol. LVIII, March 1968, pp. 1-17.

20   Note that our initial steady-state equilibrium is characterized by an inflation rate of some 1.5 percent annually.

If, with the level of unemployment returned to the natural rate (at point *E* in Figure 12-10), the government decides to renew its efforts to shrink unemployment through expansionary monetary or fiscal actions, inflation will *accelerate*. To temporarily return unemployment to the 2.5-percent target level would require a movement along a new Phillips curve (like *EF*). And, still, unemployment can be held below the natural rate only as long as labor has imperfect information.

Clearly, the *natural rate theory* implies that there is no long-run employment-inflation trade-off. This theory argues that policies aimed at reducing unemployment below the natural rate will succeed only in raising the inflation rate in the end.

An Unsatisfactory Reconciliation

Whether the long-run Phillips curve is merely a vertical line at the natural rate of unemployment or whether there is some long-run trade-off is an empirical question that has not been adequately answered. Most Keynesian economists argue, in essence, that there is some long-run "money illusion" so that labor never fully perceives the extent of price level increases. If labor does not recognize the extent of price level increases, it will never adjust its money wage demands by the full proportion of a price level rise. Thus, inflation can permanently lower the real wage, enticing employers to hire more labor. More labor is willing to work since, without fully perceiving the extent of inflation, labor thinks its money wage increases have raised real wages. If inflation can permanently lower unemployment, we could have a long-run Phillips curve like LR_1 in Figure 12-11, steeper than the short-run Phillips curve but not vertical at the natural rate of unemployment.[21]

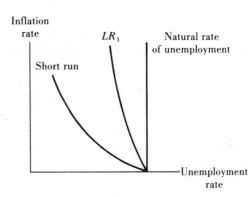

FIGURE 12-11 Competing Phillips Curves

21 See James Tobin, "Inflation and Unemployment," *American Economic Review*, Vol. 62, March 1972, pp. 1-18.

Determination of the true nature of the long-run Phillips curve remains an object of intense current research. However, with that question unsettled, what we already know about the Phillips curve has important policy implications. For example, it is clear that inflation cannot be quickly curbed without significantly increasing the level of unemployment. Indeed, if inflation has been permitted to persist for an extended time period, so that inflationary expectations are built into the decision-making process providing the inflation with substantial momentum, a quite extended period of excessive unemployment may be required to restore price stability. The least costly way to achieve price stability is clearly to prevent any significant inflation from persisting long enough to engender a wide spread of inflationary psychology. Moreover, since inflationary expectations raise the short-run Phillips curve, making the long-run trade-off between inflation and unemployment less favorable if it exists at all, the government should proceed with caution as it considers the purchase of very low unemployment rates through the application of expansionary and inflationary fiscal and monetary policy actions. The short-run Phillips curve cannot be treated as a simple menu of policy choices.

RECONCILING HIGH EMPLOYMENT WITH PRICE STABILITY

The Phillips curve evidence argues persuasively that the United States must tolerate a relatively high level of measured unemployment if approximate price stability is to be maintained. According to that evidence, if price stability is accepted as a macroeconomic policy goal, expansionary aggregate demand policies cannot be used to reduce measured unemployment below, say, $4\frac{1}{2}$ percent of the labor force. However there are policies that can shift the long-run Phillips curve leftward (whatever its slope), reducing the level of unemployment we would have to tolerate at any selected inflation rate.

It should have become clear by now that the residue of measured unemployment that remains when aggregate demand begins exerting strong upward pressure on the price level is not the same animal that Keynes was concerned with in *The General Theory* (it is not the involuntary unemployment that in our aggregate model left labor off its supply curve with the real wage above the market-clearing level). Rather than reflecting a chronic aggregate shortage of jobs, this residual unemployment is a reflection of the difficulty of matching workers with available job openings and keeping them happily employed. This residual unemployment could be reduced by: (1) shortening the search time required for a job seeker (whether a job changer or a new entrant into the labor force) to find acceptable employment, and (2) reducing job instability—the frequency of job changes.[22]

---

22   For a far more complete treatment of proposals to lower the U.S. unemployment rate, see M. Feldstein, "The Economics of the New Unemployment," *The Public Interest*, No. 33, Fall 1973, pp. 3-42.

Any program that improves the flow of information required for matching job openings and workers would reduce the time labor spends in job search and thus reduce search unemployment. Advocates of plans for regional "job banks" that keep computerized listings of job openings and applicants have such an objective in mind. To the extent that geographical barriers prevent the filling of job vacancies with qualified unemployed workers, the government could provide relocation aid in the form of loans or grants.[23]

An improved flow of job information could be of particular benefit to unskilled young workers whose average job search period is longer than for older adults. However, even with improved job information many economists feel that the search period for young workers would remain relatively high because of the effect of minimum wage laws. Young workers, particularly new entrants into the labor force, are low-skill workers. If the value of a young worker's contribution to a firm's production (his value marginal product) is less than the wage a minimum wage law requires the firm to pay for his services, he will not be hired. Thus, minimum wage laws that hold young workers' *reservation wages* above the market value of their output in some job slots limit the number of jobs available to those workers. Relaxing the minimum wage requirement for young workers would open up those job slots.

Job instability, frequency of job changes, is a reflection of job dissatisfaction. It is a characteristic common to low-skill requirement jobs (clerk, deliveryman, manual labor) that offer little hope of improved status in the future and, in many cases, scant economic advantage over the support available from public assistance programs. That unskilled workers change jobs frequently and often deliberately *choose* unemployment (or intermittent employment to take advantage of unemployment compensation) should come as no great surprise—self-interest is a potent force in rich and poor alike. In recent years, the United States has experimented with manpower training programs in the hope that with higher skill levels, previously low-skilled labor would find more rewarding, thence more stable employment.[24] As a complementary policy, some analysts have advocated raising the costs of unemployment by reducing support levels in the public assistance programs relative to the rewards from continued employment.[25] It is also worth noting that an improved flow of information in the labor market could reduce the frequency of job changes by allowing workers to better select the jobs they accept.

Special unemployment problems exist because some workers suffer from mental or physical disabilities. Many individuals, with serious disabilities that

---

23   Even now, federal income tax deductions are allowed for relocation expenses involved in a move of more than 50 miles.

24   A pessimistic view on the effectiveness of manpower training programs appears in R. Hall, "Prospects for Shifting the Phillips Curve through Manpower Policy," *Brookings Papers on Economic Activity*, 1971:3.

25   Feldstein, *op. cit.*, pp. 38-41.

limit their productive capacity, rarely find employment even in the tightest labor market. Policies which can improve employment prospects for the disabled include vocational rehabilitation programs and direct government subsidization of employment of the handicapped. The subsidy could take the form of payments to employers in private industry who use handicapped labor or could be paid directly to handicapped workers who are employed by government.

Our list of specific explanations for the extensive measured unemployment we observe in the United States, even in inflation periods, could be extended easily—for example, by pointing out that the seasonal nature of some employment (notably in construction) contributes to measured unemployment. We could also list many more policy proposals for reducing unemployment. Our brief review is sufficient, however, to demonstrate that there are programs that can improve the unemployment-inflation trade-off. The relevant question for government policy makers is whether the social benefits to be derived from implementing any selected program for reducing unemployment exceed the social costs of that program. Only if they do would society be better off with the program implemented. It is clear, for example, that vocational rehabilitation raises the skill levels of the disabled. But vocational rehabilitation is costly. In many cases, the productivity gain from rehabilitative efforts cannot cover the cost of those efforts. Society at large might be better off providing direct support to the disabled in those cases rather than depending on vocational rehabilitation to lift incomes to an acceptable level.[26]

AN ISSUE OF CONTINUING CONCERN: WAGE-PRICE CONTROLS

Probably no other action so clearly reveals the frustration policy makers have suffered from the inability of the economy to enjoy simultaneously both high employment and price stability than their well-intentioned efforts to improve economic conditions by intervening directly in the market processes which determine wages and prices. Most recently, in August 1971, the United States adopted a wage-price freeze which was followed by multiple "phases" of *controlled* adjustments in wages and prices. Those controls, which were allowed to lapse in 1973, were imposed to help end the persistent inflation that began in the mid-1960s.

The rationale for wage-price controls differs with the explanation of inflation. Many of the advocates of wage-price controls believe that recent inflation is the result of labor unions and large corporations using the monopoly power they possess to push up wages and prices—that is, that we have been suffering from cost-push inflation. They contend that if wage and price controls are employed

---

26 If the psychic well-being of disabled workers is enhanced by self-sufficiency, social welfare could be enhanced by providing vocational rehabilitation even in some cases where the market value of productivity gains falls short of the cost of rehabilitation.

to prevent the further use of that market power, cost-push pressures on the price level can be relieved.

Earlier in this chapter, we reviewed the arguments that are frequently employed to reject the cost-push explanation of inflation. But even if the arguments of the critics of the cost-push thesis are correct, we do not have to reject wage-price controls, properly applied, as an aid in controlling inflation. We have seen that once a demand-pull initiated inflation is under way, if labor and employers adapt their expectations to that experience (shifting the aggregate supply curve upward in anticipation of further price increases), inflation can continue unabated long after the economy has been purged of excess demand. Further, with well-established inflationary expectations *slow* to adjust, we have seen that a restrictive aggregate demand policy can slow the inflation rate only with a lengthy adjustment period during which unemployment is substantially increased. If, somehow, expectations could be altered more rapidly, the adjustment period during which the economy suffers the twin evils of inflation and excessive unemployment could be shortened. If, in conjunction with a restrictive demand policy, government should announce in the most convincing possible way that inflation was going to be stopped, backing up that claim by the application of strict wage-price controls, expectations might adjust far more rapidly than if sole reliance were placed on restrictive monetary and fiscal policy. Where expectations of inflation have become embedded in long-lived contracts, the inflationary wage and price increases those contracts provide can be circumvented, at least in part, with the application of wage-price controls.

To the extent that wage-price controls, by modifying inflation expectations, shorten the adjustment period required for lowering the inflation rate to the target level, they are a valuable supplement to aggregate demand controlling tools. However, they should never be looked upon as a substitute for proper control of aggregate demand. If applied during a period when aggregate demand is excessive, those controls can only *repress* the officially measured symptoms (price increases) of excess demand. More important in that case are the well-known side effects of holding prices below market-clearing levels.

Figure 12-12 shows one market in which controls hold the official product

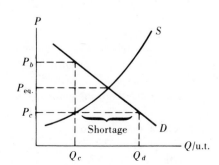

FIGURE 12-12 A Market with Price Control

price (P_c) below the market-clearing level $(P_{eq.})$. In this market, price cannot serve its normal rationing function since at the legal ceiling price the quantity supplied (Q_c) falls far short of the quantity demanded (Q_d).

If wage-price controls are imposed when there is generalized excess demand, many individual product markets (like the one in Figure 12-12) will suffer shortages. With shortages at the legal price level, waiting lines and waiting lists will form to ration the short supplies. Black markets will develop as enterprising middlemen attempt to profit from those shortages. Looking again at Figure 12-12, with supply restricted to output level Q_c by the price ceiling (in effect the supply schedule becomes vertical above P_c at output level Q_c), society would be willing to pay a black market price of up to P_b and still take the full quantity producers are willing to supply. This price ceiling would reward law-breakers while providing society with a reduced quantity of the price-controlled product.

Product quality is also likely to deteriorate as producers seek to escape the lid on prices. By reducing quality (fewer nuts in the candy bar, thinner chrome plating on auto parts, lower quality paper in books, and so on), producers can permit the increase in effective prices that market forces call for. With a host of techniques available for circumventing official price ceilings, effective prices cannot be strictly constrained for an extended time period—at least not without an army-size network of enforcement agents that would be intolerably costly (even with public cooperation spurred by patriotism, the price control program deployed in World War II required a staff of 60,000!).

Wage controls are equally difficult to enforce. With excess demand in the labor market at the legal wage rate, nonwage benefits to labor (a company car, more stock options, longer paid vacations, and so on) will rise to attract the volume of labor services firms want to hire. These alternative forms of labor compensation contribute to employers' costs (thus required prices) just as wages do.

Experience in a number of countries has shown that men can always find ways to circumvent price constraints which, for long time periods, attempt to hold prices below market clearing levels. Most economists, rather than being disturbed by that experience, find it pleasing! Why? A government cannot impose controls on the *general* price (or wage) level but must apply controls to individual prices. If those controls were effective over an extended period, then the price signals that a market economy depends on to shift resources in concert with changes in society's wants would not be operative—with individual prices controlled, *relative* prices cannot change to induce changes in the composition of production. The social loss from price-control induced resource misallocation is minimized if techniques for maintaining relative flexibility in *effective* prices (techniques for circumventing controls) can be devised.

With circumvention the likely result of an extended application of wage-price controls, and with a costly distortion of resource usage likely in the long run if circumvention does not occur, it would seem that controls should be employed strictly only for short periods (6 months, 1 year?). Reinforcing that presumption, if monetary and fiscal policy have eliminated excess demand from the economy, controls need be employed only long enough for expectations to be remolded. If controls have any effect on expectations, that effect probably is generated over a relatively short time period.[27] If monetary and fiscal policy permit the reappearance of excess demand after imposition of controls, little good (and perhaps much harm) can result from continued enforcement of those controls.

The growing dissatisfaction that emerged in the United States with phases II, III, and IV of the wage-price control program introduced in August of 1971 suggested that those controls were maintained long after the lapse of their useful lifetime—that the distortions of normal economic processes engendered by those controls outweighed any continuing beneficial influence they imposed on the momentum of inflationary forces. Moreover, since inflation continued, actually accelerated, in spite of the continued imposition of controls, their credibility—and thus their potential for affecting expectations—was sharply reduced. But, even if society in general has accepted the basic proposition that controls are no substitute for the appropriate administration of monetary and fiscal policy, there will always be those (including, always, prominent national political figures) who advocate the deployment of controls as an obvious and simple method of maintaining wage and price stability.

A Concluding Note on Incorporating Inflationary Expectations in the *IS-LM* Model

In Chapter 7, which focused on the determinants of the interest rate, we initially confronted the possibility of inflationary expectations. In the present chapter attention has once again been focused on inflationary expectations, particularly on their role in contributing to the perpetuation of an ongoing inflation. For completeness, our consideration of inflationary expectations will close with a brief demonstration of the ease with which such expectations can be accommodated in the *IS-LM* model that has been a fundamental part of our analytical apparatus.[28]

As first indicated in Chapter 7, when no inflation is anticipated no distinction need be drawn between the *nominal* rate of interest which is observed and its *real* counterpart. However, with inflation anticipated lenders will part with their loanable funds only if they receive their usual percentage interest return

---

27 An opposing view on the length of time over which controls should be maintained appears in Robert Gordon, "Wage-Price Controls and the Shifting Phillips Curve," *Brookings Papers on Economic Activity*, 1972:2, pp. 385-418.

Also see his "The Response of Wages and Prices to the First Two Years of Controls," *Brookings Papers on Economic Activity*, 1973:3, pp. 765-779. In this paper Gordon provides evidence that the wage-price controls applied in August 1971 prevented the inflation rate from being as high in 1971 and 1972 as it would have been without those controls.

28 See William E. Gibson, 'Interest Rates and Monetary Policy," *The Journal of Political Economy*, Vol. 78, May/June 1970, pp. 431-455.

plus an interest allowance sufficient to offset the impact of the expected inflation on the purchasing power of the dollars they are repaid. Hence, the nominal interest rate lenders require will be (approximately) the sum of the real rate of interest (required when no inflation is anticipated) and the expected rate of inflation. Borrowers, if they share the inflationary expectations of lenders, will agree to pay the higher nominal interest rate. They expect to repay their loans with dollars that have lost real purchasing power at the expected rate of inflation. Hence, the nominal rate of interest can be represented algebraically (as in Chapter 7) as

$$i = \rho + \frac{\Delta P^e}{P}$$

with i the nominal (observed market) interest rate, ρ the real interest rate, and $\Delta P^e/P$ the expected rate of inflation.

In Figure 12-13 a standard and familiar set of commodity and money market equilibrium schedules are sketched (IS_0 and LM_0) providing an equilibrium level of aggregate demand at output level Y_f with market interest rate i_0. For convenience, it is assumed that Y_f is the full employment level of output. If IS_0 and LM_0 represent the commodity and money market equilibrium schedules when there is a zero rate of expected inflation (as they always have up to now), the equilibrium interest rate (i_0) is identical to the real interest rate (ρ).

As a first step in accommodating the appearance of nonzero inflation expectations we must recognize that the nominal and real interest rates will diverge with the emergence of inflationary expectations (both measured along the vertical axis in Figure 12-13) and we must shift the IS curve upward. Investment is a function of the real interest rate. While the emergence of inflationary expecta-

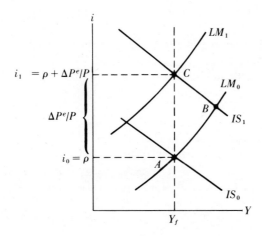

FIGURE 12-13 Inflationary Expectations in the IS-LM Model

tions raises the nominal interest cost of investment, the nominal expected returns from investment are increased by an identical percentage amount and no revision of investment plans is called for. With the volume of investment associated with any real interest rate unaltered by changes in the expected rate of inflation, the *IS* curve would be shifted upward by (measured vertically) the expected rate of inflation. Hence, for expected inflation rate $\Delta P^e/P$ the *IS* schedule would become schedule IS_1 in Figure 12-13. Along that new *IS* schedule, an unchanged level of investment, hence aggregate demand, would accompany the unchanged real interest rate, ρ, and the higher nominal interest rate, i_1. Of course, every increase in the expected rate of inflation would shift the *IS* curve farther upward and every decrease would produce a decline in the *IS* schedule. In contrast, the position of the *LM* curve is unaltered by changes in the expected rate of inflation. It is the nominal interest rate that measures the (opportunity) cost of holding money balances. Thus, any change in the nominal interest rate can be expected to change the demand for money and that response is already reflected in the standard *LM* schedule. With the nominal stock of money fixed, a change in the nominal interest rate requires a changed level of spending (a movement *along* an existing *LM* curve) for money market equilibrium to be maintained.

The Complete Adjustment to Inflationary Expectations

Beginning with the economy in equilibrium with no inflation anticipated (at Y_f, i_0 in Figure 12-13), let us trace the complete adjustment (in the *IS-LM* model) to a generalized adoption of the expectation that prices are going to rise at rate $\Delta P^e/P$ henceforth. As indicated above, with the emergence of the expectation of inflation at rate $\Delta P^e/P$ the *IS* curve is shifted upward (to position IS_1) while the position of the *LM* curve is unaffected. At the new intersection of the commodity and money market equilibrium schedules (point B) the nominal interest rate is above the original value of the real (and nominal) rate, but not by the full amount of expected inflation. Hence, the real rate of interest (the nominal rate minus the expected rate of inflation) is below value ρ. Quite simply, with prices expected to rise society's demand for money, which loses purchasing power with inflation, has declined and the resulting excess supply of money has produced a decline in the real interest rate (even though nominal rates are increased).

With the real interest rate temporarily depressed, investment is stimulated and aggregate demand at point B exceeds the full employment level of output. Prices will then rise as a direct consequence of the adoption of inflationary expectations. As prices rise the real stock of money shrinks, shifting the *LM* curve leftward until aggregate demand is reduced to equality with output. With expectations unchanged, that requires a shift of the *LM* curve to position LM_1 in Figure 12-13, providing the new "equilibrium" interest rate i_1.

While the mere adoption of inflationary expectations results in a one-shot price increase and a rise in the nominal interest rate equal to the expected inflation rate (a movement to position C in Figure 12-13), neither the inflation nor the elevated interest rate can persist unless the government validates society's expectations. Specifically, only if the government increases the nominal money stock at the rate of expected inflation can point C in Figure 12-13 remain the equilibrium point in our IS-LM model. While an increasing money supply with stable prices would shift the LM curve rightward, with prices rising at the same rate as the nominal money stock the real supply of money would be unchanged. The LM schedule would remain at position LM_1 and the IS-LM model would reflect an equilibrium at point C with a steady-state inflation at the expected rate.[29]

If the government refuses to validate the public's inflationary expectations, holding the rate of money supply growth below the expected inflation rate, the inflation rate would decline (a continuation of inflation at the expected rate would shift the LM curve leftward resulting in an excess supply of real goods and services). As inflation slows, society's inflationary expectations would be revised downward shifting the IS curve downward. If the expectation of a zero inflation rate is restored, equilibrium would be restored at i_0, Y_f in Figure 12-13 with no difference between the nominal and real interest rate.

SUMMARY

In this chapter we have reviewed the two dominant explanations of inflation, the demand-pull and cost-push theories. Demand-pull inflation, the result of excess demand for aggregate output, was shown to be self-limiting unless the government pursues fiscal or monetary policies that cause aggregate demand to grow excessively. (A continuing growth of government spending to meet a military commitment complemented with monetary expansion can surely have that effect.) Preventing demand-pull inflation requires that aggregate demand be allowed to grow only as rapidly as aggregate supply grows.

Cost-push or sellers' inflation resulted when the domestic possessors of monopoly power used that power in a way that would shift the aggregate supply curve upward or when some external shock shifted the supply curve upward. The upward shift in the supply curve raised the price level and reduced employment and output. Our model suggested that cost-push inflation would also lead to its own end, increasing the unemployment rate and reducing total sales, unless the government should validate cost-push efforts through an expansionary monetary and fiscal policy posture aimed at maintaining full employment.

While we agreed that prices are higher in markets that are monopolized, we

---

29 It would seem to be worth recalling at this point our earlier suggestion that with continued inflation in the late 1960s and well into the 1970s the "high" observed interest rates could have been expected to contain a substantial inflation premium.

sympathetically reviewed arguments that question the thesis that monopoly power (cost-push pressure) can be held responsible for sustained increase in prices such as the United States has experienced in recent years. Available empirical evidence does not indicate a sustained growth in monopoly power in the U.S. economy—a condition which the critics of the cost-push thesis claim necessary to validate the cost-push explanation of inflation.

If excessive aggregate demand must bear the bulk of responsibility for initiating inflation, the inflationary role of the supply side of the economy is in maintaining an ongoing inflation after the elimination of excess demand. Stopping an inflation when that inflation is *expected* to continue was shown to be costly, requiring an increased unemployment rate during the typically protracted adjustment period. Given the importance of the link between the inflation rate and the unemployment rate, we focused a good bit of our attention on the nature of that link—the subject of a large and growing *Phillips curve* literature. While we looked at both the short- and long-run properties of the Phillips curve, we had to leave unanswered the important question of whether there is a long-run trade-off between unemployment and inflation. It was suggested, however, that whatever the slope of the long-run Phillips curve, there are programs which can lower the "full employment" unemployment rate—shift the Phillips curve leftward.

As an addition to the standard stabilization tools that we are already familiar with—monetary and fiscal policy—we briefly reviewed the usage of wage-price controls. We observed that the failure of traditional monetary and fiscal policies to simultaneously achieve full employment and price stability has prompted a number of countries, including the United States, to adopt various forms of wage and price control policies. It was argued that those policies are not likely to be beneficial on balance except when applied for short periods during efforts to "disinflate" an economy suffering from an ongoing inflation. In this application, we must hope that the expected future rate of inflation is reduced. If expectations are so affected, disinflation may be accomplished more quickly and with a lower cost in unemployment than if such controls are not adopted.

Finally, we completed our analysis of the role of inflationary expectations by integrating such expectations into the *IS-LM* model. In so doing we verified, in a *general* equilibrium framework, our earlier *partial* equilibrium (bond and money market) argument that the existence of inflationary expectations would result in an equilibrium value of the nominal interest rate that exceeds the real rate by the expected rate of inflation.

QUESTIONS

1. Many people appear to believe that inflation is a universal evil, reducing everyone's real well-being. Briefly dispel that notion and then explain why there is such widespread concern over inflation.

2. What do inflationary expectations have to do with your answer to Question 1? Is a perfectly anticipated inflation of 50 percent per year more or less harmful than an unanticipated inflation of 10 percent per year?

3. Explain demand-pull and cost-push inflation. For policy purposes, does it matter whether an unwanted inflation is of the cost-push or demand-pull variety?

4. Explain the link between the rate of increase in money wages, the rate of growth in productivity, and inflation.

5. Can inflation continue indefinitely without an increase in the nominal money supply? Explain.

6. It is often argued that moderate inflation (say, 3 to 4 percent annually) is a small price to pay for a buoyant level of economic activity when a substantial increase in unemployment would be required to maintain price stability. Evaluate that argument in light of what you know about the Phillips curve.

7. Suggest some ways of improving the functioning of the labor market in order to reduce frictional or search unemployment.

SUGGESTED READING

Beals, Ralph E. "Concentrated Industries, Administered Prices and Inflation: A Survey of Recent Empirical Research," a report prepared for the Council on Wage and Price Stability, June 1975.

Bronfenbrenner, Martin, and F. D. Holzman. "Survey of Inflation Theory," *American Economic Review.* Vol. 53, October 1963, pp. 593-661.

Eisner, Robert. "Factors Affecting the Level of Interest Rates," *Savings and Residential Financing, 1968 Conference Proceedings.* Reprinted in William E. Gibson and George G. Kaufman (eds.). *Monetary Economics, Readings on Current Issues.* New York: McGraw-Hill, 1971, pp. 303-310.

Fisher, Irving. "A Statistical Relation between Unemployment and Price Changes," *International Labour Review.* June 1926. Reprinted in the *Journal of Political Economy*, Vol. 81, March/April 1973, pp. 496-502.

Friedman, Milton. "The Role of Monetary Policy," *American Economic Review.* Vol. 58, March 1968, pp. 1-17.

Gibson, William E. "Interest Rates and Monetary Policy," *Journal of Political Economy.* Vol. 78, May/June 1970, pp. 431-455.

Johnson, Harry G. "A Survey of Theories of Inflation," in *Essays in Monetary Economics.* Cambridge, Mass.: Harvard University Press, 1969.

Lucas, Robert E., and Leonard A. Rapping. "Price Expectations and the Phillips Curve," *American Economic Review.* Vol. 59, June 1969, pp. 342-350.

Perry, G. L. *Unemployment, Money Wage Rates, and Inflation.* Cambridge, Mass.: MIT Press, 1966.

————. "Wages and the Guideposts," *American Economic Review*. Vol. 57, September 1967, pp. 897-904.

Rees, Albert. "The Phillips Curve as a Menu for Policy Choice," *Economica*. Vol. 37, August 1970, pp. 227-238.

Spencer, Roger W. "The Relation between Prices and Employment: Two Views," *Federal Reserve Bank of St. Louis Review*. Vol. 51, March 1969, pp. 15-21.

Tobin, James. "Inflation and Unemployment," *American Economic Review*. Vol. 62, March 1972, pp. 1-18.

Yohe, William P., and Denis S. Karnosky. "Interest Rates and Price Level Changes," *Federal Reserve Bank of St. Louis Review*. Vol. 51, December 1969, pp. 19-36.

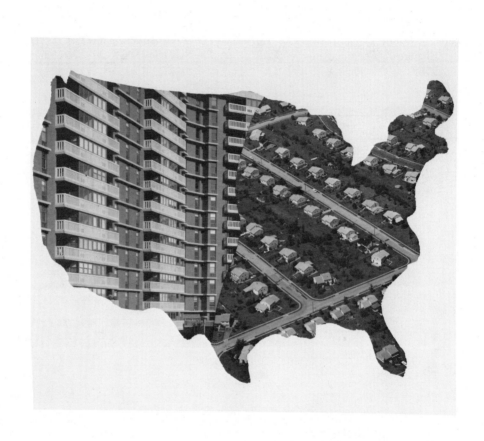

Chapter 13

Economic Growth

Up to now, our analysis has had a relatively short time perspective, focusing on the short-run behavior of the economic system. We have attempted to account for gaps between potential output (full employment output) and aggregate demand and to show how government action could close those gaps. For the most part, *potential* output was fixed because, by assumption, the time horizon with which we were concerned was too short to allow any change in the size or quality of the labor force, the state of technology, the stock of capital, or the quantity and quality of land and natural resources. However, even in our short-run model there was *net investment*—by definition, a change in the capital stock—so that at least one of our assumptions was somewhat suspect. It was necessary for us to argue that the assumption of a constant capital stock was *approximately* correct—in the short run, net investment is small enough relative to the accumulated stock of capital that the stock can be treated as approximately constant.

As the time horizon with which we are concerned lengthens, it becomes increasingly unreasonable to assume that the quantity and quality of our factors of production stay constant. With increases in the size and quality of the labor force, with growth in the stock of capital, with technological innovation, and with the exploitation of new land areas (and other natural resources), our capacity to produce grows. Indeed, production capacity in the United States has grown at a rate that has permitted transformation of a primitive, agricultural economy into a world production leader in considerably less than 200 years.

EXTENDING THE TIME HORIZON

In this chapter, the time horizon with which we are concerned is vastly extended. Instead of focusing on cyclical movements in economic activity, this chapter is concerned with the long-run growth of production capacity. We will be interested in the conditions under which economic growth takes place and with the determinants of an economy's equilibrium rate of growth.

There are a number of reasons for a country to be concerned about its rate of economic growth. With population growth, output must expand just to maintain per capita income (output). To satisfy the desire for higher levels of real per capita income, real output must grow faster than the population. Among those in the lower ranges of the income distribution, even in the affluent United States, there is no question about the desirability of per capita income growth. While, among the more affluent, it is easier to find individuals who castigate the pursuit of ever larger volumes of material goods and services, the vast majority of all income classes appear unwilling to sacrifice their color TVs, automobiles, vacation homes, beach vacations, and so on.

We also should point out that an expanding economy provides more opportunities for individuals to acquire productive employment, a distinct plus, particularly in the eyes of nonwhites and women whose unemployment rates always exceed the unemployment rate for white males by a wide margin. In addition, growth may provide for the most politically practical way for a country to provide for growing public service needs. With growth in productive capacity, increased volumes of resources can be devoted to public use, providing such public goods as schools, highways, and national defense without an absolute reduction in private resource use. Extending this line of argument, it is often contended that the conflict between rich and poor can be eased by growth since, with growth, the level of income channeled to low income groups can be raised without lowering the absolute level of income enjoyed by the relatively well-to-do. With income stagnant, the poor could be made richer only through a sacrifice of the current *absolute* living standards of the nonpoor, a requirement that is claimed to be more painful than the sacrifice of an improvement in the living standard which has not been experienced.

In the past, particularly during the 1950s and early 1960s (prior to "detente"), many analysts favored rapid growth because of our competitive relationship wtih the Soviet Union. Through growth, increasing productive capacity is made available for national defense items. Perhaps more significantly, brisk U.S. growth was called for to provide evidence to the ideologically uncommitted nations of the world that democratic-capitalistic governments can provide rapidly rising standards of living. The less developed countries have never seriously entertained the notion that higher levels of production of material goods are not essential to overall social well-being.

Of course, we must not ignore the fact that in addition to generating benefits, growth does levy some burdens (costs) on society. First and foremost, to raise future output levels, resources must be freed from current consumption use to provide the physical (plant and equipment) capital and human (skills and motivation) capital required for increased productive capacity. That is, *current* consumption must be sacrificed to provide the investment necessary for raising future output levels. A more prominent concern in recent years has centered on the possible trade-off between increases in GNP (as traditionally measured) and reductions in the *quality* of life. An extreme view of the results of growth has been offered by the British economist E. J. Mishan who blames growth for "the appalling traffic congestion in our towns, cities, and suburbs, . . . erosion of the countryside, the 'uglification' of coastal towns, . . . and a wide heritage of natural beauty being wantonly destroyed." [1] Some observers foresee even more dire consequences from continued growth. They argue that the world population is consuming the earth's exhaustible resources, including its clean air and water, at an unsustainable rate. The very survival of the human species, they claim, depends

---

1   E. Mishan, *Technology and Growth* (New York: Praeger, 1969).

on a restoration of harmony between economic activity and the demands of the ecosystem—a restoration that can be accomplished only with a cessation of growth before the "spaceship earth" is made unlivable.

The vast majority of economists are far more sanguine in their view of the impact of continued growth, for growth does not have to be as destructive of the quality of life as its harshest critics contend. Rather than denying the beneficial, productive use of our resources, most economists call for action that would promote the pattern of resource allocation—including resource use to increase productive capacity—that would be automatically provided by a competitive market economy in which the *full social costs* of production are reflected in product prices. Where production processes have the potential for generating socially undesirable by-products, the emission of those by-products can be legally restricted. Alternatively, as economists would generally prefer, the emission of negative by-products can be discouraged through tax levies that reflect the costs those by-products impose on society. If the users of such *free* resources as our exhaustible supplies of clean air and water and our uncluttered open spaces must pay user fees (tax levies) for fouling those resources there is a compelling incentive to cut back on the production that generates those by-products and there is encouragement for modification of production techniques to reduce or eliminate the effluents previously emitted.

Where production threatens to deplete exhaustible basic resources, market forces will dictate a modification of the production processes that employ those resources. As any particular resource becomes more scarce, its price will rise. The price increase will: (1) prompt efforts to find and develop additional sources of the scarce resource, (2) reduce the use of that resource by raising the cost of products manufactured using that resource, and (3) encourage the development of production processes that use the scarce resource more efficiently or that use a substitute for that resource.[2] Much of the economic progress we have enjoyed can be traced to the discoveries and innovations prompted by scarcity.

We have by no means exhausted the list of potential benefits and costs associated with the growth process. Still, our list gives a clear indication of the variety of concerns of both supporters and opponents of the growth ethic. It should be clear that what any individual picks as an appropriate growth target is dictated by value judgments, and every individual places his own weights on the specific benefits and costs he associates with growth.

In contrast to the doomsday predictions of ecologists, most economists agree that society's well-being is best served by continued economic growth. Of course, it is generally recognized that not all output growth is desirable—not all output growth makes a net positive contribution to social welfare after allowing for the

2 Among its other effects, rapidly rising world oil prices (imposed by a cartel arrangement) have: (1) substantially increased oil exploration activities, (2) slowed the rate of growth of oil usage, and (3) made small cars more popular and stimulated interest in nuclear, solar, and other forms of energy.

by-products of that growth. But, output growth that does make a net contribution to social welfare is welcomed. To adopt a no-growth policy, because output growth can produce undesirable side effects, smacks of a "throw out the baby with the bath water" policy. Indeed, only with a growing productive capacity can we maintain our current consumption standards *and* provide the capital investment needed for cleaning our air, water, and countryside; for improving our transportation system; and so on.

FIXED-PROPORTION GROWTH MODELS

The intensity of national concern over the rate of growth fluctuates with the performance of the economy. After many years of sluggish growth in the 1950s, policy actions advocated by the Kennedy administration to spur growth commanded widespread attention and support. But with output growing vigorously in the mid-1960s, growth was taken for granted and national concern turned to other issues. Since 1969, though, the rate of real output growth has slowed and inflation has accelerated. It is, once again, fashionable for society to worry about the rate of growth with that concern tempered by an awareness of the ecological implications of alternative growth patterns.

Economists themselves have always been highly concerned with economic growth. Consequently, there was only a short time lapse after the publication of *The General Theory* in 1936 before academic economists began to concern themselves with growth in a Keynesian world. In fact, a landmark in the evolution of modern theoretical explanations of growth appeared in 1939 with the publication of Roy Harrod's "An Essay in Dynamic Theory." [3]

The Harrod-Domar Model

While not identical, very similar attempts to extend the Keynesian model to analyze long-run economic growth were developed by Harrod and Evsey Domar. The basic model they developed is most often presented as the *Harrod-Domar model* in textbook reviews of the evolution of growth model analysis. While the Harrod-Domar model is quite simple, it provides some insights into the growth process that have directly affected growth planning in many countries.

The Harrod-Domar analysis focuses attention on the dual role that investment plays once we lengthen our time horizon sufficiently to let the capital stock grow significantly. On the one hand, investment expenditure, as Keynesian models emphasize, is a component of aggregate *demand*. On the other hand, net

---

3   Roy Harrod, "An Essay in Dynamic Theory," *Economic Journal*, Vol. XLIX, March 1939, pp. 14-33. See also Evsey Domar, "Expansion and Employment," *American Economic Review*, Vol. XXXVII, March 1947, pp. 34-55.

investment increases the stock of capital and, thus, increases the economy's potential *supply* of real goods and services over time. The Harrod-Domar analysis focuses on determining the (possibly restrictive) requirements for ensuring that aggregate supply and demand grow in step.

The formal Harrod-Domar model is constructed assuming a simple closed economy so aggregate *demand* is the sum of consumption (C) and autonomous investment $(\bar{I})$, as indicated in Equation (13-1).

$$\text{Demand} = Y_D = C + I \tag{13-1}$$
$$= a + bY + \bar{I}.$$

Since aggregate spending (demand) is identical to aggregate income, the equilibrium level of aggregate demand is

$$Y_D = \frac{1}{1-b}(a + \bar{I}) \tag{13-2}$$

$$\text{or } Y_D = \frac{1}{s}(a + \bar{I})$$

where s is the marginal propensity to save. The change in aggregate demand that stems from a change in investment is just

$$\Delta Y_D = \frac{1}{s}\,\Delta\bar{I}, \tag{13-3}$$

the change in investment times the simple multiplier.

To know how aggregate *supply* changes over time, we must know the nature of the relationship between output and the volume of factor inputs employed. The first production relationship in the Harrod-Domar model assumes that aggregate potential supply is directly proportional to the volume of capital stock available. That is,

$$\text{Supply} = Y_S = \sigma K \tag{13-4}$$

where K is the stock of capital and σ is the "output-capital" ratio.[4] With a constant output to capital ratio, the change in potential supply during any time period is

$$\Delta Y_S = \sigma \Delta K. \tag{13-5}$$

However, since by definition the change in capital stock during any period is net

4 If $Y = \sigma K$, $\sigma = Y/K$, the output-capital ratio.

investment, Equation (13-5) can be rewritten to show the change in aggregate supply in any period as

$$\Delta Y_s = \sigma I. \tag{13-6}$$

The dual role of investment mentioned earlier is easily seen in Equation (13-3), showing the influence of investment on aggregate demand, and in Equation (13-6), showing the influence of investment on aggregate supply.

Starting with equality of aggregate supply and demand, if full employment of the capital stock is to be maintained over time, aggregate demand must grow in step with supply. If this equality ($\Delta Y_D = \Delta Y_S$) holds over time, from Equations (13-3) and (13-6)

$$\frac{1}{s}\Delta I = \sigma I \tag{13-7}$$

$$\text{or } \frac{\Delta I}{I} = s\sigma. \tag{13-7A}$$

The term $\Delta I/I$ in Equation (13-7A) is the proportional rate at which investment itself *must grow* over time to maintain full utilization of the growing stock of capital. If, for example, the output to capital ratio is .5 and the marginal propensity to save is .1, the required rate of growth of investment for maintaining full use of the capital stock is .05 or 5 percent annually ($s\sigma = .1 \times .5 = .05$).

Should the marginal propensity to save increase to .2, the rate at which investment must grow to maintain full utilization of the capital stock becomes 10 percent. That is, the larger the fraction of any addition to output that is saved (the smaller the fraction consumed), the larger the required addition to investment if aggregate demand is to absorb the full volume of production that an enlarged capital stock can provide.

At what rate will aggregate output be growing with investment expanding at rate $s\sigma$? From Equation (13-6), output grows in absolute terms by

$$\Delta Y_s = \sigma I. \tag{13-8}$$

For the economy to be in equilibrium, saving must equal investment, and, in the long run, saving is a constant fraction of income. In this case, the average and marginal propensities to save are identical so total saving is sY where s is both the average and marginal propensity to save. Substituting saving (sY) for investment in Equation (13-8) yields

$$\Delta Y = \sigma s Y, \tag{13-9}$$

so the rate of growth of output is

$$\frac{\Delta Y}{Y} = s\sigma. \tag{13-10}$$

Thus, output grows at the rate at which investment grows.

Growth rate $s\sigma$, the rate of growth of investment and output at which the expanding capital stock will remain fully utilized over time, is what Harrod called the *warranted* rate of growth (G_W). It is the rate of growth that will result in investors' expectations being *realized* or *warranted*—all investment exactly fully utilized. There are two important lessons for growth planning implied by Equation (13-10). First, that equation indicates that the rate of growth is positively related to the saving rate. Saving frees resources for investment, and it is investment that provides for a growing productive capacity. Secondly, Equation (13-10) indicates that the growth rate is directly related to the output-capital ratio (the productivity of capital). By raising the saving rate and investing in more productive capital, it appears a country can raise its warranted growth rate.

Labor Force Utilization

To know whether warranted growth rate $s\sigma$ permits maintenance of full employment of the labor force, we need to know the rate at which the labor force grows and we need to know, from the aggregate production function, the relationship between labor utilization and output. The production relationship summarized in Equation (13-4) indicates only that aggregate supply is proportional to the stock of capital employed and tells us nothing about the labor requirement in the production process. We know though that labor inputs are required in the production process. Thus, for capital to serve as a strictly limiting variable on output, as indicated in Equation (13-4), the aggregate production function must require labor and capital to be combined in *fixed proportions*, as shown in Figure 13-1. The heavy L-shaped lines in that illustration are production *isoquants*, showing the combinations of labor and capital that can provide particular levels of aggregate output. With the production function represented by Figure 13-1, one unit of output can be produced with two units of capital and four units of labor

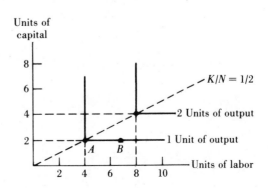

FIGURE 13-1 A Fixed-Proportion Production Function

(point A). The addition of more units of labor has no impact on output as long as the stock of capital is held constant (point B in Figure 13-1). Similarly, increasing the quantity of capital with the quantity of labor held constant, for example at the four unit level, leaves output unchanged.

The proportionate capital-labor ratio that just permits one, two, or more units of output to be produced with no surplus labor or capital is 1 to 2—one unit of capital to two units of labor. The Harrod-Domar production function clearly assumes that the ratio of required capital to labor is *fixed* for all income levels. With this highly restrictive form of production function, the economy can grow at the warranted rate only if there is surplus labor or if the effective labor supply is growing as rapidly as investment and output are growing. To return to our earlier example in which the warranted rate of growth was 5 percent annually, if the economy begins with both capital and labor fully utilized the labor force would have to grow at a 5 percent or greater annual rate to prevent labor scarcity from constraining output's growth to a slower rate. If, for example, the rate of growth of the labor force is only 3 percent annually, the rate of growth of investment and output would be constrained to be 3 percent or less annually. That conclusion holds, ultimately, even if the economy initially has unemployed labor available. Once labor is fully utilized, if the capital stock grows faster than the labor force, there will be redundant capital which, as our production function discussion has shown, has zero productivity—it simply is not used. The rate of population growth serves as a powerful constraint on the growth of output and the capital stock in the Harrod-Domar model.

Labor Force Growth

In the Harrod-Domar model, the labor force is assumed to grow at a biologically determined, constant proportional rate, $\Delta N/N$. If the rate of growth of output is constrained by the rate of population growth, there is one way in which the growth rate can be raised. If it is possible to invest in new, *technologically improved* capital (rather than just in more units of an existing sort of capital) the average productivity of labor can be increased over time so that a smaller labor input can be combined with a given "size" of capital input to produce the same output as before. Hence, with "labor-saving" technological progress, the rate at which the economy's productive capacity grows can be raised. In its effect on productive capacity, a continuous increase over time in the average productivity of labor is equivalent to having the labor force grow more rapidly with average productivity unchanged. Thus, the rate of growth of the "effective" labor force or of "augmented" labor is the sum of the rate of growth of man-hours of labor and of the rate of growth of average labor productivity. That is, "effective" labor supply's growth rate, which in the Harrod-Domar analysis is called the *natural* rate of growth, is:

$$G_N = \frac{\Delta Ne}{N_e} = \frac{\Delta N}{N} + \lambda \tag{13-11}$$

where λ is the rate of growth of average labor productivity and $\Delta N/N$, as before, is the rate of growth of manpower.

The rate of growth of output is still strictly constrained, but with labor-saving technological progress, it is constrained to equality with the warranted rate of growth $(s\sigma)$ or the natural rate of growth of *augmented* labor, whichever is smaller. Thus, the emphasis in the full Harrod-Domar model is on the important role of the rate of saving and investment as the determinant of the warranted rate of growth and on the roles of population growth and technological progress as determinants of the natural rate of growth. To accelerate growth, a country must save (invest) a larger fraction of its current output and/or must employ policies that increase the rate of technological progress.

The Razor's Edge

A full equilibrium rate of growth would be one that maintained full utilization of both the capital stock and the labor force over time. In full equilibrium, then,

$$\frac{\Delta Y}{Y} = s\sigma = \frac{\Delta N}{N} + \lambda \tag{13-12}$$

or $G_W = G_N$.

In full equilibrium, the economy would expand along a production ray like K/N in Figure 13-1, with output and the stock of capital expanding at precisely the rate dictated by the expansion of the augmented labor force.

While steady growth at the natural rate is possible, with no mechanism that coordinates the growth of the capital stock with the *natural* rate of growth (determination of s, σ, $\Delta N/N$, and λ are all independent), the probability that expansion will take place along the one *razor's edge* expansion path that maintains full utilization of labor and capital is extremely small.

Should the natural rate of growth be smaller than the warranted rate, excess capital stock will ultimately appear. Immediately the marginal product of new capital drops to zero, eliminating the incentive for investment. With investment and, thus, aggregate demand falling, excess capacity would be growing making it appear that firms had been investing at too rapid a rate when, in fact, more investment would be needed to stave off a major contraction. Conditions are little better if the natural rate exceeds the warranted rate. In that case, there would be increasing unemployment of labor over time. The equilibrium growth path represented by the Harrod-Domar model is clearly a difficult path for the economy to follow.

Happily, the real world appears less demanding in its requirements for permitting the full utilization of both labor and capital as the economy expands. Dissatisfied with the pessimistic predictions in the razor's edge model, growth theorists soon provided alternative accounts of the growth process. These alternative models of growth showed that the demanding conditions for full equilibrium in the Harrod-Domar model stemmed from the rigidity of the assumptions on which the model was built—a constant capital-output ratio, a constant saving ratio, and a constant rate of growth of the augmented labor force. By relaxing one or more of these restrictive assumptions, the razor-edge rigidity in the Harrod-Domar analysis can be eliminated.

NEOCLASSICAL GROWTH MODELS

In a seminal contribution to the new generation of growth models, in 1956 Robert Solow constructed a neoclassical growth model which: (1) generalized the Harrod-Domar analysis by employing a production function that permits substitution between capital and labor inputs and (2) focused attention on the supply of factor inputs rather than on demand as the basic determinant of the long-run growth path.[5] In conjunction with the assumption of capital-labor substitution, Solow also assumed a competitive economy (with no wage or price rigidities), providing assurance that all factor inputs would be fully utilized and that the commodity market would clear (planned investment and saving equal) at the full-capacity level of production. Since the fundamental assumptions employed in the Solow analysis are common to neoclassical theory, the resulting growth model is *neoclassical*. With full employment assured, the neoclassical growth model is concerned with the equilibrium growth rate and with the contributions that labor, capital, and technological progress make to growth.

The Generalized Production Function and Output Changes

As shown in Figure 13-2, when capital and labor are substitutes, production can take place with an unlimited number of different capital to labor ratios.[6] Each of the heavy lines in that figure is an isoquant that shows the various combinations of capital and labor that can be used to produce a particular volume of output. Two possible output expansion rays are shown in Figure 13-2, one for a capital-labor ratio of 2 to 1 and one with $K/N = 1/2$.

Examination of either of the possible expansion paths plotted in Figure 13-2 shows that an equiproportional change in both factor inputs changes output by the same proportion—for example, doubling the quantity of labor and capital employed along the $K/N = 2/1$ ray doubles output. Thus, the production function which provides the isoquants in Figure 13-2 assumes constant returns to

---

5 R. M. Solow, "A Contribution to the Theory of Economic Growth," *Quarterly Journal of Economics*, Vol. LXX, February 1956, pp. 65-94. Also see "Technical Change and the Aggregate Production Function," *Review of Economics and Statistics*, Vol. 39, August 1957, pp. 312-320.
6 The neoclassical production function that provides the isoquants (constant output schedules) in Figure 13-2 is the general form we assumed throughout our analysis of short-run income determination models.

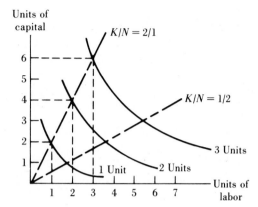

FIGURE 13-2   Neoclassical Production Isoquants—Capital and Labor
Substitutable

scale.[7] At the same time, it assumes diminishing returns to any one variable factor input. That is, adding more and more units of a variable factor input to a
fixed quantity of other inputs is assumed to raise output at a diminishing rate,
the *marginal product* of any factor input that is allowed to vary in quantity declining as additional units of the variable factor are employed.

The general algebraic form of the production function specified above is
simply

$$Y = Y(K, N) \quad s.t. \frac{\Delta Y}{\Delta K} > 0 \tag{13-13}$$

$$\frac{\Delta Y}{\Delta N} > 0.$$

Since changes in the size of either the labor force or the capital stock produce
changes in output, it is definitionally true from Equation (13-13) that

$$\Delta Y = \left(\frac{\Delta Y}{\Delta K}\right) \cdot \Delta K + \left(\frac{\Delta Y}{\Delta N}\right) \cdot \Delta N. \tag{13-14}$$

Recognizing that $(\Delta Y/\Delta K)$ and $(\Delta Y/\Delta N)$ are just the marginal products (MP)
of capital and labor respectively, the change in output is,

$$\Delta Y = MP_K \cdot \Delta K + MP_N \cdot \Delta N. \tag{13-15}$$

Since multiplying and dividing any expression by the same term has no impact
on that expression's value, Equation (13-15) can be rewritten as

7   A production function that exhibits constant returns to scale is frequently described as
linearly homogeneous or homogeneous of degree 1. For any function $Y = Y(K, N)$, if $Y(\eta K, \eta N)$
$= \eta Y$, the function is linearly homogeneous.

$$Y \cdot \left(\frac{\Delta Y}{Y}\right) = K \cdot MP_K \left(\frac{\Delta K}{K}\right) + N \cdot MP_N \left(\frac{\Delta N}{N}\right) \tag{13-16}$$

or

$$\frac{\Delta Y}{Y} = \frac{K \cdot MP_K}{Y} \left(\frac{\Delta K}{K}\right) + \frac{N \cdot MP_N}{Y} \left(\frac{\Delta N}{N}\right). \tag{13-17}$$

Equation (13-17) then defines the proportional rate of change of output in terms of the rates of change of the capital stock and the labor force. Since the neoclassical model assumes the economy is perfectly competitive, labor and capital are paid their respective marginal products. Thus, as indicated in Equation (13-17), labor's total income is $N \cdot MP_N$, capital's income is $K \cdot MP_K$, $(N \cdot MP_N)/Y$ is labor's *relative share* of total output, and $(K \cdot MP_K)/Y$ is capital's relative share of total output. If, for economy of exposition, we label capital's fractional share of output α [that is, let $(K \cdot MP_K)/Y = \alpha$] then labor's relative share is $(1 - \alpha)$ and Equation (13-17) becomes

$$\frac{\Delta Y}{Y} = \alpha \left(\frac{\Delta K}{K}\right) + (1 - \alpha) \left(\frac{\Delta N}{N}\right). \tag{13-18}$$

With the production function exhibiting constant returns to scale, if capital and labor should grow at the same proportional rate, output also grows at that rate. As we shall see, with equality of planned saving and investment maintained in the neoclassical model, there are forces that drive the growth rates of capital and output to equality with the rate of growth of the labor force which is, once again, biologically determined. In full equilibrium, then, there is only one possible output-capital ratio and one possible capital-labor ratio.

Equilibrium Growth in the Neoclassical Model

For equilibrium, planned saving must equal planned net investment. With long-run saving proportional to income $(S = sY)$ and net investment simply the change in capital stock (ΔK), equilibrium requires

$$\Delta K = sY. \tag{13-19}$$

Substituting this expression for ΔK in Equation (13-18) yields

$$\frac{\Delta Y}{Y} = \alpha s \frac{Y}{K} + (1 - \alpha) \frac{\Delta N}{N}. \tag{13-20}$$

Equation (13-20) shows that the rate of growth of output is directly proportional (*ceteris paribus*) to the output to capital ratio (Y/K). In Figure 13-3, the rate of growth of output $(\Delta Y/Y)$ is plotted as a function of the output-capital

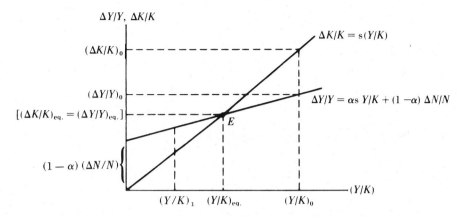

FIGURE 13-3 The Equilibrium Growth Rate

ratio for assumed, constant values of the relative income shares of capital and labor, the marginal propensity to save, and the labor force growth rate.

From Equation (13-19), the rate of growth of the capital stock is

$$\frac{\Delta K}{K} = s\frac{Y}{K} \tag{13-21}$$

showing that, for a given marginal propensity to save, the rate of growth of the capital stock rises in direct proportion to the output-capital ratio. This relationship is also plotted in Figure 13-3.

From the diagram, it is easy to see that the economy will move toward one equilibrium growth path over time. If we started with the output-capital ratio above its equilibrium value (say, value $(Y/K)_0$ in Figure 13-3), the rate of growth of the capital stock, $(\Delta K/K)_0$, would exceed the rate of growth of output, $(\Delta Y/Y)_0$, resulting in a decline in the output-capital ratio. With the output-capital ratio below the equilibrium value [as at $(Y/K)_1$ in Figure 13-3], output would be growing at a higher rate than capital, raising the output-capital ratio. Thus, there is convergence toward point E in Figure 13-3, which provides the ultimate equilibrium growth rate for output and capital $[(\Delta Y/Y)_{eq.} = (\Delta K/K)_{eq.}]$ and establishes the equilibrium output-capital ratio, $(Y/K)_{eq.}$.

Since, in equilibrium, $\Delta K/K = \Delta Y/Y$, Equation (13-20) can be rewritten as

$$\frac{\Delta Y}{Y} = \frac{\Delta K}{K} = \alpha s\frac{Y}{K} + (1-\alpha)\frac{\Delta N}{N}. \tag{13-22}$$

Substituting the value for $\Delta K/K$ given by Equation (13-21) yields

$$s\frac{Y}{K} = \alpha s\frac{Y}{K} + (1-\alpha)\frac{\Delta N}{N}. \tag{13-23}$$

Solving for $s(Y/K)$ yields

$$s \frac{Y}{K} = \frac{(1-\alpha)}{(1-\alpha)} \frac{\Delta N}{N} \tag{13-24}$$

$$= \frac{\Delta N}{N}.$$

Since $s(Y/K) = \Delta K/K$, in equilibrium

$$\left(\frac{\Delta Y}{Y}\right)_{eq.} = \left(\frac{\Delta K}{K}\right)_{eq.} = \left(\frac{\Delta N}{N}\right)_{eq.} = s \frac{Y}{K}. \tag{13-25}$$

Thus, output and the capital stock will ultimately be constrained to grow at the rate of growth of the labor force.[8]

The Propensity to Save and the Equilibrium Growth Rate

Equation (13-25) shows that, in contrast to the Harrod-Domar conclusion when the labor force is not a constraint on growth, *the equilibrium rate of growth is independent of the value of the marginal propensity to save.* This conclusion, that the growth rate cannot be raised permanently by having an increased proportion of output devoted to investment instead of consumption, rests on the assumption of diminishing returns in the production process. An increase in the propensity to save does immediately raise the growth rate of the capital stock above its previous equilibrium level and, since the marginal product of capital is positive, this lifts output's growth rate above its previous equilibrium level. However, as long as capital grows more rapidly than labor, raising the capital-labor ratio, the marginal product of capital will be falling. This reduces the rate at which output grows and, since investment is just the saving ratio times output, the rate at which the capital stock grows. Ultimately, the growth rate of output and capital would fall to equality with the labor force growth rate halting the rise in the capital-labor ratio. Thus, long-run equilibrium would finally be restored with output and the capital stock growing at the same rate as the labor force.

While an increase in the saving rate cannot permanently raise the equilibrium growth rate, it would raise the equilibrium capital-labor ratio. Since this change would provide labor with more units of capital to work with, raising the marginal product of labor, a labor force of any size would be able to produce a larger absolute level of output after the rise in the saving ratio. The economy would be placed on a permanently higher-*level* equilibrium growth path by the

8 So far, we have not allowed for technological progress in the neoclassical model. We will do so shortly.

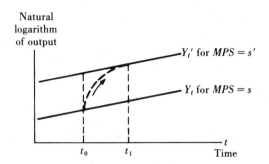

Natural logarithm of output

Y_t' for $MPS = s'$

Y_t for $MPS = s$

t_0 t_1

t

Time

FIGURE 13-4 Impact on the Growth Path of a Changed Saving Ratio

increase in the marginal propensity to save. The impact of an altered saving rate is reflected in the growth paths plotted in Figure 13-4 with the higher *absolute level* growth path corresponding to the increased propensity to save.[9]

We should be sure to note that by employing a more general and flexible production function the neoclassical model has avoided the disturbing conclusions provided by the Harrod-Domar model. In Solow's words,

> When production takes place under the usual neoclassical assumption of variable proportions and constant returns to scale, no simple opposition between natural and warranted rates of growth is possible. . . . The system can adjust to any given rate of growth of the labor force, and eventually approach a state of steady proportional expansion.[10]

Of course, to argue that capital and labor can be fully employed continuously, Solow's assumption that the economy is essentially competitive is required since under competitive conditions relative prices of capital and labor are free to adjust sufficiently to make employers willing to utilize fully the available volumes of both inputs. Even so, economic progress appears to be limited in nature. With output and labor destined to grow at the same rate in the long-run, output per capita stays constant—hardly a condition that portends a rising standard of living. But, with technological progress the long-run outlook becomes more promising.

---

9 For convenience, the natural logarithm of output is measured on the vertical axis of Figure 13-4. With output growing at a constant percentage rate, the time path of the natural logarithm of output is a straight line as drawn. The slope of the growth paths plotted in Figure 13-4 is the equilibrium growth rate which is unaffected by changes in the saving rate.

As indicated in the text, the level of the equilibrium growth path is altered by changes in the saving rate. Hence, the question arises of what saving rate and accompanying growth path for output is optimal. For consideration of that question, see Edmund Phelps, "The Golden Age of Accumulation: A Fable for Growthmen," *American Economic Review*, Vol. 51, September 1961, pp. 638-643.

10 Solow, "A Contribution to the Theory of Economic Growth," *op. cit.*, p. 458.

Technological Progress and Growth

Equation (13-18) showed the rate of growth of output as determined by the rates of growth of the capital stock and labor force with no provision for the role of technological progress. With a slight modification of that equation, technological progress can be introduced into the neoclassical model. Equation (13-26) below is the resulting expression for the rate of growth of output. In that equation r is the rate of technological progress, the annual rate of increase in output that would result from technological progress

$$\frac{\Delta Y}{Y} = r + \alpha \frac{\Delta K}{K} + (1 - \alpha) \frac{\Delta N}{N}, \tag{13-26}$$

even if the stock of capital and the number of man-hours of available labor are unchanged.[11]

To deduce the implications for the growth process of the introduction of technological progress, we can repeat the manipulations performed with the neo-classical growth model that ignored technological change. Recalling from Equation (13-21) that $\Delta K/K = s(Y/K)$, Equation (13-26) can be rewritten to define output's growth rate as a function of the output-capital ratio. Equation (13-27) does that.

$$\frac{\Delta Y}{Y} = r + \alpha s \frac{Y}{K} + (1 - \alpha) \frac{\Delta N}{N}. \tag{13-27}$$

In Figure 13-5, the relationships between the growth rate of output and the output-capital ratio are shown for zero $(r = 0)$ and positive $(r = \bar{r})$ rates of

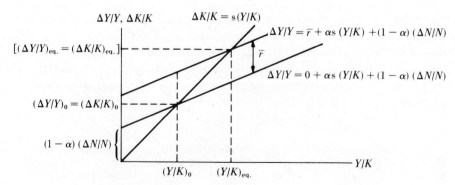

FIGURE 13-5 Equilibrium Growth with Technological Progress

11 Throughout our analysis we have failed to provide an explanation of the generation of technological progress. On that issue, see Edwin Mansfield, *The Economics of Technological Change* (New York: W. W. Norton, 1968).

technological progress. The relationship between the output-capital ratio and the growth rate of the capital stock is also plotted in that figure. The presence of technological progress clearly raises the equilibrium growth rate of output and the capital stock while the equality between those growth rates is maintained. In addition, the equilibrium output to capital ratio is raised.

What is the new equilibrium growth rate of output and capital? Since we now know that output and capital grow at the same equilibrium rate ($\Delta Y/Y = \Delta K/K$), we can rewrite Equation (13-26) as

$$\frac{\Delta Y}{Y} = \frac{\Delta K}{K} = r + \alpha \frac{\Delta K}{K} + (1 - \alpha) \frac{\Delta N}{N}. \tag{13-28}$$

Solving for the equilibrium growth rate yields

$$\frac{\Delta Y}{Y} = \frac{\Delta K}{K} = \frac{r}{1 - \alpha} + \frac{\Delta N}{N}, \tag{13-29}$$

showing that, with technological progress introduced, the equilibrium growth rate of capital and output becomes equal to the rate of growth of effective or augmented labor. Thus, output's growth rate is determined by the rate of population growth, the rate of technological progress, and the size of labor's relative share of output.[12]

---

12 Because it exhibits constant returns to scale and diminishing marginal productivity to changes in the quantity of any *one* factor input employed, a particular, simple production relation known as the Cobb-Douglas production function has been widely used in the construction of growth models. Most commonly, this function takes the form

$$Y = AK^\alpha N^{1-\alpha}, \tag{a}$$

where A and α are constants and Y, K, and N are output, capital, and labor. Differentiating this function with respect to time yields

$$\frac{dY}{dt} = K^\alpha N^{1-\alpha} \frac{dA}{dt} + \alpha A K^{\alpha-1} N^{1-\alpha} \frac{dK}{dt} + (1 - \alpha) A K^\alpha N^{-\alpha} \frac{dN}{dt}. \tag{b}$$

Dividing both sides of this expression by $Y (= AK^\alpha N^{1-\alpha})$ yields

$$\frac{1}{Y} \frac{dY}{dt} = \frac{1}{A} \frac{dA}{dt} + \alpha \frac{1}{K} \frac{dK}{dt} + (1 - \alpha) \frac{1}{N} \frac{dN}{dt}, \tag{c}$$

the percentage rate of growth of output expressed as a function of the percentage rate of "disembodied" technical progress and the percentage rates of growth of the capital stock and the labor force. If output, the capital stock, and investment all grow at constant (long-run equilibrium) percentage rates y, k, and i over time, their values at any point in time are given by:

$$Y_t = Y_0 e^{yt} \quad K = K_0 e^{kt} \quad I = I_0 e^{it}.$$

With investment identical to the rate of change of capital stock,

$$I = \frac{dK}{dt} = kK_0 e^{kt} = I_0 e^{it}. \tag{d}$$

Since in equilibrium saving, which is $s \cdot Y_0 e^{yt}$, must equal investment, our set of equalities can be expanded to

Since the rate of growth of output per worker is

$$\frac{\Delta Y}{Y} - \frac{\Delta N}{N} = \frac{r}{1 - \alpha},$$

(13-30)

there can be no increase in output per worker according to this model unless there is technological progress (r positive).

Once again, the equilibrium growth rate is independent of the saving rate. While an increase in the saving rate temporarily raises the growth rates of capital and output, diminishing returns will ultimately push their growth rates back to equality with the growth rate of augmented labor. During the transition, with capital growing more rapidly than the effective labor force, the marginal product of capital will be falling, lowering the rate of growth of output and thus of capital formation ($= sY$). This adjustment will continue until output, capital, and augmented labor grow at the same rate, $\Delta N/N + r/(1 - \alpha)$.

Agreement of Theory and Empirical Evidence on the Determinants of Growth

The neoclassical model we have developed is representative of growth theory in the mid- to late 1950s. As we have seen, this neoclassical model contradicts the Harrod-Domar conclusion that the willingness of society to forego current consumption and save is a potent determinant of the *rate* of economic growth and, thus, of society's future well-being. While the saving-investment rate remained a crucial determinant of the *level* of the growth path, changes in the investment rate could not be counted on to accelerate the long-run growth rate. This suggests that policy prescriptions for permanently altering the rate of growth would have to be focused on programs that change the quality of the factors of production—for example, on technological innovation that raises labor or capital productivity and on labor-productivity enhancing education.

Paralleling theoretical developments, by the late 1950s there had been several attempts at empirically accounting for the U.S. growth experience. The

---

$$I = \frac{dK}{dt} = sY_0 e^{yt} = kK_0 e^{kt} = I_0 e^{it}.$$

(e)

For this set of equalities to hold continuously over time, the percentage growth rates of output, investment, and the capital stock must all be equal ($y = k = i$).

With the growth rate of output equal to that of the capital stock (call the rate G_Y), equation (c) can be rewritten as

$$G_Y = \alpha \cdot G_Y + \frac{1}{A} \frac{dA}{dt} + (1 - \alpha) \frac{1}{N} \frac{dN}{dt}.$$

(f)

Solving for G_Y yields

$$G_Y = \frac{1}{1 - \alpha} \frac{1}{A} \frac{dA}{dt} + \frac{1}{N} \frac{dN}{dt}$$

(g)

which is comparable to Equation (13-29) in the text.

typical empirical study provided a statistically fitted aggregate production function that related output growth to growth in manpower and the stock of capital, and to the rate of technological progress. Such regressions provide a means of identifying the important *sources* of growth and measuring their individual contributions to growth.

The results from those studies were consistent with the conclusions of the neoclassical growth model. *Capital-deepening*—raising the capital to labor ratio by adding more units of identical capital to the existing stock of capital that labor has to work with—appeared to explain only a small part of the total growth of output per worker that the United States has experienced while technological change reigned as the primary determinant of growth in output per worker. Taking a brief look at some of those empirical results, in two different papers Robert Solow offered evidence on the sources of U.S. growth. In 1957, he fitted a production function to U.S. data spanning the period 1909-1949.[13] His regression results suggested that technological progress was responsible for a full 87½ percent of the increase in output per worker during the period analyzed while only a paltry 12½ percent of the increase could be attributed to capital-deepening.

In a later study that updated the time period covered to span 1929-1961, Solow found that U.S. output grew at a 2½ percent annual rate just as a result of technological progress.[14] Persistent growth in the labor force also accounted for substantial increases in the total volume of output over that period with an elasticity of output with respect to changes in the labor force of .89. However, the elasticity of output with respect to the capital stock was only .11 implying that a 1-percent increase in the rate of growth of capital would produce, even in the short run, only a .1 percent increase in the rate of growth of output.

Similar results were obtained by Richard Nelson. For the period 1929-1960, he found that only 18 percent of the increase in output per worker could be attributed to an increase in the quantity of capital per worker.[15] Thus, both theory and empirical evidence offered a gloomy outlook on the possibility of affecting the growth rate by employing policies that alter the investment rate. In fact, the empirical evidence cast doubt on the ability of changes in the investment rate to significantly alter the *level* of the growth path, so small were the apparent elasticities of output with respect to changes in the capital stock. Rather than depending on capital-deepening, it appeared that policies to stimulate research and education would be required to foster the productivity increases necessary for maintaining a rising standard of living.

---

13 Robert Solow, "Technical Change and the Aggregate Production Function," *Review of Economics and Statistics*, Vol. 39, August 1957, pp. 312-320.

14 Robert Solow, "Technical Progress, Capital Formation, and Economic Growth," *American Economic Review*, Vol. 52, May 1962, pp. 76-86.

15 Richard Nelson, "Aggregate Production Functions and Medium-Range Growth Projections," *American Economic Review*, Vol. 54, September 1964, pp. 575-606.

However, those pessimistic conclusions on the role of investment in altering the growth rate were probably wrong and, at best, were badly misleading. Both the theoretical and empirical results were generated using models that assumed technological progress was *disembodied*—that the rate of technological progress, which results in increased aggregate productive capacity, is *independent* of the rates at which the labor force and the capital stock are growing [look back at Equation (13-26) to see that this is the case in the neoclassical model]. Yet, much (probably most) of technological advance is *embodied* in new capital goods so that investment in newly produced capital is necessary for that technological advance to take place. As a consequence, an increase in the rate of *gross* investment brings with it an increase in the rate at which the "efficiency" of the capital stock is raised.

The need to distinguish between embodied and disembodied technological progress was clearly recognized in the early 1960s. The proponents of the resulting *new view* of investment stressed the role of investment in modernizing the capital stock as much as in deepening it. Official government recognition of the new view was reflected in a 1961 statement by the Council of Economic Advisers:

> One of the reasons for the recent slowdown in the rate of growth of productivity and output is a corresponding slowdown in the rate at which the stock of capital has been renewed and modernized. . . . As has been confirmed by more recent research, the great importance of capital investment lies in its interactions with improved skills and technological progress. New ideas lie fallow without the modern equipment to give them life. From this point of view, the function of capital formation is as much in modernizing the equipment of the industrial worker as in simply adding to it.[16]

In 1962, Edmund Phelps published a paper analyzing the properties of a growth model that makes the embodied versus disembodied distinction.[17] His model recognizes that the latest, most efficient technology can only be exploited by putting new capital goods embodying that technology in place, either to replace old capital or as a net addition to the capital stock. Since new capital is more productive than old capital, it is necessary to distinguish between different *vintages* of capital goods. The later the vintage (the newer the capital good) the more advanced the technology and, hence, the greater the output per unit of labor a unit of capital can produce. In the aggregate then, the lower the average age of the capital stock the greater is the average productivity of labor.

16 U.S. Joint Economic Committee, "The American Economy in 1961: Problems and Policies," Council of Economic Advisers, *Hearings on the Economic Report of the President*, 1961, p. 338.
17 Edmund Phelps, "The New View of Investment: A Neoclassical Analysis," *Quarterly Journal of Economics*, Vol. 76, November 1962, pp. 548-567.

The average age of the capital stock can be temporarily lowered by increasing the rate of saving and gross investment. In this way, the rate of growth of labor productivity and, thus, of output can be accelerated. However, as in the earlier neoclassical growth model, the rate of growth will ultimately return to its initial value.

Large investments today result in a large volume of old capital in the future which will tend to raise the average age of the capital stock. The average age of the capital stock will ultimately rise to its old equilibrium value and output will grow at the old rate. To obtain a permanent modernization of the capital stock would require the investment ratio to rise without limit—a clear impossibility. Thus, a once-and-for-all increase in the investment ratio is limited in the long run to increasing the capital-labor ratio with the average age of the enlarged capital stock unchanged. As in the old view model, the economy is shifted to a higher-*level* growth path by the capital-deepening a higher investment ratio provides, but grows at the old equilibrium growth rate.

It seems that our theoretical conclusions are little altered by allowing for embodied technological change. However, the empirical evidence that casts doubt on the effectiveness of investment ratio changes in altering the growth path is called into question since it was obtained treating all technological progress as disembodied or organizational.

Recent Empirical Evidence

It was expected that fitting a model which treats technical progress as embodied, so that investment is required for such progress, would reveal a far more important role for investment in controlling the economy's growth path. To test that hypothesis, Solow fitted an extreme form of the new view model that assumed *all* technological innovation was embodied. To account for embodied improvements in capital, Solow adjusted his capital stock figures to make recent additions to the capital stock more productive than older ones. This is accomplished by multiplying each vintage of capital by a productivity improvement factor $(1 + \lambda)^v$ where λ is the annual rate of technical advance and v is the vintage of the unit of capital. His model also adjusted each vintage of capital for depreciation by assuming that, from gross investment in year v of $I(v)$, the amount of capital "surviving" in year t is portion $B(t - v)$. Thus, his "equivalent stock of capital," adding up the survivors of each vintage and weighting by the appropriate productivity improvement factor was:

$$J(t) = \sum_{v = -\infty}^{t} (1 + \lambda)^v B(t - v) I(v). \qquad (13\text{-}31)$$

This measure of the effective capital stock was used in fitting an aggregate production function. The results for the 1929-1961 period indicate an elasticity of output with respect to capital stock of .51 as opposed to the .11 obtained assuming only disembodied technical change. Tangible investment in new capital goods appears to have regained some of its traditionally assumed importance. Still, since we do not have any measure of the fraction of technological advance that is embodied, we cannot know how to weight the two extreme-case results produced by Solow to find the true output-capital elasticity.[18]

Though a number of other studies by Denison, Kendrick, Jorgenson, and others have attempted to quantify the contribution to growth of changes in the quantities of factor inputs and of technological progress, the empirical results remain controversial. Yet, a policy for controlling the growth path cannot be intelligently formulated without measures of the response of output to changes in each of its determinants. As an example of the dilemma a policy maker faces, we know that technological advance is important to growth but we need to know the extent to which technical advance is embodied in new capital formation. The greater the degree of embodiment the larger the growth payoff to a policy that stimulates investment—for example, an investment tax credit. On the other hand, if the elasticity of output to changes in the capital stock is small, policies to improve the labor force (such as subsidies to education and to research to improve education) and policies to encourage basic technical research might be more appropriate.

For the time being, our best indicators of the directions in which we might profitably focus our growth-determining efforts appear to be measures of the rates of return available to alternative uses of our resources. Since a factor input's contribution to output determines the reward it receives in a market economy, the rates of return to alternative investments can be compared presuming that a higher rate of return is an indication of *relative* underinvestment. In fact, comparing the rate of return to investment in education and the rate of return on tangible, physical investment indicates that there is little difference in the rates of return to those two directions of investment allocation. For example, Gary Becker found a rate of return on investment in a 4-year college education of around 9 percent and a rate of return on tangible investment in the same range.[19] Such evidence suggests that investment in both human and tangible capital is appropriate. Currently available measures of the rate of return to intangible investment in research and development are highly tentative.[20] However, the tenta-

---

18 Some more recent studies assume various breakdowns of overall technical advance to try to identify the appropriate division. This effort has not been successful. One paper tests 36 model variations. The authors find both types of technical advance important and obtain output-capital elasticities intermediate to the extremes obtained by Solow. See L. C. Thurow and L. D. Taylor, "The Interaction Between the Actual and Potential Rate of Growth," *Review of Economics and Statistics*, Vol. 48, November 1966, pp. 351-360.

19 Gary Becker, "Underinvestment in College Education?," *American Economic Review*, Vol. 50, May 1960, pp. 346-354.

20 For a brief summary of the difficulties involved in obtaining such measures as well as some tentative estimates, see E. Mansfield, "Technological Change and Industrial Research," in E. Phelps (ed.), *The Goal of Economic Growth* (New York: W. W. Norton & Co., 1969), pp. 153-171.

tive estimates suggest that in many sectors of the economy the rate of return to additional research would exceed that on investment in physical capital.

Given current limitations on our quantitative understanding of the determinants of growth, it is difficult to formulate a specific growth policy. However, as our knowledge improves, we are likely to think more seriously about a comprehensive growth plan. In formulating such a plan, we must remain aware of the fact that *growth is not free*. The immediate and direct cost that must be borne to stimulate growth is the consumption that must be foregone in order to free resources for tangible or intangible investment. Never will our goal be the maximum possible growth rate or the highest-level growth path. Instead, we will want the *optimal* growth path—that path that, accounting for both the costs and benefits of growth, maximizes society's total well-being over time. Until our knowledge of the determinants of growth improves, probably the best positive growth policy recommendation would be to avoid short-run recessions that stifle normal expansionary forces.

Still, fiscal and monetary policy actions that are taken for stabilization purposes influence the economy's growth path in important ways that should not be ignored. An increase in taxes raises *gross* saving (private saving plus government saving in the form of a budget surplus) out of full employment income, freeing resources from consumption. If those resources are invested, the economy's capital stock is enlarged and, generally, improved in overall quality. Of course, as we already know the attractiveness of private investment can be affected by tax changes too (recall the role of corporate taxes and the investment tax credit).

On the expenditures side of the government budget, the economy's productive capacity is enlarged by greater government spending on: (1) education, including worker retraining, (2) basic and applied research, (3) transportation systems, and so on. On the other hand, monetary policy has its important influence on growth through its effect on private investment. To assess the long-run role of money in the growth process, James Tobin introduced government-issued paper money into the neoclassical growth model.[21] That paper money serves both as a medium of exchange and as a second asset in which the public can hold wealth (real capital from past investment being the other). By altering the yield on (cost of) holding wealth in money form, monetary policy has its long-run influence on investment. For example, an increase in the rate of monetary expansion that results in a continuing inflation lowers the yield on (raises the cost of holding) money balances. In Tobin's two-asset world, the increased inflation rate will induce a portfolio adjustment with wealth holders purchasing more physical assets, lowering the marginal product of capital until, at the margin, the yield on money and physical assets is equalized. With a higher capital-labor ratio, output per capita is increased—the equilibrium growth path is permanently raised. Money, then, is not neutral in the long run according to Tobin.

Since policy makers have both fiscal and monetary policy tools available, it is possible for some control to be exerted over the economy's growth path even while the primary objective of maintaining a noninflationary full employment equilibrium is pursued. If a shift toward a more restrictive fiscal posture, which would depress the economy, is accompanied by a shift toward a more expansionary monetary policy, equality of aggregate demand and supply can be maintained. At the same time, such a combination monetary-fiscal policy will result in more of current output going into investment at a lowered interest rate while less output is devoted to consumption and/or government use. A shift to such a combination policy would accelerate growth in the short run and raise the level of the equilibrium growth path in the long run. What would be the effect of a shift to a combination of restrictive monetary and expansionary fiscal policy?

SUMMARY

By historical standards, the United States has enjoyed a rapid growth rate from its inception to the present. Looking just at this century's record, real U.S. output has grown at nearly a $3\frac{1}{2}$ percent annual rate, and per capita output has grown by more than $1\frac{1}{2}$ percent annually. In this chapter, we have taken a brief look at some of the models economists have built as they have tried to unravel the mysteries of the extraordinary growth in productive capacity that the *developed* countries, like the United States, have experienced in the last two or three centuries.

The first model we looked at, the Harrod-Domar model, attached a great deal of importance to the saving-investment rate. In that model, the warranted growth rate was directly proportional to the saving ratio so that the higher the saving ratio, the greater the proportional rate at which the economy could grow. Of course, equilibrium growth required maintenance of equality between planned saving and investment, an often difficult task. In addition, output expansion was strictly limited by the rate of growth of the effective labor force since capital and labor had to be combined in fixed proportions to be productive. The Harrod-Domar model provided disturbing predictions—the economy in a Harrod-Domar world was subject to chronic unemployment if the natural rate of growth exceeded the warranted rate and to a collapse of aggregate demand if the natural rate should fall short of the warranted rate.

The dire predictions on the likelihood of steady growth with full employment of labor and capital were the result of the restrictive assumptions employed in the Harrod-Domar analysis. By the mid-1950s, a new generation of growth models had emerged which employed the standard neoclassical assumptions of capital-labor substitutability and perfect competition. In these neoclassical growth models, the conflict between the natural and warranted rates of growth was eliminated. At the same time, because production with a neoclassical production function is characterized by diminishing marginal productivity, the possibility of changes in the investment ratio altering the equilibrium growth rate was eliminated. In the neoclassical model, a rise in the investment ratio would accelerate output growth only in the short run (which could, of course, be a substantial length of calendar time). However, raising the investment ratio could, by permanently raising the capital-labor ratio, shift the economy to a higher-*level* long-run growth path.

To enable output per worker to rise when the economy was on its long-run equilibrium growth path, technological progress had to be introduced into the neoclassical model. Theoretically, it made little difference in the implications we drew from the neoclassical model whether technological progress was treated as embodied or disembodied. In either case, while the rate of growth would be accelerated in the short run by an increase in the investment ratio, only the level of the long-run, equilibrium growth path would be increased by such an investment ratio change. However, there is a substantial quantitative difference in the role the investment ratio appears to play in the growth process when production function regression models are altered to treat technological progress as embodied in new capital goods. Indeed, the traditional view of the close link between economic well-being and investment in tangible capital is far more strongly supported by models that permit investment to modernize the capital stock as well as enlarge it.

While in the 1970s, the United States is facing problems of ecological damage and resource depletion that have prompted some critics to call for a policy of no growth, majority opinion among economists and the public seems committed to the continuation of growth. A rational (welfare-maximizing) growth policy would require expansion of the use of resources in growth-enhancing activities (tangible investment, research, education) until the marginal social benefit from the last resource unit so employed is just equal to the marginal social cost (*including* environmental damage) of its use. Few think that this condition is satisfied by a zero growth rate though no technique is now available for objectively determining what growth rate would be socially optimal.

QUESTIONS

1. In what sense are Harrod-Domar models razor's edge models? To what can this property be attributed?
2. Of what importance are changes in the saving rate and the productivity of capital:
   (a) in the Harrod-Domar model?
   (b) in the neoclassical model?
3. In neoclassical growth models, the rate of growth of output is independent of the fraction of income that is saved and invested. Explain why this is so.

4. It is often alleged that the Soviet Union is now a major industrial power only because Soviet planners required a massive sacrifice of living standards in the interwar period. Evaluate that claim.

SUGGESTED READING

Britto, Ronald. "Some Recent Developments in the Theory of Economic Growth: An Interpretation," *Journal of Economic Literature.* Vol. XI, December 1973, pp. 1343-66.

Denison, E. F. *The Sources of Economic Growth in the United States and the Alternatives Before Us.* New York: Committee for Economic Development, 1962.

————. "How to Raise the High-Employment Growth Rate by One Percentage Point," *American Economic Review.* Vol. 52, May 1962, pp. 67-75.

Dernburg, T. F., and J. D. Dernburg. *Macroeconomic Analysis.* Reading, Mass.: Addison-Wesley Publishing Co., 1968, Chapters 10-11.

Hahn, F. H., and R. C. O. Matthews. "The Theory of Economic Growth: A Survey," *Economic Journal.* Vol. 74, December 1964, pp. 779-902.

Phelps, Edmund. "The Golden Age of Accumulation: A Fable for Growthmen." *American Economic Review.* Vol. 51, September 1961, pp. 638-643.

Schultz, T. W. "Investment in Human Capital," *American Economic Review.* Vol. 51, March 1961, pp. 1-17.

Solow, Robert W. *Growth Theory.* Oxford: Oxford University Press, 1970.

Swan, T. W. "Economic Growth and Capital Accumulation," *Economic Record.* Vol. 32, November 1956, pp. 334-361.

Chapter 14
The Business Cycle

While long-run trend growth in productive capacity has been a characteristic of the United States and other developed economies, the growth in economic activity has not been smooth. Indeed, economic history shows all industrial economies to have been plagued by sizable fluctuations—periods of recession following periods of expansion followed by recession in a seemingly endless *cycle*. This boom-bust sequence has been so common that virtually every U.S. citizen feels comfortable discussing the "business cycle."

Cyclical movements can be observed in any number of economic variables. As macroeconomic examples, consumption, investment, unemployment, and output all exhibit cyclical fluctuations. However, because it is a comprehensive measure of the overall level of economic activity, movements in GNP may be the best single indicator of business cycle developments.

During the *expansion phase* of the business cycle, GNP grows more rapidly than its long-run trend growth rate and more rapidly than the rate of growth of productive capacity, the proportion of productive capacity employed increasing. At some point, the GNP series reaches its *upper turning point* and the *contraction phase* of the cycle begins. In the contraction, GNP may grow more slowly than its trend rate or may even fall in absolute value. During this phase, the proportion of productive capacity utilized falls. Finally, the GNP series reaches its *lower turning point* and expansion begins. In the idealized cycle in Figure 14-1, two upper turning points (U and U') and two lower turning points (L and L') are labeled.

The amount of time required for completion of one complete cycle, called the *period* of the cycle, can be measured from cycle *peak* to *peak* (U to U') or

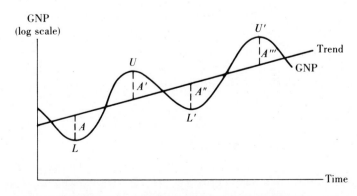

FIGURE 14-1 Idealized Cycle of GNP Around Trend

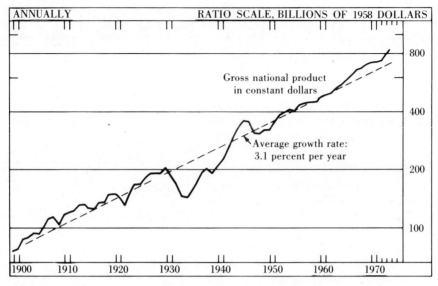

FIGURE 14-2   United States GNP, 1900-1973. Source: Board of Governors of the Federal Reserve System, *Historical Chart Book*, 1974.

from *trough* to *trough* (L to L'). The magnitude of the cycle is measured by the maximum percentage deviation of the observed value of GNP from its trend value. In our idealized graph, the cycle's magnitude, usually called its *amplitude*, would be reflected in vertical distances A, A', A'', and A''' in Figure 14-1.

Figure 14-2 shows a plot of actual U.S. GNP for 1900 through 1973 contrasted with trend growth in GNP. Clearly, neither the amplitude nor the duration of the observed GNP cycle is as regular as in our ideal cycle. In fact, the periodic expansions and contractions of economic activity have occurred with such irregularity, especially in recent years, that most modern economists feel more comfortable labeling swings in economic activity business "fluctuations" rather than "cycles"—the latter term carrying too strong a connotation of regularity. Also, as you may already know, not all sectors of the economy expand and contract in step with aggregate output. Construction, for example, generally fluctuates in a distinctly *countercyclical* pattern and industrial production is often out of step with aggregate final sales. Because of the irregularities in actual business fluctuations, it is no easy matter to identify cycle turning points (peaks and troughs). Compounding that problem, the *rate of growth* of output can decline for a time, allowing output to lag farther and farther behind productive capacity, without any absolute decline in output. In such a *growth recession* the economy suffers the undesired consequences of swelling unemployment of labor and capital but no *peak* in output is identifiable. Clearly, our scheme for labeling cycle turning points—hence expansion and contraction periods—is somewhat arbitrary.

In spite of the difficulties involved, with a frame of reference like ours the

National Bureau of Economic Research (the *NBER*) has attempted to identify the approximate dates when peaks and troughs in aggregate economic activity have occurred.[1] The turning points identified by the NBER for the postwar period in the United States are shown in Table 14-1.

TABLE 14-1   REFERENCE CYCLE TURNING POINTS

		Months in:	
Trough	Peak	Contraction*	Expansion**
Oct. 1945	Nov. 1948	8	37
Oct. 1949	July 1953	11	45
Aug. 1954	July 1957	13	35
Apr. 1958	May 1960	9	25
Feb. 1961	Nov. 1969	9	105
Nov. 1970	—	12	—

* From previous peak.
** From previous trough.
Source: U.S. Department of Commerce, *Business Conditions Digest*, June 1973.

EXPLAINING BUSINESS FLUCTUATIONS— FORMAL CYCLE THEORIES

While the rhythm of the observed fluctuations in economic activity has not matched that of our idealized cycle, it has been regular enough to suggest that fluctuations might be the result of certain systematic and recurring causes.[2] Efforts to identify those causes—to explain business fluctuations—have a long, if not impressively successful, heritage. However, since World War II confidence in the ability of the government to stabilize the economy through the active use of monetary and fiscal policy increased until interest in identifying the fundamental sources of business fluctuations virtually evaporated. Faith in the effectiveness of stabilization policy appears to have peaked in the middle 1960s and since then the belief has spread that the business cycle has only been domesticated, not eliminated. But current research continues to accord formal cycle theories a relatively low priority so that no very elaborate new formal cycle theories can be described in this brief chapter. Hence our primary focus must be restricted

1   For a detailed discussion of the identification of reference cycle turning points, see Arthur F. Burns and Wesley C. Mitchell, *Measuring Business Cycles* (New York: National Bureau of Economic Research, 1946).

2   Since 1854 the average length of the reference cycles identified by the NBER has been close to 4 years with the average expansion close to twice the duration of the average contraction. The shortest cycle lasted 28 months.

to a sample of cycle theories that have enjoyed prominence in the past. The models we will review can contribute to our understanding of some of the forces that fuel expansions and contractions. In particular, they account for momentum in expansions and contractions and indicate how cumulative movements in production may be reversed.

External and Internal Cycle Theories

There have been a great number of proposed explanations of business fluctuations. Those explanations can be grouped in a number of ways, but a basic distinction has long been made between two broad classes of models. The first class attributes cycles to forces *external* to the systematic interactions of the component parts of the economic system. Historically, these external theories of the cycle have focused attention on wars, the chance discovery of gold mines, and major innovations (like the railroad, the automobile, and the computer) as prime movers in generating fluctuations in business activity. As an interesting alternative source of fluctuations, in a frequently cited external theory (not necessarily because of its validity), the noted nineteenth century economists W. S. and H. S. Jevons attributed business cycles to changes in the level of sunspot activity. According to the sunspot theory, changes in sunspot activity affected the earth's climate which in turn affected crop yields. Fluctuations in agricultural output and prices resulted in fluctuations in the overall level of economic activity.

The second class of cycle theories, the internal theories, ascribe business fluctuations to endogenous forces—forces within the economy that automatically reverse cumulative expansions and contractions in economic activity. While there are numerous alternative *internal* explanations of the business cycle, the majority ascribe a major role to movements in investment. In order to acquire a basic understanding of what is involved in modern business cycle analysis, as our next task we will take a close look at one prominent, post-Keynesian example of an internal cycle model.

The Multiplier-Accelerator Interaction

Interaction between the income multiplier and the accelerator mechanism has played a central role in virtually all modern business cycle models. The simple accelerator, as you may recall from Chapter 6 on investment, relates the level of net investment to the rate of change of output. According to the simple accelerator, with output growing continuously net additions to the capital stock are required. For net investment to take place at a uniform *level* over time, the rate of growth of output must stay constant. As soon as the rate of output growth declines, even if it remains positive, investment falls.

The multiplier concept, relating changes in the level of income to changes in individual spending schedules, should be even more familiar since we have used it frequently in developing and manipulating our income determination models. In the late 1930s, Alvin Hansen suggested that, under some not implausible conditions, the economy might generate cyclical fluctuations internally as a result of interactions between the multiplier and the accelerator. Paul Samuelson provided a formal demonstration of Hansen's suggestion in an elegantly simple model.[3]

Ignoring the government and foreign sectors of the economy, net income (output) in period t is

$$Y_t = C_t + I_t. \tag{14-1}$$

Assuming that households' consumption responds to income with a simple, one-period lag, consumption is

$$C_t = bY_{t-1}. \tag{14-2}$$

Net investment, which takes place to provide the productive capacity necessary for satisfying aggregate consumption demand, consists of an autonomous component ($\bar{I}$) plus an *induced* component given by the simple accelerator. Net investment then is

$$I_t = \bar{I} + A(C_t - C_{t-1}), \tag{14-3}$$

where A is the aggregate accelerator coefficient. Plugging into Equation (14-1) and solving for Y_t yields

$$Y_t = \bar{I} + b(1 + A)Y_{t-1} - ABY_{t-2}. \tag{14-4}$$

For this economic system to be in *static* equilibrium, income must be constant through time. That is, it must be the case that $Y_t = Y_{t-1} = Y_{t-2} = \ldots = Y_{t-n} = \ldots$. By imposing this equilibrium condition, Equation (14-4) can be solved for the *static* equilibrium level of income, yielding

$$Y_{eq.} = \frac{1}{1-b} \cdot \bar{I}, \tag{14-5}$$

an expression that has a familiar form. However, if static equilibrium is disturbed in this model, the system *may not return to equilibrium* and, even if it does, the time path of adjustment back to equilibrium is of interest to us as it may exhibit a cyclical pattern.

To illustrate our investigation of the consequences of a shock to our simple

3 Paul Samuelson, "Interaction Between the Multiplier Analysis and the Principle of Acceleration," *Review of Economics and Statistics*, Vol. 21, May 1939, pp. 75-78.

system, we can introduce some "reasonable" numerical values into that system. To begin with, we will assume an MPC of .5, an accelerator coefficient of 2, and a value of autonomous investment of $20 billion. With these values, the equilibrium level of income is

$$Y_{eq.} = \frac{1}{1-b} \cdot \bar{I} = \frac{1}{1-.5} \cdot 20 \text{ billion} = \$40 \text{ billion.}$$

Consumption would be $.5Y = \$20$ billion. Also, since with no *change* in income there is no *change* in consumption and thus no induced investment, total investment is just the $20 billion of autonomous investment.

But now suppose there is a $10 billion rise in autonomous investment so $\bar{I}$ is lifted to a new level of $30 billion. The dynamic response of the simple economic system is traced in Table 14-2. In period 1 in that table, the system is in equilibrium with $Y_{eq.} = \$40$ billion and with both consumption and autonomous investment equal to $20 billion.

TABLE 14-2 DYNAMIC ADJUSTMENT WITH MULTIPLIER-ACCELERATOR INTERACTION *

Period	(1) $\bar{I}$	(2) $C = .5Y_{t-1}$	Induced $I =$ (3) $2(C_t\text{-}C_{t-1})$	(4) $Y = C + I$
1	20	20	0	40
2	30	20	0	50
3	.	25	10	65
4	.	33	16	79
5	.	40	14	84
6	.	42	4	76
7	.	38	−8	60
8	.	30	−16	44
9	.	22	−16	36
10	.	18	−8	40
11	.	20	8	58
12	.	29	18	77

* Figures rounded to nearest billion dollars.

In period 2, autonomous investment has increased by $10 billion so that income in period 2 (Y_2) becomes $50 billion. In the next period, consumption responds to period 2's income rise, increasing to $25 billion, and the multiplier expansion process is underway.

In isolation, the multiplier would generate an increase in income to a new equilibrium value of

$$Y_{eq.} = \frac{1}{1-b} \cdot \bar{I} = \frac{1}{1-.5} \cdot 30 \text{ billion} = \$60 \text{ billion.}$$

However, the multiplier no longer operates in isolation. Through the accelerator, the rise in consumption in period 3 *induces* $10 billion of additional investment in that period, raising income in period 3 to $65 billion. By period 4, we should note, the *rate* of increase in income has begun to fall. Consequently, the rate of increase in consumption declines in period 5 producing a smaller volume of *induced* investment in period 5. With investment falling, the stage is set for a contraction and, in period 6, income begins to fall. With the accelerator inducing net *disinvestment* beginning in period 7, a major contraction is underway.

By period 9, income has fallen well below its original equilibrium level. However, in that period the rate of decline of income slows. As a consequence, consumption's fall is slowed in period 10 and, with it, the rate of net disinvestment slows. The recovery from contraction is underway, as indicated by period 10's increase in income back to $40 billion.

If we continued to trace the adjustment path of our simple economic system, we would find income following a time path like that shown in Figure 14-3. Income would fluctuate around the $60 billion income level that the simple multiplier gives as a static equilibrium income level with *no tendency* for convergence toward that value.[4] But it should be clear that the particular path of adjustment that our example economic system traced was dictated by the values we assumed for the MPC and the accelerator coefficient (given the form of the model). For alternative values of these parameters, a rich variety of adjustment paths are possible. Figure 14-4 shows the general patterns of adjustment that may occur.

Path *A* shows a monotonic[5] adjustment of income from the original income

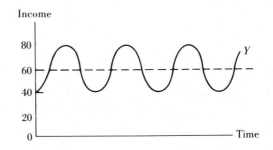

FIGURE 14-3   A Cycle with Constant Amplitude

4   A mathematician would not have to plod through the one-step-at-a-time, "iterative" process we employed in the text in order to know how our model behaves. He would recognize Equation (14-4) as a "second-order difference equation" which can be solved analytically for an expression for income in any time period. For readable expositions of the method of solving difference equations, see A. Chiang, *Fundamental Methods of Mathematical Economics* (New York: McGraw-Hill, 1975), Chapters 16-17, and William Baumol, *Economic Dynamics* (New York: The Macmillan Co., 1970), Chapters 9-11.

5   A function is monotonic if, for every point on the function, the slope (first derivative) of the function has the same sign. The function in part A of Figure 14-4 is rising (slope positive) throughout. Thus, that function shows income increasing monotonically.

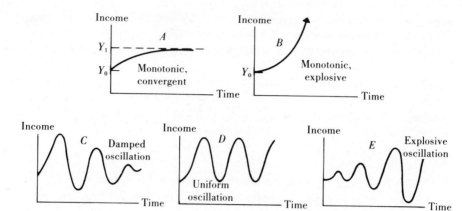

FIGURE 14-4   Possible Adjustment Patterns in the Multiplier-Accelerator Model

level (Y_0) toward the new equilibrium level (Y_1) which it approaches asymptotically. Path B is monotonic, but instead of income converging on a new equilibrium level, it grows exponentially. Path C shows income oscillating in a dampened manner (the amplitude of the cycle diminishing over time) so that income converges on its static equilibrium value. Path D is the path traced by the economy in our example—the amplitude of the cycle remaining constant over time. And, finally, path E is an explosive cycle. Clearly for an economy characterized by an adjustment path like B, D, or E, we could not expect the static equilibrium value of income to be achievable once income is disturbed.

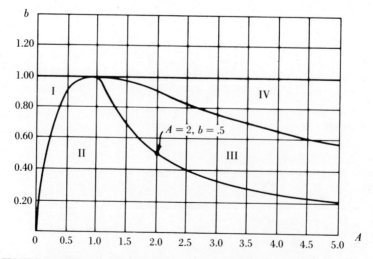

FIGURE 14-5   Regions Showing Different Adjustment Paths of Aggregate Income

Figure 14-5 summarizes the combinations of values of the MPC and the accelerator coefficient which, in the Samuelson multiplier-accelerator, yield the various forms of adjustment path shown in Figure 14-4. Area I shows the combinations that permit income to adjust asymptotically from one equilibrium income to another as shown by path *A* in Figure 14-4. Area II shows the combinations that produce damped cycles. The combinations in area III produce explosive oscillations while the combinations in area IV produce monotonic but explosive growth. The values of the MPC and the accelerator coefficient that provide the uniform cycles of our example (.5 and .2 respectively) fall on the boundary between areas II and III.

The Model's Shortcomings

The multiplier-accelerator model offers a highly simplified explanation of business fluctuations. However, it has enjoyed prominence in modern business cycle analysis because, as well as being one of the first of the post-Keynesian breed of dynamic models, it captures an interaction between the multiplier and the accelerator that is surely a basic ingredient of all *endogenously* generated cycles. Still, its extreme simplicity has compromised its validity as a complete cycle model. With values for the accelerator coefficient and the MPC in the range typically found in the United States, the multiplier-accelerator model would generate cyclically or monotonically explosive changes in income (areas III or IV of Figure 14-5). Since this kind of instability has not been observed in the United States, some modifications to the basic multiplier-accelerator model are necessary in the interest of realism. If, for example, the simple accelerator is replaced with an investment function that calls for extended lags in the response of investment to changes in the level of sales, the probability of explosive adjustments in income is moderated. But even if the simple accelerator is retained, with no lag in the response of investment to sales changes, there are logical reasons for expecting a ceiling on the upswing of income, which can halt a potentially explosive expansion and lead automatically to contraction, as well as a floor under the system's contractions which stops those contractions and leads to subsequent expansions.[6]

Ceilings and Floors

In the basic multiplier-accelerator model there is no limit on the rate of expansion until output has reached the full capacity level. But at that point output is constrained by the ceiling of productive capacity and can grow only as fast as pro-

6 The reasons for expecting a *ceiling* on income expansions and a *floor* under contractions are described in J. M. Hicks, *A Contribution to the Theory of the Trade Cycle* (Oxford: Oxford University Press), 1940.

ductive capacity grows—say, 4 to 5 percent annually in the United States. This rate of growth must be less than the rate at which output was growing prior to contacting the ceiling or that contact would never have occurred. With the annual rate of growth of sales slowed (to the rate of growth of productive capacity), the volume of induced investment called for by the accelerator falls and a contraction would be initiated in our model. Thus, the production ceiling provides an upper turning point to the time path of output even if the observed values of the propensity to save and the accelerator imply a dynamically unstable (explosive) adjustment path for the basic multiplier-accelerator model. The ceiling not only limits the expansion of output but also provides for an automatic switch to the contraction phase of the cycle.

Shifting our focus to the contraction phase of the business cycle, we now need to determine what provides a floor under output once contraction begins. According to the simple model, a fall in sales induces disinvestment in the next period, which lowers income inducing more disinvestment, and so on. However, it is unlikely that investment and income would ever fall to zero in actuality, no matter what the basic multiplier-accelerator model suggests when our best estimates of the accelerator coefficient (A) and the MPC are built into the model. As a contraction proceeds, income ultimately falls to the level where all income is consumed. At that point, even if there were no gross investment, the minimum level of gross income would have been reached. While *negative* net investment could, in theory, be so large that net income (consumption plus net investment) was zero or negative, in reality disinvestment is likely to be limited to the amount of depreciation, a value that can be much smaller (in absolute terms) than the disinvestment called for by the simple accelerator. Algebraically, if gross investment should ever fall to the zero level, minimum or *floor* net income would be $Y_{min} = C_0 - D$, where C_0 is the breakeven level of consumption spending and D is depreciation. Typically though, gross investment could never fall to zero since that would require zero gross investment for every firm. There is, most analysts would argue, a minimum value of autonomous investment that takes place independent of the level of income or its rate of change as business firms try to modernize their capital stock. In fact, to cite evidence that strengthens our belief in a floor under output, gross investment remained positive even in the depths of the Great Depression. With firm's net disinvestment plans limited to the amount of depreciation and with substantial volumes of income-independent (autonomous) investment forthcoming, contractions are constrained by a positive floor of minimum net output given by $Y_{min} = 1/(1-b) \cdot I_{min}$ where I_{min}, minimum net investment, is autonomous investment minus depreciation. Historical evidence suggests that in most contractions the volume of autonomous investment has been substantially larger than the volume of depreciation so that the floor on income has strictly limited the extent to which a contraction could proceed.

Once the floor value of output is reached, the contraction's progress is ended. With income no longer falling, the volume of induced investment called for by the simple accelerator (which was negative during the contraction) is increased (to zero) and we are returned to the expansion phase of the cycle.[7] It is easy to see, then, that even when the values of the MPC and the accelerator imply an explosive system, there are simple and sensible arguments which indicate that business fluctuations will be constrained to a pattern that accords with observed history. The basic multiplier-accelerator model just failed to explicitly incorporate the required floor of minimum output and ceiling of maximum productive capacity.

Monetary Theories of the Cycle

Multiplier-accelerator models pay no heed to the role of the financial sector of the economy in generating business fluctuations, but the business cycle literature abounds with monetary or financial theories of the cycle (most of which would fit in the more general category *expectations theories* since they rely on endogenous changes in expectations to provide cycle turning points). A prominent example of such theories was provided decades ago by R. G. Hawtrey, who attributed prime responsibility for business fluctuations to monetary instability.[8]

With the economy in recession, Hawtrey argues that banks have reserve funds with which they can extend loans and that interest rates are low. With interest rates depressed, the interest cost of holding inventories is low so inventory investment is stimulated. The increase in planned inventory investment raises production and income, raising sales. In turn, the sales increase raises expected future sales, stimulating inventory investment which raises production and income, and so it goes in a cumulative expansion. The banking system, eager to extend loans to profitable businesses operating in what is expected to be an expanding economy, supports the cumulative expansion through credit extension out of its loanable reserves. But finally the banking system's loanable reserves must be depleted and interest rates rise. The boom is ended.

With the interest cost of holding stocks of inventories increased, planned investment in inventories is cut, reducing production and income. With income reduced, sales fall, eroding confidence in future sales and further reducing inventory investment. The cumulative contraction is underway. With business firms repaying existing (high interest) loans and not borrowing additional funds to finance new inventory purchases, the volume of credit extended by the banking system falls and its loanable reserves are replenished. Interest rates then fall and the stage is set for another boom.

---

7 To be more precise about the shift to expansion, with disinvestment limited to the amount of depreciation, considerable excess productive capacity can be left by the contraction. Several periods of stagnation during which income does not grow would be required in this case, for the excess stock of capital to be depreciated away, before investment rises to a positive level (the negative D term disappearing), carrying income with it and initiating the cumulative expansion.

8 R. G. Hawtrey, *Trade and Credit* (London: Green and Co., Ltd., 1928), Chapter V.

According to Hawtrey, banks exhibit a lemming-like herd behavior which is inimical to economic stability. In the cumulative expansion, banks (collectively) extend more credit than would be required at a full-employment equilibrium output level as they share the business community's optimistic expectations about future business conditions. Analogously, after the peak in activity they allow a contraction in credit larger than that required to restore full-employment equilibrium so the cycle can continue.

Hawtrey's analysis correctly identifies inventory investment as the most volatile component of aggregate demand. Also, his concern with financial considerations broadens our perspective on the sources of economic fluctuations. But his failure to provide for any accelerator mechanism and his emphasis on the response of just inventory investment to changes in credit conditions limit the usefulness of his model. Like all cycle models, Hawtrey's is a caricature of a reality that, because of its complexity, has not yet been adequately represented in a cycle model. Our selection of specific cycle theories to describe could be vastly extended, but with little progress toward the objective of providing a general explanation of business fluctuations. As an alternative, before considering the role of government in business fluctuations we can provide a summary description of the different sorts of cycle models that have enjoyed prominence.[9] To that end, we can usefully subdivide cycle models into monetary cycle theories, nonmonetary demand theories, and supply theories, though some explanations of the cycle may overlap these categories. In the monetary theories, fluctuations in the interest rate and in the availability of loanable funds are held responsible for fluctuations in investment and, hence, in overall activity. Hawtrey's explanation of the business cycle fits this category quite well.

In nonmonetary demand theories of the cycle, expansions and contractions are generally prompted by an inconsistency between consumer demand and the existing capital stock. The investment component of aggregate demand fluctuates to provide turning points in the cycle. Many of the models that fit in this category employ some version of the accelerator principle as the multiplier-accelerator models we have reviewed do.

In supply theories of business fluctuations, it is fluctuations in operating costs and profit margins which bear the responsibility for propagating business fluctuations. Typically, changes in profit margins are held responsible for providing cycle turning points through their effects on expectations and thus investment.[10]

9 For a comprehensive treatment of cycle models the interested reader may consult any standard text on business cycles such as Louis A. Dow, *Business Fluctuations in a Dynamic Economy* (Columbus, Ohio: Charles E. Merrill, 1968).

10 The leading proponent of supply-side theories of the business cycle was Wesley C. Mitchell. See W. C. Mitchell, *Business Cycles and Their Causes* (Berkeley: University of California Press, 1941).

The Modern Role of Government in the Cycle

The introduction of a government that has the tools to control aggregate demand provides a new set of possible constraints on income fluctuations. Rather than waiting for endogenous forces (such as a production ceiling or the exhaustion of reserve funds in the banking system) to halt an expansion, the government may intervene, limiting the growth of aggregate demand in order to avoid the inflation that high levels of capacity utilization can foster. Conversely, rather than allowing a contraction to proceed until income reaches an endogenously determined floor level, the government could stimulate aggregate demand. A government that does, in fact, use its fiscal and monetary policy tools to manage aggregate demand in this countercyclical manner is pursuing a *countercyclical stabilization policy*.

In the latter stages of a buoyant expansion, whatever its ultimate cause, the government would need restrictive fiscal and/or monetary policies in force to prevent aggregate demand from outrunning productive capacity. Conversely, in a downswing (whatever its cause) the government would need to impose an expansionary monetary-fiscal program to stimulate aggregate demand. Appropriately administered, such a stabilization program would reduce the amplitude of the cycle. Figure 14-6 shows a time path of GNP with stabilization policy imposing bands (a floor and a ceiling if you prefer) on the swings in output. Unfortunately, *appropriate* administration of stabilization policy is difficult to achieve. While there are a number of reasons for government's inability to adequately employ a stabilization policy, a large share of those limitations can be classified as *timing* problems. If, to avoid inflation, the government undertakes policy actions designed to constrain demand but does so too late in the cycle, the policy actions will have their impact on demand after the peak of the cycle when income is already falling. Thus, that restrictive policy would reinforce and accelerate the contraction. On the other hand, a restrictive policy put in effect too early in the expansion phase of the cycle would stop a desirable expansion,

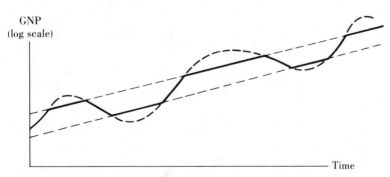

FIGURE 14-6 Cyclical Fluctuations Constrained by Stabilization Policy

limiting the growth of real output well before inflationary pressures are a serious threat. Similar timing difficulties plague efforts to limit contractions.

Clearly, poorly timed pursuit of a stabilization policy can be *destabilizing!* As Milton Friedman is fond of pointing out, the road to increased *instability* can be paved with good intentions. Most everyone would agree that our quantitative knowledge of the size and timing of impact of monetary and fiscal policy actions is, at present, too limited to make stabilization policy a straightforward administrative task. Indeed, there is little doubt but that government's stabilization efforts have, at times, been misguided and, thus, destabilizing. Still, relatively few economists are convinced that the record is bad enough to warrant rejection of the active use of stabilization policies.

In Chapters 15 and 16, more attention will be focused on the limitations on government's stabilization tools. For the time being, we should be mindful that, at least in the postwar period, government economic activity has been an integral contributor to the pattern of the observed business cycle. In fact, some economists hold the government directly and essentially independently responsible for the cyclical swings we see in economic activity.

THE DESTABILIZING EFFECTS OF GOVERNMENT POLICY IN AN INHERENTLY STABLE ECONOMY

While it remains a minority opinion, the view that the government's own monetary and fiscal actions are the major cause of economic instability has attracted growing attention in recent years. According to this view, the economy is inherently more stable than endogenous cycle models like the basic multiplier-accelerator model developed in this chapter suggest. Proponents of this view claim that history offers no evidence that ceilings and floors have played significant roles in producing turning points in economic activity. The thrust of these claims is that when a free market economy is *occasionally* pushed out of static equilibrium the economy automatically adjusts back to equilibrium, perhaps monotonically but at worst with mild and quickly damped cycles. The appearance of continuing fluctuations must be attributed to new shocks to the system that start fresh cycles or strengthen ongoing but decaying cycles. While other sources are possible, in a modern economy in which the government plays an active economic role emphasis is focused on the government's ability to produce fluctuations. An informal, modern, external theory of the business cycle results with government providing the impetus for cycle turning points.

Stop and Go Policy

Beginning with the economy in a mild recession and with no significant inflation, an activist government might be expected to use expansionary monetary and fiscal policies to raise employment and output. With no inflation expected, the expansionary policy may succeed in markedly reducing unemployment with only a moderate immediate increase in the inflation rate—along the *short-run* Phillips curve the employment-output trade-off may be quite favorable. But with any significant rise in the inflation rate, expectations will gradually be revised, shifting the short-run Phillips curve upward. Hence, maintenance of a sharply reduced unemployment rate (one below the natural rate) would require an accelerating inflation rate.

Eventually, government policy makers have to turn their attention to reducing the inflation rate, sacrificing the goal of high employment. As explained in Chapter 12, with a reduction in aggregate demand the inflation rate will recede and, with a lag, so will inflation expectations, so that the short-run Phillips curve is shifted downward. But, it is unlikely that the stabilization authorities will allow the economy to remain in a recessionary situation very long. With unemployment growing, powerful political pressures emerge pressing for a solution to the unemployment problem. With any significant reduction of the inflation rate, the focus of stabilization policy is quickly shifted from combating inflation to raising employment. Since expectations adjust with a lag, even when stabilization policy has shifted to an expansive stance, the expected rate of inflation will still be falling, shifting the short-run Phillips curve downward. Hence, the apparent trade-off between unemployment and inflation is again quite favorable. But with the shift to an expansionary policy stance, a reacceleration of inflation is unavoidable. The stop-and-go nature of stabilization policy, as government awkwardly pursued admirable goals, has produced a full cycle in economic activity and set the stage for its repetition.

As we indicated earlier, there is general agreement that the government *can* act in a destabilizing way. But few would be willing to attribute a role to the stabilization authorities as pernicious as the one just described. Moreover, the majority of economists continue to subscribe to the Keynesian notion that the economy is frequently disturbed by forces over which the stabilization authorities have little direct control. Changes in society's thriftiness as a result of spontaneous alterations in expectations; bursts of investment opportunity; swings in agricultural exports because of foreign droughts; shortfalls in domestic agricultural production because of late spring floods and early freezes; oil embargoes by the Organization of Petroleum Exporting Countries; and other shocks to the economy can generate cumulative swings in economic activity. If the economy is subjected to many small shocks that are randomly distributed over time, those shocks might be expected to cancel out over time. But apparently they do not— we observe irregular fluctuations in the economy. Notably, some cyclical fluctuations can be observed in production levels in the Soviet Union, even though there are no cycles in the central planning mechanism that dictates production targets.[11]

---

[11] For a model which shows that cycles can be generated from random shocks, see R. Frisch, "Propagation Problems and Impulse Problems in Dynamic Economics," in *Economic Essays in Honor of Gustav Cassel* (London: George Allen and Unwin, Ltd., 1933).

Engineers have theories of wave-generating mechanisms which can explain the bunching of traffic along streets and highways, the simultaneous appearance of elevators (and busses) that were dispatched at random time intervals, and so on. Economic analysis has not yet provided comparable explanations of the wave-like fluctuations in economic activity because the economic system is much more complex than the physical systems which have already yielded to engineering analysis. But research effort is currently being expended to enhance our understanding of the dynamic behavior of the economy and to ascertain the requirements for devising government policy actions that will induce the economy to expand along a desired, stable growth path. Some of that research is making use of a sophisticated set of mathematical techniques encompassed by the designation *control theory*, which in the main evolved from engineering analysis of *control problems*—the problems of optimally controlling a chemical processing plant, a spaceship trajectory, a cargo ship's course, and so on.

Formally, control theory is concerned with the analysis of systems—including mechanical, electrical, industrial, physiological, biological, and economic systems—so as to determine the manner in which control instruments may affect the evolution of that system over time and the values which those control variables would have to possess for the system to produce certain desired results. The economy is a system in which there are a number of *state* variables (indicating the state of the economy) in which we are interested—output, employment, the price level and its rate of change, and so on. Also, there are a number of control instruments available in that system, including money supply changes, government spending changes, tax rate changes, and exchange rate changes, which can be employed to modify movements of the state variables over time. It is hoped that the application of control theory will allow us to determine how available control instruments should be applied and what new control instruments (automatic or otherwise) might be employed in the pursuit of full employment, price stability, and any other policy goal. But a great deal of challenging work remains to be done before control theory will make a useful contribution to the formulation of stabilization policy. Interestingly, initial attempts at the simple task of building automatic steering devices in ships were less than an overwhelming success. Those automatic devices steered an unstable course with the ships oscillating in an undamped cycle around their desired course. Steering the economy is much more difficult than steering a ship.

System Stability and Static Macroeconomic Analysis

There remains an important implication of the dynamic analysis in this chapter which we have not yet considered. The static equilibrium level of income in the basic multiplier-accelerator model was given by the familiar expression $Y_{eq.} = 1/(1-b) \cdot \bar{I}$ [see Equation (14-4)]. This expression shows that the static equilibrium value of income is independent of the value of the accelerator coefficient. As we have seen, however, for different combinations of the accelerator coefficient and the MPC our model traces different dynamic adjustment paths and, for many combinations, a static equilibrium can never be attained—that is, the system is explosive or exhibits cycles of constant amplitude. To illustrate this point, with an MPC of .5 and $\bar{I} = \$30$ billion the static equilibrium value of income was $60 billion. However, with an accelerator coefficient equal to 2, income did not converge to that value but fluctuated around it in a cycle of constant amplitude. In contrast, had the accelerator coefficient taken the value .8 income would have followed a damped cyclical path, ultimately converging on the income level indicated by Equation (14-4) while, with an accelerator value of 3, income would have traced an explosive cyclical path.

Of the three example values chosen for the accelerator coefficient, one value $(A = .8)$ yields an adjustment path that allows income to converge on the static equilibrium value. In the other two cases, the system is *unstable*. These clear-cut results permit us to draw an important analytical rule. It is clear that there are numerous alternative models that demonstrate different patterns of dynamic behavior while yielding the same static equilibrium results. For the conclusions drawn from a static analysis (which most of this book has been devoted to) to be valid, the system must be dynamically stable. Thus, to provide a necessary condition for the conclusions we draw from analysis with static models to be valid, our models must be tested for the property of dynamic stability. The required tests involve the use of analytical techniques (differential equations, difference equations, computer simulation, and so on) which are outside the scope of this text. But the student should recognize that dynamic analysis is an indispensable adjunct to static analysis.

AN INTRODUCTION TO ECONOMIC FORECASTING

In both the last chapter on economic growth and the current chapter on business fluctuations, we have been directly concerned with tracing movements over time in aggregate income and its components. A natural *applied* extention of that interest entails the forecasting of future national economic developments.

It is in its application to forecasting that macroeconomics has its broadest audience. As our analysis has indicated already, for the federal government to make intelligent decisions on corrective stabilization policy actions, it must know what path the economy is following—it must have forecasts of future economic developments. But interest in forecasting is not limited to government policy makers. Because aggregate economic developments alter incomes, the behavior of consumers, and the behavior of other firms, economic forecasts are essential inputs in the decisions firms must make. Long-term plans for investment in production facilities, for development of distribution networks, and for acquiring and disposing of subsidiaries depend heavily on business forecasts. So, too, do financing strategies, inventory purchase plans, and hiring plans. Finally, with economic forecasts receiving widespread news media coverage, households might be expected to alter their expectations of the future on the basis of those forecasts and modify their purchase and work choices accordingly.

Forecasting with Macroeconometric Models

Following Jan Tinbergen's pathbreaking effort in 1939 to construct an econometric model of the U.S. economy, interest in the construction and application of macroeconometric models has mushroomed.[12] The U.S. central bank (the Federal Reserve System) in conjunction with a group of economists at the Massachusetts Institute of Technology has built and now operates an econometric model of the U.S. economy (the Federal Reserve-MIT model). The commerce department has its own model, too. Other models are maintained by the Wharton School of Finance and Commerce at the University of Pennsylvania, by the University of Michigan, by Princeton University, and by the Brookings Institute. Also, a number of large business firms have such models and many business firms purchase forecasts from the Wharton School model, from Chase Econometrics (a subsidiary of Chase Manhattan Bank), and from Data Resources Incorporated.

In principle, the task of constructing an econometric model of the economy is straightforward and familiar. Beginning with a theoretical model of the economy, the behavioral functions in that model are fitted to historical data. The number of behavioral functions so fitted differs depending on: (1) the model builder's interest, and (2) the degree of *disaggregation* required for obtaining *stable* regression equations (regression equations with stable parameters) which can be depended upon for prediction purposes. On the first score, a *small* model (for example, an econometric analog of the static theoretical model in Chapter 9) can be employed if predictions of movements in broad aggregates such as output, employment, the general price level, and total consumption are the concern. On the other hand, to get detailed subsector predictions on the component parts of aggregate measures such as consumption (divided, say, into nondurables and services, autos and parts, and other durables) and investment (in plant and equipment, inventories, and housing) would require a separate explanatory equation for each component variable. Similarly, added equations may be required by the desire for stable regression equations. That need arises when the behavior patterns of the component parts of some important variable differ. For example, consumer purchases of services and nondurables are far more stable over the cycle than are durable purchases. Thus, to obtain regression equations that can accurately predict total consumption spending the model builder may be required to disaggregate consumption—to divide total consumption spending into its component parts with a separate explanatory equation for each part.

Whatever the number of regression equations required, those regressions

---

12   Jan Tinbergen, *Statistical Testing of Business Cycle Theories* (Geneva: League of Nations Economic Intelligence, 1939), I.

and any accompanying identities comprise a set of simultaneous equations that can be employed for prediction purposes. Based on known or anticipated changes in factors that are exogenous to the econometric model (including monetary and fiscal policy variables) that model can be directly applied to forecasting future economic developments. Moreover, an econometric model can be used to trace the time pattern of effects of alternative policy actions (computers do the hard work of iteratively solving the system of equations for each period's solution values of the endogenous variables in the model). Since some of the behavioral relations in econometric models of the economy involve lagged responses and since the values of exogenous variables change over time, those models can exhibit cycles, reflecting (the model builder would hope) the dynamic properties of the modeled economy. It is natural that interest in formal cycle models has waned since econometric models provide a representation of the dynamic properties of the economy with far more detailed attention to the economy's structure than formal cycle models contain. (The largest econometric models of the economy contain several hundred equations while a few models contain less than ten equations.)[13]

Even though the practice of macroeconometric modeling is relatively young, there has been considerable improvement in the forecasting capability of those models. While potential for substantial further improvement remains, even now forecasts made with the more prominent existing macroeconometric models compare favorably with those made using more pragmatic techniques. Moreover, while much remains to be learned, work with those models has shed substantial light on the structure of the economy and on the effectiveness of monetary and fiscal policy weapons. Models in which both monetary and fiscal policies contribute importantly to the path of economic activity now dominate even though room for disagreement on the economy's structure and, hence, on the roles of monetary and fiscal policies remains.

Other Forecasting Techniques—
Naive Forecasts and Leading Indicators

As alternatives to econometric modeling, there are forecasting techniques that require little knowledge of the structure of the economy. The practice of extrapolating observed patterns of economic change and the use of *leading indicators* for predicting cycle turning points are commonplace examples of alternative forecasting methods.

A forecaster who relied exclusively on the simple extrapolation of observed patterns could be replaced by a parrot calling, for example, for the "same (absolute or percentage) change this period as last period." With no concern for

---

13   For a sample survey of 25 alternative econometric models, see Marc Nerlove, "A Tabular Survey of Macroeconometric Models," *International Economic Review*, 1966. Also, see M. K. Evans, *Macroeconomic Activity* (New York: Harper & Row, 1969), Chapters 15, 18, and 20.

identifying the causal forces that influence economic activity, that extrapolation technique presumes that the forces which produce each period's pattern of economic change will persist. This forecasting technique will fail to indicate every cyclical turning point in economic activity and fail to make use of any available information on changes in the economic environment which might keep past patterns from being repeated. Extrapolative models also fail to add to our understanding of the macroeconomy. Hence, they have nothing to say about the effects that monetary and fiscal policy actions may produce. Still, since cumulative swings in economic activity have a great deal of momentum, the most naive forecaster may have a respectable track record. And, with a reasonable understanding of which disturbances have an important influence on the economy and, hence, may alter the course of economic events, extrapolations may be adjusted in an *ad hoc* manner to provide an improved forecasting performance.

The practice of forecasting with leading indicators is more exotic, and comprehension of that forecasting method requires some background information. With the hope of uncovering information that would be useful in explaining and forecasting business fluctuations, several decades ago the National Bureau of Economic Research (NBER) began the task of examining more than 1,000 economic time series for cyclical patterns of movement over time. Some 400 of the series were found to vary cyclically and a number of those were identified as *leading* indicators of the business cycle. That is, cyclical peaks and troughs in a number of those variables were found generally to precede in time (lead) the peaks and troughs in overall business activity so that forecasts of cycle turning points could be obtained from following the paths of those variables.

The series of leading indicators (along with series of coincident and lagging indicators) are continuously refined and updated by the NBER. At present, a list of some 36 time series is maintained and reported in the Department of Commerce's *Business Conditions Digest*. Out of that comprehensive collection, attention is most frequently focused on a *short list* of a dozen leading indicators including the average work-week of production workers, the weekly *new* claims on unemployment insurance, net business formation, new orders for durable goods, new building permits, stock prices, and so on. In the postwar period, declines in the leading indicators have preceded, without fail, outright declines in output or slowdowns in the rate of growth of output. Of course, predicting a change in the pattern of economic events says little about the magnitude of the ensuing expansion or slowdown. Moreover, forecasting cycle developments without a firm explanation of the reasons for those developments is frustrating. Still, leading indicators are relied on extensively as crude predictors of coming economic events.

Anticipations and Intentions Data

Forecasters and the news media also devote considerable attention to *anticipations and intentions* data. The Survey Research Center at the University of Michigan compiles monthly data on consumer sentiment (economic optimism or pessimism) and on consumer intentions to purchase (a house, a car, and so on). A number of private and public organizations compile data on planned investment outlays by business firms. Of the two most frequently cited investment intentions series, one is compiled by McGraw-Hill and the other by the Office of Business Economics and the Securities and Exchange Commission. The McGraw-Hill survey is undertaken only once a year while the OBE-SEC series is available quarterly. Forecasters pay considerable attention to sizable shifts in consumer and business purchase plans as reported in the anticipations and intentions series since changes in planned spending are reflected in changes in aggregate demand for goods and services.

SUMMARY

Developed economies have experienced recurrent waves of prosperity followed by recession in a pattern that, historically, has been regular enough to be labeled the business cycle or trade cycle. In this chapter, a formal model of the economy was constructed which was capable of endogenously generating just such a cyclical pattern of movement in production activity. Consistent with traditional business cycle analysis, the model we constructed (the well-known multiplier-accelerator model) focused on the investment component of aggregate demand as the prime source of instability. With investment determined by the accelerator principle, a small percentage increase in consumption demand was seen to generate a sizable response in the demand for investment goods, initiating a cumulative expansion in output. On the other hand, with consumption demand failing to grow at a sufficiently rapid rate, the accelerator was seen to induce a drop in investment, initiating a cumulative contraction. The accelerator acted as a strong source of instability.

In fact, with plausible values for the MPC and the accelerator the basic multiplier-accelerator model suggested such an unstable system that we found it necessary to constrain fluctuations in income by the *ceiling* of full capacity and the *floor* of minimum output. Alternatively, modifications of the lag structure of the model were claimed capable of making the system behave more stably.

In working with the multiplier-accelerator, we discovered that alternative forms of a model that yield identical static *equilibrium* results can yield distinctly different dynamic adjustment paths, with some of those paths convergent and some not. From this, we were forced to conclude that the inferences drawn from analysis with static models can be valid only if the model being employed is dynamically stable.

As the financial counterpart to the multiplier-accelerator analysis, we took a brief look at a monetary theory of the cycle. In that theory, excessive credit expansions and contractions fueled the business cycle with the depletion of loanable reserve funds and their replenishment providing cycle turning points. While the role of the financial sector is no doubt exaggerated in such monetary demand theories of the cycle, cumulative monetary expansions and contractions may well reinforce cyclical movements in general business activity.

Our discussion in this chapter also recognized the potential of government, both for acting as a stabilizer and as a destabilizer. To cite recent experience, from 1961 until late 1969 the United States experienced an unbroken expansion. The active use of stabilization policy is widely credited for that favorable performance. Yet, in the latter half of that period, mistakes in the application of stabilization policy were made and the results of those mistakes still plague us.

A major increase in government spending was required, beginning in 1965, by the rapid escalation of the Vietnam War. The expansionary boom of 1966 can be directly tied to the war-induced increase in government spending which was not accompanied by an alteration of the federal tax structure. The ensuing inflation prompted the government to impose restrictive stabilization policies in 1968 and 1969. The recession of 1969-1970 was the direct result of those restrictive policies, not of any inherent cyclical forces endogenous to the economy. An easing of monetary and fiscal policy allowed income expansion to resume in 1971, clearly before inflationary forces were quelled, and restrictive monetary policy in 1974 contributed to a sharp contraction in economic activity which began in 1974.

Thus, the government's monetary and fiscal actions have been both a source of progress and of disruption. The government-managed expansion that began in 1961 and lasted until the end of the 1960s demonstrated that an endless boom-bust sequence is not inevitable—that judiciously applied stabilization policy can smooth the path of income growth. Still, our experience from the late 1960s to the present highlights the difficulties of properly applying stabilization policy, particularly when a well-entrenched cumulative expansion or contraction is underway. Cognizant of the important role government plays in the performance of the economy, we should now be ready for an intensive look at the problems of policy making—the topic of the following section of this book .

Finally, this chapter provided a brief introduction to forecasting, a natural extention of dynamic macroeconomic analysis. Our discussion of forecasting was restricted to four popular approaches: (1) forecasting with econometric models, (2) forecasts using extrapolation procedures, (3) forecasting with leading indicators, and (4) forecasting with anticipations and intentions data. All of these techniques are employed extensively by those public and private organizations that must make decisions based on expected future economic conditions.

QUESTIONS

1. Provide a verbal explanation of the way in which interaction between the multiplier and the accelerator can result in cycles.
2. Under what conditions must floors and ceilings be introduced into the basic multiplier–accelerator model?

3. With a cycle model that calls for damped fluctuations in income when the best available estimates of the system's parameters are plugged into the model, how can continued fluctuations be explained?

4. Explain and criticize the argument that the government is responsible for causing the business cycle.

5. Is it important to check any model used for policy purposes for stability? Explain your answer.

6. Briefly discuss the "inevitability" of the cycle.

7. In an earlier chapter, we argued that spending on investment goods was inversely related to the interest cost of borrowing. If this is the case, what implications are there for the multiplier-accelerator analysis?

8. Should you continue studying economics and attend graduate school, do you suppose any unsolved problems in designing stabilization policies will remain to challenge you by the time you finish your training?

SUGGESTED READING

Baumol, William J. *Economic Dynamics*, 3rd edition. London: Macmillan, 1970, Chapters 1-3, 7-10.

Goodwin, R. M. "The Non-linear Accelerator and the Persistence of Business Cycles," *Econometrica*. Vol. 19, January 1951, pp. 1-17.

Gordon, Robert A. *Business Fluctuations*, 2d edition. New York: Harper & Row Publishers, Inc., 1961.

Hicks, John R. *A Contribution to the Theory of the Trade Cycle*. Oxford: Oxford University Press, 1950.

Matthews, R. C. O. *The Trade Cycle*. Cambridge, Eng.: Cambridge University Press, 1959.

Metzler, L. A. "The Nature and Stability of Inventory Cycles," *Review of Economic Statistics*. Vol. 23, August 1941, pp. 113-129.

Samuelson, Paul A. "Interactions Between the Multiplier Analysis and the Principle of Acceleration," *Review of Economic Statistics*. Vol. 21, May 1939, pp. 75-78.

Spencer, Roger. "The National Plan to Curb Unemployment and Inflation," *Federal Reserve Bank of St. Louis Review*. Vol. 55, April 1973, pp. 2-13.

Chapter 15
Money Supply
Control-Implementing
Monetary Policy

Our analysis up to this point has assumed that the nominal supply of money is subject to precise control by an agency of the federal government. That control agency is the central bank which, for the United States, is the Federal Reserve System (popularly referred to as the "Fed"). In this chapter, we will show that the Fed does have control over the size of the money stock and will explain how it applies that control power. We will also look briefly at the shortcomings of monetary policy as a stabilization tool.

THE AMERICAN BANKING SYSTEM

To understand how the Fed controls the money stock, it is helpful to have a basic understanding of the institutional structure of the American banking system. At present, there are some 14,000 commercial banks in the United States. About one-third of these are national banks with the remainder being state chartered and supervised. (A nationally chartered bank is always distinguishable by the presence of the word "national" in its name.) All national banks are members of the Federal Reserve System, and most of the larger state chartered banks are also members. In terms of the provision of banking services, overall banking activity in the United States is dominated by those banks that are members of the Fed. At the end of 1974, nonmember banks held less than one-fourth of all bank deposits even though less than half of all the banks in the United States were members of the Federal Reserve System.

The primary functions of all commercial banks are the holding of deposits for the nonbank public (with the associated function of clearing checks drawn against *demand deposits*) and the extention of credit to the public. While a number of other financial institutions perform functions similar to those provided by commercial banks—for example, savings and loan associations and mutual savings banks make loans to the public, accept public deposits, and in practice permit the withdrawal of those deposits on demand—there is an essential difference between banks and all other financial institutions. The demand deposit (checking account) liabilities of commercial banks *are money!* By drawing a check on a demand deposit account in a commercial bank, individuals can meet their debts while all other varieties of deposits must first be converted into money (demand deposits or currency) before debts can be paid.

439

Because demand deposits are money (making up nearly 80 percent of the total money supply), the commercial banking system plays a crucial role in determining the volume of money balances in existence. The supply of money is altered whenever commercial banks *create* or *destroy* demand deposits. This is something they do every day. When a bank extends a loan, it typically does so by merely crediting an approved loan applicant's checking account (a simple book-keeping entry) with the amount of the loan extended. Since demand deposits are money, a commercial bank creates money "with the stroke of a pen" whenever it extends loans. In like fashion, commercial banks permit the money supply to shrink whenever they accept repayment of outstanding loans (wiping demand deposit liabilities off their books) without extending an equivalent volume of new loans. It is this intrinsic involvement in the money creation (and destruction) process that makes the commercial banking system important in macroeconomics.

The Need for a Central Bank

Since the commercial banking system can alter the money supply by expanding or contracting the volume of loans it extends, its actions can (at times unfavorably) affect overall economic activity. As a result, commercial banks have been subjected to increased regulation in the past several decades—regulation that has provided us with a banking system that is vastly different from the system that prevailed into the early 1900s.

In the nineteenth and early twentieth centuries the U.S. banking system was comprised of thousands of independent, private commercial banks, each operating in pursuit of profit with financial market forces providing the only central guidance on bank credit extension policy. Throughout that period the U.S. economy suffered from frequent and, on occasion, sizable expansions and contractions. From boom to bust, the profit-maximizing efforts of commercial banks produced large swings in the volume of bank loans, tending to amplify the economy's instability. During expansions, when demand for loans was strong, banks extended large volumes of new loans. This action increased the money supply, contributing to the strength of the expansion and any accompanying inflation. During contractions bank loan officers became more pessimistic about future business conditions and thus about the prudence of extending credit to loan applicants. They allowed their volume of outstanding loans to shrink, which reduced the money supply and amplified the contraction of economic activity.

Further, in the more severe contractions bank failures were commonplace. Such failures contributed to the financial ruin of countless depositors and, by adversely affecting expectations, accentuated the ongoing contraction. "Runs" on banks were commonplace, with depositors lining up to convert their deposits into "safe" currency. Unable to honor all deposit liabilities at once, additional banks folded, eroding confidence in the banking system and, thus, in the economy in general.

Aside from cyclical crises in the financial market, it is also worth noting that over the course of a normal year there are systemic "seasonal" changes in the demand for money. For example, during the Christmas season the volume of business activity, and thus of money demand, increases sharply. In the post-Christmas period business activity slumps and money demand falls accordingly. To avoid seasonal periods of money scarcity and surplus, which result in volatile movements in the interest rate, an "elastic" money supply is needed. The unregulated private banking system did not provide the needed elasticity in money supply.

The Federal Reserve System

In 1907, a financial panic in the United States precipitated the failure of an alarming number of commercial banks. Public and Congressional disgust with the apparent inadequacy of unrestricted private banking led to the creation in 1913 of the U.S. central bank, the Federal Reserve System. Among its other duties, the Fed was designed to provide an elastic currency and, more importantly, to prevent bank failures, first by setting limits on the amount of credit member banks could extend and second by serving as a *lender of last resort* to provide funds to banks that faced extraordinarily large withdrawals.

Under the Federal Reserve System, the country was divided into twelve Federal Reserve Districts, each with its own Federal Reserve Bank.[1] This geographically dispersed central bank system is administered from Washington by the presidentially appointed, seven-member *Board of Governors of the Federal Reserve System*. Direct guidance in administering monetary policy is provided by a twelve-man *Federal Open Market Committee* consisting of the Board of Governors plus five of the district bank presidents, always including the president of the New York district bank.

The Federal Reserve currently performs a variety of services for member commercial banks, the U.S. government, and the public. The array of services provided to member banks has resulted in Fed banks being labeled "bankers' banks," suggesting that these Fed banks provide, for member banks, many of the services that ordinary commercial banks provide to the public. What are these functions? The Fed provides currency to member banks on demand,[2] clears and collects checks for member banks, provides loans to member banks when necessary, and, finally, holds deposits (called *reserves*) of the member commercial banks. As a fiscal agent for government, the Fed carries the principal checking accounts of the U.S. Treasury and aids the Treasury in issuing and redeeming

---

1 The twelve Federal Reserve District Banks are located in Boston, New York, Philadelphia, Cleveland, Richmond, Atlanta, Chicago, St. Louis, Minneapolis, Kansas City, Dallas, and San Francisco. In addition to the main district bank, there are a number of branch district banks in other cities.

2 In turn, nonmember banks typically get currency from member banks.

government securities. Also, the Federal Reserve Bank of New York acts as the agent of the U.S. Treasury in gold and foreign exchange transactions.

The above list of functions is representative, not exhaustive. In fact, that list fails to spotlight the one most important function of the Federal Reserve System. That function is the regulation of the nation's money supply. We have already used our income determination models to analyze the impact of changes in the nation's money supply. We are now ready to account for the ability of the Fed to deliberately alter the money stock.

A MONEY SUPPLY MODEL

In the list of services performed by the Fed, we stated that the Fed holds deposits for member banks. In fact, member banks are *required* to maintain reserves, most of which are held on deposit with the Fed, in a fixed proportion to their deposit liabilities. The percentage reserve requirement on demand deposits we will call the *required reserve ratio* (r_d). If the required reserve ratio on demand deposits is 20 percent, a bank with $20 million in demand deposit liabilities must hold $4 million in reserves in order to meet its reserve requirement. Historically, the reserve requirement was imposed to force banks to hold a volume of reserves that was adequate to meet withdrawal demands. While under normal circumstances withdrawals and deposits pretty much cancel out, there are periods during which an individual bank suffers from an excess of withdrawals and, during the financial crises the United States has experienced historically, the banking system as a whole suffered massive net withdrawals of deposits.

Legally, a bank's reserves can be held either in the form of deposits with the Fed or as currency (called *vault cash*). Either form of reserves can support (meet the legal reserve requirement on) a multiple volume of demand deposit *money*. With a 20-percent reserve ratio, each dollar of reserves can support $5 of demand deposits. No wonder *reserve* money (including currency) is frequently referred to as "high-powered money" or "base" money. With the institutional information now on hand, we can proceed with construction of a formal money supply model.[3]

To build a money supply model, we will make use of the following definitions:

M = total money supply.

C = total currency held by the public.

---

[3] It is assumed that the student has had an introductory treatment of the banking system which has provided familiarity with: (1) simple commercial banking transactions that alter the balance sheets of the banks involved and (2) the credit expansion (contraction) process through which demand deposit money is created (destroyed). If you feel your background exposure to the banking system is deficient, review the appendix to this chapter before you proceed.

$D =$ total demand deposits held by the public.

$M = C + D.$

$r_d =$ required reserve ratio on demand deposits.

$RR =$ total required reserves.

$R =$ total reserves or high-powered money available to the commercial banking system—with increasing frequency referred to as the monetary "base."

$c =$ the fraction of its total money stock which the public holds in the form of currency.

$RA =$ total reserve money absorbed by required reserves and public currency holdings.

For simplicity, our analysis ignores the existence of time deposits against which reserves must be held and assumes that all commercial banks are members of the Federal Reserve System, hence subject to the same reserve requirement on demand deposits. It is also assumed that the public desires to hold some fraction, c, of its total money balances in the form of currency. That is, total desired currency holdings are $C = cM$, implying that desired demand deposits holdings are $D = (1 - c)M.$

There are two absorbers of reserve or high-powered money in our banking system model, required reserves and public currency holdings. Therefore, total absorbed reserves are

$$RA = RR + C \qquad\qquad (15\text{-}1)$$

However, we know that required reserves are $RR = r_d \cdot D$ with $D = (1 - c)M$, and currency held by the public is $C = cM$. Substituting these relationships into Equation (15-1) yields

$$RA = r_d(1 - c)M + cM \qquad\qquad (15\text{-}2)$$

or

$$RA = M[c + r_d(1 - c)] \qquad\qquad (15\text{-}3)$$

The Fed provides reserves to the commercial banking system (the ways the Fed can do this are described below) and we have labeled the amount provided R. Should the volume of absorbed reserves (RA) fall short of the volume of reserves provided by the Fed (R), the banking system will possess *excess reserves*—that is, the banking system will have reserve deposits or vault cash that can serve as the legal basis for the extention of loans to credit applicants.

The cost to banks of *holding* excess reserves is the foregone interest income that could be earned by lending those reserves. We will initially assume that, as profit-maximizing firms, banks always put any excess reserves to work by lending them, thus eliminating the excess. Remember, though, that these banks are legally required at least to meet the legal reserve ratio even if they must borrow reserves or call in loans to do so. Thus, a desired goal of zero excess reserves must be met for equilibrium in our simple model of the banking system. In formal terms, then, for equilibrium absorbed reserves (RA) must equal the volume of reserves (R) the central bank makes available, or,

$$R = M[c + r_d(1 - c)]. \tag{15-4}$$

Solving for the equilibrium money stock yields

$$M = \frac{1}{c + r_d(1 - c)} \cdot R. \tag{15-5}$$

If we keep our 20 percent reserve ratio and also assume that the public holds 20 percent of its money in the form of currency ($c = .20$), the equilibrium money supply is

$$M = 2.78R. \tag{15-6}$$

That is, each dollar of reserves provided by the Fed permits $2.78 of total money holdings by the public. As a simple mathematical proposition, inspection of Equations (15-5) and (15-6) shows clearly that *if the Fed can change the volume of reserves at will it can change the money stock at will*. Specifically, the change in nominal money supply that can be provided by a change in reserves is

$$\Delta M = \left[\frac{1}{c + r_d(1 - c)}\right]\Delta R. \tag{15-7}$$

which, with our sample values for c and r_d, yields

$$\Delta M = 2.78\Delta R. \tag{15-8}$$

The term in brackets in Equation (15-7) can be called a *credit expansion* or *money supply multiplier* $[\Delta M/\Delta R = 1/(c + r_d(1 - c))]$. It measures the impact on the nominal money stock of a change in the volume of reserves, assuming that, in equilibrium, the banking system holds no excess reserves.

Looking back at Equation (15-5), we also see that, with the volume of reserves fixed, the equilibrium stock of money will change with every change in the required reserve ratio (r_d). A reduction in the reserve ratio would make the denominator of Equation (15-5) smaller, increasing the size of the equilibrium money stock while, conversely, an increase in r_d would reduce the size of the equilibrium money stock. Since the Fed sets the value of the required reserve ratio, it should be able to use that ratio to control the nominal money stock.

MONETARY POLICY—THE TOOLS OF MONEY SUPPLY CONTROL

The Federal Reserve System has three important *general* instruments for controlling the money supply. They are the *reserve requirement,* the *discount rate,* and *open market operations.* With the money supply model we have just constructed it is easy to see how these instruments affect the money supply.

The Reserve Requirement

We should already feel familiar with the reserve requirement on demand deposits. Still, we will gain by carefully outlining the money supply adjustment to a change in the required reserve ratio. Let the banking system be in equilibrium (every bank has zero excess reserves) when the required reserve ratio is reduced (say, from 20 percent to 10 percent). Immediately after reduction in the reserve ratio, all banks still possess the same volume of actual reserve holdings while each bank's required reserves have been reduced (cut in half!). Each bank will have *excess* reserves which it can put to work by extending new credit.

When a bank extends a loan, it typically does so by merely crediting an approved loan applicant's checking account with the amount of the granted loan. As indicated before, since demand deposits are money, a bank creates money with such bookkeeping entries. After a reserve ratio reduction, system-wide, money creation of precisely this nature will continue as long as there are excess reserves in the system. According to Equation (15-5), after the banking system has adjusted to a required reserve ratio reduction from 20 to 10 percent, each dollar of reserves will support $3.57 of money holdings, a substantial increase from the initial $2.78 volume.

Conversely, should the required reserve ratio be increased while the banking system is in equilibrium, every bank will be faced with an unallowable reserve deficiency. Banks could respond by refusing to renew some loan commitments as loans come due, by calling in existing loans, and, temporarly, by *borrowing* reserves to meet the legal reserve requirement. As loans are repaid, banks' demand deposit liabilities are reduced, reducing the money supply. To complete the system-wide adjustment to an increased reserve ratio, total deposit liabilities would have to fall sufficiently to allow the available volume of reserves to meet the banking system's increased percentage reserve requirement.

The reserve requirement is indeed under the control of the Board of Governors of the Federal Reserve System. Thus, the reserve requirement *can* serve as a powerful tool for controlling the money supply, a reduction in the reserve ratio increasing the money supply and an increase in the reserve ratio reducing the money supply.

The Discount Rate

The discount rate is the interest rate at which member banks can borrow reserves from the Fed. When a bank borrows at the Fed's "discount window," the Fed extends the approved loan by crediting the borrowing bank's reserve account at the Fed with the amount of the loan. As we have seen, a change in reserves available to the banking system will result in a multiple change in the public's money holdings.

To encourage an increase in the money supply, the Fed can set the discount rate substantially below the short-term interest rate at which commercial banks can, in turn, lend. This strategy can normally be expected to prompt aggressive banks to borrow reserves at the Fed in order to extend new loans to the public. Conversely, the Fed can induce member banks to repay existing loans (reducing reserves in the system and thus the money supply) by setting the discount rate above the rate on short-term credit.

Open Market Operations

Open market operations are the purchase and sale of securities in the open market. In practice, the Fed conducts open market operations by having the New York branch of the Federal Reserve System buy and sell government securities through a small number of firms (around 20) that specialize in the government securities trade.[4] A purchase of securities by the Fed increases the volume of reserves available to the commercial banking system and thereby increases bank lending (creation of demand deposits). A sale of securities by the Fed drains reserves from the banking system inducing a contraction of the money stock.

The Fed may, through the New York securities specialists with which it deals, exchange securities with commercial banks or with the nonbank public. When the Fed buys government bonds from commercial banks that belong to the Federal Reserve System, payment is made, in effect, by crediting those commercial banks' reserve accounts with the Fed for the amount of the Fed's bond purchases. Should the banking system be in equilibrium prior to the open market purchase, the additional (excess) reserves resulting from that open market purchase will prompt an expansion in the money supply as commercial banks attempt to put their excess reserves to work by extending interest-earning loans.

When the Fed sells securities to member banks, the purchasing banks meet their debt to the Fed by drawing checks on themselves made out to the Fed. When the Fed receives those checks, it debits the reserve accounts of the banks on which the checks are drawn for the amount of the bond sale. If the banking system begins in equilibrium, the deficiency of reserves resulting from the Fed's open

---

4 The Federal Reserve Bank of New York has provided a clear description of the mechanics of open market operations in Paul Meek, *Open Market Operations* (New York: Federal Reserve Bank of New York, July 1969).

market sale would prompt banks to reduce their volume of outstanding loans (and, thus, the volume of "created" demand deposit money).

The money supply model we have built indicates that, when open market operations result in security exchanges between the Fed and member banks, the total money supply will change by the volume of open market purchases (or sales) times the money supply multiplier. Identical results are forthcoming when the Fed's security exchanges are with the nonbank public.

The Fed would pay for a bond purchase from the nonbank public with a check drawn upon itself. The recipient would deposit that check in his or her own bank, directly increasing the volume of demand deposits (money) by the amount of the bond purchase and creating *excess reserves* equal to the bond purchase minus the reserve requirement on the bond seller's new deposit. The banking system could then expand its deposit liabilities until the excess reserves are absorbed. Since the open market purchase increases total available reserves by the full amount of the bond purchase, total money supply can expand by the amount of the bond purchase times the money supply multiplier. You should be able to trace the impact on the money supply of a Fed sale of securities to the nonbank public.

Use of the Tools of Monetary Control [5]

In practice, changes in the required reserve ratio are infrequently used in an effort to affect the money supply. The Fed has traditionally claimed that reserve ratio changes are too blunt and crude a tool for active monetary policy use. It is argued that even a small change in the reserve ratio results in undesirably large and abrupt changes in the money supply. In addition, the Fed claims that because reserve ratio changes "announce" to the public the policy intention of the central bank they may cause unwanted, potentially destabilizing reactions from the public. Whatever the justification for a policy of disuse, the reserve ratio is altered relatively infrequently.

In contrast, the discount rate is changed fairly often. It should not be assumed, though, that this is evidence of the *active* use of the discount rate as a money supply control weapon. In fact, the discount rate is typically changed only in response to changes that have *already occurred* in the market rate of interest. A restrictive monetary stance by the Fed, implemented, say, through open market operations, would cause market interest rates to rise. If the discount rate remains unchanged in the face of such a rise in market rates, member banks have an incentive to borrow reserves from the Fed to support an increased volume of

---

5 For a complete exposition of the Fed's policy tools use, see W. Smith, "The Instruments of General Monetary Control," *National Banking Review*, Vol. I, September 1963, pp. 47-76; reprinted in W. Smith and R. Teigen (eds.), *Readings in Money, National Income, and Stabilization Policy* (Homewood, Ill.: Richard D. Irwin, 1974), pp. 236-258.

loans—loans which, by increasing the money supply, reduce the upward pressure on the interest rate. To avoid such a *slippage* in its restrictive policy, the Fed must raise the discount rate as the market interest rate rises. In fact, historical observation shows that the discount rate systematically follows movements in market interest rates, reflecting the *passive* role of discount rate changes.

The general tool that is actively employed for the day-to-day implementation of monetary policy is the open market operations tool. Since the Fed is continuously *both* buying and selling bonds in the open market, it is easy for the Fed to temporarily mask its policy objectives, preventing the announcement effects on economic behavior which it has traditionally feared.[6] Further, the Fed feels that open market operations are a precision tool—that both large and small desired adjustments in the money stock can be obtained quite precisely through open market purchases and sales. Also, the thrust of policy can be easily reversed with this flexible tool. Finally, it is argued that the initiative for a money supply change lies in the hands of the Fed with open market operations.[7] Thus, the Fed favors the active use of open market operations for monetary policy rather than variations in the reserve ratio or in the discount rate.

EXCESS RESERVES AND THE INTEREST ELASTICITY OF THE MONEY SUPPLY

To simplify matters, we constructed our money supply model assuming that all banks try to stay fully loaned, holding zero excess reserves. However, in practice we observe that banks typically hold a cushion of excess reserves. To explain that practice, we need to recognize that a bank's managers cannot know with certainty what the future holds. Without excess reserves, a period of unexpectedly heavy withdrawals or unexpectedly light deposit inflows can leave a bank with a reserve deficiency. While such a deficiency can be covered by borrowing reserves from the Fed or from other banks, the cost (primarily interest) of borrowing reserves can exceed the rate of return the bank earns at the margin on its investments. Weighing the returns from squeezing excess reserves to acquire earning assets against the costs of borrowing reserves, banks generally hold some excess reserves.

---

6 Many economists believe that the stabilization efforts of the central bank would be enhanced by clear public statements of planned monetary policy actions.

7 It is claimed that this site of rest for the initiative in money supply changes contrasts with the case of discount rate changes. A change of the discount rate would result in a money supply change only if it *induced* commercial banks to change their volume of borrowing from the Fed. "You can take a horse to water...." Of course, the Fed must also entice purchases or sales of government securities and, once it has altered reserves by doing that, the commercial banks can, as we are about to discover, limit the impact of open market operations by changing the volume of excess reserves they hold.

The Optimal Volume of Excess Reserves

If, faced with an increased risk of a reserve deficiency as they economize on excess reserves, banks determine the volume of excess reserves they want to hold by comparing the rate of return on earning assets to the discount rate, the total volume of excess reserves held by the commercial banking system will change as financial market conditions change. For example, with "tight" credit conditions, if interest rates on loans rise relative to the cost of borrowing reserves from the Fed, excess reserves would be squeezed as banks make use of available reserves to extend credit. Indeed, aggressive banks will happily expose themselves to greater risk of having to borrow reserves from the central bank if the discrepancy between the discount rate and the rate of return on earning assets is large enough. Algebraically, banking system demand for excess reserves would be given by $X = X(i - i_d)$ where i is the market interest rate at which banks lend and i_d is the discount rate at which reserves can be borrowed. This demand function simply assumes that the volume of excess reserves the banking system *chooses* to hold is a function of the gap between the borrowing and lending rate with excess reserves reduced (credit extended more aggressively) as the gap widens.

The Revised Money Supply Model

Recognition that the banking system may choose to hold excess reserves requires only a slight modification of our formal money supply model. The central bank still controls the volume of reserves (R) available to the banking system but, with banks holding excess reserves (X), only a portion of the provided reserves $[R - X(i - i_d)]$ will be used to support the commercial banking system's demand deposit liabilities. Thus, Equation (15-5) must be modified to read

$$M = \frac{1}{c + r_d(1 - c)} \cdot [R - X(i - i_d)]. \tag{15-9}$$

Our previous estimates of the volume of money that a given stock of reserves would support must now be taken as upper limit estimates—estimates that are valid only when the banking system chooses to hold no excess reserves so that

$$M = \frac{1}{c + r_d(1 - c)}[R - \overset{0}{\cancel{X(i - i_d)}}] = \frac{1}{c + r_d(1 - c)}R.$$

Equation (15-9) shows that, other things equal, the central bank can change the money supply by changing reserves just as in the simpler model. We must now recognize, however, that by altering the volume of excess reserves they choose to hold, the commercial banks can influence the response of the money supply to changes in reserves. For example, during a period of depressed economic activity with bank managers leery of loan extensions, a large portion of a central-bank engineered increase in reserves *could* be absorbed in excess reserves.

In that case, to attain the expansionary effect it desires the Fed would have to expand reserves much more than if all excess reserves were used for credit extension.

Equation (15-9) also shows that, in striking contrast to an assumption employed in all our models of the money market up to this point, we should expect the quantity of money supplied to be positively related to the market rate of interest. Other things constant, as the market rate of interest rises the gap between the rate of return on loans and the interest cost of borrowing reserves widens, enticing banks to draw down their excess reserves as they take advantage of profitable opportunities to lend. With increased lending, the stock of money is expanded.[8] This tendency for commercial bank behavior to result in an increase in the money supply as the interest rate rises may be reinforced by the nonbank public's reaction to an increased interest rate. Since currency provides no interest yield, as the interest rate rises, raising the relative attractiveness of interest-paying savings deposits and of demand deposits on which an *implicit* return may be paid (gifts for opening new accounts, preferential loan treatment for larger depositors, and so on), the public may economize on its currency holdings, swapping them for demand and savings deposits. Since currency is *reserve* money, as the nonbank public deposits some of its currency holdings in the commercial banking system additional loans will be extended, raising the money supply.[9] Thus, if an increase in the interest rate entices banks to "dishoard" excess reserves and the nonbank public to dishoard currency, the aggregate supply of

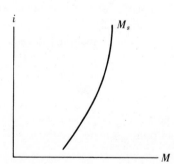

FIGURE 15-1   The Interest Rate and the Nominal Money Supply

8   Since a reduction in the discount rate (i_d) with the market interest rate unchanged would also widen the gap between the borrowing and lending rate, it is clear that the money supply also depends on the discount rate.

9   Rewriting the money supply function [Equation (15-9)], with the denominator rearranged, yields

$$M = \frac{1}{c(1 - r_d) + r_d}[R - X(i - i_d)].$$

Quite clearly, a reduction in the value of c, the currency-money ratio, increases the value of the credit expansion multiplier and raises the money supply. An increase in the value of c would induce a shrinkage of the money supply.

nominal money balances would look like the schedule in Figure 15-1, the money supply positively related to the market interest rate.

No longer can we take the nominal supply of money to be an exogenous variable that is controlled solely by the Federal Reserve. Indeed, its value is jointly determined by the actions of the commercial banking system, the non-bank public, and the Federal Reserve System.

An Interest-Elastic Money Supply

Several investigators have used regression analysis to test for the responsiveness of the money stock to interest rate changes. Their regressions have provided estimates of the elasticity of the money supply to changes in the market interest rate that range from .12 to .19.[10] These are important results, for the interest responsiveness of the money supply affects the slope of the LM curve in our aggregate model, and some modern arguments over the relative effectiveness of monetary and fiscal policy depend crucially on the shape of that LM curve. In Figure 15-2, two *real* money supply schedules are sketched (holding the price level constant), one which assumes the nominal money supply is positively related to the interest rate (M_s'/P) and one which takes the nominal money stock to be exogenous—independent of the interest rate $(\overline{M}_S/P)$. If at real output level Y_0 the demand schedule for real money balances is $(M_D/P)_{Y_0}$, the equilibrium interest rate is i_0. Since interest rate-output combination (i_0, Y_0) is a money market equilibrium

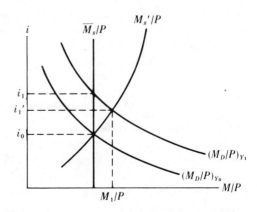

FIGURE 15-2 Money Market Adjustments with an Interest-Sensitive Money Supply

---

10 If the money supply's elasticity with respect to the interest rate is .15, a 10 percent increase in the market interest rate, say, from a rate of 8 percent to 8.8 percent, would increase the money supply by 1.5 percent. Empirical evidence on the money stock's response to interest rate changes appears in R. L. Teigen, "The Demand for and Supply of Money," in W. L. Smith and R. L. Teigen (eds.), *Readings in Money, National Income, and Stabilization Policy, op. cit.*, and in P. H. Hendershott and F. DeLeeuw, "Free Reserves, Interest Rates, and Deposits: A Synthesis," *Journal of Finance*, Vol. XXV, June 1970, pp. 599-613.

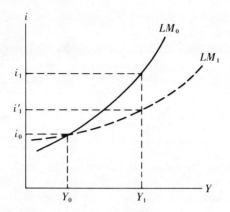

FIGURE 15-3 The *LM* Schedule with Interest-Sensitive Money Supply

combination, it can be plotted as one point on the money market equilibrium (*LM*) schedule, as in Figure 15-3.

With an increase in the level of real output, the money demand function is shifted rightward. For the higher output level Y_1, let us suppose the money demand schedule shifts to $(M_D/P)_{Y_1}$ in Figure 15-2. With the money supply fixed at $(\bar{M}_S/P)$, the money market equilibrium interest rate would rise to i_1, implying an *LM* schedule like LM_0 in Figure 15-3. But with the money supply sensitive to the interest rate increase, the equilibrium interest rate rises only to i_1'. With the money supply expanded by an increase in the interest rate, even with the volume of reserves provided by the Fed, the required reserve ratio, and the discount rate held constant, a smaller interest rate increase can restore money market equilibrium after an increase in the level of output (thus money demand). Hence, the *LM* curve is more *interest-elastic*, like LM_1 in Figure 15-3, the more interest-elastic is the money supply schedule.

The Relative Strength of Monetary and Fiscal Policy

In Chapter 9 we showed that, with the stock of money *given* and the demand for money *insensitive* to the interest rate when interest rates are at an elevated level, the LM schedule would be vertical. In that "classical" situation, any expansionary fiscal policy caused the interest rate in our model to rise until, by reducing investment expenditure, aggregate demand was restored to its original level. All an expansionary fiscal policy did in that case was raise the interest rate and reallocate an unchanged level of real output. A change in the money supply was necessary to alter the level of output.[11]

Again, the classical conclusion that fiscal policy was powerless and monetary

11   Review Chapter 9, pp. 235-239 if these arguments are not familiar. See also Chapter 10 pp. 288-291.

policy effective in altering the output level rested on the assumption that the nominal supply of money is exogenous. If the money supply responds positively to the interest rate, providing an additional source of interest-elasticity in the *LM* schedule, the classical conclusions are invalid in the *IS-LM* model even if the demand for money is insensitive to the interest rate. Unless both money supply and demand are insensitive to the interest rate, both monetary and fiscal policy can alter aggregate demand in the simple *IS-LM* model.

A Brief Summary

Our first task in this chapter was to construct a money supply model that could be used to illustrate the techniques the Federal Reserve possesses for controlling the money supply. With the help of the model we constructed, it was shown that the Fed, which provides reserves or high-powered money to the commercial banking system, can control the nominal money supply. It can do so utilizing three general control instruments: open market operations, the discount rate, and the required reserve ratio. By recognizing that the banking system holds excess reserves and that the public can alter the credit expansion multiplier by changing its currency holdings, we paid homage to the practical difficulties the Fed must deal with if it chooses a target value for the money supply and tries to hit that target. But no one said a policy maker's life is easy. The Fed must live with and compensate for the actions of commercial banks and the nonbank public, still relying on its general control instruments for pursuing its monetary policy objectives. In spite of these complications, Federal Reserve bond purchases and sales, discount rate changes, and reserve ratio alterations still change the money supply. Accurately predicting the size of money stock change from application of these policy instruments is just a more difficult and challenging task because the commercial banking system and the nonbank public are jointly responsible (with the Fed) for determining the size of the money stock.

Our last concern was to integrate our new understanding of the determinants of the money supply into the aggregate income determination model. With the nominal money supply endogenous—positively related to the market interest rate —the money market equilibrium (*LM*) schedule is more interest-elastic than it is with the nominal money stock fixed. This revelation is important because the strength of fiscal policy is increased and the strength of monetary policy reduced by an enlarged interest-elasticity of the *LM* schedule.

LAGS AND THE EFFECTIVENESS OF MONETARY POLICY

We have already devoted a good bit of attention in this text to assessing the effectiveness of monetary policy. In the aggregate model, it was shown that the impact on aggregate demand of a change in the supply of money is crucially dependent on the slopes of the commodity and money market equilibrium schedules. We have concluded that, under normal conditions, those slopes are such that

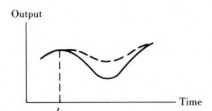

FIGURE 15-4 Smoothing the Business Cycle

monetary policy *can* be used to alter the level of aggregate demand. If the real world, like our aggregate model, were static so that adjustments to an altered money supply took place *timelessly*, we would need no further discussion of the effectiveness of monetary policy—*effectiveness* of monetary policy would mean *strength* of monetary policy. But in a dynamic world in which output and employment periodically swing in a sporadic cycle, there is more to monetary policy effectiveness than strength. In a dynamic setting, the *timing* of monetary policy's impact on aggregate demand is crucial.

Figure 15-4 shows an idealized business cycle (the solid line) in which output peaks at time t_0, declines, then begins to rise once more. If an expansionary monetary policy could begin to stimulate aggregate demand immediately after the contraction in output begins (at t_0), the severity of the contraction could be sharply reduced with the time path of output looking more like the broken-line path in Figure 15-4. Unfortunately, there is a substantial *lag* between the point in time when the need for an expansionary (or contractionary) monetary policy arises and the time when that policy can alter aggregate demand.

Recognition, Administrative, and Operational Lags

Our idealized business cycle is reproduced in Figure 15-5. From that plot, it is clear that the need for an expansionary monetary policy arises at time t_0. However, the monetary authorities may not immediately recognize that need. Data on output, employment, and so on are available only at discrete time intervals. For example, figures on gross national product, a basic yardstick of the economy's vigor, are available only at quarterly intervals. To be sure, there are other important data series, including price indexes and unemployment rates, that are available at more frequent intervals. However, one or two monthly observations do not provide the clear-cut evidence of a major change in economic developments which the Fed needs for revising its policy stance. Thus, a *recognition* lag that may last several months must be endured before the monetary authorities become convinced that a need for policy action has arisen. That lag is represented by the time lapse between t_0 and t_1 in Figure 15-5.

The solution for the delay in recognizing the need for policy action is better forecasting, and a great deal of effort has been expended toward that end. As indicated in Chapter 14, as an aid in forecasting economic developments several

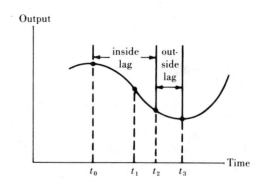

FIGURE 15-5   The Lags in Monetary
Policy

data series are available, including new orders for machinery and equipment, hiring rates, and even stock market prices, which appear to be *leading indicators* of economic activity. Over the business cycle, these data series tend to hit both peaks and troughs earlier than overall economic activity does. Data series on consumer buying intentions and business investment plans are also an aid to forecasters, and, increasingly, econometric models of the economy are being relied on for predicting the future. Experience shows, though, that in spite of our best efforts, forecasting is an uncertain affair. In 1929, a prominent group of economic forecasters predicted economic recovery within a year! As an aftermath to World War II, many economists predicted a major postwar recession. In fact, economic activity turned out to be excessively buoyant after the war.

A second lag, the *administrative lag*, is the interval between recognition of a need for policy action and the time when policy action is undertaken. Having recognized the need for an expansionary (or contractionary) monetary policy, the Fed must determine how to administer its policy action and the size of policy action that is needed. Since policy decisions are made by a compact group (the Open Market Committee) which meets at frequent intervals, the administrative lag for monetary policy is usually brief. That lag is represented by the time interval between t_1 and t_2 in Figure 15-5. The recognition and administrative lags combined are frequently referred to as the *inside lag* (t_0 to t_2), the time interval between the emergence of a need for policy and the administration of policy action.

Even after the monetary authority has undertaken a policy action, there is a sizable *operational lag* or *outside lag* before that policy has its effect on aggregate demand. For example, to stimulate economic activity the Fed can use open market operations to pump reserves into the banking system. But the commercial banking system must then transform the injection of reserves, through the multiple credit-expansion process, into an increase in the supply of money. It takes time for a general increase in available credit and the full decline in the interest rate to materialize. As that is accomplished, spending plans will be adjusted. But again, time delays are involved. Decisions to undertake a factory expansion, construct an apartment complex, or even to contract for a new home are not made overnight. Once investment decisions are made, contracts must be formalized (typically requiring an evaluation period by the capital goods suppliers and, often, the submission of competing bids) before those decisions begin to affect production.

The operational lag is represented by the time interval between t_2 and t_3 in Figure 15-5 with the expansionary monetary policy's major impact on output distributed over an interval of time after t_3. While this operational or outside lag is generally conceded to be far more important than the inside lag in delaying the effective application of monetary policy, there is no clear evidence on the length of the outside lag. Milton Friedman argues, though, that this lag is both *long* and *variable*. Empirical studies have revealed a diverse assortment of values for the outside lag ranging from 1 or 2 months to 3 years for a monetary policy action to begin to exert a significant effect on the economy.[12]

The implications for monetary policy of a long and variable lag between emergence of a need for policy and the impact of policy are clear-cut; monetary policy actions may frequently be destabilizing rather than stabilizing. Figure 15-5 illustrates that possibility. Our expansionary policy, aimed at combating the contraction that began at time t_0, does not begin to exert its expansionary effect on aggregate demand until t_3 when the contraction has ended and output is already expanding. Monetary stimulation at that point could produce an excessively strong and prolonged expansion, favoring the development of a needless inflation. Analogously, if the Fed sharply reduces the rate of growth of the money supply to stifle an expansion that it judges to be excessive, by the time that restrictive policy has its impact on aggregate demand output may have already peaked with contraction underway. Monetary restriction at that time would reinforce the contraction.

Rules versus Discretion

For many years, economists have debated whether the central bank should have a free hand in determining the growth rate of the money supply, as it now does,

---

12   For a sample of views on the length of the lag in monetary policy's effect see M. Friedman, "The Lag in Effect of Monetary Policy," *Journal of Political Economy*, Vol. LXVIII, December 1960, pp. 617-621, and R. H. Rasche and H. T. Shapiro, "The F.R.B.-M.I.T. Econometric Model: Its Special Features," *American Economic Review*, Vol. 58, May 1968, pp. 123-149.
In this vein it is worth noting that some analysts believe the operational lag in applying monetary policy could be shortened by relying on reserve ratio adjustments rather than on open market operations when a change in the money supply is desired. It is argued that open market operations have their initial impact mainly on the large New York banks (perhaps explaining why those banks are usually the first to alter their interest rates), with the economy-wide effects of the Fed's actions gradually transmitted throughout the financial system. In contrast, reserve ratio changes impinge immediately on all banks, no matter what their location. Because the first-round effects of a reserve ratio change are more widely dispersed, it is concluded that the overall lag in the effect of a monetary policy action will be shorter using that tool than if open market operations are employed.

or whether the rate of monetary expansion should be dictated by a simple rule. The majority of economists favor continuation of the discretionary implementation of monetary policy, but a vocal minority, led by Milton Friedman, favor establishment of a requirement that the Fed engineer a *steady* growth of the money supply at an annual rate approximating the long-run growth rate of real productive capacity, something between 4 and 5 percent annually.[13] That expansion rate, it is claimed, would provide the growing money stock needed to keep step with the financial requirements of an expanding economy.

A part of the rules-versus-discretion debate stems directly from differences in empirical judgment on the ability of the Fed, with its staff of professional economists, to predict the impact of monetary policy actions. Proponents of simple rules for monetary expansion argue, like Friedman, that the lags in monetary policy's impact are long and variable (thus hard to predict). As we have just seen, with the combination of a limited ability to forecast movements in economic activity and a long (not to mention variable) lag in monetary policy's impact, policy actions may be frequently destabilizing. Looking at the historical record on movements in the *money supply* and movements in *nominal output,* supporters of simple monetary rules find enough episodes of closely related, sometimes violent movements in those two variables to convince themselves that discretionary monetary policy has, on balance, been destabilizing and is likely to continue to be destabilizing in the future. This conclusion assumes, of course, a dominant role for money as an exogenous determinant of the level of economic activity—as the cause of the observed movements in output.

Advocates of discretion emphasize the endogenous nature of the money supply, pointing out that closely related movements in nominal income and money, violent or otherwise, would be observed if the money supply responds passively to money income changes (thus interest rate changes) generated by real forces. They contend that constraining the growth rate of the money supply would often be destabilizing since the monetary authority could not respond to an excessive expansion or contraction originating in the real sectors of the economy or stemming from an autonomous change in money demand. As a simple illustration of their concern, if a bond financed increase in government spending, say, for a military engagement, overstimulates the economy, adherence to a simple rule would prevent the monetary authorities from imposing a policy restrictive enough to prevent inflation. Implicit in that concern is the belief that the monetary authority can administer discretionary policy wisely: that the impact of monetary policy can be predicted accurately enough that the Fed can contribute to economic stability.

While our discussion has flirted with the issue, we should explicitly recognize

---

13 See, for example, Milton Friedman, *A Program for Monetary Stability* (New York: Fordham University Press), p. 91. For a set of arguments that supports a much lower rate of monetary expansion, see Friedman's *The Optimum Quantity of Money and Other Essays* (Chicago: Aldine, 1969), pp. 1-50.

that a second difference in judgment also plays a prominent role in the rules-versus-discretion debate. Advocates of a monetary rule typically take the classical position that the economy is *inherently stable*. They attribute a large part of the responsibility for observed fluctuations in nominal output to monetary mismanagement (which would be eliminated with a monetary rule). With an inherently stable economy, little (stability) is gained and much can be lost through the well-intentioned but inadvertently misguided use of discretionary monetary policy.

Supporters of discretion typically believe, like Keynes, that sizable expansions and contractions can be generated by nonmonetary forces and that the self-equilibrating forces in the economy are often unacceptably slow. Thus, they contend that discretionary monetary policy, properly applied, can significantly improve the economy's performance. While conceding that actual monetary policy has at times been destabilizing, proponents of discretion argue that our understanding of macroeconomic forces and our forecasting ability has improved dramatically in recent years so that policy errors now occur less frequently. They attribute the rather favorable performance of the U.S. economy from World War II till 1970 to the generally skillful use of discretionary stabilization policy and anticipate, with growing knowledge, an even better performance from stabilization policy in the future.

To close our discussion of the rules-versus-discretion issue, it is worth noting that supporters of monetary rules are frequently politically conservative (classical or nineteenth century liberals). They judge governmental intervention in human affairs to be at best inefficient and at worst freedom threatening. As a consequence, where government functions must be tolerated as necessary evils, they believe government should be strictly constrained. The advocates of discretion are much more frequently modern liberals. They typically have more faith in the ability of government agencies to skillfully and fairly administer their assigned tasks and generally do not feel threatened by active government involvement in economic affairs.

ADDITIONAL LIMITATIONS ON MONETARY POLICY

In addition to timing problems, monetary policy makers face a number of other difficulties in using monetary policy for stabilizing output, employment, and prices. If the international monetary system depends on fixed exchange rates, as it has in the past and may in the future, balance-of-payments concerns can limit the central bank's freedom to pursue domestic goals. Indeed, monetary policy was clearly constrained in the early 1960s by balance-of-payments considerations. With the economy suffering from excessive unemployment and anemic growth in the early years of the Kennedy administration, expansionary monetary policy to stimulate investment was considered but rejected. The same interest rate reduction that would have stimulated domestic investment would have lowered the yield on U.S. securities relative to those in other countries. With short-term (money) capital highly sensitive to relative returns, lowering the U.S. interest rate would have prompted a sizable capital outflow, enlarging the already worrisome balance-of-payments deficit which, by the decade's end, had led to the collapse of the dollar's international exchange value.

The Uneven Incidence of Monetary Policy

In addition to international considerations which can restrict the Fed's freedom to control the money supply and interest rates, there are a number of internal limits that arise because the interest rate changes which monetary policy actions produce can have a quite uneven impact on different groups within society. Perhaps most notably, a restrictive monetary policy that raises market interest rates can reduce the flow of funds into the home mortgage market to a trickle, dealing crushing blows to the home construction industry.

The extreme interest-sensitivity of the construction industry stems to a large extent from a set of institutional restraints imposed on interest rates. The federal government imposes ceilings on the interest rates that can be charged on VA-guaranteed and FHA-insured mortgage loans. In addition, many states enforce *usury* laws that limit the interest charge that can be levied on mortgage loans. Finally, a large portion of all mortgage lending is done by savings and loan associations—specialized financial intermediaries that channel the bulk of their deposit inflows into mortgages—and the interest rates those associations can pay on deposits is legally limited. As market interest rates rise above the level which savings and loan associations can legally offer, depositors shift their funds out of the savings and loan associations and directly into the securities market—a process called *disintermediation*—reducing the availability of mortgage funds. In addition, when market interest rates exceed the federal or state government imposed ceilings on mortgage rates, additional funds are shifted out of the mortgage market. The volatile response of the home construction industry is easy to see. As Table 15-1 reveals, in the three most recent periods of stringent monetary

TABLE 15-1   NEW HOUSING STARTS

Year	Housing Starts (in thousands of units)
1965	1,473
1966	1,165
1967	1,292
1968	1,508
1969	1,467
1970	1,434
1971	2,052
1972	2,357
1973	2,045
1974	1,338

Source: *Federal Reserve Bulletin.*

policy (1966, 1969, and 1974) housing starts have plummeted. From the year-earlier levels, housing starts dropped by more than 20 percent in 1966, by some 3 percent in 1969 in spite of sizable government support of the mortgage market, and by nearly 35 percent in 1974. These figures provide a vivid reflection of the frustrations of: (1) potential new home purchasers who cannot find mortgage funds and (2) home builders, many of whom are driven into bankruptcy as they are unable to sell the new dwellings they produce.

Of course, rising interest rates, as a signal of the pressure on scarce productive resources, must be allowed to reduce production if they are to ration scarce resources and contribute to a stable economic environment. But the response in the housing construction industry does not reflect just a price-rationed reduction in the demand for housing (a movement up a demand curve). Instead, it reflects the perverse impact of restrictions on interest rates that affect the housing industry. At allowable interest rates, the volume of funds potential home buyers would like is simply not *available* when market interest rates are at elevated levels.

To reduce the pressure that restrictive monetary policy imposes on the housing industry, the interest rate ceilings responsible for the exaggerated interest-sensitivity of money flows into that industry could be relaxed. And, since 1969 limited moves have been made in that direction. An alternative approach that the federal government has chosen to emphasize, particularly in recent years, is the funding of *federally sponsored credit agencies* which support the mortgage market directly through purchases of mortgages and indirectly through loans to mortgage-granting intermediaries.[14] But, as the 1974 data on housing starts indicates, in spite of the activities of the federally sponsored credit agencies home construction is still oppressively affected by restrictive monetary policy.

While the housing industry is the one sector of the economy that is most strongly affected by changed credit conditions, it is not the only sector so affected. State and local governments are often subject to legislative and administrative regulations that impose ceilings on the interest rates those governmental units can pay on bond debt. As a consequence, when interest rates are high, bond financing of the construction of roads, schools, parks, and so on may become impossible, even if the citizenry would be willing to pay the prevailing interest rate for the funds required to finance such projects. The impact of high interest rates is vividly apparent in survey data on the cutback in long-term state and

---

14   The federal agencies that provide support for the mortgage market are the Federal Home Loan Bank Board (FHLB), the Federal National Mortgage Association (FNMA, often referred to as "Fannie Mae"), the Federal Home Loan Mortgage Corporation (FHLMC), and, less directly, the Government National Mortgage Association (GNMA, often called "Ginnie Mae"). During 1969, the federally sponsored credit agencies provided over 40 percent of the funds borrowed to finance housing. For a more detailed treatment of the activities of these credit agencies, see Phillip H. Davidson, "Structure of the Residential Mortgage Market," *Federal Reserve Bank of Richmond Monthly Review*, September 1972. Also, see the Federal Reserve Staff Study, "Ways to Moderate Fluctuations in Housing Construction," *Federal Reserve Bulletin*, March 1972, pp. 215-225.

local borrowing in the high-interest-rate years 1966 and 1969-1970.[15] In 1966 long-term borrowing by state and local governments was reduced by approximately 20 percent of planned levels. In fiscal 1970 (July 1969 to June 1970) the cutback was about 28 percent.

It is also frequently argued that *small* businesses are particularly sensitive to altered credit conditions. Large businesses, it is claimed, have ready access to national credit markets and can borrow funds either from banks or by direct sale of their own security issues. Thus, under restrictive credit conditions banks may feel it necessary to meet the needs of its large business customers first, restricting the funds they make available to the small businesses that have no easy alternative to bank borrowing. This set of arguments is hard to assess empirically, as are similar arguments that restrictive monetary policies impose a greater burden on lower-income groups than on others. But the point is well taken that the fear (realistic or not) that a restrictive monetary policy imposes a particularly harsh burden on specific sectors of the economy can foster a reluctance to aggressively employ monetary restraint, particularly if the highly interest-responsive sectors are deemed socially worthy and politically powerful (as are the housing industry and state and local governments).

Near-Monies and Monetary Policy

In Chapter 7 money was defined as currency plus demand deposits, financial assets that are readily acceptable as a means of clearing debt. But at that time we noted the element of arbitrariness involved in defining money since many assets have some of the attributes of money. Time deposits in commercial banks; short-term government securities; and the deposit liabilities of saving and loan associations, mutual savings banks, credit unions, and other nonbank financial intermediaries are highly *liquid*—they are easily converted into money at low cost. Serving as stores of value while earning interest income, these *near-monies* are substitutes for money in financial portfolios.

In the post-war period there was a far more rapid growth in the volume of near-monies than in the money stock itself as wealth-holders substituted interest-yielding assets for money. As a long-run proposition, the increased availability of highly liquid money substitutes certainly played a prominent role in the observed post-war decline in the volume of money balances demanded (increase in velocity) at any income level. But the growing importance of near-monies has a potentially far more significant implication for the effectiveness of monetary policy. In summary form, some economists have contended that since the monetary authorities directly control only *commercial bank* reserves and deposits,

---

15 See Paul F. McGouldrick and John E. Peterson, "Monetary Restraint and Borrowing and Capital Spending by Large State and Local Governments in 1966," *Federal Reserve Bulletin*, July 1968, pp. 552-581. Also, see John E. Peterson "Response of State and Local Governments to Varying Credit Conditions," *Federal Reserve Bulletin*, March 1971, pp. 209-232.

their power to influence the economy is reduced as money holdings become a relatively smaller share of financial portfolios. This argument can easily be expanded to show exactly how the existence of near-monies may weaken a restrictive monetary policy.

In the interest of slowing economic activity, the central bank may restrict the growth of reserves and, correspondingly, the money supply. And, so far, with a restriction in money supply growth we have argued that interest rates rise, reducing aggregate demand. But, with a rise in interest rates near-monies are made more attractive so that wealth-holders may willingly exchange money for interest-yielding securities, providing the business-supporting credit that commercial banks are not able to extend. Business activity is permitted to continue at an elevated level, even though the money supply has been restricted, as the increase in interest rates induces an increase in velocity (a reduction in money demand). The restrictive effect of monetary policy appears to be blunted as each of a reduced number of dollars is used more intensively.[16]

Of course, monetary policy cannot be completely emasculated since some interest rate increase, which reduces planned spending, is required to induce the substitution of near-monies for money itself. But to the extent that the presence of near-monies, which are *close* substitutes for money itself, increases the interest elasticity of money demand (velocity), the strength of monetary policy is reduced.

The theoretical arguments we have reviewed are appealing and, in the late 1950s and early 1960s, they evoked some substantial concern over the efficacy of monetary policy. But that concern has faded in the last decade. As a practical matter, while the availability of near-monies does increase the interest-sensitivity of money demand (velocity), the evidence is compelling that money demand is still a stable (hence predictable) function of the interest rate, allowing the monetary authorities to adjust for any systematic portfolio shift from money to near-monies which restrictive monetary policy induces. The tight money periods mentioned earlier in this chapter (1966, 1969-1970, and 1974) provide ample proof that monetary policy still has a powerful influence on economic activity.

Compliance with the Treasury

With high interest rates, the interest cost to the Treasury of issuing new government debt is elevated. The interest cost of newly issued government debt can be held down though, the interest rate *pegged*, if the Fed is willing to support bond

---

16   The propositions outlined briefly in this section are most fully developed in J. G. Gurley and E. S. Shaw, "Financial Aspects of Economic Development," *American Economic Review*, Vol. 45, September 1955, pp. 515-538, and in Gurley and Shaw, *Money in a Theory of Finance* (Washington, D.C.: The Brookings Institution, 1960), Also see Lawrence Ritter, "Income Velocity and Anti-Inflationary Monetary Policy," *American Economic Review*, Vol. 49, March 1959, pp. 120-129.

prices, standing ready to buy any volume of bonds offered at the support price. Of course, Federal Reserve bond purchases add reserves to the banking system, providing the base for an expansion of the money supply.

To aid the Treasury in its efforts to bond-finance a massive volume of expenditures at a low interest cost during World War II, the Fed pegged the interest rate at its prewar (depression) level—the yield on short-term Treasury bills was held down to just three-eights of 1 percent. By the end of the war, this support policy had provided the Fed with a massive portfolio of government securities. Still, the Fed continued supporting government bond prices in the postwar period although short-term rates were permitted to rise a bit. Of course, with the interest rate pegged, the Fed had no discretionary monetary control power—it had abdicated that power to ease the Treasury's borrowing task.

With the war ended, the *voluntary* restriction on the Fed's independent power became increasingly disagreeable as the need for stabilization policy regained priority. Further, with U.S. entry into the Korean War in mid-1950, strong inflationary pressures evoked a pressing need for restrictive monetary policy. In March 1951, the Treasury and the Federal Reserve reached an "Accord" which freed the Fed from responsibility for pegging the interest rate, permitting it to resume the independent, active use of monetary policy for stabilization purposes.

Combining Monetary Control with Financial Market Stability

To complete our sample of the difficulties the Fed confronts in implementing monetary policy we need to consider the possible conflict between the Fed's pursuit of aggregate stabilization goals and the responsibility it assumes for maintaining a *stable* financial market. We indicated early in this chapter that one of the fundamental justifications for creation of a central bank was the need for an elastic currency—a money supply that would be responsive to seasonal and random fluctuations in the demand for money, expanding and contracting over short time intervals according to the *needs of trade*. If, apart from changes in money demand which stem from general economic expansions and contractions, there are day-to-day and week-to-week fluctuations in money demand, a constant money stock or one that changes along a path dictated by longer-run stabilization needs could result in volatile fluctuations in interest rates. But abrupt, sizable swings in interest rates are generally judged to be undesirable because they increase uncertainty and because they may cause inefficient, temporary shifts of resources from one use to another. Moreover, the successful marketing of new Treasury security issues which bear a fixed stream of payments depends on interest yields on comparable securities remaining below the yield on the new Treasury issue. Hence, the Fed contends that it has good reasons to stabilize interest rates on a *short-term* basis.

As we have indicated before, to stabilize interest rates the Fed must abdicate control of the supply of money. Hence, under such a policy the money supply would respond elastically to changes in money demand. But, as we also know, not all changes in money demand are random or seasonal. Some are the result of changes in the level of economic activity of the sort that must be offset if the country's macroeconomic goals are to be achieved. Unfortunately, except in the case of stable seasonal variations in money demand there is no way the Fed can tell which changes in money demand should be accommodated by a change in the money supply because of their random nature and which, because they reflect unwanted changes in economic activity, should be met with an offsetting adjustment in the money supply and interest rates. Of course, there is some latitude for the Fed to accommodate daily or weekly shocks to the money market while still giving prime consideration over a longer time horizon (such as a quarter) to the achievement of those changes in monetary aggregates and interest rates that are judged necessary for aggregate stabilization purposes. But the Fed must be on guard against the widely recognized possibility of successive "special situations" that require a money supply response cumulatively forcing the money stock and interest rates away from the paths needed for aggregate stabilization purposes. The existence of random money market disturbances to which the Fed must respond clearly complicates its control task.

No doubt, we could extend our list of the limitations that monetary policy makers must face in employing monetary policy for stabilization purposes. Our brief list, though, should leave no doubt that using discretionary monetary policy in a manner that contributes to domestic stability is a difficult task. Still the majority of economists believe that discretionary monetary policy can make a substantial contribution to the achievement of aggregate goals.[17]

SUMMARY

We know that money is important; that by altering the money supply the central bank can change the level of aggregate demand. In this chapter we have shown, with an aggregate money supply model, how the general tools available to the Fed enable it to change the money supply. At the same time, we have seen a large enough sample of difficulties in the application of monetary policy to force us to question the usefulness of discretionary monetary policy as a stabilization tool. First, there are lengthy lags between the emergence of need for policy and the time when policy has its impact and, second, the freedom of the monetary authority to pursue its domestic stabilization goals may be constrained by international financial considerations, by fear of the uneven impact of monetary restraint, and by a number of other restrictions including some that are self-

---

17 For an insider's view of the monetary management process, see Sherman J. Maisel, *Managing the Dollar* (New York: W. W. Norton & Company, 1973).

imposed. There is little wonder that the past performance of discretionary monetary policy has fallen short of the theoretical ideal.

More importantly, all economists recognize that our understanding of the influence of monetary policy on the economy is incomplete. Most fundamentally, too little is known about the precise strength and timing of monetary influences on aggregate demand and differences in judgment on such basic issues permit profound disagreements on the appropriate application of monetary policy. Clearly, there is a need for continued research in the money arena. But since money supply changes have a powerful effect on economic activity, the application of monetary policy cannot wait for a complete resolution of all the existing uncertainties on money's role. In the meantime, most economists believe that, based on what is known, discretionary monetary policy can be used to pursue important national objectives.

QUESTIONS

1. Explain the logic of the process through which the commercial banking system can use an increase in reserves to generate a multiple increase in the stock of money.
2. Build a formal money supply model. What role does the market interest rate play in determining the size of the money stock? Use your model to explain how the Fed can alter the money supply.
3. What accounts for the lag in monetary policy? What difference does it make how long that lag is?
4. Considering the current state of economic affairs, what kind of monetary policy would you prescribe for the next 6 months?
5. In what way was monetary policy emasculated in the immediate postwar period?
6. Explain how the unique aspects of residential construction can limit the use of monetary policy? Can you think of any other discriminatory effects of monetary policy?
7. Evaluate the claim that the availability of near-monies weakens monetary policy.

SUGGESTED READING

Cagan, Phillip. *Determinants and Effects of Changes in the Stock of Money: 1875-1960*. New York: National Bureau of Economic Research, 1965.

deLeeuw, Frank, and Edward Gramlich. "The Channels of Monetary Policy," *Federal Reserve Bulletin*. Vol. LV, June 1969, pp. 472-491.

Federal Reserve Bank of Chicago. *Modern Money Mechanics*. 1971.

Friedman, Milton. *A Program for Monetary Stability.* New York: Fordham University Press, 1959.

————. "The Role of Monetary Policy," *American Economic Review.* Vol. LVIII, March 1968, pp. 1-17.

Jordan, Jerry. "Elements of Money Stock Determination," *Federal Reserve Bank of St. Louis Review.* Vol. 51, October 1969, pp. 10-19.

Maisel, Sherman. *Managing the Dollar.* New York: W. W. Norton & Co., 1973.

Mayer, Thomas. *Monetary Policy in the United States.* New York: Random House, 1968.

Ritter, Lawrence. "Income Velocity and Anti-Inflationary Monetary Policy," *American Economic Review.* Vol. 49, March 1959, pp. 120-129.

Smith, Warren L. "The Instruments of General Monetary Control," *National Banking Review.* Vol. 1, September 1963, pp. 47-76.

Teigen, Ronald. "The Demand for and Supply of Money," in W. Smith and R. Teigen (eds.). *Readings in Money, National Income, and Stabilization Policy,* 3d edition. Homewood, Ill.: Richard D. Irwin, 1974, pp. 68-103.

Appendix to Chapter 15
A Brief Review of
Simple Banking
Transactions

As indicated in Chapter 7 and, again, at the beginning of Chapter 15, demand deposits—checking account deposits in commercial banks which are payable *on demand*—are the dominant form of money in the United States. Demand deposits are liabilities of banks, owed to depositors. If we concentrate our attention on demand deposit money (ignoring currency) and assume that all commercial banks are members of the Federal Reserve System, subject to the same required reserve ratio on deposit liabilities, we can easily build a model that shows how the supply of money is determined. In the process, we will illustrate a number of important bank transactions, among them transactions that *create* money.

One Bank's Response to a Deposit Inflow

Within the confines of our simple banking system, suppose you deposit $100 in your checking account at the local bank. Since that bank is an *intermediary* that generates its revenues by lending deposits—by transferring funds from primary lenders to borrowers—it will seek to profitably lend as much of your deposit as it can. If the required reserve ratio on banks' demand deposit liabilities is 20 percent, your bank can legally lend up to $80 of your deposit but must hold $20 in reserves.

In Table 15A-1, there are a set of simplified balance sheets for your bank, one for the period preceding your $100 deposit and one after. Before your deposit, it is assumed that the bank has $1,000 of demand deposit liabilities. With a 20-percent reserve ratio, the bank must hold $200 in reserves, leaving $800

TABLE 15A-1 SIMPLIFIED BALANCE SHEETS FOR A MEMBER BANK

Balance Sheet Before Deposit		Balance Sheet After a $100 Deposit	
Assets	*Liabilities*	*Assets*	*Liabilities*
Reserves $ 200	Demand	Reserves $ 300	Demand
Loans and	deposits 1,000	Loans and	deposits $1,100
Investments 800		Investments 800	
$1,000		$1,100	

free for the bank to lend and invest. Since there is an interest (opportunity) cost of holding idle deposits, for your bank to be in equilibrium we have assumed that it will hold no reserves in excess of its legal requirement. Thus, the bank is in equilibrium with a full $800 loaned and invested.

With your deposit of $100, the bank's demand deposit liabilities are increased to $1,100 and its reserves to $300. With deposit liabilities up by $100, *required* reserves are increased, but only by $20, leaving your bank with $80 of *excess* reserves which it can put to work (lend or invest).

Extending a Loan

With $80 of excess reserves, your bank can now lend $80 to any loan applicant it chooses. When the bank extends a loan, it does so by *creating* demand deposits for the loan recipient. The creation of those demand deposits requires nothing more than a set of entries in the bank's balance sheet.

Table 15A-2 shows the *changes* in your bank's balance sheet when it extends an $80 loan. This bank need not worry about holding reserves against the newly created demand deposits because the loan recipient will soon draw a check on those deposits to finance his or her spending. (Why else would he or she pay interest to borrow?) The recipient of the loan applicant's spending will deposit that check in *his* or *her* own bank.

TABLE 15A-2 CHANGES IN A BANK'S BALANCE SHEET WHEN IT EXTENDS AN $80 LOAN

Assets	Liabilities
Loans + $80	Demand + $80 deposits

An Increase in Reserves

Backtrack a moment now and look in more detail at your original $100 deposit. Suppose that the $100 represented the payment you received when you sold a government bond to the Federal Reserve System (the Fed, as you know, regularly buys and sells government bonds). In exchange for the bond, the Fed would have given you a check, drawn on itself, for $100. It was when you deposited that $100 check that your bank's demand deposit liabilities were increased by $100. By sending that check back to the Fed, your bank would have its reserve account with the Fed credited for $100 of added reserves.

By purchasing a bond from you, the Fed has increased the volume of reserves available to your bank and to the entire commercial banking system by $100. With a 20 percent reserve ratio, the volume of demand deposit *money* can

increase by a multiple of the increase in reserves—five times the increase in reserves—before all available reserves will be tied up as required reserves.

As we have already seen, with $100 of new demand deposit liabilities, $100
of new reserves, and a 20-percent reserve ratio, your bank has $80 of excess
reserves which it can lend, creating $80 more of new demand deposits in the
process. But that is not the end of the money expansion process. When our $80
loan recipient spends his loan proceeds, the recipient of that spending will deposit the $80 check he receives in his own bank. As a consequence, that bank's
demand deposit liabilities and its reserves are increased by $80. With a 20-percent
reserve ratio, this second bank has $64 of excess reserves which it can lend. On
making a $64 loan, it creates $64 of new demand deposit money which, when
spent, will be transferred to a third bank which, in turn, will have some $51 of
excess reserves, and so it goes. The total increase in money supply due to the Fed
purchase of a $100 bond would be:

$$\Delta M = \$100 + \$80 + \$64 + \$51.20 + \$40.96 + \cdots$$

or

$$\Delta M = \$100 \ [1 + .8 + (.8)^2 + (.8)^3 + (.8)^4 + \cdots].$$

The geometric series in the brackets can be readily summed [1] to give

$$\Delta M = \$100 \left(\frac{1}{1 - .8}\right) = \$100 \left(\frac{1}{.2}\right) = \$500.$$

With the reserve ratio value of .2, a $100 increase in reserves (high-powered
money) resulted in a $500 increase in the money stock. With excess reserves
available to the banking system, commercial banks literally create money with
the stroke of a pen as they extend loans. Clearly, if the central bank controls the
required reserve ratio (try a reserve ratio of .1 or .3) and the volume of reserves
available to the banking system, it can control the money stock. As a next logical
step in making our money supply model more general, we would want to take
account of the public's currency holdings and of the possibility that banks, at
times, may choose to hold some excess reserves. Those modifications are performed in the text.

---

1 Think back to the simple income multiplier process of Chapter 4.

Chapter 16
Implementing
Fiscal Policy

Until the Great Depression, the government sector of the economy was quite small. Total government receipts during the 1920s were less than 10 percent of GNP and federal government receipts were less than half of the total. The government budget philosophy was one of alleged "fiscal responsibility"—it was tacitly assumed that a government budget should be balanced annually.

It is fortunate that the government budget was small during that period. With equality between tax receipts and expenditures *required*, the decline in tax receipts experienced during a business contraction would require a reduction in government spending or an increase in tax rates, while the growth in tax receipts during expansions would call for increased government spending or reduced tax rates. This budget philosophy is clearly pro-cyclical, tending to amplify the strength of an ongoing contraction or expansion.

With government budgets of the size we have had since the Depression, attempting to maintain an annually balanced budget would have been highly destabilizing. Since the 1930s, though, there has been a growing recognition of the need, at the federal level, of *compensatory finance* policies of the type rationalized by Keynes' *General Theory*. As we already know, Keynesian analysis calls for increased government spending or reduced tax collections when income is falling and for reduced government spending or increased taxes during excessive expansions—conscious actions that lead to budget imbalances. As large as the federal government's economic role is today, such compensatory finance policies can have a powerful effect on the level of general business activity.

COMPENSATORY BUDGETS—TWO FORMS OF FISCAL RESPONSE TO INCOME CYCLES

A government that deliberately alters tax rates and planned outlays in an effort to stabilize the economy is practicing what is termed *discretionary* fiscal policy. But, in addition to discretionary adjustments in taxes and outlays, there are some *automatic* tax and outlay changes that act to dampen fluctuations in income—automatic in the sense that they occur in response to a change in the level of GNP without any deliberate (discretionary) action by government. Logically enough, these automatic changes in taxes and revenues are called *automatic stabilizers* or *built-in stabilizers*.

The Major Automatic Stabilizers

The two main automatic stabilizers for the U.S. economy are the federal income tax and the government income transfer programs, particularly unemployment compensation and welfare payments. As GNP falls during a contraction, some taxpayers find their income dropping below the taxable level, others fall into lower tax brackets, and taxes (whatever the percentage rate) are levied against a small income base. Thus, federal tax revenues are reduced as GNP falls. This is, of course, the direction in which tax collections should move to counter a contraction in economic activity. Conversely, when GNP is rising many taxpayers are shifted into progressively higher tax brackets, some who previously had no taxable income become taxable, and given percentage tax rates are levied against a larger income base. Once again, federal tax revenues move in the direction required for stabilization.

On the transfer side, the most important stabilizer is unemployment insurance. During a contraction of business activity, insured workers who become unemployed are eligible for unemployment compensation benefits. Such transfers help to maintain disposable income (thus, consumption spending) as GNP falls. During expansions of business activity employment increases and unemployment compensation declines.[1] Other forms of transfer payments (including old-age and survivors' insurance, public assistance, and other "welfare" payments) also tend to vary countercyclically, government outlays rising when GNP falls and falling when GNP rises.[2]

The existence of automatic stabilizers makes cyclical fluctuations in GNP smaller than they otherwise would be. (In terms of the models we have built, the size of any multiplier is reduced by the existence of a budget structure that includes U.S.-type tax and transfer programs.) But while they act to reduce the size of cyclical fluctuations in GNP, built-in stabilizers clearly cannot prevent such cycles since the automatic changes in taxes and transfers are *induced*— they occur only if and when GNP has already changed.[3]

---

1 Unemployment compensation is a joint federal-state program. The program is state administered but must be run in a manner that meets federal approval. Also, the federal government holds the program's accumulated reserves in the Employment Insurance Trust Fund. These transfers are available for 6 months in most states with an additional 3 months of benefits available nationwide when the national unemployment rate remains above 4½ percent for more than 3 months. Moreover, in 1974 Congress exhibited a willingness to provide additional unemployment assistance during periods of *aggravated* unemployment. In that year Congress temporarily authorized 13 weeks of "special unemployment assistance" in an area when, for 3 months, the national unemployment rate has been 6 percent or greater or the area unemployment rate has been 6.5 percent or greater.

2 While you are thinking about automatic stabilizers, you should recall that the monetary dampener also serves to stabilize the economy. For example, with output growing, the interest rate climbs, reducing investment spending and, consequently, reducing the strength of the business expansion. While our focus in this chapter is on fiscal policy, we should not forget the role of the monetary sector.

3 While the automatic stabilizers work without discretionary government action, the tax and

Automatic Stabilizers and the Budget Surplus (Deficit)

Since federal tax receipts and outlays vary automatically in response to changes in business activity, the size of the federal budget surplus or deficit changes automatically with every change in GNP. With the *rates* for tax liabilities and for transfer payments given, the federal budget will show a larger surplus or smaller deficit (due to larger tax revenues and reduced transfer payments) for higher levels of business activity and a smaller surplus or larger deficit (due to reduced tax revenues and increased transfer payments) for depressed levels of business activity.

Figure 16-1 illustrates the effect on the government budget of a change in the level of business activity, assuming that no discretionary changes in taxes or transfers occur as GNP changes. For the hypothetical budget structure reflected in Figure 16-1, an unemployment rate of 8 percent, representing a quite depressed level of economic activity, would result in a $10 billion deficit. With business activity at a less depressed level, corresponding, say, to 4 percent unemployment, the deficit would be some $2½ billion. If business activity expanded so that only 2 percent of the labor force were unemployed, assuming that such an unemployment level is attainable, the federal budget would show a surplus of some $2 billion. Because of those government tax and outlay programs that act as built-in stabilizers, net taxes (taxes minus transfers) and the actual *measured* surplus or deficit vary with the prevailing level of income and employment.

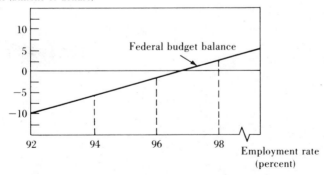

FIGURE 16-1 Employment and the Budget Surplus (Deficit)

---

transfer programs that provide automatic stabilization are the result of earlier legislation. These tax and transfer programs were established with goals other than economic stability in mind, their contribution to the smoothing of business cycles being purely a by-product of their basic function.

More on Discretionary Fiscal Policy

Discretionary fiscal policy entails a change in the *structure* of the government budget. A discretionary change in tax schedules alters the volume of tax revenues collected at any selected level of economic activity; a discretionary change in government transfer programs results in a changed level of transfer payments at any level of business activity; and so on. Thus, a discretionary fiscal policy action *shifts* the schedule in Figure 16-1 that shows the federal budget balance associated with different levels of business activity. For example, a discretionary increase in taxes (by, say, a reduction in the exemption level or by an across-the-board increase in percentage tax rates) would shift the budget balance schedule upward to reflect an increase in the surplus (decrease in the deficit) that accompanies any level of economic activity.

In Figure 16-2, there are two schedules representing, with different sets of government tax and outlay programs, the state of budget balance associated with different levels of business activity. If schedule *A* in Figure 16-2 accurately reflects the relationship between employment and the budget balance prior to a discretionary fiscal policy action, a budget shift in the direction of schedule *B* could result from a discretionary increase in taxes, a discretionary reduction in transfer payments, or a discretionary reduction in government spending. Reversing the direction of the discretionary change in tax structure or outlays would shift the schedule representing the budget balance downward (as from schedule *B* toward schedule *A*).

During an extended contraction, the appropriate fiscal response of a movement *toward* budget deficit can result, obviously, from discretionary policy actions as well as from an automatic response in tax receipts and government outlays. Conversely, during an overly rapid expansion, discretionary policy actions can produce the movement *toward* budget surplus that stabilization requires. Of the two budget postures (reflecting, again, a given set of government tax, trans-

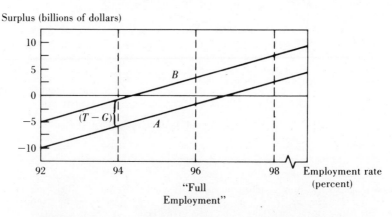

FIGURE 16-2 Discretionary Fiscal Policy and the Budget Surplus

fer, and expenditure programs) represented in Figure 16-2, budget *A* is clearly more expansionary than budget *B* since the budget deficit is larger (surplus smaller) at every level of economic activity with budget *A*.

MEASURING THE IMPACT OF FISCAL POLICY— THE FULL EMPLOYMENT SURPLUS

Historically, the degree of stimulation (or restriction) of economic activity stemming from fiscal policy has been regarded as dependent on the size of the *observed* budget surplus or deficit. The budget has been popularly regarded as stimulative when in deficit (government outlays exceeding revenues) and restrictive when accruing a surplus. A glance back at Figure 16-2 should convince us that observed surpluses or deficits are poor measures of the impact of fiscal policy. Because the observed surplus or deficit is the result both of the structure of the budget and of the current level of economic activity, it is impossible to obtain a clear-cut judgment on the impact of fiscal policy from the currently measured surplus or deficit. A budget deficit may just reflect a depressed level of economic activity rather than a stimulative fiscal policy program —hence, the very same budget structure might be judged restrictive, expansionary, or neutral depending on the prevailing level of economic activity.

The *relative* impact of two alternative fiscal policy programs can be judged by comparing the surplus (or deficit) generated by those alternative programs at a given level of employment. While this comparison can be made at any arbitrarily selected level of employment, the comparison is conventionally made at an assumed level of employment of 96 percent of the measured labor force. In the 1960s, this level of employment was assumed to approximate full employment and, as such, the resulting measure of budget posture was labeled the *full employment surplus*.

In Figure 16-2, budget *A* shows, at full employment, a deficit (negative full employment surplus) of some $3 billion while budget *B* yields just under a $4 billion surplus. With the larger full employment deficit under budget program *A* reflecting either larger government outlays or smaller tax revenues at any level of employment than under budget *B*, fiscal program *A* is *more* stimulative (or less restrictive) than program *B*. This conclusion, of course, does not rest on the observed government budget balance. Indeed, the great advantage of the full employment surplus as a measure of fiscal influence on the economy lies in its ability to separate discretionary changes in the budget from induced (automatic) budget balance changes. But the full employment surplus, while vastly superior to observed deficits and surpluses as a measure of fiscal posture, is still strictly limited—it only permits us to *compare* budgets to identify more or less expansionary budget programs. To go farther, to judge whether any particular budget program is compatible with noninflationary, full-employment equilibrium, we would need more information than is contained in a budget balance schedule.

We also would need to know the strength of private demand for consumption goods, investment goods, and net exports.[4]

When private demand is excessively buoyant, discretionary budget adjustments that provide a full employment surplus are called for. With unduly anemic private demand, discretionary fiscal policy actions that provide a full employ ment deficit are required. More specifically, if for simplicity we ignore the international sector of the economy, we know that commodity market equilibrium prevails only when planned injections into the income stream (investment and government spending) are equal to leakages (private saving plus net tax revenues) from that stream. That is, the equilibrium condition is $I + G = S + T$ or, rearranging, $I - S = T - G$. If, with output at the full employment level, planned saving exceeds planned investment (a private sector surplus), then equilibrium can prevail only if government spending exceeds net tax revenues (a government sector deficit at full employment). If full-employment planned saving falls short of planned investment (a private sector deficit), equilibrium would prevail only if net tax collections exceed government spending (a public sector surplus). For a budget structure that yields government budget balance at full employment to be compatible with full employment equilibrium, the private sector must be planning to invest and save equally (private sector budget balance) at full employment.[5]

Redirecting attention to Figure 16-2, with the budget structure represented by schedule A, were the economy in equilibrium with 6 percent unemployment, the measured budget deficit $(T - G)$ would correspond to an equal excess of planned saving over planned investment. While the budget would be permitting a sizable measured deficit, it could not legitimately be called expansionary since it permits the 6-percent unemployment level of output to remain the equilibrium level. But with a sizable increase in planned investment, the same budget would permit demand-pull inflation! The only budget consistent with full-employment equilibrium is one that fills the gap between full-employment output and aggregate demand. It goes without saying that the budget structure which fills that gap, providing full employment equilibrium, is not independent of the stance of monetary policy since money supply changes also alter private demand. Our next task is to see how budget adjustments that can contribute to economic stability are implemented.

THE BUDGETARY PROCESS

Early each year, usually in January, the President sends his budget recommendations for the following fiscal year to Congress. (Traditionally the fiscal

---

4 For a more detailed discussion of the full employment surplus concept and its limitations, see Alan S. Blinder, *Fiscal Policy in Theory and Practice* (Morristown, N.J.: General Learning Press, 1973), pp. 6-12.

5 James Tobin has clearly and elegantly explained the link between private demand and budget posture in "Deficit, Deficit, Who's Got the Deficit?", *National Economic Policy*, Yale University Press, 1966.

year ran from July 1 through June 30 of the following year but it shifted in fiscal 1976 to the October 1 through September 30 period.) His budget proposal is the result of a full 10 to 12 months of preparatory work involving the interaction of his office with the U.S. Office of Management and Budget (OMB—formerly called the Bureau of the Budget) and with affected government departments and agencies. The Council of Economic Advisers and the Treasury assist in the budget formulation process, advising on the feasibility of particular programs and on the *overall* budget impact of those programs.

Upon receipt of the President's budget recommendations, various subcommittees of the Appropriations Committee of the House of Representatives go to work separately, reviewing, debating, and revising components of the original budget bill. The resulting recommendations are reported to the full Appropriations Committee which, in turn, reports its own actions to the entire House of Representatives. After the House passes its version of the budget, it must still be sent to the Senate for consideration. In the Senate a sequence like that in the House ensues, with subcommittees, full committees, then the entire Senate considering the budget. If the Senate's version of the budget differs from that of the House, the bill is resubmitted to committee. When both houses of Congress approve a common budget bill, that bill is sent to the President who can approve (sign the bill into law), veto, or allow the bill to become law without his approval. It is easy to see why adoption of a budget proposal might take some time and how the resulting budget may be substantially altered from the President's proposed budget, both in the mix of public expenditures and in the overall size of the budget.

Once a budget bill has become law, appropriation warrants are forwarded to the affected departments and agencies who must revise their operating budgets to comply with approved appropriations. As the budgeted liabilities of the many government agencies accrue, the Treasury issues checks to cover them. Expenditure supervision is extensive—agency expenditures are reported regularly to the Office of Management and Budget with additional monitoring by the Treasury and the General Accounting Office (GAO).

Practical Limitations on Fiscal Policy— Problems of Timing and Budget Size

Our brief summary of the budgetary process indicates that a discretionary fiscal policy proposal must navigate a difficult, circuitous, and typically time-consuming course. By its very nature, this budgetary process is an impediment to the effective use of fiscal policy for stabilizing the economy. In addition, the state-constituency oriented concerns of Congress have been a serious impediment to the effective application of fiscal policy.

Fiscal policy is national in scope, the important fiscal policy variables being the overall level of tax rates and the level of planned government outlays. For stabilization purposes, changes in *specific* tax, transfer, or expenditure programs are normally important only to the extent that they affect overall tax and outlay levels. In stark contrast, a U.S. Senator or a member of the House of Representatives has as a primary concern specific tax changes and specific expenditure programs. His foremost fiscal concern is with the impact on *his constituency* of specific budget proposals—for example, with the level of government spending in his region on dams, highways, and military installations, and with the fairness to his constituency of proposed tax and transfer programs. The overall level of taxes and outlays is of distinctly secondary concern to him. Because a major budget package consists of many individual programs that have different impacts on different regions and groups, the time-consuming bargaining and compromise process in which Congress involves itself is inevitable. In that process, it is easy to lose focus on the stabilization objectives of the overall budget. As a consequence, Congress can and often has provided budgets that must be characterized as woefully inappropriate for stabilization needs.

The 1974 Reform of the Budget Review Process

In 1974, legislation was adopted to alter the Congressional budget review process. That legislation, which was scheduled to become fully effective in fiscal 1976, requires Congress to initiate its role in the budget-making process by setting an overall expenditure goal and by specifying target levels for expenditures on each major functional category in the budget. The initial budget resolution which provides those totals must be completed by May 15 each year and must also include a target for federal revenues with a recommendation for any discretionary changes in tax schedules deemed necessary.

With the guidelines provided by the first budget resolution, individual Congressional committees proceed as before in considering individual budget proposals and presenting them to appropriations committees. When the appropriations committees have completed their deliberations, the full Congress must review the overall budget results and make any adjustments required for consistency with stabilization objectives.

Timing Problems Remain

Whether, by diverting Congressional attention from the piecemeal consideration of individual budget bills to the size of the overall budget, the new budget review process will succeed in producing fiscal programs that are more appropriate for stabilization purposes remains to be seen. But even if budget bills that provide the degree of fiscal stimulus or restraint that is judged appropriate for stabilization purposes are ultimately provided, the time required for their passage can still be so long that fiscal policy's usefulness as a countercyclical weapon is seriously compromised.[6] In assessing the timing limitations on fiscal

---

6 In point of fact, the 1974 reform has probably added to the timing problems of fiscal policy. To compensate for the added Congressional review in the reformed budget process, as mentioned earlier the fiscal year will (beginning in fiscal 1976) start on October 1 instead of July 1, permitting the addition of some 3 months to the interval consumed in passage of the budget bill.

policy, we can use the same breakdown of the overall policy lag time as we did with monetary policy. The overall lag is just the sum of the three component lags—recognition, administrative, and operational—with the first two comprising the inside lag and the last the outside lag.

There is little reason to think that the recognition lag has to be much different for fiscal policy than it is for monetary policy since the same data series on economic activity are available to both fiscal and monetary authorities. But, as we have seen, the same claim cannot be made for the administrative lag. In practice, the administrative lag has been long enough to convince many analysts that fiscal policy cannot be effectively employed to combat short-run fluctuations in economic activity. However, there are techniques of providing discretionary fiscal actions which can shorten that lag. As a first step, it has long been argued that institutional reforms are needed to separate as much as possible the formulation of national income policy (overall tax and outlay levels) from the establishment of specific tax programs and from the detailed allocation of budgeted expenditures to particular programs. The 1974 reform of the budget review process reflects formal, legislative recognition of the need for that separation. With recognition of that need, it is possible to design fiscal actions that affect the level of economic activity while minimizing the involvement of Congress in debates over questions of tax equity and resource allocation. The 10-percent surcharge on income taxes adopted during the Johnson administration reflects an effort to take advantage of that separation. While a surcharge on taxes raises the entire structure of tax rates, it leaves the progressive nature of the tax structure, the distribution of tax liabilities across the population, and the allocation of government outlays essentially unchanged. Even so, it took Congress a year and a half to impose the 10-percent surcharge in July 1968 after President Johnson requested it as an anti-inflation weapon early in 1967.

In recognition of the difficulty Congress has in quickly providing the fiscal policy actions appropriate for combating short-run income fluctuations, there have been proposals to transfer that responsibility to an automatic rule or to another part of government. One set of proposals suggests that the budget should be changed by formula. For example, Congress might establish a rule that all income taxes would automatically be raised by 10 percent when the unemployment rate falls below $4\frac{1}{2}$ percent, and fall by 10 percent when unemployment rises above 5 percent. Congress could make the formulas as simple or complex as desired with taxes and outlays changing automatically when unemployment, prices, production levels, and so on move past predetermined limits. But, again, automatic (induced) changes in the budget can only reduce the size of unwanted fluctuations in economic activity, not prevent them. Moreover, constructing a rule that would provide the correct fiscal adjustment to the array of disturbances that can affect an industrialized economy is a task of awesome complexity (shades of the rules versus discretion arguments in Chapter 15). As an alternative, Congress could grant the President authority to change tax rates and expenditure levels within prescribed limits to help stabilize the economy. In fact, both Presidents Kennedy and Johnson asked for that authority during their terms in office. Perhaps the major difficulty with this proposal is political. Congress has jealously guarded its power to control taxes and expenditures. So far, it has refused to delegate any of that power to another branch of government so the administrative lag remains a major stumbling block in the successful application of discretionary fiscal policy.

The final lag in applying stabilization policy, the outside or operational lag, *can* be far less troublesome with fiscal policy than with monetary policy. A personal income tax change can alter disposable income with little delay—a change in withholding rates will be reflected in the next paycheck. Of course, as our analysis of consumption behavior demonstrated, the size of the consumption response to an income tax change depends crucially on whether the public perceives that tax change as temporary or permanent. A 10-percent tax surcharge or tax rebate that is explicitly temporary may have little impact on aggregate demand even though disposable income can be quickly altered by such a tax change.

In contrast, fiscal legislation that calls for an altered level of expenditures on public works projects directly changes aggregate demand but with a longer lag. An increase in public works projects requires a planning period, the issuance of contracts, and so on. Moreover, a cutback in public works expenditures is inefficient (should projects be left unfinished?) and often not politically feasible. To relieve partly the extended outside lag, it has been suggested that the government maintain an inventory of carefully preplanned projects. The funding for such "off-the-shelf" projects could be increased or decreased as required for stabilizing the economy.

Changes in the corporate tax rate or in the size of the investment tax credit also suffer from significant lags since they function by prompting revisions in investment commitments. But government expenditure on labor could be changed quite quickly.

Just how quickly or slowly do changes in taxes and government spending affect the economy? It should come as no surprise that the precise timing of impact of tax and expenditure changes cannot be assessed with certainty. But modern research with empirical models of the aggregate economy suggests that both tax and expenditure changes have some affect on equilibrium output within the first quarter after the policy action and that within 1 year either policy action strongly affects economic activity. The most comprehensive econometric models of the economy (the Brookings Model, the Wharton Model, and the Federal Reserve–MIT Model) exhibit general agreement on the strength and timing of fiscal policy actions. For example, the consensus from these models is that a $1 billion increase in government spending can be expected to raise GNP by $1 to $1½ billion within the quarter in which government spending rises and by some $2½ to $3 billion after 2 years.[7]

7 See Alan S. Blinder, *Fiscal Policy in Theory and Practice, op. cit.*, p. 19. Also see Michael K. Evans, *Macroeconomic Activity* (New York: Harper & Row, 1969), Chapter 18.

What overall assessment have we obtained on the usefulness of fiscal policy as an anticyclical tool? While we have noted that some analysts think our political institutions require an administrative lag that is too long to permit the use of fiscal policy for offsetting short-run fluctuations in economic activity, probably most economists are more optimistic. Indeed, the many supporters of active fiscal policy use argue that, even now, the lags involved in applying discretionary fiscal policy are often quite short and, with relatively minor institutional changes, could become inconsequential. Since empirical evidence suggests that budget changes do have a strong effect on output within a few months, they argue that fiscal policy can be relied on perhaps even to "fine tune" the economy's expansion path. With the growing recognition among members of Congress of the need for reforms that permit the active use of the budget as a stabilization weapon, we may in the future get to test the full stabilization potential of fiscal policy. In the meantime, few economists would argue against the benefits of discretionary fiscal actions when the economy is faced with a major recession or inflation.

U.S. FISCAL POLICY PHILOSOPHY

Since passage of the Employment Act of 1946, which declares that "... it is the continuing policy and responsibility of the Federal Government ... to promote maximum employment, production, and purchasing power," conventional wisdom has held that the U.S. fiscal policy philosophy is one of activism—one that accepts managed, compensatory tax and outlay changes as necessary for economic stability. While not denying the importance of automatic stabilizers, such a philosophy recognizes the need for discretionary changes in budget policy.

As we already know, if fiscal policy is to be used for stabilization purposes, the federal budget sometimes must be in deficit and sometimes must show a surplus—budgetary balance cannot be a concern. Looking at the 10 peacetime years between 1954 and 1965, we find that the federal budget was in deficit for 7 of the 10 years. Since that period was wracked by three recessions and plagued by slow growth, one might conclude that the observed deficits reflected efforts to stimulate economic activity through the active use of fiscal policy. However, during that same period the full employment budget showed a surplus *every year*—the measured deficits occurred because output remained chronically below the full employment level. Rather than representing the active application of Keynesian stabilization prescriptions, fiscal policy during that period might be termed passive at best and absolutely repressive if a less charitable view is taken.

The Era of the New Economics

President Kennedy's Council of Economic Advisers in the early 1960s recognized the drag which the sizable inherited full employment surplus imposed on economic activity. On their advice, Kennedy asked for and received Congressional approval for some modest expansionary fiscal actions in 1962. In that year, the 7 percent tax credit on investment was introduced and depreciation guidelines were liberalized to permit *accelerated* depreciation of capital assets—both of those actions designed to stimulate investment spending. In addition, there was some acceleration in the pace of federal spending. But far more importantly, in January 1963 President Kennedy asked for large reductions in both personal and corporate income tax levies even though the *observed* budget was already in deficit. After extended debate, Congress implemented that request in 1964 (a few months after Kennedy's death).

Through the 1960s, Keynesian economists lauded the major Kennedy-sponsored tax cuts as the first serious attempts at applying Keynesian fiscal prescriptions and pointed with pride at the strong, virtually inflation-free expansion in economic activity which accompanied those actions. With passage of the 1964 tax recommendations, the full employment surplus was cut by over $10 billion, and with that fiscal stimulus unemployment fell from its 1964 level of 5.2 percent until, by 1966, it was at the 4-percent level then associated with full employment. Indeed, by the beginning of 1966 the United States was entering its sixth consecutive year of uninterrupted expansion and claims that the business cycle was dead, vanquished by the application of modern, Keynesian stabilization policies, were commonplace. Unfortunately, that point in time marked the pinnacle of achievement for the *new economics* and the economy has not since enjoyed the gratifying combination of full employment, rapid growth, and price stability.

The Vietnam War and Its Aftermath

In 1965, a new source of fiscal stimulus appeared which had nothing to do with, indeed was at odds with, stabilization policy. In the 1965–1968 period, government expenditures were increased rapidly, both because of the war buildup in Vietnam and because of a sizable expansion in social program ("Great Society") outlays. In the face of quickening inflation in 1966, Congress temporarily suspended the 7-percent tax credit on investment, a modest action which was more than offset by increases in government spending. However, because monetary policy was quite restrictive, a general slowdown in economic expansion and a marked decline in construction developed toward the end of 1966. Fearful of stifling the prolonged economic expansion that had been underway since the beginning of the decade, Congress quickly restored the investment tax credit and the Federal Reserve eased monetary policy. With that policy reversal, the spectre of inflation reappeared.

Growing inflationary pressures finally prompted President Johnson to ask Congress for an income tax surcharge in January 1967. After an extended debate centering on the relative merits of an expenditure cut versus a tax increase, the Congress in June of 1968 provided a 10-percent surtax coupled with a planned expenditure cut of some $6 billion (holding outlays to $180.1 billion for the fiscal year). But the apparently strong shift toward fiscal restraint (the full employment budget shifted toward surplus by more than $27 billion from the first half of 1968 to the second half of 1969) failed to have the expected depressing effect on the economy. Unemployment remained below 4 percent and the inflation rate actually accelerated through the fourth quarter of 1969. With the tax surcharge extended for a second year, the investment tax credit once again repealed, and a strong shift toward monetary stringency beginning in the first half of 1969, a substantial slowdown in economic activity began to surface by the end of 1969. However, with well-entrenched inflationary expectations, the *deliberately engineered* slowdown in economic activity that began at the end of 1969 did not immediately slow inflation to an acceptable rate. Even so, it did lead to the elimination of generalized excess demand as the source of inflation pressure. The degree of slack introduced into the economy was reflected in an increase in the unemployment rate from the 3.5-percent average of 1969 to over 6 percent by the end of 1970.

While a tax relief and reform bill passed in December 1969, coupled with the June 1969 expiration of the surtax and an increase in government outlays, shifted the full employment budget toward a less restrictive posture, the full employment budget still showed a sizable $7.6 billion surplus for all of 1970. With a 6-percent unemployment rate judged to be intolerably high, even stronger doses of expansionary fiscal policy were applied in 1971. The expansionary policies included the introduction of more liberal capital depreciation guidelines for tax purposes, reenactment of an investment tax credit, a personal income tax cut, and a sizable increase in government outlays. It was hoped that the tightwire-walking attempt to lower unemployment and inflation *simultaneously* could be pulled off with the help of wage-price controls. Gratifyingly, through 1972 employment and output rose briskly while the inflation rate declined. Unfortunately, though, the honeymoon was short-lived. The confrontation of swelling demands, fueled by a worldwide inflationary boom, with large-scale crop failures and critically short supplies of basic materials and energy sources, put strong upward pressure on prices during 1973 and 1974. In addition, the depreciation of the dollar in foreign exchange markets raised the prices of imported goods and transferred demand to domestic production. While both fiscal and monetary authorities might have better anticipated some of the special events that renewed inflationary pressures in 1973 and accentuated them in 1974, it is hard to imagine what stabilization policies might have achieved a markedly lower rate of inflation without massively increasing unemployment. In fact, restraint on aggregate demand in 1974, achieved primarily through a marked reduction in the rate of monetary expansion, raised unemployment to over 7 percent of the labor force at the close of 1974 while "double-digit" inflation continued. Of course, theoretical arguments and empirical observations suggest that, with a lag, the slack which restrictive stabilization policies introduced during 1974 would slow inflation and in the early months of 1975 the public received the good news that inflation was moderating. The accompanying bad news was the reason! During the last quarter of 1974 and the first few months of 1975, the economy was experiencing its sharpest and most persistent contraction since the Depression. So abrupt was the contraction that it prompted a dramatically rapid reversal of stabilization strategy by the Ford administration. After calling for restrictive policies (including a 5 percent income tax surcharge) to combat inflation in October 1974, the Ford administration sensibly reversed its stance and requested a modest package of tax relief in January 1975. Just over 2 months later, Congress passed a $23 billion tax cut package that included a rebate on individual income taxes paid on 1974 income, a reduction in individual tax obligations in 1975, and an increase in the investment tax credit to a 10 percent rate for 2 years. Whether that fiscal package, in conjunction with an apparent effort by the Federal Reserve to step up the rate of money supply growth, will succeed in restoring full employment without rekindling the fires of inflation remains to be seen. When a similarly hazardous tightwire-walking task of stimulating economic activity while permitting the inflation rate to decline was faced in the 1971–1972 period, stabilization policy fell short of its goals. It must be hoped that we will not be as disappointed this time, but no one expects life to be easy for macroeconomic policy makers.

To briefly summarize the lesson on fiscal philosophy that can be drawn from our postwar experience, in just a few decades there have been major changes in accepted budget policy. From the view that government budgets should always be balanced we have come to accept the active use of discretionary fiscal policy as a basic tool of stabilization policy. It is noteworthy, as an indicator of the current commitment to modern fiscal theory, that a conservative, Republican President relied on the full employment budget concept in the early 1970s, to defend, as noninflationary, a budget that provided a sizable measured deficit. But despite the sophistication of today's *conventional wisdom* on the role of fiscal policy, much remains to be learned. More detailed information on the size and timing of impact of particular fiscal policy actions is needed. Improvements in the ability of policy makers to forecast the strength of private demand and, indeed, the level of future government spending are also essential. And, even with a much improved understanding of the influence of fiscal actions, the need for institutional reforms to permit a quicker fiscal response to economic developments remains.

FURTHER REFINEMENTS IN FISCAL THEORY— GOVERNMENT FINANCE WITH UNBALANCED BUDGETS

Recognition that stabilization policy can require a budget that is chronically out of balance forces us to be concerned with nontax methods of budget finance.

Actually, this subject was broached in Chapter 8 when we tried to distinguish carefully *pure* monetary and fiscal policies from *combination* monetary-fiscal policies. To refresh your memory by example, in that chapter a pure fiscal policy was defined as a government budget change that leaves an *exogenously* determined money supply unaltered—its impact in the aggregate model stemmed from a shift in the *IS* schedule. Now that our analysis has shown that the money supply is positively related to the interest rate, with the Fed able to exogenously control the volume of *reserves* made available to the banking system, we have to think of a pure fiscal policy as one that leaves the volume of reserves the Fed chooses to provide to the banking system (thus, the position of our *LM* schedule) unchanged. As before, the impact of a pure fiscal policy stems from a shift in the *IS* schedule. In contrast, a fiscal policy action can be financed in a way that alters the volume of reserves, such a combination fiscal-monetary policy involving a simultaneous shift in both the *IS* and *LM* schedules in the aggregate model.

At this point, we can profit by briefly reviewing and, in one new way, amplifying our earlier discussion of the ramifications of alternative techniques of financing unbalanced budgets. The amplification involves recognizing that an unbalanced budget produces a change in society's wealth by altering the volume of government debt it holds. With government purchases in excess of tax revenues, the public will acquire additional government bonds or money (interest-bearing or noninterest-bearing government debt) in the amount of the deficit. Conversely, with the government running a surplus, the public will lose ownership of government debt, bonds or money, in the amount of the surplus. If consumption demand responds positively to changes in society's wealth, the direct impact on aggregate demand of fiscal policy actions will be strengthened by the wealth effect that an unbalanced budget provides. For example, a fiscal policy action that directly increases aggregate demand (an increase in government spending, a reduction in tax collections, or both) can, through an enlarged deficit which increases society's wealth, provide additional stimulation by raising the consumption component of aggregate demand.

Deficit Finance

Turning our attention now to specific techniques of financing budget imbalances, we will first look at the consequences of financing an enlarged deficit by selling bonds to the public. When an increase in the budget deficit is financed by bond sales to the public, the public acquires government bonds in exchange for money. But when the Treasury spends the money proceeds of its bond sales it exactly restores the public's money holdings, leaving commercial bank reserves and the total money stock unchanged but leaving the public's wealth increased by the amount of the bond issue. While the wealth increase may reinforce any direct increase in aggregate demand (rightward shift in the *IS* curve) from the fiscal policy action, the *LM* schedule is unaffected by the deficit.[8] Fiscal actions that enlarge the deficit, as long as they are financed through bond sales to the public, still qualify as "pure" fiscal policies.

Our arguments are altered if the Treasury finances an increase in the deficit through bond sales to the central bank. In this case, the Treasury swaps bonds to the Fed for deposits (at the Fed) which it can spend by check. When the Treasury spends its new deposits to cover the deficit increase, it just transfers ownership of those deposits to the public by check. The recipients of the checks the Treasury draws on its account at the Fed, holders of new government debt, deposit those checks in their commercial bank demand deposit accounts providing additional reserves (in the amount of the deficit) to the banking system. Those new reserves can support a multiple expansion of the money supply. The increase in bank reserves, a debt of a government unit (the central bank), reflects the wealth increase the deficit bestows on the public. But more important is the increase in money supply that results from this technique of deficit finance. A fiscal policy action that generates a deficit becomes a combination fiscal-monetary policy if the deficit is financed through bond sales to the central bank. The rightward shift of the *IS* curve is accompanied by a rightward shift in the *LM* curve.[9]

Financing a deficit via bond sales to the central bank is equivalent to financing the deficit through the printing of new money (currency). In either case, society's wealth and the volume of reserve money available to the commercial banking system are increased by the amount of the deficit. Consequently, such bond sales are said to *monetize* the new government debt. As we already know, with a money supply increase combined with an expansionary fiscal policy, the interest rate rise that normally accompanies expansion is offset, permitting a stronger expansion than the same size pure fiscal policy would provide.

Surplus Finance

Just as fiscal actions can generate deficits, they can also generate surpluses. How the economy reacts depends in part on what the government does with its sur-

---

8   If the demand for money depends on the volume of wealth, any increase in wealth would shift the money demand schedule and, consequently, the *LM* schedule as discussed in Chapter 10. For an analysis of the impact of fiscal policy with money demand assumed to be a positive function of wealth, see W. Silber, "Fiscal policy in IS-LM Analysis: A Correction," *Journal of Money, Credit, and Banking*, Vol. II, November 1970, pp. 461-472.

9   As an example of just such a combination monetary-fiscal policy, when the Treasury offers large volumes of new bonds for sale in order to refinance maturing bond debt and cover any current deficit, the Fed pursues an "even-keel" policy of maintaining interest rates (bond prices). To maintain bond prices in the face of an increased supply of bonds, the Fed must willingly purchase bonds at the support price.

plus—on whether it is used to retire publicly held government bond debt, is used to retire bonds held by the central bank, or is just held idle.

With the tax bill, which the public pays to the government by check, exceeding government spending, the public's money holdings are reduced by the amount of the budget surplus. However, if the government uses that surplus to retire (buy back) government bonds held by the public, the same volume of money balances are returned to the public. Banking system reserves (and the *LM* curve) are left unchanged while the public's wealth is reduced by the amount of the surplus—that is, the amount its bond holdings have declined with this pure fiscal policy. Thus, a restrictive fiscal policy that generates an increased surplus is a pure fiscal policy if the surplus is used to retire publicly owned government bonds.

On the other hand, if the surplus money proceeds that the fiscal program provides are used to retire bonds held by the central bank, the money supply will decline by a multiple of the surplus. In this case, the Treasury, through a check drawn on an account it keeps in the commercial banking system, exchanges its surplus tax proceeds with the central bank for existing bonds. With that exchange, the commercial banking system loses reserves in the amount of the surplus inducing a multiple contraction of the money supply. The loss of reserves reflects society's wealth loss, but more important is the money supply shrinkage. With a reduction in reserves accompanying a restrictive fiscal policy (both *IS* and *LM* shifted leftward), the resulting contraction would be stronger than a pure fiscal policy would produce. These arguments continue to apply if the Treasury simply holds its surplus tax proceeds idle in its demand deposit account with the Fed. When the Treasury transfers deposits from its commercial banking system account to its Fed account, the banking system loses an equal volume of reserves, causing a contraction of the money supply. It makes little difference to the Treasury whether the budget surplus is actually used to retire bonds held by the Fed or is simply deposited in its account with the Fed. Each year the Fed returns its "profits" (which are substantial) to the Treasury, including interest revenues earned by the Fed on its government bond holdings.

In practice, virtually all stabilization policies are mixed monetary-fiscal policies. Still, those policy actions are separable into pure fiscal actions controlled by Congress (shifting only the *IS* curve) and monetary policy actions (shifting the *LM* curve) which are controlled by the Fed since the Fed can *independently* decide whether it wishes to be a net purchaser or seller of government bonds during any time period. Of course, the Fed may often act in a way that reinforces fiscal policy. An expansionary fiscal policy, we know, tends to increase interest rates. If the Fed wishes to hold down interest rates as an aid to economic expansion it must increase the money supply. In fact, as long as the Fed follows a policy of "leaning against the wind"—permitting the money stock to grow in an ostensibly "tight" money market in which the interest rate is rising and reducing the money stock in a slack market in which the interest rate is falling—its actions will reinforce fiscal policy.

DEFICIT FINANCE AND THE BURDEN
OF THE NATIONAL DEBT

With cumulative budget deficits that have exceeded cumulative surpluses, the difference financed largely through public bond sales, the United States has seen its *national debt* grow from just over $1 billion at the beginning of the century to around $493 billion at the end of 1974. While a large share of the existing government debt is the result of war financing, the budgetary effects of government investments and recession (particularly in recent years) have contributed substantially to the total. Should the use of fiscal policy for stabilization purposes necessitate chronic budget deficits in the future, the public debt will continue to mount.

For decades, "fiscally responsible" politicians and conservative editorialists have warned of the dire consequences of the "bankrupting" growth in national debt. If they are correct in suggesting that an increasing national debt imposes heavy burdens on society, policy makers should carefully weigh those burdens before deciding to employ fiscal policies that raise the debt.

As a background to examination of the burdens that debt finance can actually impose on society, we need to deal with a pair of ancillary issues that frequently intrude in discussions of the debt burden. First, we must disabuse ourselves of the notion that the government is just like a business firm. Too often, it seems, political commentators argue by analogy that the federal government, like a business firm, cannot indefinitely spend more than it collects in (tax) revenues without becoming bankrupt. But decidedly unlike a business firm, the federal government has virtually unlimited debt repayment power. Should it choose to fully retire the existing debt, though there is no reason why it should, it could do so through taxation or through the creation of new money—the government cannot go bankrupt. Furthermore, even the claim that business firms must have revenues that cover their full costs is patently absurd. Business firms can and often do borrow (run a deficit) as a normal practice. In fact, the growth in business debt in the United States since World War II has outrun the growth of the national debt.

The second ancillary issue arises because, historically, the debate among economists and other antagonists over the burden of debt-financed government spending has had a broad focus. In addition to analyzing the implications of bond as opposed to tax finance of a specific level of government spending, that debate has dealt with the productiveness of government resource usage. So that we can focus attention on the burdens that may result solely from the choice of bond issue as a means of financing government outlays, we first need to deal with the matter of the productiveness of government resource usage.

With the spending power gained through either tax levies or bond sales, the government can procure real resources (land, labor, and capital) for *public* use. With the economy operating at full employment, those resources have to be shifted from private use. Whether the resource transfer from private to public use imposes a burden on society depends on the benefits society reaps from that transfer. If the benefits from government resource use are greater than those that flowed from their private use, it is wrong to talk about that resource usage imposing a burden on society. If that is not the case, if government resource use is less productive than private use, a burden is imposed on society—aggregate economic welfare will be reduced. Again, this burden stems from an inefficient allocation of resources (more resources allocated to public use and less to private use than optimal allocation would call for) and is not dependent on the technique used for financing the government spending—it exists whether that spending is bond or tax financed.

On the other hand, if government spending (however it is financed) puts real resources to work which would otherwise be idle, the question of a burden from inefficient resource usage is moot. If production is raised by government resource usage (some real resources that would otherwise lie idle being used to provide goods and services) society's welfare is unequivocally enhanced by the government's spending, though some other method of mobilizing those resources might be preferred.[10]

Comparable arguments apply to concerns over the impact that current government resource usage has on the well-being of future generations—our children and grandchildren. Once again there is a burden from wasteful resource usage by government. If the government squanders real resources, some of which would have been used to enhance the economy's productive capacity, future generations inherit a reduced capacity to provide wanted goods and services. In fact, if the government's resource usage simply enhances current consumption at the expense of investment the same conclusion holds. On the other hand, if the government productively invests the resources it commands—for example, for school and highway construction, medical research, and parks—it is possible for future generations to enjoy a standard of living higher than would be provided without the resource transfer from private to public use. We must remind ourselves, though, that the burdens (or benefits) that flow to future generations as a direct result of current government resource usage are not the direct and unavoidable consequence of the technique chosen for financing government spending. Whether the government tax or bond finances the acquisition of productive resources, if it uses those resources less (more) productively than the private economy would have, future generations will be burdened (benefited).

---

10 At times stabilization actions employing government budget adjustments may be constrained (as they should be) by concern over their influence on resource allocation. See R. Musgrave, *The Theory of Public Finance* (New York: McGraw-Hill, 1959), pp. 517-520; and J. Margolis, "Public Works and Economic Stability," *Journal of Political Economy*, Vol. 57, August 1949, pp. 293-303.

Burdens from the Choice of Bond (Debt) Finance

We can now focus attention narrowly on assessing the burdens that may arise directly from the choice to finance some government outlays by bond sales rather than through tax levies. Of course, to the continuing dismay of fiscal conservatives, it is because of frequent reliance on debt issue to finance government outlays that by the end of 1974 the national debt had risen to the $493 billion level cited earlier. In their strident pleas for balancing the government budget, lay critics of deficit finance have often buttressed their offensive with emotion-packed statements of "fact." With a population of some 212 million, it could be claimed in 1974 that ". . . each man, woman, and child in the United States (even newborn babies) is saddled with more than $2300 in debt, whether he knows it or not." The intended imagery is clear. Since we as taxpayers bear ultimate responsibility for servicing the national debt, we and our children (and their children) owe for the national debt and our obligations grow with each successive budget deficit.

Fortunately, in spite of the visions of imminent economic ruin which they can evoke, the harshest critics of debt finance have clearly overstated their case for the burden of debt finance, leaving their arguments open to easy attack. It is true that as taxpayers we citizens of the United States are responsible for the national debt. And, with recurrent deficits, future generations will owe an enlarged debt. But the national debt, current and future, must be owed to someone and, for an internally held debt, that someone is the U.S. citizenry. United States citizens may face higher tax obligations because of a national debt, but in the *aggregate* those higher tax payments would be just matched by higher interest payments to U.S. citizens as long as the debt is domestically owned. For an internally held public debt, the tax obligation *burden* has often been dismissed by economists with the quip, "we owe it to ourselves"—with no externally held debt, future generations of U.S. citizens would both own (in the form of bonds) and owe (as taxpayers) the debt inherited from earlier generations. The mere creation of paper securities (bonds which are assets to the owners and equivalent liabilities to the issuer) can neither enrich nor impoverish a nation. Thus, it is far from obvious that increasing the national debt (the national *credit* held by bond-owning U.S. citizens) will alter the nation's accumulation of real wealth or its production of real goods and services.

Actual Burdens from Debt Finance

While the propositions in the preceding paragraph effectively disenfranchise the simplistic layman's notion of the manner in which debt-financing government spending may impose a burden on future generations, it would be a mistake to conclude that there are no such burdens. There are, and economists have long been concerned with them. To begin with, in response to the quip that "we owe it [the public debt] to ourselves," it is obvious that not all individuals or families hold interest-bearing government debt in proportion to the debt-servicing tax liabilities they face. Hence, even if on aggregation the taxes destined for paying interest on the inherited national debt are matched by interest receipts, there can be a distributional burden from servicing the debt. While the evidence is not clear-cut it is generally thought that bond holdings are concentrated in higher income groups so that the debt service tends to be regressive, redistributing income from lower to higher income groups (from taxpayers in general to bondholders). If servicing the debt increases income inequality, conflicting with the social objective of reducing inequality in the income distribution, a legitimate debt burden exists. However, it is usually agreed that quantitatively this burden is of relatively minor consequence in the United States.

As an additional burden, an increase in tax rates to service a growing debt may reduce national output through its "disincentive" effects. The higher are income tax rates, the smaller is the reward obtained by foregoing leisure and working more hours or working more intensively. If the federal debt grows at a faster rate than GNP, or if the interest yield government must offer on new security issues rises enough, an increase in tax rates to meet the interest charges on the debt could be required. However, the national debt has grown less rapidly than GNP since World War II (permitting a decline in the ratio of debt to GNP from 130 percent of GNP in 1945 to about 35 percent of GNP in 1974) and, in spite of an increase in interest rates to record levels in recent years, annual interest payments have barely edged above the range of 1½ to 2 percent of GNP in which they have resided for nearly 3 decades.

A third potential source of a burden which deficits can impose on future generations causes more concern among U.S. economists than the income redistribution and work disincentives which deficits may entail. To illustrate that source of burden, suppose the economy is operating at a noninflationary, full employment equilibrium with a balanced budget. Of course, for equilibrium the appropriate monetary policy stance (the correct size money stock) must prevail. Now, let government spending rise. The added expenditure would be inflationary but aggregate demand may be kept at the equilibrium level by an appropriate income tax increase with no monetary policy action. In that case, the higher use of resources by government would be at the expense of private consumption for the most part.

Alternatively, if the additional government spending is bond financed inflation can be avoided only by employing a restrictive monetary policy, which raises the interest rate to reduce aggregate demand. The higher interest rate simply frees the resources, primarily from private investment, that are required for government usage. But, with a reduction in investment spending on new plants and equipment, future generations will inherit a smaller capital stock. A burden of reduced productive capacity is transferred to future generations as a consequence of the choice to bond rather than tax finance a prescribed level of government spending.

There is general agreement among economists that the three potential burdens of (internal) debt finance that we have confronted are legitimate concerns. With somewhat less unanimity that list could be extended,[11] but with no further documentation the qualitative implications of the debt burden discussion are clear. There is some burden to debt finance and the burden may be transferred to future generations.

External Debt

So far we have restricted our discussion to consideration of a domestically owned national debt but, since a significant proportion of the U.S. debt is foreign held (approximately 12 percent at the end of 1974), the burden of an external debt deserves brief exploration. At first blush, it might seem that an external debt entails a far heavier burden than an internal debt. Rather than transferring command over an unchanged volume of productive resources among a country's citizenry, the tax levies for servicing an external debt transmit control over real resources to foreign debt holders. The output of real goods and services available for domestic use would be larger if the debt were forgiven. However, this argument ignores the international transfer of real resources that occurred when the foreign-held debt was issued. In exchange for U.S. government securities, foreign citizens gave up command (in the form of pounds, marks, yen, and so on) over foreign-owned real resources. The U.S. government used the acquired foreign currency purchasing power to acquire goods and services from abroad or exchanged that purchasing power with U.S. households and firms that wanted to buy foreign goods and services. In contrast to the internal debt case, the volume of real productive resources available for domestic use was enlarged by the debt sales abroad while no net change in the ownership of real resources occurred. In subsequent periods tax levies are required to service the foreign debt but the taxes are levied on an income that

---

11 In recent years, a growing body of adherents have adopted a fourth argument, championed by James Buchanan, in support of the claim that deficits transfer a burden onto future generations. According to this argument, whatever level of expenditures the government chooses, if it finances those expenditures through debt issue the bonds the government issues are *voluntarily* purchased by individual citizens and firms. The purchasers willingly surrender present command over real resources or privately issued securities because the return they expect to receive on their "investment" exceeds their subjective estimate of the yield foregone. Since all transactions are voluntary, it can be argued that no current burden is involved in the debt-financed transfer of productive resources from private to government use. But, according to Buchanan, the deficit does impose a burden on future generations. Since the private securities which government bond holders could have purchased offer yields that are little different from the yields on government bonds, the purchasers of the government bond issue will not be materially better off in the future because of the issuance of public debt. In contrast, the members of the future generation who are *coerced* into paying tax levies to finance the interest charges on the public debt are clearly worse off. In this sense, a burden is imposed on future taxpayers as a consequence of the choice to debt-finance current government spending. See James M. Buchanan and Marilyn R. Flowers, *The Public Finances* (Homewood, Ill.: Richard D. Irwin, Inc., 1975), Chapter 29.

is larger because of the exchange of government securities for real resources. Integrating resource allocation issues into the external debt discussion, if the imported resources were productively invested, future generations could be better off, even after allowance for the foreign debt service. In fact, governments of countries around the world regularly issue external debt expecting the resources acquired through that debt issue to lift domestic output by enough to repay the externally held debt and leave a residual for domestic enjoyment.[12] It is possible, of course, that the returns reaped from the use of resources acquired through foreign bond sales will not service the debt, leaving future generations worse off on balance. But, once again, that is because the resource usage was *unprofitable*, not because the debt was externally financed. For our purposes there is no reason to make a major distinction between internal and external debt issue.

Multiple Goals and the Coordination of Monetary and Fiscal Policies

Because debt finance does involve some burdens, it is reasonable to ask whether it is rational for the government to employ unbalanced budgets for stabilization purposes. As we know, both fiscal and monetary policy can be used to control the overall level of aggregate demand, so, in principle, it should be possible to maintain full employment equilibrium with a balanced budget. Hence, the ultimate justification for maintaining discretionary control over the state of budget balance must be the need to pursue more than just one policy goal at a time. The choice of an appropriate combination of monetary and fiscal policies must rest on the influence that choice has on secondary goals, including the economy's growth, the division of resource use between government and the private sector of the economy, the provision of housing, the maintenance of balance of payments equilibrium, and so on.

Under ideal conditions, the stabilization authorities would be able to maintain full employment equilibrium without relying on countercyclical changes in government spending. The volume of scarce productive resources which the government employs (by spending) would be determined on resource allocation grounds—however crudely the calculation of benefits must be made in practice, resources would be allocated to government production only to the extent that the benefits provided to society by government's *production* exceed the benefits that would accrue from private use of those resources. Inefficient variations in government spending (leaving projects unfinished when cutbacks occur and rushing into possibly ill-conceived projects when spending is accelerated) would be avoided. Of course, as long as discretionary control over taxes (hence over the state of budget balance) is maintained, the stabilization authori-

12 Does it make sense for business firms to finance the acquisition of capital goods externally?

ties would still have a fiscal policy tool available and the choice of a monetary-fiscal policy mix would have to be made.

As we know, whether government spending is used as a control tool or not, alternative combinations of monetary and fiscal policies have differing effects on the economy's growth path. Expansionary (restrictive) monetary policy lowers (raises) the interest rate while expansionary (restrictive) fiscal policy raises (lowers) the interest rate. If full employment is maintained by combining an expansionary monetary policy with a restrictive fiscal policy, the interest rate will be reduced. As a consequence, more of full-employment output will be allocated to investment, which contributes to future productive capacity, and less to current consumption. In contrast, a shift to a more restrictive monetary stance combined with a more expansionary fiscal policy would raise the interest rate, shifting resources out of investment and into current consumption use. The choice that the stabilization authorities make with regard to the *appropriate* combination of monetary and fiscal policy must be influenced by their preferences for current as opposed to future consumption standards and only by coincidence would the policy combination preferred on such grounds provide a balanced government budget.

Also, as indicated in Chapter 15, when designing a stabilization program consideration must be given to any restrictions that may impinge on monetary policy. Perhaps most importantly, it has been noted that monetary policy can have an uneven impact on various sectors of the economy. High interest rates have a particularly harsh effect on home construction, on state and local borrowing, and perhaps on small businesses. Concern over such side effects of countercyclical monetary policy has contributed to the growing degree of agreement in recent years that the monetary authorities should normally press for a relatively steady expansion of the money supply, avoiding excessive swings in the money stock's growth rate which would produce excessive variations in the interest rate. Moreover, with the advancing integration of world markets, monetary policy may be increasingly subjugated to the maintenance of external equilibrium. But if any constraint keeps one control tool from being used for domestic stabilization purposes, some other control device must be relied on to assume its role. In general, a separate control instrument is required for every target that must be pursued. With so many targets—full employment, price stability, rapid growth, external equilibrium, the provision of housing for a growing population, and so on—it is no wonder that the government has felt compelled to use every control instrument it has available without imposing an equality constraint on government spending and tax collections. Fiscal policy has borne and, in the foreseeable future, will continue to bear a substantial responsibility for stabilization policy. Of course, as we have explained fiscal policy has a number of limitations in the imperfect real world. In practice, the administrative lag has been a severe impediment to the active employment of budget adjustments for stabilization purposes. Moreover, variations in most lines of government spending involve an operational lag which can be quite extended unless a shelf of ready projects is maintained. As a consequence, both in principle and in practice, countercyclical variations in tax rates have received a great deal of attention in recent years. Of course, countercyclical tax changes that are clearly temporary can have a relatively weak impact on spending. But there is ample empirical evidence that tax variations which are not explicitly temporary have a prompt and substantial effect on aggregate demand. The many advocates of fiscal activism contend that the major impediments to successful fiscal policy are political rather than economic. The hope of the future is that, with continued refinements in our understanding of the macroeconomy and modest institutional reforms of the budget-changing process, we will be able to apply fiscal and monetary policy *in tandem* in the pursuit of economic welfare.

Monetary-Fiscal Policy Coordination in Practice

Since it is possible to design alternative monetary-fiscal policy combinations, which provide full employment equilibrium but impinge differently on other targets, the notion that the two types of policy action should be carefully coordinated seems obvious. But, that coordination can be hard to achieve since the responsibility for monetary control is largely separated from the responsibility for fiscal policy. While Congress has ultimate control over spending and tax collections, monetary policy is conducted by a quasi-independent Federal Reserve System—a system that was provided with statutory independence from the other branches of government, minimizing its sensitivity to political pressures so that it could employ monetary policy for the benefit of society at large.

As we have seen, in the immediate post-World War II period fiscal policy dominated monetary policy since monetary policy was directed at maintaining low interest yields (high prices) on government debt. With the *Accord* in 1951, the restriction of monetary policy to pegging interest yields on government securities was ended, and for the next several years, in fact until the 1960s, there was little overt interaction between the monetary and fiscal authorities as each followed its own course in assessing and responding to economic developments. Not until the Kennedy-Johnson era, during which improvement in the country's economic performance was energetically pursued, were conscious efforts made to coordinate monetary and fiscal policies. By the mid-1960s, systematic channels of communication had been established, and since then frequent meetings have taken place between the Chairman of the Board of Governors of the Fed and three important participants in the initiation and design of fiscal policy actions— the chairman of the Council of Economic Advisers, the secretary of the Treasury, and the director of the Office of Management and Budget (a group known as Quadriad). Of course, improved communications between monetary and fiscal authorities should not be expected always to provide agreement on what stabilization strategy is appropriate, and episodes of disagreement can be documented. During 1966, the Fed pursued a restrictive monetary policy in an effort to halt an emerging inflation. In contrast, it was not until 1967 that the Johnson administration called for fiscal restraint and more than another full year elapsed before Congress enacted restrictive legislation. Since that widely publicized disagreement between the monetary and fiscal authorities, the most dramatic indications of divergent views on needed stabilization strategies have been Congressional resolutions calling for a smoother expansion path of the money stock and, as the economy was suffering a rapid contraction, a call by Congress early in 1975 for an acceleration in the rate of monetary expansion. A variety of proposals for increasing the required degree of monetary-fiscal coordination have been aired, all of which involve some sort of reduction in the Fed's independence. Those proposals include making the tenure of the chairman of the Federal Reserve Board coincide with that of the President, requiring the Federal Reserve to maintain monetary growth rates within a spcified range set by Congress or the President, requiring the Fed to make semiannual reports to Congress of its plans for future monetary growth, and so on.

Of course, the coordination of monetary and fiscal policies need not result in correct policy actions. Following its restrictive efforts in 1966, the Fed cooperated with the fiscal authorities in 1967 and 1968, financing massive federal deficits and thus contributing to the acceleration of inflation as the money supply expanded vigorously during that 2-year period. In similar fashion, beginning in 1971 both fiscal and monetary policies were directed toward economic expansion, fueling the inflation that has persisted into the current period. Clearly, a great deal remains to be learned about the optimal strategy for economic stabilization. In the years ahead, you may contribute to improving the economy's performance by contributing to the understanding of the economy which is essential for rational policy design.

SUMMARY

In this chapter, we have tried to formalize and refine our understanding of *fiscal policy*—discretionary changes in the structure of the budget undertaken in the interest of stabilizing the economy. Our discussion showed that, once the structure of the government budget is established, changes in output automatically induce changes in tax collections and government outlays which act to damp fluctuations in output. Because of the programs that provide such automatic revenue and outlay responses—the so-called *automatic stabilizers*—if we want to compare the *relative* impact of two alternative budget structures, we have to compare the surpluses or deficits they would generate at a common output level. While this *full employment surplus* comparison provides a handy guide to the direction of change in fiscal policy, in order to go farther and determine what particular budget program is needed to provide full employment with stable prices a more detailed understanding of the structure of the private economy is needed. Only with that information can policy makers design a budget policy which, given the growth rate of the money supply, matches aggregate demand with the full employment capacity to produce.

A major complication in the active use of fiscal policy exists because of the potentially long lag between emergence of a need for fiscal stimulus or restraint and the effective application of the needed policy. While in recent years there has been a growing awareness in Congress itself of the need for streamlining the fiscal policy-making apparatus, the administrative lag remains the major impediment to the effective use of fiscal policy in countering income fluctuations. In addition, in the past the nature of the concerns of members of Congress has often left overall budget policy as a political orphan while attention was focused on the specific tax and outlay proposals that directly and intimately affect congressmens' constituents. With the budget reform of 1974, we can hope that in the future Congressional bargaining will result in an overall budget that is more closely attuned to stabilization needs.

Since the active use of fiscal policy requires the budget to frequently be out of balance, if fiscal policy is to be employed policy makers must be concerned with the implications of alternative government financing techniques. We have seen that the impact on the economy of a particular budget policy is stronger if any imbalance in the budget is financed in a way that alters the money supply. Attention was also focused on some potential burdens from deficit finance though we concluded that, in practice, the benefits from being able to pursue a larger number of targets when government can alter its spending and tax revenues independently are likely to outweigh the burdens involved in relying on debt finance to the degree that the United States has in the past. While policy makers need to be mindful of the burdens deficit spending can impose, particularly through the influence debt finance can have on capital accumulation, we would be ill advised to limit the use of discretionary fiscal policy by requiring a balanced government budget.

In closing this text, we must note that since the publication of Keynes' *The General Theory* in 1936, there has been a revolutionary change in our perception of the role of government in the economic process. The Keynesian notion that government should use its monetary and fiscal powers to influence the level of economic activity has become commonly accepted. Of course, we still have a great deal to learn about the response of the aggregate economy to policy actions. The needed improvement of our models of the economy is an ongoing task in which a large number of economists are currently involved. Only with better models and institutional reforms to make stabilization tools more effective will the government be able to improve its performance in contributing to economic welfare. But, even with the present state of knowledge, most economists believe that discretionary stabilization policy (both fiscal and monetary) has improved the performance of the U.S. economy. These feelings are well represented in a statement from Arthur Burns, chairman of the Board of Governors of the Federal Reserve System at the time this text was written. Burns argues that "Discretionary economic policy, while it has at times led to mistakes, has more often proved reasonably successful. The disappearance of business depressions, which in earlier times spelled mass unemployment for workers and mass bankruptcies for businessmen, is largely attributable to ... stabilization policies...." [13] Whether Burn's contention will appear reasonable or absurd by the time you read this text depends on the course which ongoing macroeconomic processes follow.

QUESTIONS

1. Popular wisdom apparently holds that all deficits are expansionary and all surpluses restrictive. Evaluate that belief.
2. Describe the nature of the lag in fiscal policy and explain how that lag influences the effectiveness of fiscal policy. What other impediment to the effective use of fiscal policy stems from the fact that Congress has control power over the budget?
3. Why can we not just rely on automatic stabilizers to control the economy? With those automatic stabilizers, what happens to the government budget over time and what happens to equilibrium income as a result?
4. Watch the newspapers and listen to radio and TV news for a statement on the dangers of the national debt. Evaluate that statement explaining carefully what is right or wrong with it. Are there legitimate burdens that stem from a national debt?
5. Use the full aggregate model to evaluate the effects of a stimulative fiscal policy consisting of an increase in government spending financed by bond sales to the central bank. What difference does it make how a deficit is financed?
6. Evaluate the effectiveness of a 10-percent surcharge on taxes. Be sure to address yourself to the importance of the perceived *permanence* of that tax.
7. Considering the current state of economic affairs, what fiscal policy would you prescribe for the next 6 months?
8. How would you characterize the overall stabilization program (fiscal and monetary) that has been effectuated in recent months?

SUGGESTED READING

Blinder, Alan S. *Fiscal Policy in Theory and Practice.* Morristown, N. J.: General Learning Press, 1973.

Board of Governors of the Federal Reserve System. "Federal Fiscal Policy, 1965-1972," *Federal Reserve Bulletin.* Vol. 59, June 1973, pp. 383-402.

"Budget Policy, 1958-1963," *Economic Report of the President.* Washington, D.C.: U.S. Government Printing Office, January 1962, pp. 77-84.

13 Letter from Arthur Burns to Senator William Proxmire, Vice Chairman of the Joint Economic Committee, reprinted in *Federal Reserve Bank of St. Louis Review*, Vol. 55, November 1973, pp. 15-22.

The Council of Economic Advisers. "Financing a Federal Deficit," reprinted in
W. L. Smith and R. L. Teigen (eds.). *Readings in Money, National Income, and Stabilization Policy*. Homewood, Ill. Richard D. Irwin, Inc.,
1974, pp. 312-315.

————. "The Full-Employment Budget," reprinted in A. Okun (ed.). *The
Battle Against Unemployment*. New York: W. W. Norton & Co., 1972, pp.
76-82.

————. "Toward a Flexible Tax Policy: Automatic and Discretionary Stabilizers," reprinted in A. Okun (ed.). *The Battle Against Unemployment*.
New York: W. W. Norton & Co., 1972, pp. 83-92.

Evans, Michael K. *Macroeconomic Activity*. New York: Harper & Row, 1969,
Chapter 18.

Heller, Walter. *New Dimensions of Political Economy*. New York: W. W. Norton & Co., 1967.

Lewis, Wilfred, Jr. *Federal Fiscal Policy in the Postwar Recessions*. Washington: Brookings Institution, 1962.

Musgrave, Richard A. *The Theory of Public Finance*. New York: McGraw-
Hill Book Company, 1959, Chapters 21-23.

Okun, Arthur M. *The Political Economy of Prosperity*. Washington: Brookings
Institution, 1970.

Pechman, Joseph A. *Federal Tax Policy*. New York: W. W. Norton & Co., 1971.

A Glossary of Terms and Concepts

Accelerated depreciation. A shortening of the guideline lives firms are allowed to use in calculating depreciation costs on capital assets.

Accelerator theory. An explanation of investment that links net investment to output (or its rate of change) through the production function.

Accommodating monetary policy. An expansion of the money supply to keep interest rates from rising and crowding out private spending when a stimulative fiscal policy is being applied.

Accord. An agreement between the Federal Reserve System and the Treasury which freed the Fed from the responsibility for pegging the interest rate at a low level to reduce the Treasury's borrowing costs. With the accord the Fed was able to resume the active application of monetary policy for stabilization purposes.

Adjustable peg. An international monetary system under which rates are pegged but adjustable under some circumstances. The IMF maintained such a system for almost two decades after World War II.

Aggregate demand. The total value of all planned purchases of final goods and services during a chosen period (usually a year). The sum of planned consumption, investment, government purchases, and net exports.

Aggregate demand schedule. A schedule showing the inverse relationship between the general price level and aggregate demand.

Aggregate supply. The total volume of real final goods and services provided to the product market each accounting period by businesses.

Aggregate supply schedule. The schedule, derived from the labor market and the economy's production function, which shows the relationship between the general price level and the volume of real goods and services business firms supply to the product market, holding constant the state of technology and the quantity and quality of nonlabor factor inputs.

Amplitude. The magnitude (peak to trough) of the business cycle.

Annually balanced budget. The requirement that government's outlays and tax revenues be kept equal every year.

Anticipations and intentions data. Survey questionnaire data on the expectations and purchase plans of households and business firms.

Appreciation. An increase in value. In foreign exchange, an increase in the foreign exchange value of a currency.

Arbitrage. The purchase of an item in one market for resale in a market where the price is higher. Arbitrage tends to equalize the prices of an item that prevail in different markets with allowances for transportation costs, risk, and so on.

Assets. Items that have value owned by a firm or individual.

501

Augmented labor. The affective volume of labor input in the production process adjusted for the influence of growth in labor productivity.

Automatic stabilizers. Automatic changes in tax revenue, outlays, interest rates, and so on that reduce the magnitude of the multiplier and, hence, reduce the size of expansions and contractions.

Autonomous consumption. That minimum level of consumption that is undertaken independent of the level of disposable income. In a linear consumption function, the autonomous component is the intercept.

Autonomous investment. That investment that is undertaken without regard to the level of economic activity.

Average product. Total output per unit of some variable factor input used to produce that product.

Average propensity to consume. The fraction of income that is spent on consumption goods.

Average propensity to save. The fraction of income that is saved.

Balance of payments. The difference between a country's payments to foreigners and its receipts from foreigners, reflecting all of the international economic transactions of a country and its citizens during a particular time period.

Balance of payments disequilibrium. A balance of payments surplus or deficit which cannot persist indefinitely.

Balance of trade. The portion of a country's overall balance of payments which focuses on exports and imports. A balance of trade surplus, often referred to as a "favorable" balance of trade, exists when exports exceed imports. There is a balance of trade deficit when imports exceed exports.

Balance sheet. A summary statement of a firm's financial condition showing what the firm owns (its assets), what it owes (its liabilities), and the residual net worth of the firm on a given date.

Balanced budget. A budget in which total revenues and total outlays are equal.

Balanced budget multiplier. A predictor of the impact on equilibrium income of an equal change in government spending and tax revenues. In commodity market models, the balanced budget multiplier has a value of one.

Barter. The exchange of goods and services for one another without the use of money.

Base year. A reference year employed for purposes of making comparisons.

Black market. An illegal market. With reference to wage-price controls a market in which a commodity or service is sold for more than the legal ceiling price.

Board of Governors of the Federal Reserve System. The seven-member board which supervises the Federal Reserve System. Members are appointed by the President for 14-year terms, one term expiring every 2 years.

Bond. A financial instrument entitling the holder to payments of interest and principal, generally at prescribed future dates. Both corporations and governmental units (federal, state, and local) issue bonds.

Business cycles. Periodic fluctuations in economic activity.

Capital. A produced means of further production (machinery, equipment, inventories, and structures). Human resources can be considered *human capital.*

Capital account. That part of the balance of payments that focuses on the purchase and sale of assets. The United States typically invests more abroad than foreigners invest in the United States, providing a deficit in the U.S. capital account.

Capital consumption allowance. A measure of the physical capital "used up" during the accounting period. Normal depreciation dominates this measure though the accidental destruction of capital goods is reflected also.

Capital deepening. With no change in technology, an increase in the quantity of capital employed with other resources.

Capital gain (loss). A change in the value of an asset that has not been altered.

Capital/output ratio. The amount of capital required per unit of output. This concept is applied in both a *total* and a *marginal* sense.

Cartel. An organization of producers in the same industry which regulates prices and allocates markets to cartel members with the objective of generating monopoly profits.

Circular flow. The flow of factor services and real products between households, firms, government, and foreigners and the corresponding flow of payments.

Classical economics. That body of economic thought that prevailed from the time of Adam Smith until the 1930s. Keynes attacked the classical argument that the economy was self-regulating and needed no government intervention to maintain noninflationary, full-employment equilibrium.

Closed economy. An economy which is involved in no international transactions.

Coefficient of determination (R²). A measure of "goodness of fit" which is just the proportion of the variation in a dependent variable explained by movements in the independent variable(s) in a regression equation.

Coincident indicators. Measures of particular lines of economic activity that tend to move in step with general economic activity.

Commercial bank. A federal or state chartered bank which deals directly with the public, holding deposits (primarily demand or checking account deposits) for individuals and firms and extending loans to individuals and firms. The demand deposit liabilities of commercial banks serve as money.

Comparative statics. Analysis that compares the attributes of a system at rest before and after some specific shock has disturbed that system.

Compensation of employees. The wages and salaries, tips, business social security contributions for employees, and other sources of labor compensation.

Compound interest. Interest accrued both on a principal sum and on the interest earned by that sum as of a prescribed date.

Concentration ratio. A proxy for monopoly power which measures the degree to which an industry is dominated by a few firms. Typically the percentage of an industry's sales accounted for by the four largest firms.

Consol. A bond with no maturity date which provides a set coupon interest payment each accounting period forever.

Constant dollars. Dollars of unchanged purchasing power.

Consumer price index. A measure of the average price of those goods and services bought by the "typical" urban wage earner.

Consumption. Basically, household expenditures on those durable goods, nondurables, and services which render satisfaction directly. Alternatively, when a measure of the true "using up" of consumer goods is desired, expenditures on nondurables and services plus the use value of consumer durables.

Consumption function. The relationship between income and consumption (*ceteris paribus*).

Control theory. A set of mathematical techniques which are applicable to the task of optimally controlling the adjustment path of a number of types of systems.

Coordinated policies. The simultaneous and coordinated application of two or more policy instruments in pursuit of two or more policy goals.

Cost-push inflation. That inflation that stems from an upward shift of the aggregate supply schedule. Often, organized labor and concentrated businesses are blamed for using their market power in a manner that drives up production *costs*, hence prices.

Crawling peg. A proposed foreign exchange system in which frequent and automatic *small* adjustments in the par value of a currency would occur as that currency's market value persistently pressed against the "floor" or "ceiling" of allowable exchange rates.

Credit availability or rationing. The presence or absence of a nonprice restriction on the volume of loan funds business firms can acquire for investment purposes.

Credit expansion multiplier. See money supply multiplier.

Credit markets. The financial markets in which borrowers and lenders are brought together. A complex array of financial institutions provide these markets.

Creeping inflation. A gradual (say, less than 3 percent annually) but persistent increase in the general price level.

Cross-section data. Observations across a population collected at a point in time.

Crowding-out effect. A reduction in private spending which results from and offsets the stimulative effects of an expansionary fiscal policy action. According to this thesis, an increase in government spending can reduce private investment by a like amount through increases in the interest rate.

Currency. Coins or paper money.

Current dollars. Observed, nominal values which have been subject to no adjustment for price changes.

Deflation. A statistical adjustment of nominal values to express those values in terms of base-year prices. Also, a decline in the general price level (the opposite of an inflation).

Demand deposit. An obligation of a commercial bank to pay, *on demand*, an amount specified by the customer who owns the deposit. Such deposits constitute *checkbook* money.

Demand-pull inflation. An inflation that results from a rightward shift of the aggregate demand schedule, signifying a generalized excess demand for real goods and services at current prices.

Deposit expansion multiplier. A predictor of the impact on the volume of demand deposits and money of a change in the volume of reserves or high-powered money.

Depreciation. The annual shrinkage in the stock of productive capital assets due to wear and obsolescence.

Depression. A highly depressed state of economic activity. In the Great Depression of the 1930s, the United States suffered an unemployment rate that reached 25 percent of the labor force.

Devaluation. An official reduction in the par value of a currency.

Diminishing returns. With technology held constant, as additional units of a variable factor input are combined with other factors production rises, but, ultimately, output will rise at a diminished rate (the *marginal* additions to output decline). At that point, diminishing returns have emerged. Diminishing returns to a factor and diminishing marginal productivity of that factor are two labels for the same phenomenon.

Discount rate. The interest rate at which the Federal Reserve lends reserves to member commercial banks.

Discouraged workers. Those potential workers who have quit actively seeking work because they are convinced further job search will not reveal an obtainable job. Such individuals are not counted as unemployed since one must be actively seeking work to be a part of the labor force as currently defined.

Discretionary fiscal policy. The deliberate alteration of tax rates and government outlays in an effort to stabilize the economy.

Disembodied technical change. Changes in the state of technology (such as organizational improvements) which can raise the economy's productive capacity without investment in new capital goods.

Disguised unemployment (underemployment). Unutilized or underutilized productive resources which are not counted as unemployed because of the *special* definitions employed in calculating unemployment measures.

Disintermediation. A withdrawal of funds from financial intermediaries for direct lending in the securities market when interest rates rise.

Disinvestment. A reduction in the size of the capital stock which results from gross investment falling short of capital consumption.

Disposable personal income. That income that is left after the payment of personal tax liabilities.

Dissaving. Consumption in excess of income.

Dividends. Payments by corporations to stockholders representing the reward for providing the firms with capital.

Downward rigid money wages. Money wages that do not fall at all even in the face of substantial involuntary unemployment. Downward "sticky" money wages may fall *gradually* in the face of involuntary unemployment but not rapidly enough, according to Keynesian analysis, to provide an acceptable automatic restoration of full employment.

Dynamics. An analysis in which the time path of adjustment is traced.

Dynamic stability analysis. Analysis of a system's time path of adjustment to determine whether that system will migrate to a static equilibrium position after it is disturbed by some specific shock.

Econometrics. A combination of economic theory and statistical analysis which provides a test and quantification of theory.

Economic growth. An increase in a nation's real production over time. Generally measured by an increase in real Gross National Product or per capita real Gross National Product.

Economic indicators. Time series of economic variables that are employed in analyzing and forecasting business cycles. Indicators can lead, lag, or be coincident with general economic activity.

Effective supply and demand schedules. In disequilibrium analysis, those demand and supply schedules that prevail in a market when one or more other markets are not in equilibrium.

Elasticity. A measure of *responsiveness*. Price elasticity is the percentage change in quantity demanded (or supplied) per unit percentage change in price. Other elasticities are also frequently employed in economic analysis.

Embodied technical change. Changes in the state of technology that are embodied in capital goods and, hence, require investment in technologically advanced capital goods if they are to add to the economy's production capacity.

Employment. As measured in the United States, the number of individuals who during the survey period: (1) worked any amount of time as a paid employee, (2) were self-employed, (3) worked 15 hours or more in a family enterprise, (4) did not work but had jobs from which they were temporarily absent due to illness, labor dispute, vacation, bad weather, and so on.

Employment Act of 1946. An act of Congress which declared that "... it is the continuing responsibility of the Federal Government ... to promote maximum employment, production, and purchasing power." This act formally recognizes the federal government's responsibility for employing policies which stabilize the economy.

Endogenous. Determined within the system.

Equation of exchange. The identity $MV = PY$ which relates the stock of money and its velocity with the general price level and the level of real output. This identity is fundamental to classical analysis.

Equilibrium. A rest position. A state of balance between opposing forces so that no adjustments are produced (for example, in quantity, price, income, and so on).

Equilibrium in the commodity market. The rest position that prevails when the aggregate demand for and supply of real goods and services are equal.

Equilibrium in the money market. The rest position that prevails when the supply of and demand for money (bonds) are equal.

Escalator. A formula that automatically adjusts a money flow in response to changes in the price level.

Excess reserves. The surplus of a commercial bank's actual reserves over its required reserves.

Exchange controls. Controls that limit access to foreign exchange markets by individuals and firms.

Excise tax. A tax levied on the production or sale of specific items such as liquor, gasoline, jewelry, and so on.

Exogenous. Determined outside the system and, hence, not influenced by events within the system.

Expenditure approach. A method of constructing measures of aggregate output (income) by summing the expenditures of different sectors (the household, business, government, and foreign sectors).

Exports. Sales of domestically produced goods and services to the rest of the world.

External balance (ff) *schedule.* A schedule showing all the interest rate-income combinations that provide balance of payments equilibrium.

Factors of production. Those human and nonhuman resources that are used in the production process. Can be classified in the four broad groups: land, labor, capital, and entrepreneurial talent.

Federal Open Market Committee. The chief policy making body in the Federal Reserve System, consisting of the seven-member Board of Governors of the Federal Reserve System plus five district bank representatives.

Federal Reserve System. The decentralized central bank of the United States. Created by Congress in 1913, the system includes 12 district banks (with additional branch offices) administered by a Presidentially appointed Board of Governors, the Federal Open Market Committee, and several thousand member commercial banks.

Final products. Consumer goods, government purchased production, and newly produced capital goods which are not bought for resale but for *final* use.

Financial intermediaries. Specialized, nonbank financial institutions including savings and loan associations, mutual savings banks, insurance companies, credit unions, and so on. These institutions channel savings to borrowers and may act in a manner that weakens monetary policy actions.

Fiscal policy. Stabilization policy involves changes in government spending, taxes, or transfers.

Fixed investment. Investment in plant, equipment, and residential structures. Excludes inventory investment.

Fixed-proportion production. A production process in which factor inputs (labor and capital for example) must be combined in strictly fixed proportions with no opportunity for substituting one factor input for another.

Flexible money wages and prices. Money wage rates and prices that change freely in response to changes in supply or demand schedules (as assumed in classical analysis).

Flexible or floating exchange rates. Foreign exchange rates that are determined in a free market by the interaction of supply and demand.

Flow variable. A variable which must be measured over a time period. Income, output, consumption, investment, and saving are flows.

Foreign exchange. Currency, checks, bills of exchange, and related instruments used for international payments.

Foreign exchange rate. The price of one nation's currency in terms of another.

Frictional unemployment (search unemployment). Temporary unemployment of those engaged in the process of job search. Job seekers and job slots cannot be matched frictionlessly and instantly because of imperfect information, imperfect labor mobility, and so on.

Full employment. In simple terms a situation in which a job is *available* for everyone who wants to work at the prevailing real wage. In terms of measured unemployment most economists would accept an unemployment rate in the 4 to 5 percent range as full employment.

Full employment surplus (deficit). The federal budget surplus or deficit that would prevail if the economy were at *full* employment, arbitrarily defined as 4 percent unemployment.

General equilibrium. Simultaneous equilibrium in all markets in the economy.

General price level. The "average" price level economy-wide which is probably best represented by the implicit GNP deflator though no price index can adequately measure the economy-wide price level.

GNP gap. The difference between actual GNP and the GNP that would be produced at full employment (defined as 4 percent unemployment). Often used as a rough measure of the foregone production cost of a depressed level of economic activity.

Gold standard. An international monetary system in which each nation's currency is defined in terms of a fixed weight of gold with gold bullion used to clear international payments imbalances.

Government purchases of goods and services. Federal, state, and local government expenditures on products and factor services. This total appears in the national income and product accounts as a measure of production of final goods and services.

Gross national product. The total market value of all final goods and services produced by an economy in a year.

Gross private domestic investment. Total expenditures on newly produced capital goods (including additions to inventories) with no adjustment for depreciation of the existing stock of capital.

Growth recession. A slowdown in the economy's rate of growth during which unemployment of labor and capital swells but output continues to rise though more slowly than productive capacity.

High-powered money. See reserve money.

Horizontal integration. The merging under single ownership of firms involved in the production of like goods or services.

Human capital. The mental and physical productive capabilities of the population. People invest in human capital through formal education, on-the-job training, and so on.

Hyperinflation. A very rapid, runaway inflation in which the nation's monetary system is threatened.

Hypothesis. A tentatively accepted relationship subject to refutation by observed reality.

Implicit price deflator. A *broad* measure of the general price level equal to the ratio of nominal GNP to real GNP.

Import quota. A legal restriction on the quantity of an item that may be imported during a given period.

Imports. Domestic purchases of goods and services produced abroad.

Imputations. Constructed values of economic activity employed where direct observation is impossible. Notable imputations are made for the rental value of owner-occupied houses and for farm produce consumed on the farm.

Income approach. A method of constructing measures of aggregate income (output) by summing the earned incomes of the factor inputs employed in the production process.

Income tax. A tax levied on income so that tax revenues rise with income. The personal income tax and the corporate income tax are the major examples in the United States.

Index numbers. Numbers, typically expressed in percentage form, which reveal the value of a series relative to some base period.

Indifference curve. A schedule showing all the alternative combinations of commodities, of risk and expected return on a portfolio, and so on which leave an individual equally satisfied.

Indirect business taxes. Sales taxes, excise taxes, and similar levies which are not based on firms' profits. Such taxes entail costs for business firms for which no productive services are directly rendered.

Induced spending (consumption or investment). That spending that is induced by a change in income.

Inflation. A significant and sustained rise in the general price level.

Injection. Any addition to the spending stream which does not stem directly from the income accruing to the household sector. Business investment, government purchases, and exports represent injections.

Innovation. Adoption of a new, improved method of production or of a new and different product.

Inside lag. The time that elapses between emergence of a need for a policy action and the time that policy action is undertaken.

Interest. The price of loanable funds, hence, the opportunity cost of holding money. As a factor reward, the return earned by those who provide money capital.

Intermediate products. Items purchased for resale rather than for *final* use.

Internal rate of return. The percentage rate of return a firm can expect to earn on investment in a capital asset.

International Monetary Fund (IMF). The international organization that has administered the international monetary system since the Bretton Woods conference in 1944.

Inventory. Stocks of raw materials, semi-finished goods, and finished goods which firms have on hand for further processing or for sale.

Investment. Expenditure on newly produced, physical capital goods. Expenditures on plant, equipment, residential structures, and inventory additions are included.

Investment tax credit. A credit against a business's profit tax liability based on the amount of investment the firm undertakes.

Involuntary unemployment. That unemployment (over and above normal, search unemployment) that exists when a depressed level of aggregate demand for goods and services leaves the number of jobs business firms are willing to offer at the prevailing real wage short of the number of jobs workers would willingly accept.

IS *curve.* A schedule showing all the alternative combinations of an interest rate and an income level which provide commodity market equilibrium.

Labor force. The employed plus all those individuals, 16 years of age or older, who are unemployed but are actively seeking work.

Labor services. The productive services of people.

Laspeyres. An index obtained using base year weights.

Leading indicators. Measures of particular economic activities which tend to move ahead of movements in general economic activity.

Leakages. Withdrawals from the flow of spending on domestically produced output encompassing saving, taxes, and imports.

Lender of last resort. An important duty of the Federal Reserve System as it was originally envisioned, to stand by to lend funds to member commercial banks when they were faced with extraordinarily large withdrawals during times of uncertainty.

Liability. A claim against an individual's or a firm's assets by any individual, firm, or institution (other than the owners in the case of the firm).

Linear regression equation. An equation which relates variations in a dependent variable to movements in one or more causal variables.

Liquidity. An asset is more liquid the more easily it can be disposed of without appreciable transaction costs and without loss of market value. Money is the most liquid of all assets.

Liquidity trap. A horizontal segment of the money demand schedule.

LM *curve.* A schedule showing all the combinations of the interest rate and the level of real income which provide equilibrium in the money (bond) market.

Macroeconometric models. Econometric models of the macroeconomy that are useful for explaining and predicting macroeconomic events.

Macroeconomics. That portion of economic analysis that focuses attention on the economy as a whole.

Marginal cost. The change in total costs of production stemming from a one unit change in output.

Marginal efficiency of capital (MEC). The expected rate of return on a one unit addition to the stock of capital holding constant the state of technology, the quantity and quality of other factor inputs, the prices of factor inputs over the life of the asset, and the demand for products manufactured by that asset over its lifetime.

Marginal efficiency of investment (MEI). The expected rate of return on a one unit increase in the flow rate of aggregate investment holding constant the stock of capital, the strength of demand for final goods, and the other determinants of the position of the marginal efficiency of *capital* schedule. The marginal efficiency of investment schedule slopes downward because of rising marginal costs in the capital goods producing industry.

Marginal product. The extra output that is generated by a one unit increase in the quantity of one variable input employed.

Marginal propensity to consume. The change in consumption that results from a one unit change in income.

Marginal propensity to save. The change in saving that results from a one unit change in income.

Marginal revenue. The change in revenue that results from a unit change in sales.

Marginal tax rate. The change in tax collections per unit change in income, typically expressed in percentage form.

Markets. Institutions which permit more efficient exchange by providing readily accessible lines of communication between buyers and sellers.

Measure of Economic Welfare (MEW). A measure of society's economic well-being that is broader than GNP though obtained by modifying GNP figures.

Member banks. Those commercial banks that are members of the Federal Reserve System.

Merger. The combining of two or more firms under one ownership.

Microeconomics. That portion of economic analysis that focuses on the behavior of individual economic units (individual households, firms, and industries).

Model. A theoretical explanation of some real-world phenomenon involving hypothesized relationships, interrelationships among hypotheses, and the logical implications that can be drawn therefrom.

Monetarist. A modern quantity theorist who contends that money supply changes are the dominant cause of macroeconomic adjustments while fiscal policy does little more than alter the allocation of resources.

Monetary dampener. A mechanism that tends to weaken expansions and contractions as changes in the level of income change money demand, the interest rate, and thus investment spending.

Monetary effects of fiscal policy. The money supply changes that may result from fiscal actions depending on the method the government uses to finance its spending.

Monetary policy. Stabilization policy applied through changes in the money supply.

Money. Any asset that is readily accepted as a medium of exchange. In addition to serving as a medium of exchange, money serves as a store of purchasing power and as a standard or measure of value. Money can be narrowly defined as publicly owned currency plus demand deposits.

Money capital. The funds used by business firms to buy physical capital.

Money market. That convenient market construct where money can be considered to be supplied and demanded.

Money supply multiplier. A measure of the multiple change in the nominal money supply that results from a unit change in the volume of reserves.

Money wage. The nominal wage without regard to its real purchasing power.

Monopoly. A market structure in which one seller controls market supply and, hence, has some control over market price.

Multiplier. A measure of the impact on equilibrium income of an autonomous change in spending or net tax collections.

Multiplier-accelerator model. A model that combines the multiplier and accelerator to show that cyclical fluctuations can be generated internally.

National income. A measure of income *earned* by productive factor inputs which can be obtained using either the income or the expenditure approach.

National income and product accounts. A set of data on aggregate output (income) and its components which are crucial to macroeconomic analysis.

Natural rate of unemployment. The measured rate of unemployment that would prevail when the economy is neither in a recession nor suffering from inflationary pressures. That remaining unemployment can be considered to represent *search* unemployment.

Near-monies. Highly liquid assets such as savings deposits, short-term government bonds, and the like which can be converted readily into money and which perform some of the same functions as money (for example, store of value).

Neoclassical growth models. Growth models developed in the postwar period that focus attention on the supply of factor inputs rather than on demand as the basic determinant of an economy's long-run growth path.

Net exports. Exports minus imports.

Net interest. Net interest payments from business firms to households and government.

Net national product. The economy's *net* output for the year which is available for consumption, government use, and adding to the existing capital stock. Obtained by subtracting capital consumption from GNP.

Net private domestic investment. That investment which increases the accumulated stock of capital goods. Gross investment minus capital consumption.

Net taxes. Taxes minus transfer payments.

Net worth. The difference between assets and liabilities representing an individual's or firm's owned "wealth."

Nominal interest rate. The observed, market interest rate which differs from the real rate of interest when a nonzero inflation rate is anticipated.

Nominal value. Current dollar value with no adjustment for price level changes.

Nominal wage. The wage rate measured in current dollars.

Normative economics. That economics which is concerned with what "ought to be" rather than with what "is." Ultimately rests on value judgments.

Notional demand and supply schedules. In disequilibrium analysis, those schedules that represent effective demands and supplies in a market when all other markets are in equilibrium.

Open economy. An economy that is involved in international transactions.

Open market operations. Purchases and sales of government securities undertaken by the Federal Reserve System to alter the volume of reserves and, hence, the money supply.

Ordinary least squares. A technique of fitting a linear regression equation which minimizes the sum of squared deviations of actual observed values of the dependent variable from the values predicted by the regression equation.

Outside lag. In simple terms, the time interval between a policy action and the point in time when that action has a significant effect on the economy. It must be remembered that policy actions have influences on the economy that are actually distributed in time.

Paasche index. An index obtained using latter (current) period weights.

Par value of a currency. The official exchange rate which a country was required to maintain between its currency and another country's currency under the postwar IMF system.

Partial correlation coefficient. A measure of the covariation of two variables with the influence of other variables adjusted for. The stronger the tendency for two variables to move together the closer is the value of the partial correlation coefficient to one.

Past income. In the Duesenberry model, the highest level of income attained in the past.

Period. In business cycle analysis, the amount of time required for completion of one cycle.

Permanent income. That flow of expenditures which a household believes it can enjoy in the foreseeable future without a loss in capital value or wealth.

Personal income. The total of income *received* by households without personal tax liabilities deducted.

Phillips curve. A schedule showing the trade-off between unemployment and inflation.

Positive economics. Economic *analysis* concerned with what "is" rather than what "should be."

Potential gross national product. The volume of gross national product that the economy could provide, with *full* employment defined as 4 percent measured unemployment.

Present value. The discounted, *present* worth of a stream of future receipts obtained using the interest cost of capital as the discount rate.

Price index. A measure of price level change between two periods typically expressed in percentage terms.

Prime rate. The interest rate charged by commercial banks on loans to their most credit-worthy business customers.

Private sector. That portion of the economy incorporating households and business firms but excluding government.

Product market. The market where real goods and services are bought and sold.

Production function. The relationship between output and the volume of factor inputs used to produce that output.

Profit. The residual income after payment of wages, rent, and interest which accrues to entrepreneurs.

Profit-push inflation. An inflation that is alleged to stem from monopolistic firms using their market power to push up profits by raising prices.

Progressive tax. A tax levy in which the percentage tax rate rises as the tax base grows.

Proprietors' income. Income accruing to all unincorporated businesses including single proprietorships and partnerships.

Public debt. The outstanding bond debt of government.

Pure interest rate. The conceptual interest rate that would be earned on a riskless security issue on which administrative costs are negligible.

Quantifiable. Measurable in numerical terms.

Quantity theory of money. In classical analysis the theory that argued that money supply changes bring about equal proportion changes in prices with no change in real variables. The *modern* quantity theory permits money supply changes to produce changes in real output as well as prices in the short run but still provides a proportional relationship between money and prices with output at the full employment level in the long run.

Quota. See import quota.

Razor's-edge models. Simplistic growth models which yield pessimistic predictions on the probability of the economy expanding along a path that maintains full utilization of all factor inputs.

Real gross national product. The economy's annual output of final goods and services valued in terms of base year prices.

Real income. The purchasing power embodied in a flow of money income.

Real interest rate. The observed market interest rate less the expected inflation rate.

Real wage. The purchasing power embodied in the money wage. Inversely proportional to the price level.

Real wealth effect. A change in consumption brought about by a change in the real value of society's wealth, either through a change in the general price level or through a policy action.

Recession. A period of depressed economic activity in which unemployment rises. As a rule of thumb, when real GNP declines for two successive quarters the economy is in a recession.

Recovery. The expansion phase of the business cycle in which employment and output rise.

Relative income. The value of a household's income relative to the average for its peer group.

Rent. The return received for the use of real property (land in the broad classification of factor inputs).

Rental income of persons. Rental income of those whose primary occupation is something other than the renting of real property. Included is the imputed rental value of owner-occupied homes.

Replacement investment. That portion of total investment that is required just to replace the capital that is worn out, made obsolete, or accidentally destroyed each year.

Required reserve ratio. The fixed percentage of deposit liabilities which commercial banks must hold as reserves.

Reservation wage. The minimum wage a job seeker is willing to accept.

Reserve money or high-powered money. Reserve deposits of commercial banks and currency, each dollar of which can support the existence of a multiple amount of publicly held money.

Risk. The dispersion of possible outcomes (such as gains or losses) when a particular course of action is followed. When the possible outcomes are distributed *normally*, the standard deviation of the distribution can be used as a measure of risk.

Sales tax. A fixed percentage tax levied on the retail prices of commodities and services.

Saving. That part of disposable income that is not consumed.

Say's Law. "Supply creates its own demand." The argument, fundamental in classical analysis, that there could never be a generalized glut (excess supply) of goods and services of the type Keynes claimed would send the economy reeling into recession. The proposition bears the name of French economist Jean Baptiste Say (1767-1832).

Scientific method. A method of analyzing phenomena involving the construction and testing of models that attempt to explain those phenomena.

Search unemployment. See frictional unemployment.

Shortage. An excess of demand over supply at the prevailing price.

Special classical region. The vertical segment of the *LM* schedule which emerges when both money supply and money demand become interest-inelastic. In the special classical region fiscal policy is impotent while monetary policy has its greatest strength.

Special Drawing Rights (SDRs). "Paper gold" reserves in the form of bookkeeping entries in the accounts kept by the International Monetary Fund. SDRs were created in 1969 to supplement gold as a reserve asset as world trade continued to grow.

Special Keynesian region. The horizontal segment of the *LM* schedule which reflects the appearance of the liquidity trap in the money market. In the special Keynesian region, monetary policy is impotent while fiscal policy has its greatest strength.

Speculative demand for money. The demand for money as an asset in order to avoid the capital losses that are expected on bonds as interest rates rise.

Statistical discrepancy. The difference, attributed to measurement errors, between the level of national income obtained using the expenditure approach and that obtained using the income approach.

Sterilization. The actions of a country's central bank when (using open market operations or other means) it offsets the money supply changes caused by a balance of payments surplus or deficit.

Stock. The accumulated volume of an item that is measurable at an instant in time.

Stop-and-go stabilization policy. A cyclical pattern of expansionary, then contractionary, then expansionary stabilization actions which result in inflationary booms followed by inflationary recession.

Structural unemployment. A *hard-core* residual of unemployment afflicting those whose lack of skills, location, and so on keep the value of their potential contributions to production below the wage they must be paid if employed.

Surtax. An additional tax levied on an existing tax base.

Tariff. A tax on imports.

Tax. A compulsory levy exacted by government for which no particular service is provided in turn to the taxpayer.

Technological progress. Changes in the state of technology which permit more output to be produced with an unchanged *quantity* of factor inputs.

"The rate of interest." The pure rate of interest or a weighted average of all observed market interest rates.

Time deposits. Savings accounts and certificates of deposit owed to depositors by commercial banks but legally subject to withdrawal only after a specified amount of advance notice.

Time series. A set of data with observations generated over time.

Total revenue. The product of sales price and number of units sold representing the total sales receipts of a firm.

Transactions demand. Demand for money to use as a medium of exchange, financing those transactions that occur between the points in time when income is received.

Transfer payments. Payments for which no current productive services are rendered. Pensions, unemployment compensation, welfare payments, veterans benefits, and interest on the national debt are prominent examples.

Transitory. A temporary, random, chance, unexpected increment in consumption or income.

Trend. The long-run pattern of a time series with the seasonal and cyclical influences on that series removed.

Underemployment equilibrium. A rest position for the economy with involuntary unemployment persisting in the labor market while the money and commodity markets are in equilibrium.

Unemployment rate. The percentage of the civilian labor force that is not employed.

Union. An organization of workers which, with the right to strike, has greater bargaining power with management over wages, working conditions, fringe benefits, and so on than would individual workers.

Unplanned (unintended) inventory investment. A change in accumulated inventories which occurs because aggregate planned spending differs from the volume of output firms are producing for final sales. The commodity market is in disequilibrium when there is unplanned inventory investment.

Upward bias. A tendency to overstatement as the tendency of Laspeyres price indexes to overstate the amount of inflation.

Value added. The addition to the value of an item in process as it goes through each stage of the production process.

Verification. The testing of hypotheses against observed reality to see if actual observations tend to support or refute the hypotheses.

Vertical integration. The merging under a single ownership of firms engaged in different stages of the processing of raw materials into finished products.

Vintage. Dates of origin of capital goods. The later the vintage presumably the more advanced the technology embodied in purchased capital goods.

Wage-price controls. Legal restrictions on the wages firms can pay and the prices they can charge.

Wage-push inflation. The inflation that is attributed to organized labor contracting for wage increases that exceed labor's increase in productivity.

Wages. The income earned by labor in the production process.

Wealth. An accumulated stock of valuable assets, financial or real.

Wholesale price index. An index measure of the average price of commodities measured at their first important wholesale exchange.

Yield. The return on an investment.

Index

519